W9-BGL-529

Family Identity and the State in the Bamako *Kafu*, c. 1800–c. 1900

AFRICAN STATES AND SOCIETIES IN HISTORY

Series Editors
Philip Curtin, Paul E. Lovejoy, and Shula Marks

*Family Identity and the State in the
Bamako Kafu, c. 1800–c. 1900,*
B. Marie Perinbam

*Landlords and Strangers: Ecology, Society,
and Trade in Western Africa, 1000–1630,*
George E. Brooks

FORTHCOMING

Government in Kano, 1350–1950,
M. G. Smith

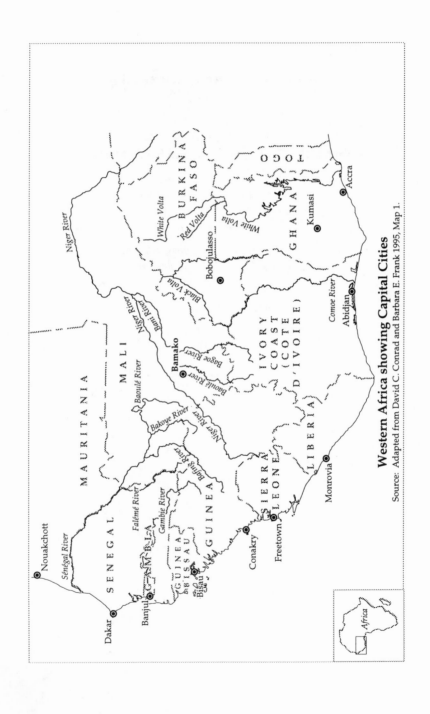

Western Africa showing Capital Cities

Source: Adapted from David C. Conrad and Barbara E. Frank 1995, Map 1.

Family Identity and the State in the Bamako *Kafu*, c. 1800–c. 1900

B. Marie Perinbam

WestviewPress
A Division of HarperCollins*Publishers*

Copyright © 1997 by Westview Press, A Division of HarperCollins Publishers

Published in 1997 in the United States of America by Westview Press, 5500 Central Avenue, Boulder, Colorado 80301, and in the United Kingdom by Westview Press, 12 Hid's Copse Road, Cumnor Hill, Oxford OX2 9JJ

A CIP catalog record for this book is available from the Library of Congress.
ISBN 0-8133-3080-7

This book was typeset by Letra Libre, 1705 Fourteenth Street, Suite 391, Boulder, Colorado 80304.

All maps adapted from sources cited by Robyn Nick.

The paper used in this publication meets the requirements of the American National Standard for Permanence of Paper for Printed Library Materials Z39.48-1984.

10   9   8   7   6   5   4   3   2   1

Contents

Preface   *ix*

Introduction   1
  Families and Identities, 1
  Contextualizing the Story, 8
  Spatializing Identity Signs, 16
  About the Book, 23
  Theoretical Paradigm, 27
  A Word About Sources, 28
  How the Book Fits into the Literature, 32
  Conclusion, 40

**1 How Identities Are Formed: The Manipulation of
  Myths and Cultural Signs**   45
  Nyakate Identities and Mande/Fulbe Articulations
    in the *Jaman'a*, 46
  Articulating Eastern Nyakate/Niare Identities, 55
  The Manipulated Wagadu Legend, 57
  Conclusions, 84
  Coda: Other Oral Accounts and Further Mythic
    Manipulations, 87

2 Material Elaborations of "The Mande Style"   95
  The Bamako *Kafu* and Regional Perspectives, 95
  The Paradigm Elaborated, 96
  Ethnic Identities Historically Contextualized, 98
  Conclusion, 136

**3 "The Family (Is) the Pivot of Sudanese Societies,
  the Center of All Organization": The Bamako *Kafu*
  and Mande States**   139
  Introduction, 139
  More Cultural Manipulations: The Roman Paradigm, 140

The Bamako *Kafu*: Contextualizing and Elaborating a
    Political Identity "in the Mande Style," 149
State Maintenance and Social Mobilization, 162
Bamako's Relationship with the Segovian Metropole, 168
Conclusion: Bamako a Minimalist and
    Semiautonomous State, 173

4 Commerce and Markets "in the Mande Style"   179
Introduction, 179
Pre-*Kafu* Regional Markets: The Samanyana
    Market Cluster and Bozo Camps, 181
Bamako Kafu and the Long-Distance Trade Market
    Operations and Commercial Identities, 185
The Gold Trade Revisited, 207
War-Time Economies and the Post-war Economic Recovery:
    Kola Nuts, Grain, and Livestock, 209
Conclusion, 216

5 "Bamako Was Not as ... We Had Supposed";
Bamako Was Not a "Nothing Country"   219
Introduction, 219
France in the Senegambia and the Advance to the Niger, 220
The Undialogue, 225
The Railway, 238
Bamako's "French" Identity: *"Votre Jolie Ville de Bamako,*
    Toute Française," 242

Conclusion: Bamako's "French" Identity or How Identities
Are Formed Revisited   247
Bamako's "French" Identity, 247
The French "Bambara" Identity, 248
The Re-Birth of the Wagadu Identity, 263

Appendix: Maps of Western Africa   275
Bibliography   283
About the Book and Author   323
Index   325

Preface

This work acknowledges a debt of gratitude to all who helped. First, I recognize the several Bamako families, the Niare, the Drave, the Ture, to mention but a few, and those of the Bamako region, such as the Kante, the Kulibaly, the Jabate, and the Keita, who graciously entered into my research, allowing themselves to be portrayed in the pages of this book. Willingly providing information, which at the time may have seemed remote, irrelevant, and downright invasive, their contributions shaped in many respects the perspectives in this book. To this extent, I acknowledge particularly Seydou Niare, Nana Niare Drave, Suleyman Drave, and Bani Toure, who were a source not only of information but also of inspiration, imagination, and hospitality. In many respects, this book is their collective portrait.

Second, beyond the circle of families, I owe special recognition to Ali Ongoïba, Archivist at the Archives Nationales Maliennes, Bamako, as well as to Thiemoko Kante, Mahmadou Sarr, Seydou Camara, and Klena Sanogo, all of the Institut des Sciences Humaines at Bamako. Generous with their time and gracious beyond compare, they not only unveiled the complexities and fascinations of the vast Mande cultural world—throwing light on the multiple regional configurations—but they also uncovered the filigreed ideographs that incised the great cultural templates, or that had slipped practically unnoticed through the cultural crevices serrating the Mande's cultural landscape. In many respects, this book mirrors their complex, conjugated minds. Also invaluable was the assistance from other personnel at the Archives Nationales Maliennes and the Institut Fondamental d'Afrique Noire at Bamako.

Third, I acknowledge with gratitude the help of members of the *jeli* (*griot* or bardic), mercantile and mining families, such as the Jabate and the Drame, the Sylla the Sisse and the Konate, the Kante the Dumbya and the Sissoko, whose oral recountings bespoke the peoples' lives, those who, since great antiquity, have heard the epic songs of the Do ni Kri[1]; or

---

1. Mande terms for the Mande plain and mountains of the middle and upper Niger.

who heed the daily call to prayer; or who, since deep time have signed Mali's wooded savannahs "Mande"; and who still say "N'Ko," or "I say." Their voices can still be heard throughout this book.

Fourth, to the librarians at the Ecole Normale Superieure at Badal-abougou, across the Vincent Auriol Bridge from Bamako, I recall the same refrain. Tirelessly affording me repeated access to the Memoires de Fin d'Etude—for the most part a cache of invaluable oral recountings and family histories compiled by young researchers under professorial super-vision—their indulgence enabled me to enrich poor findings only hither-to suggested, or to interrogate dubious inferences otherwise claiming au-thenticity, or to fill the silences left by weary, modest, or unwilling informants.

Beyond Mali and the Mande world, my acknowledgments go to the many curators, librarians, and office personnel in the offices, libraries, and archives which claimed my long research hours. In Senegal I mention par-ticularly personnel at the Archives Nationales du Senegal and the Institut Fondamental d'Afrique Noire in Dakar; in France, those at the Archives Nationales de la France, Section Outre-Mer; at the Bibliotheque Nationale; the Centre d'Etudes Africaines (CEA), Ecole des Hautes Etudes en Sci-ences Sociales; the Centre de Recherches Africaines (CRA); the Centre des Hautes Etudes sur l'Afrique et l'Asie Modernes (CHEAM); and the Centre National de la Recherche Scientifique (CNRS).

None of the above would have been possible without generous grant support from the University of Maryland's Graduate Research Board, the College of Arts and Humanities, and the History Department, as well as the United States Fulbright Commission. None of the above would also have been possible without the hospitality of friends in Paris, Dakar, and Bamako.

Finally, for Mande proper and place names I followed, where possible, the orthography suggested by the Direction Nationale de l'Alphabetisation Fonctionelle et de la Linguistic Applique (DNAFLA) in Bamako (e.g., "Futa Jallon" instead of "Fouta Djallon"). French words appearing in a French language context, such as proper names (e.g. "Brévié"), or those adopted into the French language such as place names (e.g. "Sénégal") are accented. Appearing in an English language context, they remain unaccented (e.g. Brevie), as do also the various loan words from the Mande dialects.

B. Marie Perinbam

Introduction

Families and Identities

According to Myth and Legend

This is a story about families—the Niare, the Ture, the Drave, Kulibaly, Jakite, Jara, Keita, Traore, Konate, Dembele, Sissoko, Kante, Sisse, the Dembelle, and the Konare, among others—and their articulating identities in relation to a number of phenomena, most importantly, the state and its associated political economies.[1] By "state" I mean the network of incumbent families holding political power, not families sedentarized within fixed territorial boundaries. In other words, not only were familial political and ethnographic identities derived from the family and state construct. They *were* the state. Therefore the argument is about identity as state formation, elaboration, maintenance and renewal: the history of the state was the history of its ruling families. By "identities" I mean the development of ethnic personalities within a cultural framework and associated role-plays. I also mean the relatively condensed and thus generalized way in which individuals and groups perceived themselves and the world within which they articulated and functioned. Accordingly the history of identities is also the history of perceptions.

As part of state-familial identities, this story argues additionally that clan and lineage affiliations, as well as linguistic-cultural repertoires, and the families' epic migrations were all signs of their collective ethnographic identities. Collateral signs included family legends, political

---

1. As is generally understood the structure and internal organization of African families differ from their European analogues. "Family" throughout this text denotes exogamous and endogamous polygynous consanguineous relationships, including affinals, unilinear descent, residential unity, and genuine social integration. See "The History of the African family," *Journal of African History* (hereafter *JAH*), special issue, vol. 24, no. 2 (1983). For the family and the importance of its patronym *(jamu)*, prohibitions *(tana)*, and oaths *(senankuya, siya)* and so forth see, Yves Person, *Samori: Une Révolution dyula*, 3 vols., Mémoire de l'Institut Fondamental d'Afrique Noire (hereafter IFAN), no. 80 (Dakar, 1968–1975), vol. 1, pp. 55–56, 78–79, and throughout this book.

myths, and rituals, as well as ethnographic and historical imaginations, to mention but a few. The story moreover argues that as the families migrated across transforming centuries—drawn into the vortex of one state or another—their ethnic identities functioned both as a form of definition ritually achieved and observed, and as an ongoing process of meaning sensitive to regional, political, generational, and gender challenges. Otherwise expressed, this study claims: That familial identities were *internally* reconfigured in relation to the state into which the families had integrated; that identities articulated from one ethnographic axis to another in favor of these state exigencies; and that in the process, shifting identities were perceived differently by the external Other. Taking into consideration the role of power and authority, the story relates these articulations to the several family-state-constructs within which the culturally dynamic, and interactive processes eventually occurred. Because states as a rule do not exist without political economies, this story also argues for identity as the state's political-economic elaborations and processes within cultural boundaries defining the wider Mande identity. Finally, during the latter part of the nineteenth century, when the families were inserted within the French colonial state, familial identities were further adjusted accordingly.

Principal among families in the story were the Niare (*Nyakate*: archaic *jamu*, or patronymic), clients of the powerful Bamana Segu state under the imperial hegemony of Biton (Mamari) Kulibaly (c. 1712–c. 1755). Claiming, according to legend, founder status of the Bamako *kafu*, or state—focus of the story—they owed their client status to the Kulibaly lords (see Map 2).[2] Establishing founder claims sometime during the first part of the eighteenth century within the Segovian hegemony, their decades of political power-play on the Bamako plain and upper Niger regions are also the focus of the story.[3] And although most Niare now espouse a Bamana iden-

2. *Archives Nationales Maliennes à Koulouba* (hereafter *ANMK*) 1D 33 5, Gustave Borgnis Desbordes, "Notice historique du Cercle de Bamako, 1880–1890," n. p.; *ANMK* 1D 33 2, Dr. Collomb, "Notice sur le Cercle de Bamako, 1884–1885," p. 6; *Archives Sénégalaises d'Afrique Occidentale Française* (hereafter *ASAOF*) 1G 79, Conrard, "Notice sur l'état de Bammako" (Bamako, 21 Feb. 1885), p. 3; *ASAOF* 1G 299, Jules Brévié, "Monographie du Cercle de Bamako, 1904" (Bamako, 25 April 1904), pp. 1–12; Ismaïla Soumoaro, "Etude d'un quartier de Bamako: Niarela," Mém. de fin d'Etudes, under the direction of I. M. Albassadjé, l'Ecole Normale Supérieure à Badalabougou (hereafter l'ENSUP) (Bamako, 1976–1977).

3. The chronology used here is Tauxier's based on Paul Marty. See Louis Tauxier, "Chronologie des rois bambaras," *Outre Mer* (2nd trimester, 1930): 119–130; (3rd. trimester, 1930): 255–267; and revisions made in Louis Tauxier, *Histoire des Bambaras* (Paris, 1942). See also Paul Marty, "La Chronique de Ouala-

tity, their ethnographic profile—shifting from Soninke (plu.: Soninko) to Marka-Sarakolle (plu.: Maraka) to Bamana, with a possible Fulbe interlude in between—is likewise central to our discourse (see Chapter 1).[4] Also pivotal to the *kafu*'s development were the Ture (Tawati) and the Drave (Diagina, Draoui), a Ture subgroup, both claiming "Arabic" and "Islamic" identities. Joining the *kafu* community sometime in the eighteenth century, their legends project an earlier homeland in the Saharan oases, more particularly, Tamentit in the Tawat oasis of central Algeria. Beyond Tawat, some Drave trace their identity to the Dra'a valley of southern Morocco.[5]

Of varying importance to the story were families settling in the Bamana state of Segu under the aegis of Biton Kulibaly, in the near-by Beledugu, and the old Mande (French: *Manding, Mandingue*), (see Maps 2 and 3), this latter the land of the heroic Sunjata Keita (c. 1234–c. 1260) and the "pious" Mansa Musa (c. 1312–c. 1337), both mansaw (sing.: *mansa*) of legendary proportions.[6] Somewhat peripheral were families establishing res-

---

ta et de Néma (Soudan français)," *Revue des Etudes Islamiques*, no. 3 (1927): 225–426; no. 4 (1927): 531–575. The seventeenth-century dates given by Monteil, Villien-Rossi, and Meillassoux—based on oral accounts and their chronology of the Segu Bamana state—appear to be too early. Charles Monteil, *Les Bambara de Ségou et du Kaarta* (Paris, 1924/1977), p. 102; Marie-Louise Villien-Rossi, "Bamako, capitale du Mali," *Bulletin de l'Institut Fondamental d'Afrique Noire* (hereafter *BIFAN*), sér. B, vol. 28 (1966): 249–380, see esp. 264; and Claude Meillassoux, "Histoire et institutions du *kafo* de Bamako d'après la tradition des Niaré," *Les Cahiers d'Etudes Africaines* (hereafter *CEA*), vol 4 (1964): 186–227; *ANMK* 1D 33 2, Collomb, "Notice" (Bamako, 1884–1885), p. 6; *ANMK* 1D 33 5, Borgnis Desbordes, "Notice historique," (1880–1890).

4. *Marka-Sarakolle*, in the Segovian Bamana idiom, refers to those Mande claiming a Soninke heritage. The term was also used by some Fulbe and desert-side populations.

5. Interview Suleyman Dravé (Bamako, 8–9 Jan. 1980); interview Nana Niaré Dravé (Bamako, 4–5 Jan. 1980); Meillassoux, "Histoire," pp. 186–227, esp. pp. 198–199.

6. The old Mande (what the French called *Manding* or *Mandingue*) is a region of varying delimitations. For purposes of this discussion, it enclosed the Niger's left bank as far west as the Birgo or Fuladugu, as far south as Siguiri, and as far north as the Bamako frontier: Depending on the circumstances Bamako was sometimes the northern Mande, sometimes the southeastern Beledugu. Believed to be the heartland of ancient Mali, traditions have suggested a variety of capitals for the old Mande, including Jakajalan, Tubu (Tabun), Kunfangue, Figuira, Narena, Kangaba, and Niani. See J. Vidal, "Un Problème historique africain au sujet de l'emplacement de Mali, capitale de l'ancien empire mandingue," *Bulletin du*

idences north of Bamako in the Massina (eventually the seat of power for the Islamized reformer Ahmadu Ba Lobo Sisse, c. 1775/76–1845), and more westerly in the Kaarta, country of the Kulibaly Massassi Faamaw (c. 1753–1854/56). Likewise peripheral were families in the Fuladugu with its capital at Bangasi, as well as the Khasso, Bundu, Gajaga (French Galam), and the Senegambia, in addition to the Wassulu and other upper Niger states, cities, and towns (see Maps 2 and 3).

Reaching the Bamako region from Segu on the middle Niger, and only after several hundred years in the mythical cold, the Bamako state under the Niare chiefly incumbency survived for between one hundred and fifty and one hundred and seventy-five years, until dawn on the morning of 1 February 1883, when Colonel Gustave Borgnis Desbordes, French superior commander of the upper Senegal River (1880–1883)—known as "Bourouti" in some local lore—claimed the region for the glory of France.[7] The state maintaining and renewing itself for approximately five generations, lineage identities, when realigned according to state exigencies, formed the polity's main infrastructure—the state as a sort of family affair—where power and authority (paterfamilias) within the *domus*, or private space, overlapped and articulated with its public (res publica) or state equivalent. Thus, although some officeholders, for example, the *kafu-tigi*, or chief political and administrative officer, were permanent incumbents, more commonly according to constitutional protocols, private household heads were identified as *pro tem* state-officeholders.

When the story opens in archaic time—according to myth and legend—the Mande *jaman'a*, or all the families (the Niare included), were

---

Comité d'Etudes Historiques et Scientifiques de l'Afrique Occidentale Française (hereafter *BCEHSAOF*), vol. 6 (1923): 251–268; *Idem.*, "Un Problème historique africain: Le véritable emplacement de Mali," *BCEHSAOF*, vol. 6 (1923): 606–619; Maurice Delafosse, "Le Gâna et le Mali et l'emplacement de leurs capitales," *BCEHSAOF*, vol. 7 (1924): 479–542; M. Montrat, "Notice sur l'emplacement de la capitale du Mali," *Notes Africaines* (hereafter *NA*), no. 79, (July 1958): 90–92; Raymond Mauny, *Tableau géographique de l'ouest africain au moyen age d'après les sources écrites, la tradition et l'archéologie*, Mém. IFAN, no. 61 (Dakar, 1961), pp. 121–126; Wladyslaw Filipowiak, "Contribution aux recherches sur la capitale du royaume de Mali," *Archaeologia Polona*, vol. 10 (1968): 217–232; John O. Hunwick, "The Mid-fourteenth century capital of Mali," *JAH*, vol. 14, no. 2 (1973): 195–208; David C. Conrad, "Searching for history in the Sunjata epic: The case of Fakoli," *History in Africa: A Journal of Method* (hereafter *HA*), vol. 19 (1992): 147–200, see esp. pp. 152–155.

7. Meillassoux, "Histoire," pp. 186–227; *ANMK* 1D 33 5, Borgnis Desbordes, "Notice historique" (1880–1890), n.p.

residing at Wagadu (Soninke), their mythical and ancestral homeland. This vague territory, straddling what is now the borderland of southern Mauritania and north-western Mali, is also identified with Baghana (Malinke), Bakhunu and ancient Ghana (Soninke), Wakore (Soninke), and Gumbu (see Map 3). Across the transforming centuries Wagadu has come to mean as many things to as many observers.[8] As a mythical realm, Wagadu could have been a social construct, or simply an elusive cultural concept defying time-space boundaries still surviving in collective Mande imaginations and popular cultures. As a historical reality Wagadu could have been a kingdom in the western Sahel sometime during the latter part of the first millennium and the first part of the second.[9] Indeed, as is generally known, archaeological evidence at Kumbi Saleh in the western Sahel, together with the several Arabic texts recorded between the eighth and fourteenth centuries, testify to a Soninke (Mande) state called "Ghana" with its capital at Kumbi.[10] Al-Fazari was

---

8. See Abdoulaye Bathily, "A Discussion of the traditions of Wagadu with some reference to ancient Ghana including a review of oral accounts, Arabic sources and archaeological evidence," *BIFAN*, sér. B, vol. 37, no. 1 (Jan. 1975): 1–94.

9. For different perspectives on these complex issues see Eric Pollet and Grace Winter, *La Société soninké (Dyahunu, Mali), études ethnologiques* (Brussels, 1971), pp. 25–28; Maurice Delafosse, *Haut-Sénégal-Niger*, 3 vols. (Paris, 1972), vol. 1, pp. 319–321, 418; vol. 2, pp. 12–21, 25–59; Louis Tautain, "Légende et traditions des Soninké relatives à l'empire de Ghanata, d'après les notes recueillies pendant une tournée de Bamako à Sokoto, Gumbu etc. en 1887," *Bulletin de Géographie Historique et Descriptive*, vols. 9–10 (1894–1895: 471–480; Claude Meillassoux, L. Doucouré, and D. Simagha, *Légende de la dispersion des Kusa (Epopée soninké)* (Dakar, 1967), p. 8.

10. According to the *Ta'rikh al-Fattash*, Kumbi was in Wagadu, northeast of Gumbu, en route from Gumbu to Nema and Walata. Muhammad al-Kati, *Ta'rikh al-Fattash*, trans. from Arabic by O. Houdas and M. Delafosse (Paris, 1964), p. 76. For archaeologists like Raymond Mauny, who cites a town of one square kilometer in the Sahel with houses made of stone, and a cemetery double the size of the town, Kumbi "very probably" existed (*Tableau géographique*, pp. 60, 72–74). See also, Susan Keech McIntosh, ed., *Excavations at Jenne-jeno, Kaniana, and Hambarketolo: The 1981 season* (University of California Press, Berkeley, 1995). For a further discussion see Vincent Monteil, *L'Islam noir* (Paris, 1964), pp. 65–70; see also Nehemia Levtzion, *Ancient Ghana and Mali* (London, 1973), pp. 20–22; David C. Conrad and Humphrey Fisher, "The Conquest that never was: Ghana and the Almoravids 1076," part 1. "The External Arabic sources"; part 2. "The Local oral sources," *HA*, vol. 9 (1982): 21–59; vol. 10 (1983): 53–78. For other discussions, see J. Vidal, "Le Mystère de Ghana," *BCEHSAOF*, vol. 6 (July–Sept. 1923): 512–524; Delafosse, "Le Gâna et le Mali," pp. 479–542; Charles Monteil, "Les 'Ghana' des géographes arabes et des Européens," *Hespéris*, vol. 38, nos. 3–4 (1951): 441–452; A.

the first to mention the Ghana (or Kumbi) state before 800 a.d., followed by al-Khuwarizmi before 833, by Ibn Hawqal in about 988, and al-Bakri in approximately 1068. Even the "scientific" Ibn Khaldun (d. 1406) repeated references to the Ghana state, not to mention its celebrated trans-Saharan gold and salt trade, which survived for centuries, even after the state's demise.[11]

Focus of the great "Legend of Wagadu," the lexicon of the vast Mande *jaman'a*, the myth, archetypal and "biblical" in its epic proportions, was nothing short of a Mande gnosis.[12] As the legend unfolds, we hear of a young scion squandering his birthright, and that of the *jaman'a*, refusing to sacrifice his betrothed to Bida, the sacred python at the pit-head, the monster's dreaded lair. For all the families, all cult believers, the legend is where identity began, somewhere in the deep Sahel, sometime within archaic time, and somehow within obscure recollections. Today, collective legends, fragmented into multiple versions and episodes—the form and methodology of most legends and epic genres—still turn and return, con-

---

Bonnel de Mézières, "Recherches de l'emplacement de Ghana et sur le site de Takrour," *Academie des Inscriptions et des Belles Lettres, Mémoires*, vol. 13, no. 1 (Paris, 1920): 227–273.

11. Nehemia Levtzion and J. F. P. Hopkins, eds., *Corpus of early Arabic sources for West Africa* (Cambridge University Press, 1981), pp. 7, 45, 79–87. For Ibn Khaldun also see Levtzion and Hopkins, *Corpus*, pp. 332–333; Mauny, *Tableau géographique*, pp. 24–30, 72–74; Pollet and Winter, *La Société soninké*, pp. 25–28. For a full discussion of the decline of Ghana [Wagadu, Kumbi], see Conrad and Fisher, "The Conquest," parts 1 and 2.

12. There are seventeen versions of the "Legend of Wagadu," five of which were recorded before 1900, and seven between 1900 and 1925; five were recorded between 1950 and 1975. See, for example, L. J. B. Bérénger-Féraud, *Les Peuplades de Sénégambie* (Paris, 1879); Tautain, "Légende et traditions," pp. 471–480; Charles Monteil, "La Légende du Ouagadou et l'origine des Soninké," *Mélanges ethnographiques*, Mém. 23 (Paris, 1953), pp. 361–408; R. Arnaud, "La Singulière légende des Soninké: Traditions orales sur le royaume de Koumbi et sur divers autres royaumes soudanais," in R. Arnaud, *L'Islam et la politique musulmane française en Afrique occidentale française* (Paris, 1911), pp. 144–185; M. G. Adam, "Légendes historiques du pays de Nioro," *Revue Coloniale* (1903), pp. 81–98, 232–248, 354–372, 485–496, 602–620, 734–744; (1904), pp. 117–124, 232–248, republished as a brochure (Paris Challamel, 1904), 123 pages; H. C. Lanrezac, "Au Soudan: La Légende historique," *La Revue Indigène* (1907), pp. 292–296, 380–386, 420–430; Maurice Delafosse, "Traditions historiques et légendaires du Soudan occidental traduites d'un manuscrit arabe," *Bulletin du Comité de l'Afrique Française, Renseignements Coloniaux.* (hereafter BCAFRC) (1913), vol. 8: 293–306; vol. 9: 325–329; vol. 10: 355–368. Also Chapter 1, note 32 of this book.

textualizing and recontextualizing in Mande historical and ethnographic imaginations.[13]

Dispersed from Wagadu sometime around the end of the first millennium—by a complex series of little-understood circumstances[14]—all the families later migrated throughout the western Sudan, Ja in the Massina being a major dispersal point (see Map 3). Their vast population movements have filled the better part of the present millennium. While families forming the focus of the story settled mainly west of the Niger River (Republic of Mali), most others dispersed into the far corners of the western Sudan, from the Senegambia in the west to the Volta River in the east, and from the Mali-Mauritania border in the north to the Cote d'Ivoire in the south, as well as parts of northern Ghana, Liberia, Sierre Leone, and Guinea.[15] In creating the historical "Mande world," a vast cultural crucible about the approximate size of the southeastern United States (Arizona, Texas, Oklahoma, and New Mexico combined), variable cultural indicators such as regional dialects and material cultures have textured large sections of western Africa's cultural maps (see Maps 4 and 5).[16]

---

13. See, for example, Meillassoux, "Histoire," pp. 186–227; interview Seydou Niaré (Bamako, 3–4 Jan. 1980). For other sources on further cultural manipulations see Chapter 1 herein.

14. Levtzion, *Ancient Ghana*, chap. 3 and passim. For criticisms, see Conrad and Fisher, "The Conquest," part 1, pp. 21–59; part 2, pp. 53–78; Sheryl L. Burkhalter, "Listening for silences in Almoravid history: Another reading of 'The Conquest that never was,'" *HA*, vol. 19 (1992): 103–131.

15. For Mande dispersals see, for example, B. Marie Perinbam, "Notes on Dyula origins and nomenclature," *BIFAN*, sér. B, vol. 36, no. 4 (1974): 680–689; Pollet and Winter, *La Société soninké*, pp. 19–34; Tauxier, *Histoire*, pp. 27–68; Monteil, *Les Bambara*, pp. 3–118; Jean-Loup Amselle, *Logiques métisses: Anthropologie de l'identité en Afrique et ailleurs* (Paris, 1990), pp. 119–147; Djibril Tamsir Niane, *Histoire des Mandingues de l'ouest: Le royaume du Gabou* (Paris, 1989), pp. 46–47; Emile Leynaud and Youssouf Cissé, *Paysans malinké du Haut Niger* (Edition Imprimerie Populaire; Bamako, 1979), pp. 17–37; Mamadou Diawara, *La Graine de la parole: Dimension sociale et politique des traditions orales du royaume de Jaara (Mali) du XVème au milieu du XIXème siècle* (Stuttgart, Frantz Steiner Verlag Stuttgart, 1990), pp. 21–31.

16. B. Marie Perinbam, "The Juulas in western Sudanese history: Long-distance traders and developers of resources," in B. K. Swartz and Raymond E. Dumett, eds., *West African culture dynamics: Archaeological and historical perspectives* (Mouton, 1980), pp. 458–460; *Idem.*, "Notes on Dyula," pp. 680–689; George E. Brooks, "Ecological perspectives on Mande population movements, commercial networks, and settlement patterns from the Atlantic wet phase (ca. 5500–2500 b. c.) to the present," *HA*, vol. 16 (1989): 23–40. See also notes 15, 20 of this Introduction.

Migrating in tri-partite corporate groups of *horon* or free lineages—mainly "animist" horse-warriors and their *nyamakalaw* or specialized lineages —slaves and other "minors" (mainly women and children), formed the third element in the tri-partite lineage organization. Families of Islamized traders and clerics frequently accompanied these dispersing groups.[17] Not moving in vast hordes, not in migratory waves either, and certainly not always moving, most migrations involved relatively small groups of families often extending across generations, sometimes even centuries. Families or lineage members splitting off from main groups, not uncommonly, established their own temporary—sometimes even permanent—village communities. Few migrations self-consciously conformed to exquisitely filigreed long or short-term plans. Most eventually involved rational choices in the face of practical and/or political exigencies.

However, despite pragmatic considerations producing socially fluid dynamics, the families' lives mainly followed rhythms established according to well known customary laws, traditions, belief systems, legends and myths, including those regional-cultural derivatives defining daily lives. The integrity of dominant norms therefore remained intact— even if changing across transforming centuries—as did age and gender constructs, together with social obligations and reciprocities. Thus, for example, families within the migratory process found time to fight wars, seek and obtain political power, exchange brides, birth babies, bring harvests in, trade local and foreign commodities, bury the dead, and honor the ancestors. They also found time for important ritual observances reinforcing and re-articulating their corporate identities. By way of contrast, relatively fast-paced migrations occurred more often in the wake of wars, civil disturbances, and hostile or unhealthy eco-systems, not to mention the unrelenting droughts and famines sometimes plaguing Sahelian landscapes.

Contextualizing the Story

The Historicized Mande Identity

For readers having come this far, it should be clear from the family *jamuw* (sing.: *jamu*), or patronyms, the tri-partite social organization,

---

17. For tri-partite and *nyamakala* Mande groups see below. See also George E. Brooks, *Landlords and strangers: Ecology, society, and trade in Western Africa, 1000–1630* (Westview Press, 1993), see esp. chap. 2. For Mande *nyamakala* see David C. Conrad and Barbara E. Frank eds., *Status and identity in West Africa: Nyamakala of Mande* (Indiana University Press, 1995).

and the dispersals outlined above, that this story is ultimately about Mande identities.[18] It should also be clear that much of what we know—or think we know—about Mande signs derives from myths, legends, and fluid oral traditions with porous boundaries that not only particularize substantively and chronologically, but also regionally and generationally. Contextualizing the Mande identity within a historical paradigm may therefore seem wrong-headed. I risk this historicization, nonetheless, not because empirical certainties define the field (they do not), but because Mande myths and legends became the lenses through which families ultimately mediated their identities, configured their dominant norms, and negotiated their world views, including a historical consciousness and perceptions, not to mention their social and political action. Historicizing these cardinal action-and-belief signs therefore seemed important.

Thus, we find (with the help of linguistic data) that after leaving Wagadu—the principal "sign" of the Mande identity and the original dispersal point—many families migrated to Ja (Dia, Diaka, Diagha), a secondary sign and dispersal point situated in the middle Niger's Massina (see Maps 3 and 4). Accordingly, as Wagadu was the first, so did Ja become the second signifier in the universal Mande identity: Claiming Wagadu and Ja as ancestral homelands became an authenticating principle in the universal Mande identity. Beyond the Wagadu-Ja signifiers, other families constructed equally remote identities associated with other Sahelian oases, such as the Saharan Walata and Tichit oases, aligned in oral accounts with the Nono, an archaic and obscure Soninke ethnic configuration. Still others traced identities to Tawat in the Algerian Sahara, even as far north as the Dra'a valley in southern Morocco.

Leaving these universal Saharan-Sahelian signs behind, we know that by about the eleventh century, very likely by the late fourteenth and early fifteenth centuries, several "animist" horse-warriors, and *numuw*, or blacksmith lineages, together with families espousing Islamized identities, dispersed farther south up the Niger and east toward the Black Volta River and Akan gold fields (see Maps 3 and 4).[19] Even today, many of these eastern families, whose ancestors settled in non Mande communi-

---

18. The Mande identity not only includes those who speak the language cluster which Charles Bird referred to as "Mandekan" (Bamana-Maninka-Jula (Dyula)-Mandinka-Dafin), but also speakers of the Southwestern and Southeastern Subgroups. For references and further discussion, see below.

19. As families migrated, regional dialects developed probably sometime during or after the fourteenth century (Perinbam, "Notes," pp. 680–689). For more on regional Mande dialects see notes 26, 35–38 and below.

ties, and whose cultures and identities have since been particularized in accordance with local ethnographic considerations, still trace a remote identity to Wagadu-Ja, the universal Saharan and Sahelian signs.[20]

Possibly sometime in the late fourteenth century, similar tri-partite families with Saharan and Sahelian identities dispersed south into upper Guinea, founding particularized Mande *kafuw*, or states, such as Kono and Kuranko (see Map 2).[21] By the late fifteenth century, similar families with a Saharan-Sahelian consciousness, and comparable historical imaginations, dispersed to Jaxaba (Diakaba) on the Bafing River in the Senegambia, developing particularized markets, or mercantile centers. Here, they exchanged ores from the nearby Bambuhu and Bure gold mines for food and other exchange commodities. In competition with Jaxaba, similar clans with clerical and mercantile associations developed Gajaaga (Gadiaga) on the Senegal River.[22] By the late fifteenth century, other Mande-speaking clans with a Saharan-Sahelian awareness were migrating eastward to Hausaland. Although in many instances thoroughly particularized, having even lost their Mande language, several families preserved ideologies of an archaic Wagadu identity.[23]

By the sixteenth century, Mande-speaking clans with Saharan-Sahelian signifiers, as well as Islam (in some instances), migrated into Mossi settlements in Yatenga (during the administration of Na Yedega), where they developed particularized trading centers such as Grusi. Finally, between the sixteenth and eighteenth centuries, "animist" horse-warrior lineages, together with Islamized clans dispersed into parts of the Cote d'Ivoire, such as Kong, as well as Sierre Leone, Liberia and Guinea. By the eighteenth century, therefore, Mande families, Islamized or otherwise, with Saharan-Sahelian identities (particularized for the most part) were reconfiguring the cultural templates and cosmological maps of the Mande world as we know it (see Maps 3 and 5).

Sometimes co-residing, at other times resident in neighboring locations, patterned settlements identifying "animist" and "Islamic" locations further particularized the Mande world's cultural landscapes (see Map 6). Not that identity-locations were polarized or unmistakably differentiated one from the other. They were not: But for mosques rising above savanna

---

20. B. Marie Perinbam, "The Political organization of traditional gold mining: the western Loby, c. 1850 to c. 1910," *JAH*, vol. 29 (1988): 437–462.

21. Perinbam, "Notes," pp. 681–684.

22. Perinbam, "Notes," pp. 681–684; Brooks, *Landlords*, see esp. chaps. 3, 4, 6.

23. Heinrich Barth (1850s) was among the first to draw this phenomenon to our attention (Heinrich Barth, *Travels and discoveries in north and central Africa 1848–1855*, 3 vols. [New York, 1965], vol. 3, pp. 111).

landscapes, few other clues differentiated "animist" from "Islamized" communities (see Chapter 2). Given this caveat it is however worth noting that historical articulations between highly visible "animist" identities, and those more conspicuously, or self-consciously "Islamized" were not only regionally differentiated, but also ideographically negotiated, or aligned with local configurations. For example, west and southwest of the Niger River (scene of large-scale migrations), where Islamized Mande families established *dunanw*, or stranger settlements within or alongside their "animist" counterparts, regional cultural and dialect particularizations tended to be less marked, overall Islamized (Mande) cultures more hegemonic. East and southeast of the Niger, on the other hand, especially in Yatenga, Wagadugu, the Black Volta and Akan regions, as well as in Northern Nigeria, very different cultural patterns emerged. Here, where Mande population densities were lower in relation to "animist" and non-Mande autochthones—or so it seems—a far wider range of identity signs and dialect differentials configured the eastern cultural maps. It goes without saying that within this vast east-west and north-south *jaman'a*, overall dialect differentiations and cultural particularizations were important cultural signifiers.[24]

Other factors at work within the *jaman'a's* social and ideological crevices, were also rendering the social field even more prismatic. Important among these was the presence of Fulbe families, mainly herders, who co-existed alongside Mande communities resident throughout the Mande world. In the wake of generational Mande-Fulbe intermarriages, Mande dialects, identities, and social signifiers differentiated still further in juxtaposition to the Fufulde-speakers (West Atlantic language) (see Map 7).[25] Similarly important were marriages and sacred alliances concluded with Islamized desert-side "Moors" from Tawat, who had settled in the Bamako *kafu* and the Mande world. Accordingly, Mande dialects and social identities mediated still further, as identities twisted, turned, shifted and changed in order to domesticate Fulbe and "Moorish" practices and norms, including their regionalized forms of Islam. In the Bamako *kafu*, a particularized corner of the vast Mande world, marriages and sacred alliances concluded with Bamana-speakers (a Mandekan language) differ-

24. Perinbam, "Notes," pp. 681–684; Perinbam, "The Political organization," pp. 437–462.

25. Personal communication Jean Bazin (Bamako, 9 March 1983); *ASAOF* 1G 32, "Mission Mage et Quintin: Eugène Mage à M. le Gouverneur" (Saint Louis, 21 June 1866). See also *ASAOF* 1G 2, "Voyage à Timbo par Monsieur Hecquard, 1848–1851 addressé au Monsieur le Gouveurneur," p. 14; Louis Binger, *Du Niger au Golfe de Guinée*, 2 vols. (Paris, 1892), vol. 2, p. 382. See also Chap. 1 and passim.

entiated the *kafu*'s cultural contours still further, rendering them even more prismatic.[26] Eventually, Bamako's cultural contours were aligned more specifically with the mythical-political rituals of the hegemonic Kulibaly Segovian (Bamana) state of the middle Niger (c. 1650–1861).

Finally, complicating the story further—by way of background—were the Islamic movements of the latter part of the nineteenth century, when Mande cultural landscapes came under the sword of a coercive Islam. Generally known, and widely discussed in the literature elsewhere, the first reformist *jihad* was launched by the Umarians under the authority of al-Hajj Umar Tall al-Tijani (c. 1794/96–1864), the Tukulor *shaykh* from the Futa Toro.[27] The second reformist *jihad* brought the Samorian armies under the leadership of Samory Ture (c. 1830-1900), the Mande-speaking warrior-*imam* from Konyan in Guinea and Bissandugu in the Wassulu, to within one day's journey from the Bamako *kafu*.[28] Both launching *jihads* against the "animist" and the "infidel," their imperial sub-text was signed in the name of Allah, his Prophet and the holy Koran. The wars in the end causing unbelievable suffering—not to mention loss of life and property—left sadness and grief in their cacophonous wake. As large populations turned towards the Islamic inventory of beliefs, rituals, and practices, it goes without saying that the nineteenth-century reformist *jihads* complicated the "animist-Islamic" cultural field even more (see Map 6).

In sum, wherever they settled, tri-partite Mande families remembering a larger Saharan-Sahelian heritage, not only identified with particularized signifier dialects and cultural idioms developing in their local regions, but they also identified with particularized states, civilizations and historical markers throughout the larger Mande world. Most, at one

---

26. Mandekan, according to Charles Bird, is a division of the Mande Northern Subgroup consisting of Bamana, Maninka, Mandinka, Jula (Dyula) and Dafin. See Charles S. Bird, "The Development of Mandekan (Manding): A study of the role of extra-linguist factors in linguistic change," in David Dalby, ed., *Language and history in Africa* (London, 1970), pp. 146–159; David Dalby, "The People and their language," in *Manding: Focus on an African civilization*, prepared for the Conference of Manding Studies, School of Oriental and African Studies (London, 1972), pp. 4, 7; Charles S. Bird, ed., *The Dialects of Mandekan* (Indiana University Press, 1982); see also *Ta'rikh al-Fattash*, p. 65, note 2. For an alternate terminology suggested by Valentin Vydrine, see "Who speaks 'Mandekan'?": A note on current use of Mande ethnonyms and linguonyms," *MANSA*: Newsletter of the Mande Studies Association, no. 23 (Winter, 1995–1996): 6–9.

27. See, for example, David Robinson, *The Holy war of 'Umar Tal: The western Sudan in the mid-nineteenth century* (Clarendon Press, 1985).

28. For the most comprehensive study of Samory Ture see Person, *Samori*, 3 vols.

time or another, resided as vulnerable *dunanw* (strangers) in "foreign," or even "animist" jurisdictions.

Despite this fragmentation of the universal into the particular, overall signs of a hegemonic culture endured in one form or another. Thus, by about the eighteenth century, signs of the more recent Mande world (i.e., post Wagadu-Ja) were as important to dispersed Mande-speakers as the earlier cultural indicators had been, these latter now transformed and transferred from one cultural field into another. It is also likely that the more recent signs (e.g., differentiated dialects, Islam and so forth) were as important to literate, cosmopolitan, and Islamized communities as to "animist" believers venturing no farther than thirty kilometers beyond a natal village. In addition were the *jo* power associations, especially their associated *komo* rituals (allowing for regional particularizations), both post-Wagadu signifiers of an authentic Mande identity.[29] Other universal criteria included ethnographic parsings of the great droughts and migrations, of wars fought and the Mande style of fighting them. Additional universal signs included political-ritualized marriage alliances, as well as Mande prohibitions (*tana*), and the *senankun*, the "joking relationship," really a hostility-friendship type of bonding, to mention but a few of these universal rituals.[30] Patronyms from the Mande repertoire of family names were likewise enduring universal signifiers. In fact, if some families came to share the same patronyms, it was sometimes the result of ritual alliances, which had conjugated them into "equivalencies." Among others, their *jamuw* were interchangeable, or equivalent. Not surprisingly, therefore, numerous families in these increasingly complex cultures answered to the same, similar, or related *jamuw*, even while remaining different and separate. For example, due to ritual alliances, in some instances including the *tana* and the *senankun*, some Keita families also answered to *Konate*, and some Jakite to *Kaba*; other Jakite responded to *Bari*.[31] Additional universal name-equivalencies included Kaba/Kamakakha, Ture/Drave, Ture/Samake, Koyta/Makallu, and

---

29. For a general discussion of the *komo* rituals, see Henri Labouret, "Les Manding et leur langue," *BCEHSAOF*, vol. 17 (Jan. 1934): 43–143, see esp. pp. 81–85.

30. For *tana* (pl.: *tanaw*), and *senankun, sanankun,* or *sinankun* (Bamana); *senankuya* (Maninka or Mandinka) see Chapters 1 and 3 where I discuss these ritualized relationships in greater detail.

31. The Jakite were Mande (Soninke), Tukulor, and Fulbe, especially in the Khassonke regions (i.e., all three). It is the Soninke Jakite who were *Kaba*, and the Fulbe-Tukulor Jakite who were *Bari*. In some regions the salutation for a Kaba and a Bari was also *Jakite*.

Jiop/Dembele/Traore. And if some Ture *numuw* lineages answered to *Dukure*, other Ture responded to *Drave*, some N'Diaye to *Jara*, possibly some Traore to *Kone* and so forth.[32]

Also configuring universal signifiers for the post-Wagadu Mande communities were social forms of organization. Principal among these were the tri-partite lineage formations—*horonw* (free men or horse-warriors), *nyamakalaw* (specialized lineages, also free men), and slaves (*wolosow* and *jonw*). Universal ideologies endorsed these social signs. All would have known, for example, that only *horonw* could appropriately establish a lineage, and that lineage formation was disallowed to *wolosow* and *jonw*. Or, that *nyamakalaw* were endogamous. Or, that political systems were legitimized and authenticated only after appropriate ritualization, and only after cosmic balances between the terrestrial and human; or the universal and the spiritual, had been realized. Or, that commerce was closely identified with the Islamized identity; and that stable gender relations relied on a powerful salt-gold alchemy.[33]

Finally, although fragmented by regional differentiations, particularisms, and ideographic parsings, over-arching Mande dialects reinforced Mande collective and universal identities to the extent that Mande dialects are today spoken by millions in approximately nine West African states (see Map 5).[34] Classified as sub-families of the larger Niger-Kordofanian language group (including, for example, the Niger-Congo and West Atlantic languages), Mande dialects are subdivided into: (a) the Northern Subgroup, of which the Mandekan languages are a part (e.g., jula (Dyula)/Bamana) (see Map 4);[35] (b) the Southwestern

---

32. *Archives Nationales Section Outre-Mer* (hereafter *ANSOM*) B1667, L.G. Binger, *Carnets de route*, annotés et commentés par Jacques Binger, René Bouvier et Pierre Deloncle (Paris, 1938), pp. 88–89. For further equivalencies see Chapter 1 and passim. *Jamuw* often became the same, and yet different, when they were translated from one language to the other without changing the meaning (Interview Ali Ongoïba [Kuluba-Bamako, 7 March 1983]).

33. *Wolosow* were slaves "born in the household"; *jonw* were usually trade slaves. Patrick McNaughton, *The Mande blacksmiths: Knowledge, power, and art in West Africa* (Indiana University Press, 1988), see esp. Chapter 1; and Brooks, *Landlords*, see esp. pp. 39–57; B. Marie Perinbam, "The Salt-gold alchemy in the eighteenth and nineteenth century Mande world: If men are its salt, women are its gold," *HA*, vol. 23 (1996): 1–21; Perinbam, "Notes," pp. 680–689; Perinbam, "The Juulas," pp. 458–460.

34. In 1993 more than fifty percent of Mali's population of about eight million were Mande-speakers.

35. Languages in the Northern Subgroup include Soninke (Sahelian zone and oases, Mauritania, and Mali); Susu/Jallonke/Yalunka (coastal region of Guinea-

Subgroup (e.g., Kpelle/Guerze);[36] (c) and the Southeastern Subgroup (e.g., Kweni/Guro).[37] All families in this story belonged to the Mandekan (Northern Mande) language group.[38]

This reconstruction of the hegemonic Mande identity as both universal and particular is instructive if only because similar particularized-within-the-universal templates have developed elsewhere. In his discourse on an anthropology of Islam in Korhogo (northeastern Cote d'Ivoire), Robert Launay found a similar particularized-universal phenomenon: There was no "pure" Islam at the end of the teleological rainbow extending from "pagan" to "Muslim," believers' contestations to the contrary. Instead, when embedded into "foreign" cultures, such as those of Korhogo on the periphery of the Islamic world, standard practices of the so-called global or universalizing Islam became particularized in conjunction with the host culture, transformed, in the process, into signs that were the same yet different. Thus, there was not one, but many Islams coexisting historically from Morocco to Indonesia. Binding these particularized Islamic manifestations, Launay argued, was the universalizing discourse defined by the Islamic calendar. More importantly, sealing the universal-particularized circle was the combined yet separate faith—or legal fiction—that particularized members within the Korhogo community alone possessed the pure Islam, all others blighted and standing in ignorance.[39]

As this discourse has shown, a similar—yet different, separate and more complex—calculus mediated the Mande universalism and its regional particularisms. For centuries, the two moving visions coexisted in Mande ethnographic perceptions, collective consciousness and historical imaginations. Likewise for centuries those within the particular believed

---

Conakry and northern Sierre Leone); Vai/Kono (eastern Sierre Leone and southwestern Liberia); Mandekan—subdivided into Mandinka, Maninka including Kuranko, and Bamana (spoken in the West African savanna and savanna-woodlands from the Atlantic to the Volta River)—also includes Jula (Dyula: spoken mainly in the Cote d'Ivoire), and Dafin.

36. Other languages in the Southwestern Group include Loma/Toma; Gbandi, Gbundi (Liberia); Mendi (Sierre Leone).

37. Languages in the Southeastern Group include Busa (northwestern Nigeria); Bisa, Samo, Sya (Burkina Faso); Mwa, Nwa, Kweni/Guro, Dan/Gio (central Cote d'Ivoire); Mano (north- central Liberia).

38. See footnote no. 26. See also Dalby, ed., *Language*, pp. 146–159; Dalby, "The People," pp. 4, 7; Bird, ed., *The Dialects*; see also *Ta'rikh al-Fattash*, p. 65, note 2.

39. Robert Launay, *Beyond the stream: Islam and society in a West African town* (Berkeley, University of California Press, 1992).

that they possessed the universal. Across the ages, Mande social action owed much to these signifiers of belief and action.

Spatializing Identity Signs

The Bamako Kafu

As Mande identities particularized within the universal paradigm, spatial extensions mirrored their signs. In other words, as the families elaborated their Mande identities, the manner and location of settlement sites became an enlargement of both the localized and the universal Mande identity. Even the flora and fauna were incorporated into these image-maps.

Principal among the particularized regions in our story is the Bamako *kafu* and its immediate environs, falling approximately within 11.50 and 13 degrees north latitude, and roughly 7.50 to 9.00 degrees west longitude (see Map 1). Prior to the 1880s, overall *kafu* populations approximated 4,000 to 5,000 souls. "Signed" by wooded savannas of cultural significance, among the flora identified as "Mande" were the fronded baobab, tamarind, and karite significant for their culinary ingredients, as well as the diala, or cailcedra, known for their medicinal properties. Likewise signing the Bamako and Mande regions were the flaming balansan, or acacia, an indication of political intrigue, people say, as well as the nere (or nete) trees. "Wherever the so (karite) trees grow," people also say, "there lies the Manding," land of Mansa Musa.[40] Settled in between, villages acquired spatial and architectural forms which French colonial administrators later identified as "in the Mande style" (see Chapters 2, 3).

In addition to the Niare (rulers of the *kafu*), as well as the Drave and the Ture (who further "signed" the Bamako *kafu* region with their mosques and market places), other signifier families in the Bamako region included the warrior Jara of the Manding Plateau and the near-by Beledugu, the warrior Kulibaly and Dembelle from Segu, the Konate from Khasso, and the Keita from the old Mande (see Map 3). Also among signifier families were the Fulbe marked in popular imaginations by their herding skills and animals. Many, clients of regional

---

40. The baobab *(Adansonia digitata)*; tamarind *(Tamarindus indica)*; the karite *(Butyro spermum parkii, Bassia parkii)*; diala/cailcedra *(Swietenia Mahogoni* and *S. Macrophylla)*; balansan/acacia *(Acacia albida)*. See also Djibril Tamsir Niane, "Mise en place des populations de l'Haute-Guinée," *Recherches Africaines: Etudes Guinéennes* no. 2 (1960): 40–53.

Mande lords, included the Jakite, the Sidibe, and the Sangare from the Wassulu, as well as the Jallo, the Ba, the Bari, and the So families from the Futa Jallon.[41] Later incorporated by colonial administrators into the "Bamako Circle," this signed region varied in size from approximately 10,657 square kilometers in the 1880s (slightly smaller than the U.S. state of Connecticut) to roughly 35,000 square kilometers in 1902/04.[42] Between about the 1880s and 1920, overall populations in the Bamako Circle numbered about 160,000 inhabitants distributed in approximately 400 to 500 villages including autonomous and semi-autonomous communities.[43]

The Mande-Hinterland

Beyond the Bamako *kafu*, extending further into the *jaman'a* was the "Mande-hinterland," a larger more varied unit equally signed by the savanna's wooded flora (see Map 5). Including parts of the Kaarta, as well as the Outer and Inner Beledugu (what the French called the "Grand" and "Petit Beledougou"), it was said that at the sight of the acacia or the baobab, desert-side herders descending from the north knew when they had reached the land of the Kulibaly, the Konare, the

---

41. *ASAOF* 1G 79, Conrard, "Notice" (Bamako, 21 Feb. 1885), pp. 2, 4; *ANSOM* Sén. et Dép. IV Doss. 90 Bis, François Vallière, "Expansion territoriale et politique indigène, 1887–1888: Mémoire du Cercle de Bammako" (Siguiri, 15–25 March 1888), pp. 36–40.

42. Although administrative frontiers were first organized in 1883 and 1884–1885, the Bamako Circle was officially created in 1888 by Louis-Frédéric Tautain, Commandant le Cercle de Bamako. Frontiers were reorganized between 1895 and 1899, the latter by Colonel de Trentinian, Lieutenant-Governor at Bamako (1895–1899), who played an important role in the reorganization of the western Sudan in 1899. The 10,657 square kilometers given above is Valliere's (*ANSOM* IV Sén. et Dép. Doss. 90 Bis, Vallière, "Mémoire" [Siguiri, 15–25 March 1888], pp. 1–55, see esp. p. 34). In 1884 the Circle was estimated at 50,000 square kilometers (*ASAOF* 15G 83, Ruault, "Généralités 1880 à 1920: Affaires politiques et administratives Affaires diverses, 1880–1886" [Bamako, 22 Feb. 1884], p. 8). In 1894–1895 the Circle was 35,000 square kilometers (*ASAOF* 1G 299, Brévié, "Monographie" [Bamako, 25 April 1904], p. 36; see also *ANMK* 1D 33 2, Collomb, "Notice" [Bamako, 1884-1885] p. 1; see also note 44 herein).

43. Population estimates within the Circle varied considerably. In 1920 there were about 250,000 inhabitants grouped into nearly 500 villages. *ASAOF* 1G 351, Bobichon, "Note sur le Cercle de Bamako établie par l'Administrateur en Chef Bobichon, Commandant le Cercle" (Bamako, 24 Feb. 1920), pp. 9–10; *ANMK* 1D 33 5, Borgnis Desbordes, "Bamako hier-aujourd'hui et demain," n.d. (This is an edited updated document).

Jara, and the Traore, powerful families with agriculturalist and horse-warrior identities; or that they were within a reasonable radius of the clerical Sylla and Sisse, or the maraboutic and trading Nyakate, Jakite and Dukure. Likewise within the Mande-hinterland was Segu, chiefly realm of the powerful Biton (Mamari) Kulibaly, signed by the ubiquitous acacia trees (see Map 2). Farther south were the northeast Marka towns of Banamba, Tuba, Kerowane, and Kiba, signed by mosques and market places, as well as the trading cities of the Sylla, the Sakho, and the Dukure. Still farther south, the old Mande and its Bambuhu-Bure gold fields—signed by the so (karite) trees—were penultimate icons in the Mande cosmology that travelers had reached the land of the Keita, the Camara, the Kante, and the Sissoko families. To the southeast was the Wassulu, land of the Jakite, the Bari, and the Sangare (see Map 3). Overall, the Mande-hinterland was the approximate spatial equivalent of the U.S. states of Virginia and North Carolina combined.[44]

The Mande World

Circling, while simultaneously leaning into the Mande-hinterland, was the Mande world, the approximate size of Arizona, Texas, Oklahoma, and New Mexico combined in the U.S. scale (see Map 5). Less signed as a Mande ideal—despite hundreds of families with remote Wagadu-Ja identities—this region was imposing in its spatial composition, and immensely varied in its cultural and linguistic articulations. Still somewhat recognizable, however, were Mande dialects and tripartite family organizations, as well as the variable *jo* mythical-political rituals. Also recognizable were some Mande *jamuw*, or patronyms, but with a difference. Because, while some Ture in Bamako and the Mande-hinterland were Mande-speakers, in Timbuktu (where the Songhai language is widely spoken) most Ture were Songhai; and while the Keita were Maninka in the Mande, and Bamana in the Segu heartland, in Timbuktu many too were Songhai. By that same token, if the Traore were Bamana in the Bamako region, most were Songhai in Timbuktu. Or again, while in Nioro (where there are large Soninke populations) the Sisse were Soninke, in the Massina (where many Fulbe resided)

44. *ANMK* 1D 33 2, Collomb, "Notice" (Bamako, 1884–1885), p. 1; *ANSOM* Sén. et Dép. IV Doss. 90 Bis, Gallieni and Vallière, "Délimitation des Cercles du Soudan français, Bafoulabé" (1 May 1888), pp. 1–3; *ANSOM* IV Sén. et Dép. Doss. 90 Bis, Vallière, "Mémoire" (Siguiri, 15–25 March 1888), pp. 6–36; *ASAOF* 1G 79, Conrard, "Notice" (Bamako, 21 Feb. 1885), pp. 2–3.

most Sisse were Fulbe; and if in the Kita region the Fofana were Soninke, in the middle Niger many were Bozo. In the Kaarta the Dukure were Soninke, in Banamba, Marka.[45]

Despite the vastness and variety of the Mande world, it is interesting to note that within this tri-partite spatial-cultural dynamic, articulating identities were incubated mainly in small, yet cosmopolitan worlds.[46] Bamako's relatively small population (approximately 4,000–5,000 prior to the 1880s), for example, was not unusual for many upper Niger communities,[47] likewise comparable (in the 1880s and 1890s) to Bobo-Julasso (Burkina Faso) with 3,000–4,000 inhabitants, Bonduku (Cote d'Ivoire) with 2,500–3,000, Odienne (Cote d'Ivoire), and Kankan (Guinea), both approximately 2,500–3,000. Similar estimates mark the neighboring Sikasso with about 4,000–5,000 inhabitants in 1889, about 40,000 ten years later attributable to a large refugee influx from the wars of Samory Ture, the jula-warrior-*imam* from the Konyan in Guinea (see Map 3). Not exactly bursting at the seams, Bamako's neighboring Beledugu, the most densely populated of all the Mande-hinterland, numbered between 70,000 and 100,000 inhabitants in 1888, grouped into about 40–50 *kafuw*. By way of comparison, beyond the Mande world were Kintampa (Ghana) and Salaga (Ghana) both with approximately 3,000 inhabitants. In the west, Goree housed approximately 4,000 people.[48]

---

45. See, for example, Charles Monteil, "Fin de siècle à Médine," *BIFAN*, sér. B, vol. 28, nos. 1–2 (1966): 82–172, esp. 90; Interview Alphidi Samounou (Jenne, 19 Nov. 1992); interview Ali Ongoïba (Kuluba-Bamako, 7 March 1983).

46. For a parallel shaping of the Islamic identity in relatively small communities see Nehemia Levtzion and Humphrey J. Fisher, *Rural and urban Islam in West Africa* (Boulder and London; Lynne Rienner, 1987), esp. pp. 1–20.

47. *ASAOF* 1G 79, Conrard, "Notice" (Bamako, 21 Feb. 1885), pp. 2, 4; *ANSOM* IV Sén. et Dép. Doss. 90 Bis, Vallière, "Mémoire" (Siguiri, 15–25 March 1888), pp. 36–40.

48. Population estimates very probably reflect inaccuracies. For Bobojulasso, Bonduku, Kintampa, Salaga, Sikasso, and Kong see *Archives Nationales du Ministère des Affaires Etrangères* (hereafter ANMAE), *Mém. et Doc., Sén. et Dép. 1890–1894*, vol. 123, Louis Binger, "Le Soudan français voyage du Capitaine Binger, 1887–1889, 'Le Temps'" (Paris, March 1890), pp. 68–69. See also Binger, *Du Niger*, vol. 1, p. 298; vol. 2, pp. 93, 162. For Kankan, see Djiba Diane, "Islam en Haute Guinée, 1900–1959," Thèse de Doctorat du Troisième Cycle, under the direction of Yves Person, Centre de Recherches Africaines (hereafter CRA) (Paris, 1979–1980), pp. 148–149. For Goree, and Saint Louis see *ANMAE Afrique et Colonies françaises 1780–1822*, vol. 11, "Extrait d'un Mémoire no. 93 ayant pour titre, 'Nouveau système au bien être et à la prosperité de la France par des avan-

Exceptions to the small Mande communities were middle Niger towns such as the cosmopolitan Segu-Sikoro with population estimates of 30,000 toward the latter part of the eighteenth century (Mungo Park, 1795/96), about 36,000 inhabitants in the 1860s (Mage 1867). Following Segu-Sikoro was Sinsani (Sansanding) housing between 30,000–40,000 residents (Mage 1867). West of Nyamina, Banamba numbered about 8,000–9,000 inhabitants.[49] By the nineteenth century, Jenne—already declining, wounded by the late eighteenth- and nineteenth-century wars with the Bamana Kulibaly state and the Fulbe Massina—was estimated by Caillie (1828) at 8,000–10,000 residents, smaller than Timbuktu (not a Mande town), which Oskar Lenz thought to house about 20,000–25,000 inhabitants in the 1880s (20,000–25,000 in the 1890s according to Binger), fluctuating between 8,000 and 11,000 (according to Felix Dubois in the 1890s), including Kabara its port and the city's floating population. Rivaling middle Niger entrepots was Kong (Cote d'Ivoire), a Black Volta town about 50 days' journey east of Bamako, which Binger (1889–1890) estimated at 15,000 inhabitants. In Senegal, Saint Louis was believed to house between 15,000 and 18,000 residents.[50]

---

tages réciproques, 1819,'" pp. 397–398. For a further discussion of Bonduku, see B. Marie Perinbam, "Perceptions of Bonduku's contribution to the western Sudanese gold trade: An assessment of the evidence," *HA*, vol. 13 (1986): 295–322.

49. Mungo Park, *The Travels of Mungo Park* (London, 1907), p. 195. Mage later changed his Segu estimate to 10,000 men, making no mention of women and children. For Banamba and Segu, see Eugène Mage, *Relation du voyage d'exploration* (Paris, 1867), p. 100. For Sinsani, see Eugène Mage, "Épisode d'un voyage au pays de Ségou," *Bulletin de la Société de Géographie de Paris* (hereafter *BSGP*) (Jan.-June 1867), pp. 72–101, see esp. p. 77. On his second voyage (1805), Park estimated Sinsani at only 11,000 (*ANSOM* B4, C. A. Walckenaer, *Histoire générale des voyages, ou nouvelle collection des relations de voyages par mer et par terre*, 19 vols. [Paris, 1826–1830], vol. 14, pp. 1–88, "Observations de Mungo Park." p. 14).

50. For Jenne, see René Caillié, *Voyage à Tombouctou*, 2 vols. (Paris, 1985), vol. 2, p. 148; and Binger, *Du Niger*, vol. 1, p. 298, note 1; *ASAOF* 1G 90, Binger, "Télégramme au Commandant supérieur à Gouverneur à Saint Louis" (Kayes, 8 July 1888). Here, Binger estimated Kong's population at 10,000 inhabitants. See also Victor Diabaté, "La Région de Kong d'après les fouilles archéologiques: Prospection premiers sondages," Thèse de Doctorat de Troisième Cycle, under the direction of Jean Devisse, CRA (Paris, 1979), p. 2. For Saint Louis, see *ANMAE*, *1780–1822*, vol. 11, "Extrait d'un Mémoire 93 (1819)," p. 97. Timbuktu's population is difficult to evaluate as it fluctuated greatly. Oscar Lenz, "Voyage du Maroc au Sénégal," *BSGP*, vol. 1 (1881): 199–226, see p. 217; *ANMAE*, *1890–1894*, vol. 123, Binger, "Le Soudan français," pp. 68–69; Report from the Secretary Th. Hübler on Lenz's voyage, *Bulletin de la Société de Géographie Commerciale de Bordeaux* (here-

Although these population guesstimates indicate the relatively small communities within this tri-partite Mande paradigm, it is important to remember that most towns and villages (where the majority of Mande resided) were smaller than the above. From this perspective, therefore, the figures demonstrate our point: That Mande identities were for the most part forged in small communities.

Although relatively small, the paradox is that Mande family identities were also forged in relatively cosmopolitan environments. In fact, most towns and villages, including Bamako, attracted mixed populations: "stranger" merchants en route to markets or religious fetes, transients on pilgrimage to Mecca, itinerant scholars either imparting or seeking knowledge, as well as desert-side populations on their transhumant trajectories. Bringing news not only of political affairs, of wars, raids, or interrupted routes, they were also messengers of famine conditions, not to mention social news, perhaps even gossip. Not unusually, "strangers" came from as far afield as the Senegambia, the Upper and Lower Guinea coasts, Tichit on the desert-side, more rarely from Kong in the eastern Cote d'Ivoire.[51] And news did circulate. En route to the upper Niger both Mungo Park (1795–1797) and Rene Caillie (1827–1828) were frequently apprised of trading conditions and the regional wars interrupting their respective routes. In Khasso, Park's host confirmed Major Houghton's death (1791) in the Kaarta, and at Kinytakooro on the road from Bamako, his African adventures were repeated aloud for the benefit of curious audiences (who no doubt remembered and repeated them) at the "Bentang," the town's platform or place of public hearing. It should come as no surprise therefore to learn that some thirty years later, Caillie's interlocutor at Coloni, south of Jenne, "had already learned much of (him)." At Jenne, Caillie received confirmation of Major Alexander Gordon Laing's death north of Timbuktu the previous year. Laing had been in Africa, his interlocutor explained, to "write about the land." Not infrequently Mande travelers had a passable knowledge of English and French; some even "knew about Christians."[52] And according to administrator Ferdinand

---

after *BSGCB*), vol. 25 (1881), p. 208; Oscar Lenz, *Timbouctou: voyage au Maroc, au Sahara et au Soudan*, 2 vols., trans. Pierre Lehautcourt (Paris, 1886), vol. 2, p. 149; Felix Dubois, *Tombouctou la mystérieuse* (Paris, 1897), pp. 226, 302.

51. According to traditions, many Bamana-speakers (reaching Segu from the southeast, possibly the Kong region) maintained long-standing network and familial relationships with Kong. Personal communication Jean Bazin (Bamako, 9 March 1883).

52. Park, *The Travels*, pp. 64–73, 251 and passim; Caillié, *Voyage*, vol. 2, pp. 97–98, 104, 109, 111, 116, 136, 158 and passim; *ASAOF* 1G 32, "Lettre Mage à Gou-

Rougier, Banamba Resident in 1914, the esprit, or mind-set, of these strangers was often "open," "refined," and "complex."[53]

Finally, mixed eco-systems signed the tri-partite Mande regions. For example, if average regional temperatures during the latter part of the nineteenth century varied seasonally from 35 to 45° centigrade, in the Bamako *kafu* and Mande-hinterland regions, rainfall during the wet season from May to October was between 133–260 centimeters per year in the south, less than 50 centimeters in northern portions bordering the Sahel. A long period of low rainfall between c. 1000 and c. 1630 no doubt contributed to the families' epic migrations from Wagadu and the Sahel (discussed above).[54] Land, water, and mineral resources were also variable. Farmland was mainly latasolic interspersed with laterite that had been leached of salts and silica, the upper layers containing aluminum and iron oxides. Plaguing all three identity units were diseases and parasites, more problematic for the south, including the tsetse fly (*Glossina morsitans*; the parasite: *Trypanosoma rhodesiense*) bringing sleeping sickness and other trypanosome infections to humans and domestic animals.[55] Likewise degrading regional ecosystems were the anopheles mosquito, vector of the parasite causing malaria, as well as the mosquito (*Aedes aegypti*) transmitting yellow fever, and flies spreading river blindness, ticks carrying fevers in-

---

verneur" (Saint Louis, 21 June 1866); *ASAOF* 1G 52 46, Bayol, "Télégramme" no. 314 (Saint Louis, 25 June 1880); *ASAOF* 1G 50, Gallieni, "Mission du Haut Niger 1880: Analyse au sujet des agissements des Anglais dans le bassin du Haut-Niger" (Nango, 10 Sept. 1880), pp. 2, 3; *ASAOF* 1G 52 46, Dr. Jean-Marie Bayol, "Mission de Ségou, Gallieni et Bayol: Rapport sur le voyage au pays de Bamako" (Saint Louis, 5 July 1880); *ANSOM* B1667, Binger, *Carnets de route*, p. 27; Gallieni, *Voyage*, p. 242. See also Chapter 5 herein.

53. *ANMK* 1D 33 4, F. J. L. Rougier, "Enquête sur l'Islam dans le Cercle de Bamako, Residence de Banamba" (Banamba, 31 May 1914), p. 50. For other examples of news reaching the interior about Europeans, see, for example, Major William Gray and the late staff surgeon Dochard, *Travels in western Africa in the years 1818, 1819, 1820, and 1821, from the River Gambia, through Woolli, Bondoo, Galam, Kasson, Kaarta and Foolidoo to the River Niger* (London, 1825), pp. 340–344, and Chapter 5 of this book.

54. For a wide-ranging discussion of the immense repercussions and ramifications of these climate changes, see Brooks, *Landlords*, esp. pp. 7–25.

55. The 1,000-millimeter isohyet approximately delimits the northernmost range of the tsetse fly, vector for a variety of trypanosomes lethal to animals. Animals most commonly raised in the north were camels, horses, donkeys, sheep, and zebu cattle, best suited for the tsetse-free areas of the Sahel and Savanna. The smaller *ndama*, or West African shorthorn, resistant to the trypanosomes, was also raised in the north, although it could do just as well in the south (Brooks, *Landlords*, p. 12).

cluding leprosy, and worms transmitting bilharzia among other diseases. Locusts, although not as severe as those found elsewhere—for example, in parts of East Africa—could be a scourge on the land.

About the Book

Divided into five chapters with an Introduction and Conclusion, this book elaborates on the several changing aspects of the Mande identity discussed earlier. As indicated above, the Niare families from Wagadu—eventually Bamako—are the principal focus of the story. Using their mythic and historical parsings as the basis for a case study, I argue that as the families migrated throughout the western Sudan—and across several generations—familial identities shifted from Soninke at Wagadu; to Marka-Sarakolle at Segu; to Bamana at Bamako. In between were identity variations—including combinations difficult to determine—possibly involving the pastoralist Fulbe sharing ecosystems and cultural spaces in the Mande-hinterland, and the Bamako *kafu*. In the process, I argue that the Niare families in particular, the Mande families in general, negotiated and manipulated cultural forms—in accordance with identity changes—including myths, rituals, and kin groups.

Basing my data on oral texts and recollections, as well as on the anthropological, historical, and archaeological literature, Chapter 1 critically probes mythic and legendary data that best express the families' changing identities. With respect to the Niare, I analyze and decode identity, cultural, and ideological signs—particularized signifiers in fact—as well as modulations marking cultural landscapes across about 1,000 years, or thirty to thirty-five generations approximately. Important among these last were migrations, family-alliances, lineage reproduction, rituals, cults, social stratification, and war, inter alia. Also important were power relations with the state (Wagadu, Kingi, Segu) and the language repertoires of the politically powerful, especially Segu's Bamana rulers. Non-human factors—or seemingly so—likewise affected the form and function of identities, including phenomena such as climate changes, not impossibly good luck or bad. Finally anchoring their identity in a reconstructed and negotiated ethnographic past and historical imagination, the Niare conjured their oral texts, myths, recollections and rituals into a sacred guarantee of a collective identity.

The discourse of Chapter 2 addresses Mande collective identities—of which the Niare were a part: how these identities were historically constructed, elaborated, particularized and accordingly materialized. Relying once more on the anthropological and historical literature, on oral texts and recollections, as well as on related reporting, and archival data, I further analyze identities expressed as ideological Mande particularisms, including Islam. I moreover weigh the extent to which these ideologies—historicized and materialized—affected behavior, collective identities, and material production. With respect to Islam, I show how particularized Islams transformed thousands of families into the "Other," and all within a hierarchically ordered and articulating holography. Originating in the north and diffused by Islamized northerners, I call this the "northern paradigm." I ask what the paradigm meant as an indication of identity and behavior (as perceived), how it affected identity, behavior and social relationships (as believed), and how this ideological-cultural elaboration came to take on a hegemonic life of its own. Because the paradigm pejoratively applied to the south, the other half of the northern paradigm, I furthermore examine the north-south relational outcome, relating the paradigm to the south's poverty, as well as to its gold and slave trades. Finally, by historicizing the anthropology of the Niger river—and its ritual-political role in the development of earlier Sudanese states' systems—I discuss the extent to which the river's natural disposition, ironically, contributed to the impoverishment and otherizing of the southern Other.

Examining the internal organization of familial Mande states, their political theories and constitutional protocols, as well as their mythical-political rituals, Chapter 3 contextualizes the elaboration of the Bamako state as an expression of the *jaman'a*, or global Mande identity common to the Mande-hinterland and the Mande world. As part of the contextualization, I deal with internal affairs—to the extent that the data permit—of this frontier state in relation to metropolitan Segu. I clarify state mobilization and center-periphery relations articulating between Bamako, a semi-autonomous dependency, and its powerful Segovian metropolitan patron. As an important sub-text, I examine the place of the family in state elaboration, beginning with a paradigm suggested in colonial reporting that compared Mande familial states to the Roman concept of *civitas in parvo*: When the family provides the basis for state power and authority and state structural development, it becomes "the state in miniature." While arguing persuasively for the role of the family in state formation and subsequent elaborations I, nevertheless, find the Roman paradigm wanting. Instead, working with the Mande data I devise an analysis of a minimalist semi-autonomous familial state, not in the Segovian tradition of political organization and operation but, according to another colonial reporting, "in the Mande style."[56]

---

56. *ANSOM* Sén. et Dép. IV Doss. 90 Bis, Vallière, "Mémoire" (Siguiri, 15–25 March 1888), p. 37; *ANMK* 1D 33 2, Collomb, "Notice" (Bamako, 1884–1885), p. 3. I do not treat the Bamako *kafu* as the "segmentary state" as I find the concept inappropriate. I recognize, however, that working with similar types of states others

In Chapter 4, relying extensively on oral recountings and interviews, I unravel the process that brought Bamako's markets from a relatively isolated pre-eighteenth-century Bozo riverain camp, to one of the Sudan's principal markets by the first part of the twentieth century. Manipulating the more general commercial paradigms found throughout the Mande world, and discussed in the literature,[57] I show that development of the *kafu*'s markets was essentially the negotiated product of the Islamized families: Maraka, Sarakolle, Soninko, julaw and so on. In accomplishing these commercial objectives, both the "animist" and Islamized mercantile families combined their dual identities—articulating within a fragile power equation—with the political economy and domestic ideology of Bamako's "animist" political elites.

Based mainly on French archival sources, Chapter 5 narrates the last years of the *kafu*'s decline and the French arrival in Bamako on the morning of 1 February 1883. Returning more specifically to the question of perceptions, expectations, and images of the Other—of a very different sort from that discussed in Chapter 2—I show that in their initial encounters, both the French and their Mande interlocutors were the hapless victims of manipulated news networks and misconstrued cultural forms. The result: They hopelessly misunderstood each other. Initial encounters in the 1880s and 1890s hardly went beyond colossal barriers of miscommunications, misunderstandings and misinterpretations: the dialogue of the deaf.

In the Conclusion, I summarize earlier findings, most notably those signaling shifts in the Mande identity across time and space, and especially those most commonly aligned with cultural and symbolical repertoires found in archaic time. I argue moreover that the signs were reified in the ethnographic and historical imagination through multiple processes of cultural renegotiation and remanipulation against the critical backdrop of the radically innovative colonial state. In the process, the families confronted, contested, and in some instances finally domesticated their "French" identities. No signs, however, could or would have legitimated

---

have produced useful studies. See, for example, Aiden Southall, *Alur society* (Cambridge University Press, 1953); John Middleton and David Tait, eds., *Tribes without rulers: Studies in African segmentary systems* (London, 1958); Ronald Cohen and John Middleton, eds., *Comparative political systems: Studies in the politics of pre-industrial societies* (New York, 1967); Roy Willis, *A State in the making: Myth, history and social transformation in pre-colonial Ufipa* (Indiana University Press, 1981).

57. Perinbam, "Notes," pp. 680–689; Perinbam, "The Juulas," pp. 455–475; Philip D. Curtin, *Economic change in precolonial Africa: Senegambia in the era of the slave trade* (University of Wisconsin Press, 1975); Brooks, *Landlords*.

these changes had the process not been ritualized and coded—in a way "retro-written"—into the ancient mythical-ritual text. Thus, even in the early twentieth century, this ancient yet contemporary constitution—in one form or another—was still valid, vigorous, viable, and continuously variable.

Ritual and ritualized negotiations also became the sine qua non for the manipulation and authentication of the Niare Bamana identity, as well as the identities of other Mande-hinterland families. In further deliberating the importance of ritualization in this processually changing identity, I argue that, by the late nineteenth and early twentieth centuries, *meaning* in the Wagadu mythical-ritual inventory had suffered a sea change: Accepted in deep antiquity as the ultimate symbolism, the penultimate sacerdotal, and the transcendental transcendentalism, the mythical-ritual genre had elaborated into a moralizing text for social control by the late nineteenth and early twentieth centuries. Not that myths had been transformed into a blueprint for good behavior: They had not. Rather, it is that elaborating its sacerdotal content (what the myth meant to believers) to include a functional component (what the myth could do and say), the great epic Wagadu Legend also became by the late nineteenth and early twentieth century an instrument for social control, as well. The growing influence of Islam —especially the Wahhabiyya doctrines, in addition to the increasingly invasive experience of the colonizer—clearly played a part in reshaping the myth's changing meaning and controlling function. Thus did the new colonial state influence the families' identities, especially affecting youths and women, and especially in relation to the "Bambara" identity.

I likewise argue that, about the same time, the Wagadu myth was already being transformed into a metaphor for the liminality of the *rites de passage*. Propelling this mythic parsing were unexpected—and unacceptable—changes emerging in the wake of the secular French presence (after February 1883), bringing socio-cultural and political-economic ramifications, including a social and cultural invisibility, even a social and cultural nudity in the minds of some. And while ancient fundamental powers hemorrhaged from chiefly incumbents and former elites, *kafu* youths, even women more so, were being transposed from an erstwhile status— prescribed by lineage, gender, age, and so forth—into the ranks of those newly empowered through colonial state policies and the wage labor market. The era of the "grandfathers," "the old men" and their cultural and religious identities was passing; the age of the individualized man and woman in relation to the colonial state and wage-labor considerations had not yet dawned. Hence the parallels with the *rites de passage*, liminality, and the *via negativa*, on the one hand, and the need for social controls, on the other. The distortions, tensions, ironies, and contradictions must have been unbearable.

Theoretical Paradigm

The paradigmatic framework for the study of the articulating Nyakate/Niare identity is drawn from Abner Cohen's analysis of ethnicity as a chosen variable. In his discourse Cohen argued that members of a group, interacting with others sharing common interests, tended to co-ordinate activities designed to advance and defend these interests. Depending on the circumstances, members accordingly negotiated identities by developing communal types of organizations. In the process, internal cultural forms such as kinship, myths of origin, rites and ceremonies were changed and re-ordered. To this end group ethnicity altered "in degree, depending on the importance of the interest of the group and the pressure on the members of that group imposed by other groups in the society." Ethnicity also changed internally with respect to "the type of organizational articulation developed by the group, between the associative organization at the one end and the communal organization at the other, with most groups combining these two forms in different proportions." Finally "assuming both degree and pattern of organization to be constant, ethnicity varied in the cultural forms exploited by the group in the articulation of its organization, in some cases using ... major (internal) cultural form(s), such as kinship or religion, in others using different combinations of a variety of forms."[58]

As a further elaboration of this paradigmatic framework, I draw on Charles F. Keyes' work, which similarly includes a component affecting the articulating ethnic identity. Historicizing his data more than Cohen, and in a manner appropriate to mine, Keyes perceived the process as a dialectic within a historical time perspective, beginning when people experienced a radical shift in their social circumstances, such as migration, or incorporation into a new political order. In the process they "evolve(d) new patterns of social adaptation to their changed circumstances," reassessing "the saliency of the cultural basis of their ethnic identities." As "new cultural meanings were given to their identities," internal social patterns changed accordingly.[59] Thus presenting identity and ethnicity as articulating and negotiated vari-

---

58. Abner Cohen, "Variables in ethnicity," in Charles F. Keyes, eds. *Ethnic change* (University of Washington Press, 1982), pp. 306–331; Abner Cohen, *Custom and politics in urban Africa: A study of Hausa migrants in Yoruba towns* (University of California Press, 1969). For a critique of Cohen's paradigm see David D. Laitin, *Culture and hegemony: Politics and religious change among the Yoruba* (University of Chicago Press, 1986).

59. Keyes, ed., *Ethnic change*, pp. 3–32 and passim.

ables operating internally and externally in relation to changing circumstances and adaptive goals, both Cohen and Keyes pointed to the
necessary social adjustments, cultural manipulations, and internal
social-group ramifications inherent in the process. Finally, while Cohen emphasized the communal and associative organizations set in
place in order to achieve specific goals, Keyes historicized his paradigm by situating it within the dialectic.

On reviewing Niare data in relation to the above theoretical constructs, I find that as recounted in their myths and legends, Niare group
organization and collective behavior combined with internal and external exigencies—some, derivatives of political and mythical-ritual ideologies—to advance and defend very specific common interests: the
establishment of a suitable state-homeland in the wake of the families'
Wagadu dispersal. In the process, communal groups manipulated internal cultural forms, above all their great myths, kinship groupings,
and rituals. Most notable were manipulations within the great Wagadu
myth and rituals where, reshaped across time and space, both constantly modified and re-organized the articulating Niare identities. The
reverse was also true: As Niare identities changed so were their myths
and rituals conjugated (see Chapter 1). Similarly demonstrating the
manipulation of elite and popular epistemes—likewise serving collective interests—was the Islamized northern paradigm (see above and
Chapter 2), this latter equally articulating in meaning and function
across time and space.

Accordingly, throughout the transforming centuries, both the Wagadu myths and the Islamized northern paradigm became hegemonical,
shaping and reshaping the families' attitudes, consciousness, historical
imaginations, and behavior in relation to their vast migrations, political state exigencies, and encounters with the supernatural. The rest of
the story plays out these identity, mythic, and ritual parsings as family
interests intersected and/or conflicted with regional configurations
including the Other, most often Mande, sometimes non-Mande
(Fulbe). Identity, myths, and rituals likewise intersected and/or conflicted with the families' material environments and production criteria, ultimately with the states of Wagadu, Kingi, Segu, and not least of
all Bamako. Identities, self-perceptions, consciousness, and behaviors
shifted accordingly.

A Word About Sources

Large bodies of formal Bamako traditions are now rare. Common instead are numerous fragments and floating episodes, hardly surprising
really given the character of the oral genre. On examining archival ver-

sions of Niare legends— oral accounts in their late nineteenth- and early twentieth-century forms—records treating the *kafu*'s founding span nearly twenty-five years, from 1880 to about 1904. Most accounts thereafter abandon reflections on the founding families and their little *kafu*'s origins.[60] Among the first to recount the *kafu*'s mythical past in a European idiom were members of the Gallieni Mission (1880-1881) who, traversing the region en route to the Umarian Sultanate at Segu, sojourned briefly at Bamako. Too short a period for in-depth observations, mission reports nonetheless opened the first European window on the founding Niare lineage and its legends.[61] Bamako's conqueror, Borgnis Desbordes (1883) provided later versions. Very problematic, "Bourouti" (as he was known in some local lore) was out of his depth as ethnographer and cultural analyst. Frustrated, moreover, by fluidities defying positivistic historical and racial categories, Bourouti noted that the region's history had already collapsed into "myth and mystery." Besides, believing that the various mythic versions served only the "narrators' interests," he dismissed them as valueless. Subsequent accounts remained more or less faithful to these earlier insights (or lack thereof). And it is only with the turn of the century, and the reporting of Jules Brevie (1904), Bamako's administrator adjoint, that fuller and critical—if arguable—commentaries on Bamako's founding and subsequent development appear in archival holdings. Even so, equally frustrated by the genre, Brevie was impatient with local myths: nothing more than "unconnected episodes," he thought.[62]

In addition to French administrative accounts on the *kafu*'s founding, also proliferating in bureaucratic profusion are archival accounts (in France, Senegal, and Mali) affecting French governance in the Bamako region and its Mande-hinterland. Traditional types of documen-

---

60. Most other founding accounts appearing after these dates repeat much of the earlier data.

61. Although Mungo Park was in Bamako in the latter part of the eighteenth century, he left no record of the families, nor their lineage histories (Park, *The Travels*, pp. 181–182). For the Gallieni Mission see, Joseph S. Gallieni, *Voyage au Soudan français: Haut-Niger et pays de Ségou 1879–1881* (Paris, 1885); *ASAOF* 1G 50 20, "Mission du Haut-Niger, Lettre Gallieni à Gouverneur" (Nango, 7 July 1880); *ASAOF* 1G 50 77, "Mission du Haut-Niger, Lettre Gallieni à Gouverneur" (Makajambugu, 26 April 1880); *ASAOF* 1G 52 46, Brière de L'Isle, "Télégramme" (Dakar, 25 June 1880); *ASAOF* 1G 52 46, Bayol, "Télégramme" no. 314 (Saint Louis, 1880) n.p.; *ASAOF* 1G 52 46, Bayol, "Mission de Ségou," (Saint Louis, 5 July 1880), and throughout this book.

62. *ANMK* 1D 33 5, Borgnis Desbordes, "Notice historique" (1880–1890), n. p.; *ASAOF* 1G 299, Brévié, "Monographie" (Bamako, 25 April 1904), pp. 1–12.

tation therefore follow: French political and military accounts devising the region's "conquest" and "pacification"; purchases for military campaigns; and the abolition of domestic slavery as labor recruitment and the beginnings of a large free-labor market began to emerge. Also appearing in archival accounts are political treatises on the annihilation of the Umarian and Samorian political power-blocks, the humbling of the wayward Beledugu chiefs, the "threat" of "l'Islam noir," and the consolidation of the French administrative machine. Reports on the ethnographic labeling of the "Mande races" are ubiquitous, including their "characteristic" facial, hair, body, and intellectual features, as well as "superstitions," "sorcery," behavior, and identity. Related characteristics affecting the regional flora and fauna are juxtaposed, as are the reopening of long-distance and domestic markets, road-building and Bamako's urban reconstruction, including the establishment of secular schools. Above all, archival accounts bulge with data on the Kayes to Bamako railway (ultimately linked to Dakar), the reorganization of the French Sudan and creation of L'Afrique Occidental Française (AOF) in 1904, and the transfer of the French sudanese seat from Kayes to Bamako (1906–1908). Similarly overflowing in archival holdings are data affecting France's role in the scramble for West Africa, not to mention the endemic and widespread fear of British regional maneuverings and intentions. In other words, archival information predictably treats matters germane to French interests in what was once the Bamako *kafu* and its Mande-hinterland.

Secondary accounts pertaining to Bamako's founding families—critiqued and annotated by anthropologist-ethnographers such as Viviana Paques (1953), Claude Meillassoux (1963), and Marie-Louise Villein-Rossi (1966)—were published in the 1950s and 1960s.[63] Relying for the most part on members of the Bamako Niare clans (as well as archival and secondary sources), Meillassoux and Villein-Rossi in particular drew on the recollections of Amadu Kumba Niare (1883–1964), scion of the *faamaya*, or Niare chiefly lineage. The *kun-tigi*, or *doyen* of the Niare family, product of the Ecole des Otages and functionary in the colonial educational system, Amadu Kumba was neither a *jeli* (*griot* or bard), nor a *buruju gosila* (professional genealogist), nor an official family informant. Not formally memorizing family records either, nor following a literary choreography, he simply recalled personal reminiscences of texts intended primarily for

---

63. Viviana Pâques, "L'Estrade royale des Niaré," *BIFAN*, sér. B, vol. 15, no. 4 (Oct. 1953): 1642–1654; Villien-Rossi, "Bamako," pp. 249–380; Meillassoux, "Histoire," pp. 186–227.

internal consumption at family fetes and ceremonies, such as funerals and celebrations of the *inese*, or cult of the ancestors. Not surprisingly, given the genre, Amadu Kumba's "factual" data in the hands of Meillassoux and Villein-Rossi—who both consulted the *doyen*—vary and are conflictual. Moreover, there are problems with Meillassoux's chronology. Following Delafosse (1912) and Monteil (1924)—rather than compilations by Marty (1927), and Tauxier (1930), now for the most part adopted by the academy—Meillassoux placed Mamari (Biton) Kulibaly's Segu administration between c.1660—c.1710 instead of the more widely accepted c. 1712–c. 1755.[64] His chronology is therefore open to question.

In addition to the above, between the 1960s and 1980s, published and unpublished oral versions were recorded, summarized, or cited—in European and Mande idioms—by professionals and students from French research institutes, such as the Centre de Recherches Africaines, the Centre d'Etudes Africaines and the Ecole des Hautes Etudes en Sciences Sociales.[65] Similar work has been done at the Ecole Normale Superieur at Badalabougou, on the Niger's east bank, across the Vincent Auriol Bridge (800 meters long) from Bamako.[66] Deep and richly textured, these sources

---

64. Meillassoux, "Histoire," pp. 186–188, 222–233. See Monteil, *Les Bambara,* pp. 35–36, 44–45, 102, 118; Tauxier, "Chronologie," pp. 119–130, 255–267; Marty, "La Chronique," pp. 255–426. More recently both Pageard, and Pollet and Winter subscribe to the Marty-Tauxier chronology. Robert Pageard, "Une Tradition musulmane relative à l'histoire de Ségou," *NA*, no. 101 (Jan. 1964): 24–26; Pollet and Winter, *La Société soninké*, pp. 28–34. For other variations, see Delafosse, *Haut-Sénégal-Niger*, vol. 1, p. 319; vol. 2, p. 25–26; Tautain, "Légende et traditions," pp. 472–480; Pâques, "L'Estrade royale," p. 1644.

65. See, for example, Mousso Dosso, "Histoire du pays Malinké de Côte d'Ivoire: Evolution politique, économique, et sociale 1898–1940," Mém. de Maîtrise, under the direction of Yves Person (Paris, 1971); Monique Chastenet, "L'Etat du Gajaaga de 1818 à 1858 face à l'expansion commerciale française au Sénégal," Mém. de Maîtrise, under the direction of Yves Person (Paris, 1975–1976); Diabaté, "La Région de Kong"; Alphonse-Ignace Aikpévi Patinon, "Contribution à l'histoire du sel alimentaire dans le Soudan précolonial (fin Xe au début XXe siècles)," Thèse de Doctorat de Troisième cycle en histoire under the direction of Jean Devisse, 2 vols., CRA (Paris, 1986); Mohmadou S. Bathily, "Les Soninké dans l'histoire du Fuuta Tooro: Introduction à la mise en place et à l'insertion d'une minorité ethnique régionale," Mém. de D. E. A., under the direction of Claude-Hélène Perrot (Paris, June 1987); Massa Makan Diabaté, "Essai critique sur l'épopée mandingue," Thèse de Doctorat de Troisième Cycle under the direction of Yves Person (Paris, n.d.).

66. See, for example, Sidy Diabaté, "Kankan Moussa, Empereur du Mali," Mém. de fin d'études, under the direction of Ly Madina Tall, l'ENSUP (Bamako,

provide insights into little-known cultural interstices. Finally a collection of oral texts recorded in the 1980s from regions beyond Bamako, such as the Manding Plateau, the Beledugu, and the Kaarta (Lambidu: Dunbel-li)—with references to Kingi, the Gidiume, Yelimane, and even the Gambia—speak of the *jaman'a*, or larger Niare identity, beyond Bamako. All of the above I have supplemented with fieldwork in Mali, Senegal, France, and the Cote d'Ivoire (1979, 1980, 1981–1983).[67] It goes without saying that library collections in the United States, France, Senegal, and Mali have been invaluable.

How the Book Fits into the Literature

Given its scope, range, and argument, this book can be contextualized in two ways. First, it belongs to that part of the historiography contributing to the growing interest in a changing ethnographic identity: how peoples' identities shifted, or appeared to shift, from one configuration to another. Basically, it addresses issues involving the kinds of people likely to experience identity shifts and under what circumstances—including a complex array of options and choices, a calculus more complicated than the simple who/what equation may suggest. *External* cultural boundaries framing identities, their openness and articulative capabilities, are also taken into consideration, as are the multiple processes of *internal* shifts within the changing identity: The data show that while ethnographic identities may be seemingly invariable,[68] they are in fact highly variable,

---

1973–1974); Naïny Touré, "L'Amenagement de la ville de Bamako de 1945 à 1973," Mém. de fin d'études, under the direction of Daniel Bléneau, l'ENSUP (Bamako, 1973–1974); Yanoco Traoré, "La Zone industrielle de Bamako," Mém. de fin d' études, under the direction of Daniel Bléneau, l'ENSUP (Bamako, 1973–1974); Soumaoro, "Etude d'un quartier de Bamako"; Seydou Camara, "Le Manden des origines à Sunjata," Mém. de fin d'études, l'ENSUP (Bamako, 1977–1978).

67. See for example Oudiary Makan Dantioko, "La Légende des Nyaxate," photocopied manuscript, Direction Nationale de l'Alphabétisation Fonctionelle et de la Linguistique Appliqué (DNAFLEA), Bamako, n.d., 36 pp.; Jayi Maadi Nyaxate, "La Dispersion des Nyaxate," in Oudiary Makan Dantioko, *Soninkara tarixinu: Récits historiques du pays soninke* (Niamey, 1985), pp. 220–237; Sanba Jabate, "La Légende des Nyaxate du Kaarta," in Dantioko, *Soninkara tarixinu*, pp. 238–329. See also Anonymous, "Chronique historique de la ville de Bamako," trans. from the Arabic by Mallick Yattara, *EM*, no. 20 (Jan. 1977): 62–66; fieldwork includes eighty-two interviews with family members, as well as archival work in Mali, Senegal and France.

68. Clifford Geertz, "The Integrative revolution: Primordial sentiments and civil politics in the new states," in Clifford Geertz, *The Interpretation of cultures* (New York, 1973), see esp. pp. 259–260.

almost continuously responding to the push and pull of internal and external exigencies, positive and/or negative. How these considerations are mediated, conjugated, and negotiated when confronted with the Other relates to the degree of manipulation within the articulating identities. Second, as with the historiographical considerations, this book also addresses the historical ramifications of identity changes, knowing that the calculus is far more complex than a win/lose equation may imply.

Within this first context, my work resembles that of Thomas Spear and Richard Waller, although in some respects it is very different. Dealing with the East African Maasai as "prototypical pastoralists" within an eco-system and cultural space, the authors assume ethnicity to be a function of economic activity: When "at home" the Maasai are Maasai because they are pastoralists (and not, for example, agriculturists). However, because eco-systems and cultural spaces articulate with those of other regional and neighboring identities, overlapping boundaries are porous. The outcome, the authors argue, is not a featureless cultural landscape, but the actual positioning of boundaries across which differentiated peoples negotiate their constantly changing identities.[69]

However, while my story does treat matters affecting articulating and overlapping ethnicities—especially with respect to Mande/Fulbe alliances (Chapter 1 particularly)—and while the story does materialize ethnic identities according to economic function (Chapter 4 particularly), the focus lies elsewhere. Instead, upstreaming some thirty to thirty-five generations (approximately 1,000 years) into archaic myths and legends, I show how, across time and space, the identities of Mande families in general, and the Niare families in particular, suffered a sea change: By the twentieth century, their identities had been radically changed; and yet they remained the same. My story is also more mythically and historically instructed than Spear and Waller's study; it deals more with large cultural identities that become hegemonic; it is more specifically focused on familial identities and more concerned with long-term changes within one set of collective identities than is the Maasai study. Although dealing with Mande/Fulbe relations, my treatment is also less boundary oriented. It is also more focused on state power, as well as on those who own, use, and inherit it.

Second, by historicizing the analysis, this discourse also belongs to the historiography contributing to the growing interest in paradigmatic distortions that shape our mis/understanding of the processes

---

69. Thomas Spear and Richard Waller, eds., *Being Maasai: Ethnicity and identity in East Africa* (London: James Currey; Ohio University Press, 1993), see esp. introduction.

of the variable ethnic identity. Within this anthropological-historio-graphical context, I show that not only were Europeans responsible for otherizing the Other, but that within the Mande-Fulbe-Islamized ethnographic context, a certain amount of otherizing likewise oc-curred. With respect to the European otherizing, a growing critique al-ready exists. Among these is V. Y. Mudimbe, whose hermeneutical work on Africa invented examined the European episteme imposing its analogical modes on African culture histories. Mis/understanding Africa, the reader is left, according to Mudimbe, not with insights into the African identity, but with an image of Europeans in the process of inventing the African identity.[70] In order to correct these proliferations, Mudimbe argued for the development and ordering of knowledge ow-ing little to European epistemes. Probing these distortions from anoth-er perspective is Maria Grosz-Ngate. Historicizing and contextualizing her discourse especially in relation to the Mande, Grosz-Ngate demon-strated the methodological and paradigmatic heresies obscuring the Mande identity since the eighteenth century. Critiquing the reflections of European travelers such as Mungo Park and Rene Caillie, or those of military-administrators and ethnographer-administrators such as Joseph S. Gallieni, Maurice Delafosse, Charles Monteil, and Henri Labouret, Grosz-Ngate's analysis revealed the holographic structures on which their recountings were based, including individual concerns, not to mention the European mis/conceptions of external relationships (*Weltanschauung*), and mis/perceptions of realities (*Weltansicht*).[71] Finally, undertaking a longer critique of the historical obscuring of the Mande identity, Jean-Loup Amselle showed how in mis/understand-ing the Mande historical identity and its articulations, the colonial state imposed a "raison ethnologique," an inappropriate structuralist and un/changing "racial" identity—mis/applied in the interest of colonial state interests. Within the colonial experience different com-munities were thus fragmented, combined, pluralized, or inap-

---

70. V. Y. Mudimbe, *The Invention of Africa: Gnosis, philosophy, and the order of knowledge* (Indiana University Press, 1988). For a more general and theoretical dis-course, see Robert P. Scharlemann, *On the Other: Dialogue and/or dialectics* (Univer-sity Press of America, 1991). See especially Roy Wagner, "Dif/ference and its dis-guises," pp. 42–52, and M. E. Brint, "The Politics of difference," pp. 53–70.

71. See Maria Grosz-Ngaté, "Pouvoir et savoir: La Répresentation de monde mandé dans les oeuvres de Park, Caillié, Monteil, et Delafosse," *CEA*, vol 28 (1988): 485–511. For a reply see Ed Van Hoven, "Representing social hierarchy: Administrators-ethnographers in the French Sudan: Delafosse, Monteil, and Labouret," *CEA*, vol. 30 (1990): 179–198.

propriately juxtaposed. Substituting "logiques metisses" for the disconnecting and decontextualizing of ethnic identities, Amselle argued for the reconnecting of the historically disconnected.[72]

In other words, signaling competing positions on the nature of knowledge, the authors appropriately claim that knowledge can be differently constructed or construed; that in so doing it changes not only its nature, but also its content, meaning, and perspective; and that in the last analysis the creation of knowledge relates in varying ways to power relationships (colonial in this context) and their cultural filiations. Works cited above have also signaled that a new discourse on the nature of order exists: that it too changes; and that in changing, it can be differently represented and differentially studied and construed. Thus, new questions find different answers. Still wanting in the reconstruction and re-representation of order and knowledge, however, are theories and methodologies treating Mudimbe's problematic: That newly ordered knowledge of Africa should owe little to its Western epistemological filiation. The same might be said of Amselle's argument for the reconstruction of ethnic identities historically disconnected by the "raison ethnologique" of colonialism.[73]

As a historian-anthropologist trained in the Western tradition, I have made no attempt to reconstruct the Mande past without consulting and critiquing the contents of the colonial archives and other Western collections. By that same token, in reconstructing this story I have relied on oral accounts and other forms of knowledge construed and ordered by Mande interlocutors. It is obvious that cross-cultural methodologies—appropriate to an understanding of a universalized knowledge about Africa—are a necessity. In the process, I confirmed that universalizing knowledge out of Africa in general, and about the Mande in particular has been part of world history since about the fifteenth century, when the

---

72. Amselle, *Logiques métisses*; see also Jean-Loup Amselle, "Un Etat contre état: Le Keleyadugu," *CEA*, vol. 28 (1988): 463–483; Jean-Loup Amselle, "L'Ethnicité comme représentation: à propos des Peul du Wasolon," *Annales; Economies, Sociétés, Civilisations*, vol. 42, no. 2 (1987): 465–489. For studies providing a similar treatment see Michael Jackson, *Paths toward a clearing: Radical empiricism and ethnographic inquiry* (Indiana University Press, 1989).

73. Mudimbe, *The Invention*, pp. 19, 24–97, and passim; Amselle, *Logiques métisses*, pp. 235–248. See also Richard M. Rorty, ed., *The Linguistic turn: Essay in philosophical method* (University of Chicago Press, 1992); Idem., *Objectivity, relativism and truth: Philosophical papers* (Cambridge University Press, 1991), vol. 1; Idem., *On hermeneutics: General studies and teaching*, selected papers from Synergos Seminars, vol. 2 (George Mason University, 1982), pp. 1–43.

Portuguese navigators first rounded Cape Bojador (1434). It was, after all, Duarte Pacheco Pereira (1506–1508) who introduced the "Banbarranaa" to the European world:[74] Pereira's attempt (albeit a crude one), was in effect a harbinger of the ways in which cross-cultural knowledge (in many respects) has since come to be constructed. He got it all wrong. Yet, his universalizing of knowledge-out-of-Africa is a prototype of contemporary cross-cultural investigations, a methodology which we now consider commonplace.

It is therefore not the reliance on Western knowledge and how it is construed that have made this cross-cultural universalizing problematic, as Mudimbe, Amselle and others have reflected. Rather, it is that while European epistemes and methodologies became more varied and archaeologically complex—vis à vis civilizations of European origin—those applied to Africa (and the non-European world) remained as rude and childish as the era of the first encounter, and as distorted as the nineteenth-century discourses of the social Darwinists. Ensuring the survival of these misshapen knowledge remnants were the power relationships forging African-European encounters, especially those which marked the late nineteenth, and the better part of the twentieth century. Many disfigured remnants still survive in popular and learned epistemes, despite the changing global configurations of the mid- and late-twentieth century.

Thus if investigators appropriately call for a new knowledge-out-of-Africa that is differently parsed, severing its construction and ordering from a European filiation may not necessarily solve the problem. Because, as the previous constructs—misconstrued in Europe—proved unequal to the universal mission of an open discourse on knowledge and how it is generated and ordered, a one-dimensional knowledge-out-of-Africa would likewise fail in its universal mission. The age of generating local knowledge exclusively from within national or local boundaries and perspectives that is nationally or locally owned, is already over. An interdependent and universal African scholarship, universally owned, already exists. Universalizing, rather than reconnecting Africa's past according to

---

74. One of the earliest references to the Mande in the European literature is Duarte Pacheco Pereira, *Esmeraldo de situ orbis (c. 1506–1508)*, ed. and trans. Raymond Mauny (Bissau, 1956), p. 67. Jean-Baptiste Labat was among the early published French authors. *Nouvelle relation de l'Afrique occidentale: Une description exacte du Sénégal et des païs situés entre le Cap Blanc et la Rivière de Serrelionne, jusqu' à plus de 300 lieuës en avant dans les terres. L'Histoire naturelle de ces païs, les differentes nations qui y sont répanduës, leurs religions et leur moeurs*, 5 vols. (Paris, 1728); vol. 3, pp. 334, 359; vol. 4, p. 85, 87.

a more contemporary European paradigm; and globalizing rather than disconnecting knowledge out of Africa from its European filiation; and integrating Mande theoretical and empirical constructs into a universal discourse, already exists. Theoretically, the process ascribes as much to the African voice—Mande in this case—as to any other. Thus, rather than assembling the history of the Mande according to some little remembered or forgotten paradigms; or worse, according to a new or contemporary European paradigm, it seems more appropriate to enrich existing methodologies—in search of the archaeologically complex and compound epistemes—that situate Africa in the universal and cross-cultural discourse. Pereira's universalized "Banbarranaa" was a false start; yet it is with him that the universalizing of the Mande began.

As part of this universalizing and cross-cultural learning, this work most specifically resembles Jean Bazin's treatment of the internal creation of the Bambara identity, "Bambara" in this instance the sobriquet for "animist," "fetishist," "pagan," and *dolo*-consuming "farmer," even "metaphysician." Rejecting the essentialist "Bambara" and its corresponding ethnonym in favor of a relative and shifting identity—what he called "à chacun son Bambara"—Bazin argued that the Bamana identity was first the product of an internal otherizing of the ethnographic Other, only later incorporated into external European evolutionary designs.[75] A ubiquitous terminology (*Banmana, Bamana, Bamanan, Bambara, Banbara*) found throughout the western Sudan—from the Senegambia to the eastern Cote d'Ivoire, and from the Niger bend to northern Guinea—Bazin showed that even Mandekan sharing the same eco-system and cultural spaces as the Other were also prone to holographic dancing (my term): The "Bambara's" identity in the Mande-hinterland, and consequently in European texts, was designed not by himself/herself, but by local Mande and non-Mande residents—differentially situated—whom Europe's pioneers encountered in Western Africa. Prior to their arrival, Sudanese jula (Islamized long-distance traders) and Maraka merchants were most responsible for diffusing this human and social geography in the form of

---

75. Jean Bazin, "A Chacun son Bambara," in Jean-Loup Amselle and Elikia M'Bokolo, eds., *Au Coeur de l'ethnie: Ethnies, tribalisme et état en Afrique* (Paris, 1985), pp. 87–127 see esp. pp. 94–112. The first internal written references in the Arabic language and script to this pejorative "Bambara" identity comes from the author of the *Ta'rikh al-Fattash* pp. 20 and note 7, 86 and note 2, 87, 107. *Bambara* (*Banbara*) is used by some Fulbe, Songhay, Soninke, and desert-side "Moors" of the Timbuktu and Niger bend regions. In some instances *Bambara* is the equivalent for *Bamana*. The Bamana of the Segu and Bamako regions called themselves *Bamana*. By the late twentieth century they were *Bambara*.

ethnic and cultural stereotypes, Bazin argued, later leaving impressions in the minds of early French travelers (e.g., Caillie and Mage) that an essentialist "Bambara" existed, even if difficult to recognize. Then projecting their European images on to pre-existing European mis- and pre/conceptions, the double analogies were doubly confounded.

I need hardly remind readers that otherizing the ethnographic Other is as old as the Greek and Chinese civilizations, possibly older.[76] As noted above, it is also not exclusively a Western cultural disorder either, appearing in epistemes as remote from those of Darwin and Marx as the Acropolis was from The Forbidden City. Likewise noted above is that otherizing is both an internal and external exercise, occurring *within* the same cultural boundaries, as well as *between* seemingly discrete cultural configurations, a phenomenon that Robert Wagner overlooked in his critique of the anthropologists' holographs and analogizing.[77] Even participant observers self-consciously parsing data—according to internal considerations applied by people to themselves—may not altogether escape these proliferating ironies. Thus, on finding paradigmatic distortions (in the northern paradigm) among seventeenth-century Islamized elites in Niger bend towns (see Chapter 2)—similar to those that Bazin found elsewhere in the Mande-hinterland—I conclude that perhaps the Acropolis may not have been that far from the Forbidden City, nor Mecca that distant from Rome or Canterbury.

Finally, if my study more readily aligns with Bazin's notion of the internal paradigm, its time-space correlations correspond most closely to Igor Kopytoff's *The African Frontier*. This work, informed by several theses, argues that frontier societies and states shared multiple defining features, the work of frontiersmen, many of whom had been ejected from kin groups, communities, and polities. Although the mythical genre spoke of culture-heroes opening "new" lands for settlement, "frontiersmen" was often the coded term for disengaged groups. Claiming that even if settlement occurred in the so-called "institutional vacuum" open to legitimate intrusion, there were usually organized settler communities with which

---

76. Chinese ethnographic formulations developed during the T'ang (c. 618–c. 907), Sung (960–1279), Yûan (1260–1368), and (c. 1368–c. 1642) Ming Dynasties. J. J. L. Duyvendak, *China's discovery of Africa* (London, 1949), pp. 12–15. For a revisionist view of the contribution of the Greek episteme to the intellectual categories of Western Europe see Sarah P. Morris, *Daidalos and the origins of Greek art* (Princeton University Press, 1992); Martin Bernal, *Black Athena: The Afroasiatic roots of classical civilization*, 2 vols. (Rutgers University Press, 1987–1992); and Bernal's critics in *Arethusa: The challenge of "Black Athena,"* special issue (Fall, 1989).

77. Wagner, "Dif/ference and its disguises," pp. 42–52.

frontiersmen had to negotiate. Moreover, when constructing their own state or societal system, frontier groups usually replicated political cultures and legitimate social orders transposed from pre-existing and remembered paradigms. Because frontier social construction called for entrepreneurship and specialized skills, those in public office frequently elaborated their political power-base by "attracting and retaining adherents and dependents" into an integrated kinship political relationship. At a later level of political maturity, if indeed the state survived initial vicissitudes, the integrative political group altered its constitution and/or fundamental law to emphasize an interdependence between rulers and subjects. Although "firstcomers" legitimated state and societal authority, the principle later adapted to acknowledge the de facto domination of entrepreneurial and specialized in-migrants.[78]

Frontier states were often on the cusp of an ideological duality, he continued: Since the state was a direct expansion of the founders' frontier hamlet, the rulers' patrimonial model became the basis for their constitutional ideology; by way of contrast, the subjects' domestic ideology parleyed the ruler into their own creation. Hence the "sacred chieftainship" was a bonding device between ruler and ruled: the chiefly presence was a guarantee of the collective well-being. As the polity matured, "the subject-ruler division and inter-dependence were incorporated into the integrative symbolism of royal ritual." In seeking an expanding legitimacy, that is, one beyond the patrimonial domain, rulers drew on regional values, traditions, and legitimizing themes. Within its historical process, the state either expanded at the expense of regional polities, or disintegrated under the weight of internal stresses, or was absorbed into a larger frontier, regional, or metropolitan polity.[79]

Presenting characteristics remarkably similar to Kopytoff's paradigm of the frontier state, the identities of the Niare and other Mande families were forged in a Bamako polity that moved in and out of varying political phases. Political elites, entrepreneurs, and specialized workers bonded to the ruling lineage through various alliances, while developing the state's political economies. Mythical-political rituals, ceremonies and organized beliefs further bonded this form of political and social organization. It was thus that the state's interactive dynamic endured for approximately 150 to 175 years. The rest is sometimes history, oftentimes myth.

---

78. Igor Kopytoff, ed., *The African frontier: The reproduction of traditional African societies* (Indiana University Press, 1987), see esp. pp. 3–84.

79. Kopytoff, *The African frontier*.

Conclusion

Ultimately, if my work resembles to some extent that of Bazin and Kopytoff, the overall analysis finishes by attempting something quite different. First, I argue theoretically for the almost limitless articulation of Mande ethnic identities within cultural contexts historicized at the outset within the Wagadu state affiliation, later at the Kingi, Segu and Bamako states. And while I differentiate the particular articulation from the universal, I also show how identities collapse into the same, yet different, and separate entities. Second, I demonstrate the extent to which the Bamako-state paradigm, organization and dynamics were embedded in the family structure, function, and relationships. It is almost as if without the family the Bamako state could not have been summoned into existence. With important modifications, the same may be said for the development of market economies, the right to own, maximize, and transfer material property, as well as other aspects of the collective political economies. Third, unlike the previously cited studies, I focus on oathings and rituals (most importantly ritualized marriage alliances) as integral to identity formations, functions and articulations, as well as the great myths and legends, landscapes and ecosystems, languages and dialects, not to mention belief systems and cosmologies. I similarly demonstrate these changing phenomena as sensitive to and transformed by generational and gender challenges.

Fourth, going beyond the Mande world and into the New World, this discourse implies by extension that the essentialist or syncretic "Mandinga" persona punctuating historiographies of New World slavery, like the earlier European distortions, has similarly proved unequal to the universal mission of an open discourse on how knowledge is generated and ordered, or how identities are formed in this case. Not always listening to the African voice, nor appreciating the particularisms mediated in the West African cultural field, some slave historiographies have collapsed the complicated Mande identity into the "Mandingo," "Mandinga," or "Mandinka," even applying these terms, as if generic, to all Mande speakers. Even worse, others seem unaware that Mandingo, Mandinga, Mandinka, are but the tip of the iceberg, and that in the vast Mande world an incredible variety of other Mande speakers exists. The Mande's complex social organizations have likewise been frozen into monolithic and homogeneous "tribes." Often, the Mande's esoteric power associations and associated rituals have either been diminished as "primitive religions," or ignored as unimportant figurations. It may therefore come as a surprise to learn that throughout the vast Mande world, only the Maninka called themselves *Mandinga*, and that other Mande speakers called them *Mandinka, Mandingo, Manding*, and *Malinke*. It may also come as a surprise to learn that because the Mande past was reconstructed mainly from within by traditionalists (*jeliw*), *Mandinga* had no internal sociocultural context, no interior social meaning, and no domestic sociohistory beyond Maninka country; or that those who spoke for the Maninka could have been otherizing them.

Additionally, the New World slave discourse has also seemed unaware of situational ethnic identities commonplace to many Mande cultural fields: That human agency often functions within a range of identities seems to have been insufficiently problematized; or that many West Africans spoke one or more of the Mande dialects, in addition to a mother tongue (and could therefore have been mistaken for "Mandinga"); or that "Mandinga" and "Bambara" are not necessarily synonyms, when in fact the term "Bambara" has a very complex and different history; or that the Mandinga identity could have been the construction of a West African dealer; or more banal, that a slave-ship's employee could have created a market concept of "the Mandinga" largely for convenience ("à chacun son Mandinga" to paraphrase Bazin), or as a New World market designation to attract quick sales. And while learned discourses have reified this rigid Mandinga, some fictional representations have popularized these essentialist distortions to an even wider audience.[80]

Thus replacing ethnic articulations with misplaced rigidities, many New World slave discourses have imprisoned the Mande in an old fashioned essentialist argument reminiscent of Park and Caillie, Gallieni and Borgnis Desbordes, Delafosse and Tauxier, and the "raison ethnologique," which Amselle appropriately critiqued (1990). The "Bambara" has likewise suffered the same fate: Both "ethnies" not only appeared in the slavers' logs as an essentialist diagram, but he or she also survived the experience of capture and/or sale in West Africa, the transatlantic sea change, the "seasoning" in the West Indies, and the subsequent resale on North American marts, not to mention the centuries of slavery in multiply-differentiated regions of the Americas.

As was the malformation of the European "raison ethnologique," at the heart of the New World misrepresentations is a misunderstood ethnicity and misconceived concepts of race, most of which have little meaning beyond the social and political contestation for power, the accumulation of wealth, and/or competition for scarce resources. Many aspects of the slave past and histories have uncritically bred these problematics. Thus,

---

80. For example, Gwendolyn Midlo Hall, *Africans in colonial Louisiana: The development of the Afro-creole culture in the eighteenth century* (Louisiana State University Press, 1992); Alex Haley, *Roots* (Double Day, 1976).

authenticating the "racial" survival of the Mandinga, as well as his "racial" and "ethnic survivals," her "cultural traits" and "characteristics" may have been more the product of sociopolitical and socioeconomic power considerations and control than their creators suggest, more necessary for continued social inequalities than their supporters admit, and more remote from the universal discourse about Africa than their propagators are aware. Worse, as others have shown, privileging allegedly unchanging traits and characteristics within a social field of inquiry favors the a-historical over the historical.[81]

Finally, it would be unfortunate—and ironical—if the historical articulations and ambiguities within the West African Mande identity had played simplistically into New World rigidities. My previous discussion drew attention to the dynamics of this interplay that was both particular and universal, as well as the same yet different. In the case of the New World slave historiographies, was the particular—disconnected and decontextualized—distorted into the universal? Did the disembedded part speak for the whole? Did its New World elaboration lead to a disfiguration in need of a universal discourse? Although answers are difficult to determine, it should be clear from my remarks, both here and throughout this book, that the variable West African Mande identity bears little resemblance to the New World's frozen "Mandinga." The irony is that whereas Mande social organizations—the inclusive family not the least— mediated difference into sameness, and sameness into unchange, the West African Mande identity was constantly changing. If the Mande *jeliw*'s recountings are any guide to a collective awareness, most selfconscious Mande seemed aware that this changing-unchange was the same-yet-different. A further irony is that when decontextualized, ambiguities of this sort may well have played into the images of the essentialist Mandinga, and the New World "raison ethnologique." Which may partly explain, at any rate, why the invariable Mandinga has survived in the New World slave discourse, not as an ambiguous concept (as in the Mande-hinterland and Mande world), but as a clear misunderstanding of these ambiguities. Or why the different-yet-the-same-yet-changing Mande argument was collapsed into the essentialist Mandinga diagram.

---

81. For further critique, see, for example, Stephan Palmié, "Africa in colonial Louisiana," *Africa*, vol. 64 (1994): 168-171. See also *Idem.*, "Against syncretism: 'Africanizing' and 'Cubanizing' discourses in North American *orisa*-worship," in Richard Fardon, ed., *Counterworks: Managing diverse knowledge* (London; Routledge, 1995), pp. 73–104; *Idem.*, "Ethnogenetic processes and cultural transfer in Afro-American slave populations," in Wolfgang Binder, ed., *Slavery in the Americas* (Würzburg; Königshauser and Neuman, 1993), pp. 337–364.

These, then, are my contributions to the field. That they can be contested is without question. That others can and will produce more cogent arguments goes without saying. If building on these findings today, others can go beyond them tomorrow, I would not have labored in vain.

1

How Identities Are Formed: The Manipulation of Myths and Cultural Signs

The Introduction presented the families in this story, briefly indicating their cultural-linguistic, ritual, and socio-spatial identities, together with their mixed eco-systems. All, to one degree or another, contributed to the formation of the Mande-hinterland's differentiated identities. I likewise observed that although Mande families eventually imposed their manipulated cultures over large areas of the western Sudan—from the Senegambia in the west to the Black Volta regions in the east, and from the Niger bend in the north to towns and villages north of the forest zone throughout Guinea, Sierra Leone, Liberia, and the Cote d'Ivoire—most identities were forged in relatively small communities (see Map 5).[1] In the process, further regional particularizations emerged. To this extent Bamako, the centerpiece of this story, did not stand alone; like thousands of relatively small and larger communities, the *kafu* was integrated into the wide screen Mande-hinterland and the larger Mande world. A semi-autonomous state (state: families holding political power), Bamako was ruled by its founding chiefly family, the Niare (Nyakate: archaic *jamu* or patronym) from Wagadu. Established during the eighteenth century on the periphery of the Bamana Segu state hegemony, the metropole further redirected identity shifts through wide-ranging public policies (see Map 2).[2] Through wars, the development of *tonjonw* armies, marriages and

---

1. The term "manipulated" here refers to the process and artful manner with which people handled or managed their myths—consciously or otherwise—adapting them in accordance with changing ethnic identities. We cannot always verify meaning behind every mythic manipulation.

2. Tauxier, "Chronologie," part 1, pp. 119–130; part 2, pp. 255–267; Tauxier, *Histoire.* See also Marty, "La Chronique," no. 3, pp. 225–426; no. 4, pp. 531–575. Mon-

other alliances, Segu's hegemonic endeavors ultimately affected vast sections of the upper Niger region falling within its tributary range. Language repertoires and *jo* rituals embellished and consolidated these far-ranging considerations. Finally, the Umarian and Samorian wars of the latter part of the nineteenth century, mainly *jihad*s with an imperial subtext, introduced a serious ideological discourse into state-society relations, producing conflict as a forge for still further identity negotiations, manipulations, and modifications.

Returning to the cultural data and its mythic past, in this chapter I probe somewhat further the extent to which cultural signs and symbols were manipulated and/or negotiated in search of the Mande identity in general, its Niare counterpart in particular. More specifically, I argue (as Cohen's paradigm suggests) that while the Soninke families reshaped their ethnic identities within the dispersal, and in relation to the state, and that later identities were no doubt "revised" with the colonial authorities in mind, the search for a more general Mande identity was a historical necessity. Dispersed from their Wagadu homeland—possibly since about the end of the first and the second millennium—Soninke families wandered a mythical landscape in search of a homeland. In the process—approximately a thousand years in some instances—they "documented" and "signed" their presence across what was to become the Mande-hinterland and the Mande world, manipulating cultural forms and kinship groups, not least of all their great myths and legends (see Map 5). Today, many Soninke families have espoused different identities, some even no longer Mande.

Nyakate Identities and Mande/Fulbe Articulations in the *Jaman'a*

Although the Niare (Nyakate) and their Bamako state are the focus of this discourse, it became apparent during my initial research that a larger Mande-Niare/Nyakate identity existed in the Mande-hinterland, well beyond Bamako, which needed to be addressed. Here, I am referring to the global (*jaman'a*) Nyakate family which left Wagadu after the dispersal. Most, probably numbering several hundreds originally, if not thousands—along with other Soninko (sing.: Soninke)—eventually settled west of Bamako, in cultural spaces forged in the

---

teil, *Les Bambara*, p. 102; Villien-Rossi, "Bamako," pp. 249–380, see p. 264. See also Meillassoux, "Histoire," pp. 186–227; *ANMK* 1D 33 2, Collomb, "Notice" (Bamako, 1884–1885), p. 6; *ANMK* 1D 33 5, Borgnis Desbordes, "Notice historique" (1880–1890), n.p.

Kaarta (Lambidu) and beyond, as well as in the Gidiume, Yelimane, Jafunu, and Keniareme regions, even southwest in Khasso, Gajaga (the French Galam), and the Gambia (see Maps 2 and 3). Of those migrating east from Wagadu,[3] many eventually settled in the Massina in the Ja region (Jakha, Jaghara or Jagari), creating cultural spaces along the middle Niger zones, especially in the Segu and Nyamina regions, finally founding Minkungu on the Manding Plateau overlooking Bamako. While many migrating west retained their older Soninke identity, including their language and archaic Nyakate patronymic, most of those migrating east toward Segu and the Niger were eventually absorbed into complex processes involving other ethnic identities.[4] As a matter of interest (although not part of this story) other families migrating still farther east toward the Black Volta experienced additional identity shifts, as they settled among the region's autochthones (see Map 4).

It remains unclear why the western Nyakate branches tended to retain an earlier Wagadu identity when their eastern counterparts, including the Bamako Niare, shifted theirs. It isn't that westerners were removed from the cross-cultural discourse: As mainly maraboutic and trading clans, they were in frequent contact with desert-side Sanhaja and other Berber-Arab identities. They were also the axis of regular exchanges with the Jallonke and Mandinka-speakers of the gold-bearing Bambuhu region, as well as the Fulbe of Fuladugu (Fadugu) and the Birgo (see Maps 3 and 7). Neither did they escape the eighteenth- and nineteenth-century Kaartan and Senegambian wars, not to mention earlier debacles. They likewise shared an ecosystem with the western Fulbe and were in contact with Tukulor and Mandekan from the Futa Toro and the upper Senegambia, respectively.[5]

---

3. In this discourse, Mande-speakers migrating east from Wagadu should not be confused with other Mande who migrated farther east to the Black Volta region. For the Southeastern Mande see, Perinbam, "The Political organization," pp. 437–462.

4. Interview Seydou Niaré (Bamako, 6 Jan. 1980); interview Mahmadou Sarr (Bamako, 8 Jan. 1980); *ASAOF* 1G 32, "Lettre Mage à Gouverneur" (Saint Louis, 21 June 1866).

5. *ASAOF* 1G 8, "Exploration du Kaarta 1824 à 1829, Rapport de M. Duranton, 1824," pp. 47; *ASAOF* 1G 8, "A Messieurs des membres de la Société de Galam, rapport de M. Duranton, 1824" (Bakel, 2 April 1824), p. 1; *ASAOF* 1G 22, Hecquard, "Voyage à Timbo" (1848–1851), p. 14; *ASAOF* 1G 32, "Lettre Mage à Gouverneur" (Saint Louis, 21 June 1866). Many Fulbe are said also to have come from

On the one hand, most western Nyakate tended to retain an earlier Wagadu identity, because possessing greater numbers and denser cultural-linguistic boundaries, their social groupings were more compact than those found among easterners.[6] On the other hand, we should leave open the possibility that some western Nyakate identities did in fact shift. As former Nyakate they may now be known by other *jamuw*, a hypothesis applied to some western branches of the Jakite families, some of whom may have been originally Nyakate (see below). Or some western Nyakate could have otherwise "disappeared," now quite "unrecognizable." We recall Heinrich Barth's surprise in the 1850s at finding ex-Mande farther east in northern Nigeria—the "Wangara" had migrated there sometime during the fourteenth century—with completely new identities, having "entirely forgotten" their mother tongue, some speaking Fulfulde, "even Hausa."[7]

However, if some western Nyakate retained a reasonably clear Wagadu signature, their eastern identities remained more complex, involving the pastoralist Fulbe and Bamana, all ultimately informed by the Segovian and Kaartan (both Bamana) state hegemonies. Today, many eastern Niare families, likewise Bamanized and claiming affiliation with the Bamako Niare, are still found in Nyamina, Kulikoro, Markala, and Segu.[8] Not just the Niare were found there however: Other Soninke families migrating east—the Sakho and Kone of Nyamina, the Sisse from Kerowane, the Dukure of Kiba, the Sylla from Tuba, and the Simpara from Banamba, to mention but a few—were likewise drawn into the Segovian state hegemony, ultimately espousing a Marka-Sarakolle, eventually a Bamana, identity by the late nineteenth century. Complicating the matter, many Fulbe in the Segu and Bamako regions had also bamanized by the late nineteenth century, and vice versa[9] (see Map 3).

Wagadu (*ASAOF* 1G 248, Captain Pérignon, "Généralités sur les régions du Haut-Sénégal et du Moyen-Niger: Monographie des Cercles de Kita et de Ségou, 1899-1900," pp. 233–235).

6. Even today, the western families are more "closed" than their eastern counterparts. Interview Ali Ongoïba (Kuluba-Bamako, 4 Feb. 1983).

7. Barth, *Travels*, vol. 3, p. 111.

8. Interview Seydou Niaré (Bamako, 15 Dec. 1982).

9. *Marka-Sarakolle* in the Segovian Bamana idiom refers to people claiming a Soninke heritage. The term was also used by some Fulbe and desert-side populations. The above towns, all Marka-Sarakolle, lie to the northeast of Bamako. Most were officially founded in the late eighteenth and nineteenth centuries. B. Marie Perinbam, "Islam in the Banamba region of the eastern Beledugu, c. 1800 to c. 1900," *IJAHS*, vol. 19, no. 4 (1986): 642–646. See also *ASAOF* 1G 32, "Lettre Mage à

But if many eastern Nyakate bamanized, what of those *jaman'a* Nyakate sharing in-between or truly mixed cultural spaces with the Fulbe in the east, in the Massina, in or around Ja, a region still signaled by most Mande-speakers as a major dispersal point after Wagadu? (see Map 7). Or those *jaman'a* Nyakate establishing in-between lineage-locations among Fulbe on the Kaarta's eastern fringes, in the Massina, the Kingi and Kani-aga regions, ecosystems which they also shared with Fulbe?[10]

The data, few and consequently difficult to interpret, are nonetheless sufficient to allow a hypothesis for further investigation. First, the data clarify that in-between Nyakate-Fulbe co-residencies in the west, at Lam-bidu in the Kaarta and at Kaniaga (near Kingi) were long-standing since about the fourteenth century Malian state hegemony.[11] Under these cir-cumstances, many Nyakate could have "tilted" to a Fulbe identity. Second, as part of this process the data especially particularize a close as-sociation between the Soninke-Nyakate and the Fulbe-Jakite—especially in the Massina, Gidiume, Kita, and Kaniaga regions—to the extent that an equivalency existed between the Soninke-Nyakate *jamu* and the Fulbe-Jakite patronym: Both families were entitled, in other words, to the Nyakate and/or Jakite salutation, interchangeably (see Maps 2 and 3). Similar patronymic alternates found elsewhere in the Mande-hinterland are usually explained by close, long-standing ritual alliances between families, very likely including marriage on an intergenerational basis.[12] Applied to the Soninke-Nyakate and Fulbe-Jakite families, interchange-able salutations and patronyms likewise suggest long-standing clan asso-ciations bonded by marriage and further alliances. The evidence once

Gouverneur" (Saint Louis, 21 June 1866); *ASAOF* 1G 52 46, Bayol, "Mission de Sé-gou" (Saint Louis, 5 July 1880); *ASAOF* 1G 79, Conrard, "Notice" (Bamako, 21 Feb. 1885), p. 3.

10. According to the French colonial administration Kaniaga was a province midway between Gumbu (Wagadu) and the Beledugu. According to Mande speakers, however, Kaniaga was a large region including Kaniaga properly speak-ing, Wagadu, Bakhunu, Kingi (region of Nioro and Jara), the Gidiume, Jafunu, perhaps even the Gidimaxa and Gajaga (a corruption of *Kaniaga*, the French Galam) in the upper Senegal (Bakel) region (*Ta'rikh al-Fattash*, p. 68, note 3).

11. Interview Seydou Niaré (Bamako, 4 Jan. 1980); Nyaxate, "La Dispersion," p. 225; Delafosse, *Haut-Sénégal-Niger*, vol. 1, pp. 124 137, 266–267 and passim. Fieldwork (Mali, 1980, 1981–1983).

12. I. G. Boyer, *Un Peuple de l' ouest soudanais: Les Diawara* (Dakar, 1956), pp. 24–25; Pollet and Winter, *La Société soninké* p. 31–32. For the Niare in the Massina, see Jabate, "La Légende," pp. 241–327. See also Nyaxate, "La Dispersion," p. 225; Delafosse, *Haut-Sénégal*, vol. 1, pp. 124, 137, 266–267 and passim. For other equiv-alencies (mainly Mande/Mande) see Introduction.

again suggests that some Soninke-Nyakate could have tilted to a Fulbe-Jakite identity. Third, if the eastern Nyakate-Jakite (Mande/Fulbe) axis was an articulating one, compounding the issue was the observation that some Fulbe-Jakite in other Mande cultural spaces (e.g., the Mande Khassonke of the southwest; the Wassulunke and people of Buguni) conjugated a similar axis with other families, notably the Soninke-Kaba, as well as with the Bari, who were Fulbe. Farther south within the Samanyana, Dalakana, and Faraba cultural spaces, other Fulbe-Jakite—associated with the Futa Jallon—may also have "tilted" toward a Mande identity (see Maps 3 and 7).[13]

Accordingly, whether in the east, southwest, or south, clearly these four identities (Soninke-Jakite, Soninke-Kaba, Fulbe-Bari, and Fulbe-Jakite) were variable and "open": Through long-standing marriage and other alliances, these four ethnographic identities articulated on a moving cultural axis, sometimes tilting toward a Mande identity, at other times toward a Fulbe (e.g., Wassulunke).[14] On turning to a chronology, although uncertain, articulating identities probably began sometime during and after the Malian fourteenth century state hegemony, probably between the thirteenth and nineteenth centuries, the process very likely still continuing. By the eighteenth and nineteenth centuries, several of these Mande-Fulbe families had reached the Bamako region mainly from the Massina and Kingi. Others arrived via Gajaga and the Futa Toro, some migrating further southeast to the Wassulu.[15]

Thus if, when focusing on the Niare and their Bamako state, I suspected the existence of a *jaman'a*, or global Nyakate identity, in the Mande-hinterland well beyond Bamako, it is because there was one.

---

13. The Jakite from Samanyana, Dalakana, and Faraba should not be confused with the Jakite (Fulfulde-speakers), a major clan found throughout the old Mande and the Wassulu, also originally from the Massina and the Fula Jallon, related to the Jallo and the Kone by the *senankun* (Bamana: "joking relationship"; Maninka: *sanankuya*). For the *senankun* see note 19 herein. For Jakite in the Buguni region who have tilted toward a Bamana (Kulibaly) identity, see Brahima Diarra, "Du Banimonotie au Cercle de Bougouni: Contribution à l'histoire d'un canton 1667–1914," Mém. de fin d'études l'ENSUP (Bamako, 1974–1975), pp. 5, 9–11, 18. For the Mande, see Niane, *Histoire des Mandigues*, pp. 46–47; E. Leynaud, "Clans, lignages, et cantons," paper presented at the Conference on Manding Studies (London, 1972), pp. 5, 25–34; Leynaud and Cissé, *Pays malinké*, pp. 32–137, 155–159; interview Modibo Diallo (Paris, 23 June 1982).

14. Amselle, *Logiques métisses*, p. 212 and passim.

15. The Jakite-Sabashi probably reached the Wassulu sometime after the sixteenth century. See Amselle, *Logiques métisses*, p. 78, see also pp. 119–147. See also Brooks, *Landlords*, pp. 107–108, 127–128, 172–173, 199–200.

And if I speculated that some *jaman'a* Nyakate families had interacted with Fulbe ethnic identities, it is because they had: The *jaman'a* family leaving Wagadu after the dispersal settled in Fulbe regions, later in particularized Bamana zones across the Mande world, from the Senegambia in the west to the Niger in the east, and from the Massina in the north, to beyond Bamako in the south (see Maps 4, 5 and 7). And if many westerners retained a Soninke-Nyakate identity many easterners—especially those who fell under the Bamana Segovian hegemony, including the Bamako Niare-Nyakate—ultimately became Marka-Sarakolle-Bamana (Niare) and Fulbe (Jakite).

However, "open" lineages were not only found among the Nyakate-Jakite and the Kaba-Jakite families (i.e., a Mande [Soninke] and Fulbe connection). Open lineages could also be found throughout the Mande-hinterland, even the Mande world wherever Mande- and Fulfulde-speakers co-resided. In fact, similar articulations were commonplace from Bakhunu and the Massina in the north, to the Futa Jallon in the south, and from the Senegambia in the west, to Buguni, the Wassulu, the Kong and Black Volta regions in the east, including the Kaarta-Beledugu-Bamako regions and the Bafulabe-Kita-Kayes-Gajaga cultural spaces. Some Fulbe lineages in the Kaarta, for example, are said to have completely "lost their language" and are now Bamanakan. As a matter of further interest, many Mande-Fulbe combined with the Tukulor of the Futa Toro. In some northern regions Mande-Fulbe identities also fused with desert-side signs, including language.[16] Similar open lineage articulations likewise occurred in the Khasso-Fuladugu (Bangasi)-Kita, and Birgo regions, where Fulbe-Soninke and Mandinka co-resided. Known by different regional ethnonyms in the popular cultures, peoples of these ambiguous Mande-Fulbe (or Fulbe-Mande) identities were called *Fulanke* in the Kayes-Kita regions, *Fulanka* or *Fulga* in the Segu regions, *Wassulunke* in the Buguni areas, and *Maninka-Fula*, or *False Peul*—especially the Jakite, Sidibe, Sangare and Jallo—in the Buguni-Wassulu ecosystems. In the Bafulabe region, moreover, *Souare*, *Sisse*, *Jiango*, and *Jiaka* have been identified as *Fulanke* patronyms; similar variations have also been found farther west in the Futa Toro.[17] Identity articulations were even occurring

---

16. *ASAOF* 1G 32, "Lettre Mage à Gouverneur" (Saint Louis, 21 June 1866); *ASAOF* 1G 52 46, Bayol, "Mission de Ségou" (Saint Louis, 5 July 1880); *ASAOF* 1G 248, Pérignon, "Monographie" (1889–1900), pp. 233–235; *ASAOF* 1G 8, "Rapport de M. Duranton, 1824," pp. 47; *ASAOF* 1G 22, Hecquard, "Voyage à Timbo" (1849–1851), pp. 14–15; Dantioko, *Soninkara tarixinu*, pp. 235, 325.

17. *ASAOF* 1G 248, Pérignon, "Monographie" (1889–1900). Other Maninka-Fulbe (e.g. Jakite) were found in Siby, Kirina, Kinieroba, and Samalen, all in the

in "animist" Bure regions where Soninke-Mandinka and Jallonke co-resided, and where by the mid-nineteenth century, Jallonke-speakers had shifted their idiom to Mandinka.[18]

Adding his voice to this discourse on the articulating Mande/Fulbe, Fulbe/Mande identity was Louis Binger (1892). According to his linguistic data, a 25 percent component of Fulbe and Arabic loan words had been incorporated into the Soninke idiom by the late nineteenth century. Binger's quantification can no longer be verified; neither did he mention the word-categories: Herding? Islamic sciences? Textile work? Yet his findings are compelling: In non-writing cultures, loan-words were likely to transfer from one language system into another after considerable articulation, suggesting power relationships and marriage alliances with pre-selected groups. Oathing alliances reminiscent of the *siyah* oath and the *senankun*, a "joking relationship" combining friendship/hostility, seem also likely.[19] Processing data about the negotiated

---

northern Mande, as well as the Sidibe from the Wassulu. See also *ANMK* 1D 32 5, "Etude sur les marabouts du Cercle de Bafoulabé, 1894" (Bafulabe, 5 July 1894), p. 2; Tauxier, *Histoire*, preface, pp. 8, 15, 29, 35, 51; N. S. Hopkins, "The Social structure of Mali (Kita and Bamako) in the 1880s," unpublished Master's thesis, University of Chicago, 1960, p. 3; *Idem*, "Kita, ville malienne," *EM*, no. 6 (July 1973): 1–26; Diarra, "Du Banimonotie," p. 5; Bathily, "Les Soninké dans l'histoire du Fuuta Toro," pp. 26–27; see also note 67 herein. The Maninka are otherwise known as *Mandinga*.

18. *ASAOF* 1G 32, "Lettre Mage à Gouverneur" (Saint Louis, 21 June 1866).

19. The *siyah* was a binding interlineage alliance of mutual help frequently involving intergenerational marriages and reciprocal assistance, including war. Examples of *siyah-nyogow* include the Camera of Siby and the Keita of the old Mande. *Senankunw* varied, including blood brotherhoods instituting peace between warring groups, political and diplomatic relationships, and so forth. Similar kinds of "joking" oaths were also found among the Songhay, the Fulbe, and the Wolof, even in parts of southern Africa, as among the Tonga. The frequency of *senankunw* between *numuw*, or blacksmiths, and the Fulbe is striking. Examples of the *senankuya* include the Tunkara and Sisse who were *senankuya* of the Mande Keita. So were the Jara/Traore, the Kuyate/Keita, and a range of *garanke* families: the Sylla/Jawara, Makalu/Simaga and so forth. Tal Tamari, "The Sunjata Epic as evidence for ancient Manding social structure," paper presented at the African Studies Association (St. Louis, 26 Nov. 1991). See also R. Pageard, "Notes sur le rapport de 'Senankouya' en Soudan français particulièrement dans les cercles de Ségou et de Macina," *BIFAN* sér. B, vol. 11 (1958): 123–141; *Idem.*, "La Parenté à plaisanteries en Afrique occidentale," *Africa*, vol. 12, no. 3 (1959): 244–253; McNaughton, *The Mande*, see esp. pp. 11–12; Labouret, "Les Manding," pp. 100–104. See also Binger, *Du Niger*, vol. 2, p. 382. See also *ANSOM* Sén. et Dép. IV 90 Bis,

identity from a different perspective, Tauxier reached similar conclusions with respect to the articulation of Mande/Fulbe or Fulbe/Mande identities, also a matter of negotiation and perspective within mixed language and dialect repertoires.[20]

Approaching linguistic data more recently from a different perspective, Tal Tamari's study of sixty-seven "caste," or *nyamakala*, designations in use in eleven West African languages likewise suggests Mande/Fulbe linguistic borrowings, although borrowing directions in every case are not always clear.[21] For example, among the four (only) West African languages (Mandekan, Soninke, Wolof, and Fulfulde: Fulani and Tukulor) with collective designations for "caste people,"[22] Tamari traces their derivation to two possible etymons: Manding *nyamakala* and Wolof *neeno*. Arguing moreover that "Manding, Soninke, and Wolof caste institutions may have each evolved independently," she finds that "caste institutions of other peoples were heavily dependent on those of other groups for their development," among these—not surprisingly—the Fulbe. Thus, for example, her data suggest that the Mandekan and Soninke *garanke* (leather worker) is the source of the Fulani *garanke*, *garankejo*, and *garankebe*; and while the Mandekan *jeli* (griot or bard) is the root of the Fulfulde *jeeli(be)*, the Fulfulde *gawlolawlube* (bard) is the basis for the Mandekan *gawulo* and *gawule*; or again, she finds that the Fulfulde *maabo* (bards specialized in epic poetry) is the source of the Bamana *maabo*. In weaving communities the Mandekan *maabo* is derived from the Fulfulde *maabo/maabuube*, where the terms denote "musician-weaver." Furthermore if, as indicated above, the Fulani terms *garanke(jo)/garankebe* (leatherworker) are derived from the Mandekan and Soninke *garanke*, the Fulfulde *sakke(jo)/sakkebe* (leather worker) is related to the Soninke *sakke* (woodworker), although borrowing directions remain unclear. Among woodworkers more generally, although *kule* (Mandekan) exists, the Mandekan *la(w)ube* and the Fulfulde *labbollawbe* are clearly related; the Bamana *segi* and *surasegi* are related to the Soninke *sakke* and the Fulfulde *sakke*.[23]

Vallière, "Mémoire" (Siguiri, 15–25 March 1888), pp. 2, 3, 18–19, 36–37, 46 and passim; *ASAOF* 1G 32, "Lettre Mage à Gouverneur" (Saint Louis, 21 June 1866).

20. Tauxier, *Histoire*, preface.

21. Tal Tamari, "Linguistic evidence for the history of West African 'castes'," in Conrad and Frank, eds., *Status and identity*, pp. 61–85, see esp. pp. 65–73.

22. *Nyamakala* (Manding), *naxamala* (Soninke), *neeno* (Wolof), *nyeenyolnyeenybe* (Fulfulde: Fulani and Tukulor), *nyaamakala* (Fulfulde: Tukulor only) (Tamari, "Linguistic evidence," p. 65).

23. "In most Fulfulde-speaking areas, bardship is thought of as the primary activity, and weaving as a secondary one, but in some Manding areas, *maabo* are thought of primarily as weavers" (Tamari, "Linguistic evidence," p. 65).

Further evidence substantiating the linguistic data comes from comparable social organizations where Mande *nyamakalaw*, or specialized endogamous families, have their Fulbe counterpart especially in the *wambabe*, or Fulbe *griot*. Both groups have likewise developed similar power associations (secret societies), political rituals and religious symbolism, including Tyanaba, a Fulbe python image figuring in textile designs, the equivalent of Bida the sacred Mande python.[24] Proverbs and sayings in the popular cultures also reflect these affinities, such as the Mande proverb recalling that "wherever a Manding (i.e., Bamana and Mandinka) establishes his residence in the morning, he is joined by a Fulbe in the evening." Not surprisingly, when the Niare founded their Bamako *kafu*, they were joined by Fulbe and Jawambe (sing.: *jawando*) herders, the latter a Fulbe subgroup. Others migrating into the Bamako *kafu* region hailed mainly from Gumbu, Sokolo, and Segu.[25]

Thus across the centuries (according to linguistic and cultural data), negotiated Mande/Fulbe identities emerged, most probably "processed" through marriage and other ritual negotiations including the *siyah* and *senankun* alliances. Residual cultural and linguistic traces, apparent even today, suggest Mande-Fulbe or Fulbe-Mande continua— depending on the region—where identities continue to articulate differently, and separately, the cultural semicircle linking Segu, Sikasso, Koutiala, and Kong the most striking example of this seemingly collapsing phenomena (see Maps 5 and 7). Yet in what is now an indecipherable and elliptical way (as discussed in the Introduction) they also appear to have been the "same" within the historical-particular-within-the-mythical-universal. By that same token, depending on the region, not only were the Nyakate-Soninke, Jakite-Fulbe, Kaba Soninke, and Bari-Fulbe identities variable, articulating, and separate, but they too sometimes appeared to be the same. Which may explain why even today seemingly different people in the Mande-hinterland still insist that they are the same.[26]

---

24. Pâques, "L'Estrade royale," pp. 1643–1647.

25. *ASAOF* 1G 299, "Sénégambie-Niger: Cercle de Bamako, généralités frontières, Bamako ville, définitions administratives et géographiques, 1903–1904," n.p.

26. Interview Nana Niaré Dravé (Bamako, 5 Jan. 1980); interview Marabout Bani Touré (Bozola-Bamako, 4 Jan. 1980). For studies of articulating and shifting identities elsewhere in Africa, see, Justin Willis, "The Makings of a tribe: Bondei identities and histories," *JAH*, vol. 33, no. 2 (1992): 191–208; Saul Dubow, "Afrikaner nationalism apartheid and conceptualization of 'race,'" *JAH*, vol. 3, no. 2 (1992): 209–237.

Articulating Eastern Nyakate/Niare Identities

Cultural-Mythic Manipulations

The Myth. On turning more specifically to the smaller Bamako-Niare families, we ask how their identities were articulated and/or expressed; or what complex circumstances engendered their shift from Soninke-Nyakate to Marka or Sarakolle, to Bamana-Niare, with possibly a Fulbe type interlude in between? The myth, beginning with societal strivings, ends with state initiatives and ideology. Thus both familial corporate groups and the state played a role in the Niare identity negotiations and their further manifestations.

Those studying myths and legends know that, by its very nature, the oral genre is not only episodic, contradictory, conflictual, and overlapping, but also highly manipulable: We recall that on first hearing the Bamako legends, both Borgnis Desbordes in 1883 and Brevie in 1904 found their "unstructured" and "episodic" forms maddening, the former in particular believing them valueless, serving only the "narrator's interests." Echoing similar sentiments more than half a century earlier Anne Jean-Baptiste Raffenel (1840s), the French voyager, had dismissed legends as nothing but a "swarm of contradictions." Accordingly, as information is moved from one literary stratum to another, or the traditionalist shifts his sliding focus from one family to another, narratives can be reorganized, re-contextualized, and/or overlaid with themselves and one other, not to mention deformed and confused.[27]

We also know that textual variations often represent different voices speaking from particularized perspectives, intended for still more variable audiences, the latter lending their involved imaginations in the interest of an "authentic performance." Thus providing an authenticity which the genre allows, seemingly conflictual and contradictory voices speak for different identities. And if particularized variations appear to be manipulated, negotiated, overlapping, conflictual, and even contradictory, it is because they are. Also known is that within the mythic process, narrative lines—which serve different ends—can develop fluid chronological boundaries, sometimes extending beyond several generations, at other times collapsing into one lifetime. Still otherwise, fluid chronologies co-opt events from one time frame, inserting them into another; not infrequently, the same or similar events appear and reappear in different time

---

27. Anne Jean-Baptiste Raffenel, *Nouveau voyage au pays des nègres*, 2 vols. (Paris, 1856), vol. 1, p. 169. For some critiques of oral histories, see Joseph C. Miller, ed., *The African past speaks: Essays on oral tradition and history* (Kent, England, 1980), and note 29.

frames, organizing, reorganizing and legitimizing events according to compelling ideological necessities.[28]

We likewise know that while the genre creates culture heroes, larger-than-life icons with biblical life spans, they are often there to legitimize change. Accordingly, great iconic persona—a Sunjata Keita, a Sumanguru Kante, a Mansa Musa, a Dembele *numu* (or blacksmith)—shift around the genre, sometimes niched in historical crevices, at other times concealed in the ethnographic imagination as venerable ancestors legitimizing socio-political action, favoring ritual innovation, and sanctioning violators of sacred cultural symphonies. By that same token, culprits of sullied fame—passed over briefly in some bardic refrains—are oftentimes "excused" in one text, only to be justified in another as partisan voices speak. Under-standing the manipulability of the oral genre, it was the *jeli* (bard) Baba Sissoko who noted that "a story that is told for a long time and never written down may be told in many ways."[29] More than a hundred years earlier—and equally cognizant of the genre's fluidity—Raffenel noted that "rarely do legends and oral traditions (after many recountings), survive without alteration."[30]

Not surprisingly, on turning to the Bamako Niare myths, we find multiple overlays with the Segovian and Wagadu traditions of which seventeen versions (of the "Legend of Wagadu") are extant.[31] Moreover, not only have the Niare appropriated the Wagadu legend as their principal identity signifier, but so have all the Wago (plural form), or leading Soninke families—the Sakho, the Sisse, the Jaby, and the Dokote.[32] Mani-

---

28. Thomas Spear, "Oral traditions: Whose history?" *HA*, vol. 8 (1981): 165–181; Jan Vansina, *Oral tradition as history* (University of Wisconsin Press, 1985); David Henige, *The Chronology of oral tradition: Quest for a chimera* (Oxford at Clarendon, 1987).

29. For Baba Sissoko see Conrad and Fisher, "The Conquest," part 1, pp. 21–59; part 2, pp. 53–78.

30. Raffenel, *Nouveau voyage*, vol. 1, pp. 169, 183. Recall that Gallieni had similar reactions (Gallieni, *Voyage*, p. 464; and personal communication, Ali Ongoïba [Kuluba-Bamako, 18 Jan. 1983]).

31. For references, see Introduction note 12, and note 32 of this Chapter. For a discussion, see Conrad and Fisher, "The Conquest," part 2, pp. 53–78; Pollet and Winter, *La Société soninké*, pp. 22–28. A separate *Ta'rikh Niaré* is also said to exist.

32. The Wago are those families who it is said best upheld the ethics and honor codes most identified with "Soninkeness." Supposedly four in number, names cited from different sources add up to more than four. Those cited above are drawn from Meillassoux, "Histoire," p. 189, note 2. For those recording the Sakho version, see G. Tellier, *Autour de Kita* (Paris, 1898), pp. 207–209; Delafosse, "Traditions historiques," vol. 8, pp. 293–306; vol. 9, pp. 325–329; vol. 10, 355–368; De-

pulating the genre further, all the Wago claim to have been Wagadu's (Ghana's) ruling lineage.[33] Not surprisingly, so have the Niare who, in addition, claim Wage (sing.) lineage status.[34] It is no longer clear how or why these early traditions became so enmeshed, overlaid, and interlocking, or why they embody conflicting, ambiguous, and contradictory claims. Raymond Mauny, on the one hand, estimated that families customarily embellished their lineage status mainly for the colonizer's benefit. On the other hand, Ali Ongoiba supposed more generally that lineage enhancement very often belonged to local competition and political power plays.[35]

The Manipulated Wagadu Legend

The Disaster Episode

Principal episodes of the signature "Legend of Wagadu" are well known. Recounted in mythic time (the continuous present), we hear the story of the ancient Soninke kingdom of Wagadu lost because a scion of the ruling dynasty refuses to sacrifice his betrothed to Bida the sacred python (*milimini*). Observed in accordance with a renewable mythical-ritual-political alliance with earth spirits (representatives of a fundamental law) and entered into in mythical time at the original land settlement, this rite, calling for a sacrificial virgin, has been observed annually since archaic time. From the signature myth we know that Bida is symbolic of fertility, light (the sun), water (rainfall), brightness (gold), and power (political power).[36] Thus through the alliance the ser-

---

lafosse, *Haut-Sénégal-Niger*, vol. 1, pp. 261–262; Monteil, "La Légende," pp. 361–408. For the Jaby-Sisse version, see J. H. Saint-Père, *Les Sarakollé du Guidimaka* (Paris, 1925), p. 13; and for the Dokote version, see Adam, "Légendes historiques" (1903), pp. 81, 232, 354, 485–496, 602–620, 734–744; (1904), 117–224, 232–248. See also below and Introduction herein note 12.

33. For a history of Ghana, see Levtzion, *Ancient Ghana*, pp. 16–22. For a discussion of sources see Conrad and Fisher, "The Conquest," part 1, pp. 21–59; part 2, pp. 53–78. For archeological findings affecting Kumbi, see Mauny, *Tableau géographique*, pp. 72–74, and the Introduction notes 10, 11 herein.

34. Others dispute the Nyakate rulership claim. See Diawara, *La Graine*, p. 35, and below.

35. Personal communication Raymond Mauny (Paris, 2 Dec. 1982); personal communication Ali Ongoïba (Kuluba-Bamako, 15 Jan. 1983).

36. The widespread incidence of mythical-magical snakes in ancient epistemes is remarkable, for example, ancient Egypt, Hebrew mythologies, in sub-Saharan Africa as far south as the Bemba of South Africa, as well as some pre-Colombian civilizations. In some cultures they represent pure energy.

pent has guaranteed a ritual access to political state power, its resources, and a collective well-being. By way of a reciprocal exchange, Wagadu's rulers are obligated to obedience, a responsible stewardship, and a just governance.[37] Their alliance is not, however, a contract; rather it is a renewable bonding between the Soninko and the fundamental law violated only with devastating penalties. In the signature myth, the rite is the original process creating the Soninko and their "Soninkeness."

As episodes of the manipulated Niare version (as opposed to the generic or signature myth) open, we hear that the Nyakate, the endogamous ruling dynasty with its capital at Kumbi Saleh, has already been ruling Wagadu for a formulaic 450 years. Renewal of the alliance is at hand; and standing by is Sya Nyakate, the beautiful maiden whose hour has come. She is, at midnight, to be sacrificed to Bida at his sacred lair. Unknown to the elders and the waiting crowd, however, is Fata Maghan Nyakate, scion of the 450-year ruling dynasty, Sya's cousin and betrothed who, in defiance, has decided to abort this sacrificial rite. Stealing to the serpent's pithead under cover of darkness, concealed in the loose folds of his beloved's veil, Fata Maghan abrogates the ritual-political alliance. He severs the sacred serpent's head.[38] According to most versions, Fata Maghan's unauthorized action—a political crime against the elders, the ancestral spirits, and the fundamental law—is perpetrated not in the collective interest, but directed at individual gain. The third time he is required to sacrifice his betrothed to the python, Fata Maghan, neither a revolutionary nor a culture hero in the oral texts, decides to end his "victimization" by violating the ritual

---

37. Information on this institutionalized sacrifice to Bida varies: According to Monteil, the sacrifice to Bida was an annual affair, with a total of 441 sacrifices across the centuries; according to Tauxier, the sacrifice was every seven years with a total of 287 sacrifices. See also Jean Bazin, "La Production d'un récit historique," *CEA*, vol. 19 (1979): 435–483.

38. According to this Niare version recorded by Meillassoux, the python had one head. According to Paques, whose version makes greater use of Mande imagery, the beast had seven heads. The python, moreover, according to Paques, was the masculine element, while Bida's pit (a well) was the feminine element. As a consequence, the python (*Boidae pythoninae*) became the Niare *tana*, or prohibition, an animal (or some other living creature) the Niare were prohibited from killing or harming on pain of serious penalties (Pâques, "L'Estrade royale," pp. 1643, 1644, 1649). According to other reports, other Niare *tana*w include the fromager tree (*Ceiba pentandra*), the lion (*Panthera leo*), and the gray pigeon (genus *Columbidae*). See notes 88 and 95 for further discussion of the *tana*.

alliance, risking political chaos for the entire collectivity. He thereby triggers the automatic penalty, worse than a father's curse: the curse of Wagadu.

In the wake of this ritual-political crime—the crowd converging in wrath—Fata Maghan flees. Speeding southwest through the night on a trusty steed, the legend takes a surprising turn when the malfeasant is unexpectedly, and inexplicably, joined by Mana Maghan his older brother, the last ruler of Kumbi (Wagadu). Mana Maghan, who lost his realm and kingly birthright at the hands of a deviant cadet, strangely seems to condone the condemned.[39] The brothers' flight heralds disasters, droughts, the disappearance of gold, the disintegration of the state, and the permanent dispersal of the Soninko from Wagadu, their ancestral home-land.[40]

---

39. In Paques' account the two Niare brothers are Fusseni and Lassana, twin sons of Dignan, the latter a nomad from Guimbala (L'Estrade royale," pp. 1643–1644). According to the *Ta'rikh as-Sudan,* Maghan was the name of a Wagadu ruler; *Maghan* meaning "large," was adopted from the Fulbe idiom into Soninke and Bamanakan. The *Ta'rikh al-Fattash* identifies *Kaymaga* (Maghan) as a title, among other things (As-Sadi, *Ta'rikh as-Soudan,* trans. O. Houdas [Paris, 1964], p. 18, note 2; *Ta'rikh al-Fattash,* p. 42, note 4).

40. According to other sources the drought lasted a symbolic seven years, seven months, and seven days. The python had been responsible for rain showers of gold falling on the land (Pâques, "L'Estrade royale," p. 1644; Bugari Kanadji, "La Légende de Wagadou," in Dantioko, *Soninkara,* pp. 102–144). Another Niare fragment claims that the drought incident occurred at Lambidu in the Kaarta, and not at Wagadu (Soumaoro, "Etudes," p. 2).

In addition to the Nyakate, other lineages to flee Wagadu included the Jakite who settled near Tango in the Gidiume, Kaniaga, and Nioro, where they have been closely associated with the Nyakate. Those in the Tango region were eventually driven out by the Soninke speaking Jambu who imposed their hegemony on the remaining Soninko communities. In the Nioro region the Jakite settled near the old Nyakate state of Kingi (Pollet and Winter, *La Société soninké,* p. 30). Other lineages to leave Wagadu after the crisis were the Sisse, the Ture (with whom the Sisse are closely associated), the Sylla, and the Jarissi (alternates Yarissi, Bacilli, Bathily, Batchily, Bakari). According to tradition, these latter settled in Gajaga (French Galam). Other lineages included the Kumma, the Berote, the Jaby, the Kone, and the Dukure, most of whom settled between the regions of Mema, Ja, Nono, Sinsani (Sansanding), and Guimbala—in the Niger Delta and Lake Debo regions—as well as in Gajaga. The Dukure settled at Diengei, south of Bakhunu, and in Jafunu, a grain-producing region. Some Soninko even settled as far afield as the Black Volta region. Pollet and Winter, *La Société soninké,* pp. 28–34, 47–49; Delafosse, *Haut-Sénégal-Niger,* vol. 1, pp. 252–278. These Soninko are frequently known by different ethnonyms according to regional idioms. See Perinbam, "Notes," pp. 687.

The Nyakate's 450-year rule at last comes to an end. Embellishing the story, other versions depict Bida's head plunging south to the Bure, where shedding his sacred hide, gold ores fall upon the earth.[41] From our perspective, the dispersal from Wagadu marks the first manipulation in a set of Soninke-Niare identity signifiers. After such disasters the Nyakate transform their internal social system, abandoning endogamy, an arcane identity marker.

Critique

An interesting aside, the endogamous control over marriage was a key element in the development of Mande political linkages and power alliances. However, as Claude Meillassoux has shown, endogamy, or the procurement of brides from within a community, tended to threaten elders' authority from *within*, because, encroaching on their power over matrimonial management, institutionalized endogamy weakened internal political alliances (i.e., internal contradictions arose because too many families had become part of the organization of power). Moreover, offering fewer opportunities for internal coalitions and transactional relations, endogamy could in the long run decrease elders' rights over production and reproduction (i.e., internal contradictions developed because too many families had rights in progeny and property). By restricting their outward power-elaboration through political or diplomatic agreements, endogamy could similarly weaken the elders' external political leverage (i.e., external exchange of brides was important for foreign and diplomatic relations).[42]

Finally, leaving Wagadu were the Fulfulde speakers, settling in the northern Mande, where collective identities changed over the centuries becoming "Maninkized" (Maninka-Fula). Wa Kamissoko and Youssouf Tata Cissé, eds., *L'Empire du Mali: Actes du Colloque*, Deuxième Colloque Internationale de Bamako (12–22 Feb. 1976), 2 vols. (Bamako, 1977); vol. 2, p. xvi. For a discussion of the origins of the Mande clans according to oral texts, see Germaine Dieterlen, "The Mande creation myth," *Africa*, vol. 27 (1965): 124–138. See also Tauxier, *La Religion*, pp. 114–138.

41. Interview Guimba Djakité (Bamako, 3 Jan. 1983); interview Diarra Sylla (Bamako, 15 March 1983).

42. Endogamy was apparently most prevalent in ruling lineages where the families were subject to different reproductive norms, as well as in patrimonial societies anxious to preserve their wealth (Claude Meillassoux, *Maidens, meal, and money*, trans. from the French [Cambridge University Press, 1981], pp. 25, 74–77, 127–130, 133–134 and passim).

It is therefore possible that "the Disaster Episode" at the pithead could simply have been spectacular imagery to explain Nyakate attempts in this manipulated version to recover a loss of internal power and authority, and to enlarge their external diplomatic range, as well as enhance all overall power and authority. The Nyakate could also have been reinforcing their political and ritual authority and power-base in the face of internal challenges. Or perhaps the fundamental law—the state's ritual-constitutional and ritual-political integrity—and its ritual-social theory were being called into question. And clearly the younger generation was out of control. However, although circumstances point to an internal crisis, as the secondary literature has shown, it is also likely that external exigencies played a role. Conceivably, the clans were driven from the Sahel by droughts and increasing regional desiccation.[43] Should this have been the case, it implies—in the mythical genre at any rate—a ruptured alliance between fundamental law (Bida) and the Soninko, producing grave environmental degradation. Or possibly Wagadu's ruling dynasty lost access to trade routes—important for state revenue. Should this have been the case, their rivals would have been the Almoravids, who, seizing Sijilmasa in the north and Awdaghost in the south by about 1054, were controlling Ghana's (Wagadu) gold trade.[44] Or perhaps Ghana was conquered by the Almoravids, a hypothesis currently losing ground.[45]

Given the above, it is now academic to ask whether or not Wagadu existed. As a social construct, Wagadu could have been no more than a survival or revival in the Soninke historical imagination, or simply an elusive cultural concept without time-space boundaries, although a location in the western Sahel seems feasible.[46] And while the serpent's murder provides the imagery and mythical explanation for the state's decline and the Soninko dispersal, not surprisingly, the historical record offers no such assurance. As to chronology, it defies comprehension, especially the

---

43. Brooks, *Landlords*, pp. 1–57 and passim.

44. B. Marie Perinbam, "Social relations of the trans-Saharan and western Sudanese trade: An overview," *Comparative Studies in Society and History*, vol. 15, no. 4 (Oct. 1973): 416–436.

45. See Conrad and Fisher, "The Conquest," see esp. part 2, p. 69. Other accounts to question the conquest theory include A. Bathily, "A Discussion ... Wagadu," pp. 1–94; Burkhalter, "Listening," pp. 103–131.

46. For different perspectives on these complex issues see Pollet and Winter, *La Société soninké*, pp. 25–28; Delafosse, *Haut-Sénégal-Niger*, vol. 1, pp. 319–321, 418; vol. 2, pp. 12–21, 25–59; Tautain, "Légende et traditions," pp. 472–480; Meillassoux, Doucouré, and Simagha, *Légende de la dispersion*, pp. 8, 11.

Nyakate formulaic 450-year rule.[47] Despite few empirical and chronological boundaries, however, it cannot be ruled out that events of this, or a
similar nature, could have been occurring in the western Sahel sometime
during the latter part of the first millennium and the first part of the
second. Not altogether mythical, archaeological evidence at Kumbi Saleh
and the several Arabic accounts recorded between the ninth and fourteenth centuries do, in fact, testify to a Soninke state with its capital at
Kumbi.[48] I stated in the Introduction that al-Fazari was the first to mention the Ghana (or Kumbi) state before a.d. 800, followed by al-Khuwarizmi before 833, by Ibn Hawqal in about 988, and al-Bakri in approximately
1068. I noted that even the "scientific" Ibn Khaldun repeated references to
the Ghana state, not to mention its celebrated trans-Saharan gold and salt
trade, which survived for centuries even after the state's decline.[49]

Less academic is the question of Niare dynastic claims: Did the
Nyakate rule Wagadu? That no historical evidence supports any Wago
dynastic pretensions, let alone Niare claims, contests their and all other
dynastic conjurings, calling all into question. No other mythical "evidence" weighs in the Niare's favor, or in anybody else's either. By way of
contrast with respect to the Niare, two legendary sources state otherwise.
First, in his Kingi study, Mamadou Diawara places the Nyakate not
among the Wago as they themselves acknowledge, but among the "Son-
ninkannu," or lesser nobility of Wagadu, freemen with no access to political power, the latter otherwise claimed by the "Sonininkaxooro" (pl.), the
grand nobility, such as the Camara and Kamissoko families. On Diawara's
authority it is therefore unlikely that the Nyakate ruled Wagadu.[50]
Second, in his study of Ghana and Mali, Nehemia Levtzion identified the

---

47. While Delafosse traced Wagadu's demise to the latter part of the eighth
century, Tautain suggested the middle of the tenth century. In the Niare-Meillas-
soux version, the mid-twelfth-century date may have some validity (Meillassoux,
"Histoire," p. 223). See also Delafosse, *Haut-Sénégal-Niger*, vol. 2, p. 25–26; Tautain,
"Légende et traditions," 472–480; Pollet and Winter, *La Société soninké*, pp. 22–34;
Pâques, "L'Estrade royale," p. 1644.

48. Mauny, *Tableau géographique*, pp. 60, 72–74; Levtzion, *Ancient Ghana*, pp.
20–22; Conrad and Fisher, "The Conquest," part 2, p. 53; Introduction herein,
notes 10, and 11. See also, McIntosh, *Excavations at Jenne-jeno*.

49. Levtzion and Hopkins, *Corpus*, pp. 7, 45, 79–87, for Ibn Khaldun see pp.
332–333; Mauny, *Tableau géographique*, pp. 24–30, 72–74; Pollet and Winter, *La Société soninké*, pp. 25–28. For a full discussion of the decline of Ghana (Wagadu,
Kumbi), see Conrad and Fisher, "The Conquest," parts 1 and 2.

50. Diawara, *La Graine*, p. 35. For a similar reference to the *miskin* of Gumbu,
see Claude Meillassoux, "Etat et conditions des esclaves à Gumbhu (Mali) au XIXe
siècle," *JAH*, vol. 14, no. 3 (1973): 429–453, see esp. p. 429.

Nyakate as the first rulers of Jara (Diara) in the Kingi, and not at Wagadu. Following the Wagadu dispersal, according to this account, "Malinke bands from the south" raided the region, obstructing trade routes and creating civil unrest. It is at this point that one Mana Maghan Nyakate, a Soninke merchant frequenting the region, according to this version, organized an army of followers consisting of local Soninke and Jawambe, a Fulbe sub-group. Defeating the "Malinke," Mana Maghan consolidated gains by establishing a state with himself as "king," Jara (Kingi) as his capital. On later becoming vassals of the Soso, subsequently of Mali, the Nyakate ruled Jara jointly with a Malian "commissioner" as guarantor of their loyalty. Third, on Boyer's authority, likewise, the Nyakate were not rulers at Wagadu.[51]

In the apparent absence of historical or mythical substantiation, why then did the Niare claim to be Wagadu's rulers? Empirical data beyond further investigation, contextual events, and circumstances suggest that in advancing these claims—also made by all Wago or leading Soninko families—the Niare were enhancing and legitimizing sacred leadership rights at Bamako, tracing a chiefly identity to Wagadu. Should this have been the case, and it appears feasible, their manipulation of the signature Wagadu legend would have authenticated their "grand nobility," justifying chiefly legitimacy in the face of political contestants (see below). More importantly from our perspective, mythic manipulations authenticated Nyakate-Soninke identity claims when faced with the Bamana and Fulbe Other, whether in the Massina, in Kingi, at Ja, or at Segu.

Finally, there remains the question of a relative chronology for which little historical evidence exists. But because Wagadu's (Ghana) state development and decline may have occurred toward the latter part of the first millennium and the early part of the second, in approximate world or universalizing time, events in the Wagadu state could have coincided with the Arab expansion beyond the Arabian peninsular region (634–641). And, in what would become France, Charlemagne of the house of Pepin (771–814) was expanding his rule to include the Germans. In al-Andalusia, the Iberian peninsula, the Muslim conquest between 711–715 could also have been occurring "during the time of Wagadu"; and in England, the Norman invasions (1066) would have been a decade earlier than Kumbi's much-contested destruction by the Almoravids (1076). Further east, the decline of Wagadu could have coin-

---

51. Levtzion, *Ancient Ghana*, pp. 48–49, 81. See also Adam, "Légendes historiques" (1903), pp. 81–98, 232–248, 354–372, 485–496, 602–620, 734–744; (1904), pp. 117–124, 233–248. See especially 1903, pp. 232–233; Boyer, *Un Peuple*, pp. 24–26; *Ta'rikh al-Fattash*, pp. 62, 70–74.

cided with the Age of the Crusades (1096–1291) and the final disintegration of the Byzantine Empire (1025–1204); while the Magna Carta (1215)
could have been signed just about the time of, or not long after, Wagadu's demise. In East Asia, the illustrious T'ang Dynasty (618–907)
may have been centralizing its rule "in the time of Wagadu," together
with paper printing for the first time (868 the earliest extant printed
book). Of particular interest is that during the same era in Japan, the imperial line, concerned with dynastic legitimacy, was extended to include
"mythical time" and equally "mythically ruling ancestors." And the *Ko-
jiki* (712), or written history for this timeless age, was being written
down for the first time (Chinese orthography was introduced in the seventh century).

The Sacrifice Episode

On returning to the Niare texts (and mythic time), we hear of a "Sacrifice Episode,"[52] where the two Nyakate brothers in flight from Wagadu—
now beyond pursuit—arrive at Kingi north of Kaarta (see Map 3). Exhausted, and believing it safe to abandon flight, the young culprit Fata
Maghan sinks to rest under a drame tree (*Laennea acida*). Unsuccessful in
a quest for venison to assuage his sibling's hunger, the compassionate
doyen, Mana Maghan—he whose realm is lost by a wayward sibling—
severs a morsel from his calf (other versions indicate it was from his
thigh). On braising it over live coals, Mana's ravenous sibling eats. Later
learning of the sacrifice, Fata Maghan's voice rises in song, swearing to
spend the rest of his days in praise of the *doyen*'s magnanimity. By this
sacrificial act, the cadet Fata Maghan marks the beginnings of new social
relationships and differentiations within the Niare social organization:
the creation of a *jeli*, or bardic lineage (*geseru:* Soninke), adopting the
Drame (Darame) *jamu*, or patronym, in commemoration of the heroic
sacrifice. For us, the act marks the second in a manipulated set of signifiers in the emergence of a variable Soninke identity, its social stratification and transformative process.

Critique

Not always subscribing to the popularly held *jeli* epistemology embedded in this Sacrifice Episode, other informants extrapolate a more general

---

52. "Sacrifice" is not used here in the religious sense as was the case at Wagadu, although bloodletting of any sort, usually part of a ritual to unite earthlings
with the spiritual universe, was significant. "Sacrifice" here probably means the
surrender of something of value for the sake of a greater gain.

"social stratification theory," allegedly explaining dubious social differentiations within Soninke lineages, perhaps even the precarious delineation of social "castes," which may or may not be just another "colonial" epistemology. On the one hand, the implication here—often misleading—is that as part of a "cultural coding," sacrificial formulae invariably explained, sometimes covered up, a wide range of social "slippages" of one sort or another, wherein families lost face or were disgraced by alleged acts or deeds considered socially reprehensible. On the other hand, in conflict with this more general social-stratification theory (which is often misleading) is an equally questionable "punishment theory," where the *nyamakalaw*, or specialized workers, are said to have come by their (despised) status because, not matching expectations (i.e., holding up cherished values to ridicule), they were finally held accountable. Slippages according to these likely "colonial explanations" were thus more causally and specifically related.[53]

Whatever the theories—and many abound—more appropriate from our perspective is the view that families "slipped" into a number of different conditions having nothing to do with the *nyamakala*, some for general, others for more specific, reasons. A more general slippage could have occurred in the event of war bringing slavery, or a slave interlude for a family, as was the case many times over during the Umarian and Samorian wars of the latter part of the nineteenth century. Escaping slavery, others lost wealth and social status during the wars, becoming just plain poor, and not necessarily "slipping" into *nyamakalaw* ranks (not that incorporation into *nyamakalaw* ranks necessarily meant slippage). The French Lieutenant Collomb (1884–1885) noted in the wake of the Samorian wars, for example, that several families became poor: The loss of so many able-bodied family members had deprived them of a labor force.[54] The loss of political power, or a drought, could likewise bring disaster, hence further slippage. Even more specifically, a recalcitrant wife could be sold into slavery, or a debtor cast into the slaver's irons, which could cause more social slippage. Slipped families, it is said, covered up or explained their misfortune through metaphors, imagery, and symbols, their "secret" frequently known only to insiders and to trusty *jeliw*. Which is why a *jeli*'s lacerating tongue is so greatly

---

53. Social stratification and punishment theories no longer find support in current Mande scholarship. For a good discussion, see Conrad and Frank, eds., *Identity and status*.

54. *ANMK* 1D 33 2, Collomb, "Notice" (Bamako, 1884–1885), p. 15. For a discussion of poverty as the paucity of a labor force, see John Iliffe, *The African poor: A history* (Cambridge University Press, 1987), see introduction.

feared, people say.[55] Thus, a sacrifice episode—any sacrifice episode within the oral repertoire —expressed a variety of social phenomena (and not necessarily a misleading "slippage" into *nyamakala* ranks) believed to have universal application in the Mande identity.[56]

In the case of the Drame or Nyakate bardic lineages—frankly puzzling—the Sacrifice Episode hardly provides a satisfactory explanation for social stratification within the Nyakate families, especially since other accounts (see below) offer a conflicting calculus for a variety of other slippages, perhaps even disgrace. Possibly, Niare manipulations in the Sacrifice Episode explain some kind of internal organizational change within familial social relationships without, however, clarifying its full nature or intent. Moreover, that sacrifice stories are common to myths within other familial identities, even differentiated ethnic identities, suggests a general formulaic imagery implying, without explaining, important social changes occurring within Soninke lineages in general. From another perspective, sacrifice episodes could simply be "explaining" considerable suffering, even bad luck occurring within families during the dispersal, suggesting a threat to collective and individual identities, a kind of cultural nudity and social invisibility. Or their metaphorical and parabolic vagaries could simply be a manifestation of the sort commonly found in middle portions of the mythic genre. In any event, the Sacrifice Episode clearly represents a third identity marker in the manipulated Niare texts, an experience relating them to Wagadu and archaic time.

The Kingi Episode

On returning to the Niare oral texts, we hear of the Kingi Episode, when the Nyakate and their Drame, or bardic lineage, establish their

---

55. Personal communication Ali Ongoïba (Kuluba-Bamako, 5 April 1983). The *jeli* Wa Kamissoko expresses a similar view (interview Sidy Diabaté with Wa Kamissoko in Diabaté, "Kankan Moussa," p. 53). Although not related, Fulbe traditions at Kingi record a similar cover up of "family secrets." According to one story Jata Jallo, a common herder, is said to have sacrificed his life to save that of Haren Makan (his Jawara chief), a sixteenth-century ruler of Kingi. Before Jallo's death, the grateful Jawara is said to have concluded an alliance with him, thereby institutionalizing Jallo's lineage status as "herders of the chiefly animals." On subsequently recounting their family history, the Jato Jallo produced a "useful history" by suppressing their "common" origins, tracing instead the family heritage exclusively to "the pact" and their elevation as "chiefly herders" (Diawara, *La Graine*, pp. 74, 77; Pageard, "Notes ... 'Senankouya'," esp. pp. 134–136).

56. Personal communication Ali Ongoïba (Kuluba-Bamako, 5 April 1983).

second state at Kingi with Jara (Diara) as its capital. Resorting to yet another formulaic imagery, some versions claim that the Nyakate rule Kingi for another 450 years.[57]

The Adultery Episode

But eventually all is not well in the state of Kingi. Another young Nyakate scion, this time Bemba (Benba, Bamba), son of Seribadia Nyakate, Kingi's ruler, has violated another sacred alliance, again involving a woman: Stealing into the night, Bemba compromises his brother's wife.[58] Instead of contrition, other versions say, Bemba worsens matters by posturing before his accusers, killing the "morality squad" sent against him, simultaneously disappearing from the mythic record. Still other versions exclaim that Bemba, a "tyrant," is overthrown by his Fulbe subjects; or that asleep, he is trapped during an unidentified enemy attack on Kingi, similarly disappearing from the mythic record; or that a "sickly" fellow, he was left behind when the Mana Maghan Nyakate dynasty was overthrown at Kingi. Bemba's deviancy looms even larger in the Lambidu (Kaarta) accounts where voices portray a kind of "bogey man," a "turbulent child," and a "troublemaker" responsible for the Nyakate dispersal, this time from Kingi. His dispute with the Fulbe of Kaarta is likewise profiled in Lambidu accounts where, in the imagery which the genre allows, Bemba "burnt the millet"; a further debacle elsewhere is once more attributed to the work of Bemba[59]

But if Bemba's deviancy looms larger in the Lambidu accounts, we also hear the voice of his defender: A Lambidu *jeli*-version excuses him on grounds that he is only "a child who (knows) ... nothing" better.[60] This defense is to no avail, however, because, once more suffering the collective consequences of a youthful offense, the Nyakate lose their Kingi realm, at which point Seribadia Nyakate, Kingi's last ruler, flees under the shadow of another family disgrace. He is accompanied by Delbafa, the aggrieved son whose wife Bemba has compromised, eight

---

57. Meillassoux, "Histoire," pp. 189–190.

58. Meillassoux, "Histoire," pp. 190–191. According to Soumaoro, the act was committed at Lambidu in the Kaarta (Soumaoro, "Etude," pp. 1–2). See also Villien-Rossi, "Bamako," p. 264. Adultery stories also appear in Fulbe legends.

59. Adam, "Légendes historiques," p. 103; Delafosse, *Haut-Sénégal-Niger*, vol. 1, pp. 271–275; Pâques, "L'Estrade royale," p. 1644. Different scenarios occur in other Bemba stories (Boyer, *Un Peuple*, pp. 24–26).

60. Nyaxate, "La Dispersion," pp. 223, 225, 227, 229; Jabate, "La Légende," pp. 243.

brothers, and a handful of retainers including two marabouts, Muhammad Fassi and Sidi Muhammad Tabure.[61] Other Nyakate, according to an Islamized Kaarta version, flee west to the Gidiume, and even the Gambia (see Map 3). Those remaining in Kingi adopt Drame—often a *jeli* patronym—as their *jamu*. At the conclusion of this episode, the leadership of Kingi passes to Jamangille of the Kingi legends, who later adopts a Soninke identity and the Jawara (Diawara) patronym.[62] From our perspective, the Kingi and Adultery Episodes become the third in a manipulated set of identity signifiers.

Critique

The leanest and most challenging of all the legendary episodes, Kingi texts are the most difficult to interpret. They are certainly not wanting in signs of violence, legitimacy, and power struggles. We begin by wondering: Did the Nyakate establish a state at Kingi? If global Nyakate accounts speak of a Nyakate Kingi state, they were unavailable. Other indications suggest that an Arabic text and fragmented legends may be circulating in the Nioro region.[63] This, seemingly a silence in the global Nyakate accounts, is surprising, given that if the Nyakate had ruled Kingi, the larger western branches would probably have preserved this information in oral records—given also that western accounts indicate that Kingi was a dispersal point in the migrations of the *jaman'a*, or global clans. Yet the sole oral reference—or seemingly so—comes from the eastern Nyakate branch.

Six other accounts in the literary strata throw further light on the subject. First, the *Ta'rikh al-Fattash*—oral accounts recorded in the Timbuktu region during the seventeenth century—does substantiate Niare claims: that one Suleyman Bana Nyakate ruled Kingi, a semiautonomous Nyakate state within metropolitan Mali, and who accompanied Mansa Musa on a Pilgrimage to Mecca circa 1325. Kingi, according to this ac-

---

61. Tabure recollections identify Sidi Muhammad Tabure as a merchant, not a marabout (Meillassoux, "Histoire," p. 190, see also note 5; p. 192, see also notes 4, 5).

62. Jabate, "La Légende," pp. 243, 245, 247. See also Diawara, *La Graine.*

63. An Arabic text from the Nioro region apparently maintains that after the Nyakate fled Kingi, "until now, no one has had news (of them), not of Mana Makhan (Kingi's last Nyakhate ruler), nor of any of the members of the Nyakhate clans" (Delafosse, "Traditions historiques," p. 304). See also, Boyer, *Un Peuple,* p. 24.

count, survived as an independent state after the Nyakate fall from power in about 1350.[64]

Second, relying on the Timbuktu *ta'rikh* inter alia the French administrator Maurice Delafosse—some 200–250 years later (1912)—supported the view that the Nyakate did in fact rule Kingi. Providing a different context, however, Delafosse's data spoke of a Kingi settlement by the Soninko—from Ja in the Massina—toward the latter part of the seventh century. Kingi was later incorporated into the Ghana state as a semiautonomous polity. After Ghana's decline (in the latter part of the eleventh century, according to Delafosse), Kaniaga, Bakhunu, and Kingi became independent successor states, ruled by the Jarissi, the Dukure, and the western Nyakate families, respectively.[65]

Third, two versions (Boyer, 1953; Pollet and Winter, 1971, who obtained their information from the *Ta'rikh al-Fattash*, Delafosse, and the Arab geographers inter alia), provided additional support for the Nyakate rule at Kingi. Contextualizing Kingi as a semiautonomous client state—ruled by the Jara Kante of the Soso Jarissi family of the Kaniaga polity—they traced the state to the early twelfth century. With the rise of Sunjata in the thirteenth century, Kingi fell to Mali. On later regaining independence, its ruler, one Mana Maghan Nyakate, became the *chef de guerre* within the Malian state hegemony. Under Mana Maghan Nyakate, Kingi extended its hegemony over the Keniareme, the Gidiume (ruled by the Jakite), and Jafunu (ruled by the Dukure), both incidentally grain-producing regions (see Map 3). As his military power increased Mana Maghan, it is said, held hegemonic sway farther afield, in Kaarta, Jangunte, and Bakhunu. Confounding the situation further, Boyer's patronymic for the ruling Nyakate dynasty was *Jakite*.[66]

Fourth, according to the *Chronique du Fouta Sénégalais*, the Nyakate ruled Kingi. Differently contextualized, we hear that the Jyaogo chiefs of the Tekrur state on the lower Senegal River were overthrown toward the late tenth century by the Islamized Manna. The Manna, according to this story, were none other than a branch of the Nyakate, the latter, rulers of Kingi, clients of the Soninke of Ghana ruling from their capital at Jara. Thus whether acting on their own, or on Ghana's behalf, the Manna-Nyakate had elaborated their power over the Futa Toro into a Kingi state hegemony. After Ghana's eleventh-century decline, the story continued,

---

64. *Ta'rikh al-Fattash*, pp. 62, 70–74.

65. Delafosse, *Haut-Sénégal-Niger*, vol. 2, pp. 154–161, 270. For another Delafosse version based on the Arabic text from the Nioro region, see "Traditions historiques," pp. 303–304.

66. Boyer, *Un Peuple*, pp. 24–25; Pollet and Winter, *La Société soninké*, pp. 31–32.

the Manna-Nyakate state fell tributary to the Kaniaga Soso rulers, later to the Mali state after Sunjata's defeat of Sumanguru Kante at Krina in about 1235. Toward the late fourteenth century, the Nyakate lost Kingi to Jamangille (who later adopted the Jawara patronym), father of the conqueror Mahmud.[67]

Fifth, we already heard Levtzion's story based on Boyer's account: that the Nyakate were the first dynasty to rule at Jara (Kingi) and that the state was founded by the Soninke merchant Mana Maghan Nyakate. The family became vassals of the Soso, later Mali. But unhappy with their ruler, the people of Kingi rose against the Malian hegemony, killing the "amir." Taking "advantage of internal dissensions, and of the weakness of the Mali kings" toward the latter part of the fourteenth century, the Jawara (Jamangille) seized power establishing a new dynasty, their capital at Jara.[68]

Finally, in conflict with all the above is Mamadou Diawara's version of the Kingi story (1990). Gathering data exclusively from Kingi residents—descendants of the Jawara (Jamangille or Daman Gille) ruling lineage, Kingi residents (Soniko), *nyamakala* groups such as metal and leather workers, bards, and slaves—Diawara has dismissed Nyakate claims. Confirming the existence of a Kingi state from the fifteenth to the nineteenth century, the ruling dynasty was not Nyakate, according to Diawara, but Jawara (Diawara). The Nyakate were present at Kingi. But not as rulers. They were *sodoga*, or official orators, praise singers, or "people of the word." We recall from the Meillassoux-Niare text that the young (and ravenous) Fata Maghan Nyakate sang out the praises of Mana Maghan Nyakate, his *doyen*, on learning of the latter's sacrifice. The Kingi episode, according to that text, occurred under the shadow of the drame

---

67. As a matter of interest, the Islamized Manna—Soninke ruling elites from Silla—were, according to the Futa chronicle, independent of the Ghana state. Negotiating new identities, they are now the Pular-speaking Silbe and the Soninke-speaking Sylla, "people of Silla," residing at the confluence of the Faleme and Senegal Rivers. The Manna were overthrown during the early fourteenth century by Wolof *tonjonw*, suggesting Malian slaves of the age-group associations (Siré Abass Soh, M. Delafosse and H. Gaden, eds., *Chronique du Fouta sénégalais* [Paris, 1913], cited in J. Spencer Trimingham, *A History of Islam in West Africa* [Oxford University Press, 1962], pp. 26, 43 note 2, 45 and notes 1 and 2, p. 46). See also Bathily, "Les Soninké dans l'histoire du Fuuta Tooro," pp. 26–27.

68. Levtzion, *Ancient Ghana*, pp. 48–49, 81; Adam, "Légendes historiques," (1903), pp. 81–98, 232–248, 354–372 485–496, 602–620 734–744; (1904), 117–124, 233–248, see esp. 1903, pp. 232–233; Boyer, *Un Peuple*, pp. 24–26. See also *Ta'rikh al-Fattash*, pp. 62, 70–74.

tree.[69] As indicated above, Mana Maghan Nyakate adopted the Drame *jamu* as his patronym.

Thus did the Nyakate rule Kingi? Manipulated data are clearly conflicting, serving objectives now beyond further investigation. On the one hand, five of the six sources cited above (Boyer, Pollet and Winter are combined) substantiate the Niare claim to have ruled Kingi, at least three following the seventeenth century *Ta'rikh al-Fattash* (Delafosse, Boyer, Pollet and Winter), one following the *Chronique du Fouta Sénégalais* (Trimingham), and one fashioned after Boyer (Levtzion). According to these written accounts, therefore, the possibility exists that the Nyakate could have ruled Kingi, eventually ousted by the Jawara, the latter's partisan claims notwithstanding. Particularly persuasive are data from the seventeenth-century *Ta'rikh al-Fattash*, this most self-consciously Islamic of texts: Not only were the Nyakate Islamized, according to this account, but in accompanying Mansa Musa on Pilgrimage to Mecca circa 1325, Suleyman Bana Nyakate performed this function not as an individual, but as "ruler" of Kingi.[70]

On the other hand, had the Nyakate ruled Kingi, why the silence on this in the global Nyakate oral records? Could the silence be covering up the families' overthrow at the hands of the Jawara? Diawara's account lends some credence, if not substantiation to this supposition. Or was Bemba the metaphor simultaneously explaining and covering up their misfortunes? He "committed adultery"; he "was asleep"; he "burned the millet"; he was a "tyrant"; he "killed his accusers"; he "was a turbulent child"; he was a "troublemaker." Or again, he was a "loathsome bandit"; a "cruel prankster"; a "whiner"; he sliced open pregnant women; he killed the Fulbes' cattle; finally, he was only "a child who knew nothing" better. Ongoiba's insights suggest the probability, if not substantiation, for this hypothesis. Or did his lineage adopt

---

69. For an explanation of how the Drame *geseru* (bards) became Kingi bards (*sodoga*), see Diawara, *La Graine*, pp. 38–44, 73–74. Incidentally, not all those bearing the Drame *jamu* were Kingi *jeliw*: This patronym was apparently also common among Kingi marabouts. See also A. Bathily, "A Discussion ... Wagadu," pp. 11, 49–71; Dantioko, *Soninkara tarixinu*; Bokar N'Diayé, *Les Castes au Mali* (Bamako, 1970), pp. 97–98.

70. The *Ta'rikh al-Fattash* was never ambiguous when referring to the "fetishist" or "pagan." If the Kingi Nyakate escaped the unfriendly sobriquets, it is likely that their Islamization passed the test. This may not have been true of those Nyakate families migrating east to the Bamako region. According to Marabout Touré, the Bamako Niare were not Islamized until the nineteenth century (Interview Marabout Touré [Bozola-Bamako, 5 Jan. 1980]).

a Fulbe identity artfully disappearing from Mande mythic records? According to Boyer, those Kingi-Nyakate who remained adopted the Jakite (Fulbe) patronym.[71] Heinrich Barth's findings for northern Nigeria—where Mande-speaking migrants had "entirely forgotten" their idiom, speaking Fulfulde and even Hausa—provide a worthwhile analogy, if not empirical assurance for this speculation. Or could it be that Bemba and his lineage remained at Kingi as *sodoga* or Drame bards, even after the Jawara advent to power toward the early fifteenth century? His troubled episodes support this possibility, given that both the Niare and Diawara accounts intersect at the formation point of a Kingi bardic lineage. Both, moreover, identify the *geseru/jeli* lineage as Drame, claiming Mana Maghan Nyakate as the lineage ancestor.[72] Both suggest a family "disgrace" at Kingi, Bemba committing adultery among other offenses in the various Bamako Niare accounts, the sodoga-Nyakate sleeping through an enemy attack in the Diawara records.[73] Both accounts likewise imply altercations and power struggles. Accordingly, if the historical realities of a Niare rule at Kingi are beyond empirical reach, it is possible that one or more familial branches remained—possibly as Drame-*sodoga*, possibly as Jakite-Fulbe—in Kingi's ruling circles.

Finally, although intersections between the Niare and Diawara texts seem compelling, more importantly from our perspective is that the manipulated texts signal a Kingi association, a known historical dispersal point after Wagadu, and a further Soninke marker. All provide an appropriate genealogy—fictive or otherwise—for chiefly legitimacy at Bamako in the face of further power struggles, the *kafu* once founded.

As to chronology, Jamangille may have assumed the Kingi chieftainship sometime in the thirteenth century while Sunjata was still ruling Mali, according to Delafosse and related legends, or in the mid- to late fourteenth century, according to Arnaud and Boyer, or the latter part of the fourteenth century according to Lieutenant Conrard of the Senegalese *tirailleurs*, or the late sixteenth century, according to Adam. Collecting data at Kingi, Mamadou Diawara, the latest to probe this fluid

---

71. Boyer, *Un Peuple*, pp. 24–25.

72. Barth, *Travels*, vol. 3, p. 111. The Arabic text from the Nioro region maintains that after the Nyakhate rulers fled Kingi, only the *sodoga* Nyakhate remained behind, see Delafosse, "Traditions historiques," pp. 303–304.

73. References to "sleep" in Mande thought usually suggest unawareness, not in a state of consciousness. In other mythic accounts, Bemba migrated to Lambidu, to Yuri, and so forth in the Kaarta (Jabate, "La Légende," p. 243).

chronology, suggests the early fifteenth century.[74] Given that the Nyakate ruled Kingi for a formulaic 450 years, the Kingi events could thus belong to the first part of the second millennium A.D. In approximate world or universalizing time, the episode may thus have coincided with the later Norman and Plantagenet kings of England (1066–1377), perhaps declining during the early Chinese Ming Dynasty (1368–1644), or perhaps the early Safavid rule in Persia (1448–1736). The Nyakate-Kingi rule (historical or mythical) could also have coincided with the Crusades (1096–1291), or it was declining before the early Moghul Empire in India (1526–1858) would reach its zenith under the emperor Akbar (1556–1605). The Azuchhi-Momoyama or Japanese period of "national unification" (1568–1600), one of the more dynamic in Japan's history, may have begun after the Nyakate-Kingi decline. The same may be said of the Ottoman Turks consolidating their imperial hegemony toward the late fifteenth century (c. 1463–c. 1566). In England the Tudor kings would ascend the throne (1485–1603). Across the Atlantic, "Indians" will hear that one Christopher Columbus, or Cristobal Colon, in search of Cathay and the Great Khan, has entered their hemisphere from the east, arriving in tall ships (1492). Within decades the Atlantic slave trade will begin.

The Segu Episode

On departing Kingi during the next episode we hear that Seribadia, the last ruler of Kingi, has migrated east toward the Niger, arriving at Segu Koro during the administration of the Bamana ruler Biton (Mamari) Kulibaly (c. 1712–1755). We hear, moreover, from the Niare-Meillassoux version that on attaining Segu, Niare legends intersect with the more numerous, better preserved, and more formal Segu traditions.[75] Thus with a more or less stable chronology at hand we can, for the first time, trace events to a date in the universal chronology: the eighteenth century between c. 1712 and c. 1755, the Segovian state's apogee, according to the Marty, Tauxier, Pageard, and Pollet and Win-

---

74. Boyer, *Un Peuple*, pp. 24–25; Delafosse, *Haut-Sénégal-Niger*, vol. 2, p. 270; *ASAOF* 1G 79, Conrard, "Notice" (Bamako, 21 Feb. 1885), n.p.; Diawara, *La Graine*, pp. 21–25, 40–41.

75. For some of Segu's traditions see Conrad, *A State*; Gérard Dumestre, *La Geste de Ségou* (Paris, 1979); Lilyan Kesteloot, *Da Monzon de Ségou épopée bambara*, 4 vols. (Paris, 1972); Lilyan Kesteloot, "Un Episode de l'épopée bambara de Ségou: Bakari Dian et Bilissi," *BIFAN*, sér. B, vol. 35, no. 3 (1973): 881–902; *Idem.*, "Le Mythe et l'histoire dans la formation de l'empire de Ségou," *BIFAN*, sér. B, vol. 40, no. 3 (1978): 578–681.

ter chronology.[76] Sojourning at Segu, a new chapter opens in the shifting Nyakate identity. Seribadia and his entourage are at first welcomed by head-of-state Biton; and on concluding a Nyakate-Kulibaly *siyah* alliance, a marriage between Seribadia and Sumba, Biton's sister, is arranged.[77] On sealing the *siyah*-marriage alliance (see below) with Bamana state power, the Segovian Faama offers the Nyakate "four hundred slaves" (presumably *jonw* or captives) as bridewealth—a guarantee of permanency within the alliance—to remain in the *balimaaya*, or uterine line of the Niare patrimony.[78] But then we hear that Seribadia and Biton are feuding, and before long the Niare are, for the third time, in flight destined for Nyamina and Gringume in the Manding Mountains. These events occurring before Biton's death in around 1755, the families rescatter even farther afield, some returning west to the Kaarta, founding settlements in Lambidu, others to the Nioro region (Yelimane, the Gidiume, Khasso), and even as far west as the Gambia (see Maps 1 and 3).[79] Not surprisingly, the Nyakate-Segovian experience becomes a fourth set of recontextualized and manipulated identity signifiers.

Critique

Like the Kingi episodes, the Segovian counterparts have been equally recontextualized and manipulated. Once again we ask: Did the Niare arrive at Segu Koro? No, according to Delafosse (1912): The Nyakate were received instead by the Massassi Kulibaly at Kaarta. Also no, according to Paques (1953), who has even failed to mention Segu at all, arguing instead that the families migrated directly from Jara (Kingi) to Gringume in the Manding Mountains overlooking the Bamako plain.[80] Thus, whether or not the Nyakate reached Segu

---

76. For Meillassoux's questionable chronology, see, Meillassoux, "Histoire," p. 223. Also see Introduction.

77. For a brief discussion of the *siyah* see, note 19 herein and Chapter 3.

78. Meillassoux, "Histoire," p. 192. In Paques' more stylized account, there are 100 male and 100 female slaves ("L'Estrade royale," p. 1645).

79. Meillassoux, "Histoire," p. 192. The Lambidu Niare, said in other sources to be the parent lineage of the Bamako Niare, all claim "the same (Lambidu) father" (Dantioko, *Soninkara tarixinu*, pp. 237, 244; interview Seydou Niaré [Bamako, 3 Jan. 1980]).

80. Delafosse, *Haut-Sénégal-Niger*, vol. 1, pp. 286, 288, 289; Pâques, "L'Estrade royale," p. 1644. According to another account, the Niare sojourned at Sokolo, reaching Bamako directly from Lambidu in the Kaarta, bypassing Segu altogether (Soumaoro, "Etudes," pp. 1, 2, 3, 4, 5–8). While not claiming that the Niare ruled Segu

remains arguable. What seems more likely is that while some Nyakate remained at Kingi, others, bent on redispersing, went their separate ways, some to Segu, others to the Kaarta, some even migrating directly to Gringume and the Manding Mountains. What also seems more likely is that if Kingi was a western dispersal point, Segu became the dispersal juncture for the eastern Nyakate families. Most importantly, therefore, the Segu episodes mark the beginnings of a decisive spatial-cultural separation between the western Nyakate familial identities and the Bamako-Niare eastern identities.

Likewise significant in the Niare repertoire of identity markers is the role of the state in the marriage alliance between Seribadia Nyakate and Sumba Kulibaly, which has an interesting twist (references to Seribadia in the myth are of course to his lineage; at this point he would have attained a great biblical age). Already known is that bridewealth in the Mande identity is usually the function of a groom's family. Yet according to the Niare-Meillassoux version there is a double twist: Bridewealth is offered by Biton, the bride's "brother" (possibly a biological or affinal brother). As Meillassoux has demonstrated elsewhere, bridewealth *(furunafolo)*, usually offered by a groom's family, was a sign of political control over production, reproduction, and progeny among women and minors. In patrilineages (such as the Kulibaly), it was also a sign of claiming the descent-group-membership of the groom's progeny, together with initiating alliances, coalitions, and transactions between matrimonially designated groups, establishing exchange patterns likely to survive across generations. Through preselected matrimonial areas and the fiduciary nature of bridewealth—an "insurance" that designated groups would seek brides from the same matrimonial areas—whole communities could thus establish lasting social relations of a highly productive, reproductive, and political nature.[81]

In initiating the marriage alliance—and here is the meaning of the first twist—Biton could not have made his regional power intentions more clear (we recall from the Introduction that Biton extended the Segovian hegemony to towns and villages of the upper Niger region and beyond).

Kingi, Lieutenant Conrard of the *tirailleurs* indicates that in about 1385, the Nyakate left Kingi for a settlement on the Niger banks (see *ASAOF* 1G 79, Conrard, "Notice" [Bamako, 21 Feb. 1885], p. 3). For further interpretations, see notes 63, 72 herein.

81. Meillassoux, *Maidens, meal*, esp. pp. 97–103, 105–115, 194. For another perspective on Mande marriages see, Sarah C. Brett-Smith, *The Making of Bamana sculpture: Gender and creativity* (Cambridge University Press, 1994).

First, according to this Niare-Meillassoux text as indicated above, Biton—not the groom but the bride's brother—was the one to offer bridewealth. In this gesture Biton thus demonstrated his intentions to maintain political control over Sumba's progeny, now members of his, and not Seribadia's descent-group, by virtue of the bridewealth. He was also making sure that marriage transactions between these matrimonially designated groups would be continued, to survive across several generations. Political, kinship, and territorial alliances between Bamako and Segu were thus likely to survive generationally with Segu as the senior and hegemonical partner. Seemingly, Biton had it made. But then these stories and their interpretations are never that stable: According to one set of sources Sumba, supposedly Biton's sister, is a male. In yet another, she is Biton's daughter; and in still yet another, it is Seribadia's son (Jamusadia Nyakate) who marries Sumba, (and not the aged Seribadia).[82] Not too amazingly, these conflicting accounts—seemingly innocent of serious intent—do, in fact, render a different construction on Biton's reach for power. For, had Sumba been a male member of Biton's biological or affinal household marrying a Niare female, on the one hand, Biton's power-reach would have been considerably weakened: a male Sumba could have established his own potentially competing lineage. And were he (Sumba) from a senior lineage, his threat would have been even greater. Were Sumba Biton's daughter (not sister), on the other hand, Seribadia (the groom) would have been liable for bridewealth, both the slave and the free progeny therefore his, thereby establishing another threat to Segu's power base. By identifying Sumba as Biton's sister, for whom Biton contributes the bridewealth, the Niare-Meillassoux text acknowledged the Niare as Biton's junior affinals.

Second, assuming that Sumba was a female member of Biton's domestic society, as the Niare text indicates, Biton's bridewealth of 400 slaves made yet another statement of his regional-power intentions. Intended as the principal labor force for the new *cike-bugu*—or agricultural slave village which the Nyakate were expected to establish as a Segu dependency (see below)—the slaves could only be inherited through the *balimaaya*, or uterine line. There was another twist, however: According to established procedures the inheritance transmitted through the female passed indirectly through the female's male affiliate, a husband, a father, a brother, a son, and so forth . Only in the absence of all these, probably a rare occurrence, could an inheritance pass directly through the female line.[83] Thus

---

82. Soumaoro, "Etude," pp. 1–3, 8.

83. *ASAOF* 1G 248, Pérignon, "Monographie" (1899–1900), p. 325; *ANMK* 1G 299, Brévié, "Monographie" (Bamako, 25 April 1904), pp. 27–29.

by inheriting directly through the female line, the slaves remained Kulibaly property, producing and reproducing in a Segovian client state, while Niare males became the managerial clients.

According to the double twist in the Niare-Meillassoux version, therefore, Biton's marriage alliances with the Niare not only enabled him to extend Segu's state hegemony into the upper Niger region in the form of the Bamako agricultural slave settlement, but the double twist also provided the political-kinship power structure, the managerial cadre, and the labor unit. Above all, this version of the mythic manipulation—to which Bamako's leading Niare families subscribe—not only enabled them to claim a remote Soninke Wagadu (Mande) identity, but also a more recent Bamana-Kulibaly (Mandekan) identity associated with the Segu state; all this most probably for the benefit of the contesting Other. As to the various legends disputing Sumba's gender, they suggest a range of other, more remote political rivalries, now lost even to myth.

With respect to the *siyah* sworn over Segu's three most potent oracles, the oath enforced a ritual-political alliance (resembling a marriage and diplomatic alliance combined) entered into in the presence of the supernatural. Symbol of obligations, reciprocities, and mutual sharing of good fortune and ill, such as marriage celebrations, baptisms, and funerals, the *siyah* was also a defensive and offensive alliance in war and peace. The obligations and reciprocities remained in force even after the death of the *siyah-nyogow* (participants to the sacred oath), or even if *siyah-nyogow* progenies permanently migrated outside the region. Therefore, among *siyah-nyogow* could be numbered families, lineages, and clans of absolutely no acquaintance, nor even mutual knowledge, but whose remote ancestors had once oathed this alliance. Moreover, creating familial alliances, the *siyah* intentionally opened opportunities for further marriages, in this case between the Niare-Kulibaly lines. Once more Biton had it made.

Indubitably, the Marka-Sarakolle-Bamana identity-process began among eastern Nyakate families in the wake of this marriage-*siyah* alliance, together with the formation of the Bamako *kafu*, if not before. Entering what could conceivably have been a third identity shift in the Segu-Niger region (the second possibly a Fulbe "tilt" during the Kingi episode), it was from this point that the Nyakate officially acquired a Marka-Sarakolle, later a Bamana, identity. Also at this point linguistic-cultural differentiations between the western and eastern Nyakate identity began to widen. Thereafter, the Nyakate patronymic was transmitted into the Bamana idiom, becoming "Niare," meaning "magnanimous," a likely reminder of Mana Maghan's magnanimity toward his famished brother-image at Kingi. With the closing of the Segovian Episodes, the Niare temporarily come in from the mythic cold with Seribadia—the patriarchal culture-hero—associated with the identity change and the creation of a new state power. The newly negotiated Soninke-Nyakate/Bamana-Niare identity had met with ancestral approbation.

That the Niare dialect shift from Soninke to Bamana occurred in relation to state power is interesting. It could hardly have been that Kulibaly rulers rationalized the state idiom (Bamana), restricting the language repertoire of populations within their hegemonical range, as was the case, for example, in France, Spain, and Japan between the sixteenth and nineteenth centuries. The predominantly non-writing Bamana cultures, and the relatively small communities, would have made this improbable. More likely, as David Laitin noted (and Cohen implied), rulers, through their policies, frequently influenced the language repertoires of the ruled who, in turn, engaged in language shifts—learning language(s) other than a mother tongue—when choices were perceived as instruments of fulfillment of socioeconomic and political goals. In the case of the Bamana idiom, the language diffused beyond Segu to the south and west of the Kulibaly state primarily through migrations, marriage alliances, Islamized trading clans, and an enabling state system facilitating and controlling metropolitan-wide commercial networks.[84]

More significantly, the language diffused through Biton's most powerful instrument of state-control: the professional armies of *tonjonw* (slave armies) and *sofaw* (armed cavaliers) where, through the open recruitment of war captives, young men were groomed—away from the influences of home—for long periods of time.[85] Through state rewards (e.g., brides, booty) and punishments (e.g., public floggings, even death), *tonjon* armies articulated rational choices in relation to realizable social and political goals, thereby manipulating new identities. It is possible that across the decades Niare youths were among the *tonjonw* and/or *sofaw* serving the Segovian state—more certain given that Bamako was founded as a *cike-bugu*, or slave village—that Segu's *tonjonw* were stationed there, and that youths were drawn into the armies from all over the state.

Thus were the Niare drawn into the bamanization process through a series of cultural signifiers including dispersals, migrations, sacrifices and

---

84. Perinbam, "Notes," pp. 676–690; Bird, "The Development of Mandekan," pp. 146–159. For a more general discussion, see David D. Laitin, *Language repertoires and state construction in Africa* (Cambridge University Press, 1992), pp. 12–14, 47, 52, 82–83; Cohen, "Variables in ethnicity," pp. 306–331.

85. Biton's armies may have totaled about 40,000 men or more, according to Kare Tammoura, Monteil's Islamized informant at Segu (Monteil, *Les Bambara*, pp. xi, 50–51).

disasters, marriage alliances, mythical-political oathing and rituals, client status, dialects, and conceivably service in the Segovian armed forces. Even the wayward actions of youthful "delinquents" became signals explaining the process. Furthermore, in adopting the Bamana idiom, acquiring a new patronymic, and acknowledging Segu's right to "own" the progeny of both slave and free in families involved in marriage alliances, the Niare were identified as Biton's affinals. Finally, in refashioning state power (Bamako's), the families entered into a relationship with the ultimate in political-cultural signifiers: the state and state power. In creating an enabling environment for these developments, the Kulibaly chieftainship subsequently and reciprocally consolidated, elaborated, and amplified Biton's original intentions, while expanding their patronage, protection, and hegemonical domestic ideology.

Because Niare textual manipulation has caused a narrative intersection with the more formal and better-preserved Segovian traditions, we are reasonably sure that the Segovian Episodes occurred during the first half of the eighteenth century. In world or universalizing time, the English had just consolidated a united Great Britain through the Act of Union with Scotland (1707), and the Union Jack (the Crosses of St. George and St. Andrew) were adopted. In 1714, two years after Biton came to power, the British Parliament was settling its crown on the Protestant Hanoverian House. On the European continent, the Spanish Succession War (1701–1714), the Polish Succession War (1733–1735), and the Austrian Succession War (1740–1748) involving marriage and diplomatic alliances all overlapped with Biton's administration (c. 1712–c. 1755). In China, the Segovian "golden age" coincided with the Ch'ien Lung rule of Kao Tsung (1736–1795), imposing imperial hegemony throughout Central Asia. It likewise coincided with Tsung's invasion of Tibet (1751), establishing control over succession and the Dalai Lama's temporal acts. The Segovian golden age was probably occurring about the same time as the Maratha state in India was consolidating its hegemony over the Deccan (c. 1715–1760). In Japan, Yoshimune (d. 1751), among the ablest of the shoguns of the Tokugawa house of Kii—and Biton's (d. 1755) nearest contemporary —was consolidating economic, feudal and military reforms, simultaneously disseminating Confucian values and scholarship (1716–1745). About the same time, Japanese language rationalization was forcing out regional dialects *(hogen)* favoring instead the capital city's idiom. Within decades the French (1789–1815) and American revolutions (1763–1788) would begin.

The Bamako Kafu Episode

When we return to the Bamako legends, we hear in a "Bamako *Kafu* Episode" that Jamusadia, son of Sumba Kulibaly and Seribadia Nyakate,

is out hunting on the Bamako plain.[86] On encountering a resident crocodile called Bamakoni, he kills the beast, subsequently rendering himself
the region's ritual master.[87] In another Niare account, Jamusadia wrestles
the beast for a year inside a well, a violent image suggesting a power
struggle for regional control over the *numuw*, whose *tana* was/is the crocodile.[88] On killing the beast Jamusadia founds the Bamako *kafu* as a
Segovian client state. Concluding a ritual-political alliance with supernatural forces (fundamental law) within the ecosystem, Jamusadia buries live
pythons (reminiscent of Wagadu and now a Niare *tana*, or prohibition) as

---

86. The *dia* suffix is a clue to Seribadia's impressive height. Niare males might
indeed have been given to height. When on mission to Segu (1880–1881), Gallieni
met a "gigantesque" Niare male (Gallieni, *Voyage*, p. 337). Recall that according to
the *Ta'rikh as-Sudan*, "Maghan" was the name of a Wagadu ruler, meaning "large,"
adopted from the Fulbe idiom into the Soninke and Bamana. See herein note 39.

87. According to one folk etymology, "Bamakoni" (*bama*: crocodile; *ko*: river; *ni*:
diminutive) gave his name to the *kafu*. According to others, *Bamako* derived from
Bamba-Kong, *Kong-Bamba*, Bamba in this case being Bamba Sanogo, the unidentified persona discussed below, who some claim (erroneously it seems) inhabited
the region prior to the *kafu*'s founding by the Niare. Other accounts associate Bamako's name with *Bamba-ko*, or "behind Bamba's back," Bamba in this case being
the same Bamba Sanogo. Yet another account suggests that Bamako derived its
name from Samake Bamba, supposedly a Mande chief extending his hegemony
over the region prior to the Niare arrival. Others suggest *Bamako* derived from *ban*:
palm; *ko*: river, hence "river of palms," and "river of crocodiles" (*bam*: crocodile).
The reliability of these folk etymologies is unknown (field work Bamako, Jan.
1980, Oct. 1982 –May 1983). See also Dominique Traoré, "Une Seconde légende relative à l'origine de la Ville de Bamako," *NA* no. 40 (Oct. 1948): 7–8.

88. According to Tauxier, *Bamana* meant "the people of the crocodile." Tauxier
(*Histoire*, p. 43). Bamako, it is said, was established over the site of the well. In addition to being a prohibition, a *tana* demonstrated the spiritual and material continuity between the animal and human worlds. Examples of *tanaw* include: the cat
fish (*mpolio*) for the Segu Kulibaly; the lion or panther for some Kone clans; the
lion and the black monkey for some Jara clans; the python, the lion, and the gray
pigeon for the Niare, the tortoise for the Dumbya. *Tanaw* were not usually contex-
tually linked to a clan *jamu*, or patronym, and more than one clan could adopt the
same *tana*. The *tana* is widespread throughout the western Sudan: Among the
Wolof, it is called *bang*; *ouada* among the Fulbe; *kossée* among the Soninke; *kabi*
among the Songhay; and *kisgu* among the Mossi. Delafosse, *Haut-Sénégal-Niger*,
vol. 1, pp. 285; vol. 3, pp. 101, 107–109, 162–163, 171–172, 178–182. For the importance of the *tana* (and its *jamu*) in Mande cultures see Person, *Samori*, vol. 1, pp. 54,
57; Binger, *Du Niger*, vol. 2, p. 375–377. For the Niare's *tanaw*, see note 38 herein;
see also note 95.

well as gold objects in the newly consecrated earth, thereby becoming the *dugu-kolo-tigi*, or "master of the earth."[89]

In addition to the aforementioned 400 bridewealth-slaves, Bamako's population initially includes Jamusadia's lineage, those of his brothers, the *jeliw* lineage (Drame), and others within the entourage including Islamized clients, said to be Niare associates since Kingi—their great ages notwithstanding. As one of Segu's many *cike-buguw*, or agricultural slave villages, Bamako plays an important role on Segu's upper Niger, or southern metropolitan periphery, producing food, markets, slaves, and militia assistance during Segu's expansionist wars and other endeavors. As Segu's hegemony extends south beyond Bamako to Samanyana, local chiefs, including the Fulbe chief Bassy Jakite, fall within the Segovian matrix, as do the Beledugu chiefs, some chieftaincies along the Niger's east bank, and most of the Mande and the Wassulu—all under the surveillance of resident Segovian *tonjonw*.

Critique

As is often the case with the genre, the last episodes of a mythic story are usually fuller, more complete, and less susceptible to manipulation. Thus given this ferocious crocodile imagery, the collective historical imagination was probably reenacting the sacred ritual reminiscent of the Wagadu-Bida alliance, or the power struggle between Sunjata and Sumanguru Kante at the battle of Krina (c. 1235), where the former worsted the blacksmith king, or any other power struggle for that matter. In any event, as the reconstruction and recontinuation of a sacred alliance, the ritual consolidated bonds with the Segu state. The crocodile imagery underscored a relationship which we know to exist between *numuw* (blacksmiths) and state builders in the Mande theory of state building.

Whether or not settlers—in addition to the *numuw*—were already in the Bamako region prior to the Niare arrival remains problematic, although it is highly likely that riverside camps for transient Bozo and/or Somono families were already in place. Oral accounts, moreover, speak of hunters in the Minkungu region (on the Manding Plateau overlooking the Bamako plain), who may have been associated with Niare lineages. An all-too-slender discourse in the archaeological literature substantiates this with claims of fifteen archaeological sites in or near the Bamako region,

---

89. This ritual act also decreed that *somaw* (priests) mediating between terrestrial and supernatural powers be drawn from the Niare lineages. In Bamana cosmology, there was no such thing as a "free right" to natural resources, which could only be accessed through ritual (Monteil, *Les Bambara*, pp. 228, 230–233).

some Neolithic, possibly related to hunters, traders, and/or to initiation ceremonies, which would explain the *numuw*-crocodile imagery.[90] Other voices (non-Niare) punctuate the silences and uncertainties with further propositions having doubtful historical validity.

The Suraka Episode

It is at this point in the legends that four groups of Islamized "strangers" join the *kafu* as Niare clients. Among them are the "Arab" or Suraka Talmamane family (later adopting the Ture patronym) with a mercantile identity, from Tawat, the southern Algerian oasis,[91] as well as their

---

90. Personal communication Mamadou Sarr (Bamako, 4 Jan. 1980). Some of these have been tumulus excavations, involving surface collections, under nominal or no-control conditions. Considerable work remains on these and other sites. See G. Szumowski, "Notes sur la grotte de Bamako," *Congrès Panafricanist de Préhistorique, Actes de la IIe Session* (Alger, 1952 [1955]), pp. 673–680; see also *Idem*, "Notes sur la grotte préhistorique de Bamako," *NA*, no. 58 (April 1953): 35–40; *Idem.*, "Sur une gravure rupestre du Niger à Bamako," *Bulletin de la Société Préhistorique* (1955): 651–654; *Idem.*, "Fouilles de l'abri sous roche de Kourounkorokalé, *BIFAN*, sér. B (1956): 462–508; P. Creach, "Sur quelques nouveaux sites et nouvelles industries préhistoriques en AOF, "*Conférence Internationale des Africanistes de l'Ouest* (Dakar, 1945) (1954), pp. 397–430; G. Vuillet, "Note sur une caverne au nord de la gare de Nafadié," *BCEHSAOF* (1924): 735–736; R. Guitat, "Carte et répertoire des sites néolithiques du Mali et de la Haute-Volta," *BIFAN*, sér. B, vol. 34, no. 4 (1972): 896–934; H. Hubert, "Grottes et cavernes de l'Afrique occidentale," *BCEHSAOF*, vol. 1 (Jan.–March 1920): 43–51.

91. The Ture probably reached Bamako sometime during the eighteenth century. Their *jamu* and its different identities (see Introduction) are found throughout the western Sudan from the Futa Toro to the upper Senegambia and the Sahel. Numerous in Ja, Jenne and elsewhere in the middle Niger, Ture are also in Timbuktu. Farther south they settled mainly in Buguni, about 160 kilometers southeast of Bamako; they are also found in Kankan and Odienne. Still farther south they scattered toward the kola forests, as well as toward the Jallonke and the Susu in the Kuranko and the Konyan. In the east the Ture are found mainly in Bobo-Julasso, Bonduku and Kong. Although many still espouse an "Arab" identity (due most probably to their long-standing Islamized orientation), other traditions trace the Ture descent to the mythical Dinga of Wagadu, implying a remote "animist" Soninke identity. Still others claim that *ture* is a religious-literary title, much as *modi*, or *karamoko*, which makes more sense than the popular etymology (that *ture* is a corruption of *tawati*) (Cissé, Youssouf Tata, ed., *Histoire et tradition orale: Projet Boucle du Niger: Actes du Colloque*. Troisième Colloque International de l'Association SCOA [Niamey, 30 Nov.–6 Dec. 1977], p. 17; Person, *Samori*, vol. 1, p. 237; Monteil, "La Légende," pp. 361–408).

mercantile Drave (Draoui, Digina, Diagina) affiliates from Adrar, the latter reaching Bamako from Timbuktu, possibly originally from the Dra'a valley in Morocco.[92] Also taking their place as members of the new community are the Islamized Bozo-Somono fisher-folk maintaining a riverain identity all the way from Segu on the middle Niger to Kurusa in Guinea (in the Timbuktu region they are known as Soroko). The Jawambe, Islamized Fulbe sub-groups with Islamized identities, follow. Other Islamized families also join the *kafu*, followed in the nineteenth century by refugees from the Umarian and Samorian wars. Relying on wholesale desert-side commercial networks, the Surakaw soon extend trading interests throughout and beyond the Mande-hinterland, from Tichit to Timbuktu, Bamako to Bure, Kulikoro to Kankan, and Moribadugu to Medine (see Chapter 4). By the late eighteenth century, their commercial enterprises interact with those within the Mande world from the Senegambia to Sierra Leone, later with Liberia. Other Ture functioning as marabouts and teachers introduce Islam into Niare ruling circles and the community at large. It is they, the voices continue, who build the Bamako Dabanani mosque, still extant in reconstructed form near the old colonial marketplace.[93] Otherwise concluding oathing alliances with their patrons, both the Ture and Drave marry into the ruling Niare families, strengthening lineage bonds and patron-client alliances. Needless to say all Islamized clients become Bamana-speakers, integrating new identities into older counterparts: "Islamic" and "Arab" in the case of the Surakaw reminiscent of their desert-side origins; "fisherfolk" and "river transporters" in

---

92. The Drave probably also reached Bamako sometime in the eighteenth century. Their identity and place of origin are obscure. According to the Drave, they came from the Ouad Dra'a in southern Morocco via Timbuktu; clans from the Adrar came originally from the Ouad Dra'a (interview Suleyman Dravé [d. 1986], *doyen* of the Drave clan [Bamako, 5 Jan. 1980]; interview Nana Niaré Dravé [Bamako, 4 Jan. 1980]). According to other sources, *Draoui* is the generic term for peoples of the Ouad Dra'a in southern Morocco (*Tedzkiret en-Nisian fi Akbar Molouk es-Soudan*, trans. O. Houdas [Paris, 1966], p. 225, and note 2). Other sources attribute Hassanic origins to the Drave, but this has not been substantiated (*ANSOM* Sén. et Dép. IV 90 Bis, Vallière, "Mémoire" [Siguiri, 15–25 March 1888], p. 37). Contrary to Marty and the popular traditions, Meillassoux identified the Drave not with the Ouad Dra'a but with the Adrar, about 10 kilometers from Tamentit (the latter in the Tawat) (Meillassoux, "Histoire," p. 199, note 4; Paul Marty, *Etudes sur l'Islam et les tribus du Soudan*, 4 vols. [Paris, 1920], vol. 4, pp. 65–66. See also *ASAOF* 1G 79, Conrard, "Notice" [Bamako, 21 Feb. 1885], p. 3).

93. Interview Seydou Niaré (Bamako, 3 Jan. 1980); Perinbam, "Muslim minorities in the Bamako *kafu*," paper delivered at the meetings of the African Studies Association (Baltimore, Nov. 1991), p. 15; Meillassoux, Histoire," pp. 198–203.

the case of the Bozo-Somono; and "Fulbe herders" in the case of the
Jawambe (see Chapter 3).

Conclusions

First, readers will have noticed that threading through this discourse
from Wagadu to Bamako is the negotiated ethnic identity found in Cohen's paradigm. Here, Cohen's "group members," interacting with others
sharing common interests, coordinated activities designed to advance and
defend their interests. Depending on the circumstances, members negotiated identities manipulating, in the process, internal cultural forms such
as kinship, rites, ceremonies, and above all myths. To this end group ethnicity changed in response to both internal and external pressures, forming and re-forming associative and communal organizations in the
process. Reknitting the families' unraveling lives, restoring ethnographic
identities through key turning points established at Wagadu, Segu, Bamako, and more ambiguously Kingi, readers will likewise note that
Keyes' dialectic within a historical time-space perspective came to prevail.
Through a historical articulation with Fulbe identities at other key turning
points throughout the western Sudan (the Massina, the Kaarta, etc.), familial identities continued to twist and turn as radical shifts in social circumstances, such as migration and/or incorporation into a new political order, intersected their lives. In the process, the families evolved new
patterns of social adaptation to changing circumstances, simultaneously
rearguing the saliency of the cultural basis of shifting ethnic identities,
consciousness, and behavior. As new cultural meanings became attached
to oscillating identities, internal social patterns were parsed accordingly,
producing social adjustments, further cultural manipulations, and oscillating internal social-group organizations.

Thus, in successfully negotiating their cultural forms, from Soninke to
Marka-Sarakolle, to Bamana, and from Wagadu to Kingi to Segu to Bamako, identity shifts occurred within approximately 1,000 years, or across
about thirty to thirty-five generations—all this in the quest of a homeland
and a reconstructed ethnographic identity. By the late nineteenth century,
when members of the Gallieni Mission (1880–1881) and Borgnis Desbordes (1883) heard their story, family signs and episodic myths were revealing a "current" version—fully internalized—of the image which Niare
families now wanted to project. Paramount among Niare more recent
signs were new ancestors (Kulibaly); an old/new patronym (Niare); and a
different if related dialect (Bamana). Additional negotiated signs included
differently arranged mythical-political rituals and ethnographic cults (*jo*
associations including the *komo* and *nama* rituals, etc.), replacing Wagadu's python cult. Also included were altered marriage traditions

wherein endogamy was abandoned, replaced by exogamy. New marriage partners articulating with kinship forms included the Kulibaly and the Ture/Drave, both now Niare preselected marriage groups. Modifying social organizations further—creating a stratified society (the Sacrifice and Kingi Episode?)—the Niare went on to create the tri-partite social groups found in all Mande societies: *horonw*, or families free to establish lineages; the *nyamakalaw*, or endogamous specialized lineages; and *jonw, wolosow*, or slaves born in the household.[94]

Second, reprieved from a social invisibility following the dispersal, mythical-political alliances and rituals not only became signals of the new identity negotiations: They were the axis of the entire mobilizing process. Particularly important for the Niare/Kulibaly ritual bonding was the *siyah* alliance with its open-ended and designated marriage component: Through these rituals, different groups of people were collapsed into the "same" (see Introduction)—something rather like identical twins, the same, but different, and separate; but then again, not like identical twins, not having been originally the same—but different. *Siyah* relationships, moreover, obliged *siyah-nyogo*, or alliance partners within the sacred *siyah* circle, to a reciprocal observance of each others' ritualized *tana*w, incumbent on pain of penalties. The *tana*, or prohibition, was an object—usually animal, sometimes vegetable or mineral—that in the structure of beliefs had once saved an ancestor's life; or, providing succor, had released him/her from dire consequences. Many Mande families (especially those with *nyamakala* identities such as the *numuw*) had at least one *tana*, many, in addition, espousing the *tana* together with their *jamu, siyah*, and *senankun* (ritualized joking relationship), although no overall patterned association or grouping of *jamu, tana, siyah*, and *senankun* exists. Not infrequently, families sought several partners and/or *tana(w)* within the circle of sacred alliances.

Thus, across the *siyah* alliance, the Niare came to respect the Kulibaly *tana*w (a sheat-fish, *Silurus glanis*: large cat-fish), and the Kulibaly the Niare gray pigeon (genus *Columbidae*), python (*Boidae pythoninae*), fromager tree (*Ceiba pentandra*), and lion (*Panthera leo*)—Niare multiple *tana*w probably reflecting the varied processes through which their identities were negotiated across the centuries.[95] Whether or not a Nyakate/

---

94. There were unsubstantiated reports throughout my fieldwork that the Jamusadia Niare founding lineage was a *numu* lineage, which would make perfect sense, as many Mande founding lineages elsewhere were said to be *numuw*. (Mali 1979, 1980, 1982–1983).

95. Pâques, "L'Estrade royale," pp. 1643, 1644, 1649. Similar exigencies were required by other Mande families within the process. Among the Kante, for exam-

Fulbe alliance per se was concluded in the Kingi region remains unclear, although we know that other open Mande lineages *did* exchange marriage alliances and other reciprocal relationships with Fulbe families, for example, the long-standing *senankun* between the Fulbe and Mande blacksmiths.[96]

Third, while ritual alliances, prohibitions, and oaths signaled the passage from a Soninke to a Marka-Sarakolle, ultimately a negotiated Bamana identity, the state and domestic ideologies (Islam and the *jo* association), also played a role, providing stable institutionalized processes and procedures. The state's role is hardly surprising: State power, resources, leverage, and authority not only created enabling circumstances, such as the army in the Segovian state, but the state also renewed, institutionalized, and ritualized these negotiations. When Ngolo Jara seized the Segovian *faamaya* in about 1766, after the decline of the Kulibaly dynasty, predictably, they renewed oaths, especially the *jo* oath, with the Niare[97] and all other clients in the Mande-hinterland.

Finally, there was Islam as an identity signifier. Although the Bamako Niare were not officially Islamized until the late nineteenth and the early twentieth century (after the Umarian and Samorian wars), the global Nyakate identity had for centuries been part of the Mande-hinterland's dynamic Islamized process, as indicated according to the seventeenth-century *Ta'rikh al-Fattash*. Across the centuries, the western Nyakate in particular clung to their maraboutic and trading identities, the ultimate in Islamic signs. Among the Bamako Niare and the more easterly families, an Islamized identity was less clear, differentiating "Muslim" from "animist" frequently much more ambiguous (see Map 6).

What seems more likely in Bamako, and elsewhere in the Mande-hinterland and Mande world, is that Islam and/or particularistic Bamana ideologies, forged in the same cultural crucible, also came to resemble each other: the same, yet different, and above all, separate. Thus if, on the one hand, some Islamized communities followed the *Shari'a*, prayed, gave alms, and fasted, others espousing an "animist" identity revered the local marabout, his prayers, ablutions, and dress as power signs, even acquiring prayer beads—without knowing the prayers—as a sign of accessing

---

ple, the white pullet was espoused as their *tana*, the Kuyate the lizard (*Sauria*), the N'Diaye the boa constrictor (*Constrictor constrictor*), and the iguana (genus *Iguana*), while certain *garanke* (leather workers) adopted the jackal (*Canis aureus*). See also notes 38, 88 herein.

96. N'Diayé, *Les Castes*, p. 67. For further examples of *senankun*, see note 19 herein.

97. Meillassoux, "Histoire," pp. 197–198.

power. And if the pious observed the *habus*—holding inalienable lands in trust for charitable purposes—neighboring "animist" fetes coinciding with Islamized feasts were widely tolerated. Finally, if some communities founded mosques and Koranic schools—the "animist" Bamako *kafu* boasted nine mosques—particularisms (magic, divination, and other non-Islamic features) were very likely integrated into local Islamic rituals.[98] On another level, when Islamic-"animist" tensions threatened a community's integrity—as had occurred in Bamako during the Samorian wars— or when "mixed" marriages created strife with respect to family law and property rights, Islamic law was often shaped and reshaped in order to restore accord.[99] Accordingly, not only had Islam entered the *kafu*'s ideological episteme—through particularized "receptors" such as feasts and prayers—but in the wake of long co-residencies with Islamized populations, signs of particularized "animist" identities were also contextualized within the universal Islamic discourse. Of considerable interest is that Titi Niare, the incumbent *kafu-tigi*, when posturing ideologically before Bourouti (Borgnis Desbordes) in 1883, defined his position not in animist terms (i.e., he observed the *jo* rituals), but according to a well-established Islamic holograph: He was a regular *dolo* consumer.[100]

Coda: Other Oral Accounts and Further Mythic Manipulations

Were oral texts simple, our story would have ended here. But because of predictable complexities and further manipulations inherent to the genre, other oral texts have formulated conflicting founding claims. Conceivably, in manipulating, defining, and redefining their identities—while tracing a dynastic heritage to Wagadu, Kingi, and Segu—the Bamako Niare may in fact have also been responding to counterclaims and overt contestations. Most common among these are recognizable Islamized versions disputing Niare state-founding suppositions. One Islamized claim sometimes heard is that the Niare held power, not through the grace of

---

98. For a discussion of similar processes elsewhere, see Launay, *Beyond the stream.*

99. *ASAOF* 1G 299, Brévié, "Monographie" (Bamako, 25 April 1904), pp. 1–21; *ANMK* 1D 33 4, Rougier, "Enquête sur l'Islam" (Banamba, 31 May 1914); Marty, *Etudes*, vol. 4, pp. 176–179; Perinbam, "Islam," pp. 654–656.

100. *ANMK* 1D 33 5, Borgnis Desbordes, "Notice historique" (1880–1890); *ASAOF* 15G 83, Ruault, "Généralités 1880 à 1920" (Bamako, 22 Feb. 1884), p. 18; *ANSOM*. Sén. et Dép. IV 90 Bis, Vallière, "Mémoire" (Siguiri, 15–25 March 1888), p. 40. *Dolo* (a millet beer) is about 40 to 50 percent alcohol.

God and His holy Prophet Muhammad—the only way to legitimize power—but through their *gris-gris*. Thus notable among the contestations are
Suraka Ture versions reversing the founding order, asserting the Ture clan
as the *kafu*'s historical founders: Going against what appears to be overwhelming evidence, Ture accounts purport that it was they, as state-
founders and resident merchants, who welcomed the "animist" Niare to
Bamako as clients. Similarly, a conflicting Niare account from Lambidu in
the Kaarta attributes Bamako's founding to one Bamba Ture with whom
the "animist" Niare later settled.[101] Despite the frequency with which
these Ture stories reappear, it seems unlikely that these desert-side
marabouts and traders were ever Bamako's "animist" state-founders, if
only because no account has verified their *dugu-kolo-tigiw* or "master of
the earth" status, the ultimate in Mande state formation. And ironically,
because many Ture/Drave espoused a strong Muslim and "Arab" identity, it is difficult to reconcile their claims with an "animist"/*soma* or priestly past, the sine qua non of Mande chieftainship.

Conflicting "Islamized" oral texts, most probably crafted within a late
nineteenth-century Niare/Ture political power struggle—possibly even
for the colonizer's benefit—may have opened more windows on Ture
posturings than on the shifting Niare identity. We recall that on first reporting these ambiguously Islamized versions in 1883, poor Bourouti, be-
fuddled on his own admission by the "myth and mystery" therein, wondered if narrators were serving only "partisan interests." Of considerable
interest for us is that although members of the Gallieni Mission
(1880–1881) reported Niare/Suraka power struggles, none questioned
Niare chiefly legitimacy. Ambiguously Islamized Ture mythic manipulations may therefore be specified to sometime within the nineteenth century's last two decades.

The stories vague, crudely episodic, and really bent out of shape,
their distortions and manipulations hardly conform to settlement paradigms found throughout the Mande-hinterland and Mande world, although exceptions exist. More common among Mande political configurations—as Kopytoff pointed out—was a "first settlement" by

---

101. See, for example, the problematic Anon., "Chronique historique," pp.
62–66 and the equally problematic Arabic text of the Ture *Ta'rikh*. See also
Soumaoro, "Etudes," pp. 1–16; Nyaxate, "La Dispersion," pp. 229, 324; Villien-
Rossi, "Bamako," p. 264; *ASAOF* 1G 79, Conrard, "Notice" (Bamako, 21 Feb. 1885),
p. 3; *ANMK* 2D 132, "Organisation administrative de la ville de Bamako, liste
chronologique des Commandants de Cercle de 1883 à 1902, notes sur les chefs de
villages, population, 1902" (Bamako, Nov. 1902), pp. 7, 9, 11; *ANSOM* Sén. et Dép.
IV 90 Bis, Vallière, "Mémoire" (Siguiri, 15–25 March 1888), p. 37.

autochthonous clans that, as *dugu-kolo-tigiw*, produced the *somaw* (priestly lineage), sometimes the *faamaya* (chiefly lineage), and sometimes the *kafu-tigiw* (*kafu* chiefs), allowing for regional variations. In related paradigms, autochthones sometimes ceded the office of *dugu-kafu-tigi* to outside conquerors, thereby creating a dynamic tension between the sacred and secular political powers. Desert-side or Islamized trading lineages joining the community usually did so as *dunanw*, or "stranger" clients of the constitutionally recognized political incumbents. Thus, for example, in the Mande-hinterland and Mande world, historicized settlement paradigms show (as discussed in the Introduction) that throughout the centuries which brought them into the western Sudan's wider reaches, Mande-speakers integrated as strangers into autochthonous communities—some "animist," most non-Mande—which they ultimately transformed. Our earlier discourse demonstrated these features in upper Guinea, where Islamized stranger families developed *kafuw* in locations such as Kono, Konyan and Kuranko by forging alliances with "animist" autochthones (see Map 3). Similar developments occurred in and around Kong in the eastern Cote d'Ivoire, the Voltaic region, Sierre Leone, Liberia, and Guinea, where commerce and urban development followed. Likewise, eighteenth and nineteenth-century migrant Marka lineages, joined by Islamized Soninke clans—mostly from Guidimaka in the Senegal River region—settled as stranger-clients among autochthonous "animist" Bamana of the eastern Beledugu, establishing trading centers such as Banamba, Tuba, and Kerowane. And in the Bambuhu and Bure gold-mining regions, where residents were mainly autochthonous Mandinka-speakers, Islamized desert-side trading clans established stranger residency rights.[102] In light of this general settlement paradigm where Islamized traders settled among mainly non-Muslim autochthones, the Islamized Ture claims, manipulations, and distortions appear fragile.

More specifically, variable versions of these ambiguously Islamized accounts attribute the *kafu*'s founding to one Bamba Sanogo. The first French reference, appearing in Borgnis Desbordes's history of Bamako, attributes the *kafu*'s founding to Bamba Sanogo, identifying him as a trader from Kong and Baguinda (implying an Islamized identity), who later welcomed the Islamized Tali Mahamane Ture, marabout and salt merchant from Walata. A second Borgnis Desbordes version identifies Bamba

---

102. Perinbam, "Notes," pp. 680–689; Perinbam, "The Juulas," pp. 548–560; Perinbam, "Islam," pp. 642–646; Perinbam, "The Political organization," pp. 448–450, 452–455.

Sanogo as a hunter (implying an "animist" identity) from the Belekunu, the southern province of the Beledugu.[103]

But if the Bamba Sanogo identity is obscure in French written accounts, it is all but unrecognizable in fragmented oral texts, because, if Bamba Sanogo's alternate names and ethnonyms are Samake Bamba and Bamba Sananogo, he is also Kong Bamba, Samalen Bamba, Banba Sakho, and Banba Sarhanorho, a floating silhouette of unknown identity, hence a *sina* (without a lineage), although his identity could be anything from Soninke (Sakho or Sarhanorho), to Bamana (Sanogo, Sananogo, Bamba, Samake), possibly even Marka-Sarakolle.[104] In these accounts he also possesses a contradictory, overlapping and/or collapsed social identity, ranging from marabout, hunter, chief, kola nut, and long-distance trader, to slave originating variously from the Mande, Manfara, Maninkura, Moribadugu, Baguinda, the Belekunu, and even from Kong in the Cote d'Ivoire etc. Even his burial site remains ambiguous: Kong, Samatiguila, and Maninkura among others.[105] Two Niare oral texts from Kingi and Lambidu respectively (rival family branches?) claim a slave identity for Bamba, while an altogether different oral text associates him with the *woloso* Kulibaly and Saganogo slaves of the Mande, which would also technically render him a *sina*, or one without a lineage.[106]

A third series of seemingly unrelated legends speak of "invasions": a seventeenth-century invasion of the Segovian settlements by Kong warriors; an eighteenth-century invasion (1725?)—associating Bamba with Seku Wattara from Kong and/or Samanyana Jakite—against the Kene-

---

103. *ANMK* 1G 33 5, Borgnis Desbordes, "Notice historique" (1880–1890); Anon., "Chronique historique," pp. 62–66. According to Amadu Kumba Niare, Bamba Sanogo was a marabout from Maninkura whom Jamusadia invited to Bamako, but who left in the wake of a false prophecy. See Meillassoux, "Histoire," p. 193, notes 2, 5.

104. Only one source provided Bamba (possibly) with kin. Dominique Traoré, "Une seconde légende," p. 8, note 8. See also herein note 87.

105. According to some accounts it was the Saganogo who established a mosque at Manfara in the Mande. Cissé, *Histoire et tradition*, pp. 7, 8–9. For Bamba Sanogo, see Dominique Traoré, "Sur l'origine de la ville de Bamako," *NA*, no. 35 (July 1947): 26; Traoré, "Une seconde légende," pp. 7–8; Anon., "Chronique historique," pp. 62–66; Institut d'histoire d'art et d'archéologie africaine, *Actes de la table ronde sur les origines de Kong*, Kong, 1–3 November 1975, Annales de l'Université d'Abidjan, 1977, sér. J, vol. 1 (Kong, 1975), pp. 68–70; interview Marabout Touré (Bozola-Bamako, 5–6 Jan. 1980).

106. According to Boyer, the Nyakate had a slave at Jara (Kingi) named Bamba. For the Kaarta (Kingi) traditions, see Boyer, *Un Peuple*, p. 24; for Lambidu traditions see Nyaxate, "La Dispersion," pp. 220–237.

dugu (Sikasso), the Minianka, the peoples of the Bani valley, Sofara, and even the Macina; and a nineteenth-century invasion (1820s?) by Kong against the Kenedugu (Sikasso) and the subsequent murder of seventeen Traore "brothers" from Sikasso, on a peace mission to Kong. In expanding westward toward the Niger, the Wattara, it is said, sought easier access to Jenne's salt trade.[107] Reverse population movements from the Bamako to Kong regions likewise seemingly occurred: "Sekou Wattara was not the first to establish a settlement at Kong," according to a Kong informant, "It was Maghan (Traore) who (first) came from Di (i.e., Bamako). Maghan's father was Dabla."[108]

Complicating the situation still further are other ambiguously Is-lamized Bamba identities: Samake (one of Bamba's patronyms) is an alter-nate salutation for Ture; and according to another oral record, one Samake Bamba, a Mande chief, is said to have extended a hegemony over the Ba-mako region prior to the Niare arrival. In an additional oral record, Bam-ba Saganogo (another of Bamba's *jamuw*) from Kong was also identified with a settlement at Demeni, in the Morila *kafu*. With respect to Kong, it is of considerable interest that among the first Mande *numuw* to migrate from Ja in the Massina to the Kong region—in about the eleventh-century—were the Ligby, whose *tana* was *bamba*, or crocodile, and patronym Bamba. Because *numuw* frequently preceded agriculturists and herders when founding new Mande settlements, it is not inconceivable, therefore, that Bamba Sanogo's image could be all that is left of a power struggle between Segu and Kong—that is, the Kulibaly and the Wattara—in the early eighteenth century, for control over the Bamako plain and the old Mande. The Niare and the Bamba Sanogo could have been their re-spective pawns and proxies, the Bamako Ture the "devil's advocate": They had after all betrayed the Niare several times, albeit unsuccessfully: during the Samorians wars they invited in Samorian lieutenants to over-

---

107. For the seventeenth-century invasion, see *ASAOF* 1G 320, "Notice sur le Cercle de Ségou, 1904," pp. 1–2; *ASAOF* 1G 322, "Monographie du Cercle de Sikasso, 1904"; for Seku Wattara, see *Table ronde*, pp. 64–70; Robert Pageard, "La Marche orientale du Mali en 1644, d'après le Tarikh es-Soudan," *Journal de la So-ciété des Africanistes* (hereafter *JSA*), vol. 31, no. 1 (1961): 81; Antoine Dincuff, "Kong et Bobo-Dioulasso: Capitales Dyoula," Thèse de Doctorat de Troisième Cycle under the direction of Yves Person (CRA, Paris, n.d), p. 19; personal com-munication Mamadou Sarr (Bamako, 4 Jan. 1980).

108. Dincuff, "Kong et Bobo-Dioulasso," p. 34. According to traditions, many Bamana-speakers (reaching Segu from the southeast, possibly the Kong region) maintained long-standing network and familial relationships with Kong. Person-al communication Jean Bazin (Bamako, 9 March 1883).

throw the Niare chiefly incumbents; despite Niare outrage they sold slaves to Samorian lieutenants during the war; they sent their sons to serve in Samorian armies against the Niare; Niare displeasure notwithstanding a Ture son piloted the Gallieni Mission to Bamako; even after the French arrival in 1883, the Ture were hatching fecund schemes with the Samorians to overthrow both the Niare *and* the French. In league with the Samorians, negotiations with Borgnis Desbordes in February 1883 would have been ripe for a power struggle against the Niare overlords.[109] Bourouti's befuddlement could have played into their hands. The brouhaha could have been just another Bamba Sanogo story.

Typically—according to these voices—Bamba Sanogo, authorized by a regional chief (Moriba Jara, also known as Baguinda Moriba), establishes the Bamako settlement, the leadership of which he subsequently surrenders to the Niare on their late arrival. In some accounts, Bamba Sanogo accedes to this self-denial because of "family reasons," in others, because he has been recalled to assume Kong's chieftainship.[110] Kong texts fail to substantiate the Bamba claims, the only Bamba reference being to Bamba Wattara of Kong, said by some to be of slave ancestry, who, equipped with a slave army known as Bambajonw, carried military campaigns into distant lands to the north and west, which could have included Bamako. Raids from the nearby Samanyana into the Bamako region have also been suggested as possible explanations for the floating Bamba identity.[111] None of this seems plausible largely because (like the Ture stories) no account verifies Bamba Sanogo as Bamako's *dugu-kafu-tigi*.

---

109. *ANMK* 1D 33 5, Borgnis Desbordes, "Notice historique" (1880–1890); *ASAOF* 15G 83, Ruault, "Généralités 1880 à 1920" (Bamako, 22 Feb. 1884), pp. 3, 9; *ASAOF* 1G 50 49, "Lettre Piétri à Gallieni" (Bamako, 9 May 1880), pp. 1–2; *ASAOF* 1G 52 46, Bayol, "Télégramme" (Saldé, 29 June 1880); *ASAOF* 1G 52 46, Bayol, "Mission du Ségou" (Saint Louis, 5 July 1880); *ASAOF* 1G 50 20, "Lettre Gallieni à Gouverneur" (Nango, 7 July 1880), pp. 17–20; *ASAOF* 1G 50 77, "Lettre Gallieni à Gouverneur" (Makajambugu, 26 April 1880), pp. 2–3; *ASAOF* 1G 79, Conrard, "Notice" (Bamako, 21 Feb. 1885), pp. 3–4; *ANSOM* Sén. et Dép. IV Doss. 90 Bis, Vallière, "Mémoire," (Siguiri, 15–25 March 1888), pp. 24–25, 32; Person, *Samori*, vol. 1, pp. 398–399; Gallieni, *Voyage*, pp. 174–176, 236–239, 246–250.

110. Claims in some accounts that Bamba Sanogo was the chief of Kong are very unlikely, the Kong incumbents being the Wattara (Traoré, "Une Seconde légende," p. 8, note 8).

111. E. Bernus, "Kong et sa région," *Etudes Eburéennes*, vol. 8 (Direction de la recherche scientifique, Ministère de l'Education nationale de la République de Côte d'Ivoire, Abidjan, 1960); 242-319, see esp. p. 253; Kathryn Lee Green, "The Foundation of Kong: A study in dyula and Sonongui ethnic identity," Doctoral dissertation (Indiana University, 1984), pp. 324–335; *Table ronde*.

And so this ubiquitous persona, whom oral texts cycle and recycle, remains an unknown silhouette in historical imaginations and in popular voices. And while one hypothesis relates Bamba Sanogo to the early eighteenth-century power struggle between Segu Kulibaly and Kong Wattara for control over the Bamako plain and the old Mande, another links him to (related?) Niare/Ture power struggles in the Bamako region. In either case, his persona would have tested and contested Niare mythic and historical claims as Bamako's founders. Under these circumstances— although the process is far from obvious—those claiming a relatively clear Wagadu-Kingi-Segu-Bamako state identity before Bourouti on the morning of 1 February 1883, as opposed to an ambiguous Kong-Segu counterpart, clearly gained the historical advantage.

2

Material Elaborations of "The Mande Style"

The Bamako *Kafu* and Regional Perspectives[1]

Identity, Spatial Forms, and Relations

On constructing the *kafu*'s nucleus, Bamako town—as opposed to the *kafu*—was built around four *kindaw*, or city quarters, facing north-north-west and east-southeast. Differing architectural styles marked each *kindaws*' ethnic identity. For example, Niarela, the Niare urban quarter and seat of the *kafu-tigi*, or head of state, was recognizable by its round structures and conical thatched roofs. Situated where the French later constructed the Société Commerciale Ouest Africaine (SCOA), the quarter was modestly appointed, the Niare apparently not consumer-rich. As a further sign of their agricultural and husbandry identity, Niare *kindaw* included orchards and pastures. Toward the city's east, marked by two-storied flat-roofed houses—"in the Segu or Moorish style" (according to archival reporting) imaging their Saharan identity—was Tawatila (Touti-la, Tavatila, or Tourela), residence of the large mercantile and Islamized Ture family from Tawat in the Algerian Sahara. More numerous, richer, and more consumer-conscious than the Niare clans, the Ture were *dunanw*, or protected client-strangers, of the ruling Niare chiefs. Dravela housed the Drave, an Islamized mercantile Ture subgroup, also from Tawat (or the Adrar, or the Ouad Dra'a in southern Mauritania depending on the source), whose *kinda* faced west. As a mark of both their "Arabic" and "Islamic" identities, Dabani, the Ture-Drave mosque, since reconstructed and still extant, was located in the city's "Moorish" quarter. For

---

1. As indicated in the Introduction, "regional perspectives" in this context refer to Mande-speakers east and southeast of Nioro and the Senegambia, e.g., the Segu, Beledugu, Bamako, and Mande regions. It does not refer to those Mande who migrated farther east to the Black Volta region.

defense and privacy each *kinda* was enclosed within a *jifutu* (*jin, djin*), or inner wall. All three *kindaw* were surrounded by a *banco tata*, or outer wall made of packed earth about 4.5 meters high and 2 meters thick. To the southeast outside the city walls was Komola, the fourth or Bozo *kinda* with identifying straw structures, home of the Sinaba (Sinayogo) Bozo attached through ritual alliances to the Niare family. Mainly fisherfolk and water transporters, Bozo families moved inside the city walls after the 1883 attack on the *kafu* by Samorian *sofaw*.[2]

Flanked by twenty angle-towers, the city's principal road led northeast to Kulikoro, the old river town, about sixty kilometers downriver. Enroute was the Niare sacred grove (*jetu*) where the *jo* ceremonies, especially the *komo* and other political-religious rituals, were observed. After 1906–1907, Kulikoro became the termination of the Kayes-to-Bamako rail line where a French shipbuilding yard was subsequently constructed. The westerly road led to Kati, a small town cresting the Manding Plateau, later the site of a French slaughterhouse and military post. In the southeast the road led to Kangaba (Kaaba), the Mande's heartland about a three- to four-day journey from Bamako;[3] after a ten to fifteen day journey, the northeast route culminated at Segu, metropolitan capital of the *kafu*'s Kulibaly lords. Making room for the Dakar-Kayes-Bamako railway, the old *kindaw* were razed to the ground at the turn of the century.

The Paradigm Elaborated

Materialized and Regionalized Development

If the previous chapter demonstrated how Nyakate/Niare ethnographic identities were negotiated, and cultural forms manipulated

---

2. Other terms for *kinda* were *kabila, sukula,* and *bösö*. Lineages, or *luw* , were grouped into these lineage-locations (Person, *Samori*, vol. 1, pp. 54, 57). See also Gallieni, *Voyage*, p. 245; *ASAOF* 1G 50 49, "Lettre Piétri à Gallieni" (Bamako, 9 May 1880), p. 3. Paques claims that more recent accounts of the old city have been kept secret because of ancestral graves within ("L'Estrade royale," pp. 1645, 1654). Touré, "L'Amenagement," pp. 2–5; Soumaoro, "Etude," pp. 17–23; Claude Meillassoux, "The Social structure of modern Bamako," *Africa*, vol. 35, no. 2 (April 1965): 125–127; Claude Meillassoux, *Urbanization of an African community: Voluntary associations in Bamako* (University of Washington Press, 1968), pp. 3–6; Meillassoux, "Histoire," pp. 203, 223–225; Interview Marabout Mohammed Touré (Bozola-Bamako, 4 Jan. 1980).

3. Interview Seydou Niaré (Bamako, 2 Jan. 1980). Kangaba was said to be one of Mali's capitals along with Jakajalan, Mani or Manitomo, Jeribatomo, Niani or Nianiba. See Introduction, note 6.

across the mythic past, it also discussed the ritual process by which these identities were ultimately legitimized in relation to the state. Contextualizing the Nyakate/Niare communities first within the universal Wagadu ideal in archaic time, I later showed how across thirty to thirty-five generations, the families' identities shifted to the Bamana Segovian mythical-political and ritual particularisms indigenous to the Bamako *kafu* and upper Niger worlds.

Building on the previous chapter, the present one historicizes the earlier findings drawn primarily from myth, critiquing the families' accounts in relation to French archival resources, and vice versa. In the process, I elaborate on the political economies that did develop historically. The chapter, furthermore, interrogates domestic ideologies that *also* emerged; it critiques the extent to which historically patterned ways of thinking shaped collective political economies, simultaneously molding the families' collective behavior and consciousness. Thus, as this critique binds history to myth, so does the discourse of the shifting identity parse the transition from one to the other. Not so amazingly, Mande identities, historically reconstructed were strikingly reminiscent of the mythologized past.

Additionally, this chapter builds on a set of patterned perceptions broadly elaborated: In asking how families perceived themselves, and how they were perceived by others, I develop the "northern paradigm," a mainly northern and Islamized construct that analogized southern families as the "animist" Other. In other words, if Jenne—the middle Niger entrepot—was the "city blessed by God," southern urban communities in the old Mande were "kaffir" towns at the world's nether reaches. Or, if the north was "urban," "mercantile," and "civilized," the south, rich in gold ores and "animist," was the Muslim's Other, accordingly a reservoir for slaves.[4] A vast ideological and cultural gap—or so some believed—separated the one from the other. Moreover, I historicize the anthropology and political economy of the Niger River. I argue that because southerners related to the river primarily through ritual rather than through a political economy, opportunities to develop the south's material resources were delayed for centuries: In relation to the north, the south's political economies languished in an underdeveloped marginality. Thus, given this ritual-religious relationship—and the south's corresponding underdevelopment—ironically, the Niger's life-giving force contributed to the northern disposition of otherizing the "animist" Other.

---

4. As, for example, in the Wassulu, see Amselle, *Logiques métisses*, pp. 222–224.

Finally, when the archives speak—for the better part of the eighteenth
and nineteenth centuries—the historian learns that across the mythic
vagaries, the families had been signing their land and ecosystems unambiguously Mande; and that by the eighteenth century when the Bamako
kafu was founded, and the families in place, the south, the whole south,
had already become the land of Do ni Kri.[5]

Ethnic Identities Historically Contextualized

The Mande-Hinterland Before the Niare

A rocky landscape, Bamako's Mande-hinterland curved westward toward the Manding Mountains incorporating the Beledugu to the northwest, a mass of undulating protrusions extending across differentiated
ecocultural systems toward the drier savanna. This vast region the French
later divided into the Guemene-Jedugu, and the Petit and Grand Beledugu (see Maps 2 and 3). Farther west the Mande-hinterland enclosed the
Nioro and Kita regions, while east-northeast it extended to the Segu heartland incorporating Markadugu, Nyamina, Mercoya, Murdia, Damfa, and
Sokolo. In the south the hinterland's ecocultural delineations enclosed the
old Mande and the gold-rich Bure and Bambuhu regions. Delimiting administrative colonial units after 1883, the Bamako Circle was created in
1888, later modified between 1895 and 1899. In the process, the French
identified large areas within the Mande-hinterland as "Bambara," "agricultural," and "herding."[6]

---

5. According to D. T. Niane, the land of Do was the Mande-hinterland's plain
extending as far north as Segu. The Kri was the mountainous regions to the west
of the Mande-hinterland (Djibril Tamsir Niane, *Recherche sur l'empire du Mali au
moyen âge* [Paris, 1975], p. 87, note 13). For archival references, see throughout this
book. For other examples of parallel "ethnographic signs" see Charles Bailleul,
Contes bambaras (Paris, 1975); Martha Kendall, "Getting to know you," in David
Parkin, ed., *Semantic anthropology* (London, 1982), pp. 197–209.

6. ANSOM Sén. et Dép. IV Doss. 90 Bis, Vallière, "Mémoire" (Siguiri, 15–25
March 1888), pp. 1–55, see esp. p. 34; *ASAOF* 1G 79, Conrard, "Notice" (Bamako,
21 Feb. 1885), p. 2–3; *ASAOF* 1G 299, Brévié, "Monographie" (Bamako, 25 April
1904), p. 36–46, 61; *ANMK* 1D 33 2, Collomb, "Notice" (Bamako, 1884–1885), p. 1;
ANSOM Sén. et Dép. IV Doss. 90 Bis, Gallieni and Vallière, "Délimitation des Cercles" (Bafulabe, 1 May 1888), pp. 1–3. See also *ASAOF* 1G 32, "Lettre Mage à Gouverneur" (Saint Louis, 21 June 1866), and this Introduction herein, notes 42 and 43.
Louis-Frédéric Tautain, Commandant le Cercle de Bamako created the Circle in
1888.

As events would have it, the Niare and their clients—the desert-side Ture/Drave families, the Fulbe/Jawambe herding families and others—were latecomers to the Mande-hinterland, settling into regions already parsed by families dispersed from Wagadu, Kingi, Ja, and Segu sometime between the twelfth and the seventeenth century.[7] Although unclear, the northern Mande-hinterland's earliest settlers probably included Soninke *horonw*, or free families from Wagadu (that is, those without a trace of slavery, and therefore free to create lineages). Likewise among the region's earlier residents were the Kagoro families, perceived sometimes as having close Soninke associations, at other times Bamana affinities. Also already in the pre-*kafu* region were Bozo and Somono (also Northern Mande Subgroup-speakers), having frequented the southern Mande-hinterland since archaic time, establishing riverain camps extending from Segu on the middle Niger to Kurusa in Guinea.[8] Not always clearly differentiated, these river nomads were more "Somono" in the north, more "Bozo" in the south. Claiming Islamization since deep antiquity, possibly since the eleventh century—before the Kulibaly Bamana arrival in the Segu region, and certainly before the *kafu*'s founding—both Bozo and Somono were historically filiated through marriage alliances and communal organizations, including labor units, with terrestrial Mande lords.[9]

Many originally from Wagadu, among these early families were the Keita of Kangaba, who settled along the Sankarani River, and the Camara of Siby (and Kangaba) with whom the Niare are said to have a blood oath

---

7. Personal communication Ali Ongoïba (Kuluba-Bamako, 7 March 1983).

8. According to Germaine Dieterlen, numerous locations along the river from its source to Lake Debo were sites for important Bozo and other rituals ("Mythe et organisation sociale au Soudan français," *JSA*, vol. 25 [1955/1956]: 38–76, 376–389; vol. 29 [1959]: 119–138).

9. There may be about four Bozo identities on the river: (1) Pondo Sorogo Bozo of the Lake Debo and flood region, who speak a Bozo dialect closely identified with the ancient Sorko language; (2) Tie Ceye, or the Nuhun Bozo of Massina; (3) the Kelenga Bozo in the Segu region, largely Bamanized and now identified with the Marka. The Kelenga are now spending less time on the river and more in commerce and agriculture; (4) the Sonogo Bozo in the Jenne, region (Seminar, Professor Jean Bazin, Ecole des Hautes Etudes [Paris, 10 and 17 May 1982]). Seydou Niare subscribes to the view that the Bozo of the Bamako region were originally Soninke-speakers as a result of some ancient alliance with the Niare family. It is likely that the Bozo have been associated with several identities, which explains why their background is so difficult to trace (Interview Seydou Niaré [Bamako, 6 March. 1983]).

sworn at Lambidu. Also among early residents were the Konde from the Segu region and Sisse, as well as the Berete, Traore, and Ture from the old Mande. Perhaps earliest among all the arrivals were the Dumbya and the Sissoko, both monopolizing the forge, as well as the Kuyate *jeli*, or bards to the Konate, the Keita, the Traore, and the Kone.[10] Their stories are told in the "Epic of Sunjata"—all twenty or thirty versions of it including fragments—which, like the "Wagadu Legend," can still be heard a thousand times: how the Malian state was won for the Keita families and their clients; how, at Kurugan Fugan the spacious clearing beyond Kangaba (Kaaba), another version continues, the thirty-three clan elders received their lands, *jamuw*, and *tanaw* at the hands of their Sunjata lord, acknowledging in return a sacred alliance with the new state; and how the "twelve kings" of "the bright savanna country" with their "twelve royal spears" acknowledged Sunjata as Mansa, while the crowd cried "Wassa, Wassa ... Aye."[11] The epic also tells how lineage-locations and cultural spaces were authorized and negotiated between and/or within lesser lineage heads (*kun-tigiw*), on the one hand, and village chiefs (*dugu-tigiw*), on the other hand; and how ritual access to the wider hinterland's natural resources was guaranteed. By the late nineteenth century most families, like the Niare, were or had become Mandekan, having negotiated a range of identities with regional lords including the Mansa, or rulers of old Mali (c. 1200–c. 1450).

The Northern (Mande) Identity and the Northern Paradigm

The Islamized North. Extending political economies into the desert-side commerce, by the nineteenth century many of these pre-Niare families had also elaborated their commercial identities to include the European entrepots at Sierre Leone and the Gambia.[12] Agricultural undertakings similarly embellished their northern latitudes, adapted in this instance to the north's inferior soils, light, sandy, and rocky, especially clay and ferruginous in some regions, depending on the location, for example, the Grand Beledugu, the Guemene-Jedugu, and the Kaarta (see Map 3). The north's considerably lower rainfall complicated developmental problems:

---

10. Those Konate, who later became known as *Keita*, according to some southern traditions apparently were the first to settle the south (Diabaté, "Kankou Moussa," pp. 9–11, 21; Camara, "Le Manden," p. 18; Djibril Tamsir Niane, *Sundiata: An epic of old Mali* [Longmans, Green & Co., 1965], pp. 77–78; Jabate, "La Légende," p. 243; Niane, *Recherche sur l'empire*, pp. 11–13).

11. Niane, *Sundiata*, pp. 73–79.

12. *ASAOF* 1G 32, "Lettre Mage à Gouverneur" (Saint Louis, 21 June 1866).

Seasonal aridities were frequent, aggravated by slash-and-burn agricultural techniques. By the early twentieth-century some French observers were comparing northern landscapes to a "lunar desolation" menaced by the Harmattan.[13]

Given these problematics, northern families signaled their presence with dry-climate political economies, focusing mainly on drought-resistant cereals, such as fonio (*Fanicum longiflorum*), sorghum (*Pandropogu sorghum*), and millet (*Millet pennissetum*), the latter adapting best to the varied and inferior soils. Producing also tobacco (*Nicotiana rustica*), sesame, and groundnuts, northerners simultaneously signed themselves as herders, breeding sheep, goats and cattle—both the humped *zebu*, and the shorthorned *ndama*—as well as camels, horses, and donkeys. Distinctively northern was the fact that these animals found survival difficult below the 1,000-millimeter isohyet, due to tsetse infestation, and fly parasites.[14].

In addition to agriculture and herding, northerners also signed themselves as "mercantile," and "urban," the mostly Soninke city of Jenne their pride and joy, "the city blessed by God," according to the *Ta'rikh as-Sudan*. Also associated with the ancient and Islamized city of Ja in the Massina floodplain, by the eighteenth and nineteenth centuries Soninko and Maraka traders had developed markets throughout riverain towns such as Segu, Sinsani (Sansanding), Nyamina, and Kulikoro, as well as the Marka towns north and east of Bamako—primarily Banamba, Tuba, and Kiba, and Kerowane (see Map 3). Soninke-Sarakolle families identified as urban included the Sakho, a clerical family that, according to their traditions, had adopted an Islamic identity from as early as the eleventh century in association with the so-called Almoravid invasions. Also settling these

---

13. *ANSOM* Sén. et Dép. IV 90 Bis, Vallière, "Mémoire" (Siguiri, 15–25 March 1888), pp. 6–36; *ANMK* 1D 96, "Notice sur le...Cercle de Bamako, 1902" (Kati, 7 July 1905), p. 9.

14. The Sarakolle produced the largest quantities of millet sold in the markets. Consumers distinguished between the "large" and the "small" millet, but in reality several varieties were produced, which adapted to the different types of soils: sandy, clay, rocky, or ferruginous. Grains were for the most part exchanged for slaves and salt brought by julaw and other traders into the region (*ANMK* 1D 33 1, "Notice historique et géographique du Cercle de Bamako, 1880-1890," pp. 3–19; *ASAOF* 1G 299, Brévié, "Monographie" [Bamako, 25 April 1904], pp. 63–66 and passim; *ASAOF* 1G 305, "Monographie du Cercle de Djenné" [Jenne, 10 March 1904], pp. 28–38; *ANMK* 1D 33 2, Collomb, "Notice" [Bamako, 1884–1885]. See also Brooks, *Landlords*, p. 12. personal communication Mahmadou Sarr [Bamako, 7 Jan. 1980]).

northeast Marka towns were the Islamized Sisse developing Kerowane, according to their traditions, followed by the Dukure, another clerical family, which elaborated Kiba. And while the clerical Sylla are said to have been among the first Islamized households in Tuba, Banamba's development has been attributed, sometime in the 1840s, to the Simpara family.[15] Integrated into the desert-side and Sierre Leone and Gambian commercial enclaves by the late eighteenth century, some urban Soninko-Maraka families from Nyamina and Sinsani in particular are said to have amassed "great fortunes" by the mid-nineteenth century.[16]

But if northerners forged identities as agriculturalist, herders, merchants and urban dwellers, their northern identity was ultimately redefined in relation to the Other: incoming Bamana migrants reaching the middle and upper Niger from an easterly and southeasterly direction.[17] Noted for the first time in the European literature by Pacheco Pereira (1506–1508) and Pere Labat (1728), their earliest reference in the Arabic sources is none other than the two seventeenth-century Timbuktu *ta'rikhs*:[18] The "pagan Bambara"—whose identities the Niare eventually adopted—were "newcomers." Moving toward the Inland Niger Delta and beyond during the sixteenth and seventeenth centuries, Bamana in-migrants established settlements in the Massina, the Beledugu, the Kaarta, and regions west in Nioro.[19] While some invaded cultural spaces once claimed by the Soninko, others settled with previously arriving congeners. Not surprisingly, many previously settled Soninko and/or Maraka families lost ground to the new Bamana in-migrants; so did the Kagoro

---

15. Perinbam, "Islam," pp. 437–657.

16. *ASAOF* 1G 32, "Lettre Mage à Gouverneur" (Saint Louis, 21 June 1866). Residents also prepared textiles during the dry season, working at their craft four out of every seven days, completing a strip about 0.15 meters wide and 15 meters long per day. Raw cotton prices at the turn of the nineteenth century were about 0.55 francs per kilo in the market, and 0.9 to 0.10 francs per kilo at the place of production, usually at the weaver's home. Textile prices varied, but a strip measuring 0.15 meters wide and one meter long sold for about 0.10 francs in most of the Circle (*ANMK* 1D 33 1, "Notice historique" [1880–1890], pp. 5–12).

17. Bazin, "A Chacun son Bambara," pp. 87–127, see esp. p. 104. Tauxier, *Histoire*, pp. 6, 33 –35, 49, 53, 54–55, 57; Raffenel, *Nouveau voyage*, vol. 1, pp. 363–365.

18. Pereira, *Esmeraldo de situ orbis*, p. 67; Labat, *Nouvelle relation*, vol. 3, pp. 257, 334, 359; vol. 4, pp. 85, 87; *Ta'rikh as-Soudan*, pp. 172, 223, 274, 276, 280, 411, 418, 420; *Ta'rikh al-Fattash*, pp. 20, 86, 87, 107.

19. For wet-dry climate changes affecting north-south migrations, see Brooks, *Landlords*, esp. pp. 1–5.

especially those of the Kaartan northwest said also to be among the region's earliest inhabitants.

Overall consequences of Bamana in-migrations, and the ways in which they re-shaped northern identities were considerable. First the Bamana brought comparably higher population densities—especially in the Beledugu where the Jara and the Traore settled, higher also when compared to the more humid south, even the more hospitable Bamako plain, which the Niare settled in the eighteenth century. The precise fate of these early Soninko and Kagoro settlers—and their Fulbe clients—in the face of the Bamana in-migrations is unknown. On the one hand, a fair assumption is that as the Soninko and Kagoro Bamanized (in the wake of the overwhelming Bamana presence), many probably adopted Marka and Sarakolle identities. On the other hand, most Fulbe herders, never far from settled Mande patrons, maintained their herding and veterinarian identities, the latter associated with "women's work." With respect to continuing Mande-Fulbe articulations (see Chapter 1), it is worth noting that by the nineteenth century at least, Fulbe lineage specializations resembled their Mande counterparts to the extent that while some were textile producers (*maabuube*; sing.: *maabo*), others were bardic (*wambabe*; sing.: *bambado*). Several Fulbe families, in addition, engaged in trade, suggesting overall Fulbe production capacities ranging well beyond their celebrated herding skills (see Map 7).[20]

Second, not tardy in advancing their interests (or their image), the mere presence of the "idolatrous Bambara" required northerners to adjust their collective consciousness, perceptions, and corporate identities. Because, ravaging the land—or so it seemed to northerners—the Bambara destroyed villages, pillaging, sowing seeds of disorder, and seizing free women as concubines. Forcing the state of Jenne into tributary status, even sacking the city of Jenne "blessed by God," their raids continued into the eighteenth century, especially against the Massina and surrounding regions. In their wake famine stalked the land, although the "Bambara" were not entirely responsible for this and subsequent disasters. But to no avail, because by the seventeenth century, indelible in the northern episteme were images of the Bambara as "pagan," "idolatrous," and "fetish-

---

20. Pollet and Winter, *La Société soninké*, pp. 44–148. During initiation ceremonies Fulbe youths learned the medicinal qualities of herbs useful for their animals. *ANMK* 1D 32, Lieutenant Monziols, "Notice historique de Cercle de Bafoulabé" (Bafulabe, 1 May 1889); *ANMK* 1D 32 2, Administrateur G. Mary, "Précis historique et géographique du Cercle du Bafoulabé" (Bafulabe, 1 Nov. 1890); *ANMK* 1D 32 5, "Etude sur les marabouts" (Bafulabe, 5 July 1894); Camara, "Le Manden," pp. 17, 20.

ist" destroyers of property and sackers of towns and villages, "stone by stone." Worse still, from east to west and north to south, the Bambara were "ravagers" of women who raised "pagan" children, the faithful calling on God to preserve them from these calamities. Not acting alone, they sometimes formed heinous alliances with allegedly treasonous northern populations sharing the Bambara's despicable values and lack of shame, or so it seemed to some contemporary northern observers. But God was good. He had used the Moroccans and their victory at Tondibi (1591) over the north's "pagans" as a veritable chastisement. And His mercy for ever enduring, the Moroccans, rounding up the pagans in the middle of a large forest in the Massina, slaughtered them one by one most deservedly. Even venturing beyond the Mande-hinterland, in about 1670, Timbuktu, the Sudan's premier entrepot and focus of the western Sudan's higher learning, was sacked by the Bambara. Although not signed a Mande city, Timbuktu had long since hosted Mande scholars such as the Mandinka al-Abbas Mandawiyya, the Soninko Turi Kuri and Sissi Kuri, and the Mande author of the *Ta'rikh as-Sudan*.[21]

Third, Bamana in-migrants also brought new elaborations on a state identity based on war, slaves, market economies, and the *jo* cult and rituals. I am here referring to the Kulibaly Bamana Segu state (c. 1600/1625–1861), and its "brother state," the Kulibaly Bamana Massassi polity in the Kaarta (eighteenth and nineteenth centuries). Of the two, the Segu state was pivotal to Soninke identity shifts in general, and the Niare identity shifts in particular. Further ramifications followed, including the rise of the Jara and Traore horse-warriors, especially during Segu's eighteenth-century expansionist wars. In keeping with their warrior image, Beledugu clans, for example, came to be identified with well-known patronymics such as Jara and Traore (Tawari, Tarawele), the region's two largest and most powerful warrior families. Since wars and raids could enrich a community, bringing captives, women, grain, and animals into circulation, Beledugu horse-warriors were therefore important to Bamana state development. Likewise following the Bamana state hegemony was the expansion of market infrastructures linking middle Niger and Beledugu families, the two combining to form the region's largest middle and upper Niger populations, larger by far than those on the Bamako plain and *kafu*: A population estimate of the late 1880s suggests approximately 70,000–100,000 Beledugu inhabitants, between

---

21. *Ta'rikh as-Soudan*, pp. 221–222, 223, 274, 276, 280, 411, 418, 420; *Ta'rikh al-Fattash*, pp. 20, 86, 87, 107; *ASAOF* 1G 305, "Monographie du Cercle de Djenné" (Jenne, 10 March 1904), pp. 5, 10, 54.

seventeen and twenty times larger than Bamako's 4,000–5,000 *kafu* residents, suggesting a far larger consumer capability.[22]

Finally, important to the reconstruction of the besieged northern identity was the role of Islam. No reliable statistics on Islamized populations exist. In any event we no longer risk the problematics of differentiating "Muslim" from "animist" in a region where Islamic and "animist" particularizing made differentiation difficult, or where ideological and religious identities could alter within one generation, and where the colonial criteria for evaluating Muslims and "animists" are no longer acceptable (see Map 6). This caveat said, French records nonetheless support the growing northern perception—as expressed in the Timbuktu *ta'rikhs*—that if the north was Islamized, the south was not. Thus, on the one hand, at the turn of the century in the northern colonial circle of Jenne, 75 percent of the 70,000 residents was "Muslim." Islamized populations also resided in the Massina, especially in Ja where Ibn Battuta (1352–1353) had noted the existence of a long-standing Islamic tradition of learning.[23] Sizable Islamized populations were also in Nyamina and Sinsani, as well as in the Marka towns of Banamba, Kerowane, Kiba, and Tuba.[24] Sticking out like a sore thumb in this Islamized configuration was the Segu state, a "bastion of animism," only 35 percent "Muslim" of an overall population of 170,000 residents at the turn of the century."[25] In the south, on the other hand, only 5 to 10 percent of Bamako's *kafu* population of 4,000–5,000 inhabitants was "Muslim" in 1883, only 4 to 5 percent in Satadugu of a total population in 1905–1906, and only 5 to 6 percent in Sikasso of a total population of 101,500 residents.[26] Even if the statistical data are misleading, of

22. Estimates have been rounded out. *ANSOM* Sén. et Dép. IV 90 Bis, Vallière, "Mémoire" (Siguiri, 15–25 March 1888), pp. 34, 51.

23. *ASAOF* 1G 305, "Monographie du Cercle de Djenné" (Jenne, 10 March 1904), pp. 5, 10, 54; *ANMK* 1D 38 3, "Etudes générales: Monographie du Cercle de Djenné, 1909," pp. 3–24 and passim; *ANMK* 1D 38 2, "Djenné historique: Cercle de Mopti" (1930), pp. 5–7.

24. *ASAOF* 1G 189, "Rapport du Capitaine d'Artilllierie de Marine MacLeod adjoint au Commandant de Cercle de Bamako, sur une tournée faite dans le Maracadougou" (Bamako, 1 Oct. 1894).

25. *ANMK* 5D 51, "Soudan 1905–1906, Statistiques de la population: Tableau d'ensemble du Haut-Sénégal-Niger, 1905–1913."

26. *ANMK* 5D 79, "Recensement, Statistiques annuelles: Cercle de Satadougou, 1905–1914"; *ANMK* 5D 53, "Cercle de Bamako: Etat numérique de la population indigène par religion"; *ASAOF* 1G 351, "Monographie du Soudan 1921: Bamako ville et Cercle de Bamako," p. 11; *ANMK* 4E 36, "Politique musulmane: Rapport sur l'Islam et les ... Musulmans, Cercle de Bamako, 1897–1911"; *ANMK* 5D 51,

growing importance to the argument is that in the world of imaging, the south, compared to the north, was being stamped with "animist's" signs.

Accordingly in the north, a hegemonical paradigm associated with this Islamized presence began to stabilize during the seventeenth century (if not before), about the time when the two Timbuktu *ta'rikhs* were written. Imaging northerners as Islamized elites, the paradigm was really an internal construct to promote a northern identity in relation to the Other: the "pagan" and "animist Bambara." There had been earlier attempts to define the northern identity. But previous endeavors had been associated with the Islamic traditions at Ja and with prominent Mande scholars such as the Mandinka al-Abbas Mandawiyya and the Soninko Turi Kuri and Sissi Kuri. Similar traditions were later reflected in the teachings of the fifteenth-century Tawati *alim* Muhammad Abd al-Karim al-Maghili and the Cairene *alim* Jalal al-Din al-Suyuti (d. 911/1505). Jenne's scholarly community was likewise well known throughout the western Sudan, glorified in the *Ta'rikh as-Sudan*'s peon of praise.[27] As-Sadi (to whom the authorship of the *Ta'rikh as-Sudan* has been attributed), was himself a Jenne *imam* and judiciary (1629–1643). Previous Islamic traditions (proselytizing and reformist) had been associated with either the more aggressive al-Maghili (d. 1504) or the quietist al-Suyuti (1445–1505), the latter more compatible with the thirteenth-century Suwarian traditions at Ja in the Massina.[28]

"Soudan 1905–1906: Statistiques de la population"; *ANMK* 1D 38 3, "Monographie du Cercle de Djenné" (Jenne, 1909)," p. 102. See also *ANMK* 4E 39, "Politique musulmanes: Rapport sur l'Islam et les confréries musulmanes, Cercle de Beyla, 1896"; *ASAOF* 1G 299, Brévié, "Monographie" (Bamako, 25 April 1904); *ANMK* 2E 43, "Politique indigène: Notes et fiches de renseignements sur les chefs et notables de Cercle de Bamako, 1897–1908."

27. *Ta'rikh as-Sudan*, pp. 22–28.

28. The Suwarian tradition, traceable to al-Salim Suware, a semi-legendary persona, was associated with the Islamic traditions of Ja in the Massina. Another tradition associates al-Salim Suware with Dinga, Bida's father (Bida, we recall, was the sacred python of Wagadu), and hence with an "animist" identity. John O. Hunwick, "Ahmad Baba and the Moroccan invasion of the Sudan (1591)," *Journal of the Historical Society of Nigeria*, vol. 2, no. 3 (1962): 311–328; Elias N. Saad, *Social history of Timbuktu: The role of Muslim scholars and notables, 1400–1900* (Cambridge University Press, 1983), pp. 7–8, 22–46, 59, 68, 131, 134, 147–148; Ivor Wilks, "The Transmission of Islamic learning in the Western Sudan," in Jack Goody, ed., *Literacy in traditional societies* (Cambridge University Press, 1968), pp. 162–195; Lamin Sanneh, "The Origins of clericalism in West Africa," *JAH*, vol. 17 (1976): 49–72; Mervyn Hiskett, *The Development of Islam in West Africa* (New York and London, 1984), pp. 15, 16, 34, 36–38, 41, 42, 47, 85, 161, 248, 246, 272, 314, 316, 317.

Islamized traditions reemerging in the form of a mid-seventeenth-century paradigm were timely. In addition to the presence of the offending Bambara, the north's humiliating defeat at Tondibi (1591) at Moroccan hands coincided with deep fluctuations in the trans-Saharan trade, bedrock of the north's larger political economies. Boding even more ill for future generations were famines and epidemics devastating the north from the sixteenth to eighteenth centuries, not to mention northern literacy and learning now in decline.[29] The northern paradigm thus emerged at a time when northern elites and literati were on the defensive against "Bambara invaders" violating their cultural spaces. The *dar al-Islam* had been dishonored before, by the equally "pagan Mossi," burning Timbuktu between 1332–1336, sacking it again in about 1338, attacking Sunni Ali (d. 1492), Songhay's founder and ruler (1469 and 1470, and again between 1477 and 1483), even raiding as far west as Walata in 1483. Also attacking were the Akil and Maghcharen Tuareg, who roamed the desert steppes menacing caravans, seizing Timbuktu, Arawan, and Walata in 1433, subordinating it to tributary status between 1433 and 1468.

But the "Bambara" seventeenth and eighteenth-century menace was different: Now having a clearer sense of its own identity, the Islamic north was prepared to defend its image. More importantly, the north's internal paradigm had acquired hegemonic proportions, extending west and south into the Senegambia and upper Guinea, where Mande-speakers had settled since about the fourteenth century, if not before, even to Black Volta towns and mining communities, likewise settled by Mande-speakers between the eleventh and seventeenth centuries.[30] So powerful was this internal paradigm that it survived well into the late twentieth century, ironically "matching" French holographs of the Muslim/pagan, Muslim/uncivilized and Muslim/animist.

Accordingly, the Mande-hinterland, even more so the Mande world, were theologically divided according to a hegemonic north/south paradigm analogically bound into Muslim/kaffir, Islamized/infidel, civilized/Bambara, free/slave, trader/animist farmer, and trader/warrior oppositions in defense of the ideal Mande identity and its Islamized arsenal. Reinforcing the paradigm was the *Ta'rikh al-Fattash's* well-known

---

29. Saad, *Social history*, pp. 46, 59, and chap. 3; Sékéne Mody Cissoko, "Famines et épidémies à Tombouctou et dans la boucle du Niger du XVIe au XVIIIe siècle," *BIFAN*, sér. B, vol. 30 (1968): 806–821.

30. Perinbam, "Perceptions," pp. 295–322," see esp. pp. 308–309; Perinbam, "The Political organization, pp. 437–462, see esp. pp. 456–457; Binger, *Du Niger*, vol. 2, pp. 375, 382, 385–386.

observation that "if you ask what difference exists between the Malinke (southerner) and Wangara (northern Soninke), know that the Wangara and the Malinke are of the same origin, but that 'Malinke' designates 'warrior' (*dolo* consumer), while 'Wangara' (abstainer) designates a trader who travels long-distance from country to country."[31] Less well known is that in preparing his monumental work, al-Kati, the author of the *Ta'rikh al-Fattash*, collected those oral traditions associating the north's Islamized literati with an Arab or Hebrew identity; and that this "semitic" argument—in circulation since the sixteenth century—had been used by northerners to justify the region's socio-political organization. According to Madina Ly Tall, the traditions crystallized in the seventeenth and eighteenth centuries, when the Mande had declined and a "glorified past" became important.[32] Far from developing the idea on his own, therefore, al-Kati was drawing on conventional wisdom.

Thus it was that a man who consumed the much-maligned alcoholic beverages—the *dolo* or millet beer (40–50 percent alcohol)—became the "Bambara" and "animist" image (the pagan sobriquet) in pious Muslim eyes. So compelling was this hegemonic paradigm that southeast in the Sikasso region Islamized Dioula slurred "animist" Senufu by naming them "Bambara," and the Soninke of the Odienne region stereotyped "pagan" Mandinga or Maninka as "Bambara." Farther west, pious Muslims in the Circle of Tuba (Guinea) sneered at those Bambara who set aside "drinking days" as well as "market days" with the same regularity, while farther east Islamized Mande-Jula in the Black Volta region dismissed the "kaffir" Gbanian and Dagari as Bambara. Farther north in the Timbuktu and Massina regions, many Bambara were generally known as slaves: Throughout vast quarters of the western Sudan, "Bambara" had come to mean "animist farmer," "pagan," "fetishist," "primitive," "inferior being," and "slave."[33] Recall that many of these "pagan Bambara,"

---

31. *Ta'rikh al-Fattash*, pp. 20, note 6, 40, note 2, 65, and note 2.

32. Djibril Tamsir Niane, "Mythes, légendes et sources orales dans l'oeuvre de Mahmoûd Kâti," *Recherches Africaines: Etudes Guinéennes*, new ser. no. 1–4 (Jan–Dec. 1964): 36–42; Cissé, *Histoire et tradition*, pp. 8–9, 12–13, 17–20, esp. p. 19; Madina Ly "Quelques remarques sur le *Tarikh el-Fettach*," *BIFAN*, vol. 34, no. 3 (1972): 471–493.

33. Charlotte Quinn, *Mandingo kingdoms of the Senegambia* (London, 1972), p. 53; Bazin "A Chacun son Bambara," pp. 87–125. *ASAOF* 1G 194, "Dossier sur Tombouctou: Notice sur la région de Tombouctou historique" (c. 1896); *ANMK* 1D 173 C1, "Notice ethnographique et historique: Circonscription de Séguela Cercle de Touba 1900" (Seguela, 31 May 1900), p. 3.

"Malinke and "Mandinga" were among those sold into New World slavery (see Introduction).

Not surprisingly, analogical modes forged in the paradigm filtered into the historical-ethnographic imaginations as well as popular cultures. Thus, for example, cereal production, associated with the Islamized Soninko and Sarakolle, and destined for "Islamic" desert-markets was included in the repertoire of a northern identity, even although cereals were widely produced and consumed throughout the Mande-hinterland, even by non-Soninko, even by "animists." Privileging cereals in the northern paradigm was the belief that grain production was a chiefly sign.[34] The paradigm likewise reinforced the Islamic image of northerners as tobacco producers and snuff consumers (both also said to be chiefly signs), as well as groundnut farmers, despite the fact that all four commodities were widely produced and consumed elsewhere in the Mande-hinterland, although admittedly to a lesser extent in the south where soils were less suitable. Even husbandry became a sign in the northern paradigm, the horse especially signifying nobility introduced into the Mande-hinterland by Soninke migrants "riding in from the east." The Arabic horse, seldom bred by northerners and most often imported from Algerian oases, was notably expensive and "sickly." Yet this exotic steed was preferred over domestic "Bambara" (Beledugu) mounts, cheaper and hardier. It was also preferred over Bandiagara (Sanga) breeds, a cross between Mossi mares and Fulbe stallions, other males said to be "weak and malnourished." Farther south, where horses hardly tolerated the humidity and disease environment, northern Sarakolle merchants traded horses against southern Bambara slaves. By that same token, the larger Massina sheep useful for its wool and the Sahelian sheep bred for its milk were chosen over "Bambara" breeds, even though the latter produced good wool and meat, admittedly smaller milk yields.[35] As to Saharan rock salt, it had, since antiquity been signed unambiguously northern and Islamic.

A developmental ideology also filtered into the paradigm, where northerners, especially Soninko (the Wakore of an earlier era) were identified with trade rather than war. Admittedly a destroyer, war was nonetheless, a means of enrichment, raising tribute, earning revenue, exacting

---

34. Personal communication Mahmadou Sarr (Bamako, 6 Jan. 1980).

35. *ANMK* 1D 33 1, "Notice historique" (1880–1890), pp. 10–12, 15; *ASAOF* 15G 83, Ruault, "Généralités 1880 à 1920" (Bamako, 22 Feb. 1884), p. 7; *ANMK* 1Q 202, "Renseignement sur les maisons de commerce Cercle de Bandiagara, 1907–1911: Renseignements sur la situation économique de la residence de Sanga" (May 1907), n.p.; Camara, "Le Manden," pp. 17, 52, 53, 54.

punitive taxes, acquiring slaves, and appropriating large quantities of grain, women, and animals if planned in a timely manner and effectively implemented. It goes without saying that the north's "Bambara" population elaborated state systems through war, otherwise an abomination (in pious Muslim eyes) unless undertaken as a *jihad*. The paradigm likewise identified the north with Islamic sciences and learning, implying that the south's "animist" theology of the occult—the sacred fundamental law—was nothing but a "pagan" discourse; and that the *numuw* 's abilities to manipulate the natural and spirit world through ritual was hardly a scientific endeavor.

It remains unclear where this analogic and paradigmatic naming of the "Bambara" Other originated. The northern Soninke and Fulbe, cultural brokers and the region's Islamized state-builders since the eleventh century (especially those of the Massina and Segu regions) appear among the earliest conjurers: After all, Arabized Fulbe and Soninke had been the main interlocutors and translators to adventuring Arab geographers prior to the sixteenth century.[36] By the seventeenth century (noted above), Fulfulde (and Hausa) loan words were clearly widely used in the Timbuktu and desert-side regions to identify Mande-speakers: *Mali, Malinke, Wangara, Wakore,* and *Bambara* have all been associated with the northern Fulbe, who, incidentally, also claim to have "converted" the "pagan Bambara" to Islam. Differentiating further, it is believed that while the Fulfulde term *Wangara* was a universal coinage identifying Islamized Mande-speakers in general, *Wakore* referred more specifically to Soninko and Sarakolle. Thus, by applying the naming terminology, *Bambara*, to southerners, northerners laid the cornerstone of the "southern identity." It goes without saying that these ethnonyms were rarely used south of middle Niger regions, except by those subscribing to the paradigm. In the south, Bambara named themselves *Bamana*, while the Maninka called themselves *Mandinga* (the French often used *Malinke*, the Fulbe terminology). In the Senegambia, Mande-speakers named themselves *Mandinga*; *Mandinka* was their local Fulbe name.[37]

Beyond the Fulbe and desert-side influences, others adopting the northern paradigm included Islamized Marka, Sarakolle and Soninko

---

36. Diabaté, "Kankou Moussa," p. 29.

37. *Ta'rikh al-Fattash,* pp. 40, note 2; p. 65, note 2. *Soninke,* the western equivalent of *Bambara,* was in use in the Senegambia. Quinn, *Mandingo,* p. 53; Bazin, "A Chacun son Bambara," pp. 87–125; *ASAOF* 1G 248, Sén. et Dép., Pérignon, "Monographie" (1899–1900), p. 259; *ASAOF* 1G 305, "Monographie du Cercle de Djenné" (Jenne, 10 March 1904). See also Introduction herein, note 75.

slavers, traders, and literati identifying more readily with cereal production, urban development, "civilized" merchants and scholars—whose Koranic, commentaries, and scriptural exegeses stocked northern libraries. Similarly dealing in Tichit-Taodeni rock salt and northern herds, their commodities were exchanged for "kaffir" gold and "Bambara" slaves. Instructors in Koranic schools and institutions of higher education also, no doubt, shared the paradigm and its Islamic episteme where knowledge of writing and the language of God were transferred by "People of the Book." Aside from Jenne, Timbuktu, and Ja in the Inland Niger Delta region, most of the north's Koranic schools and intermediate institutions of higher instruction were in Marka towns such as Tuba (Sylla), Kerowane (Sisse), Nyamina (Sakho), Kiba (Dukure), Banamba (Simpara), and Sinsani, numerically fewer schools in the Beledugu, the latter altogether lacking in institutions of higher learning.[38]

Within this northern paradigm, it was the Maraka (sing.: Marka) from middle and upper Niger towns who came to dominate, diffusing their political institutions, ideologies, cultural forms, historical imaginations, and commercial blueprints, establishing *kafuw* and/or residing in Bamana jurisdictions.[39] Ubiquitous under the Umarian "Islamic umbrella" after the 1860s, they could be found throughout the western Sudan proselytizing, slaving, producing cereals, breeding sheep, goats, and horses, even working their fields alongside slaves[40]—clearly an uneasy alliance, especially in Banamba, one of the Sudan's principal salt and slave markets. By the turn of the century, the "Banamba incident" of 1905, involving slave flights and violence, made no secret of the "profound disdain" in which Marka owners held their "Bambara" slaves.[41] Finally aligning with

---

38. Perinbam, "Islam," pp. 652–653.

39. *Ibid.*, pp. 537–657.

40. *ANMK* 1D 33 4, Rougier, "Enquête sur l'Islam" (Banamba, 31 May 1914); *ASAOF* 1G 229, Brévié, "Monographie" (Bamako, 25 April 1904); *ANMK* 4E 32, "Politique indigène: Rapports sur la situation de l'Islam dans le Haut-Sénégal-Niger, 1908"; see also *ANMK* 4E 32, "Politique musulmane 1903–1912," correspondence and reports nos. 1, 3–9; *ASAOF* 1G 189, McLeod, "Rapport ... Marcadougou" (Bamako, 1 Oct. 1894); *ANSOM* Sén. et Dép. IV Doss. 90 Bis, "Rapport de la mission de la compagnie dans le Bélédougou" (Kita, 26 Feb. 1888); *ASAOF* 1G 83, "Mission Caron à Tombouctou, 1887–1895, Le Lieutenant de vaisseau 'Caron' commandant le canonnière à M. Le Chef de bataillon " (Aboard the "Niger," 31 Oct. 1887), p. 32.

41. *ASAOF* 15G 170, "Rapport sur le conflit markas à M. Le Gouvernenr Général, affaires politiques: Incidents de Banamba dossier du Commandant Laverdure" (Gorée, 15 June 1905), pp. 2–3; *ASAOF* 15G 170, "Cercle de Bamako in-

the north's Islamized paradigm were Bozo and Somono families, fisher-folk and river nomads.

Ignored by the Islamized paradigm however was the fact that north-erners particularized belief systems according to ethnographic considera-tions. Residing in "animist" jurisdictions since antiquity under the autho-rity of *dugu-kolo-tigiw-* ("masters of the earth")—as indeed was the case in Bamako—ethnographic parsings occurred as Islam was contextualized and recontextualized within particularized jurisdictions. Even Islamized residents in the Jenne Circle (land of the "city blessed by God") particu-larized their beliefs through the *jo*, more particularly the *komo* and *nama* rituals.[42] Farther west many Muslims danced and sang by moonlight, drank the much-maligned *dolo*, and scarred themselves. Dressed to kill for the *salintchini* (feast to celebrate the end of Ramadan, the tenth day of *dhu al-hijja*), they created mayhem, firing shots, beating drums, feasting and visiting neighbors, avoiding mosques, preferring instead to pray in way-side *bonlon-nin*, or shrines associated with ancestral cults. Eschewing the *muezzin*'s cry, they summoned the faithful to prayer with drums, blowing elephants' tusks hollowed to resemble bugle horns; and beseeching good harvests, invoked the rain powers. Muslims further particularized beliefs by relying on magic, divination, and "animist" sciences, calling on the powers of talismans, amulets, and *gris-gris*. Conversely, Bamana "ani-mists" showing too great familiarity with the prayer, or Islamic rites, were shunned when seeking brides. And ever since that day in Segu when Biton Kulibaly's (the Segu Faama) mother, a "pious Muslim," allegedly sold millet beer (40–50 percent alcohol) to the *tonjonw* (supposedly the ori-gins of the *disongo*, or general tax), pious gossips have never ceased their clucking.[43]

Similarly, northern Bozo and Somono lineages particularized rituals and ideologies even while clinging to an Islamic identity and the hege-monical paradigm. In the service of terrestrial Mande lords, their *ji-tigi* (*ji-*

cident de Banamba dossier du Commandant Laverdure, 1905: Rapport sur le con-flit markas" (Gorée, 26 June 1905); *ASAOF* 15G 170, "Cercle de Bamako, Incident de Banamba dossier du Commandant Laverdure, 1905: Rapport sur le conflit markas" (Gorée, 11 July 1905), pp. 1–20.

42. *ANMK* 1D 38 3, "Monographie du Cercle de Djenné" (Jenne, 10 March 1909), pp. 10, 24, 102; Gallieni, *Voyage*, pp. 429–430.

43. Perinbam, "Islam," pp. 639, 651, 655; Jennifer C. Ward, "The French-Bam-bara relationship, 1880–1915," Ph.D. dissertation (University of California, Los Angeles, 1976), p. 36; Park, *The Travels*, (1971), pp. 96–97; Raffenel, *Nouveau voyage*, vol. 1, pp. 423, 428; *ANMK* 1D 33 4, Rougier, "Enquête sur l'Islam" (Banamba, 31 May 1914).

tu) or supernatural powers—as "masters of the water"—corresponded to those of the *dugu-kolo-tigi*, "master of the earth." Accordingly committed to their patrons' ancestral cults, the Islamized Bozo and Somono were also important players in the *komo* mythical-political rituals: In the Bamako region, Komola, the original Bozo urban quarter, was situated outside the city walls en route to the *komo*'s sacred grove. Oral texts moreover link the Islamized Bozo, in particular, through blood oaths and joking relationships to the "animist" Dogon of Jafabare in the Massina and the Bandiagara escarpments.[44] More ubiquitous in the Segu and Inland Delta regions, Islamized Somono invited to Segu by the "animist" Biton (according to oral accounts), served both their Kulibaly and Jara lords, sharing their patrons' ritual-magical and ritual-political cults.[45]

The Southern (Mande) Identity and the Northern Paradigm

Perspectives on an "Animist" Mythic-Ritual-Political Identity. However, it wasn't just the northern Bambara who was the "animist" Other within the northern paradigm: In fact the south, the whole south, especially

---

44. Interview Alphi Samounou (Jenne, 19 Nov. 1982). Samounou's testimony is supported by Griaule claiming that the Dogon graphics or ideograms have been influenced by the Mande, including Bozo *glaw-so*, or signs. His claim has also been supported by Seydou Camara, who argues that Dogon oral traditions associate them with the Mande; and by Wa Kamissoko, that the Dogon and the Mande share the *sigui*, a ceremony celebrated every sixty years. Marcel Griaule, *Introduction: Signes graphiques, soudanais* (Paris, 1951), p. 6. See also Germaine Dieterlen and Youssouf Cissé, *Les Fondements de la société d'initiation* (Paris, 1972), esp. chap. 1; Delafosse, *Haut-Sénégal-Niger*, vol. 1, pp. 253–254; Youssouf Tata Cissé and Wa Kamissoko, *La Grande geste du Mali, des origines à la fondation de l'empire* (Traditions de Krina aux colloques de Bamako) (Paris, 1988), p. 181, note 47; Cissé, *Histoire et tradition*, p. 12; Diabaté, "La Région," p. 27; Camara, "Le Manden," p. 34; *ANMK* 1D 38 3, "Monographie du Cercle de Djenné" (Jenne, 10 March 1909), pp. 3–4, 6, 20; *ASAOF* 1G 305, "Monographie du Cercle de Djenné" (1904), pp. 2–3.

45. Some Somono traditions allege a servile heritage, still others that all Somono from Kankan to Timbuktu were of the "same family." *ASAOF* 1G 79, "Le Capitaine chargé de travaux: Renseignements divers sur Bamako et le pays environnant, 1885" (Bamako, 21 Feb. 1885), pp. 22–23; *ANSOM* Sén. IV Doss. 90 Bis, Vallière, "Rapport sur l'opération de Minamba-Farba" (Bamako, 9 March 1888), pp. 2, 6, 9. *ANSOM* Sén. et Dép. IV Doss. 90, Vallière, "Mémoire" (Siguiri, 15–25 March 1888), pp. 45–46; *ANMK* 1D 33 1, "Notice historique, 1880–1890," pp. 15–16; *ANMK* 1D 38 3, "Monographie du Cercle de Djenné" (Jenne, 10 March 1909), pp. 3–4, 8, 20. For Mage's account of the Somono, see *Relation*, pp. 257–258. See also J. Daget, "Notes sur Diafarabé et ses habitants Bozo," *N A* (July 1948): part 1, 31–34; part 2, 24–25; N'Diayé, *Les Castes*, pp. 13–52, 66, 83–97.

the *Mandekalu* (the external name for the people of the Mande), were also unambiguously identified as "animist," sometimes even as "Bambara" regardless of language or ethnic identity.

It seemed of little importance that like the north, the south's developmental process was heavily ritualized; or that the same karite and nete (nere) trees opened on to southern landscapes; or that on voyaging south from Segu—pockmarked by the "treacherous" balansan—northerners identified with southern horizons shaped by the culinary karite; or that the south's historicization of material and ethnographic signs resembled their northern counterparts; or that southerners also produced the same grains—fonio, millets, and sorghum—as found in the Islamized north; or that they also grew maize, but admittedly more tubers (*Dioscorea alata, Colens-coppini, Helmia bulbfera*) and cabbages (*Colocasia antiquorum*).[46] True, southerners excelled at "dry" and "wet" rice (*Oryza glaberrima*: *Malo-le, malo-ba*, and *Kuma-malo* respectively) production; true, also that their "white" rice was even more "beautiful than Jenne rice." And yes, they mined the Bambuhu and Bure gold that northerners exchanged for rock salt and grain in lean years when harvests failed.[47] And while no written texts compare with the north's Islamized manuscripts—not least of all the Timbuktu *ta'rikhs*—and for written sources we rely mainly on Ibn Battuta's *Tuhfat al-Muzzar* (1353–1354) and Ibn Khaldun's *Histoire* (1390),[48] the south's oral texts were incontrovertibly rich beyond compare.

It also seemed of little importance that the author of the *Ta'rikh al-Fattash* had spoken: Northerners and southerners were "the same." The Mandekaluw were not only Mande-speakers, but they also identified

---

46. *ANMK* 1D 33 1, Notice historique" (1880–1890), pp. 5–7, 9–10, 13, 16; *ASAOF* 1G 299, Brévié, "Monographie" (Bamako, 25 April 1904), pp. 69–70 and passim.

47. For food shortages in the Bambuhu, see *ANMK* 1D 33 2, Collomb, "Notice" (Bamako, 1884–1885), p. 11; *ANMK* 3Q 12, "Rapport sur le mouvement minier dans la colonie du Haut-Sénégal-Niger, 1909." For ritual observances in Bambuhu similar to those in Bure, see *ANMK* 3Q 3, "Mines: Renseignement sur les régions aurifères du Bambouk 1896"; Niane, *Sundiata*, p. 81; Cissé and Kamissoko, *La Grande geste*, p. 245.

48. We, of course, also rely on the Portuguese voyagers. See, for example, Gomes Eanes de Azurara, *Chronique de Guinée* (1453) (Dakar, 1960); Alvise da Cadamosto (c. 1468), *The voyages of Cadamosto and other documents on western Africa in the second half of the fifteenth century*, ed. G. R. Crone (London, 1937); Valentim Fernandes (1506–1510) *Description de la côte occidentale d'Afrique (Sénégal au Cap de Monte Archipels)*, trans. and annotated Th. Monod, A. Teixera da Mota and R. Mauny (Bissau, 1951); Pereira, *Esmeraldo de situ orbis*.

with the mythical Wagadu dispersal, the old Malian state hegemony (elaborated after the battle at Krina [c. 1234]), the rituals revealed at Kurugan Fugan, as well as the tri-partite social organization. It likewise seemed of little importance that both northern and southern myths were similarly parsed into related mythical-political rituals associated with the six (male only) great *jo* associations. Allowing for particularized articulations, doctrines formulated on a cosmological and mythical template did integrate the south's intellectual and spiritual universe into a configuration resembling the north's.

But then, the author of the *Ta'rikh al-Fattash* had spoken otherwise: Islamized northerners and "animist" southerners *were* different. While the one was an abstemious long-distance trader, the other was a *dolo*-drinking warrior.[49] Not just the Timbuktu *ta'rikh*, even popular discourses parsed these differences. For example, some Fulbe believed that the Maninka (Malinke), lacking sensibilities, was prone to violence; he resisted Islam, placing only one foot at a time on the prayer mat. Conversely, many southerners believed the Fulbe too remote; he was hypocritical; he was two-faced: "If you see a Fulbe, and you don't see his other side, you haven't seen a Fulbe" (Maninka proverb). The Bambara indulged in indirection; he used double-speak: "If a woman gives birth to a female child … the Bambara will tell you that the infant is not a boy." The Wassulunke was garrulous: "The word was conceived in the Mande, born in Bambara, and baptized in the Wassulu." The Khassonke was lax; he was prone to false consciousness; he believed the Christian missionaries' doctrine of the Holy Trinity. The Maninka respected power; "only people without power believe it unimportant". Even the landscape spoke the language of the south: Wherever the so (karite) tree grows (in the south) people say "N'Ko" for "I say."[50] While popular discourses of this sort could be heard throughout the Mande-hinterland, both north and south, pejorative connotations just below the surface in popular exchanges emphasized the underlying sense of ideological and behavioral difference.

But if northern identities were the same yet different, it was the south's archaic occult that ultimately compromised its image in pious Muslim eyes. In privileging the *numuw* and the *jo* cult above the marabout and the Book, southerners forged a recognizably different identity in gold and iron ores that the north, lacking the abundance and high quality of gold and iron ores, could not emulate. Southerners *were* different. It was moreover not unusual for whole southern lineages to espouse a *numu* identity

---

49. *Ta'rikh al-Fattash*, p. 65, and note 2; see also p. 40, note 2.
50. Diabaté, "Essai critique," pp. 9–13; Niane, "Mise en place," pp. 40–53.

and a *komo* adherence (e.g., some Camara and Keita lineages in the Bure) because, if *komo* rituals required ecological obligations, they also guaranteed safe mining procedures and producer well-being. As a matter of interest, the Bamako *kafu* had about 50 *numuw*, one for approximately every eighty to a hundred residents. As a much larger "animist stronghold," not surprisingly, the Beledugu had a great many more.[51]

With respect to the *jo* rituals, we still know little, still relying for the most part on the work of earlier scholars such as Louis Tauxier, Henri Labouret, Germaine Dieterlen, Charles Monteil, Moussa Travele, Youssouf Cisse, and more recently, Patrick McNaughton.[52] Divided into six male only associations, they were: the *ntomo* (*ndoma*) or association for uncircumcised youths (*bilakori*) where entry marked the beginning of the long initiation process; the *komo* (for circumcised males only) honoring the ancestors; the *nama* protecting magicians and sorcerers; the *kono* governing human relationships; the *tyawara*, the sign of the youthful male *ton* (association) functioning as agricultural labor units; and the *kore*, the ultimate association marking deep self-knowledge, enlightenment, and spirituality capable of manipulating energies within the universe.[53] Chief

---

51. *ASAOF* 1G 32, "Lettre à Gouverneur" (Saint Louis, 21 June, 1860); *ANMK* ID 33 2, Collomb, "Notice" (Bamako, 1884–1885), p. 12; *ASAOF* 1G 79, Conrard, "Notice" (Bamako, 21 Feb. 1885), pp. 18–20; *ASAOF* 1G 52 46, Bayol, "Mission de Ségou" (Saint Louis, 5 July 1880), p. 11.

52. For Bamana ritual see Tauxier, *La Religion*; Germaine Dieterlen, *Essai sur la religion bambara* (Paris, 1951); *Idem.*, "The Mande creation myth," pp. 124–138; *Idem.*, "Mythe et organisation sociale en Afrique occidentale (suite)," *JSA*, vol. 29, no. 1 (1959): 119–138; *Idem.*, "Contribution à l'étude des forgerons en Afrique occidentale," *Annuaire de l'Ecole Practiques des Hautes Etudes*, vol. 73 (1965–1966): 1–28; Dieterlen and Cissé, *Les Fondements*; Monteil, *Les Bambara*, p. 404; Moussa Travélé, "Le *Komo* ou *Koma*," *Outre-mer*, vol. 1, no. 2 (1929): 127–150; Béatrice Appia, "Les Forgerons du Fouta-Djallon," *JSA*, vol. 35, no. 2 (1965): 317–352; Labouret, "Les Manding et leur langue," pp. 7–147, see esp. pp. 81–95, 113–134; Maurice Delafosse, "Terminologie religieuse au Soudan," *L'Anthropologie* (Paris), vol. 33 (Dec. 1923): 371–83; Dominique Zahan, *Sociétés d'initiation bambara, le N'domo, le Kore,* (Paris-La Haye, Mouton, 1960), pp. 12–13, 20–22, 438; *Idem, Religion, spiritualité, et pensée africaines* (Paris, 1970), esp. chaps. 8, 9; McNaughton, *The Mande*, pp. 13, 15–19, 41, 48, 59, 68, 71, 103, 112, 119, 149; Cissé and Kamissoko, *La Grande geste*, pp. 135, note 6, 239. For Gallieni's and Valliere's mangled accounts of the *nama* rituals in Nango (Beledugu) and at Siby, home to the Camara, as well as elsewhere, see Gallieni, *Voyage*, pp. 324–327, 328–329, 428–440.

53. Denise Paulme, "Bambara," *Dictionnaire des civilisations africaines,* ed. Georges Balandier and Jacques Maquet (Paris, 1968), pp. 58–60, see also pp. 21–22. Tauxier's list of *jo* associations varies somewhat (Tauxier, *La Religion*, pp. 272–355).

custodian of the south's universal structure of occult meaning, expressing a continuity between the physical and human world and the *nyama*
(*nyana, gnena*), or pervasive spirit or energies of action, the *jo* enforced
scrupulous observance, invoking dread and awe. Observed within collectivities revering obligations, reciprocities, and social solidarity, few
defied the *komo*'s categorical imperatives, least of all women (especially
unfaithful wives), minors, and slaves. Manifested only after dark
through complex rituals under the leadership of a *komo-tigi* (ritual head,
usually a dreaded *numu*) and particularized through Islam in some jurisdictions, *komo* observances included music, dance, masks, sacrifices, sacred objects, and "sorcery."[54]

Also a teaching institution commanding control over moral meaning,
the *komo* further shaped identities through value transference of societal
and juridical rights-and-duties, reciprocities and obligations. Knowledge
of the autonomy of words-signs emanating from the *jo* as energy-in-action
was accordingly revealed,[55] not as a rule divulged beyond the sacred circle of initiates, and never to women and minors, although women had
corresponding associations. Originally regulated according to the solar
year—but sometimes made to coincide with Islamized fetes in circum-

According to some oral accounts from the Mande, the seven associations originated in Mecca and were introduced to the Bamana, the Maninka (Mandinka), and
the Minianka (Cissé, *Histoire et tradition*, p. 12). According to Dieterlen and Cissé,
jo by extension had multiple meanings including *ton* or association for initiating
young males, a cult, and a cult secret, hence *jo-jo* the "truth," "that which is vigor-
ously exact," and "to purify," etc. (Dieterlen and Cissé, *Les Fondements*, p. 17, note
1). Other sources suggest that the *jo* was a meteorite employed as an altar (Cissé
and Kamissoko, *La Grande geste*, p. 181, note 47, 215, note 24). See also *ASAOF* 1G
299, Brévié, "Monographie" (Bamako, 25 April 1904), p. 98. Elsewhere *jo* was
translated as "fetish" (Camara, "Le Manden," pp. 48, 56).

54. *Nyama* may also be translated as "wind," "breathing," or "soul" of an otherwise inert object (Tauxier, *La Religion*, pp. 8–9; Delafosse, "Terminologie religieuse," pp. 376–377). *Komo* rituals were also observed among the Minianka and
the Senufo of San, Kutiala, and Sikasso. See also Dieterlen and Cissé, *Les Fondements*, pp. 9–10, 15–17.

55. McNaughton, *The Mande*, p. 42. According to Dieterlen and Cisse, the *jo-
baw* had a total of 266 secret primordial signs (*ti -baw*: great signs), representing the
glaw (*gla-zo*), or the Bamana graphic system. We are not told how they arrived at
this estimate. The primordial signs also corresponded to other symbolic knowledge, for example, the "great master" (*ma ba*), "that which astonishes" (*koni*), the
"master of all things" (*bema*), etc. (Dieterlen and Cissé, *Les Fondements*, pp. 10–17,
18, 21, 263–295; Dieterlen, *Essai sur la religion*, pp. 142–165; Cissé, *Histoire et tradition*, pp. 5, 17).

scriptions where the prayer was heard—*komo* ceremonies were usually observed in sacred locations: a consecrated ground, or sacred grove (*je-tu; dje-tu*), most southern jurisdictions possessing a *komo* site. In Bamako, chicken corpses and crocodile teeth hung deep within the *kafu* 's sacred grove, not only to assure good harvests, but also to discourage disobedient and unfaithful wives.[56]

Some legends have it that the Dumbya *numu* lineage was the first to receive the secret "sign of the anvil" revealed by *nyama* (energy) at Jakajalan, believed to be one of the old Malian capitals. Said to trace their identity to Dinga (Bida's father) and the Wagadu *numuw*, some say it was the Dumbya who led the Mande peoples out of the Sahel after the Wagadu dispersal. In a more ambiguous version, manipulating and recontextualizing the myth within an Islamized episteme, Dumbya is said to have returned from the *hajj* with *boliw*, or sacred *komo* altars, masks, and "1,440 fetishes," and that at Sama, en route to the Mande, he carved the first *komo* mask.[57] An equally ambiguous Islamized account from Segu, associates the *komo* with Mansa Juru Kali Nani, a man "from the east."

The Place of Gold in the Southern Identity

Whether or not the Dumbya were *komo* originators, important from the north's perspective was the place of gold ores—"royal" and "divine"—in the south's mythical-political identity. Extracted from the Bure and Bambuhu mines exclusively by empowered *numuw* (this exclusivity had ceased by the latter part of the nineteenth century), the ores were bestowed at Wagadu, thereafter in the Mande by Bida, according to particularized oral accounts. Slain at his pithead by the wayward Nyakate youth in Niare manipulated legends, Bida's decapitated form plunging south, we recall, came to rest in the Mande's Bambuhu and Bure gold fields (see Chapter 1). That is why people still say that the south's gold outcroppings, no common variety, are Bida's scales falling from his sacred hide.[58]

---

56. *ASAOF* 1G 299, "Définitions administratives, Cercle de Bamako, 1903–1904."

57. The Dumbya are also known as Fakoli, Koromaka, and Sissoko (Conrad, "Searching," pp. 152–155). Later, in the company of the Maraka and Kagoro, Dumbya allegedly composed the most important songs for the *komo* initiation (Cissé, *Histoire et tradition*, p. 5; for another version see p. 12). See also Person, *Samori*, vol. 1, p. 80, note 44.

58. Interview Guimbu Djakité from the Mande (Bamako, 3 January, 1983); interview Diarra Sylla (Bamako, 15 March 1983); interview Massa Makan Diabaté (Bamako, 21 March 1983). See also P. Siossat, "Les coutumes des orpailleurs indigènes du Maramandougou," *BCEHSAOF*, vol. 20 (1937): 336–349.

Thus the *jo* (sacred anvil or alter) was covered with gold, most often Bure gold, the "prettiest of the lot," representing "purity of spirit," and kept in *jo-sanuw* (sacred jars) or a *so diyah* (place of the cult).[59] More importantly, gold in the *jo* guaranteed a wholesome equilibrium between human and supernatural powers. Thus as a "sacred divine knowledge," and "perfect purity," gold entered the inventory of the *komo* rituals. Not surprisingly in many jurisdictions, including the Bamako *kafu*, gold rarely entered domestic markets much before the eighteenth century.[60]

Following ritual exigencies, only persons identified with a legitimate mythical-ritual and political power-authority, such as a *komo-tigi* , usually a *numu* or *mansa* (ruler), could preside at *komo* ceremonies. Sacrifices to *kongoba*, "mother of the bush," and the killing of a white ram, were de rigeur. None, moreover, could with impunity manipulate gold's powers until "killed" (neutralized) by the *sanun-fagala* (he who kills gold), usually a redoubtable *numu*. A hapless fool stumbling unexpectedly on gold ores along a riverbank, on exposed roots of a great tree felled by powerful storms, or simply under large rocks in deep bush, hastened to rebury the dreadful find, on pain of death.[61] And only the "master of the mine" could remove an interdiction, only after ritual sacrifices over which regional marabouts sometimes presided. The south's *soma*, or priestly Camara family, was most identified with the ultimate in gold mining and *komo* rituals. In fact it was even said of the south that Camara *numuw* were closer to a state of ritual purity than their northern counterparts, the latter sullied by Islamized "compromises."[62]

Thus, when appropriately accessed by authorized intermediaries, *komo* gold could unleash untold secret terrors against offenders, even death. And if gold rarely entered the region's domestic markets, none dared steal

---

59. To most observers Bure gold meant "the purity of spirit," "the arc of the sky"; it was "prettier" than Bambuhu gold. See for example, Cissé and Kamissoko, *La Grande geste*, p. 241; interview Thiémoko Kanté (Bamako, 4 Jan. 1983); *ASAOF* 1G 50, Gallieni and Vallière, "Notes sur la situation politique des peuplades des vallées du Bafing, du Bakoy et du Haut-Niger" (Bamako, 9 May 1880), p. 30; Cissé, *Histoire et tradition*, p. 13.

60. Interview Thiémoko Kanté (Bamako, 4 Jan. 1985). Gold in international markets was of course a much older phenomenon.

61. This, and the following section draw on Perinbam, "The Salt-gold alchemy," pp. 1–21; *ASAOF* 1G 32, "Lettre Mage à Gouverneur" (Saint Louis, 21 June 1866).

62. Interview with miner Famale Cissoko (Bamako, 20 April 1983); Niane, *Sundiata*, p. 78; interview Massa Makan Diabaté (Bamako, 21 March 1983).

komo gold for fear of certain death before dawn (in order to ensure death some mining operations were surrounded by armed slaves); and no *komo-den* (initiate) pronounced gold's name (*sanu, sani, sanuya*), "the purity of spirit," after sundown for fear of an unbearable fate.[63] It was therefore with sorrow and anger that the bard Wa Kamissoko of Krina in the Mande recounted the oft-repeated stories of Mansa Musa's "misappropriation" of Mali's *komo* gold, squandering it with impunity while on pilgrimage to Mecca in around 1325.[64] Offering a different perspective, Tauxier suggested that the *komo* spirit provided "interest-free loans" bound with dire consequences, should debtors default.[65]

But if gold was central to the south's mythical-political and ritual identity, it also symbolized a cosmology of origins and the moral order even beyond sacred *komo* circles. Humans were once custodians of both good and evil, an ancient legend goes. A wayward hunter—abrogating a sacred oath with gold's spirit—brought disaster into a universe now besieged by evil, gold, a "bad dream," the demon perpetrator. Order eventually reconfigured the universe, the legend continues, but only after gold had appropriated the power over good and evil.[66] Becoming the magical catalyst with terrible powers, gold's presence therefore represented the good, its mere absence predicating evil.

When gendered, gold became a female principle guaranteeing fecundity: Given to brides, it safeguarded reproductive continuity. Juxtaposed in Mande cosmological inventories with salt, the latter gendered as a male principle, it was said that male semen was "marinated" in this magical alchemy and that a salt-gold equilibrium maintained harmonious gender relations. Thus if women were the "gold" of the earth, men were its "salt"; which is why women expect metal workers to heat gold ores in salt solu-

---

63. Interview with miner Famale Cissoko (Bamako, 20 April 1983).

64. Elsewhere Kamissoko calls Mansa Musa's identity into question, claiming that three Mali chiefs of that name have survived in the traditions (Ibn Khaldun names only two). According to Ibn Khaldun, it was one of the Mansa's successors, who died in 1373–1374, who squandered the nation's patrimony (Cissé, *Histoire et tradition*, pp. 8, 12–13, 15, 17, 20, 21; Cissé and Kamissoko, *La Grande geste*, pp. 25, 30, 181, and note 47, 199, note 12, 215, note 24, 237–243; interview Sidy Diabaté with Wa Kamissoko c. 1973–1974, in Diabaté, "Kankan Moussa," pp. 52–53). See also Dieterlen and Cissé, *Les Fondements*, p. 39; Ibn Khaldun, *Histoire des Berbères et des dynasties musulmanes de l'Afrique du septentrionale*, trans. de Slane, 4 vols. (Paris, 1969), vol. 2, pp. 114–116.

65. Tauxier, *La Religion*, p. 280.

66. Legend attributed to Wa Kamissoko of Kirina, recounted by Thiémoko Kanté (Bamako, 4 Jan. 1983).

tions prior to transformation. And if one never stole *komo* gold, and rarely sold it on domestic markets, the moral imperative was to avoid wasting salt, or risk unhinging the universe.[67]

Finally, as part of the south's mythical-political and ritual identity, gold's presence was de rigeur at fetes, oathings, and sacrifices, whether of a political, agricultural, or familial nature, including births, baptisms, initiation rituals, marriages, and funerals. Chiefly powers and political stability depended on its sacred alchemy. Gold was even cast into the Niger, when appropriate, in order to ensure the good will of Ba Faro, a powerful water spirit (*mire*) making his home downriver from Bamako. By that same token, gold was always present at *komo* rites, and invoked before launching important collective endeavors: hunting expeditions, or a war. As to burials, no male left this world (in theory, at any rate) without obsequies marked by gold.[68]

Given this discourse of the south's gold identity and its ritualized relation to the archaic occult, were architects of the northern paradigm correct in assuming southern congeners as the "animist" Other? Mali's fourteenth and fifteenth-century state decline suggested the south's "return to animism," "evidence" circulating in multiple forms.[69] Among these were stories affecting Mansa Musa's (fl. 1312–1337) "Islamic" image and his alleged pilgrimages to the Holy City. On returning from the first *hajj*

---

67. Interview Massa Makan Diabaté (Bamako, 21 March 1983). According to Raffenel, a vigorous man was said to be "a salt eater" (Raffenel, *Nouveau voyage*, vol. 1, p. 453). Elsewhere in the old Mande, the perspective varied depending on the region: In some, gold was a masculine principle, while silver was the female counterpart (Camara, "Le Manden," p. 56).

68. Agricultural fetes at Bamako (sometimes calling for gold to be cast into the Niger) usually involved encounters between a virgin and the Niger crocodiles, the blacksmith's *tana*. See also Cissé and Kamissoko, *La Grande geste*, pp. 79, note 43, 99, note 12, 241, and note 16, 177, 179, 181, 199–201, 203, 205, note 17, 211, 249, 291; Niane, *Sundiata*, pp. 67, 73–78, 94, note 66; Delafosse, *Haut-Sénégal-Niger*, vol. 1, pp. 292, 321; vol. 2, pp. 168–170, 179. For Ba Faro the river spirit, see Dieterlen, *Essai sur la religion*, pp. 40–55. For the place of gold in family rites, see Tauxier, *La Religion*, pp. 289–302, 355–470.

69. According to some, only two Mansaw made the *hajj* after Mansa Musa's pilgrimage (1325). See also *ANSOM Sén. et Dép.*, IV Doss. 90 Bis, Vallière, "Rapport sur l'organisation politique donnée aux états de Mambi" (Kangaba, 5 March 1888), n.p.; *ASAOF* 1G 32, "Lettre Mage à Gouverneur" (Saint Louis, 21 July 1866); Niane, *Recherches sur l'empire*, pp. 40–47; for the Arab authors' observations of "animist" practices in ancient Mali, see al-Bakri, and al-'Umari in Levtzion and Hopkins, *Corpus*. For an account of Mali's decline, see Ibn Khaldun, *Histoire*, vol. 2, pp. 115–116.

(date unknown) for which the Mansa received gold from his mother, according to this story, southern *komo* (Kulibaly) officials, jealous of their "animist" identity, obliged the Mansa to imbibe, *publicly*, four alcoholic beverages, a "proof," some say, that *his* conversion was but a fickle one. His more serious offense, the second pilgrimage celebrated according to al-Umari (c. 1325), and which Sudanese Islamized traditions have also glorified—left local *numuw* so enraged, oral reports continue, that they stalked from the region in a huff, threatening to toss the Mansa down a well (*mini-minin-kolon*): They were not there to mine gold for "turban wearers."[70] Not just the *numuw*, but other citizens equally enraged, accused the Mansa of wasting gold on unproductive marabouts and of impoverishing the land.[71]

A third manipulated version of the *hajj* stories, more ambiguous or more assuring depending on the perspective, claims that the Mansa (and not the Dumbya) returned from the *hajj* with 1,440 fetishes. A fourth version less ambiguously declares that, outraged with the Mansa for having undertaken the *hajj* in the first place, *numuw* placed both the pilgrimage and the 1,440 fetishes "in taboo" (beyond discussion), which may explain why some "animist" texts are altogether mute on the Mansa's *hajj*; and why the slurs on "turban wearers" and "unproductive" Muslims—who "pass their time praying" only to "beg millet from a neighbor"—circulated in "animist" circles; or why some southern traditions still evoke the Mansa's "great hunter" (i.e., "animist") image at the expense of the "pious" Islamized one.[72] And whether or not the south *was* the "animist" Other, understandable was the *numuw* outrage with their sovereign lord for visiting the Holy City in the first place, given their role and sacred articulation with gold ores in *komo* rituals and the Mande's archaic occult.

---

70. Madina Ly Tall does not think that the Mansa made two pilgrimages. Cissé, *Histoire et tradition*, pp. 8–9, 12–13, 19–21. Ibn Khaldun mentions only one (Ibn Khaldun, *Histoire*, vol. 2, p. 112). Other southern traditions speak of two of Sunjata's sons (Mansa Ule and Sakuro) who went on pilgrimage (Diabaté, "Kankou Moussa," pp. 21–24). See also Ibn Khaldun, *Histoire*, vol. 2, p. 111. See also note 69 herein.

71. Cissé, *Histoire et tradition*, pp. 8, 15, 17, 21; interview Sidy Diabaté with Wa Kamissoko c. 1973–1974, in Diabaté, "Kankou Moussa," pp. 52–53.

72. Diara, "Du Banimonotie," p. 26. Interview Massa Makan Diabaté (Bamako, 21 March 1983); Diabaté, "Kankou Moussa," pp. 6, 21–24, 26–28, 39–43. See also *ANMAE, 1780–1822*, vol. 11, "Projet d'un nouvel établissement en Afrique, 1816," pp. 345–346.

More importantly from our perspective, however, was that if northerners were parsing Islamic beliefs with "animist" rituals, southerners—despite numu militancy—were particularizing *their* "animist" doctrines, cults, and rituals with Islam. Acknowledging that Mande belief systems were ethnographic particularisms possessing open epistemological boundaries and that they had been interacting with Islam across the centuries—both parsings within the same ethnographical and epistemological contexts—revisions and recontextualization seemed unavoidable. For example, it is said in some southern communities, that the "animist" Malinke originated variously in Saudi Arabia, in Egypt, in Yemen, and in North Africa, depending on the interlocutor; that the Keita descended from Bilali, the Prophet's faithful servant; that Islam was "just another formula for expressing animism"; that similarities between Islam and "animism" far outweighed the differences; and that on returning from Mecca, the eldest of three Simbon brothers (the "animist" hunter's penultimate icon) brought to the Mande the gift of Bida's gold.[73] Of particular interest: In the "animist" Beledugu, the Mande, and Wassulu some *komo* propagators were known by the Islamic title of *moriba*, or *marabout*.

Opening a window for Europeans on the ambiguities, contextualizations, and particularisms within the southern identity was Mungo Park (1796), who visited the Koranic school at Kamalia in the Mande (the south). Here, on the one hand, under the guidance of Instructor Fankuma, "pagan" children and "sons of Kaffirs," whose parents schooled them for "improvement," were reading the Koran and reciting prayers. On the other hand, as "watch dogs" of the cult, the Mande's *numuw* were in a flurry: Defending the south's mythical-ritual-political integrity and identity was the sole way to balance the sociopolitical axis.[74] From a doctrinal and cosmological perspective, theirs was no idle consideration. Not only was an entire belief system at stake—and not just human gender relationships—but also at risk were the ancestral and sacerdotal spirits, the moral universe, the fate of entire lineages, and all future access to the mines.

A century later a similarly threatening disaster prevailed farther west: At Manfara, a sacred Islamized city in the western Mande (Bafulabe Circle) (see Maps 2 and 3), Chief Nyonko Sisse was conspicuously offering public prayers persuaded, some said, by "predatory" marabouts. So

73. Camara, "Le Manden," p. 16; Diabaté, "Essai critique," pp. 7–8; Niane, *Recherches sur l'empire*, pp. 13, 19, for accounts of the south's ritual "mixing," see pp. 42–27; interview Ali Ongoïba (Kuluba-Bamako, 7 Feb. 1983).

74. Park, *The Travels* pp. 240–243. There were other Islamized populations in the south.

deafening was the "fetishist" outcry, that the humiliated Nyonko was obliged to ban all the region's marabouts.[75] Thus, for Park's militant *numuw*—as for all "fetishists" throughout the Mande-hinterland and Mande world—a moral universe compromised by the competing beliefs of "turban wearers" claiming autonomous status could foment conflict in the human condition, heralding disasters of cosmic proportions. But *numu* militancy, notwithstanding, "compromises" with Islam persisted. Elsewhere in the Bafulabe Circle, for example, "animist" families fostered marriages with Islamic practitioners; while in the Kita Circle, Islamic Maninka and Jallonke who "imbibed the *dolo* one day, said the Prayer the next" were tolerated despite partisan posturing. Similar Islamized arrangements even occurred farther south, even in the Mande's gold-bearing regions.[76]

Thus, by the eighteenth and nineteenth centuries, at least, the south's Islam and Mande belief systems had been so ethnographically parsed that regional ambiguities and manipulations were commonplace. So were the seemingly contradictory manifestations combined into a single complex of mutually defining and sustaining elements. Accordingly, "mixed" knowledge was constantly being generated, culturally derived, together with dynamic systems upon which the proper ordering of society and social action depended. Moreover, whether revealed by God or derived from "pagan" norms, southern beliefs forged states and sociopolitical rituals similar to—and different from—those that had developed in the north. The rate at which *komo* elites lost ideological ground to the Islamized Umarian-Samorian proselytizing elites during the latter part of the nineteenth century suggests that southerners, used to open epistemological boundaries, moved across them with greater ease than did many northerners, who were bound by the holy writ: We recall that the Niare family, our case study, negotiated religious identities across the centuries from the python cult at Wagadu, to the *komo* and *nama* cult-rituals of Segu and Bamako. Today, Niare elites are for the most part Muslim.

---

75. The French took from this the lesson that "fetishists" could be counted on to betray "conspiratorial" marabouts to the proper authorities, especially if a marabout's *gris-gris* had lost its potency (*ANMK* 4E 35, "Politique musulmane" [Bafulabe, 1897–1914]). The mosque at Manfara was allegedly built by the Saganogo (Sanogo) (Cissé, *Histoire et tradition*, pp. 8–10, 12).

76. *ASAOF* 1G 248, Pérignon, "Monographie" (Bamako, 1899–1900).

Poverty and the South's Slave Identity

If the south's engraved occult and richly embossed *jo* image differentiated it from the north, the Islamized paradigm, eventually self-serving,
persisted, even among Islamized southerners. Profiting most were commercial elites—mainly Soninke, Sarakolle and desert-side merchants—for
whom the "kaffir" gold and Bambara slaves were important. And if Islam
justified a livelihood, ironically it also protected the south's "animism":
Northerners and Islamized southerners could well have been holding
their breath, fearing "conversions" and the subsequent disappearance of
the precious ores at the sound of the *muezzin*'s call to prayer.[77] They could
also have feared the loss of a legitimate reservoir, according to Islamic law,
of "animist" slaves.

Among principal slavers were the Islamized Soninke, Sarakolle, and
desert-side traders, including Bamako's Ture and Drave families. Likewise attracted by the Bambuhu-Bure gold, and the allegedly rich inhabitants, neighboring warriors and chiefs such as the "animist" Camara and
the Keita could hardly resist the tempting raids. With some frequency oral
texts report the "era of slave raiding" following the Malian state's decline,
when the unwary were spirited away, mainly Mandinka (Maninka, Malinke) captives, to Sahelian slave marts. Bought eventually by Islamized
Marka and desert-side traders, they were often exchanged for salt. The
"secret" route along which captives were supposedly spirited away eventually passed through the Manding Plateau and Bamako plain en route to
the Niger bend, the Beledugu, the Kaarta, and the Sahel. Villages built
near caves and mountain outcroppings provided the best security; and
when under siege in the Bambuhu region, for example, women and children, the likely victims, concealed themselves in mines. Those with no
such hiding places, dreading the slavers' irons, fought with the same fero-
city as men.[78]

Slave hunting in the south was still commonplace in the eighteenth
century, some 300 to 400 years after Mali's decline, according to Park
(1795–1796). Noting that "slaves ... are nearly in the proportion of three to
one to the free men," and that "a state of subordination and ... inequalities
of rank (are) ... carried to ... great length(s)" in Africa, Park drew attention to the large numbers of captives of the Segu-Kaarta war (1796), which

---

77. The reference here is to al-'Umari's observations (Levtzion and Hopkins,
Corpus, pp. 262, 269–271). See also Cissé and Kamissoko, *La Grande geste*, pp. 25,
30, 181 and note 47, 199, note 12, 215, note 24, 237–243.

78. *ASAOF* 1G 12, "Voyage dans le Bondou et le Bambouk par M. Tourette,
mineur 1828–1829."

coincided with his visit. These recent captives, he noted, were on sale not only in the Mande's southern markets—such as Kangaba, Kamalia and Kankaree—but also farther north in Bamako, and Nyamina.[79] Short of one hundred years later (1850s), the northern slave commerce was still lucrative, even before the Umarian and Samorian wars brought the unexpected bonanza: Louis Faidherbe (governor at Saint Louis) noted that a slave worth "practically nothing" in the upper Niger region was sold for 400–500 francs in Morocco. Some thirty years later (1880), one of Valliere's jula interlocutors, a "convert" to free market principles, assured him that but for the risk of unsafe routes, the slave trade would have been more profitable than the gold commerce. Pathetically carrying out the heinous practices commonplace in the northern paradigm, according to Valliere, was another slave caravan of "animist" children: The little ones were jumping about, gamboling, and swimming in the river, shrieking with childish delight while chasing insects, even fish, seemingly unaware of their great "misfortune."[80]

Four years later (1884) slavery was still "flourishing"—even in the "animist" Beledugu, according to Ruault—where social boundaries between "fetishists," "Muslims," "captives," "slaves," "domestic servants," and "wives" were confusedly blurred, and where slaves became friends and confidants to needy masters, as was the case in ancient Rome, Ruault editorialized. Reports in the "Affaires Indigènes" of a decade later (1890s) confirmed that nothing much had changed: Mamadu Camara sold five free orphans into slavery; Fade Jakite disposed of free refugees seeking asylum in his territory; Mamadu Sakho sold his brother's free wife for grain "in order to feed his family"; and Jan Jakite disposed of his nephew's captives without his knowledge; not to mention the numbers fleeing the slaver's irons, seeking refuge in the French liberty villages.[81]

Given that southern slave raiding persisted—an acknowledged virtue, according to the northern paradigm—a certain ambiguity nonetheless prevailed. For example, there were, on the one hand, those forswearing slave raiding, attributing its heinousness to rulers with

---

79. Park, *The Travels*, pp. 197, 220–228, 243–244 and passim. See also Cissé and Kamissoko, *La Grande geste*, pp. 193, 207; Camara, "Le Manden," pp. 53–54.

80. Louis Faidherbe, *Le Sénégal: La France dans l'Afrique occidentale* (Paris, 1889), p. 319; Faidherbe's gubernatorial administrations were: 1854–1856, 1856–1858, 1859–1861, 1863–1865; Gallieni, *Voyage*, pp. 320–321.

81. *ASAOF* 15G 83, Ruault, "Généralités 1880 à 1920" (Bamako, 22 Feb. 1884), p.7; *ASAOF* 15G 168, "De Kayes à Bamako (1853–1913): Région est (chef-lieu Bamako) 1894 à 1895 affaires indigènes," nos. 634, 837, 838, 839, 846, 847.

powerful "animist" identities, especially warrior-sorcerers such as Sumanguru Kante, who met his destiny at Krina (c. 1236).[82] Slaving practices ceased, the argument ingenuously avowed, with Sunjata's rise to power, historically associated with the first part of the thirteenth century. On the other hand were northern apologists, who shared the views of Al-Hajj Muhammad al-Mokhtar from the Tagant (Algerian) oasis: that "slaves are given by God to believers as a mark of His favor, so that they (slaves) may lead more pious lives." Besides, he continued, although disposable "when ceasing to please," perhaps even exchanged for a horse, "a good slave enjoy(ed) his master's trust, and (was) treated as a friend." In the south, an Islamized Fulbe chief was voicing similar sentiments: "It is the Law," he informed Winterbottom (1794), who was in the Futa Jallon: Slavery was the proper penalty against "kaffirs."[83] Ambiguities and manipulations notwithstanding, it is generally known that Islamized traders continued to slave in the south, justifying their actions on grounds that the south's identity was still "animist," and that it was better to lead "idolaters" into slavery as God's children than to leave them free in a state of nature.[84]

Commenting on the slave identity imposed on the south, and its internal abuse by those with opportunistic agendas, the bard Wa Kamissoko of Krina noted that: "If today (1976) the Mande is depopulated, we wonder who exterminated the inhabitants of this country! Well, it is the Malinke (Maninka) who have fallen over themselves to sell one

---

82. Gallieni, *Voyage*, pp. 27, 29, 193–195, 199–203, 205, 207, 209, 211, 225, 267; *ASAOF* 1G 50 20," Lettre Gallieni à Gouverneur" (Nango, 7 July 1880), pp. 34–35.

83. *ANMAE, 1890–1894*, vol. 123, "Etude géographique sur le Tagant" (Alger, 2 Feb. 1891), pp. 180–181; *ANSOM* B4, Walckenaer, *Histoire générale*, vol. 7, "Voyage de M. M. Watt et Winterbottom à Timbo et à Laby dans le pays foullahs en 1794," p. 261.

84. There is considerable evidence of raids (*jadow*) on the Bure (and Bambuhu) by regional people, a common means of acquiring gold and slaves. See *ANSOM* Sén. III Doss. 1, "Compte rendu du journal du voyage éxecuté par Monsieur Mollien dans l'intérieur de l'Afrique" (Paris, 8 July 1819), pp. 9–11; *ASAOF* 1G 8, "Rapport de M. Duranton, 1824" (Bakel, 2 April 1824), p. 17; *ASAOF* 1G 8 13, Duranton, "Examen de la situation présente...au Sénégal" (Feb. 1826), p.14; see also *ASAOF* 1G 32, "Mission Mage et Quintin 1863" (Medine, 1 Nov. 1863), p. 5; *ASAOF* 1G 50, Gallieni and Vallière, "Notes sur la situation politique" (Bamako, 9 May 1880), esp. pp. 15–31. For similar conditions in Bambuhu, see *ANMK* 3Q 3, "Mines" (1896), n.p.; *ANMK* 3Q 13, "Rapport sur l'industrie minière du Haut-Sénégal-Niger, 1910," pp. 3–4. For a discussion of the *jadow* or raids, see Jean Bazin, "Guerre et servitude à Ségou," in Claude Meillassoux, ed., *L'Esclavage en Afrique précoloniale* (Paris, 1975), pp. 146–147, 150.

another" into slavery, leading captives north along the "little route of betrayal" concealed behind southern villages and which passed through the Manding Plateau and Bamako plain en route to the Sahel. It was in the Mande, he continued, that the greedy and covetous "shoved the bit of slavery into the mouths" of their own people. Then manipulating the historical evidence—as the bardic genre permits— Wa Kamissoko poetically (but incorrectly) noted that "no war ... had (ever) been fought" in the Mande "since the world began," with the exception of the Samorian wars. Passing over the wars and raids bedeviling the old Mande since the thirteenth century, if not before—not to mention later wars including Segu's raids in the eighteenth and early nineteenth centuries, the Umarian wars of the nineteenth century, and the countless raids in between—the bard attributed population losses and "extermination" to self-inflicted social wounds. Not entirely the case, serious losses had also been occasioned by famines and other civil disturbances. When in the Mande as a member of the Gallieni Mission (1880), and noting the region's devastation, Valliere believed that the population had declined from about 20,000 to 4,000 souls since the 1860s. So disastrous was the situation, apparently, that even the steely Gallieni drew attention to the "sad villages of the Manding," the Bure particularly bereft due to declining populations.[85]

Mis/representations notwithstanding, the south's rich gold-slave, and "animist" identity persisted in the northern paradigm. The image not always matching the reality, southern populations were oftentimes poorer than most in the Mande-hinterland, agricultural yields sometimes so low that one failed harvest, it is said, could lead to three or four months of famine. Explanations were apparently quite rational: Bambuhu, and particularly Bure inhabitants, produced little food, sometimes even less gold, for fear of endemic slave raids from covetous neighbors and voracious enemies. The reverse dilemma was such that producing so little gold and grain, long-distance Islamized traders feared entering the region, finding costs considerably outweighing benefits. In fact, food production was so low during the Umarian and Samorian wars that Bure inhabitants were even purchasing grain at high prices from desert-side Moors, themselves food purchasers buying grain from northern Soninko and Sarakolle traders. The situation in neighboring Bambuhu seemed correspondingly precarious where, even as late as 1896, inhabitants were exchanging large

---

85. Cissé and Kamissoko, *La Grande geste*, pp. 195, 203–205, 207, 225; *ASAOF* 1G 50, Gallieni and Vallière, "Notes sur la situation politique" (Bamako, 9 May 1880), pp. 14–32; Gallieni, *Voyage*, pp. 297, 305, 336, 338.

quantities of gold for meager food supplies.[86] And as to fending off the covetous, the mean, and the rapacious, most seemed resigned to a fearful destiny. Unaware of contextual ramifications affecting the south's gold/slave and rich/poor identities—and expecting to see more developed political economies—the author of an official French report (1909) was at a loss to explain why, after centuries of participating in the northern gold trade, the south was "still so poor."[87]

But the south's historical poverty, as opposed to its rich gold-slave-"animist" identity in the northern paradigm, could not be attributed exclusively to frequent raids and low productivity, neither to poor soils and relatively small populations in comparison with the north. Nor could historical poverty be causally related to the south's "animist" identity, its belief systems, or its cosmology. Above all, it could not be said that the south lacked corporate organizations designed to advance collective interests, nor that its political economies were insufficiently ritualized. In fact, to the contrary: so exigent were southerners in aligning themselves with the ritual occult that the outcome should have been very different. But events proved otherwise.

The Anthropology of the Niger River and the Southern Identity

An irony in all this is that stabilizing the pattern of the south's historical poverty—somewhat overlooked in the northern paradigm—was none other than the Niger, this life-giving force: Aggravating the ideological

---

86. For eighteenth-century references, see Labat, *Nouvelle relation*, vol. 4, pp. 45, 60. In the latter part of the nineteenth century grain prices at Bamako were 10 to 20 centimes per kilo, while at Bure the same grain was being sold for 1 franc per kilo *ANSOM* Sén. III Doss. 1, Mollien, "Journal du voyage" (Paris, 8 July 1819), pp. 6–7; *ANSOM* Sén. et Dép. IV Doss. 90 Bis, Vallière, "Rapport...Mambi" (Kangaba, 5 March 1888), p. 6; *ANSOM* Sén. et Dép. IV Doss. 90 Bis, Vallière, "Mémoire" (Siguiri, 15–25 March 1888), p. 43. For food shortages in Bambuhu, see *ANMK* 3Q 3, "Mines" (1896); *ANMK* 3Q 12, "Rapport" (1909), p. 2; *ANMK* 3Q 13, "Rapport" (1910), pp. 3–4; *ANSOM* Soudan V Doss. 2 d, Marillier, "Expeditions militaires 1890–1893: Reconnaissance en Bambouk" (March 1894).

87. *ASAOF* 1G 12, "Voyage dans le...Bambouk par M. Tourette" (1828 à 1829); *ANMAE, 1780–1822*, vol. 11, Mém. no. 4, "Moyens par lesquels le Gouverneur de la Concession du Sénégal pourra exécuter avec plus de facilité les vues du Ministère pour cette Concession," pp. 35–45; *ANMAE, 1780–1822*, vol. 11, Mém. no. 32, "Sur le Sénégal, Galam et Bambouc," p. 148; *ANMAE, 1780–1822*, vol. 11, "Projet d'un nouvel établissement en Afrique 1816," pp. 344–345; *ANMK* 3Q 3, "Mines" (1896), n.p.; *ANMK* 3Q 12, "Rapport" (1909), p. 3; *ANMK* 3Q 13, "Rapport" (1910), pp. 3–4.

north-south divide was the river's physical rupture markedly differentiating the north-south images and identities. Snaking like Bida across the western Sudan for some 4,000 diagonal kilometers (2,500 kilometers navigable depending on flooding) the Niger, or Joliba as the Mandekan called it, flowed from about the ninth parallel north of Timbi Kunda in the Futa Jallon—to the floodplains of the Inland Niger Delta and beyond.[88] Flooding its upper and middle course for about 100 kilometers with an interannual flood deviation of between 100 and 10,000 cubic meters during the wet-season from April to November, Niger waters usually peaked between July and September. Like the Nile, interannual flooding contributed to the earliest material culture-agglomerations of the Inland Niger Delta and Jenne-Timbuktu regions, long before the trans-Saharan trade developed toward the ninth and tenth centuries.[89] Also like the Nile, state foundations in the upper and middle Niger regions began with the river, a material as well as a ritual-cultural resource. In acknowledgment of its sacerdotal presence, when Sunjata "divided the world" at Kurugan Fugan, according to the epic, the sacred pebbles (*konkon-berew*) with which Mali's thirty-three clans were identified (and numbered) were secured by *numuw* from the Niger's bed where the spirit Ba Faro resided. During agricultural fetes, Bamako residents regularly consigned gold ores to the Niger's watery wastes. In the early nineteenth century, Gordon Laing found inhabitants in awe of the mighty river and its wondrous power.[90]

---

88. The Delta is believed to be the remnant of an inland lake in which the upper Niger once terminated. In prehistoric times, the Delta region is said to have overflowed during the wet season to join the Tilemsi River which once drained from the now arid Adrar des Iforas to the middle Niger course north of Bourem (*Africa south of the Sahara*, 20th ed. [London, 1991], p. 668). See also *ANMK* 1D 5, "Notice sur la région sud, 1895–1899."

89. For a discussion of the early Inland Niger Delta agglomerations see Roderick J. McIntosh, *The Pulse theory: Genesis and accommodation of specialization in the Inland Niger Delta of Mali*, working paper no. 4 (Houston, TX: Center for the Study of Institutions and Values, School of Social Sciences, Rice University, March 1988), p. 1. See also Roderick J. McIntosh, "The Inland Niger Delta before the empire of Mali: Evidence from Jenne-jeno." *JAH*, vol. 22 (1981): 1–22; McIntosh and McIntosh, *Prehistoric investigations*; S. K. McIntosh, "Archaeological reconnaissance," *National Geographic* (1986), pp. 302–319; S. K. McIntosh, ed., *Excavations at Jenne-jeno*. See also Jean Gallais, *Le Delta intérieur du Niger: Etude de géographie régionale*, Mém. IFAN, no. 79, 2 vols. (Dakar: IFAN, 1967). For the upper Niger, see *ANMK* 1D 5, "Notice sur la région sud, 1895–1899," pp. 1–16.

90. Niane, *Sundiata*, pp. 73–78; *ANSOM* B4, C. A. Walckenaer, *Histoire générale*, vol. 7, Gordon Laing, "Travels in Timanae, Kooranko, and Soolima countries in western Africa (London, 1825)," p. 305.

Fractured, however, in its upper course about 10 kilometers down-river from Bamako—for approximately 60–70 kilometers along the line forming the Sotuba and Maniabugu (Manambugu) Rapids—the *fada* (rapids) created a physical north-south divide. Not of serious concern to most shipping during the wet season—when several craft could scale the rapids with minimum risk—dry season shipping proceeded only with caution. Mungo Park (1796), Staff Surgeon Dochard (1819), and Rene Caillie (1827) had all noted this phenomenon.[91] North of the rapids, on the one hand, a wide navigable flow along a gentle down-river incline marked the approximately 1,000 kilometers from Kulikoro to middle Niger towns, the Inland Delta, and Timbuktu. Ideal year-round for commercial river traffic, even large, covered, salt-laden barges pulling 1.20 meters of water could navigate the river's middle course, especially during the interannual flooding from July to December, when Jenne was surrounded by water. South of the rapids in the river's upper course, on the other hand, it was a different story for the 374 kilometers separating Bamako from Kurusa in Guinea. Here, a narrower, more rapid flow created year-round difficulties for all but the region's smallest craft, even during the wet season when the river's breadth sometimes extended to approximately 2 kilometers.[92]

This north-south differential in the river's course, depth, and interannual flooding produced long-term consequences for the region's political economies, ultimately confirming the south's rich/poor identity within the northern paradigm. Little used during the Soninke hegemony at Wagadu (Ghana), largely due to its remoteness from the state's

---

91. Park, *The Travels*, p. 181; Gray and Dochard, *Travels in western Africa*, p. 255; Caillié, *Voyage*, vol. 1, 329–330; Faidherbe, *Le Sénégal*, pp. 323–325, 347–349.

92. Exiting from the southern region at Nafaji, the Niger flows north to Siguiri and Bamako. The high water season in the upper Niger flow is longer than its counterpart on the Senegal River. Of the west-bank tributaries the most important are the Tinkisso (explored in 1899 by Lieutenant Hourst of the Marine), joining the Niger at Siguiri in Guinea, and the Sankarani (or Gouala) in the east, joining the Niger about 10 kilometers from Kangaba. The Sankarani—navigable only for a part of its course—flows through the Wassulu. Downriver, the Baoule and the Bani join the Niger at Jenne, and Mopti. The Bani is navigable for about 300 kilometers during high water (*ANMK* 1D 5, "Notice sur la région sud, 1895–1899," pp. 1–15); *ANMK* 1D 38 3, "Monographie" (Jenne, 1909), p. 31; *ASAOF* 1G 299, Brévié, "Monographie" (Bamako, 25 April 1904), pp. 56–57. For the Niger, see M. Tymowski, "Le Niger voie de communication des grands états du Soudan occidental jusqu'à la fin du XVIe siècle," *Africana Bulletin* (Warsaw University), vol. 6 (1967): 79–85.

main commercial arteries, the river was of greater importance to the
Malian hegemony (c. 1250-c. 1355). Here, in the interest of state development, elaboration, and maintenance, ruling elites combined land and
water routes from Timbuktu to the south: Once on board at middle
Niger ports, Somono craft plied upriver to Jenne's floodplains (the Bani
a navigable tributary, was known in Mande cosmology as the "male"
river, the Niger the "female"). From there, watercraft proceeded farther
upriver to the Nyamina-Kulikoro-Manambugu regions, the upper
Niger's main ports[93] (see Maps 2 and 3). At the Kulikoro-Massala lay-
overs, where approximately the rapids began, river transport became
dangerous for some 60–70 kilometers, especially for large flat-bottomed
barges, even during the interannual high-water flooding. Malian administrators avoided what was really an engineering challenge—which
would have altered their ritual relationship to the river—by developing
north-south land routes approximately between Kulikoro, Bamako, and
the Mande towns, even though commodities such as grain traveled best
by water. Once in the Mande regions of Siby, Samanyana, Samalen, and
Niani—Bamako's Mande neighbors to the south—merchants returned
to the river-route, transshipping goods on smaller covered *pirogues*, or
the region's year-round light craft, heading as far south as Kankan on
the Milo and Siguiri (see Map 3).[94] Eventually much of the salt and grain
were destined for markets of the Bure mining regions where they were
exchanged for gold.[95]

---

93. The Bani was designated male because its interannual flood waters "pene-
trated" the Niger between July and December (*ASAOF* 1G 305, "Monographie du
Cercle de Djenné" [Jenne, 10 March 1904]).

94. The upper Niger's main east bank tributary is the Milo with its fertile, well-
populated valley, joining the Niger at Jelibacoro (Dialibacoro). Sections of the Milo
are navigable all year round. Standing a few kilometers to the northwest of the
Milo is Kankan. A *pirogue* can carry 200–300 bars of salt. These boats were about
8–10 meters long, "sewn" together (in the style reported by Caillié) by local *numuw* (*ASAOF* 1G 79, Conrard, "Notice" [Bamako, 21 Feb. 1885], p. 22). Interview
Massa Makan Diabaté (Bamako, 21 March 1983); Patinon, "Contribution," vol. 2,
pp. 668–673; interview Tiémoko Coulibaly (Kangaba, 13 April 1983); *ANMK* 1D
97, "Notices géographiques historiques: Topographiques et statistiques, Cercle de
Bamako, poste Bamako-Kati-Koulikoro, 1902," p. 1.

95. Patinon, "Contribution," vol. 2, pp. 668–673. Mauny argues that southern
stretches of the river most in use were between Kurusa in the south (Guinea), and
Koukia or Bentia (Mali) in the north (Mauny, *Tableau géographique*, p. 409); Gallieni,
Voyage, pp. 546–547.

However, although this ritual solution to an engineering problem was in harmony with Ba Faro and the south's occultism, its material consequences were long-term: By avoiding the challenge—that would have altered the ritual relationship to the river, and that could, conceivably, have opened the south's political economies to more complex uses—the Niger's interrupted course continued to impact the south's political economies, including its rich/poor identity, for centuries. Thus while the river's middle course was well utilized year-round and regional political economies reasonably well developed—as indicated by as-Sadi who knew the districts well (undertaking several voyages upriver between Timbuktu and Sinsani during the seventeenth century), and that Caillie confirmed some 200 years later—the Niger's upper regions remained marginalized, and under-utilized by all but the small covered Bozo and Somono craft. Correspondingly, the south's political economies remained relatively underdeveloped for centuries. Establishing an administrative seat at Kangaba on Mansa Musa's return from Mecca about 1325—only eight- to ten-days' journey from the future Bamako site—did little to encourage the region's foreign trade potential beyond its salt, gold, slave, and luxury imports-exports. And with the Malian state's decline in the late fourteenth century, the international flow of travelers and trade all but disappeared. True, the pre-Bamako *kafu* site remained the river's fording point, which, in theory, could have been the focus of further material development.[96] But so infrequented was the upper river by the larger commercial craft that regular river users were mainly pilgrims en route to the Holy City. Or, they were observers of the Ba Faro cult and its great spirit.

The ubiquitous obligations of Malian elites to invest primarily in private material consumption—mainly luxury goods—at the expense of public enterprises contributed to the south's rich identity in the northern paradigm, and a deepening poverty in the historical reality. Even Ibn Battuta (1352–1353), the only fourteenth-century Arab author to visit the south, left images reinforcing the south's riches, without mentioning its poverty: For example, Mansa Musa, he of pilgrimage fame, was generous; he gave 4,000 gold *mithqals* to Abu Ishaq al-Sahili "in a single day" because the Mansa "liked white men" (he was a northerner); he gave 3,000 *mithqals* to Mudrik b. Faqqus (another northerner), the Mansa wishing to "treat (him) kindly"; and 700 *mithqals* to Ibn Shaykh al-Laban from Tlemcen (Algeria).[97]

---

96. *Ta'rikh as-Sudan*, pp. 392–394, 422–423; Caillié, *Voyage*, vol. 2, pp. 152, 165–206; ANMK 1D 33 2, Collomb, "Notice" (Bamako, 1884–1885), p. 3.

97. A *mithqal* according to the same author was approximately 4.72 grams of gold, equal to about 1,150 cowries (Levtzion and Hopkins, *Corpus*, pp. 283, 289–297).

During the Songhay hegemony (c. 1468-c. 1591)—when demands for southern grains increased in the Timbuktu and central Saharan regions—southern traders did little to alter their ritual relationship to the river. Moreover, for reasons not entirely clear, Songhay administrators paid little attention to the underdeveloped Beledugu and Kaarta regions, establishing no viceroys in the equally underdeveloped "Banduk," a vague term referring to Songhay's southern hegemony. From French sources we learn of a successful Songhay raid on the Malian "capital" in the mid-sixteenth century, with surprising consequences, as the raiders (the Askia Issiak) departed without even demanding a tribute.[98] One short-term explanation for Songhay's apparent indifference to the south's tributary potential is that its gold was reaching northern markets anyway, in fact in such large quantities that for a long time Jenne and Timbuktu merchants realized a favorable balance of trade at the expense of desert-side traders. Jenne in the Inland Delta thus became the focus of Songhay's domestic and international economy, together with Ja and Kabura in the Massina, while Timbuktu and Gao at the Delta's nether edge virtually monopolized the foreign commerce with Morocco, Tawat (Algeria), Tripoli, and Egypt. Songhay's northern trade orientation was masking the growing north-south disparities in regional identities; developmental infrastructures in the Mande-hinterland's southern political economies were lagging behind their northern and even southwestern counterparts.

The Stabilized River and the Shifting Paradigm

If easy access to gold had configured Songhay's short-term relationships with the "animist" south, shifting trade patterns—occurring during the long dry period between 1100 and 1630—were pushing a lucrative commerce further south, beyond Songhay's reach, even before the state's defeat in 1591 at the hands of the Moroccans. In fact, by the late sixteenth century, Mande traders and blacksmiths, establishing conquest states

---

98. Delafosse, *Haut-Sénégal-Niger*, vol. 2, p. 215. See also Patinon, "Contribution," vol. 2, pp. 672–673. Throughout the Songhay territory the range of administrators included four viceroys: (1) Dandi in the east around Lake Chad; (2) Banku between the Timbuktu and Gao regions as far north as Tawat; (3) Bal or Balma in the northwest from Timbuktu to Taghaza; (4)Kurmina the most important (capital at Tindirma), which supervised the regions of Baghena, Barra (capital at Sa), Dirma (capital at Jira), the Massina and Danka. No viceroys were appointed to Jenne, Banduk (later the Bamako region), Kala (Sokolo), and Hombori. See also Dubois, *Timbouctou*, pp. 132–134; Tymowski, "Le Niger," pp. 79–85

south and west among West Atlantic and Gur-speakers, had already been integrated into the European coastal trade.[99]

However, despite the river's anthropology, which restricted the growth of the south's political economies, the northern paradigm began to shift southwards anyway. Driving these new developments were the coastal trade, and the rise of the Bamana-Segu and Kaarta states. Now the paradigm's more economic dimensions came to play a larger role. Even "animists," not least of all Segu's and Bamako's elites, were trading "kaffir" slaves. It isn't that regional political economies were becoming more "rational" and/or secularized, nor that the Segovian state and its Bamako *kafu* had openly embraced Islam. Rather, it is that Kaarta's, and especially Segu's, southern elaboration as war-based polities dependent on *jonw* armies had introduced a different model of state development, different at any rate from the older Mande tri-partite state organization, the latter family-based. Thus, although not "converting" to Islam in the formal sense, in the interest of state elaboration Kaarta's, Segu's and Bamako's elites created further differentiations within the northern paradigm by identifying with its material basis within a particularized Islamic episteme.[100]

Fortunately for posterity, Park (1796) and Gray and Dochard (1825) were eyewitnesses to the changing paradigm. From the former, drawing attention to the Segu-Kaarta wars, and the latter to the Segu-Massina and Kaarta-Bundu wars, we learn that a profitable slave trade was driving middle and upper Niger political economies linking them to the Atlantic trade via the Kaarta, the Senegambia, and upper Guinea. Park in particular drew attention to Segu's heavy shipping pushing south toward the upper Niger, the river's dysfunctionality and rapids notwithstanding, although it is fair to say that Park was visiting the south in August during the wet season. Trade with the south was still in evidence when Dochard reached Bamako in February 1818, the dry season, when land routes were still in evidence.[101]

---

99. Brooks, *Landlords*, pp. 4–5.

100. The comments above, and the following affecting slavery and the northern paradigm are a contribution to the ongoing discussion on the impact of the Atlantic slave trade on West African domestic slavery. For further discussion, see E. Anne McDougall, "In search of a desert-edge perspective: The Sahara-Sahel and the Atlantic trade, c. 1815–1900," in Robin Law, ed., *From slave trade to 'legitimate' commerce: The commercial transition in nineteenth-century West Africa* (Cambridge University Press, 1995), pp. 215–239.

101. Park, *The Travels*, pp. 167–170; 237–238; Gray and Dochard, *Travels in western Africa*, pp. 180, 189–207, 254–255, 344–345, 346, 349–350.

As political economies within the northern paradigm pushed south—the ideologies becoming domesticated and particularized with ambiguous twists and turns—doctrinal stirrings were even heard among the remote valleys of the Konyan in Guinea. There, in about 1830, a baby boy was born to the Ture family (no apparent relation to the Bamako Ture). They called him Samory. Coveting a jula identity in his "animist" youth—the ultimate sign of Islamized, Mande-speaking, long-distance traders—by the 1850s, Samory was stockpiling European firearms. Later yielding more directly to Islamic influences, by the 1870s his military prowess forged a state-by-conquest, its capital Bissandugu (Guinea); by the 1880s, he was the south's unchallenged master. Purchasing British arms—now on sale even in Timbuktu—from traders in their Sierre Leone enclaves, Samory was exchanging them for "kaffir" gold and "Bambara" slaves. In the Senegambia where the northern paradigm had long since been particularized, another baby boy was born to the Tall family (not a Mande family) of the Futa Toro. Approximately thirty-six years Samory's senior, they called him Umar Ibn Sa'id. Spending his youth in pious pursuits, like Samory, Umar later became a warrior in the Prophet's holy name, eventually establishing a state-by-conquest, its capital Segu. Purchasing European arms from the Senegambian enclaves, Umar likewise exchanged them for "kaffir" gold and "Bambara" slaves. As the nineteenth century unscroled, southern identities were about to be further negotiated. Southern poverty and devastation deepened.[102]

Conclusion

First, where the data permit, this chapter historicized the political economies and material elaborations of the families who first appeared in

---

102. *ANMK* 1D 5, "Notice de région du sud, 1895–1899," pp. 17–18; *ASAOF* 1G 50, Gallieni, "Analyse...agissements des Anglais" (Nango, 10 Sept. 1880), pp. 2–4. After the Conference of Brussels (1889–1892), the French made several attempts to curtail the flow of arms into the interior. *ANMAE, Affaires diverses Afrique,* "Conférence de Bruxelles, 1889–1892," Carton 2. For the sale of slaves and arms, see *ANMAE, 1780–1822,* vol. 11, Mém. 5, "Moyen de tirer ... commerce considerable" (1780), pp. 47–48; *ANMAE, 1780–1822,* vol. 11, Mém. 29 (May 1782), p. 120; *ANMAE, 1780–1822,* vol. 11, Mém. 34 (1783), p. 160; *ANMAE,* vol. 11, Mém. 39 (1783), pp. 191–201; *ANMAE, 1780–1822,* vol. 11, "Expédition de Galam" (6 Nov. 1819), vol. 37, p. 303; *ANMAE, 1856–1867,* vol. 47, p. 177; *ANMAE, 1843–1885,*" vol. 74, p. 22; *ANMAE, 1892–1894,*" vol. 124, pp. 21–22, 35, 218, 277–278, 332–335, 336–337; *ANMK* 1D 5, "Notice sur la région sud, 1895–1899."

this story in myth and legend (see Chapter 1). I argued that negotiated identities in the historical argument paralleled the manipulated and shifting identities initially inscribed in myths and legends. And if family myths spoke of centuries of ethnic articulations across the Mande-Mande dialect-cultural fulcrum, or Mande-Fulbe and Fulbe-Mande continua, French eighteenth and nineteenth century archival sources not only documented these transformations in the families' political economies and domestic ideologies, but also in their languages and dialects, cults and rituals as well. By the time the Niare and their clients arrived on the Bamako plain and Mande-hinterland—in the mid-eighteenth century—ethnographic and flora signs from horizon to horizon had already signaled, "in the Mande style," that this land was the Do ni Kri.

Second, both the legendary and historical data demonstrate Islam's activist political and sociological agenda in the Mande-hinterland between the seventeenth and nineteenth centuries. I called this the northern paradigm. Here, in both the clerical and popular discourse, a self-conscious northern Islam was reordering knowledge, defining perceptions, raising consciousness and regulating behavior that discriminated against the "kaffir," usually identified as a southerner, most often as the "Bambara," and always as the Other. In otherizing the Bambara, the northern paradigm justified slaving, not only in the Bamako *kafu* region, but also in the Mande-hinterland. As the paradigm shifted and turned, pushing south in response to both internal and external changes; and as material incentives jostled with ideological considerations, even "kaffirs" began trading "kaffirs." At the same time, an articulating Islam was parsing a theological discourse with "animism" in ways that were sometimes acknowledged, at other times denied, but at most times effective when serving an ideological or material end.

Third, I argue that although theologians within the northern paradigm divided the Mande-hinterland culturally and theologically into the Islamized north and the "animist" south, materially and material-historically no clear divide existed. Ambiguities notwithstanding, Islamized traders, slavers, and proselytizers kept the bifurcated vision alive—for centuries—even while the historical record denied its clear existence. Both the north and the south were "the same" in that Mande dialects and cultures, cults, oaths and rituals, lineages and patronyms, family structures and social organization, political economies and domestic ideologies, as well as architectural styles, cuisine and so forth, were all Mande. Moreover, all owning Mande dialects as their first language, traced their identities to the Wagadu legend and that mythical land somewhere in the Sahel, somehow in archaic time. Accounting for "difference" within this universal template were the regional particularizations that appeared to signify discrete templates. An activist northern Islam, seeking to define a distinct identity, and a "semitic" agenda conjugated the seeming difference into the Other difference.

Finally, although the north and south were the same, and that the south only appeared to be different, this chapter ultimately argues that historically the northern and southern identities were really different. Underscoring the southern identity were the gold ores found in greater abundance than anywhere else in this Mande-hinterland. The difference then was between those who produced gold (an "animist" function), and those who consumed it as a market commodity (an Islamized function). At that point Islam and "animism" could not, would not intersect, despite the wide-ranging articulations affecting social relations elsewhere. Due to the ideological rigors of the occult and the sacerdotal nature of gold, southern *numuw* would not, could not stand in water—knee deep—in order to mine gold for "turban wearers." The cultural pollution would have been unbearable.

The ideological lines defining identities were thus drawn. To the "animist's" icons of the hunter and his whistle, the dolo-consumer and his drinking days, and the warrior and his gain, one should therefore add the gold-producer and the *jo*: The *jo* was important because of the gold ores, and not that the gold ores were important because of the *jo*. So important was the *jo* that even some Islamized communities tried to access or appropriate its power, in much the same way as animists sought to access Islamic might without knowing the prayer. It stands to reason, therefore that differentiating the southern identity further was its analogous "kaffir"-slave image, followed by the vicious cycle of slave raids, wars, and political instability. I argue eventually that despite its life-giving force, the ritualistic relationship which bound the Niger River to its southern users gave rise to a dysfunctional anthropology, and a marginalized political economy. The palpable irony is that in choosing a ritual relationship to the river instead of an economic one, for example, southern identities became historically mired in an indelible poverty.

3

"The Family (Is) the Pivot of Sudanese Societies, the Center of All Organization":[1] The Bamako *Kafu* and Mande States

Introduction

By the mid-nineteenth century the Bamako *kafu*, ruled by its Niare *kafu-tigiw*, had already been in existence for about 100 years, possibly more. Integrated into the Mande-hinterland specifically, the Mande world more generally, *kafu* families were becoming Bamana, an identity shift similarly affecting thousands of regional families. Articulating identities were, for the most part, negotiated through the manipulation of cultural forms (e.g., lineage, language, myths/legends, ideology, etc.). Sacred state rituals (Wagadu, Kingi, Segu, Bamako) authenticated and legitimated these modulations, the sine qua non of identity realization and consolidation. Within this long process, the families materialized and historicized regional identities through political economies—in the Mande style—whether found in the Bamako *kafu*, in the Islamized middle and Inland Niger "industrial" towns, or in the south's fructuous heartland and occult gold fields. Shifting identity processes notwithstanding, distortions developing within the northern paradigm manipulated regionalized epistemes. In the long run, they influenced political economies, consciousness and behavior.

If the previous chapter dealt with materialized and historicized elaborations of Mande mythic identities, the next two chapters carry the discourse still further, treating politico-commercial-cultural developments found therein. I examine these phenomena first in relation to the Bamako *kafu* (the present chapter), and second within the framework of the state's so-

---

1. Jules Brévié, Administrative Assistant to the Colonies (Bamako, 1904).

cio-commercial elaboration (Chapter 4). Once again, "state" hardly refers to territorial boundaries, but to families holding political power where political incumbents *were* the state. On observing this phenomena in the Mande-hinterland, French colonial administrators in the late nineteenth and early twentieth centuries, likened the Mande political organization and governance to the *civitas in parvo* of the early Roman monarchical state.[2] I critique this Roman paradigm in the present chapter attributing its creation more to the French nineteenth-century episteme and the ways in which their young were socialized than to Mande historical realities.

Accordingly, I characterize the Bamako *kafu* as a "minimalist state" in the Mande style, to the extent that state officials managed the res publica (public, or state affairs), with the minimum of separate, independent, and bureaucratic state law and/or institutions. In other words, while not the *civitas in parvo* ascribed by the French, most public business in Bamako was conducted through existing family institutions, the Mande common law, and corporate social organizations. Except under specially preselected circumstances (e.g., war, hunting, decisions affecting the entire collectivity, etc.), functionally differentiating the family from the state was, for the most part, unnecessary. The same may be said for political-mythic-ritual ceremonies and ideologies where private and public belief systems, as well as social behavior, remained mainly undifferentiated. It isn't that public duties and responsibilities were unspecialized functions; they were. Rather, it was that flexibilities and elasticities within family groups and social organizations were such that public officeholders could legitimately articulate—ad hoc—in and out of public and private identities through ritualized sociocultural manipulations. State, society, and families were therefore of a whole; functional transitions from one to the other were smooth, when appropriately ritualized.

More Cultural Manipulations: The Roman Paradigm

Paterfamilias and Civitas in Parvo[3]

On reviewing the data from our present perspective, it is clear that offending northerners were not alone in developing false paradigms affect-

---

2. *Civitas in parvo*: the state writ small, meaning that in monarchical Rome, early state organization was modeled after the family, the principal social institution, and not vice versa; and that in the absence of differentiated and/or autonomous state institutions, the family became the principal political institution both in the *domus*, or private domestic space, and in the *publicus*, pertaining to the state.

3. Paterfamilias: father/male head of a household/family.

ing identities and imagery in the Mande-hinterland. The French, the region's newest in-migrants—settling there possibly some 800 years after the first Wagadu arrivals—were likewise quick to misread the region's signs and symbols. Arguing as if Rome's style of governance had by sleight of hand reached the Niger's bank, French "chiefs"—appropriately ritualized by *their* state authorities—analogized the elaboration of Mande political systems and identities as something akin to early monarchical Rome: the *civitas in parvo*.

Given the manner in which French children were socialized and schooled through "progressive" curricula, the mistake was explainable, if false. Because ethnographic imaginations bred on social evolutionary paradigms and classical school texts had identified Frenchmen as inheritors of the glory that was Greece and Rome, and because classical pedants were assuring posterity of the validity of governance in the "ancient world," recognizing the early signs of "classical governance" on the Niger's banks was but an artful (if wrong) next step.[4] With respect to early Rome, French schoolboy texts—the source of their "initiatic wisdom"—would have borne out these evolutionary "truths." Perpetuating an authoritarian ideology forged during the Napoleonic and Restoration eras, Roman families—as every schoolboy would have known—were not only the center of decision-making, but also of familial morality. If true for the early Roman Republic (c. 509 b.c.–c. 31 b.c.), familial authority was even more central to the monarchy (c. 753 b.c.–c. 509 b.c.) when societal relationships were relatively fluid and frequently changing. The paterfamilias, usually the oldest surviving male, was also the virtual lord of his lineage domain.[5] Beyond his patriarchal realm was regnal Rome's much looser governance of state affairs (res publica), bound by fluid alliances between the *gens* (groups of families), the elective king, the advi-

---

4. For example, in a controversial analysis of the nineteenth-century historiography, Martin Bernal revealed the extent to which nineteenth-century historians limited European "origins" to the Dorian/Ionian Greeks, to the exclusion of other Indo-European peoples (especially Semites), and the Egyptian influences on the ancient world, *Black Athena*.

5. As among Mande societies, the pater was not necessarily the *genitor*. As state power grew during the first two centuries of the Principate, the state initiated interventionist policies into a family's internal affairs, for example, most emperors urged on the Romans the virtues of large families, with mixed results. The state also sought to regulate marriages and to discourage celibacy, no doubt with the army and public service in mind, again with mixed results (Beryl Rawson, "The Roman family," in Beryl Rawson, ed., *The Family in ancient Rome* [London and Sydney, Australia, 1986], pp. 1–57, see esp. pp. 6, 9–11, 16, 20–26).

sory senate of 100 elders (known as *patres*, or state "fathers"), and the popular assembly of the curiae, or metaphorical "clans." "Fathers" and "groups of families" conferred the king's imperium, or the authority of the paterfamilias, over the entire res publica. According to Roman law, furthermore, patrilineages and patriarchal clans also defined the discourse for descent and succession, both for the res publica, as well as the res privata, or *domestica*.[6]

Even more compelling, evolving Roman law not only identified the civil magistrate as the paterfamilias whose state power, or *patria potestas*, was likewise informed by a patriarchal discourse, but by the early empire, the magistrate's father image had coincided with his state power.[7] The paterfamilias had become the *patria potestas*. In other words, the social organization and governance of the familial *civitas in parvo* had been transferred to the state, albeit greatly elaborated, empowered, and legalized. The model of the state and the *patria potestas* had evolved from the *civitas in parvo*. Where gerontocracies prevailed, a freeman's right to public and private authority, to hold office, or to formulate judicial and political decisions went to male family heads whose age and rank rendered them eligible. And, respectful of the natural material order and its spiritual energies, early Roman canons observed religious rituals to Mars—an agricultural deity before becoming a war god—in which the *numen*, or divine prerogatives, were invoked in the interest of the state.[8] Finally, lest any schoolboy forget, Rome, according to myth and legend, had been founded by two brothers, Romulus, the son of Mars, and Remus, the two suckled by Fera the she-wolf.

Given the form and organization of early Roman governance as summarized above, I hardly suggest that the paradigm was appropriate. In-

---

6. On marriage and the succession question under the Roman Republic and Empire, see Archie C. Bush, *Studies in Roman social structure* (University Press of America, 1982), especially chapter 6.

7. A harbinger of this growing state power was that until the late Republic (c. 31 b.c.), hereditary (familial) paternal power was the dominant custom. With growing state power, Roman family names began to be handed down in exact form from father to son, suggesting an increasingly interventionist state (W. K. Lacey, "Patria potestas," in Rawson, *The Family*, pp. 121–144, see esp. pp. 123, 138–139).

8. However, by the third and second centuries b.c.—as Rome's external expansion (among other things) became too problematic for the uninformed and unwieldy comitia—the consolidation process of internal rule into the hands of a series of *patricio-plebeian* alliances and coalitions began to win support. See also Lacey, "Patria potestas," pp. 121–145, esp. pp. 138–140.

stead, I ask why French ethnographers and administrators associated Mande governance in Bamako and the Mande-hinterland with the *civitas in parvo* of regnal Rome. Three case studies throw some light on the mistaken parallels.

Case Study 1: The "River Sierra Leone": "Their Government and Their Laws Appear to Have Been Originally of the Patriarchal Kind." Visiting the "River Sierra Leone" between 1785 and 1787, Lieutenant John Matthews of the British Royal Navy—sojourning for several months on the West African Guinea Coast—noted that among the region's "Mandingoes" (Mandinka) and "Suzee" (Susu?), "government and ... laws appear to have been originally of the patriarchal kind, where the elder of every family was priest and judge." However times changed, he continued, and "at present the prevailing form in these parts of Africa is a kind of mixed monarchy, elective, and extremely limited both in external and internal power." The word *mungo*, which Europeans translated as king, he continued, "only signifies head man." Yet despite this, the king "is always addressed by the title of *fasee*, or 'father,' not necessarily the genitor, but he who nourishes, protects, and controls, and who in turn expects a labor contribution, and a share of dependents' surplus value. Every separate district, in the same nation, has a separate king (father), ruler, or chief." Although executive power and final decisions rested with him, "every head, or principal man of a village, thinks himself sole lord within his own town. Neither can the king command, but only intreat (*sic*), except in matters which have been debated and determined in full council." As to laws, Matthews concluded, "handed down by tradition from father to son," they are "merely the local customs of the country," differing little from one district to the next. All capital offenses were punished with fines, slavery, even death. Finally, Matthews noted that eligibility for chiefly office called for "a thorough knowledge of the local customs of the country"; the qualities of "a good orator"; a "good head," understood to mean "a clear understanding"; a predilection for soberness (as opposed to drunkenness); and "attentive(ness) to hear the complaints and redress the grievances" brought before him.[9]

Although Matthews seemed unaware of this, of interest to us is that the "Mandingoes" whom he had observed on the "River Sierra Leone" were none other than the southwestern Mande who, like the Niare and the

---

9. John Matthews, *A Voyage to the River Sierra-Leone, on the coast of Africa* (London, 1788/1966), pp. 73–79, 80. For a further discussion of the father's socioeconomic and political role, see Meillassoux, *Maidens, meal*, pp. 47, 80, 86, 87.

Mandekan in the Mande-hinterland, had also migrated from Wagadu sometime in deep antiquity.

Case Study 2: Kita Region: "Political Organization Derived Naturally from That of the Family." Working in the 1890s among the Khassonke (Mandekan) in the Kita region, about a fifteen- to twenty-day journey west of Bamako, colonial administrator G. Tellier noted in accordance with the Roman paradigm that among the Mande, "political organization derived naturally from that of the family." Expressed otherwise, it was said that outside the family, relationships "lacked cohesion."[10] Further elaborating the family-state concept (which we now recognize as tri-partite), Tellier noted its "two estates": the free or *horon* estate; and the *nyamakalaw,* or specialized workers estate. Invested with less political power were slaves, wives and other minors, people whom Tellier inappropriately referred to as the "lesser sub-divisions" (Tellier also failed to understand that slaves [*jonw* and *wolosow*] were likewise an "estate"). The term "fa," or "father," applied not only to all biological fathers, but also to fathers' brothers (i.e., patrilineal uncles) as well. Senior household heads (*ton-tigiw*) and heads of grouped families (*lu-tigiw*) were likewise "fathers."[11] Business affecting the patrilineage was always conducted in the *ton-tigi's* or *lu-tigi's* name even if he was a minor, or too old and infirm, or blind, or unable to comprehend, or even communicate. Fathers were, moreover, responsible for the well-being of the entire household (i.e., land distribution, food, and spouses for youths of marriageable age), including minors and slaves, even temporary residents. The private paterfamilias in domestic council (*privatum consilium*) was expected to rule with justice and mercy. De jure succession to public and private power was through the collateral line in the senior patrilineage (*fasiya*). All Mande families were identified according to this internal organization, Tellier thought, differences more apparent than real.[12]

---

10. Tellier, *Autour de Kita,* pp. 17, 82–95. Kassonke is a Mandekan language of the Mande Northern Subgroup (see Introduction, notes 26, and 35–38); *ANMK* 2D 133, "Programme d'action politique, administrative et économique pour la période 1912–1922 du Cercle de Bamba, 1918." It is worth noting that according to some Niare accounts, the family migrated to Bamako from the Khassonke region (Soumaoro, "Etude," p. 4).

11. Tellier, *Autour de Kita,* p. 82. Among the Mande, "family" in some respects also means *badenya,* "mother-childness," or belonging to the mother's side of a polygynous household. The term derives from *den-baya*: mother (Camara, "Le Manden," p. 63).

12. Collateral succession from brother to brother marked the transfer of the *doyen's* prerogatives to male producers who succeeded each other in the produc-

On matters affecting the state, little differentiated the "ruling dynasty" from civil society, Tellier continued. In this multilateral, multicentric lineage state, the public paterfamilias in council (*publicum consilium*) was to the state what the private paterfamilias was to the household. Assuming this to be a balanced equilibrium (as with the smaller domestic system), the *faama*'s or "father's" state powers were balanced or restricted by those of his semiautonomous "sons," the *dugu-tigiw*, or village chiefs, themselves "fathers" within their own public and private jurisdictions.[13] Usually required, according to constitutional protocols, to deliberate within circles of family intimates, *nyamakalaw* and slave representatives also carried a certain political weight and moral authority, especially *jeliw* (bards) and *numuw* (blacksmiths).[14] Finally, with state power (*patria potestas*) intersecting his private powers, the *faama*'s authority even extended over matters affecting life and death where the entire patrilineage was concerned, while "sons" retained the final authority over *their* individual households, including matters affecting property, life and death. In an attempt to "domesticate" Tellier upon his arrival in Kita in the 1890s, "fathers" from surrounding jurisdictions made him *their* father, thereby elevating him to the rank of "father of *all* fathers."[15]

Case Study 3: Bamako and the Mande-Hinterland: "The Family (Is) the Pivot of Sudanese Societies, the Center of All Organization." Product of the same "initiatic wisdom" and the Roman paradigm, Jules Brevie,

---

tion cycle (Tellier, *Autour de Kita*, pp. 81–83, 86–88, 91–92). Lineages or *luw* were grouped together into a quarter or *kabila* [*sukula; bösö*] Person, *Samori*, vol. 1, pp. 54–57). See also Meillassoux, *Maidens, meal*, p. 48. For a similar discussion on the Mande in general see Labouret, "Les Manding," pp. 55–61, 65–73.

13. Tellier, *Autour de Kita*, pp. 92–93. Compare again with Matthews: "Every district, in the same nation, has a separate king, ruler, or chief," who "thinks himself sole lord within his own town" (Matthews, *A Voyage*, pp. 74, 77).

14. Tellier, *Autour de Kita*, pp. 83–89. In 1850, Lunéville found similar consultative relationships in the nearby Bambuhu states inhabited by the Mandinka (*ANSOM* Sén. et Dép. Doss. 54 1817–1856, "Maréchal de Lunéville à Monsieur le Président du pouvoir éxecutif, au citoyen, Président du Conseil de Ministre, Chef du pouvoir éxecutif" [Paris, 1850], p. 8). So did Marillier some forty years later, also in Bambuhu (*ANSOM* Soudan V Doss. 2, no. d, Marillier, "Reconnaissance en Bambouk" [March 1894], pp. 2, 5, 8). Compare again with Matthews: "Neither can the king command, but only intreat, except in matters which have been debated and determined upon in full council"; the king "had not authority to compel" (Matthews, *A Voyage*, pp. 77–78). For *numu* political roles among the Bamana, see *ASAOF* 15G 83, Ruault, "Généralités 1880 à 1920" (Bamako, 22 Feb. 1884), p. 9.

15. Tellier, *Autour de Kita*, pp. 17, 82–97.

administrative assistant to the colonies stationed in Bamako at the turn of the century (1904), interpreted the signs of elaborated governance somewhat similarly. Focusing more on a political theory than Matthews and Tellier had previously essayed, Brevie noted that the family was "the pivot of Sudanese societies, the center of all organization." It was, moreover, the sole operational unit for the state's entire social, economic, judicial, and military organization and process. *Ton-tigiw* (household heads) spoke exclusively for their patrilineages.[16] As a mark of state identity, domestic ideologies, highly persuasive, described an "internally oriented" and "relatively closed" social order—more so than Matthews and Tellier had noted among states along the River Sierre Leone, and the Kita region respectively. Individual identities were, moreover, "grouped around the oldest (male) family member who, in gathering all authority into his hands, represent(ed) the entire patrilineage and its interests." Unchallenged patriarchal ideologies justified exploitation in addition to domination, Brevie thought.

As a unit, Brevie continued, "the family has its own personality (identity) independent of its members": An individual's identity, especially that of juniors, was absorbed into the group's; and "in the case of the *tontigi, his* (emphasis added) personality (identity) became an emanation of the collectivity which he represented and directed." In a word, Brevie concluded, "without saying that the individual's interests are absolutely sacrificed to internal group objectives, they (nonetheless) are completely subordinated." Morality, both public and private, was a family affair.[17] Finally, believing (wrongly) that both state and family were ideologically closed, Brevie defined the elaboration of political identities in upper Niger states as conservative, where adherence to Mande values and behavior was de rigeur, the moral environment palpable. Developing a juridical argument suggested by Tellier, Brevie concluded (again wrongly) that so deeply were these norms embedded within the moral order that only in extremes were constitutional conventions subject to change. Offending members—that is, those departing from the *manikaya*, or behavioral

---

16. *ASAOF* 1G 299, Brévié, "Monographie" (Bamako, 25 April 1904), pp. 18, 22–36. Raffenel found similar strong family ties in the Kaarta where the patriarch's role was preeminent (Raffenel, *Nouveau voyage*, vol. 1, p. 459). Ruault and Vallière found similar phenomena in the Beledugu (*ASAOF* 15G 83, Ruault, "Généralités 1880 à 1920" [Bamako, 22 Feb. 1884], p. 9; see also *ANSOM* Sén. et Dép., IV Doss. 90 Bis, Vallière, "Rapport sur l'opération de Minamba" [Bamako, 9 March 1888], pp. 24–25, 32).

17. *ASAOF* 1G 299, Brévié, "Monographie" (Bamako, 25 April 1904), pp. 18, 22–36.

norms within the Mande identity—were socially excised so that the status quo ante could be restored. Thus, even while evaluating observations from different perspectives, and differing on their detailed observations, Matthews, Brevie, and Tellier all had similar findings: The family was key to all forms of social and political organization; according to the political elaboration of the Mande identity both public and private chiefly authorities were undifferentiated, the father-chief even having power over life and death.[18]

Given these three case studies, had observers appropriately identified Mande social organizations and governance as rule by the paterfamilias and the *civitas in parvo*? Seemingly unaware of its broader historical significance, observers, on the one hand, were in fact identifying a universal phenomenon: That where political centers and alliances were multiple, fluid and frequently changing, social institutions also tended to be fluid and articulating. Given these circumstances, it is hardly surprising that families, familial institutions, and associated conventions did in fact provide the most stable societal core. In the past, moreover, the family was—and in some instances still is—the most important custodian of domestic ideologies, societal behavior, and moral categories important for a collective well-being, not to mention control over women, minors, and slaves. Whether in ancient Rome, nineteenth-century France, twentieth-century Japan, or the present-day kingdom of Saudi Arabia, for that matter, the word of the paterfamilias within his household could carry the weight of law. And of considerable importance: Of all the kinship terms, the one most securely established in most languages is "father."[19] Thus, given the nature of human societies across time, space, and differentiated cultures, families have been among civil societies' most important institutions, a given only recently challenged in the latter part of the twentieth century.

Moreover, with respect to the Mande and the Romans, kin-group social organizations and the role of the paterfamilias were, both in form and function, a kind of *civitas in parvo*, the res publica conducted *as if* a "family affair." In both, patrilineal gerontocracies prevailed, vesting "freemen elders" with rights to public and private authority, to hold office, and to

---

18. As a matter of interest, in pleading his case in Bamako in February 1993, Moussa Traoré, president of Mali (1968–1991), referred to himself as "father of the nation" who "accepted political and moral responsibility (for) ... the nation" (*African Research Bulletin*, vol. 30, no. 2 [1993]).

19. Emile Benveniste, *Indo-European language and society* (University of Miami Press, 1969/1973), p. 169.

formulate judicial and political decisions. Belief systems took cognizance of spiritual energies in the physical universe, especially acknowledging agricultural deities. Both types of states took augurs and seers seriously before reaching important collective decisions; and in both, the "high priest" (*pontifex maximus*) in Rome, the *kafu-tigi* (*kafu* chief), *soma* (priest), and grand *numu* (blacksmith) in the Mande-hinterland enjoyed great spiritual authority. Finally, mythic formulations concerning both states' origins by two sets of brothers were strangely similar in some respects.[20] It is understandable among French administrators therefore, if mistaken, that the elaborated identity of a Mande "father" and his household should have been analogized as a signifier of the paterfamilias, his family and household a *civitas in parvo*.[21]

Likewise mistaken was the inappropriate contextualization of the Mande states, situating them in a European episteme and paradigm, as mistaken and misleading as the northern paradigm had been. We recall that by contextualizing the south as "animist" and "fetishist," contributors to the northern paradigm expected southern Mandekan to be the endless suppliers of slaves and gold (see Chapter 2). Now, by contextualizing Bamako within an ontological, social-evolutionary framework, framers of the teleological Roman paradigm were suggesting that Bamako could one day be to the Niger what Rome was to the Tiber. That these latter visions coincided with perspectives of some French imperial "seers"—the Saint Simonists, the positivists, mercantile communities from Bordeaux and Marseilles—not to mention the military and policymakers from the Ministry of Foreign Affairs and Ministry for the Colonies, is probably no coincidence. In both instances miscontextualizing was to misconceive, misunderstand, and misrepresent.

---

20. There were other similarities. Legal conventions, for example, were designed in both instances for "insiders," or for a limited group of ascriptive citizens born to a civic heritage, combining religious ceremonial and ancestral formulates, thereby excluding outsiders from political power and direct citizenship. Within these relatively small communities, moreover, patron-client relationships negotiated the advent of the "stranger," the "guest," and the potential "enemy" (the *dunan* in Mande conventions; the *externus*, the *alienigena*, the *hostis*, and later the *barbarus* in Roman law); and in both polities, patron-client ties or fictive relationships retained their fundamental importance for centuries.

21. In fact, so hegemonic was the Roman paradigm that even the analogy of a "pax Romana" for Africa was construed in public documents recalling its earlier counterparts in "barbarian" Gaul and Britain (H. Busson, "La Partage de la boucle du Niger," *Bulletin de la Société d'Alger*, vol. 2 (1898): 111–112.

The Bamako *Kafu*: Contextualizing and Elaborating a Political Identity "in the Mande Style"

Part 1: The Core-State and the Collateral Succession

Having critiqued both the northern and the Roman false paradigms, resounding somewhat absurdly would be claims that my analysis of Bamako's state was paradigm-free. The idea of contextualizing and elaborating a political identity "in the Mande style" in fact comes from Valliere (a member of the Gallieni mission), who, on reaching Bamako in 1880, noted that political entities in the Mande-hinterland formed "loosely articulated state(s), or confederation(s) ... in the Mande style."[22] Valliere was, of course, referring to the Mande tri-partite familial and state organization later noted by Tellier when visiting the Khassonke polity at the turn of the century. In other words, although Bamako had been marked with Segu's metropolitan signifiers—the balansan, or acacia trees not the least of these—the *kafu*'s internal organization and governance had been elaborated more in accordance with the old Mande paradigm of the semi-autonomous state—operating within Segu's larger, more centralized imperium—than by Segu's *tonjon* or governmental organization. In effect, the Mande style to which Valliere referred was more the norm than the exception found throughout the Mande-hinterland. Accordingly cleaving to its variation on the Mande style of "peaceful" tri-partite settlements, Bamako remained primarily a trading, agricultural, and herding *kafu* with little interest in warfare.[23] As a military *tonjon* state organized for war, it was Segu's political identity that was among the exceptions.

In pointing to the signs of governance in Bamako and throughout most of the Mande-hinterland, it is noteworthy that following family concepts, public officials became legal officeholders by virtue of private lineage affiliations, birth order, and social rank, and not, for example, by war or military coups or prowess. Public political behavior and choices likewise derived from the conventions of private family filiations. Central to the *kafu*'s authenticity and political integrity was the *kafu-tigi* and

---

22. *ANSOM* Sén. et Dép., IV Doss. 90 Bis, Vallière, "Mémoire" (Siguiri, 15–25 March 1888), p. 37; *ANMK* 1D 3 2, Collomb, "Notice" (Bamako, 1884–1885), p. 3.

23. Traditions, as reported by Amadu Kumba Niare, spoke of Bamako's pre-French military prowess (Meillassoux, "Histoire," pp. 192–195, 215–217). In archival accounts, however, Bamako was better known for its commercial and textile traditions. See *ASAOF* 1G 52 46, Bayol, "Mission de Ségou" (Saint Louis, 5 July 1880), pp. 9–10; *ASAOF* 1G 50 49, "Lettre Piétri à Gallieni" (Bamako, 9 May 1880), p. 2; *ANSOM* Sén. et Dép., IV Doss. 90 Bis, Vallière "Mémoire" (Siguiri, 15–25 March 1888), p. 37; *ANMK* 1D 33 2, Collomb, "Notice" (Bamako, 1884–1885), p. 3.

his family (Jamusadia Niare's lineage) comprising the core-state, the latter an articulating axis where important decisions affecting the res publica were made. As head of state, members of the Jamusadia lineage were "fathers of the fathers." Likewise as "masters of the earth"—in addition to being state-founders—the Niare chieftaincy was "sacred," Jamusadia (the state's founder) having concluded an alliance with the earth's spiritual energies through the ritual sacrifice of live pythons, gold, and other sacred objects (see Chapter 1).[24] The alliance, in the lexicon of Mande constitutional protocols, formed the basis for the ruler's authority and sacred ideology. That a chief's sacerdotal persona was inviolate only in relation to his ability to manipulate the supernatural—in the collective interest—was also a consideration within the Mande style of governance. And as the *ton-tigi* or *lu-tigi* "owned" his family, so was the state a chiefly patrimony, an elaboration of the *kafu-tigi's* familial identity. Both chief and state were assisted by an ad hoc council of *dugu-tigiw* (core-state "sons"), or chiefly advisors, reinforced by Segovian representatives, most often resident *jonw*. Observing this conciliar figuration when a visiting member of the Gallieni mission in 1880, Captain Pietri confirmed that all important *kafu* decisions required consultations with core-state *dugu-tigiw*.[25] Moreover, as the "father of fathers," Niare *kafu-tigiw* were the highest juridical voice throughout the land.

Unfortunately, little information with respect to historical Niare chiefs has survived. No unbroken "king-list" is extant, the mythical Jamusadia (c. 1742–?) and the historical Titi Niare (c. 1864?–September 1898), the first and last preconquest incumbents, respectively. Broader strokes outlining Madiugu Seriba Niare's warrior identity (c. 1796?–c. 1838?), especially in the Niare-Meillassoux text, could conceivably be due to his state-elaborating capabilities as a Segovian client. His more clearly defined warrior identity could also suggest a well-developed special purpose organization for state formation and initial maintenance. Other sources attempting king-lists, including Borgnis Desbordes, provide little by way of usable information.[26]

24. To the best of my knowledge there was no other priestly family in the Bamako *kafu*. See also Meillassoux, "Histoire," p. 193.

25. Camille Piétri, "Note topographique sur l'itinéraire suivi par la mission du Haut-Niger, de Kita à Bammako (Nango, 10 June 1880)," *BSGCB* (1881), pp. 565–573.

26. For variations on dynastic lists see Meillassoux, "Histoire," pp. 194, 201–202, 214–217; Anon., "Chronique historique," pp. 62–63; Soumaoro, "Etude," p. 8; *ANMK* 1G 33 5, Borgnis Desbordes, "Notice historique" (Bamako, 1880–1890).

Few data are similarly extant on how the collateral succession operated historically in the Niare senior patrilineage. As is generally known the collateral, or "Z," succession outlined protocols by which a *ton-tigi*, or family head of a polygynous household, was succeeded not by his son, but by the oldest male in the senior patrilineage (i.e., the ruler's lineage "brother," sometime a nephew in reality), assuming him to be able-bodied and of sound mind.[27] Continuing through the male line (real or fictive) until all eligible, able-bodied "brothers" had served according to birth order, only then did the *ton-tigi's* or *lu-tigi's* office pass to the eldest "son" of the next generation: hence the "Z." According to the Mande style, collateral succession in the state, or res publica, should have imaged its family, or private counterpart traceable to the Sunjata Keita patrilineage and the old Mali state, according to Ibn Khaldun.[28]

With respect to the Bamako *kafu*, only fragmentary data suggest that state-founder Jamusadia was succeeded by his son, Fabile (Fable), or that the latter in turn was succeeded by his brother, Malassa Bakary Niare (mid-eighteenth century?). Several other "brother" successions may have followed, according to the anonymous author of the "Chronique historique," although the data are far from clear.[29] No further usable data extant, our next source is the Gallieni Mission to Segu (1880–1881), some of whose members noted—while sojourning briefly in Bamako—that Titi Niare was ruling in place of his "brother" Biramou (supposedly old and

---

27. According to the *fasiya* (collateral succession through the senior patrilineage), fathers took precedence over sons, and older brothers over younger (Tellier, *Autour de Kita*, pp. 82–92). Note that while private political succession passed through the *fadenya* (i.e., father-childness), inheritance of personal material wealth was through the *balimaya*, or uterine line, where *badenya* (i.e., mother-childness), or siblings of the same mother, inherited private material wealth directly from their mother (*ASAOF* 1G 48, Pérignon, "Monographie" [1899–1900], p. 325). Although material property was inherited through the female line, theoretically the male household head could dispose of property.

28. Apparently as a way of consolidating power in a new dynasty, sons succeeded lineage founders. For example, Sunjata Keita (c. 1234–c. 1260) was supposedly succeeded by three sons, followed by the collateral succession in the chiefly patrilineage, according to Ibn Khaldun. Ibn Khaldun made similar claims for Mansa Musa Keita (c. 1312–c. 1337, Sunjata's nephew), whose son succeeded him, the succession thereafter passing to the Mansa's brother's son (his nephew) (Ibn Khaldun, *Histoire*, vol. 2, pp. 111, 114; Niane, *Recherches sur l'empire*, pp. 15–18, 37–38, 45). See also, Diabaté, "Kankou Moussa," pp. 15–16, 18, 31–34.

29. Anon., "Chronique historique," pp. 62–66.

infirm).[30] Clearly the richer of the two, Titi had acquired a modest capital accumulation from the production and marketing of *dolo*, as well as his foreign trade (including slaves) at the Sierre Leone enclaves: hence the possible source of his material leverage over an "older brother." Annoyed by the Gallieni Mission, Gallieni found him feisty—"most impudent" in fact. Seeking wider political opportunities after 1883 when Borgnis Desbordes (known as "Bourouti" in some local lore) arrived in Bamako, Titi's circle of intimates made it known that their lord intended to be master of the Beledugu, and with Bourouti's blessing, no less. Alarmed, the Beledugu chiefs hunched into a stony silence. Titi was still guarding his "animist" turf in 1884, a full year after Bourouti's conquest. Still quick to assert power, he kept male relatives at bay, excluding them (especially Jyonko, his "brother" and successor) from state affairs, ironically relying on the Ture and Drave—his Islamized Surakaw clients—who, although richer, powerful, and apparently quite overbearing, were legally excluded from the succession. That the French favored two Niare "nephews," even including them among local hires could not have irritated Titi more. Quick to assert his "animist" identity before both Gallieni and Borgnis Desbordes, Titi had boasted that as a *dolo* consumer, he could hardly be mistaken for a "shaved head" Muslim.[31]

Related data from near-by Mande-hinterland states throw more light on the collateral succession. In the Beledugu *kafuw*, for example, Gallieni, Delanneau, Ruault, and Rougier noted a strict collateral observance in the patrilineage—as a means of checking local rivalries and political factionalism—even at the risk of marginalizing the youth in state affairs. For example, the Traore chief of the Beledugu Kumi *kafu*, Gallieni noticed, seemed especially successful at keeping competitors at bay. Ruling in the

30. Gallieni, *Voyage*, p. 246–249, 595; *ASAOF* 1G 50, "Lettre Gallieni à Gouverneur" (Makajambugu, 26 April 1880), p. 3; *ASAOF* 1G 50 49, "Lettre Piétri à Gallieni" (Bamako, 9 May 1880), pp. 1–2; *ASAOF* 1G 52 46, Bayol, "Mission de Ségou" (Saint Louis, 5 July 1880), pp. 9–10; *ASAOF* 1G 50 20, "Lettre Gallieni à Gouverneur" (Nango, 7 July 1880), pp. 10–35. According to later sources Titi was ruling in the place of another brother, Batigi Niare (*ANMK* 2E 43 "Politique indigène" [1897–1908], n.p.); see also, *ANMK* 2D 132, "Organisation administrative … ville de Bamako" (Bamako, 1 Nov. 1902), pp. 3–5.

31. When Gallieni complained to Titi Niare about the attack in the Beledugu at Jo (11 May 1880), Titi apologized despite his high dudgeon informing Gallieni that Bamako was not a "nothing country" (Gallieni, *Voyage*, pp. 246–250; *ASAOF* 1G 52 46, Bayol, "Mission de Ségou" [Saint Louis, 5 July 1880]; *ASAOF* 15G 83, Ruault, "Généralités 1880 à 1920" [Bamako, 22 Feb. 1884], p. 18; *ANMK* 1D 33 2, Collomb, "Notice" [Bamako, 1884–1885]).

name of an "infirm elder," he wielded a "certain authority in the cantons and a ... far reaching influence in the neighborhood" without involving members of the younger generation. In Daba and Kumi (also in the Beledugu), Delanneau found chiefly brothers to be of considerable importance; and both in the Beledugu and northeast in the Moribugu regions, Ruault was struck with the widespread observance—"according to the Bambara custom"—of the collateral succession, which left government in the hands of the most experienced (a practice that European monarchies should consider, he editorialized). Among the Islamized Maraka of the Banamba region, Rougier found some irregularities in that rich brothers tended to muscle their way in at the expense of legal but poorer claimants. Finally, in Nonkon (Nango, where Gallieni had been detained at Segu's pleasure from 1 June 1880 to 29 March 1881), Chaman Nyuaman, younger brother of the Beledugu Nonkon chief (and his intended successor), lost his claim to the chief's son masquerading as a nephew.[32]

Metropolitan Segu followed similar de jure collateral considerations, power seizures by *tonjonw* between 1757 and 1766 considered quite illegal. The principle at any rate was enshrined in constitutional protocols: "When a Bamana dies" the legacy "goes to the eldest son." "If that one leaves it," the convention continues, "then it goes to the next eldest son. If that one also leaves it then it is given to the next eldest son. Each has to wait for his turn, right up to the last one. Even if you demand to share the legacy a Bamana legacy is not something to be shared. Each must wait ... the blade of the gravedigger's hoe."[33]

In practice the first Segovian succession appeared regular, in that according to constitutional protocols Suma Kulibaly, the lineage founder, was succeeded by Biton, his son, in approximately 1712. Irregularities thereafter apparently occurred to the extent that Biton (1712–1755) was not succeeded by "brothers," but by two sons, Dekoro (1755–1757) and Ali

---

32. Gallieni, *Voyage*, pp. 246–247, 595; *ASAOF* 1G 80, "Mission Delanneau dans le Cercle de Bamako, 1885"; *ASAOF* 15G 83, Ruault, "Généralités 1880 à 1920" (Bamako, 22 Feb. 1884), pp. 3, 6–7, 18; *ANMK* 1D 33 4, Rougier, "Enquête sur l'Islam" (Banamba, 31 May 1914), p. 43; see also *ASAOF* 1G 52 46, Bayol, "Mission de Ségou" (Saint Louis, 5 July 1880), p. 10; Piétri, "Note topographique," p. 572; *ANSOM* Sén. et Dép. IV Doss. 90 Bis, Vallière, "Rapport sur l'organisation ... Mambi" (Kangaba, 5 March 1888); *Archives Maliennes Fonds Anciens*, Affaires politiques, 1E 18, "Rapport politique, Cercle de Bamako, Rapport sur la tournée fait par le Capitaine Besançon, Commandant de Cercle de Bamako" (Bamako, 30 Oct. 1897), cited in Ward, "The French-Bambara," pp. 54, 244–245, 285; *ANMK* 2D 132, "Organisation administrative ... ville de Bamako" (Bamako, 1 Nov. 1902), pp. 3–5.

33. Conrad, *A State*, p. 146.

(1757), the latter a serious student of Islamic Law (and ironically head of an "animist" state), who had studied at Timbuktu under Shaykh Sidi Moktar. It can be argued that power elites aimed to secure the Kulibaly dynasty. There may have been further irregularities after Monzon Jara (1787–1808: the Jara had seized power from the Kulibaly in about 1766), when Da Jara (1808–1827), Monzon's son, seized office from his older brother, Nyenekoro.[34] Thereafter the succession regularized, following the collateral "Z": Despite Da's numerous sons, none ruled until 1870 (Nyanemba II Jara, 1870–1878), eight of his brothers ruling instead between 1827 and 1870, even after the Umarian conquest in the early 1860s, and even after 1878, when Nyanemba was succeeded by his brother, Massatomo Jara (1878–1883). Collateral rule persisted in the Segovian patrilineage even after the French arrived at Bamako (1883), when the Segu *ton-jonw* installed Karamoko Jara (1883–1889), Massatomo's brother, although by now the Segu state was in disarray and the Jara incumbents in exile. In Kaarta—Segu's "brother" state where the Massassi Kulibaly ruled—Raffenel found the collateral succession strictly observed, with "brothers" following according to age.[35]

As with Segu, de facto deviations also occurred in the old Mande: If the collateral succession ("the Manding law," Peroz noted) had ever worked as a "safety device," by the nineteenth century the system was breaking down. Here the *fadenya*, or competing Keita "brothers," kept interclan rivalries *(fadenkele)* endemic—between the Kaniba Mambi Keita the elder Niagassola patrilineage, and the Mambi Kumu Keita the younger Kangaba branch—for the greater part of the nineteenth century.[36] Aggravated by destabilizing political conditions, young contenders contributed to the turmoil with appeals for outside help, the Niagassola Keita calling in the Umarians, while their Kangaba kin re-

34. For variations on the Segu succession, see Tauxier, *Histoire*, pp. 96–102; Konaté, "Monographie," pp. 22–23, 28–29, 30–34. (We recall that Mungo Park's two visits, 1796 and 1805, coincided with Monzon's administration.)

35. Tauxier, *Histoire*, p. 97; Ward, "The French-Bambara" pp. 33, 48–49; *ASAOF* 1G 320, "Notice sur le Cercle de Ségou 1904," pp. 1–3, 14–15; Raffenel, *Nouveau voyage*, vol. 1, pp. 379, 387, 439.

36. Diabaté, "Kankou Moussa," pp. 15–16, 18, 31–34. The collateral had apparently worked better in the past, see note 28. See also, Etienne Péroz, *Au Soudan français: Souvenirs de guerres et de mission* (Paris, 1891), pp. 241–242. For a discussion of the *fadenya* see Jean-Loup Amselle, "Un Etat contre l'état: Le Keleyadugu." *CEA*, vol. 28 (1988): 463–483; Claude Daniel Ardouin, "Une Formation poliltique précoloniale du Sahel occidental malien: Le Baakhunu à l'époque des Kaagoro," *CEA*, vol. 28 (1988): 443–461, esp. pp. 450–452.

cruited the Samorians. Making matters worse, according to Valliere, the Kangaba Keita, numbering about 600 "brothers" eligible for the *faamaya*, were also in a state of internal rivalry. Eventually all clan branches supported the French. At Siby (the Camara homeland and Bamako's neighbor in the northern Mande) the collateral gerontocracy likewise did not always prevail, Valliere observing—as John Matthews had done on the Guinea Coast a century earlier—that the "best speakers" and "renowned warriors" usually dominated.[37] And a century earlier in the Bambuhu and Niumi regions of the Senegambia, Goldberry (1785–1787) noted that on a ruler's death the oldest male always inherited the power. The collateral still configured the succession ritual approximately thirty years later throughout the entire gold-mining and Bundu regions, according to Gaspard Mollien (1819). It was still operative seventy-five years later according to Marillier (1894), a military officer on tour in the mining regions. However, a devastating deterioration in the political environment—attributed to the late nineteenth century Umarian and Samorian wars and the south's great poverty—subsequently tore whole communities apart. The result as we know it was a deadly political anarchy.[38]

Given the above insights into the Mande-hinterland's collateral succession, fratricidal strife, and factionalism (*fadenkele*), we have little reason to suppose that succession in the Bamako *kafu* might have functioned differently.

Finally what seems clear in this family calculus is that while constitutional protocols privileged the collateral succession, the historical praxis allowed for deviations on the part of ambitious brothers; so did the loose interpretation of the "brother" terminology in the Mande style. Under these circumstances, for example, an incumbent deviating from the collateral succession could be a father's biological son (i.e., direct father-son descent, although this seemed legal if the father had been the state

---

37. *ANSOM* Sén. et Dép. IV Doss. 90 Bis, Vallière, "Rapport sur l'organisation … Mambi" (Kangaba, 5 March 1888), p. 17; Gallieni, *Voyage*, p. 330. For other discussions of the collateral succession, see Person, *Samori*, vol. 1, pp. 54–56, 79.

38. *ANSOM* B4, Walckenaer, *Histoire générale*, vol. 5, "Voyage de Goldberry en 1785, 1786, et 1787, et ses observations sur les contrées comprises entre le Cap Blanc et Sierre Leone," pp. 349, 454; *ANSOM* Soudan V Doss. 2, no. d, Marillier, "Expéditions militaires" (Bambuk, March 1894), pp. 2, 5, 8, 12, 13. Farther south in the Circle of Tuba (Guinea), the collateral was also observed in private inheritance (*ANMK* 1D 173 C1, "Notice ethnographique et historique de Séguela" [Seguela, 31 May 1900], p. 2; *ANMK* 1D 175 C1, "Rapport ethnographique et historique de la Circonscription de Touba, 1900" [Tuba, 7 June 1900], pp. 8–9).

founder). Or, he could be a father-brother's son (i.e., patrilineal nephew of the deceased or deposed ruler), the successor in each case ruling in *his own* lineage right. Thus, depending on the number of eligible lineages, incumbents could be drawn from several brother-lineages, while at other times, any suitable elder of a ruling patrilineage could be an appropriate choice given the circumstances. The rule of one brother and not another could decisively shift the locus of power from one branch of the family to another. Hence the power struggles, as Wa Kamissoko observed: Not infrequently, rivals opportunistically sold a brother into slavery. Given the deadly stakes, it is hardly surprising that "mothers" also competed on behalf of ambitious "sons"[39]

Other variations persisted in the collateral calculus. For example, in some instances a brother's age was symbolically computed, in that on becoming a "father," or the "father of fathers," a chronologically younger "brother" became a metaphorical or political "father." Not surprisingly, the Islamic principle of direct patrilineal succession likewise introduced other variations, especially in families where one branch was "animist" and collateral, and the other Islamized and following the direct succession. Ultimately, as with the *faamaya*, the uterine (*balimaya*) inheritance operated exactly as it did on the domestic level, with sons inheriting material wealth from mothers, giving rise to further power struggles endemic in household and state relationships.[40]

The French eventually altering the Mande style of succession, it is worth noting that between 1883 and 1958, when only French approved Niare chiefs were appointed, incumbents were chosen more for their compliance than for collateral lineage filiations. At the same time, although deprived of the right to determine foreign policy, somewhat ironically, Niare elders exercised greater *internal* power as "native chiefs" within the colonial construct than they had at any other time in their known dynastic past. In fact it was only after October 1898, when colonial circles were recreated and Niare canton chiefs appointed according to French signs of governance, that the elaboration of "Niare chiefly power" extended be-

---

39. Camara, "Le Manden," p. 64.

40. Diabaté, "Kankou Moussa," pp. 31–32; Camara, "Le Manden," pp. 62, 72; *ANSOM* B4, Walckenaer, *Histoire générale*, vol. 5, "Voyage de Goldberry," pp. 349, 454; *ANSOM* Soudan V Doss. 2 no. d. Marillier, "Expéditions militaires" (Bambuk, March 1894), pp. 7, 9, 12, 13. If traces of the collateral succession were unclear among those in public office, it seemed to have worked better among private inheritors (*ANMK* 1D 32 2, G. Mary, "Précis historique" [Bafulabe, 1 Nov. 1890], p. 3).

yond Bamako city for the first time. Niare power-range and leverage had
been hitherto restricted by familial contours and constitutional protocols.[41] Images of Niare chiefly power vested in Jamusadia's lineage survived officially until 1958 when, with Amadu Kumba Niare, the last internal incumbent, the office was abolished. Theoretically, his private internal
powers remained unchanged until his demise in 1964.

Part 2: Spatial Organization in the Core-State:
Consanguinity as an Expression of Political Relationships

Second, if the Mande style of governance had shaped both the organization and operation of the collateral succession in the *kafu-tigi*'s office, it
also choreographed the spatial organization of family members in relation
to the core-state. Not that space was diagramatically or graphically designed; it was not. Rather, it was that since consanguinity was an expression of political relationships, blood and family ties *were* important when
determining spatial lineage-locations. In other words, the ratio of political
status to kin-group ties was expressed as a spatial calculus. Accordingly,
the closer the blood alliance with core-state families, the closer-in spatial-
ly was the lineage-location, together with its corresponding political identity and entitlements. Therefore, not surprisingly, located closest to Niare
families of the core-state were the Sumbala, or slave families: Slaves were
not only Segu's state property—creating surplus value for the metropole—but slave women were also the basis for Niare lineage elaboration
(see Chapter 1).

Internal workings within these slave-family villages are not well
known, although it is clear—according to the Mande style—that each was
under the aegis of a *faama*-approved *dugu-tigi*, and that land tenure laws
were oftentimes shaped more by the numbers of slaves owned (Niare
slaves in this case), than by free lineage relationships. Neither can we be
certain of Sumbala-village nomenclature and/or locations—so conflicting
are both the oral and written texts—although Niare slave families have
been associated with Gringume, Kuluniko and Minkungu on the Manding Plateau, as well as Lasa, and Dogodima on the eastern slopes of the
Manding Mountains.[42] Particularly important from our perspective are

---

41. Anon., "Chronique historique," pp. 64–65. In May 1908, when Bamako
became the seat of the French Sudan under Governor Clozel, it was the administrative center of twenty-two civil circles, and a vast military territory of thirteen
Circles.

42. Verifying names and locating the twenty or thirty-something *kafu* villages
has proven problematic, as sources provide considerable variation. For various

the Niare *jamuw*, or patronyms, still found in Minkungu, associated with families of an otherwise obscure identity.[43] Subject to the Niare *kafu-tigiw* and other chiefly incumbents prior to 1883, the extent to which the French altered the Niare-Sumbala spatial organization and governance in the late nineteenth century, remains unclear, although we know that residences were razed to make way for the Kayes to Bamako railway at the turn of the century. That Niare chiefly authority continued to operate in the Sumbala villages in one form or another until 1958 seems likely, especially since Sumbala villages had formed an important branch of the families' labor force prior to 1883.

Part 3: Spatial Organization Between the Core-State and the Periphery

Third, balancing the core-state—in accordance with the Mande style and its political elaboration—were alliances and relationships extending from the center state to the periphery, where spatial positioning was once again determined by consanguineous, affinal, and filial relationships, political alliances accordingly defined. Therefore, following the familial paradigm, those closest to the Bamako core-state and slave villages were descendants of Jamusadia's, Delbafa's, and Seribadia's patrilineages establishing their own semiautonomous village-households. While only Jamusadia's lineage was eligible for the *faamaya*, or state chieftaincy, both Jamusadia's and Delbafa's descent lines were exempt from the *disongo*. Seribadia's line, excluded from the *faamaya*, but still entitled to advisory and deliberative status, was liable for the *disongo*.[44] Historically actualized

lists of villages, see Anon., "Chronique historique," pp. 63–65; *ASAOF* 1G 52 46, Bayol, "Mission de Ségou" (Saint Louis, 5 July 1880), p. 12; Soumaoro, "Etude," pp. 10–11; *ANSOM* Sén. et Dép. IV Doss. 90 Bis, Capt. Fortin, "Rapport sommaire sur les opérations exécutées par la colonne de la Gambie, pendant la campagne contre le marabout Mahmadou Lamine" (Senudebu, 6 Jan. 1888); *ANSOM* Sén. et Dép., IV 90 Bis, Vallière, "Mémoire" (Siguiri, 15–25 March 1888), pp. 38–39. According to Amadu Kumba, Gringume was founded by Seribadia (Meillassoux, "Histoire," pp. 191, 195). According to Paques, it was founded by Seribadia's sons Bemba and Delbafa (Pâques, "L'Estrade royale," p. 1644). See also Gallieni, *Voyage*, pp. 594–595.

43. Personal communication, Mamadou Sarr (Bamako, 5 Jan. 1980; 6 Nov. 1982).

44. The *disongo* was a tribute paid by political entities incorporated into larger states. Determining the exact *disongo* is unlikely as quantities varied regionally, and from one period to the next: It could have varied from the equivalent of 200 to 40,000 cowries. *Disongo*, usually remitted by each family head, was often paid in slaves, gold, cloth, and horses; later *disongo* came to include cowries. So common

villages within this first degree of political, spatial, and consanguineous relatedness—that is, those established by Jamusadia's immediate descendants—were the founding villages at Mankono, Donfara, Meke-Sikoro, and N'Tuba, according to some sources. Delbafa's brother-lineage founded seven other settlements at N'Gomi, Sirakoro, Banambani, Sorokolo, Turodo, Donegebugu and Wagudu-Sikoro on the eastern fringes of the Beledugu.[45] Because the process affected the res publica, even among these semiautonomous villages the appointment of local officials required the *kafu-tigi*'s approval.

Situated farther out on the *kafu*'s periphery, expressing a certain political and affective remoteness, was another "layer" of semiautonomous villages comprising mainly political refugees. Originally established by eighteenth-century Kulibaly refugees fleeing the Ngolo Jara power seizure at Segu sometime after 1766, by the nineteenth century, peripheral lineage-locations were providing asylum for refugees from the Umarian and Samorian wars. Reversing the earlier patron-client power relationship, the Segu Kulibaly were now within Bamako's jurisdiction.[46] In establishing a residential presence, the Kulibaly were fully within their rights. Conjugating their *siyah-nyogo*, or alliance status, with the Niare (we recall according to the Niare-Meillassoux version of the Wagadu Legend, that Jamusadia Niare married Sumba Kulibaly: see Chapter 1) the Kulibaly families accordingly, established seven villages on the outer periphery in the Grand Beledugu, at Jago, Joko, Fanafiekoro, Safo, Sogolobugu, Dabani and Donyumana. Segovian Kulibaly refugees were later joined by subbranches of the Traore, Jara, and Konate families. As a function of their political, lineage and affective "remoteness," these semiautonomous villages on the state's outer periphery, including the Kulibaly *siyah-nyogow*, were liable for the *disongo*.[47] And although still within Bamako's political sphere of influence, it is worth noting that peri-

---

was this levy that by the nineteenth century *disongo* became a synonym for all taxable commodities, even in situations where taxes were not liable, such as market exchanges where cowries facilitated monetary flows. *Disongo* was sometimes based on the *talikise*, a gold-based unit of account: 1 *talikise* (grains from the "bois rouge": *Erythrophloeum guineense*) was valued at one gram of gold, or 400 cowries. For local purchases, 6 *talikisew* were worth 1 *minkalli* (a weight); 1 *talikise* could buy a chicken, 3 a sheep, 6 a bullock etc. Poor villages paid the *disongo* according to their resources. Konaté, "Monographie," p. 40; Park, *The Travels*, p. 234.

45. Localizing some of these villages has not been possible.

46. Several Segu Coulibaly families still reside in the Kulikoro and Bamako regions (Interview Ba Moussa Coulibaly [Mansala, 6 May 1983]).

47. Meillassoux, "Histoire," pp. 196–197.

pheral villages were more exposed to cultural borrowings—from the neighboring Segu, Beledugu, and Maraka states—than from the Bamako core-state.

Part 4: Political Appointments Are Binding Moral Commitments

Finally, because core-state villages were either family-based or linked through sacred alliances, meaning in political appointments and processes went well beyond contract "professionalism." Political appointments were instead binding moral commitments based on lineage relationships, obligation, and reciprocity, sometimes redistribution. Thus avoiding the land-holding equation—which would have defined a vertical land-based relationship closer to the Sunjata paradigm established at Kurugan Fugan (c. 1234)—interactions based on kin-group and sacred alliances allowed for a greater internal-horizontal discourse within the political process. Vertical hierarchical orders within the system therefore hardly prevailed. Farther out on the periphery—among the Kulibaly, Jara, and Traore families of the Grand Beledugu—where kin-group and sacred alliances with core-state families were less intense and probably not so complex, residents retained a greater internal autonomy, especially during the Umarian and Samorian campaigns when war stresses loosened the *kafu-tigi*'s political hold on the state's periphery. Here, where lineage ties were less dense, and ritual oathing lacking the same intensity, a modified hierarchical order did prevail: Relationships were more temporal embodying a certain patron-client and land-related implication, although this was not at all secular and not overtly hierarchical. Moreover, given the density of sacerdotal relationships within Mande cultures, internal affiliations and belief systems, it was generally believed that land relationships were shaped more by the sacred and the ritual than by the secular political-power discourse.[48]

Thus, avoiding political elaborations resembling those of Segu's *jon* war-based state, or of Sunjata's old Mali realm for that matter—with its hierarchical land-related organization as expressed in some versions of the Sunjata epic—Bamako's political identity elaborated its own version of the Mande style. It might be of interest to note that in accordance with the *civitas in parvo* considerations, additional legal provisions were made for the *dunan* (stranger) in much the same way as the Romans had made room for the *externus*, the *aliengena*, the *hostis*, and the *barbarus*.

---

48. Interview Marabout Touré (Bozola-Bamako, 5 Jan. 1980); interview Suleyman Dravé (Bamako, 5–6 Jan. 1980).

In effect the Bamako state, a variation on hundreds found throughout the Mande-hinterland, was an integrated web of multiple power centers. Governance was based on overlapping family relationships, and/or associational bonds, wherein each *dugu-tigi*, or incumbent in his own power-center, exercised a semiautonomy in relation to the core-state. Overlapping, interconnected, and permanently articulating relationships often intersected at the point where the same groups—many consanguineous—were intergenerationally interdependent for a wide variety of permanent obligations, social mobilizations and observances, such as cults and mythical-political rituals, labor units, funerals, marriages, baptisms, and fetes to celebrate the harvest. Bound, moreover, by reciprocal ritual alliances that were also permanent, many family members were simultaneously separated by equally enduring prohibitions, especially in cases where relationships were close, frequent, and patterned, and where conflictual distortions could easily enflame potentially tense situations. For example, the violation of an oathed *tana*, instead of respect, could create internal conflict between groups that were otherwise permanently allied. So could hostility within the *senankun* that exceeded the delicate fulcrum between hostility and friendship; or *siyah* obligations that were more burdensome than reciprocal; or deteriorating marriage alliances between powerful families. Moreover, conflict under certain circumstances—involving for example "stranger" brides, defiant youths, and adultery or incest within the family—could likewise give rise to internal conflict requiring ritual cleansing before the status quo ante could be restored.

However, despite real potentials for societal conflict, a moral commitment to the maintenance of law and order—as guarantors of the Mande identity—were expected to prevail. And while Bamako's residents acknowledged Segu's Faama as metropolitan overlord, within the *kafu* similar constraints were likewise intended to prevail within a community where hierarchical considerations were operative only in relation to the core-state and its outer periphery. That the authority of Bamako's *dugu-tigiw* was only restricted by the *kafu-tigi*'s ratification of their appointments, was more a managerial policy than a political power-play, and certainly not an overarching authority or control. That local surplus value (i.e., agricultural yields, *disongo*, tribute etc.) and labor obligations were regularly owed to the core-state, was more a revenue and redistributive device to enhance state maintenance and stability, than an extractive or exploitative governance, although the potential for chiefly abuse was ever present. Above all, despite this constitutional balance of power and authority between the core-state and the multiple semiautonomous power-centers, the *kafu-tigi*'s overall authority and sacred chieftaincy was expected to prevail, in theory at any rate.

State Maintenance and Social Mobilization

The Family

As a multicentric and semiautonomous state in the Mande style surviving for more than 150 years on the elaborated Segovian periphery, the *kafu*'s identity was maintained and renewed primarily through internal mobilization, including preparations for war. During later decades offensive warfare most often gave way to defensive strategies including flight.[49]

As might be expected, the *kafu*'s internal mobilization relied almost exclusively on families, their internal organization and alliances with differentiated collectivities, reminiscent of Tellier's observation that the state's "political organization derived naturally from that of the family,"[50] and of Brevie's comment that the family was "the pivot of Sudanese societies, the center of all organization."[51] Specialized lineages, age cohorts, gender units, and their prearranged divisions of labor were the keys to social mobilization. When combined with the familial/state tri-partite organization—likewise organized accordingly to pre-selected divisions of labor—operationalizing *kafu* residents required only an occasion, such as war, raids, the hunt, fishing, or herding enterprises that mobilized action, in theory at any rate. More importantly, social mobilization was generated from *within* respective organizational sectors, each with its labor unit, work ethic, and gendered and operational identity. The *kafu*'s "400 Sumbala" slave units, for example, were mobilized from within for intensive agriculture. Within easy access to lineage fields, they worked their masters' fields, as well as the *kafu-tigiws*', trading surpluses on domestic markets. The Sumbala, in addition, performed other functions, maintaining routes, repairing the *tata* and *jin* walls or those of private residences after the wet season.[52] Not just the Sumbala, but also slaves of other free families, such as the Jara, the Kulibaly, Traore, and Kone, as well as those of the Ture and the Drave (these latter two large slaveholders), were mobilized for similar operations at their masters' behest. Like the Niare slaves, Ture and Drave agricultural slaves worked the land in their masters' names.

49. *ANSOM* Sén. et Dép., IV Doss. 90 Bis, Vallière,"Mémoire" (Siguiri, 15–25 March 1888), p. 37; *ANMK* 1D 33 2, Collomb, "Notice" (Bamako, 1884–1885), p. 3.

50. Tellier, *Autour de Kita*, pp. 17, 82–95.

51. *ASAOF* 1G 299, Brévié, "Monographie" (Bamako, 25 April 1904), pp. 22–36.

52. Gallieni, *Voyage*, p. 245. Paques mentioned three walls, one outer and inner, borne out by other evidence; she claims that the site of the old *tata* has been kept secret because of gravesites within its walls (Pâques, "L'Estrade royale," pp. 1645, 1654); *ASAOF* 1G 50 49, "Lettre Piétri à Gallieni" (Bamako, 9 May 1880), p. 3.

Slaves were also mobilized for herding and commerce, suggesting the development of specialized organizations with an organized labor force.[53] When warring or raiding, mainly on Segu's behalf during the *kafu's* founding era, both *tonjonw* and Sumbala were accordingly mobilized. *Kafu horonw*, or free men, likewise operationalized in discrete groups, performed similar work depending on need, filiations, and local exigencies. Ineligible for public political representation, women were also permanently mobilized into labor units where, producing food and other domestic commodities for household consumption, they exchanged surpluses in domestic and foreign markets.[54]

Beyond the tri-partite corporate groups, but still within the familial community, were the *kafu's* clients, likewise preexisting identity units mobilized in the interest of state maintenance and renewal. I am referring here specifically to the Surakaw, the Bozo, and the Jawambe lineages—as well as the various resident *dunanw* or trading "strangers"—all of whom espoused an Islamized and a specialized identity. All attached to *kafu* patrons, mainly *horonw* lineages, patron-client bonds were most often realized through ritual oathing and/or blood and marriage alliances. Also participants in the mobilization process—and similarly beyond the ruling tri-partite paradigm—were refugee families fleeing the Ngolo Jara at Segu (after 1766), as well as from the Umarian and Samorian wars.

Powerful Ritual Alliances

But if families, age cohorts, specialized lineages, and gender groups were the principal focus for internal state mobilization, operationalizing units on an even deeper cultural level were the powerful rituals galvanizing entire societies from within. Perhaps it can even be said that ritualization was the engine driving both societal and state mobilization. Of all alliances consolidated through ritualization, marriage proved the most comprehensive, dynamic, and reliable for state maintenance and renewal. When historicized, marriage alliances and associated obligations, including reciprocal exchanges and redistributive processes, could be sequentially negotiated from one generation to the next. Historicized marriage alliances, including provisions for brides from preselected

---

53. Interview Suleyman Dravé (Bamako, 7 Jan. 1980). Slave labor remained officially in force until 1904 when, by the colonial decree, captives in French West Africa were freed (Richard Roberts and Martin Klein, "The Banamba slave exodus of 1905 and the decline of the western Sudan," *JAH*, vol. 21, 3 [1980]: 375–394).

54. Interview Suleyman Dravé (Bamako, 9 Jan. 1980).

groups, could also operationalize stable power alliances, as important for long-term internal mobilization as for the state's historical elaboration and survival. As noted earlier above, Niare-Kulibaly marriage alliances provided the ritual and historical basis for the Bamako state formation, maintenance, and renewal in the first place. Later, marriage alliances institutionalized between the Niare-Ture-Drave families reproduced the system of obligations and reciprocities, as indeed did subsequent alliances between *kafu horon* and Bozo families, on the one hand, and similar combinations with slave lineages on the other. For example, while the Niare, it is said, developed intergenerational marriage alliances with Bozo and Niare slave lineages, the Drave, established similar slave-free affiliations. Expressed otherwise: Without the obligations and reciprocities inherent within marriage alliances, mobilizing families in the first place would have been difficult, perhaps even impossible, given the small body of autonomous state law existing independently of families and familial law.

Also important as the modus operandi of social mobilization from within were the *siyah* and *senankun* ritual alliances, bonding groups and individuals on an intergenerational basis. Where ritual alliances overlapped with state power, they became the engines of internal state mobilization in the interest of the res publica. The *siyah*, or blood oath sworn over the *numuw*'s sacred anvil, mobilized *siyah-nyogow* (paired groups) to reciprocal action on each other's behalf. *Siyah-nyogow* were expected, for instance, to reciprocate loyalty and responsibilities, and to acknowledge shared obligations and rituals, including the exchange of brides (e.g., the Niare-Kulibaly *siyah-nyogo* relationships). Or, the *senankun*, mobilizing participants at a fixed point in "normal" relationships, required participants to strengthen interclan articulations (especially when internal conflicts threatened), while attending to reciprocal and obligatory commitments, including regular labor exchanges.[55]

Additional and reciprocal obligatory modes mobilized both public and private morality in the interest of property preservation and an obligatory presence at familial ceremonies such as baptisms, rites of passage, weddings, and burials. Some *senankunw* called for self-abnegation, others a blood brotherhood forswearing war between old enemies, still others triggering political and diplomatic relationships. Strengthened by the *senankukun*, according to Amadu Kumba Niare, the ritual motivated Bamako's participants to regulate hereditary rights in minors and property

---

55. For more on the *siyah*, see Chapter 1, and note 19; for the *senankun*, see Chapter 1, and notes 19, for the *tana*, see Chapter 1, and notes 38 and 88, 95.

in accordance with tradition, and under specially prearranged circumstances.[56] Mentioned in the Sunjata epic, we learned that at Kurugan Fugan the Tunkara and the Sisse became *senankun*, or "banter brothers," of the Keita. Sharing the same bonds were the Jara and Traore, the Kuyate, Keita, Kaba, and a range of *garanke* families with the *Sylla, Jawara, Makalu* and *Simaga* patronyms. Beyond Bamako in the Segu and Massina regions Pageard found that not only was the *senankun* observed among the Keita, the Konate, the Ture, and the Tangara, but the ritualized oath likewise existed among several Bamana, Fulbe, Somono, Bozo, Minianka, Songhay, and Mosse families. As mentioned above, the frequency of *senankunw* between Mande *numuw* and the Fulbe in the Mande-hinterland is striking. Finally, there was the *tana*, a ritual prohibition, already discussed above. Handed down at Kurugan Fugan, according to legend, the *tana* mobilized participants to protect the *tana* or prohibition of a "brother" clan or individual. In practice, the *tana* also limited conflict between families: As a taboo, it discouraged harmful reciprocal relations. The prohibition, on the other hand, could also apply to the self: Under certain circumstances a subject eschewed objects and animals harmful to his or her dignity and/or destiny.[57]

Likewise mobilizing the community from within was Islam, which, by strengthening the ritual oathing, reinforced the call to social mobilization in both public and private endeavors. On the public level, despite differences on matters affecting diplomacy and foreign affairs, Niare chiefs in particular mobilized the writing skills and science of the Islamized community in the interest of the res publica. On private levels within their own *kabilaw*, or urban quarters, Islamized communities mobilized their families internally for other forms of collective pursuits, including labor contributions in the interest of the whole, and institution building. They traded extensively, for example, enriching and diversifying the community, while attracting "stranger" co-religionists participating in similar mercantile enterprises. Maintaining the Islamic Law, Koranic schools, courts, and mosques, of which there were nine in the *kafu* (two in Kulikoro and twenty in Banamba), Islamized families were

---

56. Fieldwork (Bamako, 5–9 Jan. 1980; 25 Oct. 1982); (Kangaba, 5–6 Feb. 1982); (Banamba, 28 Feb. 1992); Meillassoux, "Histoire," p. 199, see esp. note 3.

57. Delafosse, *Haut-Sénégal-Niger*, vol. 1, p. 285; vol. 3, pp. 101, 106, 107–109, 151, 162–163, 171–172, 178–182; Tamari, "The Sunjata epic," (St. Louis, 26 Nov. 1991). See also Pageard, "Notes sur les rapports de 'Senankouya'," pp. 123–141; McNaughton, *The Mande*, see esp. pp. 11–12; Labouret, "Les Manding," pp. 100–101, 104; Niane, *Sundiata*, p. 78; Person, *Samori*, vol 1, p. 79. See also herein note 55.

also textile producers, some even serving as silversmiths with the aid of slaves, many of the latter *wolosow*. Given the Mande tri-partite social order, it is important to remember that Islamized smiths (i.e., "Moors") were not *nyamakalaw*.[58]

Also mobilized by the sacred oathing, and responding to an Islamized mobilization, were the river nomads who served terrestrial lords. Usually enjoying more cordial relationships with "animists" than land-bound Muslims, the Jire in particular, a Somono family, was introduced from the Segu region. Together with local Bozo counterparts, these riverfolk were singularly mobilized for state maintenance and renewal in a variety of ways. For example, providing fresh and dried fish, as well as a building-lime produced from the shells of crustaceans, above all river transport, inter alia, river nomads not only served the Bamako state but also, incidentally, the various polities from Jenne-Segu in the north to Siguiri-Kurusa in the south.[59] Organized since antiquity, no state-complex along the middle and upper Niger could mobilize resources without the labor and skills of these river nomads. Few in number (there were only about 400 Bozo on the river between Bamako and Siguiri in the latter part of the nineteenth century), Bamako's Niare and other free lineages, among them the Traore and Kulibaly, married their captives to the Jire, thereby expanding their lineage base, integrating them into those of the river nomads. By that same token, progeny of the Bozo-Sumbala unions, known as the Sinayogo or Sinaba Attiukuru Bozo, acknowledged the Niare Faamaw as their overlords.[60] Also enjoying more cordial relationships with "animist" lords were those of the Jawambe identity migrating, as they did from the Bangasi (Kita), the Massina, and the Futa Jallon in the eighteenth century, or from the Kaarta sometime during the nineteenth cen-

---

58. Generally speaking, Islamized smiths (i.e. "Moors") were not *nyamakalaw*. There were, however Mande smiths who were *nyamakalaw*, and who also observed Islamized rituals (as a personal preference?) (Béatrice Appia, "Les Forgerons du Fouta-Djallon," *JSA*, vol. 35 [1965]: 317–352; *ANMK* 4E 36, "Rapport sur l'Islam et les ... Musulmans, Cercle de Bamako" [1897–1911]; interview Suleyman Dravé [Bamako, 9 Jan. 1980]; interview Mamadou Sarr [Bamako, 4 Jan., 1980]).

59. Meillassoux, "Histoire," pp. 200–221.

60. *ANSOM* Sén. IV Doss. 90 Bis, Vallière, "Rapport sur l'organisation ... Mambi" (Kangaba, 5 March 1888), p. 6; *ANSOM* Sén. IV Doss. 90 Bis, Vallière, "Mémoire" (Siguiri, 15–25 March 1888), p. 46; personal communication Seydou Niaré (Bamako, 3 Jan. 1980); interview Marabout Touré (Bozola-Bamako, 5–6 Jan. 1980). See also *ANMK* 1D 33 2, Collomb, "Notice" (Bamako, 1884–1885), p 8. For a variation on this see Meillassoux, "Histoire," p. 200.

tury.[61] Just about every village in the *kafu* had at least one Jawando family mobilized for the care of community animals and the production of
dairy commodities, these latter either consumed domestically or exchanged for needed commodities. Finally, it should be pointed out that if
a quasi-hierarchical order existed between the Bamako core-state and its
most remote and semiautonomous periphery, a similar relationship between the *kafu-tigi* and Islamized strangers also prevailed, although such
inequalities were seldom reflected in public policy.

But however beneficial Muslims were to a state's internal mobilization,
we know that an Islamic presence could sometimes derail mobilization
processes, especially when conflicting corporate interests were at stake.
Serving the state, enriching and diversifying its material cultures and domestic ideologies—but legally excluded from public office—ambitious Muslims rarely eschewed power politics or political factionalism. With respect
to Bamako, their anti-Niare machinations during the Samorian wars nearly
brought the *kafu* to its knees; their later efforts facilitated the French arrival
on the Niger's banks. Fearing these "trojan horses," it is said that farther
west, the Mandinka of Bafulabe were Islam's "sworn enemies," while the
more radical Bambuhu residents could be relied upon to kill *their* Islamized
"intruders."[62] Beyond the Mande-hinterland, analogous problematics prevailed throughout the "animist" Mande world. Here, Muslims were accused of mobilizing conflict, depending on the circumstances. Conflict mobilization was even more widespread in the eastern Mande world (eastern
Côte d'Ivoire) among, for example, the "animist" Jomande and Camara
families who barely tolerated their Mande-Jula;[63] or among the "animist"
Pakhalla (or Kulango) and Lobiri, Wule, Birifor, and Dagari-speakers in the
Black Volta towns of Buna and Kong "burdened" with their Mande-Jula.
And it is said that among the Mossi of Wagadu, similar distortions in the
mobilization process had virtually paralyzed the Naba's (paramount chief)
administration by the late nineteenth and early twentieth centuries.[64]

---

61. *ASAOF* 1G 248, Pérignon, "Généralités" (1899–1900), pp. 233–235; *ANMK*
1D 38 3, Charles Monteil, "Etudes générales: Monographie des Cercles de Kita et
Ségou" (Kita, 1899–1900), pp. 233–235.

62. *ANMK* 1D 32 5, "Etude sur les marabouts" (Bafulabe, 5 July 1894), pp. 1–13;
ANSOM B4, Walckenaer, *Histoire*, vol. 5, "Voyage de Goldberry," pp. 446, 459.

63. Y. Person discusses some of these problems in *Samori*, vol. 1, pp. 215–216;
vol. 2 p. 807. See also *ASAOF* 15G 83, Ruault, "Généralités 1880 à 1920" (Bamako,
22 Feb. 1884), p. 11.

64. *ANMK* 1D 168, Lieut. Greigert, "Notice géographique et historique sur la
circonscription de Bouna, Cercle de Bondoukou" (Buna, 1902); *ANMK* 1D 5, "Notice sur la région sud, 1895–1899," pp. 38–39.

Bamako's Relationship with the Segovian Metropole

On turning to Bamako's relationship with Segu, we are already familiar with several aspects therein. As one of Segu's *cike-buguw*, or agricultural slave villages—where metropolitan *tonjonkun-tigiw* (*tonjon* chiefs) resided as "protectors" of Segu's interests and identity—it was said that wherever a Bamana traveled within the Segu state hegemony, a *tonjon* associate would be there to receive him, quite an achievement, really, given that Segu's overall land ratio may have been about 1,000,000 square kilometers) (see Maps 2 and 3).[65] We also already know that although the metropole never imposed Segovian political institutions on local jurisdictions, many Bamako residents eventually identified with Segu's mythical-political cult and the six great *jo* associations. Here, doctrines formulated on a cosmological and mythical epistemology integrated the *kafu*'s intellectual and spiritual universe.[66] Of particular interest: By regularly outmarrying females to regional chiefs, the Kulibaly—later the Jara Faamaw—employed brides as metropolitan spies, thereby further amplifying, reinforcing, and protecting Segu's peripheral state power and integrity. Conceivably, brides exchanged between Bamako and Segu, according to the Niare-Meillassoux text, could therefore have been Segu's "women in Bamako" assuring chiefly loyalties to the metropolitan identity. Segovian *tonjonkun-tigiw* had probably been resident since about 1755 in each of Segu's sixty provinces, their number varying according to the metropole's political fortunes. Conversely, provincial officials residing at Segu were thought to be "hostages" to the sacred alliances aimed at preserving a Bamana identity. Segu's representatives, accordingly, reviewed policy implementations, especially the collection of taxes, the *disongo*, and the raising of armies and militia.[67] All adults—some Niare village chiefs

---

65. At its apogee, Segu's realm extended from Bure to Wahiguya in Burkina Faso, and from Odienne and Tengrela in the Cote d'Ivoire, to Timbuktu. See Monteil, *Les Bambara*, pp. 296–298. For Bamako's local *tonjonw* and other miscellaneous information, see *ASAOF* 1G 248, Pérignon, "Monographie" (1899–1900), p. 239; *ANMK* 1D 33 2, Collomb, "Notice" (Bamako, 1884–1885), pp. 2-3; *ASAOF* 1G 52 46, Bayol, "Mission de Ségou" (Saint Louis, 5 July 1880), p. 9; *ASAOF* 1G 50 20, "Lettre Gallieni à Gouverneur" (Nango, 7 July 1880), pp. 18–21; Konaté, "Monographie," p. 42.

66. Paulme, "Bambara," pp. 58–60, see also pp. 21–22.

67. Interview Ismael Fane (Tesserela, 25 March 1975); see also interview Koke Coulibaly (Segu, March 21 1975), in Ward, "The French-Bambara," pp. 33, 61, note 35. After the Niare-Kulibaly marriage, Bamako observed close ties with Segu and the Beledugu chiefs (*ANMK* 1D 33 2, Collomb, "Notice" [Bamako, 1884–1885], p. 2). Later, Umarian slaves were stationed in some Bamana precincts as a precaution

excluded—paid the *disongo*, refusal to pay a punishable offense. While not required to intervene in local affairs, Segu's *tonjonkun-tigiw* were nonetheless expected to advance metropolitan considerations, even to influence the appointment of the "king's men" as local officials.[68] A Segovian *kele-tigi*, or war chief, was also resident in Bamako—as indeed were counterparts residing elsewhere in the Segovian war-state—where, it is said, the *kele-tigiw* numbered thirty-five, corresponding to military jurisdictional variables. Depending on the role-play, some *kele-tigiw* apparently exercised considerable powers, including power over life and death under certain circumstances. All were supposedly accountable to regional administrators of which there were five, Biton's sons the first incumbents in this elaborated Segovian state structure. And while armies were voluntarily recruited in peacetime, the *levee en masse* prevailed during war, recruits identified by the two-pointed bonnet worn by Biton's men.[69] As Segu's gateway to the Mande, Bamako identified with the metropole's war aims during the *kafu*'s early years. Reasonably secure behind the city's outer wall (measuring about 1,700 meters in circumference, 3–4 meters high, and 2 meters thick)[70] during these early decades, Bamako's residents were subject to the discipline of expansionist wars, raiding the neighboring Solokono Jara families of Nyamina, of Megueta, of Guemene in the Beledugu, and of Murdia. In further carrying out metropolitan intentions, Bamako's *tonjonw* and *sofaw* (armed cavalry) extended Segu's wars into the old Mande, as far south as Kurusa in Guinea, bringing the entire region, including Worodugu (kola nut forests) under Segu's tributary (*disongo*) hegemony (see Maps 2 and 3).[71] With Bamako's help during these early

---

against revolt (*ASAOF* 1G 83, "Mission Caron à Tombouctou, 1887–1895" [Aboard the *Niger*, 31 Oct. 1887], p. 32.

68. Monteil, *Les Bambara*, pp. 296–298. See also *ASAOF* 1G 248, Pérignon, "Monographie" (1899–1900), p. 239; *ANMK* 1D 33 2, Collomb, "Notice" (Bamako, 1884–1885), pp. 2–3; *ASAOF* 1G 52 46, Bayol, "Mission de Ségou" (Saint Louis, 5 July 1880), p. 9; *ASAOF* 1G 50 20, "Lettre Gallieni à Gouverneur" (Nango, 7 July 1880), pp. 18–21; Konaté, "Monographie, p. 42.

69. For Bamako's *kele-tigi* see Meillassoux, "Histoire," p. 206; Konaté, "Monographie," pp. 43–45; Gray and Dochard, *Travels in western Africa*, pp. 354–355, 346.

70. According to another source, the wall was 4.5 meters high (Touré, "L'Amenagement," p. 4; *ASAOF* 1G 50 49, "Lettre Piétri à Gallieni" [Bamako, 9 May 1880], p. 3). See also Chapter 2, note 2.

71. For *disongo*, see note 44. While the Bamako *faamaya* apparently kept some tribute for maintenance of the *sofaw* (e.g., from Mpiebugu, Nafaji, Kati, Dugabugu), other *disongo* (e.g., from the Mande) was shared between Bamako, Segu (a third), and Murdia (interview Marabout Touré [Bozola-Bamako, 4 Jan.

decades, Segovian authority was also extended to Dugabuga and the Jara villages of Mpiebugu and Kati, both brought under the *kafu*'s tributary jurisdiction. Other settlements incorporated through this early warfare included the Traore villages of Bla and Kurale, as well as the Fulbe Jakite polity of Samanyana in the northern Mande. According to some reports, Bamako was assisted in its struggle against Samanyana by the Beledugu warrior chiefs of Kolokani (Traore and Kulibaly), Massantolo, Jiji, and Nossombugu (Konare). Possessed of an armed militia under the ad hoc leadership of the *kele-tigi*, and the *muru-tigi* ("master of the sword") according to the Niare-Meillassoux text, Bamako's armed forces were also swelled by *dosonkew* (warrior-hunters).[72] Armed with bows (*kalaw*) and arrows (*bienw*) as well as knives and lances, firearms perhaps blunderbusses and single-barreled guns were either bought from the British at Banjul and Saint Louis or they were locally produced. Guns, locally manufactured on a large enough scale, were also used in defensive and offensive wars. Together with Bamako's young men, most Mande-hinterland youths also participated in Segu's early wars.[73]

On further historicizing the data, we know that with the defeat of the Segovian state by the Umarians in 1861, southern Mande-hinterland states—the Bamako and Beledugu *kafuw* included—technically became clients of the Umarian state hegemony subject, in some instances, to an Umarian state presence.[74] Not for long, however, because within two years the Beledugu and the southern Mande-hinterland were wresting their autonomy from their new Umarian overlords, within less than twenty years, from the Samorian state. Before long, thousands of refugees from Segu the Beledugu the Mande, and the Niger's east and west banks had joined the *kafu*'s community.

Finally, it is worth repeating that as a regional superpower, Segu used war to negotiate the Mande-hinterland's local and regional identities. I mentioned elsewhere (see Introduction) that Segovian wars—

1980]; Meillassoux, "Histoires," pp. 193–196, 203-207, 215–218). See also *ASAOF* 1G 248, Pérignon, "Monographie" (1899–1890), p. 239; *ASAOF* 1G 52 46, Bayol, "Mission de Ségou" (Saint Louis, 5 July 1880), p. 9; *ASAOF* 1G 50 20, "Lettre Gallieni à Gouverneur" (Nango, 7 July 1880), pp. 18–21; *ANMK* 1D 33 2, Collomb, "Notice" (Bamako, 1884–1885), pp. 2–3.

72. Ward, "The French-Bambara," p. 74, note 88; Meillassoux, "Histoire," pp. 93, 205–206.

73. Interview Marabout Touré (Bozola-Bamako, 4 Jan. 1980); interview Bu Traore (Segu, 27 Nov. 1974); interview Koke Coulibaly (Segu, 21 March 1975), in Ward, "The French-Bambara," pp. 33–34.

74. *ASAOF* 1G 52 46, Bayol, "Mission de Ségou" (Saint Louis, 5 July 1880).

calling for long absences from home spent in professional armed forces subject to metropolitan ideologies, military disciplines and cultures— had accelerated the Bamanization of the region's youth. Now, we acknowledge that Segu's wars and tribute policies provided a further acceleration of the Bamanization process, especially in the south. For example, between the 1720s and 1850s, Segu launched no less than about eight military expeditions toward the south, mostly against Samanyana, the Beledugu, the Mande, Wassulu, Fuladugu, and Bure regions, according to oral texts (see Maps 2 and 3). Many seemed to have been tax and tribute-raising ventures: Segu evidently took tax and tribute-collecting seriously.[75] More specifically, according to one account, during the late eighteenth or the early nineteenth century, Monzon Jara, the Segu incumbent (c. 1787–c. 1808), ravaged west and south in the Mande-hinterland to within seven-days' journey northwest of Bamako. We know from Park (1796) that Monzon's wars in the Kaarta and Wassulu "harvested" large slave contingents, as much as 900 in one day.[76] According to other traditions, the old Mande town of Samanyana became a target of more than one attack—one apparently in the late eighteenth century during the *faamaya* of Ngolo Jara (1766–1790)— when Samanyana Bassy, the chiefly incumbent, was refusing to pay taxes.[77] A second expedition may have been launched sometime later by Da Jara (1808-1827), poor Bassy liable for another tax offense. The message could hardly have been lost on Bamako's residents, especially since the expedition reportedly passed on the east bank in what is now Badalabugu, in full view of *kafu* citizens.[78] By the nineteenth century, several neighboring regions (the Beledugu, Nyamina, Kulikoro, Banamba, Wassulu, the Mande, the Bambuhu-Bure gold fields, and Fuladugu), had all at one time or another felt the sting of Segu's sword, or they had been drawn into the metropole's tax or tribute and cultural range, or plundered for non-compliance and other liabilities (see Maps 2 and 3).

---

75. Segu apparently took tax collecting seriously, but apparently not excessively (*ASAOF* 1G 299, Brévié, "Monographie" [Bamako, 25 April 1904], pp. 33–34). See also Konaté, "Monographie, pp. 42–43.

76. Park, *The Travels*, pp. 194, 196–197, 222, and passim; see also Konaté, "Monographie," p. 30; Tauxier, *Histoire*, p. 9.

77. Personal communication Mamadou Sarr (Bamako, 4 Jan. 1980; 16 Dec. 1882); Leynaud and Cissé, *Paysans malinké*, pp. 22, 33, and note 26.

78. Dominique Traoré, "Samaniana Bassi," *NA*, 34 (April 1947): 1–3; personal communication Mamadou Sarr (Bamako, 5 Jan. 1980; 6 Nov. 1882).

While war and tax/tribute policies became the modus operandi for the Mande-hinterland's Bamanization, additional processes included forced labor, public humiliations and floggings, and hostage taking, not to mention the fear of death.[79] By the latter part of the nineteenth century, however, after decades of Segu's wars, its considerable resources and enormously effective military machine had been virtually exhausted. As Binger later observed, reliance on wars, raids and slave populations hardly augured well for state maintenance and renewal, as neither provided infrastructures, nor viable political institutions, nor corresponding political economies.[80]

Yet, if state resources had been depleted in pursuit of war aims, among the long-term consequences of Segu's war games was a diffusion of the Segovian markers or signs: the Bamana language and its patronyms; Segu's mythical-political rituals; oathing alliances; power associations; cults; and the domestication and particularizing of Segovian oral epics and traditions. Also diffused and elaborated was Segu's commercial system, its operational mode and market networks extending from desert-side marts in the north to the Mande, Wassulu, and Worodugu, the south's exchange-centers. Trading networks even extended beyond to the European enclaves in the Sierra Leone and Guinea regions (see Chapter 4). Likewise, Segu's east-west commercial systems included markets reaching from Senegambian marts in the west, to Kankan and points east in Guinea. And if metropolitan governmental forms and organization were never diffused on quite the same scale, it was because Segu's imperial authority was indivisible. Accordingly, while the Segovian political presence was officially marked by metropolitan representatives (including spy-brides), and provincial institutions bore signs of the metropole, balansan, or acacia, trees opening across the land unambiguously signified that this was Segu's imperium.

---

79. Interview Marabout Touré (Bozola-Bamako, 6 Jan. 1980); Konaté, "Monographie," pp. 42–44. In the last analysis Segu evidently had a great deal to show for its energetic wars and tax policies: By the 1860s it is said that its rulers had amassed more than 20 million francs in gold ores. Small wonder that on two separate occasions (c. 1720s) Segu was obliged to defend its integrity against the Kong Wattara chief laying siege to Biton's capital. See *ASAOF* 1G 32, "Mage à Gouverneur" (Saint Louis, 21 June 1866); Tauxier, *Histoire*, pp. 8, 30–36, 101–102; Konaté, "Monographie," pp. 5–8, 16–17, 19–21, 33 and passim.

80. *ANMAE, 1890–1894*, vol. 123, Binger, "Le Soudan français, 'Le Temps'" (Paris, 1890), pp. 68–69.

Conclusion: Bamako a
Minimalist and Semiautonomous State

First, on the basis of this discourse, it seems clear that the Bamako *kafu*—indeed most states in the Mande-hinterland, and especially in the Bambuhu and Bure regions—were minimalist states: Beyond a lineage organization favoring elders in a nonhierarchical political order, state elaboration and constitutionality were minimalized. Familial institutions, their power and authority, all overlapped with state institutional power and authority, and vice versa. To this extent, Bamako's governmental organization, decision-making, and the chiefly role-play more closely resembled governance "in the Mande style" (as Valliere had noted) than that of the Segovian metropole where a more centralized, bureaucratized, autonomous, and authoritarian state prevailed. And although bearing a remote resemblance to the Roman *civitas in parvo*, Bamako's governance was in reality both familial and conciliar. Not only did Titi Niare— Bamako's last chief, and the only one for whom we have usable data— consult chiefly councils, but internal palavers also included the client Surakaw, as well as heads of senior *nyamakalaw* lineages. Even *wolosow* were included in conciliar circles.[81] Beyond the tri-partite establishment and its inherent de jure state right, were the families whose de facto empowerment imposed further boundaries on Niare chiefly power. Most important were the Suraka families with their material wealth and spiritual power, the latter reified in mosques and Koranic schools, not to mention their writing skills, their capacity to transfer knowledge, universal perspectives, and ability to relate to the external world. Finally, further establishing boundaries to chiefly powers were families on the state's farther periphery, each possessing the right of grievance over enforcements that displeased them.

Second, unlike Segu's governance, power and authority in the Bamako *kafu* were divisible: The *kafu-tigi* shared important state powers with separate and differentiated corporate identities. Important among them were the leading *nyamakalaw* families, especially the *numuw* and *jeliw*. Powerful because of monopolistic knowledge and powers over the "word," *jeliw* families frequently provided advisors, councilors, and emissaries for the Niare and other chiefs.[82] Even more powerful, the *numuw*, whose knowledge of the esoteric, the occult and the sacerdotal was formidable, presided at oathing ceremonies, always providing the sacred anvil on which oaths

---

81. Piétri, "Note topographique," p. 572.
82. Interview Marabout Touré (Bozola-Bamako, 4 Jan. 1980); personal communication Tiémoko Kanté (Institut des Sciences Humaines, Bamako, 5 Feb. 1983).

were sworn. To prevent an oathing abrogation, its amendment or future forswearing, it is said that *numuw* tossed "ritual" anvils into the Niger's watery wastes, oathing ceremonies once concluded. If these costly procedures outweighed more material considerations, such as anvil production costs (which were high), it was because state cohesion, internal integrity, and ritual mobilization called for a spiritual valuation over a material one.[83] And while a *numu* presence was essential to the integrity of male initiation ceremonies and *jo* rituals, leading lineages from both *nyamakalaw* identities (*numu* and *jeli*) officiated at the state *sa wolo-ula seli*, or seven year fetes.

Third, as a minimalist state, the *lex familiaris*, or internal family law, considerably restricted the state's interventionist powers. Within the *kabila*, or family unit, family law was supreme. "People power" was enhanced because, although powerful alliances bound state and society into viable corporate identities, no collective contract submitted citizens to an overarching state agreement in the public interest—which is what Sunjata is said to have accomplished at Kurugan Fugan with the creation of the Mali state (c. 1234). It follows, therefore, that in the Bamako *kafu*, the *jus publicum*, or public law, was relatively small compared with the *jus privatum* governing private rights and property.

Neither could the state exert leverage in the religious affairs of civil society beyond the jurisdiction of Bamako city; and only rituals associated with the res publica—such as rain ceremonies, or those mitigating earth spirits, or agricultural/planting (*zerinin-kuru*) rituals—fell within the core-state's jurisdiction. Such ceremonies, it is said, were usually conducted either at Komola, the *komo* site near the old Bozo quarters, or at the *jetu*, the sacred grove where the *boli*, or altar, was located. With respect to *jo* rituals, the Bamako Faama presided officially only in ceremonies affecting the core-state, while *dugu-tigiw* held sway over their communities' moral and spiritual well-being. Otherwise, statewide economic planning involving the spirit world was the work of *nyamakalaw* (e.g., annual planting and harvesting), the Bozo (e.g., fishing) and Jawambe (e.g., herding), their decisions usually guided by lunar cycles, seasonal changes, and political exigencies inter alia.[84] Finally, aside from

---

83.According to Arnaud, Ngolo Jara (1766–1790), on taking office as Segu Faama, swore loyalty to the office and Segu notables on an anvil and two alters (Arnaud, "La Singulière légende," p. 183); Meillassoux, "Histoire," p. 213.

84. According to Paques, the appropriate time to plant was with the appearance of the *ningu-ningu*, or the *seba nadie*, or the Pleiades, a conspicuous group of stars in the constellation Taurus, commonly spoken of as the "Seven Sisters," although only six are visible ("L'Estrade royale," pp. 1645–1646).

state-imposed market operations (e.g., collecting the *wusuru*, or market tax), both domestic and foreign commerce were almost exclusively in private hands. In fact, as indicated above, it was only with the recreation of colonial circles in October 1898, and the appointment of the Niare as canton chiefs, that Niare authority extended for the first time beyond Bamako city.[85]

Fourth, a loose body of administrative law testified to a marginal state autonomy. It is true that public offices remained separate from their officeholders and that institutional continuity prevailed even after an incumbent's term of office had ended. Yet countervailing administrative law and limited state interventionism was the internal familial system of alliances and marriages, which, if anything, loosened rather than tightened state autonomy, tightened rather than loosened familial power over the res publica. The state's autonomy was therefore marginal. Thus internal political efficiency and stability remained problematic, frequently mirroring the vicissitudes of leading families. We already know the extent to which the collateral succession, fratricidal conflict, and factionalism could threaten a state's internal stability. Or, to take another example, the state's collection of miscellaneous taxes—market fees and customs-dues owed by julaw and Maraka itinerant traders, as well as gifts from other strangers, such as the Bozo and Somono—was customarily the work of public officials, only partially differentiated from their familial roles within civil society. Tax collectors could therefore have been playing conflicting public/private roles when enforcing the state's tax-collecting authority. Similarly, the absence of a permanent *dux* (war chief; *kele-tigi*) separate from the permanent *rex* (king) opened doors for families with opportunistic agendas, especially with respect to foreign policy. We saw above how the Keita *fadenyaw*, vying for power, sought external support from the Umarians, the Samorians, and later the French. Related problematics with Bamako's Suraka families developed in the Bamako state (a subject already discussed herein and in Chapter 2). Accordingly, potential threats to the minimalist state often came from within, from competing *fadenyaw*, from ideologically differentiated identities (Islam and "animism"), and from discrete power centers in this multicentric state where power and authority overlapped and *were* divisible.[86]

---

85. Anon., "Chronique historique," pp. 64–65.

86. For the *fadenya* see Amselle, "Un Etat contre l'état," pp. 463–483; Ardouin, "Une Formation politique," pp. 443–461, esp. 450–452.

Finally, in contextualizing governance in the Mande style—admittedly as seen through French eyes—I have argued for the validity of the Bamako familial state. Given the fluidity of Mande ethnographic identities, social relationships, and alliances, together with their long migrations, and scattered lineage-locations, a certain internal stability *did* derive from the powerful corporate groups with slower changing identities, such as families. Moreover, with relatively restricted material cultures and resources, low-level technologies, and low population densities—considerably lower than the Beledugu and middle Niger population densities—a larger state elaboration may well have been unnecessary, unsustainable, and even dysfunctional. And given Segu's political ambitions, ubiquitous spy brides and resident *tonjonw*, it is hardly likely that the Segovian war-state would have tolerated a larger, more aggrandized client-state on its southern periphery, especially during its eighteenth-century state hegemony. Thus given the contextualization, the minimalist state elaboration and political behavior of Bamako's chiefs were normative and "in the Mande style." As Segovian clients, the *kafu-tigiw* accomplished apparently what was expected: In reinforcing Bamako's mythical-political-ritual identity, they sought legitimacy in the eyes of their metropolitan lord and respect from regional peers.

As to the internal stability and/or instability endemic to Mande states, especially smaller polities in the southern Mande-hinterland, the matter may bear some relationship to the way in which male children were socialized. Raised to compete (*fadenya*), half-brothers of the same father, were permitted—indeed expected—to fight for a father's inheritance; hence the fratricidal conflict (*fadenkele*) and instability found in the collateral or "Z" succession throughout the Mande, the Beledugu, the Bambuhu, the Khassonke states, and elsewhere in the Mande-hinterland. Sometimes countervailing conflict was the *badenya* (mother-childness), or behavior and consciousness of siblings of the same mother socialized to eschew conflict, to cooperate, and to display affection. Further limiting internal conflict was the assurance that siblings inherited material wealth directly through the *balimaya*, or uterine line. It was probably, thus, very difficult within these *fadenya/badenya* somewhat oscillating relationships (triggered by circumstances) to limit conflicts endemic to young men socialized for *both* conflict *and* cohesion, especially when housed for the greater part of their lives within the same or proximate compounds, and on an intergenerational basis.

In expressing these articulating relationships, the figurative idiom noted that while siblings of the same mother were assured the safety of a mother's household (sleeping quarters), "the greater the distance from one's mother's (house), the greater the social dislocation and potential disaster."[87] Or, that while "a battle between milk brothers (*badenya*) smokes but never flames," war was more likely to break out between the *fadenya* or brothers of the same father. We recall that referring to the old Mande, rife with succession conflicts for the greater part of the nineteenth century, Krina's bard (Wa Kamissoko) noted: "Every little king fearing that...one of his blood brothers (might) overthrow him, lost no time in having his slaves spirit (the brother) away." Perhaps it may be no coincidence, as Tellier discovered, that in Mande cosmology, *badenya* came to mean "cooperation," and *fadenya* "chaos."[88]

---

87. John W. Johnson, "The Epic of Sun-Jata: An attempt to define the model for African epic poetry," Ph.D. dissertation (Indiana University, 1978), pp. 95–97, cited in McNaughton, *The Mande*, p. 17; Camara, "Le Manden," p. 63.

88. Conrad, *A State*, pp. 119, 146, 150–151; Kamissoko and Cissé, *La Grande geste*, p. 193–195; Tellier, *Autour de Kita*, pp. 82–92.

4

Commerce and Markets "in the Mande Style"

Introduction

The previous chapter demonstrated the extent to which the Bamako state was an elaboration and extension of the ruling families' identities. I argued that while the Roman analogy of the *civitas in parvo* (or state writ small) was inappropriately applied by French administrators schooled in the classical tradition, in other important ways the state did function as if a family affair. With a fluid bureaucracy overlapping familial structures and organization, and a *jus privatum* (governing private rights and property) often taking precedence over the *jus publicum* (public law), I demonstrated that unlike the model of the Segovian imperium, the Bamako *kafu* was not an invasive, but rather a minimalist state elaborated "in the Mande style."

Building on the "family argument," the present chapter examines the extent to which similar family networks provided the infrastructure and the organizational system for the development of related markets and their wider commercial linkages. Unlike political power relationships, however, the *jo* rituals played no official or state role in commercial articulations. Instead, the power and imagery for long-distance commerce derived from Islam. On the one hand, so important was Islam in trading relationships that those aspiring to a commercial identity frequently coveted Islamic signs as a "membership ticket" to the community of traders and its moral perspectives.[1] On the other hand, because Islam was not central to the *kafu*'s political identity, commercial pursuits were there-

---

1. Abner Cohen, "The origin of trading diasporas," in Claude Meillassoux, ed., *The Development of indigenous trade and markets in West Africa* (Oxford University Press, 1961), pp. 276–278. For a discussion of trade, Islam and the *ulama* (scholars and clerics) see Levtzion and Fisher, *Rural and urban*, pp. 21–54.

fore less focused on de jure state power. Finally, because Islam in the Bamako *kafu* and Mande-hinterland had been particularized and shifting
identities so skillfully conjured, we once more face another series of prismatic social constructs historically devised. More clear is the sense that
interactive collectivities—mainly families—articulated within the range
of shared interests, coordinating activities, and defending common goals.
Communal organizations notwithstanding, individuals sometimes operated on their own. And almost all, if not all, traders were private investors, all either Maraka-Sarakolle, Soninke, or Kooroko according to the
period, region, and evidence. Some were also julaw, many in their trader
role coveting an Islamized identity. Commercial and other taxes and *disongo* once paid to the state, profits remained with private investors.[2]

The chapter also argues that although Bamako had become a complex,
high-level market on Segu's southern periphery by the late eighteenth
and early nineteenth century, the region's commercial transformation was
slow: Prior to the *kafu*'s eighteenth-century founding, material exchanges
in the pre-*kafu* region—an "animist" space within the imagery of the
northern paradigm—had hardly elaborated beyond simple low-level exchanges between Bozo river nomads and Bamana hunters frequenting the
Manding Plateau. Despite the ancient gold, salt, and slave exchanges ani-
mating the south since antiquity, no data suggest the pre-*kafu*'s regional
involvement.[3] When *kafu* traders finally accessed regional and international markets during the eighteenth century, success came through the
salt exchanges and the slave commerce, and not the gold trade: Gold was
still too closely identified as the *jo*'s "sacred purity" (see Chapter 2).

Accordingly, by the late eighteenth century at least, Bamako's trading
families had extended their interests from the desert-side salines of Tichit
(Sbakh-Ijil) and Taodeni in the north, to the Senegambia and upper and
lower Guinea coasts in the south and west (see Map 3). It is of interest to
note that once family members had gained access to southern markets,
they found southern commercial networks in the hands of Northern and
Southwestern Mande-speakers who, like themselves, had once dispersed
from Wagadu. Southern and coastal families had also been joined by West
Atlantic-speakers.

---

2. *Kooroko* was the local name for the itinerant, Islamized, Mande speaking,
long-distance traders, known west of the Comöe River in the Cote d'Ivoire as *jula*,
and in the Segu region as *Marka*.

3. Generally speaking, traditionalists do not record commercial data, preferring instead to manipulate the images of political authorities (interview Mahmadou Sarr [Bamako, 6 Jan. 1980]).

Finally in this chapter, I argue that Bamako's breakthrough linkages into the southwestern Mande-hinterland and coastal trade articulated along the same or similar kinds of kin filiations found elsewhere in the Mande world. Not surprisingly, these southwestern systems intersected wider networks extending from the Senegambia to Wassulu, and from Kankan to Timbuktu. Thus, despite modest beginnings as low-level exchange centers in a relatively remote upper Niger region, by the eighteenth century Bamako's high-level, complex markets were within reach of all major commercial centers of the western Sudan and western Africa. The nineteenth century, prior to the Umarian and Samorian wars brought further elaboration and regional inclusions.

Pre-*Kafu* Regional Markets:
The Samanyana Market Cluster and Bozo Camps

As the southern element in the paradigm's holography (i.e., the northern paradigm), it still remains unclear when pre-*kafu* regional markets began to develop and by whom. Oral recountings recall that prior to the Segovian state hegemony, small- and medium-sized markets operated on or near the pre-*kafu* site. Among these was the Samanyana urban cluster in the northern Mande (e.g., Samalen Samalia and Siby), about two to three days' journey south of the future *kafu* site (see Maps 2 and 3). These towns are of interest if only because—like Beyla, Kankan, Sikasso, Odienne, and Kong—they developed within the same ecological latitudes subsequently favoring Bamako.[4] Within these low-level markets, pioneering traders exchanged salt, captives, and kola nuts, not surprising really, given that the towns defined a north-south axis roughly equidistant between the Worodugu kola forests and the Inland Niger Delta towns. That the pre-*kafu* region was known as "Samanyana Sira," or "on the road to Samanyana," suggests associations with the ruling Jakite family, one of whose alternate patronymics was *Nyakate*, the Niare's archaic *jamu*, that is, before they negotiated a Bamana identity with Biton, the Segovian Faama (see Chapter 1). Later allies of the Niare, several members of the Jakite family still reside in Niarela, the Niare quarter of modern Bamako.[5]

---

4. Bakary Traore, "Contribution à l'histoire du peuplement du Kala: De la fin XVIe au XIXe siècle," Mémoire de fin d'études under the direction of J. B. Konare, l'ENSUP (Bamako, 1981–1982), pp. 28, 34, 45.

5. Interview Marabout Touré (Bozola-Bamako, 3 Jan. (1980); personal communication Raymond Mauny (Paris, 3 Dec. 1981); personal communication Ma-

In addition to the Jakite, Bamana and Mandinka hunters—these latter roaming the Bamako plain and Manding Plateau—were probably also among early participants in pre-*kafu* market exchanges, most likely purchasing salt and/or grain, possibly slaves. Given this linkage with the south, the future *kafu* site may therefore have been a relay center on a lesser west-bank route no doubt leading from the Kaarta-Beledugu and middle Niger towns to the Samanyana market cluster, the Mande, and later the kola forests of Worodugu: hence "Samanyana Sira." In addition to these early hunter families were the Bozo river-nomads. Often a precursor of market developments, Bozo riverside camps had been established along the Niger's entire length—from Siguiri (Guinea) to Timbuktu (Mali)—well before the eighteenth century, where the Bozo fished, supplementing food supplies with grain, most probably fonio (*Digi-taria exilis*) and sorghum (*Dourra*). Bozo families also exchanged crocodile skins, fish, and grains in upriver markets, especially those in the Mande, where the grain trade had been operationalized at least since the fourteenth century. It is likely that integrative currencies, even in these low-level markets, included salt and slaves, possibly even gold in the Bure-Bambuhu regions where the precious metal was sometimes exchanged for food. Thus were local markets tangentially linked to the larger Niger, desertside, and North African marts.[6]

Given these exchanges, the question is: Was gold on sale in these southern markets?[7] Our only perspectives come from an earlier version of the northern paradigm where, even prior to the seventeenth century, gold had an unambiguous market value.[8] We know, for example, that since

---

madou Sarr (Bamako, 6 Jan. 1980; 5 Nov. 1982); see also *ANMK* 2D 132, "Organisation administrative ... ville de Bamako" (Bamako, 1 Nov. 1902), p. 13.

6. Interview Mamadou Sarr (Bamako, 4 Jan. 1980); interview Marabout Touré (Bozola-Bamako, 6 Jan, 1980); interview Seydou Niaré (Bamako, 6 Jan. 1980; 15 Dec. 1982); Meillassoux "Histoire," pp. 188–198; *ASAOF* 1G 12, Tourette, "Voyage dans ... Bambouk" (1828 à 1829); *ASAOF* 1G 32, "Lettre Mage à Gouverneur" (Saint Louis, 21 June 1866).

7. Gold deposits were widespread throughout parts of the western Sudan, i.e., north of the fourteenth north parallel longitude, and west of the Greenwich meridian: for example, in the Beledugu (Mali), the Galam-Bambuk-Tambaura regions, in the Southern Rivers, Sierre Leone, northern Guinea, the Guerze country in the western Cote d'Ivoire, the Pura mines of Burkina Faso, the mines of northern Benin and Nigeria, as well as in the Black Volta regions of the eastern Cote d'Ivoire, and the Akan mines in Ghana.

8. According to Raymond Mauny, the trade's beginnings can be traced to sometime during the last millennium; Timothy Garrard traces it to the late third or

deep antiquity, many Timbuktu, Jenne and desert-side dealers had been aware, however vaguely, that gold had a market value both in North Africa and beyond the desert's northern shores. We also know from the previous discourse that the south was a very different story: Here, gold belonged primarily to a "sacred purity," or to the south's mythical-political-ritual identity (see Chapter 2). The Arab authors had found these dual valuations—both market and cosmological—treacherously confusing. For example, al-Dimashqi (1327): "Gold is abundant in their country (Ghana)" (i.e., gold's market value), "but they do not use it" (i.e., making no sense). Or, al-Idrisi (1154): In "Wangara," the king "tethers his horses" to a large "gold brick" weighing about 30 *ratls* (also making no sense). Or, al-Bakri (1068): In wearing necklaces and bracelets, the "king (of Ghana) adorns himself like a woman" (making no sense); he dresses up his dogs with gold ornaments. Or, al-'Umari (1337–1338): "At the sound of the *muezzin*'s call to prayer gold disappears" (magical-cosmological value), only to reappear "in neighboring heathen countries" (magical-cosmological value). Or, Abu Hamid al-Gharnati (1169): "Gold of extraordinary (purity) grows in the sand" (market value); and al-Qazwini (1275): Growing in the sand, it was plucked at sunrise in the same manner as carrots (market value).[9] Further confounding these confusions and misinformation were the tombal silences enshrouding gold. Originally proscribed by the *jo* (as a matter of life and death), silences continued, in some instances well into the twentieth century, although by then the *jo* had come to resemble the tax man.[10]

Given gold's sacred purity, it therefore seems reasonable to surmise—for the time being—that the farther south one traveled from the Timbuktu-Jenne markets, the more gold's identity became complex and ambiguous in relation to market values. Thus while gold was secure as a market-exchange commodity in middle Niger inventories, in the south it remained ambiguously embedded in subcultures permitting foreign gold

---

the early fourth century of the present era (Raymond Mauny, "Essai sur l'histoire des metaux en Afrique occidentale," *BIFAN*, sér. B vol. 14 [Jan.-April 1952]: 550-552; Timothy F. Garrard, "Myth and metrology: The early trans-Saharan gold trade," *JAH*, vol. 23, no. 4 [1982]: 443–461). See also, Levtzion and Hopkins, *Corpus*, p. 13; Mauny, *Tableau géographique*, pp. 300–301; Herodotus, *Histories*, Book IV, p. 196.

9. One *ratl* equals 397.2 grams (Levtzion and Hopkins, *Corpus*, pp. 80, 110, 132, 177, 212, 262; interview Thiémoko Kanté [Bamako, 4 Jan. 1983]). For further references to the Arabs' Wangara mines, see Levtzion and Hopkins, *Corpus*, pp. 38, 107, 108, 110–111, 112, 116, 120, 128–129, 186, 287, 320, and passim;

10. Interview Tiémoko Coulibaly (Kangaba, 13 April 1983).

market exchanges, on the one hand, (gold dust: *al-tibre al-daqiq*),[11] while denying domestic trade, on the other hand; or gold circulated within the repertoire of official uses in chiefly administrations and political economies, on the one hand, while it was hoarded on the other hand.[12] Penultimately for cult believers, gold was cherished as a profoundly sacerdotal mystery-without-end. Because "owning" properties that could bring good, forestall evil, combat the sorcerer's wrath (even bring his death), and guarantee female fecundity, gold ores could never be sold in domestic markets. Among cult believers, gold could only be exchanged for nonmarket purposes. And if conservative ritual conventions cautioned against selling gold, imperatives of the power associations forbade revealing its secrets. As a vestige of these sacred associations, not surprisingly many gold dealers in contemporary Bamako still "exchange," rather than buy and sell gold.[13]

Given the pre-*kafu*'s low-level markets, and the infrequency of local gold exchanges, we wonder why the site seemed important to political visionaries, such as Biton Kulibaly: Not only was the region almost commercially invisible before the eighteenth century, but all major western Sudanese routes virtually bypassed these quiet fields, the Sotuba *fada* partially impeding river communications (see Chapter 2). Even as late as the early eighteenth century (1728), probably within a decade or two of Bamako's founding, Pere J. B. Labat was advised that merchants traveling north from Galam (Gajaga) to "Bambara" (i.e., Kaarta and the middle Niger towns) usually passed via the Manding Plateau, west of Bamako, or south via Dinguiray, Labe, Kankan, Beyla, and the Futa Jallon (Guinea) approaching Segu from the Niger's east bank (see Map 2). A hundred years later, little had changed. Following a north-south caravan en route from Kankan, Tangrela, and Bancusi (Guinea) to Jenne and Timbuktu (Mali), Rene Caillie (1828) notably bypassed Bamako on the Niger's east bank.[14]

---

11. Levtzion and Hopkins, *Corpus*, pp. 81, 267. It is also likely that gold had a non-market value in certain types of exchanges even in Timbuktu.

12. Gold may have been the base in some regions for the *talikise* on which the *disongo* or tribute was based (see Chapter 3, note 44). *ANMAE, 1780–1822*, vol. 11, "Mémoire servant à donner de renseignement sur le pays des mines que nous appelons Bambouk," pp. 24–25.

13. Personal communication Mamadou Sarr (Bamako, 3 Nov. 1982); personal communication Massa Makan Diabaté (Bamako, 21 March 1983); interview Diarra Sylla, metalworker (Bamako, 15 May 1983).

14. See Labat *Nouvelle relation*, vol. 1, pp. 297–298; vol. 3, pp. 334, 364–365, 368; Caillié, *Voyage*, p. 36 map.

Although seemingly marginal to metropolitan interests, Bamako's commercial potential was, however, more real than immediately apparent: In many respects, the *kafu*'s location was ideal, an observation that would hardly have escaped Biton's ambitious political imagination: Bamako was only about eight to ten days' journey from the Bure gold mines, only slightly more from their Bambuhu counterpart.[15] A mere fifteen to twenty days from the Worodugu kola nut forests,[16] Bamako was also only forty to fifty days from the desert-side salines of Tichit (Sbakh-Ijil) and ninety days from Taodeni.[17] Most importantly, Bamako was only about a thirty- to fifty day journey from European coastal enclaves along the Gambia and Cacheu Rivers, as well as the Grande and Pongo Rivers (the Cacheu and Grande in Guinea Bisau, the Pongo in Guinea). Rubber forests, the French later realized, were within a thirty-day journey to the south. Once developed it was local traders—working through private business procedures—who seized commercial initiatives, first in the old salt, slave and possibly gold trades, later diversifying their inventories.

Bamako *Kafu* and the Long-Distance Trade Market Operations and Commercial Identities

Paucity of evidence prevents an effective operationalizing of Bamako's eighteenth- and early nineteenth-century markets. Confounding the data problem is the manner in which business deals were concluded, many in private—in the Mande style—with the equivalent of a gentleman's handshake. Moreover, across the decades many merchants be-

---

15. *ANMK* 1D 33 5, Borgnis Desbordes "Notice historique" (1880–1890); *ANMK* 1D 33 2, Collomb, "Notice" (Bamako, 1884–1885), p. 2; Jacques Méniaud, *Haut-Sénégal-Niger*, 2 vols. (Paris, 1912), vol. 2, p. 166, for a full discussion of the mines, see pp. 166–195. See also McIntosh, "The Inland Niger Delta," pp. 1–22; McIntosh, "A Reconsideration," pp. 145–158.

16. Al-'Umari (fourteenth century) was the first Arab author to mention the kola nut trade, and Leo Africanus (c. 1515) the first to describe it. Al-Maqqari (seventeenth century) reported its sale in Tlemcen in northern Algeria. Cadamosta (1455–1457), Pacheco Pereira (c. 1506–1508), and Valentim Fernandes (1506–1507) also mention it. For an account of the kola trade, see Paul E. Lovejoy, "Long-distance trade and Islam: The Case of the Hausa nineteenth-century trade," *Journal of the Historical Society of Nigeria*, vol. 5, no. 5 (June 1971): 537–548.

17. For a discussion of the Saharan salts, see E. Anne McDougall, "Salts of the western Sahara: Myths, mysteries, and historical significance," *IJAHS*, vol. 23, no. 2 (1990): 231–257. See also Mauny, *Tableau géographique*, pp. 321–335.

came invisible, if only because "commercial identities" per se frequently collapsed into familial identities and/or small corporate group equivalents, thereby disappearing from the oral record. That no great power associations (e.g., *komo*) lent their formidable presence to these commercial pursuits means that no stories of irascible *numuw* threatening chaos, or *jeliw* with lacerating tongues appear in the oral recollections of trading families.[18]

However, while gentlemen's agreements leave few traces, it seems clear that commercial identities were forged and operationalized through Islam: contracts and partnerships, such as the Maliki proprietary partnership including the *ijara* and the *commenda* (*mudaraba, qirad, muqarada*). While the *ijara* was a hire contract, the *commenda*, combining advantages of a loan-with-partnership, regulated the use of capital, trading skills, and labor in the interest of mutual gain. The principal formulae by which long-distance trade was undertaken in the Muslim world, both the *ijara* and the *commenda* enabled investors, or groups of investors, to entrust capital or merchandise to a hire in the case of the former, to an agent-manager in the event of the latter. On trading *ijara* capital, hired agents were usually entitled to an equitable remuneration (*air mithluhu*) in addition to specified expenses. On trading *commenda* capital, agent-managers returned the principal and previously agreed-upon share of profits to investors, subtracting a remuneration for time and labor. Within the articulation of *commenda* agreements, agent-managers were considered trustworthy: They were not held accountable for losses occurring in the normal course of business exchanges, unless proven otherwise. *Commenda* under most circumstances were either unilateral or bilateral, the investor the sole source of capital in the case of the former, the agent-manager contributing a part in the case of the latter.

The extent to which partnerships were applied varied. The Kooroko of Bamako, formerly of Wassulu, found them useful for contractual agreements between *jula-baw* (senior partners), and *jula-denw* (juniors), in a formalized trading relationship. Trading partnerships were also common among merchants joining caravans, especially for security during the Samorian wars, when salt, kola, and grain dealers divided profits at the conclusion of an enterprise. In Bamako, Collomb found that while large dealers made use of the *ijara*, or trader for hire contracts, they oftentimes

---

18. Working with the idea that political icons were more important than commercial images, it is of interest that prior to 1883, many families saw the French as "only merchants," which may partly explain the considerable misunderstandings that followed (see Chapter 5).

required agents to leave as pawns a slave, a horse, a wife, or a daughter. Only on concluding the contract to the manager's satisfaction was the pawn returned.[19]

Once the market was operationalized, Bamako's Islamized identities came to dominate. Although a potential source of conflict in local "animist" jurisdictions (as noted earlier), a Muslim identity was invariably tolerated on the assumption that the presence of a *karamoko* (Koranic scholar) or *moriw* (marabouts) "upgraded" a jurisdiction's moral environment, perhaps even adding an aura of "blessedness" reminiscent of as-Sadi's encomium to Jenne, the "city blessed by God." Itinerant merchants were thus emboldened to risk the hazards of bandit-infested roads in the interest of collective gain. There were also reverse expectations: that robbers dreading Islam's holy powers and deft spirits would desist from their iniquitous ways.[20] Primary among Bamako's "Muslim" merchants were the Ture and Drave families projecting a Qadiriyya Sufi identity, who, as all-purpose *ja-tigiw*, were among the region's most numerous hosts attracting co-religionists. Following the signifiers of commercial prosperity, Islamized clients sought Bamako's markets from as far afield as the Kaarta (fifteen to twenty days), Sokolo and the middle Niger towns (fifteen to twenty-five days), Odienne (fifteen to twenty days), the Wassulu (ten to fifteen days), Kankan and the Mande (eight to ten days), and the northeast Marka towns, such as Banamba and Tuba (seven to ten days), as well as the Beledugu towns (three to ten days) (see Map 3).

In operationalizing their markets—eventually affecting both salt and slave transactions, as well as gold, livestock, grain, and kola nut exchanges—Bamako's commercial elites established six markets: the *dogo-ba* (*dogo*: market; *ba* large), or large weekly market to which traders brought grain, livestock, chickens, and textiles, as well as imported merchandise; local domestic markets provisioning daily supplies of grain and household necessities; the gold market usually conducted in dealers' homes, open only to those "who knew someone"; the salt market operationalized outside the city, especially important in the dry season; the slave market, a daily occurrence while supplies lasted; and the kola commerce brought by

---

19. *ANMK* 1D 3 2, Collomb, "Notice" (Bamako, 1884–1885), p. 12; Perinbam, "The Juulas," pp. 465–466; Jean-Loup Amselle, "Parenté et commerce chez les Kooroko," in Meillassoux, ed., *The Development*, pp. 253–265. *ASAOF* 1G 50 49, "Lettre Piétri à Gallieni" (Bamako, 9 May 1880); *ASAOF* 1G 299, Brévié, "Monographie" (Bamako, 25 April 1904); interview Tiémoko Coulibaly (Kangaba, 13 April 1983).

20. *Ta'rikh as-Sudan*, p. 22; interview Tiémoko Coulibaly (Kangaba, 13 April 1983).

Maraka and julaw traders from the Worodugu forests. The *dogo-tigi* (market official), often a *woloso* or slave born in the household and appointed by the *kafu-tigi*, supervised market proceedings and protected the state's prerogatives. Like that of the *jo-tefe*, or slave dealer, the *dogo-tigi*'s office brought obliquity. Currencies most commonly used in the Bamako *kafu* and Mande-hinterland were cowries, together with grain, textiles, horses, honey, and slaves, with gold usually the preserve of the rich; outside the Bamako region iron bars were customary.[21]

The Salt and Slave Breakthroughs

Because there is considerable literature on western Sudanese markets and the long distance trade, I refer interested readers elsewhere.[22] Alternately, this discourse examines the process by which Bamako's commercial elites upgraded and extended their trade from the pre-eighteenth-century low-level exchanges to the complex high-level markets of the late nineteenth and the early twentieth century. Although merchants dealt in the full range of commercial inventories, it was the salt trade and the slave trade—rather than the gold or kola nut exchanges—that created breakthrough opportunities into wider and more complex markets.[23]. However, although both salt and gold were sold within the same political economies, they were not paired exclusively. To the contrary: Hedging their risks, merchants most often preferred diversified inventories.[24] It

---

21. Meillassoux, "Histoire," p. 211; interview Suleyman Dravé (Bamako, 5 Jan. 1980); interview Abdoulaye Touré (Bamako, 8 Jan. 1983).

22. See, for example, Curtin, *Economic change*; Anthony G. Hopkins, *An Economic history of West Africa* (New York, 1973).

23. During the Umarian and Samorian prewar years, Bamako traded extensively with the Wassulu, the Mande, and the east bank, also with the Beledugu, Fadugu, Tichit, and Timbuktu. Salt was most often exchanged for captives (*ANMK* 1D 33 2, Collomb, "Notice" [1884–1885], p. 2; *ASAOF* 1G 50 20, "Lettre Gallieni à Gouverneur" [Nango, 7 July 1880], pp. 17–18). It is of interest to note that like gold, salt had its own subculture, said to be an organizing principle together with gold in harmonious gender relations. And if gold was a woman's mineral, salt was gendered male, signifying masculine strength and the chemical basis for male semen (Interview El Hajj Mamadou Makadji [Banamba, 12 April 1983]); Perinbam, "The Salt-gold alchemy," pp. 1–21.

24. Interview El Hajj Mamadou Makadji (Banamba, 12 April 1983); interview Abdoula Gueye (Bamako, 10 March 1983). Abdoula Gueye, born c. 1920, was a salt trader in the Bamako region. Interview Massa Makan Diabaté (Bamako, 21 March 1983); interview Suleyman Dravé (Bamako, 8 Jan. 1980). There is considerable material on the salt trade. For a selection published between 1932–1990 see Col. Man-

goes without saying that slave supplies increased notably during the Umarian, and especially the Samorian war years between the 1860s and 1880s, when prices plunged to their lowest level. Taking advantage of increasing supply-demand ratios, Maraka from Banamba, as well as Bamana traders from Bamako, extended slaving farther afield into the Mande-hinterland. In the early 1880s, Bamako dealers in particular were exchanging slaves for firearms with Samory's lieutenants, sometimes for salt, for as little as one salt bar per captive.[25] By way of contrast, slave purchases for domestic uses remained relatively small, largely attributable to local reproductive capacities.[26]

Bamako's elaboration into the wider southern markets via salt and slave exchanges—both icons in the northern paradigm—should not be surprising. The *kafu*'s southern latitude was ideal for desert-side salt dealers traveling south, very advantageous for southern slave merchants traf-

geot, "Le Problème du sel en Afrique occidentale française," *BCAFRC*, vol. 42 (1932): 254–257; Capt. D. Brosset, "La Saline d'Idjil," *BCAFRC*, vol. 43 (1933): 259–265; Henri Lhote, "Les Salines du Sahara: La Saline de Teguidda N'Tissemt," *La Terre et la vie* (Paris), vol. 3 (Dec. 1933), pp. 727–735; *Idem.*, "Le Cycle caravanier des Touaregs de l'Ahaggar et la saline d'Amadror: Leur rapports avec les centres commerciaux du Soudan," *BIFAN*, sér. B, vol. 31 (1969): 1014–1027; J. Génévière, "Les Kountas et leurs activités commerciales (commerce du sel)," *BIFAN*, sér. B, vol. 2 (1950): 1111–1127; Th. Monod, "D'ou provient le sel d'Idjil?" *NA*, vol. 47 (July 1950): 89–90; J. Clauzel, *L'Exploitation des salines de Taoudenni* (Algiers, 1960); Paul E. Lovejoy, "The Bornu salt industry," *IJAHS*, vol. 4 (1979): 629–668; *Idem.*, "Commercial sectors in the economy of the nineteenth century Central Sudan: The trans-Saharan trade and the desert-side salt trade," *African Economic History* (hereafter *AEH*), vol. 13 (1984): 85–116; *Idem.*, *Salt of the desert sun: A history of salt production and trade in Central Sudan* (Cambridge University Press, 1986); Michel Museur, "Un Example specifique d'économie caravanière: L'Echange sel-mil," *Journal des Africanistes* (hereafter *JA*) vol. 47 (1977): 48–80; Dominique Neunier, "Le Commerce du sel de Taoudeni," *JA*, vol. 50, no. 2 (1980): 133–144; E. Anne McDougall, "The Sahara reconsidered: Pastoralists, politics, and salt from the ninth through the twelfth centuries," *AEH*, vol. 12 (1983): 263–286; *Idem.*, "Camel caravans of the Saharan salt trade: Traders and transporters in the nineteenth century," in Catherine Coquery-Vidrovitch and Paul Lovejoy, eds., *The Workers of African trade* (Sage, 1985); *Idem.*, "Salts of the western Sahara" (1990), pp. 231–257.

25. McDougall, "Salts of the western Sahara," pp. 240, and esp. p. 242, note 31. Interview Mamadou Sarr (Bamako, 4 Jan. 1980); interview Suleyman Dravé (Bamako, 8 Jan. 1980); interview Tiémoko Coulibaly (Kangaba, 4 April 1983); Meillassoux, "Histoire," pp. 208–209; Gallieni, *Voyage*, pp. 320–321.

26. Interview Marabout Touré (Bozola-Bamako, 3 Jan. 1980); interview Suleyman Dravé (Bamako, 8 Jan. 1980).

ficking with the Sahel, and favorably situated for slave vendors with eyes
on the more southern and coastal trades. With respect to *both* trades, our
earliest European recollections come from Mungo Park. Overnighting in
Bamako on 23 August 1796, Park, a well-informed traveler—having acquired the Mandinka idiom in the Gambia—opened a window (for Europeans) on Bamako's salt trade. Disappointed at "Bammakoo's" "middling" size, having "heard (it) much talked of as a great market," Park
nonetheless noted that considerable salt and slave breakthroughs had
already occurred.[27] Lodging with a *ja-tigi* identified as "Serawoolli"
(Sarakolle), their exchanges on the banks of the Niger are now history:
The "Moors" brought salt to Bamako through "Bambarra" (the Segu, or
Massassi state) where, on arriving, "they constantly rest(ed) a few
days."[28] From there, salt was trans-shipped throughout regional markets
by "the Negro merchants ... well acquainted with (its market) value in
different kingdoms, frequently purchas(ing) by wholesale, and retail(ing)
it to great advantage." Of Bamako's "Moors," Park noted their "very good
(knowledge of) Mandingo," suggesting either that they were bilingual (to
say the least), or that by the late eighteenth century "Moorish" families
were already Mandekan. One "Moor," having traveled to the "Rio
Grande" was respectful of "Christians," while another, an unidentified
slave dealer, had resided for years in the Gambia.[29]

Kulikoro, about 60 kilometers downriver and one of Bamako's salt-
trading partners where Park overnighted on 20 August, was "a considerable town ... a great market for salt." Some twenty years later Dochard
also found it "considerable." Here, as posterity knows, Park's "Jatee" (*ja-
tigi*) was "Bambarran turn(ed) Mussulman," a former slave of a "Moor"

---

27. Park, *The Travels*, pp. 181–183. The British surgeon Dochard, who
overnighted in Bamako some twenty-three years later on 20 June 1819, thought
Bamako "small" (*ANSOM* B4, Walckenaer *Histoire générale*, vol. 7, "Travels in
Western Africa, in the years 1818, 1819, 1820 and 1821. From the River Gambia ...
Kaarta and Follidoo to the River Niger, by Major William Gray and the late Staff
Surgeon Dochard [London, 1825]," pp. 140–141).

28. Park did not quantify, but according to observers Bamako's old salt market
at Santile attracted as much as 200 to 300 camel loads annually during the nineteenth century, i.e., about 36,000 to 54,000 kilograms (Meillassoux, "Histoire," p.
208). As a matter of interest Bamako's old salt market at Santile, en route to Kulikoro, is now an urban quarter of modern Bamako.

29. Park, *The Travels*, pp. 181–182. Despite this bamanization, some members of
this large Ture family still claim an "Arabic identity (interview Marabout Touré
[Bozola-Bamako, 4 Jan. 1880]; interview Suleyman Dravé [Bamako, 8 Jan. 1983];
interview Nana Niaré Dravé [Bamako, 6 Jan. 1980]).

on whose account he had conducted a "considerable trade" in salt and cotton cloth, traveling regularly to the desert-side towns of Arawan, Taodeni, and "many other places in the Great Desert." Kulikoro's chief may also have been a salt dealer as, on learning that Park was a Christian with writing skills, he requested a *gris-gris* to "procure wealth."[30] Overnighting at "Marraboo, a large town" (Moribabugu?, Manabugu?) on 21 August—also downriver from Bamako—Park noted that like "Koolikorro," "Marraboo (was) famous for its trade in salt." Park's host, "Jower," was a member of the Jara family. Not only was Jara a salt dealer, but he also traded slaves having acquired "a considerable property" including a house, thereby adding to his preeminence: a "sort of public inn for all travelers." Jara expected at least to cover his expenses, as lodgers were required to hand over "money" (quantity and currency not specified). In the event of indigent guests, among whom Park was numbered, Jara provided what "he thought proper" lodging the Scottish adventurer with "seven poor fellows," one a trader from Kangaba in the Mande upriver from Bamako.[31]

Whether or not Bamako's commercial identity included the "great" salt market that Park had been led to believe, remains unclear. The data are mixed. My investigations suggest that Bamako's salt markets were smaller than Kulikoro's, "Marraboo's," and Banamba's. First, data demonstrate that Sarakolle traders from the Kaarta and Nioro regions—Bamako's trading partners—preferred Banamba for salt and slave operations, many finding Bamako too small and poor, although by the turn of the century preferences were reversed.[32] Second, Banamba favored by a more northern latitude, northern breeders preferred its lower humidity and fewer risks of disease and parasites, an early pluvial onset far less dreaded. Finally, shipping desert-side animals on Bozo or Somono craft to the east bank in search of wider markets, should Bamako be experiencing a poor season, was a breeder's nightmare. Commercial and ecological factors therefore seemed to favor Banamba—and possibly its

---

30. Park, *The Travels,* pp. 146, 179–180. It may be of interest to note that Arawan did not become an important salt market until the eighteenth century, when its trade connections with Timbuktu (and indirectly the Segu state) were stabilized.

31. Park, *The Travels,* pp. 179, 181.

32. Moors, however, continued to come south with their herds to Banamba (interview El Hajj Mamadou Makadji [Banamba, 11 April 1983]; interview Tiémoko Coulibaly [Kangaba, 13 April 1983]). See also, *ASAOF* 1G 79, Conrard, "Notes" (Bamako, 1885), pp. 4–5; *ANMK* 1Q 24, "Correspondance commerciale Cercle de Nioro: Lettre le Capitaine de Lartigue Commandant la région du Sahel à Monsieur au Gouverneur à Kayes" (Nioro, 25 Dec. 1895).

neighboring towns such as Tuba and Kerowane—over Bamako as Park's great salt market. But then, according to Captain Fortin (Artillery of the Marine), Banamba and Tuba formed part of the old *kafu*'s commercial markets. Thus Park's informants could indeed have been referring to the Bamako region's larger commercial identity beyond the *kafu*, including west- and east-bank villages, together with those on the Manding Plateau. Altogether, this "greater Bamako region" comprising Kulikoro, Banamba, Tuba, and possibly Moribabugu would indeed have yielded a "great" salt market.[33]

Regardless of the argument, Bamako's identity as a great salt market is not the primary focus of this discourse. Of greater importance is that entering the regional trade via salt and slave exchanges, Bamako's commercial elites had effectively projected their presence as far north as Arawan, the Taodeni and Tichit salines (the journey from Tichit-Sbakh-Ijil to Kaarta was between forty to fifty days, possibly twenty to twenty-five days from Taodeni to Timbuktu), and as far south as the "different kingdoms" of the old Mande and upper Niger (between one to ten days south of Bamako) (see Maps 2 and 3).[34] These different kingdoms were, above all, where "the greatest of all luxuries is salt," according to Park, and where only a rich man ate his food with salt, children sucking it like sugar. In contrast with Bamako, and probably because of its ancient association with the international gold trade, salt in the old Mande heartland was primarily exchanged for gold, especially during Segu's expansionist wars. The price of both rock and sea salt (now reaching the

---

33. Looking ahead we might say that French demands for salt and livestock for the military campaigns of 1887–1889 expanded both the desert-side and sea-salt commerce considerably, although by the end of the century sea-salt was throwing local traders into a tizzy: Bamako, consumers were turning up their noses, preferring desert-side salt instead. *ANSOM* Sén. et Dép. IV Doss. 90 Bis, Fortin, "Rapport ... la Gambie" (Senudebu, 6 Jan. 1888), pp. 24–26; *ANSOM* Sén. et Dép. IV Doss. 93 Bis, "Governor General à Gallieni, service vétérinaire, Rapport de fin de campagne, 1888 à 1889" (Paris, 11 Oct. 1889), p. 5; *ANSOM* Soudan XIII Doss. 11, "Le Lieutenant Gouverneur du Soudan français à M. le Ministre des Colonies à Paris" (Kayes, 4 July 1898), n.p.

34. From Ijil in the west, routes led south to Kouga on the Senegal River, while those from Wadan, Awdaghost, and Walata terminated at Jara in Nioro and the old Soninke state at Wagadu. Trunk routes branching east joined those from Taodeni. Varying in size according to the mineral type—usually 1–1.5 meters long, 0.30–0.40 meters wide, and 0.60–0.15 meters thick—salt slabs reached the western Sudan on the backs of camels (170–189 kilograms per camel), bullocks or draft oxen (100–140 kilograms per animal), and donkeys (50–70 kilograms each).

region) Park thought considerable, each in relation to the distance from its source.[35]

On turning to Bamako's slave trade, we note that if the salt commerce facilitated the *kafu*'s breakthrough into the wider market, the slave trade—also closely identified with the northern paradigm—brought similar advantages. As is now generally known, the legal procurement of captives was commonplace, expedited by wars (*killiw*) and raids (*tegerew*) on unsuspecting villagers, lone traders, women and children, or simply by clapping into irons adulterers, debtors, criminals, and famine victims. Also known is that entering the trade was not very difficult: At its simplest, commercial elites could claim a market share by simply gaining the attention of the local *jo-tefe*, or slave dealer. The Umarian and Samorian wars brought nothing but good fortune to those perceiving the trade through northern eyes, many getting a start in business during the late nineteenth century.[36] Therefore, not necessarily calling for considerable capital outlays, nor storage space, nor long-term planning, nor sophisticated management skills for that matter, slave dealers could get by with far less organization than their analogues in most other western Sudanese commerce. Certainly less organized than the salt and kola trades, the trade was accessible even to small dealers. Even the *jo-tefe's* position, apparently a sordid one at best, was open to all, including *numuw*; and offering no opportunities for an official monopoly, *jo-tefew* were known to keep competitors at bay by "strong-arming."[37]

---

35. According to Park one salt slab sold for about two pounds ten shillings sterling; the regular price he thought ranged from one pound fifteen shillings to two pounds. Prices for sea salt varied according to demand-supply ratios (Park, *The Travels*, pp. 214, 229, 233–234).

36. For example, Tiémoko Coulibaly, born in Bamako (c. 1910), was a kola and salt merchant trading between Kankan, Siguiri, and Mopti; he was the fourth generation in this commerce. His great-grandfather started the family business as a slave dealer traveling to Mauritania with caravans escorted by armed slaves. His grandfather (born c. 1856 in Guinea) and his father (born c. 1883) expanded the trade to include kola nuts and salt, as well as dried fish purchased at Mopti and sold in Bamako, Kulikoro, Guinea and the Cote d'Ivoire. (Interview Tiémoko Coulibaly [Kangaba, 13 April 1983]). El Hajj Mamadou Makadji was also a fourth generation trader involved in the salt-gold-kola trade, whose family business began with slaves. Makadji was born in Kabida in the Sahel (c. 1913) of Suraka ancestry. He traveled mainly between Banamba and Kulikoro (Interview El Hajj Mamadou Makadji [Banamba, 12 April 1983]). See also, *ASAOF* Sén. et Dép. 1G 50 77, "Lettre Gallieni à Gouverneur" (Makajambugu, 26 April 1880), pp. 2–3; Faidherbe, *Le Sénégal*, pp. 326, 339; Person, *Samori*, vol. 1, p. 398.

37. Park, *The Travels*, pp. 222–228; Meillassoux, "Histoire," p. 204.

There were, however, considerable advantages to the trade: Slaves could be exchanged for salt and horses, two of the western Sudan's most prestigious purchases, according to the northern paradigm.

Given the relatively steady demand in both northern and southern markets for salt and slave exchanges, we wonder why commercial elites passed over opportunities to operationalize the slave commerce on a more complex and stable basis. At the heart of the problem were matters affecting procurement, or methods by which slaves could be legally obtained. Given legal boundaries, slave procurement was either too expensive (wars were costly), too risky (raids could be dangerous), or domestic supplies were too small (debtors, adulterers, troublemakers too few in number). Unless vended in distant markets, involving middlemen and additional expenditures, by the nineteenth century profits were also too small except in cases involving large dealers, such as Segu's Faamaw, or where ideology (Islam) was placed above material gain.[38] Moreover, institutionalizing the office of a slave *ja-tigi* would have been difficult, given the numerous problems associated with slave lodgings and maintenance. Besides, what *ja-tigi* would hold himself accountable for runaway slaves, mutinous slaves, sick slaves, pregnant slaves, not to mention dead slaves? That domestic slave reproduction remained high also reduced the need for a large market organization. Prior to the French arrival, according to the Niare-Meillassoux text, Bamako markets had three *jo-tefew* representing various ethnic identities or *kafu* interest groups.[39]

Farther south in the old Mande and the Wassulu, commercial elites operationalized slave markets with even fewer procedures, probably because supplies were even more readily available. Of the south's eighteenth-century (1796) slave trade, Park reminds us that the Mande in particular had become the land where slaves were procured: Large numbers of captives had reached the region in the wake of the Segu-Kaartan wars, apparently as much as 900 in one day according to Park. Probably avoiding expenditures, not to mention risks of maintaining sizable quantities of war captives in one jurisdiction, Monzon Jara's (Segu Faama, c. 1790–c. 1808) prisoners had been shipped to upper Niger towns where, instead of salt, most were exchanged for gold dust.[40] During Segu's nineteenth-century decline, slaving, now com-

---

38. For Islam's justification of slavery in the northern paradigm, see Chapter 2.

39. Meillassoux, "Histoire," p. 209; interview Marabout Touré (Bozola-Bamako, 3 Jan. 1980); interview Suleyman Dravé (Bamako, 8 Jan. 1980); personal communication Mahmadou Sarr (Bamako, 7 Jan. 1980).

40. Park, *The Travels*, pp. 194, 196–197, 209, 220–228, 248 and passim.

monplace in the Mande, required even less capital outlay and planning, slaves sometimes even exchanged for dogs, much coveted by "animist" hunters. And, as with slaving elites farther north, the Umarian and Samorian wars brought a slave bonanza. Reminding listeners of "the little route of betrayal" along which slaves were scurried away to the Sahel, the bard Wa Kamissoko upbraided listeners for their dog-slave exchanges, hardly a prestigious exchange. Those exchanged for dogs, he warned, risked mockery. And if perchance "you exchange your child for a dog, make sure to redeem him (later) ... otherwise people will say of your progeny 'here comes a person descended from one exchanged for a dog.'"[41]

Commenting further on the easy availability of southern slaves, especially in the Wassulu, Valliere noted that julaw, often traveling between French trading posts in the Senegambia where they purchased cloth, subsequently exchanged cloth for Tichit salt in the Nioro region. From thence, trans-shipping merchandise to upper Niger towns, they exchanged salt for slaves. Transactions were simple, he explained: Three captives could be obtained for as little as 25 francs. Commenting on similar trading patterns, Binger noted that the farther north a Wassulunke slave traveled, the greater the market value, while Gallieni noticed the Wassulunke's ubiquitous presence on slave markets.[42]

Beyond salt and slaves, it goes without saying (as we saw above) that other commodities also formed part of Bamako's trading inventories. Most important during the greater part of the nineteenth century was the livestock trade (also important in the northern paradigm), bringing horses, donkeys, mules, sheep, and goats, locally produced or obtained from Mossi (donkeys) and northern dealers. Likewise important to Bamako's widening commercial elites were the grain and kola nut trades, more significant for the nineteenth and twentieth centuries. In all these exchanges, elites traded with neighboring jurisdictions.[43] Finally, as Segu's military star waned during the nineteenth century, so did Bamako's, its earlier horse-warrior identity giving way to an image of peace-loving weavers, traders, farmers, and herders. European armaments that had been reaching middle and upper Niger towns no longer had the same priority. Later, drawn unwillingly and in self-defense into the Umarian and Samorian

41. Kamissoko and Cissé, *La Grande geste,* pp. 55, 193–195, 203–207, 267.

42. Binger, *Du Niger,* vol. 1, p. 130; Gallieni, *Voyage,* pp. 320–321, 597–598.

43. Interview Marabout Touré (Bozola-Bamako, 3 Jan. 1980); interview Suleyman Dravé (Bamako, 7 Jan. 1980).

wars, Bamako developed defensive alliances with the powerful Beledugu horse-warriors, as well as with those of Fadugu and the Messekele.[44]

Some Principal Ja-tigiw and Their Work

Residing mainly in Bamako city, the Ture, owners of three *kafu* villages and among Bamako's principal *ja-tigiw*, hosted primarily slave and salt dealers, trading with counterparts in the Tichit or Sbakh-Ijil salines, as well as others identified as "Islamized Sarakolle" originally from Wagadu. On gold eventually becoming a market-exchange commodity, the Ture also hosted gold dealers in their homes and family compounds. Among larger Ture clients were the Islamized Sylla from Jafunu in Nioro, many of whom dealt in cloth, salt, gold, and slaves, as well as Moroccan and European merchandise. Larger Ture clients also included the Jawara from Kingi (near Nioro), the Nyakate state (according to some oral accounts) founded after their Wagadu dispersal, later lost to the Jamangille Jawara. Ture clients also included the Simpara from Banamba.[45] Beyond the Mande-hinterland, the Ture likewise attracted desert-side Islamized "strangers" who, while seeking gold, slaves, and hides (inter alia), also expected their co-religionists' protection in the interest of mutual gain and personal security. Not political incumbents, but rich and controlling considerable resources, Ture *ja-tigiw* best known in the early 1880s (which is as far back as our data permit) were Abderaman Ture, or Ule, and his four uncles (some say three) of the Karamoko Drave clan, descendants of the Surakaw, or Saharan clans from the Tawat oasis settling in Bamako in the eighteenth century. Within the last fifty years, Ture *ja-tigiw* renowned for their business acumen and managerial skills included Lahaou Ture, Sidi Mohammad Ture, Abdul Ture, and al-Habib Ture, whose descendants are still among the city's principal *ja-tigiw*.[46]

Projecting similar commercial identities were the Islamized Drave (Diagana, Draoui) from the Adrar in the Tawat. Slave dealers-owners on a lesser scale—possessing only one slave village as opposed to three Ture

---

44. By the nineteenth century, Bamako, was better known for its commercial and textile image than for war. *ANSOM* Sén. et Dép. IV 90 Bis, Vallière, "Mémoire" (Siguiri, 15–25 March 1888), p. 37; *ANMK* 1D 33 2, Collomb, "Notice" (Bamako, 1884–1885), pp. 2, 3.

45. Interview Marabout Touré (Bozola-Bamako, Jan. 5–6, 1980); *ASAOF* 1G 50 20, "Lettre Gallieni à Gouverneur" (Nango, 7 July 1880), p. 17; *ASAOF* 1G 79, Conrard, "Notice" (Bamako, 21 Feb. 1885), p. 5.

46. Interview Marabout Touré (Bozola-Bamako, 5 Jan. 1980); personal communication, Seydou Niaré (Bamako, 15 Dec. 1982).

slave villages, some in the deep Beledugu—Drave slaves were largely agriculturists. Migrating from the north, the Drave, as noted above, had entered the salt and slave trades in Timbuktu during the eighteenth century, even before reaching Bamako. Stationing representatives in Timbuktu, Gao and Jenne in the north, also south in the Mande towns, Drave trade relations with these and other representatives in Gao, Jenne, and the Mande were more individualized and autonomous than the Ture corporate presence, the latter usually far more structured and tightly controlled by Bamako elders. Dealing in European goods, salt, and slaves, both the Jenne-Drave and the Bamako-Drave sent representatives annually on purchasing missions to Kita, Kayes, and Rufisque, as well as entrepots in Sierra Leone and Liberia. While on mission in 1880, Gallieni noted that a Drave (or Ture?) scion had arrived at Bakel, having accompanied a slave caravan along the jula route via Bure and Medine. At the turn of the century the Jenne-Drave were earning about 150,000 francs per year according to estimates; and like the Ture, they welcomed marabouts and traders of the Qadiriyya tradition.[47]

Likewise accessing the trades as *ja-tigiw* were the Niare chiefly incumbents, officially "animists," but as slave traders coveting Islamic signs. Opting for simpler lifestyles than those of the more flamboyant Ture— much to Gallieni's dismay when there in May 1880—the Niare were nonetheless rich, possessing several hundred slaves housed in four or more "Sumbala" slave villages. Initially part of the Niare-Kulibaly eighteenth-century *siyah*-marriage alliance (see Chapter 1), by the following century domestic reproduction pointed to manifold increases not only within slave lineages, but also among slave-free Niare alliances. Together with Bamako's Islamized and Mande-hinterland trading elites, Niare traders supplied slaves both to the desert-side and Atlantic commerce, the *faama/ja-tigiw*—Titi Niare himself—pursuing this trade.[48] Traveling to the salt and slave markets of Kulikoro, Nyamina, and Markala, even as far afield as Segu, Nioro, Sierra Leone, and the Southern Rivers (upper

---

47. Interview Suleyman Dravé (Bamako, 8, 9 Jan. 1980); *ANSOM* 1G 50 20, "Lettre Gallieni à Gouverneur" (Nango, 7 July 1880); *ASAOF* 1G 305, "Cercle de Djenné" (Jenne, 1904), pp. 48–49.

48. Interview Marabout Touré (Bozola-Bamako, 3 Jan. 1980); interview Mamadou Sarr (Bamako, 4–5 Jan. 1980); interview Seydou Niaré (Bamako, 6 Jan. 1980; 15 Dec. 1982). The Gallieni Mission attributed only one voyage to Sierra Leone on the part of Titi Niare. According to Gallieni, Biramou was the nominal Faama eclipsed by Titi, his more "take charge" and loquacious brother (Gallieni, *Voyage*, p. 246; *ASAOF* 1G 50 49, "Lettre Piétri à Gallieni" [Bamako, 9 May 1880]; *ASAOF* 1G 52 46, Bayol, "Mission de Ségou" [Saint Louis, 5 July 1880], p. 9).

Guinea), Titi shared *ja-tigi* honors with his "son," as well as with other Niare notables.[49] Scattered throughout *kafu* villages such as Nikomi, Sikoroni, and Minkungu, Niare *ja-tigiw* best remembered for business acumen and managerial skills within the last fifty years included Biramon, Jyokolo, and Bomboli Niare.[50]

But although it is the Niare, Ture, and Drave *ja-tigiw* whose identities are best remembered in local lore, Bamako's largest slave dealers were none other than the "animist" warrior families, more specifically the Kulibaly, Jara, and Traore lords mobilizing junior males in dependent clans. Identifying with the northern paradigm—and clearly interested in material gain as well—they extended the slave trade to Buguni, the Mande, to Wolessebugu, Tenetu, Sambatigila, and Nanankoro, many eventually accessing the Atlantic slave trade. Controlling production costs, these "animist" Bamana families not only sold captives on the open market, but trading in other commodities, used slaves-pending-sale to porter market-bound grains, later cotton cloth and rubber as well. Slaves accordingly not only "paid" their keep and owners' transport costs, but facilitating a larger profit margin, they provided capital for the next investment. Likewise using slaves as currencies (in addition to cowries, honey, and karite oils, etc.), credit, and collateral, these "animist" lords also gained access to "foreign exchanges," this latter necessary for high-level purchases in the region's more complex and differentiated markets. Ironically the French sometimes conformed, in practice at any rate, to these slave-credit-collateral exchanges—even while tut-tutting the principle in public policy statements. They also discouraged "exchanges in kind," including cloth, expecting instead to monetize regional economies according to metropolitan guidelines.[51]

Finally breaking through into the Bamako and Mande-hinterland trade, especially the salt-slave trades, was another commercial Islamized elite, a stranger *ja-tigi* whom local recollections identify as Abdul Kadar of Weyaweyanko, now a Bamako suburb known as the "jula

---

49. *ANMK* 1D 33 2, Collomb, "Notice" (Bamako, 1884–1885), p.6 ; *ASAOF* 1G 50, "Lettre Piétri à Gallieni" (Bamako, 9 May 1880). See also Person, *Samori*, vol. 1, p. 387. The south was fairly densely populated affecting the size of markets, especially in the Rio Grande area (Labat, *Nouvelle relation*, vol. 5, pp. 157, 248–249, 257–258).

50. Interview Marabout Touré (Bozola-Bamako, 4 Jan. 1980); personal communication Seydou Niaré (Bamako, 15 Dec. 1982).

51. Interview Suleyman Dravé (Bamako, 9 Jan. 1980); Interview Mamadou Sarr (Bamako, 4 Jan. 1980); interview Marabout Touré (Bozola-Bamako, 3 Jan. 1980).

quarter." Originally a small settlement, 2–3 kilometers southwest of the old *kafu*, Weyaweyanko was the battle site where the Samorian "3,000" (probably an exaggeration) were worsted by Borgnis Desbordes, and the "242 Bambara" *tirailleurs* in April 1883. Possibly maintaining interests in Sanankoroba and Timbuktu (variously, according to oral recountings), Abdul Kadar's identity drifts in and out of oral records. Despite his silhouette persona, it is likely that Abdul Kadar hosted mainly kola nut traders—more specifically Bamana and Maninka itinerant *julaw*. In addition, the *kafu*'s Islamized Fulbe, or Jawambe families, although occupied mainly as herders and leather producers, made similar commercial breakthroughs into the slave trade, even having their own *jo-tefew*, or slave dealers, some of whom may have come from a local Jakite clan.[52]

None of the above operations would have functioned in the Mande style, however, had comparable reciprocities, overlapping and interconnected networks, not prevailed. In fact, the networking was a work of art, because if the Jafunu-Sylla were principal clients of the Bamako-Ture, at home in Jafunu they cultivated representatives from Bafulabe and Kita, about a fifteen to twenty-day journey from Bamako, as well as from Tuba and Banamba. And if the Banamba-Simpara were clients to the Bamako-Ture, at home in Banamba they hosted traders from the Marka towns of Tuba and Kerowan, as well as from the Inland Delta towns, a journey of about eight days. The Sylla-Simpara-Ture axis therefore connected all three families to the European trade in the Senegambia (southwestern Mande), the desert-side salt trade in Banamba, the Inland Delta towns, and the upper Niger markets in the Bamako Mande-hinterland. From the Adrar in the Tawat, Drave *ja-tigi* networks connected them to the Timbuktu-Drave, the Gao-Drave, and the Jenne-Drave, with other networks extending to Kita, Kayes, and Rufisque. Ture networks, the largest of them all, extended from the Senegambia and the Mande to the desert salines.[53]

It is not clear when all these regional networks were first in place, although they were already there by the end of the eighteenth century

---

52. Bayol, *Voyage*, pp. 121–122; *ASAOF* 1G 79, Conrard, "Notice" (Bamako, 21 Feb. 1885), pp. 2–4; interview Marabout Touré (Bozola-Bamako, 4 Jan. 1980); Meillassoux, "Histoire," p. 209.

53. Niare *ja-tigi* networks, which ran southwest to the upper Guinea Coast, are less clear; so are those affecting the Kulibaly, Jara, and Traore slave lords "harvesting" captives in the Mande regions and beyond. The same might be said for Abdul Kadar of Weyaweyanko, the kola nut dealer, who would have hosted mainly traders from the south.

when Park passed through Bamako. When corresponding networks in the Senegambia and Guinea coastal areas (Southwestern Mande speakers) began their northward expansion into the Bamako region and Mande-hinterland also remains unclear. Southwestern Mande networks were probably in place within decades after the Portuguese established their forts at Arguin (c. 1443), or at the Cabo Verde archipelago (Cape Verde, c. l460s), or at Sao Jorge da Mina (El Mina, c. 1482). They would probably have extended further north during the fifteenth- and sixteenth-century expansion of Cabo Verdian commercial enterprises into upper Guinea, from Rio Fresco, Portudal, and Joal (Casamance), extending eastward along the Sierre Leone coast. By the seventeenth century, Mande traders were also expanding towards French establishments at Saint Louis (c. 1638), the Senegal River and the Senegambia (c. 1630s to 1670s), and at Rufisque, Portudal, and Joal (c. 1670s) after Dutch posts had been established there (albeit briefly). More breakthroughs in the Senegambian and Guinea Coast networks followed during the two centuries marked by British and French competition on the Gambia River (c. 1618–1690s), the Senegambia, and Sierre Leone (c. 1700–1780s). Similar phenomena would have developed once French joint-stock companies had established their forts (temporarily as events subsequently proved) at Saint Joseph (1699) and Saint Pierre (1715)—on the Senegal and Faleme Rivers respectively— and at Podor (1743) in the Futa Toro. These expanding trades occurring over approximately one hundred years prior to Bamako's founding would have justified Biton's eighteenth-century southward expansionist designs.[54]

Southwestern Networks: Articulations with Bamako, the Mande-hinterland, and the Mande World

Given this northward expansion from the Senegambia and the Guinea Coast, what trading groups were most responsible for these developments? The new networks of trading communities into which the Bamako families were being integrated were none other than the Northern and

---

54. Some of these early Europeans visited the Galam-Bambuk-Tambaura mines. See also, Labat, *Nouvelle relation*, vol. 4, p. 32–56; vol. 5, pp. 124–125, 157, 195–220, 248–249, 250–251, 257–258; *ANSOM* B4, C. A. Walckenaer, *Histoire générale*, vol 8, Sieur Villault et Sieur de Bellefond, "Relations des côtes d'Afrique, appelées Guinée, avec la description du pays, des moeurs, des usages, des productions (1666–1667)" (London, 1670), pp. 28, 29; *ANSOM* Sénégal III, Doss. 1, Mollien, "Journal du voyage" (Paris, 8 July 1819).

Southwestern Mande speakers who, like their Bamako counterparts, had been dispersed from Wagadu since antiquity. Many had settled in these southern and southwestern regions since the fifteenth century, at least. Together with autochthonous overlords, they had elaborated relayed trading networks north, east, and west into the interior.[55]

Few voices call their names, although they would probably have answered to particularized variations of Kante, Kulibaly, Konate, and Ture. However, especially remembered among them, in the European sources at any rate are groups of dependent strangers—living along the full length of the upper and lower Guinea coasts, and identified as Americo-Africans (Sierra Leonians?, Liberians?), Anglo-Africans, Portuguese, Cabo Verdians, and Luso-Africans.[56] Among these were the Luso-African Fernandez family from Bramaya in upper Guinea and their Americo-African counterparts, the Curtis family, from Kissing. Other strangers, the Wilkinson and Lightburn families, were settled along the Rio Pongo (both in upper Guinea). Powerful, Lightburn elders were sometimes co-signatories with local chiefs in treaty-signings; Curtis notables were sometimes advisors to local chiefs at Thia in upper Guinea. Likewise powerful was the Sierre Leonian (Americo-African?) Charles Heddle family, and one Mr. Fabes, an Anglo-African, head of another trading family, who consulted regularly with chiefs of the Futa Jallon on local political affairs. Although family names have not always survived, other records speak of "French," "Portuguese," "white," "black," and "mulatto" advisors who, had become domesticated according to regional customs. A "black Englishman" from Sierra Leone identified among them, this young man served as translator to the Samorians, while exchanging slaves for British arms in the Siguiri region. Elsewhere, reports recur of "mulattos in league with the British, stirring up trouble for French traders"; or of "Moors and mulattos" in opposition to the French, obstructing the gum trade; or of "Portuguese" and "mulattos" engaged in serious trade. Or, we hear of "lazy Portuguese" in pantaloons—who neither worked nor hunted—practicing the same religious rituals as their African hosts, who had children with African women, and who passed their days in idleness, sitting around on vestibule mats, smoking and chatting with friends, only moving about for

---

55. Perinbam, "Notes," pp. 676–690; Perinbam, "The Juulas," pp. 455–475. See also Curtin, *Economic change*.

56. *ANMAE, 1780–1822*, vol. 11, "Mémoire: Moyens à employer par le Ministre pour assurer à la France touts les avantages qu' elle peut tirer d'un établissement près des mines en Bambouk, 1780," pp. 29–34.

necessities. Later observers were surprised to find a great many Portuguese loan words in these local language repertoires[57]

Central to these family networks were women playing important roles, especially in Luso-African communities, where as wives, concubines, and slaves, they mediated between strangers and their lords. At Kayes (western Mali), for example, William Gray and surgeon Dochard (1825) noted a Luso-African woman trader "exercising a considerable influence throughout the region." Known as Madam Eliza Tigh, all Kayes' inhabitants (a total of fifty residences) were either dependents and/or related to Madam. In the Rio Pongo (Guinea), Faidherbe likewise noticed a Luso-African businesswoman, one Madam Leyboun, managing a large trading company of about 2,000 slaves. About sixty years of age, according to Faidherbe, Madam was assisted by her daughter, a Ms. Campbell and her descendants, together with Madam's mother, nearly one hundred years old, altogether five generations of the Leyboun family involved in the slave and kola nut trade. Also working with indigenous overlords, but less clearly identified, were other Euro-Africans (mainly Luso-Africans) and Mande families around the Rio Pongo (Guinea) and Bure regions, some resident since the seventeenth century in Bure's case.[58]

Other families had been in the region for between five to seven generations (since 1710, allowing thirty years per generation). Traveling extensively and controlling vast interests, their trading networks extended into the eastern Mande-hinterland beyond the Futa Jallon to Worodugu. Several of these Euro-African families, trading directly with the Fulbe of the Futa Jallon, were buying cattle, sheep, gold, slaves, grain, and groundnuts. Children in the families were sent to French and British mission

---

57. Labat, *Nouvelle relation*, vol. 1, pp. 12–16, 19–24, 36–151, 160–165, 234–250, 253–270, 305; vol. 5, pp. 248–251; see also *ANSOM* B4, C. A. Walckenaer, *Histoire générale*, vol. 5, "Voyage de Pelletan au Sénégal en 1787 et 1788," pp. 310–311; vol. 8, Villault et de Bellefond, "Relations des côtes d'Afrique," pp. 11, 13–14, 28–29; Odile Göerg, *Commerce et colonisation en Guinée, 1850–1913* (Paris, 1986), pp. 20, 26–27; *ASAOF* 1G 26, "Voyage du Gouverneur Faidherbe à la côte occidentale de l'Afrique 1860"; *ANSOM* VI Doss. 1, "Affaires diplomatiques, 1889 à 1895, Liberia: Délimination de la Côte d'Ivoire du Soudan et du Liberia 1892" (Siguiri, 24 Feb. 1892); *ANMAE, 1773–1820*, vol. 37, "Mémoire sur l'expédition de Galam, 6 Nov. 1819," pp. 294, 295. Other corresponding communities included the Biafada-Sapi, Banyun-Bak, and Kruan (West Atlantic languages), whose coastal and riverain networks extended from Cape Verde and Casamance Rivers (Senegal), to the Malaguetta Coast and Cape Mount as far east as the Cestor and Cavalla Rivers (Liberia). Brooks, *Landlords*, pp. 49–197 and passim.

58. See note 56.

schools established in coastal regions. Many of them clients of the chiefly Mande speaking Susu of the Rio Pongo, these southern Euro-Africans (Portuguese, British, French, American) were paying rent to the "masters of the earth." Other Euro-Africans in league with indigenous traders were also at Gajaga, where, to the disgust of the French, they were trading extensively with the British.[59]

Also among these southwestern family networks—we should hardly be surprised—were John Matthews's "Mandingoes" (Mandinka) and "Suzee" (Susu?) of the "River Sierra-Leone" whose governmental procedures he described sometime between 1785 and 1787 (Chapter 3). In his discourse on their governance, we recall, Matthews believed "Mandingoes" to have "a kind of mixed monarchy," and that every little "king," known as *fasee*, or "father," believed "himself (the) sole lord within his own town." Their laws, we also recall, were "of the patriarchal kind, where the elder of every family was priest and judge." Now, Matthews informs us that these industrious communities, traded extensively with hinterland networks, as well as with European traders, exchanging primarily slaves for firearms and a laundry list of European luxury commodities: silk handkerchiefs, taffetas, scarlet cloth, coarse and fine hats, worsted caps, sabers, lead and iron bars, iron pots, beads of various kinds, paper, British and foreign spirits and tobacco—the usual European inventory. As elsewhere along the Guinea Coast, Euro-Africans, in this case Anglo-Africans—"and there are not a few of them," according to Matthews—spoke only their mothers' idiom.[60]

With politically unstable communities separating Bamako family networks from those of the southwestern Mande, trade linkages between the two could hardly have been easy. For example, in the south during the sixteenth century, the Mani-Sumba migrations ("invasions," others called them) brought large groups of horse-warriors, blacksmiths, settlers, and Islamized trader-groups into hinterland areas, competing for land and

---

59. *ASAOF* 1G 26, "Voyage du Gouverneur Faidherbe" (1860); *ANMAE, 1733–1820*, vol. 37, no. 1, "Lettre Charles Stuart à son Excellence le Marquis Dessolle" (Paris, 23 Aug. 1819), pp. 290–291; *ANMAE, 1773–1820*, vol. 37, "Mémoire: Expédition de Galam" (Paris, 6 Nov. 1819), pp. 294–314; *ANSOM* B4, Walckenaer, vol. 5, "Voyage de Goldberry," pp. 441, 459; vol. 7, Gray and Dochard, "Travels in Western Africa," p. 112; vol. 8, Villlault et de Bellefond, "Relations des côtes," pp. 11, 13–14, 28–29.

60. Other items on sale included: linen goods, Indian cotton, coarse blue woolen cloth, coarse red woolen cloth, sabers, basins, linen ruffled shirts and caps, copper kettles, earthen and glassware (Matthews, *A Voyage*, pp. 52–55, 57, 59, 73–74, 77–78, 80–82, 139–159, 170 and passim).

trade, pressing the autochthones before them, eventually devastating whole regions. Their migrations are still little understood. Likewise rendering commercial linkages no easier were the eighteenth-century wars in the Futa Jallon, Kissidugu, Timbo, and Labe, disquieting otherwise peaceful settlements, and further destabilizing trade. In addition were the unsettling seventeenth- and eighteenth-century European wars when European "strangers" competed with one another other—and with autochthonous families—for commercial superiority throughout the Senegambia and coastal Guinea regions. Facilitating easier linkages were the same-yet-different cultural articulations that subsequently brought several southwestern families, including the autochthones, into the Wagadu circle of the particular and the universal (see Introduction and Chapter 1). The same was true of some of the Mani-Sumba in-migrants. Settling in Liberia and Sierra Leone among previous occupants, some of them southwestern Mande, many of these newcomers not only adopted a Mande dialect, but Mande power associations as well, including the mythical-political rituals, appropriately contextualized, particularized and manipulated to form the Poro and Sande/Bunde associations.[61]

Difficult as this sociopolitical nightmare may have been, neither the southwestern Mande families nor their northern counterparts—at least judging from ultimate initiatives and successes—appear to have taken flight.[62] By the eighteenth century, as we know from the record, the Segovian state hegemony was pushing south, institutionalizing access to trade centers, enclaves, and southern networks, taking wives in a number of instances. Participating in these new found endeavors, upper Niger families contributed to Segu's commercial and political expansion.

Given that Mande, especially Sarakolle, came to dominate these large commercial networks, what network articulations integrated Bamako's elites into this expanding commercial universe? To say that a neat pattern of layered articulations developed would be to oversimplify. Yet some kind of concentric layering did occur, first incorporating families engaged in the gold and slave producing regions of the Mande, the upper Niger, and the Bambuhu-Bure towns.[63] Note that the Bambuhu-Bure

61. Matthews, *A Voyage*, pp. 182–185. Others not part of our story migrated east beyond the Mande world along the coast, possibly as far as present day Ghana.

62. Brooks, *Landlords*, pp. 286–299; ANSOM B4, Walckenaer, vol. 5, "Voyage de Goldberry," pp. 441, 457; vol. 7, Laing, "Travels in Timanae," pp. 340–343.

63. ANSOM B4, Walckenaer, *Histoire générale*, vol. 5, "Voyage de l'Abbé Demanet à l'île de Gorée, au Sénégal et à la Gambie en 1763 et 1764" (1767), pp. 178–180; vol. 5, "Voyage de Pruneau de Pommegorge, en Nigrite, de 1743 à 1765"

towns were only between eight to ten days' journey from the Bamako *kafu* (see Maps 2 and 3).

Extending south, a second east-west layering articulated around the western, and southwestern family networks centered on the Rio Pongo. Other families branches extended from the Southern Rivers east to the Futa Jallon including Labe, an "island" of Islamic clerisy, libraries, and sciences, ideologically committed to the slave trade. Further extensions ran east to Worodugu. Within an articulating axis, the Futa Jallon and Worodugu were approximately fifteen to twenty days' journey from the Bamako *kafu*.

Farther west, a third combination of articulating layers extended to the families of the upper Niger, including centers with access to European trading ports in the Senegambia: Albreda in the Gambia; French posts on the lower Senegal River; as well as those in the Bambuhu goldfields. This third linkage-layer later came to include Gondiuru, principal town of Gajaga, replaced by the French post at Medine in the mid-nineteenth century. In fact, so successful were the western families' articulations with European entrepots that in 1817, some Mande traders were petitioning the French to reopen earlier Senegambian forts—Saint Pierre and Saint Joseph, abandoned in 1759 and 1782, respectively—under their management. Eventually all roads led to the trading families of Timbo in the Futa Jallon and to counterparts in Kankan in Guinea.[64]

Kankan, like Labe, renowned for its Islamic clerisy, was the hub of yet another combination of families articulating and integrating the upper Niger into the Mande world, their commercial interests extending from the Senegambia to Wassulu, from Kakondy (Southern Rivers) to Timbo

---

(1789), p. 29–30, 32–33; vol. 5, deBouffler, "Fragment d'un voyage en Afrique," 2 vols. (1802), p. 346; vol. 8, Villault et de Bellefond, "Relations des côtes d'Afrique," pp. 28–29; vol. 8, Jean Matthews, "Voyage à Sierre Leone de 1785 à 1787," pp. 177, 180, 186; Labat, *Nouvelle relation*, vol. 4, pp. 210–215; vol. 5, pp. 248–249, see also pp. 195–220; *ANMAE*, 1780–1822, vol. 11, Mém. no. 5, "Moyens de tirer tous les avantages … Bambouk … 1780." *ANSOM* Sén. et Dép. XIII Dos. 55, L. Faidherbe, "Agriculture, commerce, industrie, 1856 à 1860: Mines du Bambouk, exploitation 1856–1857" (Gorée, 12 July 1856), pp. 1–32.

64. Abela de la Rivière, *Les Sarakolé*, pp. 69, 122; *ANSOM* Sénégal III Doss. 1, Governor Schmaltz, "Instructions pour les seigneurs Brédif, ingénieur de 1ère classe au Corps Royal des Mines et de Chasselus ingénieurs-géographe, envoyés par sa Majestie pour explorer le cours du Sénégal et l'intérièure de cette partie de l'Afrique, jusques aux Royaumes de Galam, Bambouk et Bondou inclusivement" (Saint Louis, Oct. 1817), pp. 3–4; Caillié, *Voyage*, vol 1, pp. 325–327; *ASAOF* 1G 22, Hecquard, "Voyage à Timbo" (1849–1851).

(Futa Jallon), and from Segu to Timbuktu.[65] Kankan was about ten to fifteen days' journey from the Bamako *kafu*. A fourth combination of layered articulations focusing on present-day Guinea would have again included Timbo's trading families and those of Beyla, the latter a rapidly growing polity, involved in the gold, ivory, wax, animal, and slave trades. Shipping commodities regularly to their counterpart families in Jenne and Timbuktu, Beyla dealers, in particular, also handled salt, tobacco, cowries, and European merchandise, while Timbo's merchants traded slaves destined for the coast, as well as firearms and textiles. Timbo was within fifteen to twenty days' journey from Bamako. Finally, the same century that saw Bamako's foundation also witnessed the development of corresponding southern regions involving, most importantly, the trading families of Buguni, Odienne, and Wassulu. Buguni, initially a commercial outpost of the Bamana Segu state, where trade was in the hands of its Kooroko dealers was, by the nineteenth century, a transit point between Segu, the Wassulu, and Odienne (Cote d'Ivoire). Buguni, about ten days' journey north of Kankan, was only about two to three days south of Bamako[66] (see Maps 2 and 3).

Linkage families integrating Bamako and upper Niger towns into the wider trading networks of the southern Mande-hinterland and Mande world, therefore, ranged from those in Buguni (three days), to their counterparts in Bambuhu-Bure (eight to ten days), to Kankan (ten days), and to Timbo (ten to fifteen days). Family networks leaving all these centers intersected with the wider system extending from the Senegambia to Wassulu, and from Kankan to Timbuktu, focusing particularly on Bakel, Medine, Fattatenda (on the Gambia River), the Rio Nunez, and Sierre Leone enclaves. When combined with their northern trading networks, Bamako's families were thus within reach of all major commercial centers of

---

65. It was on realizing this widespread commercial network that Gaspard Mollien recommended reopening French commerce with the Senegambia (Galam and the Faleme) (*ANSOM* Sénégal III Doss. 1, Mollien, "Journal du voyage" [Paris, 8 July 1819]); see also *ASAOF* 1G 32, "Mage à Gouverneur" (Saint Louis, 21 June 1866); *ANMK* 1D 5, "Notice sur la région sud, 1895–1899." British trade, especially in arms, was also reaching far into the interior. *ASAOF* 1G 50, Gallieni, "Analyse … agissement des Anglais" (Nango, 10 Sept. 1880), pp. 2–6; *ASAOF* 1G 50 46, Bayol, "Mission de Ségou" (Saint Louis, 5 July 1880), p. 15.

66. *ANSOM* B4, Walckenaer, *Histoire générale*, vol. 7, "Voyage de M. M. Watt et Winterbotton à Timbo," pp. 257–261. For Kankan and Buguni, see Diané, "L'Islam," pp. 154–156, 159–168; Diarra, "Du Banimonotie," pp. 7–9. For Wassulu, Odienné, and Tuba, see Dosso, "Histoire," p. 85.

Western Africa: from the Senegambia in the west to Timbuktu in the east, and from the desert salines in the north to the Guinea Coast in the south.[67]

The Gold Trade Revisited

What in the meantime was occurring in the gold trade? By the late eighteenth century, if not before, gold's sacred purity was clearly giving way to market forces, persistent ambiguities notwithstanding. I am informed that when Bamana and other Mande traders finally parted with gold destined for international markets, unaware of market values, the families sold it "dirt cheap." We recall that when in the Gambia River approximately four hundred years before, Cadamosto had likewise noticed that although the peoples of "Battimansa" held gold in "high esteem," regarding it as "extremely precious," they sold it cheaply; and that about three centuries later, Park's host (the Almamy of Bundu) was apologizing for the small "trifle" of gold (five drachmas), which he had exchanged for his guest's beads and writing paper.[68] It could have been that since deep antiquity middlemen in the long-distance trade had been making a killing. (Were these the silences in the so-called "silent trade"?)

The process transforming the ores from the *jo*'s sacred purity into a market exchange commodity remains unclear. However, an early dating (if not processual) clue comes from Park. In January 1797 while visiting Kamalia in the Mande (Kamalia was Park's base from August 1796 to April 1797 after leaving Bamako), he learned that in the wake of Faama Monzon Jara's (c. 1790–c. 1808) Segu-Kaartan wars, captives were sent upstream from Segu "for sale at Yamina, Bammakoo, and Kancaba, at which places the greater number ... were bartered for gold dust." Clearly the institutionalized gold and slave articulations were in place. Our next reference comes from Rene Caillie. Bypassing Bamako on the east bank some thirty years later in the early 1820s, Caillie heard of Bamako's involvement in the gold commerce, attributing it to commercial diversions due to the "Segu Jenne war." In what seems like a windfall, even merchants from as far afield as the Senegambia, Gajaga, Bundu, Futa Jallon, and Kong, avoiding the Segu Jenne war zone, were buying gold along

---

67. Gallieni, *Voyage*, p. 435. Binger likewise indicated the widespread reach of the entire region. See the several items in *ASAOF* 1G 90, "Mission Binger et Treich-Laplène à Kong, 1887–1888," and passim.

68. Cadamosto, *The Voyages*, p. 160; Park, *The Travels*, p. 42. Even in the late 1980s gold sold in Mali was well below world market prices (fieldwork in Mali, 1970s, 1980s).

the middle and upper Niger, at Nyamina, Sinsani, and even Bamako.[69] Now, Caillie's Segu Jenne war was none other than the Segu-Massina war between Da Jara (1808–1827), the Segu Faama, and the Massianke Ahmadu Lobo (1810–1862), Islamic reformer of the Fulbe Bari family. The war beginning in about 1816, or shortly thereafter, it was still waging when Dochard visited Segu in 1819,[70] a regional catastrophe by the time Caillie passed through in the early 1820s. Jenne eventually recovered from its war wounds. But in the meantime, advantages redounded upriver to towns like Sinsani, Nyamina, and Bamako.[71] Thus, Bamako's dealers had commoditized gold by at least the latter part of the eighteenth century, if not before.

But if gold was going dirt cheap, what was happening to mining rituals and procedures? More to the point, what was occurring within *numu* communities, those monopolistic power associations that had refused to mine for turban wearers, or whose members had blanched at standing knee-deep underground in water only to hear the *muezzin*'s horn; or who, according to oral accounts, left town enraged when the Mansa returned from his first pilgrimage (date unknown) threatening to toss him into a well on presumably returning from the second (c. 1325) (see Chapter 2).

---

69. Interview Suleyman Dravé (Bamako, 5 Jan. 1980); Park, *The Travels*, p. 244; Caillié, *Voyage*, vol. 2, pp. 153–154.

70. *ANSOM* B4, Walckenaer *Histoire générale*, vol. 7, Gray and Dochard, "Travels in Western Africa," pp. 274, 345. To contextualize the war more broadly, Caillie's "Segu Jenne war" belonged to the nineteenth-century Islamic reforms against "animists" and "backsliders" occurring first in the Futa Jallon in about 1725, when the Fulbe, Karamoko Alfaya, overthrew the Mande-speaking Jyalonke creating an Islamized state at Timbo under the Alfaya and Soriya; second, in the Futa Toro in about 1776, when Abd al-Qadir and the Tukulor *torod'be* triumphed over the Jenyanke, founding an Islamized confederation; third, in the Sokoto Caliphate (1830s–1900/06) under the leadership of Uthman dan Fodio (1754–1817) against corrupt practices; and finally, the imperial *jihad* of 'Umar Tall (1794–1863) against "animist" of the upper and middle Niger. The Segu hold over Jenne may have occurred between 1712 and 1803 (Monteil, *Une Cité*, pp. 102–105; Tauxier, *Histoire*, p. 32). See also *ASAOF* 1G 305, "Histoire du pays de Djenné depuis les temps les plus reculés jusqu'au 12 avril l893," pp. 10, 12, 13; Bintou Sanankoua, *Un Empire peul au XIXe siècle: La Diina du Massina* (Paris, 1990), pp. 51–57, 66–76; C. A. Walckenaer, *Recherches géographiques sur l'intérieur de l'Afrique septentrionale* (Paris, 1821), pp. 92, 94, 477–481; Mage, *Voyage*, p. 403.

71. *ASAOF* 1G 305, "Cercle de Djenné" (Jenne, 10 March 1904), p. 19. Mage's reference to gold traded along the Niger by the 1860s in exchange for cloth makes no reference to Bamako (*ASAOF* 1G 32, "Mage à M. Le Gouverneur" [Saint Louis, 21 June 1866]).

Once too powerful to defy, by the late nineteenth and the early twentieth century, *numuw* power associations were losing their sacred terror: Gold mining was opening to the secular and profane. By the twentieth century, "all who were interested" were permitted to mine gold. Under these changing circumstances, market-oriented miners worked either as a "company of one," or in groups. Most mined and traded part-time in the dry season from October to May. And it was not long before market-driven entrepreneurs appeared in their own right, ostensibly owing nothing to the *jo* or to the sacred *komo* rituals.[72] The precious ores were being deritualized and commoditized. By the early twentieth century, gold had taken its place in Bamako's market inventories along with salt, slaves, herds, grains, kola nuts, and varieties of European merchandise.

War-Time Economies and the Post-war Economic Recovery: Kola Nuts, Grain, and Livestock

By the time the French reached Bamako in February 1883, the Mande-hinterland's political economies, in deep depression since the 1860s, lay in ruins, thanks mainly to the Umarian and Samorian wars. Few merchants ventured forth; and fearing to risk investments, desert-side salt and livestock merchants ceased traveling south, returning instead to desert-side locations from points well north of Bamako. Even worse, the establishment of Umarian garrisons in the Marka towns of Tuba, Nyamina, Banamba, Kerowane, and Kiba, as well as their east bank occupation, had isolated Bamako both economically and politically. Further Umarian raids against the Bamana of Fadugu, Messekele, and Doeribugu brought additional economic disasters. Only the most intrepid kept merchandise circulating during the war-torn decades.[73] Local food production, moreover, virtually ceased: Farmers fearing exposure abandoned their fields to dust. In several regions, but especially in the Mande, famine stalked the land. In the Wassulu and Worodugu—where cholera ravished the impoverished—decimated populations devoured horses and donkeys for fare. Devastating more than the Umarians, Samorian armies made extraordinary demands on local resources. So did the French after 1883, requiring

---

72. Interview Massa Makan Diabaté (Bamako, 21 March 1983); see also, *ASAOF* 1G 46, "Mission Solleillet 1878 à 1879: Rapport sommaire sur le commerce adressé à M. le Gouverneur du Sénégal et dépendances," pp. 4–8.

73. *ASAOF* 15G 83, Ruault, "Généralités 1880 à 1920" (Bamako, 22 Feb. 1884), pp. 9–13; *ASAOF* 1G 79, Conrard, "Notice" (Bamako, 21 Feb. 1885), pp. 4–6; Gallieni, *Voyage*, pp. 199, 200.

tirailleurs, engineers, craftsmen, cooks, porters, interpreters, and inform-
ers, not to mention livestock and grain. Unsettled conditions elsewhere
brought unprecedented numbers of refugees from the Beledugu, the
Mande, the Wassulu, the right bank—even Segu—adding to the chaos.[74]
Similar conditions prevailed in neighboring jurisdictions, in the Beledugu
and Kaarta, as well as middle and upper Niger political economies, all
struggling to restore political economies in ruin.

Even the salt and slave traders lost their share of the market. When reviving, it was the kola nut (*Stercullia macrocarpa*), grain, and livestock
trades that now drove Bamako's economic recovery during the latter part
of the nineteenth century. Not hitherto unimportant, we recall that all three
commodities were traded in the old Mande-hinterland markets, desert-
side dealers exchanging animals and rock salt for grain, slaves, and kola
nuts. Specifically cultivated in the Wassulu, so cherished were these fruits
that dealers not uncommonly traveled as far afield as fifteen days in search
of suitable leaves for kola wrapping.[75] Accordingly, it was not long before
increased demands, spearheaded by the French after 1883 ignited producer response, many traders expanding inventories to include grains and
livestock, much needed by the French. Population increases—mainly war
refugees, new migrants, *tirailleurs*, "foreign" wage laborers, many of them
Wolof from Senegal—created a large kola nut market, almost overnight.[76]

Steeped in a ritual subculture—as with gold and salt—kola nuts were
not only ingested as a stimulant and thirst-quencher, but were also consumed by Muslims identifying with the northern paradigm in lieu of the
much despised *dolo*. Symbols of vigor and power, kolas were presented as
gifts, particularly when ratifying alliances, the latter including Islamized
commercial partnerships. Family ceremonies and fetes were invariably
associated with kola nuts, presented at marriages, naming ceremonies,
and burials, almost as important as gold under certain circumstances.[77]

---

74. Numerous reports bear this out. See, for example, *ANSOM* Sén. et Dép. IV
Doss. 90 Bis, "Gallieni à M. Le Capitaine Roiffé" (Siguiri, 5 April 1888), p. 2; *ANMAE,
1892–1894*, vol. 124, "Télégramme no. 165" (Saint Louis, 22 Sept. 1893), pp. 321–322.

75. *ANMAE, 1890–1894*, vol. 123, Binger, "Le Soudan français, 'Le Temps'" pp.
68–69. See also Thadeus Lewicki, *West African food in the middle ages* (Cambridge
University Press, 1974), pp. 122–123. For the place of the Kooroko in the kola nut
trade see Amselle, "Parenté et commerce," pp. 253–265.

76. Interview El Hajj Mamadou Makadji (Banamba, 12 April 1983); interview
Tiémoko Coulibaly (Kangaba, 13 April 1983); interview Massa Makan Diabaté
(Bamako, 21 March 1983).

77. The kola nut culture is very old, and may even predate the introduction of
Islam in the region (interview Mahmadou Sarr [Bamako, 6 Jan. 1980]). Symbolic

On the industrial level, kola nuts were much in demand, especially in Segu's textile industry, one of the region's most developed, where the fruit's yellowish-brown properties were utilized in dyes. Thus in response to consumer demand, merchants elaborated and expanded grain, livestock, and kola nut markets northward, particularly to Nioro, Gumbu, Jenne, and Timbuktu, where both kola nuts and grains were highly prized. By the turn of the century, the salt trade was reviving.[78] Bamako, in the meantime, was becoming a warehouse for merchandise coming from well beyond the Mande-hinterland: from Timbuktu and beyond in the north, from regions surrounding the southern Niger tributaries (Tinkisso and Sankarani), from the Senegambia in the west, and Siguiri and Kurusa in the east (see Map 3).

As dealers operationalized political economies in combination with regional investors and French commercial houses, the economic recovery first focused on reopening the old, later, pioneering new routes and markets well beyond the Mande-hinterland.[79] In search of kola nuts, many traders pioneered more southerly routes for the first time, including major roads converging on Odienne (Cote d'Ivoire), and Kankan (Guinea), even farther south to Kani and Zuenula in Guru country (Cote d'Ivoire), site of kola nut production. They also elaborated major roads to Kissi and Beyla (Guinea) in Toma country, to Danane (western Cote d'Ivoire), Tuleplu (northeast Cote d'Ivoire), and Tappi (eastern Liberia) in Guerze country. Farther west, kola networks extended northeast from the Southern Rivers to centers such as Kono, Kissi, and Konyan—producer regions in Sierra Leone and Guinea. In the north,

---

meanings for the kola nut varied. Frequently in the Bamako, region, the white kola signified happiness, the red, misfortune.

78. Kong's textile industry likewise had a great need for kola nuts (Diabaté, "La Région," pp. 63, 65; Boubacer Konaté, "Monographie," pp. 17, 27, 28, 30, 31, 33, 34, 40, 42, 43); Diarra, "Du Banimonotie," p. 7. The numerous quarterly commercial reports likewise substantiate this claim of economic recovery. See especially *ANMK* 1Q 44, "Rapports commerciaux, 1886–1919: Etat récapitulatif des patentes de dioulas délivrées à Bamako, pendant l'année 1898 avec les diverses destinations et le détail des marchandises emportées" (Bamako, 20 Jan. 1899).

79. In 1905 there were about eighteen European commercial houses in Bamako, twenty-one in 1906. French commercial houses included Maurel et Prom, Compagnie Française Africaine Occidentale de Teyssère [sic.], Ch. Peyrissac et Compagnie, Devès et Chaumet, Société Commerciale, Buhan et Teissière [sic.], Société Niger Soudan, Cohen Frères, et Compagnie Française de Commerce Africain (COFCA); companies came mainly from Marseilles, Bordeaux, Le Havre, and Paris.

Mopti, hitherto marginal to the older trades, entered the kola markets by exchanging dried fish. And in the Jenne regions, focus of the old northern paradigm, both Maraka and Bamana farmers moved aggressively into grain production.[80]

As markets widened and competition increased in the kola nut and grain trades especially, Bamana and Maninka *jula den*, or younger southern scions, were dispatched farther afield as regional representatives. Among these were juniors from the Kulibaly, Jaby, Traore, Gassama, Wattara, Sylla, Sisse, Fonfana, Samake, and Sanogo families. Establishing businesses in Bamako's urban quarters, the first to prosper were Bozola and Weyaweyanko. Also attracting dealers from elsewhere, other juniors came from Dravela and Tawatila (Bamako's Ture quarter), notably scions from the Kone, Drave, and Ture families.[81] The turn of the century heralding further operations in the north-south kola trades, increasing monetary flows encouraged merchant-families to exploit Guinea's kola forests more fully, those of Liberia and the Gold Coast as well. By 1904 about 10 million kolas per annum were transiting Bamako, worth about 50 francs per kilogram (about thirty kolas to the kilogram), suggesting markups of between 100 and 300 percent.[82]

Expanding kola markets notwithstanding, the grain and livestock trades also led Bamako's economic recovery. With both French and Samorian armies competing for identical resources—as well as growing numbers of railway and engineering crews, not to mention war refugees—local dealers and producers lost no opportunity to control both the grain (millet, maize, rice, barley) and livestock (horses and mules) trades, albeit briefly, during the early 1880s and 1890s. The same

---

80. Gallais, *Le Delta intérieur*, vol. 1, pp. 476–478; Perinbam, "The Juulas," p. 462; interview Tiémoko Coulibaly (Kangaba, 13 April 1983); interview Kalifa Coulibaly (Bamako, 30 Oct. 1982); interview Abdulhai Diallo and Mahmadou Diallo (brothers) (Mopti, 17 Nov. 1982). See also ANMK 1D 33, "Monographie" (Jenne, 1909), pp. 34–35, 51–67, 69.

81. Interview Marabout Touré (Bozola-Bamako, 4 Jan. 1980); interview Kalifa Coulibaly (born c. 1907) (Bamako, 30 Oct. 1982); interview Karamogo Touré (Bamako, 8 April 1983); interview Tiémoko Coulibaly (Kangaba, 13 April 1983); interview Suleyman Dravé (Bamako, 8 Jan. 1980).

82. Diarra, "Du Banimonotie," pp. 7, 50; Hammadoun Diallo, "La prise de Djenné par Archinard au avril 1893," Mém. de fin d'études under the direction of Kagnoumé J. B. Konaré, l'ENSUP (Bamako, 1976–1977), pp. 13–14; Traore, "Contribution," p. 35; ANMK 1D 243, "Mission du Chef de bataillon Digue: Chemin de fer entre Bamako et Niamey, 1905," pp. 77–80; ANMK 1Q 44, "Rapports commerciaux, Cercle de Bamako, 1886–1919," see report for Bamako, 1903.

might be said for the sale of groundnut straw used for animal forage.[83] Grain, forage, and livestock markets thus became a seller's paradise, attracting breeders, especially those from both Niger banks, the Mande, the Beledugu, and the Kaarta, even as far afield as Kayes, and the Moorish desert-side communities. While some were quick to dispose of animals in local markets before the pluvial onset, others, like the powerful Beledugu chiefs, used grain and livestock as political weapons against the French, withholding produce until political demands had been heeded. They also slowed supplies by clapping into irons—and selling into slavery—intrepid julaw making their way to French forts.[84] With increasing demands for grain in neighboring markets, by the late 1880s, Bamako and its Mande-hinterland were becoming the Sudan's grain (and arms) storage and market centers. By the 1890s, northern Fulbe and Maraka farmers from the Massina and middle Niger, reinventing their earlier northern paradigm, had become the principal grain and livestock producers, while desert-side Moors—although not producers—were vending cereals and herds in "kaffir lands," as far south as Guinea, the Cote d'Ivoire, and the Gold Coast. Indigenous successes were, however, relatively short-lived. Within a few decades, when Lebanese merchants were installed in the Bamako region and

---

83. *ANMK* 1Q 44, "Rapports commerciaux 1886–1919: Cercle de Bamako" (Bamako, Jan. 1886); *ANSOM* Sén. et Dép. IV Doss. 90 Bis, Vallière, "Rapport ... Minamba-Farba" (Bamako, 9 March 1888), p. 2; *ANSOM* Sén. et Dép. IV Doss. 90 Bis, Soudan français, décision no. 80, Vallière, "Recolte des fourrages dans les postes du Soudan français" (Siguiri, 6 April 1888), n.p.; *ANSOM* Sén. et Dép. IV Doss. 90 Bis, "Rapport no. 5 du Lieutenant-Colonel Gallieni Commandant Supérieur du Soudan français sur le service administratif du Soudan français pendant le campagne, 1887–1888" (Bafulabe, 10 May 1888), pp. 9–10; *ANSOM* Sén. et Dép. IV Doss. 90 Bis, Gouverneur Général à Gallieni, "Rapport" (Paris, 11 Oct. 1889), pp. 1–5; *ANSOM* Soudan 1 Doss. 9, Louis Edgar de Trentinian, "Affaires politiques et indigènes: Exposé de la situation politique intérieure et extérieure des cercles au 1 juillet 1895" (Kayes, 10 August 1895), pp. 4–5; *ANMK* 1D 33 5, "Notice historique" (1880–1890), pp. 7–18.

84. *ANSOM* Sén. et Dép. IV Doss 90 Bis, "Le Sous-Secrétaire d'Etat (i.e., Vallière) au Ministère de la Marine et des Colonies au Gouverneur du Sénégal" (Paris, 20 Oct. 1886), p 5; *ANSOM* Sén. et Dép. IV Doss. 90 Bis, Vallière, "Rapport ... Minamba-Farba" (Bamako, 9 March 1888), pp. 17, 36; *ANSOM* Sén. et Dép. IV Doss. 90 Bis, Vallière "Rapport ... Mambi" (Kangaba, 5 March 1888), pp. 21, 25; *ANSOM* Sén. et Dép. IV Doss. 90 Bis, Extrait no. 2, Tautain, "Extraits des rapports politiques venus de Cercle de Bamako" (Bamako, 4 March 1887), n.p.

Mande-hinterland, a large share of the region's grain commerce passed into their hands.[85]

In the meantime it goes without saying that the French, the region's newest in-migrants and major purchasers, were annoyed by the local competition, no doubt also the Samorians, although no trace of their displeasure has survived.[86] In a high dudgeon, the French talked of establishing a permanent marketing board for animal purchases at Kayes and Bamako. To this end, they also recommended that purchases of the more elegant, more expensive, and less efficient "Arab" horse imported from Algeria (an icon in the northern paradigm) be abandoned in favor of the hardier Sudanese mule, better adapted for drudgery and the cacophony of war.[87] By the late 1880s, when Bamako became the principal base for French campaigns against the Umarians at Segu, northern breeders were sending large shipments south to Kayes and Bamako—a trend that continued—trading 15,000 heads in 1904 of sheep, goats, horses, cattle, and

---

85. Interview Suleyman Dravé (Bamako, 5 Jan. 1880); interview Marabout Touré (Bozola-Bamako, 5 Jan. 1980); *ASAOF* 1G 351, Bobichon, "Note sur le Cercle de Bamako" (Bamako, 20 Feb. 1921); *ANSOM* Sén. et Dép. IV Doss. 90 Bis, Vallière, "Expédition dans le Grand Bélédougou" (Bamako, 1 Feb. 1888), p. 36; *ANMK* 1D 33 5, Borgnis Desbordes, "Notice historique" (1880–1890), p. 7; *ANMK* 1Q 44, "Rapports commerciaux 1886–1919: Cercle de Bamako" (Bamako, see reports from 1905–1910, 1913, 1st trimester).

86. *ANMAE, 1886–1889*, vol. 122, "Clauses exécutoires annexes au traite du 28 mars 1886 reglant la paix entre les Français et Samory," arts. 1, 2, pp. 31–32.

87. In addition to carrying less and suffering higher losses (as much as 95 percent in the military campaigns of the 1880s as opposed to mule losses at 48 percent for the same period), horses were more expensive, 1,000 francs per head in 1888 as opposed to 900 francs for the dowdy mule. The military had spent 500,000 francs at least on "Arab" horses for campaigns between 1892 and 1898, considered exorbitant. *ANSOM* Sén. et Dép. IV Doss. 90 Bis, "Le Capt. Patriarche, C'dant de la compagnie de régiment de tirailleurs sénégalais au Chef de bataillon…Kayes" (Bamako, 1 March 1888), p. 1; *ANSOM* Sén. et Dép. IV Doss. 90 Bis, "Campagne 1887–1888: le Chef de bataillon Vallière au Lieutenant Colonel Gallieni C'dant Supérieur du Soudan français" (Siguiri, 1 April 1888), p. 26; *ANSOM* Sén. et Dép. IV Doss. 90 Bis, "Comptes des dépenses de la colonne du Haut Niger, campagne 1887–1888, 10 dec. 1887 à avril 1888" (Kayes, 12 May 1888), pp. 3, 6; *ANSOM* Sén. et Dép. IV Doss. 90 Bis, "Campagne 1887–1888: Rapport no. 3 du Lieutenant-Colonel Gallieni Commandant Supérieur du Soudan français sur le service vetérinaire, le service du train et la remonte des saphis dans le Soudan français" (Bafulabe, 10 May 1888), pp. 2–8; *ANSOM* Sén. et Dép. IV Doss. 93 Bis, Gouverneur Général à Gallieni, "Rapport" (Paris, 11 Oct. 1889), pp. 1–5, 13–15 and passim.

donkeys in Bamako-Buguni markets.[88] Similarly irked by grain competition and inevitable price increases—despite the larger than expected cereal harvests in the Bamako region and Mande-hinterland—the French craved more grain production. And if the elegant "Arab" horse in its heyday had savored the large millet, it should also be fed to old nags and mules.[89]

Thus by the end of the military campaigns of the 1880s and 1890s against the Samorians—after the latter's troops had moved east to Kong and Bonduku—and the Umarians defeated, Bamako's political economies were showing signs of recovery for the first time, after a forty- to fifty-year very deep depression. By the turn of the century, Somono transporters were once more regularly on the river. As before, other commodities were also on Bamako's domestic and foreign markets, not least of all commodities of local manufacture. With the exception of the Beledugu and right-bank communities—where cowries were still widely used—most economies were becoming monetized by the late 1880s; a labor market was developing (labor, however, remained a scarce commodity for several years thereafter). And while protesting merchant voices could be heard against taxes, custom dues, and rail tariffs, others brought charges of abusive treatment at the hands of French merchant houses including gross dishonesties and public floggings.[90] Thus, Bamako's economic recovery,

---

88. *ANSOM* Sén. et Dép. IV Doss. 90 Bis, "Vallière au Gouverneur du Sénégal" (Paris, 20 Oct. 1886); *ANSOM* Sén. et Dép. Doss. 90 Bis, Vallière, "Rapport … Minamba-Farba" (Bamako, 9 March 1888), p. 17; *ANSOM* Sén. et Dép. IV Doss. 90 Bis, "Patriarche … au Chef de bataillon" (Bamako, 1 March 1888), p. 1; *ANMK* 1D 33 5, Borgnis Desbordes, "Notice historique" (1880–1890); *ANMK* 1D 243, Digue, "Chemin de fer" (1905), pp. 80–81; (*ANSOM* Sén. et Dép. IV Doss. 90 Bis, Gallieni, "Rapport sur les opérations militaires" (Aboard the *Siguiri,* 22 May 1888), pp. 4–5.

89. The French were importing barley, millet, and other forage. In the 1887–1888 military campaigns alone, 15,000 kilograms of barley cost 4,400 francs, and 25,703 kilograms of millet, 4,369 francs, bringing the total cereal invoice to 8,769 francs. *ANSOM* Sén. et Dép. IV Doss. 90 Bis, "Comptes des dépenses" (Kayes, 1888), pp. 3, 6; *ANSOM* Sén. Dép. IV Doss 90 Bis, Vallière, "Récolte des fourrages" (Siguiri, 6 April 1888), n.p.; *ANSOM* Sén. et Dép IV Doss. 90 Bis, "Rapport no. 5 du Gallieni" (Bafulabe, 10 May 1888), pp. 2–8, 10; *ANSOM* Sén. et Dép. IV Doss. 90 Bis, Gallieni, "Rapport" (Aboard the *Siguiri,* 22 May 1888), p. 16; *ANSOM* Sén. et Dép. IV Doss. 93 Bis, Gallieni, "Rapport" (Paris, 11 Oct. 1889), pp. 1–5, 13–15 and passim.

90. *ANSOM* Sén. et Dép. IV Doss. 90 Bis, "Rapport no. 5 du Gallieni" (Bafulabe, 10 May 1888), pp. 9–10; *ANMK* 2L 8, "Télégramme, Correspondance navigation de Bamako, 1901–1915" (Bamako, 10 Jan. 1901), n.p.; *ANMK* 1Q 17, "Corre-

at first war related, had by the turn of the century taken on new dimensions in preparation for the unprecedented role as the French capital of the western Sudan. The transfer from Kayes, the former capital, to Bamako was finalized in 1908.

Conclusion

During the approximately 150 years of the *kafu*'s existence, Bamako's elites elaborated the region's political economies in three different ways. During the first, the pre-*kafu* era, pioneering families (Bamana horse-warriors, Bozo river nomads) exchanged commodities in small, low-level markets. Although local exchanges were probably linked to the Samanyana cluster of older market towns (e.g., Samalen Samalia, Siby), exchanges revealed no marks of elaborated Mande political economies, in what Valliere would have identified as "in the Mande style." The second level of development came with the *kafu*'s founding sometime during the first half of the eighteenth century. Although Bamako was marked by a warrior identity in its initial stages, Islamized commercial elites later developed commercial networks—in the Mande style—articulating principally around families. Unlike the south's earlier gold and salt trade (the means by which families in a previous era had entered the formative trans-Saharan trade), Bamako's access to international trade was primarily through the salt and slave domestic and international markets. Gold, still important in the *jo*'s inventory of sacred signs and symbols, was late in acquiring a market value. By the late eighteenth century, Bamako's elites had accessed the Senegambian and Guinea Coast trades, interacting

spondance commerciale 1882–1907: Cercle de Kita, lettre Commandant du fort à Kita, à resident à Niagassola" (Kita, 17 April 1882); *ANMK* 1Q 17, "Correspondance commerciale 1882–1907: Cercle de Kita, lettre le Captaine Tellier Commandant le Cercle de Kita à Monsieur le Gouverneur" (Kayes, 19 April 1897); *ANMK* 1Q 22, "Correspondance commerciale 1887–1907: Cercle de Médine, lettre Monsieur le Commandant supérieur à Kayes" (Kayes, 27 April 1887); *ANMK* 1Q 22, "Correspondance commerciale 1887–1907: Cercle de Médine, lettre à Monsieur le Colonel Archinard" (Medine, 6 March 1891); *ANMK* 1Q 22, "Correspondance commerciale 1887–1907: Cercle de Médine, lettre d'Aly Gueye au Gouverneur du Soudan français" (Medine, 13 May 1894); *ANMK* 1Q 22, "Correspondance commerciale 1887–1907: Cercle de Médine, lettre à Monsieur l'Administrateur du Cercle de Médine" (Medine, 8 Oct. 1896); *ANMK* 1Q 24, "Correspondance commerciale 1892–1911: Cercle de Nioro; *ANMK* 1Q 29, "Correspondance commerciale 1899–1907: Cercle de Ségou"; *ANMK* 1Q 44, "Rapports commerciaux 1886–1919: Cercle de Bamako," see esp. 3rd quarter, 1909; 4th quarter, 1910.

for the first time with the networks of counterpart families speaking other Northern, and Southwestern Mande languages. Important among these southwestern identities were women and families espousing Euro-African identities.

Commodities exchanged throughout this 150-year period approximately, represented the usual inventory associated with the western Sudanese trades. By the eighteenth century, a growing quantity of European consumer goods—armaments to a lesser extent—were reaching the upper Niger. Mande-hinterland political economies, ruined by the Umarian and Samorian wars, and in a totally depressed state for about forty to fifty years, finally recovered slowly with the French entry into these wars. The kola nut, grain, and livestock trades led the economic recovery.

5

"Bamako Was Not as … We Had Supposed"[1]; Bamako Was Not a "Nothing Country"[2]

Introduction

We are nearing the end of the story. The Bamako *kafu* has been in existence for approximately 150 years in a universalizing chronology, about thirty to thirty-five generations in lineage time. There have been good times and bad; good, bad, and worse harvests. Some years the rains came; in others the animals died. There have been famines, devastating wars, and rumors of wars. Babies have been born. Many have died. The "grandfathers" lie buried. The Segu state hegemony has come and gone. The families have become more or less Bamanakan. And now the "Rumi" are coming.[3] Because the French advance to the Niger between the 1850s and 1880s has, like the families' stories, been retold many times, this chapter provides the merest background. Neither does it treat the politics of the scramble that brought the British and French into West Africa, perspectives already recounted several times over. Instead, the chapter opens windows on further manipulations—this time French cultural manipulations—together with misleading imagery generated in Mande-French

---

1. *ANMK* 1D 33 5, Borgnis Desbordes, "Notice historique" (1880–1890).

2. "Titi replied (to Gallieni, who complained about the attack at Jo, 11 May 1880) that he regretted this aggression, but that (Bamako) was not a nothing country, adding that … he proved his friendship by permitting (the French) … to remain under the walls of the village" (*ASAOF* 1G 52 46, Bayol, "Mission du Ségou" [Saint Louis, 5 July 1880], p. 10).

3. Terminology for the French among some North African, Sahelian and Saharan communities.

sub-texts during the late nineteenth and early twentieth centuries, imagery which ultimately conjugated misconstrued political policies into
misshapen political behavior.

France in the Senegambia
and the Advance to the Niger

It was generally known by many upper Niger families that the French,
"strangers" and "clients" of the various Senegambian lords, had been on
the West African coast since the time of the "grandfathers" in lineage
time, since the seventeenth century in universal chronology. Their domesticated image and contextualized behavior were "understood": The
French were julaw interested mainly in long-distance trade, their guns
and trinkets amusing and interesting. Besides, whites were hardly a military threat, living as they did in ships with no country of their own.[4] Alliances and coalitions were, accordingly, concluded in line with customs
of the region, or so it seemed: Building on agreements with local chiefs,
French policies articulated around commercial and military "understandings." Joint policies, it was believed, could be made to serve common interests, with which goal-oriented West African chiefs could identify. Although the French claimed that alliances and coalitions between "friends"
should carry the weight of legal contracts, local chiefs, including upper
Niger Mande lords, believed otherwise: Contractual agreements—not being sacred ritual alliances between families, as marriage exchanges
were—carried no long-term consequences and no unbearable penalties.
Or so it seemed. By the 1850s the client French, restless and overbearing,
were training their sights on the upper Senegambia and Niger, their behavior going well beyond the boundaries of earlier agreements, and certainly unacceptable within the paradigm of patron-client relationships.
Umarian reactions, swift and sharp, were to remind the French that they

---

4. We recall that Park had also been domesticated as a jula. In Bundu (upper
Senegambia), he was told "that every white man must of necessity be a trader"
(Park, *The Travels*, p. 40; see also *ANSOM* B4, Walckenaer *Histoire générale*, vol. 7,
Gray and Dochard, "Travels in western Africa," p. 349). More than half a century
later, Bozo fisher people on the upper Niger were also of the impression that the
French were "only merchants" (*ASAOF* 1G 83, "Mission Caron à Tombouctou,
1887–1895," pp. 5, 15). The term *jula* acquired widespread use during the colonial
era. It refers to a long-distance, Mande-speaking, Islamized itinerant trader. Not
all jula had a Mande idiom as a mother tongue; some came from a Fulfulde or Sen-
ufu-speaking heritage and so on. Those west of the Comöe River were however
still known as *jula* (Perinbam, "Notes," pp. 676–690).

were "only merchants" (the Umarians were in the Senegambia region from the 1850s; see Introduction). Warships could not be brought into the River, neither could forts be constructed. The price for the client status—and the right to exchange merchandise—was tribute.[5]

Known to many Senegambian and Guinea Coast families, if not always by name at least by image and identity, were France's architects of empire during the latter part of the nineteenth century: none other than military-technical advisors and administrators from the Ministry of Marine in Paris, such as Louis Faidherbe ("Fitiriba" to some Mande-speakers) who, save for eighteen months, was governor in Senegal from 1854 to 1865. Similarly known were the identities and powerful images of like-minded colonial architects, such as Colonels Jean-Bernard Jaureguiberry, and Louis Briere de L'Isle both governors of Senegal in 1861–1863 and 1876–1881, respectively, Juareguiberry later Minister of the Marine in Paris (1879–1880, 1882–1883). Bamako's families were soon to internalize a similar imagery of an expansionist power, summarized not least of all in the persona of "Bourouti," otherwise known as Colonel Gustave Borgnis Desbordes, the *kafu*'s conqueror in 1883. Also known was Joseph S. Gallieni, "the French chief of all the country between Bakel and Bammako," who led the mission to Bamako in May 1880, and who, as commander of the upper Niger from 1886 to 1888, successfully directed military operations in the western Sudan from his Bamako base. By the early 1890s, Gallieni was sending his "friend" (Gallieni's term) Captain Louis Binger, who would speak of nothing but "peace, friendship, and good fortune," to the "commercial establishment at Bamako."[6] By that same token, traders from the Birgo (Maninka and Fulbe) were paying homage to Valliere, their "chief" from the French trading posts in Senegal (Valliere was exploring the Birgo and the old Mande, May 1880); while less than a decade later, Umarians were collapsing the Rumi's powerful identity into the imagery of Colonel Louis Archinard, Segu's conqueror in 1890–1891. All imagery was associated with a powerful state.[7]

Over the decades, these architectural images had committed time and resources to expand and maintain French interests, building forts, prospecting for gold in the Bambuhu-Bure regions ("more riches here than the Spanish and Portuguese have in Mexico, Brazil, and Peru," an

---

5. Faidherbe, *Le Sénégal*, pp. 19–114, 170, 252,–270 and passim.

6. It was Gallieni who described himself as "the French chief," when sending Binger into the interior (Binger, *Du Niger*, vol. 1, p. 9; Soumaoro, "Etude," p. 10).

7. Some members of the Niare family still speak of these French soldiers. For Valliere see Gallieni, *Voyage*, pp. 274–275.

enthusiastic observer estimated), granting mining concessions to French businesses, and concluding treaties with Senegambian chiefs.[8] Cross-cultural conflicts and misunderstandings distorted Franco-Senegambian relations for decades. But the Rumi almost always prevailed. Of their early investors, one of the two most responsible for shaping policies was Chambonnea, director of the Compagnie du Senegal (1682–1695) who, in 1693, sketched ambitious plans for territorial expansion, including agrarian and immigration schemes, as well as policies to establish contact with the Niger interior, not to mention the fabled city of Timbuktu.[9] Similarly, Andre Brue, director of the Compagnie Royale du Senegal (1696–1709), and later of the new Compagnie du Senegal (1709–1719), advanced French interests in Cayor and the Gambia region.[10] The Brakna Moors and the Tukulor of Dimar and Toro in the Futa Toro likewise established commercial interests with him. Following moderately expansionist schemes, the *numuw* and their families in the lower Bambuhu watched as Brue's profane teams reconnoitered regions known for their gold deposits, the *jo*'s "sacred purity."[11] On the other hand, many southwestern

---

8. Curtin, *Economic change*; ANMAE, *1780–1822*, vol. 11, "Mémoire servant à montrer l'importance de la possession de la rivière du Sénégal," n.d., pp. 10–12.

9. See Labat, *Nouvelle relation*, vol. 1, pp. 12–30, 34–36, 45–55, for Labat's discussion of early French commercial endeavors in the Senegambia. See also *ANMAE, 1780–1822*, vol. 11, "Mémoire ... mines en Bambouk 1780," pp. 29–34.

10. For French competition with the Dutch on the Senegambia coast, see Labat, *Nouvelle relation*, vol. 1, pp. 36–151, 160–165, 234–250, 253; vol. 4, pp. 210–215. See also *ANMAE, 1780–1822*, vol. 11, "Mémoire no. 21 sur le droit qu' à la forme de commerce dans tout le cours de la rivière de Gambie ce que les Anglais veulent lui refuser depuis long temps 1780," pp. 95–97.

11. It took approximately 130 years for these and other experimental forms to become official policies (Abdoulaye Ly, *La Compagnie du Sénégal* [Paris, 1958], pp. 263–275; Faidherbe, *Le Sénégal*, pp. 28–34). Dates for early French companies vary according to the source. Of the following approximations, important chartered trading companies brought into existence between 1626 and 1719 included: (1) 1626–1664: Compagnie Normandé or l'Association des Marchandes de Dieppe et de Rouen; (2) 1664–73/74: Compagnie des Indes Occidentales; (3) 1674–1679: (first) Compagnie Royale d'Afrique; (4) 1679–1684: (second) Compagnie Royale d'Afrique; (5) 1684–1884 (sic): (third) Compagnie Royale d'Afrique; (6) 1684–1692: Compagnie du Sénégal; (7) 1692–1694: reorganization of the third Compagnie Royale d'Afrique; (8) 1694–1709: Compagnie du Sénégal, Cap Nord et Côte d'Afrique; (9) 1709–1719: Compagnie du Sénégal; (10) 1719–1738: Compagnie Royale des Indes; (11) 1784–1785: Compagnie Royale de la Guiane; (12) 1783–1791: Compagnie Royale du Sénégal. Of twenty directors, ten died in Senegal (Raffenel, *Nouveau*, vol. 2, pp. 35–44). Faidherbe has a slightly different list; see Faidherbe, *Le*

and Guinea coastal families—the Lightburn, the Curtis, the Leyboun, the Wilkinson, and others—were in fact reacting to similar European initiatives (Chapter 4).

However, according to this well-known story, early French policies had little to show for decades of blood, sweat, and tears; and by the latter part of the eighteenth century, the Senegal colony was in decline. Faidherbe attributed the colony's downturn to the abolition of slavery (1794), and to the Napoleonic Wars, which reduced France's holdings to Goree, Rufisque, Portudal, and Joal.[12] However—no doubt influenced by the Government Commission of 1850, as well as by French investors and merchants—Faidherbe enunciated what later became public policy: that lacking financial reserves and managerial savior faire, most companies needed state support, including a military infrastructure. Spelling out new policies, Fitiriba made his well-renowned statement: "Commerce without protection from the barbarians (i.e., the families) is a thing which has long since been known to be impossible."[13]

Sénégal, pp. 19–20. The companies traded mainly gum—used for confectioneries—from the desert-side populations of the Senegal River. In about the early 1850s, dextrin replaced gum and prices fell. Gum prices fell again in the 1880s to 1 franc per kilogram, largely the result of competition from gum production in Darfur, Kordofan, and Arabia sold in Egypt (Faidherbe, *Le Sénégal*, p. 35); see also Robinson, *The Holy war*, p. 143; James L. Webb, *Desert frontier: Ecological and economic change along the western Sahel, 1600–1850* (University of Wisconsin Press, 1995).

12. Although the French slave trade had been abolished by the Convention in 1794, it had virtually stopped in 1789. Napoleon reimposed and legalized the trade, which was technically outlawed in 1814–1815. The Treaty of Paris, 30 May 1814, restored to France all its territories between Cap Blanco and the Gambia River. In return for relinquishing rights at the mouth of the Niger, the Gold Coast, Sierre Leone, and the Gambia, the French turned toward Senegal and the upper Niger, the areas of earlier monopolistic concerns. In 1818, a fort was built at Bakel, and both Governors Schmaltz (1817–1818; 1819–1820), and Roger (1822–1824; 1825–1827) sent unproductive missions into the gold-bearing Bambuhu regions. Planned expeditions to Timbuktu (1824–1826) were never realized, and early proposals to establish a consul at Bamako, came to nought. The Compagnie du Galam (1824–1835; 1844–1848), which handled the gum trade, was virtually kept out by desert-side producers and eventually had to leave. Governor Protet (1850–1853, 1854), who had been slow to follow up on the French initiative against the desert-side gum producers, was replaced by Faidherbe.

13. So concerned was Faidherbe with developing markets that at one point he was prepared to pay the 5 or 10 percent customs dues to local jurisdictions. Even so, until about 1870 he aimed to achieve commercial objectives by peaceful means, despite the Umarians, still a threatening force between Medine and the Niger

But going beyond mere protectionism, and training his eyes on the Kayes to Bamako-Kulikoro railway (about 553 kilometers and nearly 50 million francs according to some estimates), Faidherbe sent the Lieutenant Eugene Mage Mission (1863–1866) to the Umarian capital at Segu.[14] Among other things, the mission was charged to connect French establishments on the upper Senegal with Bamako, and to create a line of posts about 15 to 20 kilometers apart between Medine and Bamako, the latter most "suitable for the creation of a commercial center on the River."[15] Although intending to, Mage never reached Bamako, and additional plans—to create a "Senegambian Triangle" by securing a line of forts from Saint Louis to Bamako, and along the coast from Saint Louis to Sierre Leone—were likewise abortive.[16] Although respective French governments dragged their feet, it was primarily British competition (German to a lesser extent) that ultimately provided the catalyst, transforming earlier monopolistic trading traditions into commercial and imperial policies.[17]

(Faidherbe, *Le Sénégal*, pp. 2 note 1, 3, 8). The Government Commission (1850) recommended retention of the existing forts at Richard-Toll, Dagana, and Bakel, as well as reinforcements for the post at Senudebu, and the reconstruction of the old fort at Podor.

14. The Umarians overthrew the Jara administration at Segu in 1861. For the railway, see *ANMK* K 40, "Chemin de fer Kayes au Niger tarifs généraux et spéciaux pour les transports à grande vitesse et à petite vitesse 1903." See also Chapter 4, notes 82, 88 and below.

15. Faidherbe, *Le Sénégal*, pp. 2, 6–7, 121, 299–300, 304; Mage, *Relation*, pp. 1–4, 9–14. Faidherbe in addition wanted posts at Bafulabe, Kita (Makajambugu), Murgula or Bangasi, and Bamako. The construction of a new fortified post at Podor on the Senegal in 1854 was the merchants' long looked for reward.

16. Schemes of this nature were outlined from as early as the first part of the eighteenth century. Labat, *Nouvelle relation*, vol. 1, p. 368, see also pp. 363–365. Faidherbe's policies won no support at the Ministry of Marine because the minister, the Marquis de Chasseloup-Labat, disapproved of the Senegambian Triangle project, doubting whether the Gambia would be worth the loss of Gabon, or that it would be possible to compensate the Portuguese for the loss of their Guinea enclave (Louis, Faidherbe, *L'Avenir du Sahara et du Soudan* [Paris, 1863]). See also Mage, *Relation*, p. 221; *ANSOM* Sénégal 150 C, "Ministre au Marine Chasseloup à Faidherbe" (Paris, 24 Dec. 1863); A. S. Kanya-Forstner, *The conquest of the western Sudan: A study in French military imperialism* (Cambridge University Press, 1969), p. 44.

17. For early competition among the British, Portuguese, and Dutch, see *ANMAE, 1780–1822*, vol. 11, pp. 4–20, 30–32, 82–97, 164–165, 393–411 and passim; *ANMAE, 1773–1820*, vol. 37, pp. 32–37, 43–46, 290–291; *ANMAE, 1856–1867*, vol. 47, pp. 26–29, 69–70, 71–74, 84–85, 99–100, 111–114 and passim; *ANMAE, 1892–1894*, vol. 124, pp. 21–22, 23–24, 35, 192–197, 215, 217, 230–231, 277–278 and passim.

Political and military follow-ups developed slowly; and it was not until the late 1870s that French military expansion in the interest of commerce and political domination was once more favored—to one degree or another—by public policymakers.[18] In the meantime, Rumi economic adventurism was transformed into the new-age imperialism abstracted from Saint Simon's (1760–1825) vision of a reorganized society.[19]

Following Faidherbe, later military commanders spelled out the General's policies, most eventually affecting the small *kafu* on the Niger's west bank. The military campaigns launched after the French fort was established at Bamako in 1883 brought glory to France (nothing but infamy, others said); and the names of men such as Bourouti, Fitiriba, Boileve, Combes, Gallieni, Caron, Frey and Archinard still bring encomia from the lips of partisans.

The Undialogue

Part 1: Understanding/Misunderstanding Identities and Images

On returning to cultural distortions, ambiguities, and subtexts, we recall those of the northern paradigm, an internal construct through which northerners mis/understood southerners (see Chapter 2). The analogy of the Roman *civitas in parvo*, which some French administrators applied to Bamako's family-state, equally mis/understood some of the historical realities (see Chapter 3). Now we find a very different combination of mis/perceptions that likewise led to a mutual mis/understanding of identities, images, and intentions. And if the northern paradigm confounded rather than clarified Islamized identities—and the *civitas in parvo* analogy a misleading one—further articulations of Mande-French images and mis-images across cultural and political boundaries produced the dialogue of the deaf, more appropriately the undialogue.

On the one hand were the Bamako families and those Mande-speakers of the Mande-hinterland who, by the late nineteenth century, had developed particularistic ways of conducting both public and private business within variations on the Mande style. With respect to this latter, we re-

---

18. For French expansionist policies, see note 17 above; see also, for example, Faidherbe, *Le Sénégal*, pp. 315–316, 321–349 and passim; Colonel Frey, *Campagne dans le Haut-Sénégal et le Haut-Niger, 1855–1856* (Paris, 1887), p. 406; Joseph Gallieni, *Deux Campagnes au Soudan Français 1886–1888* (Paris, 1891), pp. 618–633.

19. *ANMAE, 1780–1822*, vol. 11, marks the formation of the Société de l'Afrique intérieure, 1801, pp. 313–320; *ANMAE, 1780–1822*, vol. 11, "Extrait d'un Mémoire 93" (1819), see pp. 393–411.

call—by way of summarizing the analysis discussed earlier (see Chapter 3)—that constitutional protocols required families and political power-holders to renegotiate, on a recurring basis, matters affecting the res publica: Renegotiated alliances—sacred in intention and purpose—reconnected the Mande identity to the spiritual universe, thereby both guaranteeing and recreating it. Societal observances of prescribing and proscribing rituals were a further guarantee of harmonious social relationships. Within these provisions conjugated in the Mande style, penalties and punishments were not wanting. And while further alliances bound families within sacred and inviolable circles, not to mention generational cohorts, related provisions limited the social conflict generated therein. Obligations and reciprocities mobilized the community's life, renewing and reproducing its inner integrity according to Mande considerations.-And if the state's moral environment was as palpable as Brevie believed (1904), it is because values and identities were said to be non-negotiable (except that this was not the case). In elaborating the Bamako state's political identity, we moreover recall that the state was neither autonomous nor interventionist. On the contrary, I identified the familial state as "semiautonomous" and "minimalist," meaning that officeholders were not required to separate state power from family filiations. And if matters affecting the collective identity were in the hands of the "father of fathers," the state's everyday life was in the care of the paterfamilias in the Mande *civitas in parvo*.

On the other hand were the Rumi, French speakers of the French state, who, by the late nineteenth century, had likewise developed very specific ways of conducting both public and private business within variations on the French style. Unlike familial states of the Mande-hinterland and the Mande world, however, the Rumi state was territorial in its boundaries, bureaucratic in structure, and both militaristic and imperialistic in its foreign policies, not to mention the industrializing and globalizing of the state's identity. And although familial identity and imagery were important to the French state, especially to those families bearing aristocratic and bureaucratic signs, by the nineteenth century, state and family identities had been significantly differentiated and separated.

Even more interestingly, the Rumi state was coming of age in an era soon to fall under the spell of technological change. Bureaucratic and elite cultures as well as the popular idiom reflected these transformations, including the introduction of machine-age signifiers: The Paris Exposition of 1889, for example—for which Gustave Eiffel designed the tower—has remained one of France's enduring signs. In literature and the arts, contributions of foremost symbolists—such as the Belgian-born poet Maurice Maeterlinck (1862–1949)—to French culture were likewise confirmed. We recall that French and Belgian symbolist poets and writers of the late nineteenth century were identified among those rejecting naturalism, turning instead to evocative images and associations as conveyors of being and experience. Sharing a similar fascination for technology—as well as a facility for manipulating signs and images as measures of identity—many Mande families, were, however, disturbed by the Rumi's mechanical identity: Machines were signs of autonomous and intrusive power. Not surprisingly, the Dakar-to-Bamako railway line was to become the great signifier of the invading Rumi.

Part 2: Imagery in the Bamako Region and the Mande-Hinterland

However, although the families found Europeans and their merchandise interesting—even amusing, according to Park and Raffenel—that the French were also Scriptuaries from a strange writing culture was menacing. The centuries-long exchanges with Islamized peoples, their writing, and *their* Book, had made this threat even more real: Scriptuaries possessed powers to appropriate the word through writing. Like sorcerers, *jeliw*, and marabouts, Scriptuaries with writing skills could access resources of the occult. Writing-on-paper was a secret power. It extracted, accumulated, and thereby controlled knowledge and its uses. Worse, in the lexicon of cultural identities and imagery, extracted knowledge stored in writing became a threat beyond control to the Mande identity. While in Bamako on the Gallieni mission (May 1880), Captain Camille Pietri learned from Karamoko Ule, a Bamako Ture elder—whose "delicate sentiments" according to Gallieni, "were unknown in the Sudan"—how much the "ignorant Bambara" feared the very sight of paper.[20]

Underscoring this subtext, which passed for understanding, was the fact that *seben* in the Mande idiom not only meant "writing" as in "accumulated knowledge," but, in invoking the image of the marabout, *seben* also meant "amulet," or guardian against the sorcerer's wrath. Thus, as the *jeli* 's word took energy, becoming its own word-action, so did the marabout's writing take power, empowering its own writing-intentions. We recall that not only Islamized peoples, but also "pagans" frequently wrapped themselves in written amulets extracted from the holy Koran, including the "animist Bambara," before joining battle with a foe—although according to Captain MacLeod the marabout's IOUs at Nyamina were frequently withheld until the "pagan's" safe return. We also recall that the word out in Niger towns that Park was a "saphie writer" (i.e. marabout)—and therefore "a man of too great consequence to be long concealed"—the Scottish adventurer was soon conjuring amulets "to

20. Gallieni, *Voyage*, pp. 242, 247–248, 280, 374, 379.

procure wealth," his grateful clients licking the board on which his magic signs appeared, having literally consumed its contents with gulps of
water and appropriate prayers; or, that at Kulikoro, Park's "Bambarran"
ja-tigi, on "turn(ing) Mussulman," requested a "Christian" prevention
against misfortune; or, that earlier, when in Khasso in the upper
Senegambia, Park had also been required to reproduce these powerful
signs. And possibly with the same subtext in mind, Mollien's (1819) interlocutor in the Futa Toro wondered if he could write; was he a
marabout? In other imagery, the marabout was expected to be abstemious. On showing little enthusiasm for a drink (*dolo*) while in the
Kaarta, Raffenel's (1840s) host wondered if he was a "marabout, drinking
only when alone, and only in private."[21]

Nearly a quarter century later—amid persistent rumors of the Rumi's
"sorcery"—respect and awe of writing had turned to dread. While exploring the course of the Baoule River (west of the Beledugu), Pietri was advised against writing reports: His scribblings were magic spells; he was
poisoning the wells; his *gris-gris* could ensure a certain death. Not surprisingly, miscellaneous misfortunes occurring in the Beledugu after the Jo
attack in 11 May 1880 were attributed to French sorcery and the paper
gris-gris. Little had changed some twelve years later: In Mossi country,
Binger was "almost accused of sorcery" because of nefarious scribbling.[22]

But not all Europeans were mistaken for julaw, or marabouts or even
sorcerers. Here, in a sub-text that recognized the machinations of a secular political power, writing in the hands of Europeans was understood
as a rational means to a conquering end, justly to be feared. Which may
explain the slap on Gallieni's wrist by his hosts when detained at Nango in the Beledugu (1 June 1880–29 March 1881): "We have noted," his
host began, "that when a white man arrives in our country, he writes all
that he sees; and we have noticed that after this white man (leaves),
others arrive ... who know our routes, and our *tata* (city defenses)."
Correct in his assessments, not only had Gallieni relied on Park (1796),
Dochard (1819), Caillie (1827), Raffenel (1840s), Mage (1863) and others,
but so had Binger (1892), the latter adding to his working bibliography

21. ASAOF 1G 189, MacLeod, "Rapport du Capitaine d'Artillierie" (Bamako, 1
Oct. 1894); Park, *The Travels*, pp. 57, 179–180; Raffenel, *Nouveau voyage*, vol. 1, p.
191; Gaspard Mollien, *Travels in the interior of Africa*, trans. from the French (London, 1820), p. 108.

22. Gallieni, *Voyage*, pp. 242, 247–248, 280, 374, 379; Binger, "Du Niger au Golfe
de Guinée," *BSGP*, vol. 10 (1889): 329–371, see p. 345; Camille Piétri, "Rapport sur
la reconnaissance du Ba-Oulé," *BSGCB* (1881), pp. 709–717. See also Caillié, *Voyage*, vol. 2, pp. 61–62.

Barth (1857), Borgnis Desbordes (1882), Gallieni (1885), and Peroz (1888), not to mention the two seventeenth-century Timbuktu *ta'rikhs*. Not the first to be chastised either, British Major William Gray (1819) had earlier been upbraided by another suspicious chief for writing "geographical knowledge," and to what end?: "Are there no rivers in the country you say you inhabit," queried his curious interlocutor—no doubt remembering what may have seemed like Park's absurd obsession with the obvious. Park (1796), we recall, was at pains to explain his mission: "When (my interlocutor) was told that I had come from a great distance ... to behold the Joliba (Niger) river, (he) naturally inquired, if there were no rivers in my own country, and whether one river was not like another." A similarly perplexed interlocutor in Bundu "thought it impossible ... that any man in his senses would undertake so dangerous a journey," apparently for nothing. Suffering similar reproaches from his host, the botanist Lecard, on mission in 1880, was informed that he should quit taking notes because "the whites are (only) writing about our country so that they may later return to take it." Not wishful thinking, and not a self-fulfilling prophecy either, the curious interlocutor could not have been more correct: Writing a memo from Nango (10 Jan. 1880), Pietri noted: "This note, exclusively military (in content), is intended to furnish the expeditionary column with information needed for its march through the Beledugu"! In the meantime, among the Tukulor of Murgula, southwest of Bamako, Valliere, whose reception was nothing short of menacing, was informed of a suspicious looking "white" in the Sitakoto region "seen writing, examining trees, mountains, and reading from his mysterious little instruments"—and what did all this mean?[23]

In Bamako, ruling elites likewise understood writing's rational power as a means to a conquering political end. We recall that in 1883 Titi Niare, Bamako's last *kafu-tigi*, turned to the writing method of the powerful, when warning Bourouti against what seemed like a pro-Umarian French policy. Relying no doubt on one of the *kafu*'s Islamized literati, Titi instructed the conquering image, whose conquering flag had been hoisted behind the *kafu* that all Franco-Umarian alliances were forbidden, because if "the friend of a friend is a friend, the friend of an enemy is an enemy" (the Gallieni mission had promised "friendship"). Moreover, should the

---

23. Gray and Dochard, *Travels in western Africa*, p. 349; Park, *The Travels*, pp. 40, 153; Gallieni, *Voyage*, pp. 248, 280, 374; M. Lécard, "La Vigne du Soudan," *BSGCB* (1880): 593–594, see p. 594; Piétri, "Note topographique," p. 573.

French persist with their Franco-Umarian agreements, the guaranteed enmity of the powerful Beledugu chiefs would be unbearable.[24]

Finally, there were those who understood writing's market power. Within an indecently short period after the ambush at Jo in the Beledugu (11 May 1880), Gallieni, to his chagrin, was purchasing *his own notes* and papers from a Soninke dealer at Kulikoro whose innocent-looking inventory included slaves, salt, and gunpowder. The dealer, whose "considerable price" betrayed an astute market awareness, traveled regularly between the Niger's right bank and the Beledugu.[25]

But if writing had created a subtext that passed for understanding, the image of women and family alliances gave rise to even further misconstructions. When in the Bambuhu region, British Major William Gray was offered "one of (the prince's) sisters" sent to "make (him) comfortable and at home," and to "teach (him) to speak Bambarran." From Gray's perspective, the chief's action seemed a kindly gesture; an unlikely probability however, given the chief's next question: Were he to visit England, would "the king (of England) give him one of his daughters to wife?" Assuming in the Mande style (as we saw in Chapter 3), that family alliances were of the ultimate importance both in the long and short term, and that brides and marriage agreements were the basis for ritualized bonding, the Bambuhu chief may have been expecting to palaver Gray and his secret powers into a potent domestic alliance, especially if the possibility of some reciprocity with "the King of England" existed. Teaching Gray "Bambarran," and making him "comfortable and at home" was, as we saw in Chapters 3 and 4, the Mande way to naturalize the stranger. Except that Gray apparently misunderstood. Now it was the chief's turn to misunderstand when he observed that: "White women were ... completely mistresses of the(ir) men," and that "the whole care and labor of supporting (their) ... families depended on (men) who dare not even speak to any woman save their wives" (what was he thinking?; had he collapsed Christian monogamy, "the mistress," and Western patriarchy into one overall concept?). Elsewhere, a Guinina chief (south of Bamako) was inappropriately applying the family paradigm to Pietri. He would have Pietri as a "brother," but not as a "friend." Earlier, Park's appearance had been the source of great hilarity, especially "the whiteness of (his) skin, and the prominency of (his) nose, both of which observers insisted were artificial,

---

24. *ASAOF* 15G 66, "Correspondence" (Bamako, 1880), n.p.; *ASAOF* 1G 52 46, Bayol, "Mission de Ségou" (Saint Louis, 5 July 1880), pp. 9–10; *ASAOF* 1G 50 20, "Lettre Gallieni à Gouverneur" (Nango, 7 July 1880), p. 28.

25. Gallieni, *Voyage*, p. 374.

the first the result of daily milk baths, the second of daily pinching. Elsewhere, observers said he had cat eyes. [26]

But as the subtext that passed for understanding deepened in this Mande-French undialogue, very high political gains and losses were at stake. Believing, for example, that the French were "only julaw," as well as sea nomads "liv(ing) exclusively in ships on the sea"—having no country of their own—some Beledugu warrior lords, locked in their rocky fastness, could hardly be persuaded to take the French seriously. Yes, the Rumi like the Umarians—the other Scriptuaries—could not be trusted. But, it would be easy "to rid the region of them. "They"would not dare bring their cannons here," Beledugu warriors in the Kumi, and Siracoroba *kafuw* were heard to say. The rocky Beledugu was too remote and too secure. So as the days passed the warrior lords sat around drinking *dolo*, confident of a favorable outcome. In the meantime, the Samorian intelligence—riding high on successful military campaigns—was spreading the word that the Rumi had no intention of advancing to the Niger, nor even venturing beyond Kita, so formidable were barriers and obstacles into the interior.[27]

Not all Beledugu lords were as insouciant as those in Kumi, and Siracoroba. Deeper in the Beledugu, Samba Bile, the Massantolo lord, was brooding on possible sinister consequences. Preemptively clapping into irons those Mande julaw still rash enough to reach French trading posts, Samba Bile made it known that "we do not like those who like the French." Farther west in the Kaarta, they were likely to lose their heads. Equally astute was one of Da Jara's "slaves" (Da Jara: Segu Faama, 1808–1827) stationed at Bamako in 1819. In conversation with British surgeon Dochard, he wondered: Did the British intend to do with the Niger what the French had done with the Senegal River valley?[28] Similarly aware was the old chief of Wuloni in the western Beledugu. Hardly concealing hostility when granting Gallieni an audience (5 May 1880), the chief's response to the lieutenant's friendship and commerce conjuring was that the Umarians, two decades earlier, had juggled similar promises

---

26. Gray and Dochard, *Travels in western Africa*, p. 303; Gallieni, *Voyage*, p. 240; Park, *The Travels*, pp. 41, 98.

27. *ANSOM* Sén. et Dép. IV Doss. 90 Bis, Vallière," Rapport … Minamba-Farba" (Bamako, 9 May 1888), pp. 3, 7; Laing, "Travels in Timanae," pp. 342–343, 349; Person, *Samori*, vol. 1, p. 399.

28. *ANSOM* Sén. et Dép. IV Doss. 90 Bis, Extrait 2, Tautain, "Extraits … Cercle de Bamako," (Bamako, 4 March 1887), n.p.; *ANSOM* Sén. et Dép. IV Doss. 90 Bis, "Rapport de la mission de la première campagne dans le Bélédougou" (Kita, 26 Feb. 1888), p. 9; Gray and Dochard, *Travels in western Africa*, p. 353.

with betrayals, raids, war, and seizure of women and animals: "We were forced to take refuge in the mountains," he conceded. Now "you pass through my territories loaded with costly gifts," and for the Umarians? Given recent memories of broken promises, "who can prove that you speak the truth ... who assures us that you will not deceive as the Umarians once did?" Harboring a similar subtext, we recall that Titi Niare had warned Gallieni to watch his manners: Bamako was not a "nothing country." Not the only chief to doubt Gallieni's integrity, by 1881 Amadu Tall, the Umarian Sultan whose father had seized Segu (1861–1862) from the Bamana-Jara rulers (c. 1766–1861), was volubly critical: Why assume Gallieni more trustworthy than Mage had been to his father some twenty years before? Elsewhere, exchanges fraught with menacing demeanors and the atmosphere thick with brooding threats, muffled voices throughout the western Mande-hinterland were fearing a French betrayal, in turn, promising a fearful revenge. In the meantime, Pietri in Bamako was selling the Niare chiefs the same "peace and friendship" story.[29]

But brave talk was easy. Always menacing was the haunting subtext of the Rumi's sorcery: After Park's Segu departure (1805), Monzon Jara and "other great personages" died "immediately" (Monzon actually died three years later in 1808). And following Dochard's Bamako arrival (1819), Segu's resident "governor of Bamakoo" and other "chief men" gave up the ghost "suddenly" within a few days. We recall that miscellaneous misfortunes occurring in the Beledugu after the Jo attack against the Gallieni Mission in 11 May 1880 were attributed to French sorcery and the paper *gris-gris*. Not surprisingly, the old chief at Sambabugu in the western Kaarta excused himself when Pietri requested a demonstration of the *numu*'s iron forge.[30]

By the late 1880s, most Beledugu chiefs were "cold against the French." Appearing to warm to Valliere's sugared words that the French had come as "peacemakers" and "friends"—as well as "masters of the country," Valliere had added somewhat ominously—the Beledugu chiefs were dismayed with continuing Franco-Umarian relations, the latter seemingly amicable: Gallieni (1880) had talked only of friendship and commerce, swearing anti-Umarian sentiments, they said. Why then had the French placed trade with the Umarians above doing "the right thing"? Why had the Commandant Superieur not received orders to attack the Umarians?

---

29. *ASAOF* 1G 52 46, Bayol, "Mission de Ségou" (Saint Louis, 5 July 1880); Gallieni, *Voyage*, pp. 209–212, 247, 462 note.

30. Gray and Dochard, *Travels in western Africa*, pp. 345–346; Camille Piétri, "Rapport sur la reconnaissance," pp. 709–717.

Diplomatic understandings, that the friend of a friend is a friend, the friend of an enemy, an enemy, seemed outrageously violated. Confused imagery was confounding value and meaning. In their anger, the Beledugu chiefs stalled, "insulting" Valliere by refusing "to recognize his presence ... as a powerful chief in passage" through their territory. That there were no marabouts in the Beledugu to assist as interpreters and scribes, Valliere complained (or is it that none came forward?), hostile gossip and rumors had poisoned official exchanges. His response was Lieutenant Bonnacorsi's punitive expedition and the taking of chiefs' "sons" as hostages.[31] Clearly misunderstanding the meaning of the "Z" succession (see Chapter 3), Bonnacorsi's hostage taking would have been more effective had he seized the chiefs' "brothers" instead. Finally, as if the Beledugu chiefs were not sufficiently put out, the air was brisk with rumors that the Keita families in Kangaba were "buying" French support with a payoff in gold.[32] By 1915 Beledugu chiefs were once more in arms against the French, opportunistically taking advantage of the fact that their overlords were engaged in a vicious European war.

Part 3: The French in the Western Sudan

If the families' subtexts were fostering ambiguous mis/understandings of French identities images and intentions in this undialogue, a misleading French subtext of a different sort was reaching the Quai d'Orsay (Foreign Ministry) and the Rue Royale (Ministry of the Marine), as well.

Fueling a wide range of false expectations and misconceived identities since the seventeenth century, the French had subscribed to the mistaken image of great wealth in Bamako and its upper Niger towns, an image incidentally also shared by subscribers to the northern paradigm. Born of investors' expectations and adventurers' dreams, this enduring identity was based on nothing less than the fabled wealth of the "Bambouk" and "Bure" mines[33] (not to mention the legendary wealth of Timbuktu), the gold none other than the *jo's* "sacred purity," the *numuw* its jealous guardians. The region's "golden" image also based on misleading market evaluations, needless to say, the French were astonished to find a relatively small, poor Bamako *kafu* surrounded by a devastated region, the

---

31. *ANSOM* Sén. et Dép. IV Doss. 90 Bis, Vallière, "Rapport ... Minamba-Farba" (Bamako, 9 March 1888), pp. 7–9, 16–19, 33–35; Gallieni, *Voyage*, pp. 209–210; *ASAOF* 1G 351, "Note sur le Cercle de Bamako" (1920), n.p.

32. *ANMK* 1D 33 5, Borgnis Desbordes, "Notice historique" (1880–1890).

33. Numerous reports and exchanges reflect this unrealistic view of the region's riches. See, for example, selections from *ANSOM* Sén. et Dép. XIII Doss. 55.

equally "rich" Mande now impoverished beyond their imaginings. Earlier images of Bamako had been formulated around Park's account (1796) and later Caillie's (1827), the latter among the first to suggest Bamako as a location for a French post. Caillie never visited Bamako, bypassing it on the east bank. Yet his recommendations were taken seriously, more so than Goldberry's (1780s) and even Raffenel's (1840s) urgings that Sansanding in the Bambuk region was a more appropriate choice (not that they were justified in these recommendations either).[34]

By the 1850s sage administrators such as Fitiriba (Faidherbe) were urging a French advance up the Senegal River, believing that the French flag "ought to be respected at Bamako." Yet reservations persisted: By 1859 doubts were overheard at the Ministry of the Marine; it was eight months since receiving word from "le haut pay" beyond Medine; the heavy losses of men and mules were perhaps due to "hasty" and "pele-mele" planning. By the 1860s Mage, who never reached Bamako either, but sufficiently afflicted with Faidherbe's more public railway imagery, was recommending Kita as the French point of departure to the Niger.[35] Enthusiastic about prospects of the trans-Saharan railway when himself on mission in 1878–1879, Solleillet—a "jula" with an engineering turn of mind—ventured that the Niger from Bamako to the Busa Rapids, beyond Gao, could become a "French river" were a canal built from Bafulabe (on the Senegal) to Bamako. Other expectations or visions dancing in administrative heads were that Bamako would one day recover its "ancient splendor."[36]

On mission in 1880, Gallieni at first spoke enthusiastically about attaining Bamako "at all cost," even at the expense of other plans. Yet later whistling a different refrain, within three months he seemed embarrassed at the "penury" of available information on the little *kafu*—no more than Mage's recountings despite the seventeen years separating

---

34. Caillié, *Voyage*, vol. 1, p. 330; *ANSOM* Sén. et Dép. XIII Doss. 54, 1817–1859 "Lunéville, à Monsieur le Président" (Paris, 1850), pp. 7, 9; *ANSOM* Sén. et Dép. XIII Doss. 55, Faidherbe, "Agriculture ... 1856 à 1860: Mines du Bambouk ... 1856 à 1857" (Gorée, 12 July 1856), p. 14.

35. Faidherbe, *L'Avenir*, pp. 110–112; *ANSOM* Sén. et Dép. XIII Doss. 55–55c, Faidherbe, "Réponse à la dépêche du 9 juillet 1859" (Saint Louis, 14 August 1859), pp. 1–2; Mage, *Relation*, p. 59.

36. *ASAOF* 1G 46, "Mission Solleillet 1878 à 1879," p. 7; *ANMAE, 1879–1881,* vol. 75, "Transsaharien Mission Flatters, Solleillet et Choisy, Correspondence, 5 aôut 1879–oct. 1879," pp. 16–61; see also 118–132, 154–171, 208–261, 293–294, 301–302, 322, 324, 328, 341; *ASAOF* 1G 52, "Brière de L'Isle, Télégramme" (Dakar, 25 June, 1880).

their two endeavors, he confessed. But even more troubling, Gallieni thought, were the "vague" responses that met his inquiries: Did the *kafu*'s image match the reality? Had the Umarian wars so isolated the region? Was the *kafu* in decline? Why did some interlocutors profess never to have heard but the "vaguest rumors," and others that their news was at least twenty years out of date? Why had Park and Mage been "somewhat mute" about Bamako in their reporting? When himself in Bamako in May 1880, or lamenting his woeful misfortunes at Nango (1 June 1880–29 March 1881), Gallieni wondered why evidence of its "large" and "celebrated market"—according to Park—was not apparent: Could the French have nurtured a false identity all these years (or what he called a "false appreciation") of the city's political and commercial importance? More importantly, if the Niare chiefs had been all that powerful, and the swaggering Abderaman (their Ture guide) all that influential, why had they not prevented the mission's ambush at Jo in the Beledugu on 11 May 1880? In the meantime, en route through the Beledugu Pietri found the villages "tightly closed," and the information "very vague." Guides who came forward deceived them.[37]

When in Bamako in May 1880 as a vanguard member of the Gallieni Mission, Pietri seemed equally perplexed: The image was not matching the reality. "What!" he exclaimed. "Is this the much vaunted town, the market so renowned?" True, he estimated the Bamako *kafu* and city population at between 7,000 and 8,000—one of the largest assessments (1,000 for the city). Yet most puzzling was the collective amnesia: No one could remember the alleged prosperity of the salt trade of which Park had spoken some sixty years before. (We recall that having heard of "Bammakoo ... as a great (salt) market," Park was "disappointed" at the sight of a "middling" town). Was Park's information correct? More baffling: None in Bamako had even heard of Park, nor of his visit, insisting that he (Pietri) was the first European to set foot in town! A likely case of political amnesia, we know that staff surgeon Dochard of the British Navy had visited both Bamako and Segu in about 1818–1819. And as to having never heard of Park (1796 and 1805), Dochard (1819), Raffenel (1856), Mage (1863), Pietri (1880), Gallieni (1881, 1885), and Dubois (1897) all reported having met people who spoke of Park's visit, approximately 100 years

37. *ASAOF* 1G 50 77, "Lettre Gallieni à Gouverneur" (Makajambugu, 26 April 1880), pp. 2–3; *ASAOF* 1G 50 20, "Lettre Gallieni à Gouvernenr" (Nango, 7 July 1880), pp. 10–15. See also *ASAOF* 1G 50, "Lettre Gallieni à Gouverneur" (Nango, 20 August 1880); Gallieni, *Voyage*, pp. 236, 339–340, 594–595; Piétri, "Note topographique," pp. 567–569.

after the fact in Dubois' case. Park himself had predicted that the year 1796 would be remembered for generations as the *Tubab tambi sang,* or "the year the white man passed." That is exactly what appears to have happened. An old woman trying to lift Gallieni's gloom (1 Jan. 1881) while imprisoned at Nango assured him that "the year (of Park's arrival) ... was for a long time in the region known as 'the year the white man came.'" Finally, at Guinina, south of Bamako, Pietri chatted with "several old men" who had heard about Park's visit.[38]

In the meantime, Dr. Jean-Marie Bayol of the Marine, a thoughtful man and member of the Gallieni Mission, observed that Bamako was small, only 600 inhabitants—the smallest estimate offered—a "dependency" of the Beledugu and "without importance from the political and commercial perspective"; the Mande and the Bure region, he suggested, were more central to French interests.[39] Five years later Conrard, lieutenant of the Senegalese *tirailleurs,* who estimated Bamako's population at 4,000 to 5,000 inhabitants, insisted that the city was hardly worth its salt, important only after the 1860s as a refuge haven from the Umarians. In any event, he thought the citizens a fickle lot, opportunistic to the point of allying with any partisan promising the greatest fortune; and they never stayed to fight, throwing in the towel at the drop of a hat.[40]

Colonel Henri Frey, charged with an expedition in 1885–1886 in the Haut-Senegal, was even more scornful, arguing that the Sudan was mainly good for "catching slaves" and "making war," hardly appropriate for a French post. Besides, Frey continued with a materialistic turn of mind, better cotton, indigo, rubber, and animal skins were produced elsewhere in the western Sudan. Piqued that "our enterprise" had been publicly criticized, Fitiriba dismissed Frey's as "a personal opinion ... not

---

38. Piétri, "Note topographique," pp. 572–573; see also *Idem.,* "Rapport sur la reconnaissance," pp. 709–717; Vallière, "Situation politique" (1881), pp. 451–468; Park, *The Travels,* p. 210; Gallieni, *Voyage,* pp. 240–242, 245, 421; Gray and Dochard, *Travels in western Africa,* pp. 254–256, 271, 274, 346, 353.

39. Bayol was here referring to the gold deposits of Bure and the caravans that regularly visited the region (*ASAOF* 1G 52, Bayol, "A Monsieur le Commandant Supérieur" [Bakel, 12 June 1880]; *ASAOF* 1G 52 6, Bayol, Télégramme no. 314 [Saint Louis, 25 June 1880]; *ASAOF* 1G 52, Bayol, "Télégramme" [Saldé, 29 June 1880]; *ASAOF* 1G 52 46, Bayol, "Mission de Ségou" [Saint Louis, 5 July 1880], p. 10); Piétri, "Note topographique," pp. 567–573; Gray and Dochard, *Travels in western Africa,* p. 239; Raffenel, *Nouveau voyage,* vol. 1, p. 360; Gallieni, *Voyage,* pp. 225, 244–245; Dubois, *Tombouctou,* pp. 45–46.

40. *ASAOF* 1G 79, Conrard, "Notice" (Bamako, 21 Feb. 1885), pp. 2–4; *ASAOF* 15G 83, Ruault, "Généralités 1880 à 1920" (Bamako, 22 Feb. 1884), p. 4.

shared by the majority of people." But Dr. Louis-Frederic Tautain apparently shared Frey's scorn, arguing in 1887 that Bamako and the Petit Beledougou (Inner Beledugu) offered "nothing in particular." Even as late as February 1888, five years after Bourouti's conquering flag was fluttering on the Niger's bank, Valliere was arguing to downgrade Bamako to a "provisioning post" for grain and livestock, favoring instead a command seat perhaps in the Beledugu where population densities were higher and the Bamana warrior-chiefs more powerful. That same month, an officer from the Beledugu was complaining of Bamako's "unhealthy" location, advocating instead the Merkoya in the Grand Beledugu as a more important and suitable location.[41] About two years later Bourouti was sheepishly admitting that perhaps "Bamako was not the commercial town with the large hegemonic range that one had (previously) supposed." Once believing it "the most accessible and advantageous (interior) point," Borgnis Desbordes had now downgraded Bamako to "the capital of a former little state ... rich, it is true, but destroyed since the (Umarian) conquests through the loss of commerce with Timbuktu" and other Niger towns. And in 1890 the Departmental Commission to advise on the future of French policy in the upper Niger called for the fort's evacuation and the choice of Bafulabe as the colony's political capital and military headquarters.[42]

As the debate wound down, the imagery seemed to be matching the reality. According to Captain Guegan, chief of an artillery squadron stationed at Kayes in 1894, the reasons previously favoring Bamako as a Sudanese seat no longer existed: It was too far from the Circle's more densely populated sections, too distant from the major trade routes; otherwise the problems seemed too many to enumerate. Perhaps the city should be downgraded to a provisioning and military post, and an administrative seat established at a more central location such as Kumi in the Beledugu. Finally in 1911, Marie-Francois Clozel, the newly appointed

---

41. *ASAOF* 1G 52, Bayol, "Télégramme" (Saldé, 29 June 1880), n.p.; *ASAOF* 1G 52 46, Bayol, "Mission de Ségou" (Saint Louis, 5 July 1880); *ASAOF* 1G 50 20, "Lettre Gallieni à Gouvernenr" (Nango, 7 July 1880), pp. 10–11, 17–18, 21; *ANSOM* Sén. et Dép. IV Doss. 90 Bis, "Rapport de la Mission" (Kita, 26 Feb. 1888), p. 9; Faidherbe, *Le Sénégal*, pp. 106, 111; Piétri, "Note topographique," p. 573; *ANSOM* Sén. et Dép. IV Doss. 90, Tautain, "Extraits des rapports politiques venues du Cercle de Bamako" (4 June, 1887).

42. *ANSOM* Sén. et Dép. IV Doss. 90 Bis, "Rapport de la mission" (Kita, 26 Feb. 1888), p. 14; *ANMK* 1D 33 5, Borgnis Desbordes "Notice historique" (1880–1890); Kanya-Forstner, *The Conquest*, pp. 171–172.

governor, wondered how the Bamako region was going to become "one of
the world's granaries" when it was 1,800 kilometers from the sea.[43]

The Railway

Despite the undialogue, and the misleading sub-texts, by 1908 the capital of the Haut-Senegal-Niger was moved from Kayes to the upper Niger
with Bamako as the Sudanese seat. No longer appealing to the region's
fabled gold, revising and reviving the earlier image was the Kayes-to-
Bamako railway, on Faidherbe's expansionist agenda since the 1850s.
More pressing was the revived age old fear of British competition (to a
lesser extent the German) in the upper and middle Niger: French intelligence had learned that the British had even opened negotiations with
Timbuktu and were believed to be selling arms (earlier voices had fretted
about a possible "volte face [on the part of the upper Niger populations]
favoring the British").[44] In a different kind of undialogue, where officer
voices from the Sudan seemingly went unheard at the Quai d'Orsay (Foreign Ministry) and the Rue Royale (Ministry of the Marine), railway
plans went ahead. Imaged in accordance with visions for the trans-Saharan railway, from the 1850s and 1860s Bamako had been intended as an
upper Niger command post for shipping and commerce between the
southern Sudan, Timbuktu, and France's North African territories. As
railway policies began to crystallize, mixed images emerged: France, the
"master" of the Niger, was becoming the "mistress" of the western Sudan
with Bamako its "pearl."[45]

Competing successfully against the more downgrading representations of "men on the spot," plans went forward for the intrusive railway
extension into the interior. In September 1879, a preliminary credit of

43. *ASAOF* 15G 168, "Traités 1821–1899: Le Chef d'escadron d'artillerie Guégan, Commandant la région à Monsieur le Gouverneur du Soudan français," (Bamako, 19 Oct. 1894), pp. 1–3; Delafosse, *Haut-Sénégal-Niger*, vol. 1, preface: Marie
François-Joseph Clozel, pp. 11–12.

44. *ANMAE, 1886–1889*, vol. 122, "Lettre au Président du Conseil, Ministre des
Affaires Etrangères, 1 mars, 1886," pp. 12–16; see also most of vol. 122; *ANMAE,*
"Conférence de Bruxelles 1889–1892: Lettres du Vice-Consul de France à Liège à
Monsieur le Ministre" (Paris, 15 Nov. 1890, 3 Dec. 1890); *ANMAE, 1773–1820*, vol.
37, "Mémoire sur l'expédition de Galam" (Salde, 6 Nov. 1819), pp. 294–314.

45. *ANMAE, 1886–1889*, vol. 122, (1 March 1886), pp. 12–16; Pierre Jagu-Roche,
"Bamako, la perle de l'Afrique occidentale française," *AOF Magazine*, vol. 20, no.
17 (1956): 14–18; Faidherbe, *Le Sénégal*, pp. 2–3, 6–7, 116–117, 121, 299–300,
303–305, 319, 325.

500,000 francs had been announced for the Senegal-Niger railway, closely associated with the name of Charles de Freycinet, Minister of Public Works, the Artillery of the Marine, and the noisy railway lobby. About the same time, Jaureguiberry won approval for a similar credit to the tune of 1,300,000 francs, authorizing a railway line from Medine to Bafulabe (where the Bafing and the Bakoy Rivers join to form the Senegal): Construction on the Kayes to Bamako line was supposed to move forward. Supposedly helping it along was the creation on 26 January 1880 of the "Superior Commander of the Upper River," Bakel its headquarters. In that same year, the Gallieni Mission to the Umarian Segu capital was authorized inter alia to survey the route to the Niger and, in anticipation of a railhead at Bamako, to sign a protectorate treaty with Bamako's chiefs.[46]

Political policies were faithful to the revised imagery, as well as to power politics within the metropolitan armed services. In 1881, Borgnis Desbordes established a new military command at Kita in the upper Senegambia. By November 1882, he was en route from Kayes to Bamako with his small expeditionary force, images of the railway dancing in his head. Passing through the Beledugu, scene of the Gallieni mission's humiliation in May 1880, warrior chiefs afforded him the "proper respect," except for the old Daban chief, instigator of the earlier mischief against the Gallieni mission at Jo. This time suitably humbled, "the Bambara ... will remember that," Marc Maurel, president of the Bordeaux Geographical Society, later informed its members. But the railway project had stalled, even after Borgnis Desbordes had reached Bamako. Begun in 1878, by 1882 there were only 4 kilometers of rail line, only 53 in 1884 against a total expenditure of 14 million francs; in 1887 there were 94 kilometers.[47] No immediate action followed. And between about 1884 and 1891 no further credits were voted for its continuation, merely 125 million

---

46. The Dakar-Niger railway was intended to develop in three stages, the first two from Dakar to Saint Louis, with a branch line to Medine, to be financed by private investments, while the third, from Medine to the Niger, to be financed by the state. In its initial stages, the main Kayes-to-Bamako line stopped at Bafulabe; passengers had thus to undertake the 175-kilometer stretch to Jiubaba (Dioubaba) by *décauville*, the narrow-gauge railway named for Décauville, its inventor. The route to Bamako, passed southeast through the basin at the headwaters of the Senegal and Niger Rivers (Kanya-Forstner, *The Conquest*, pp. 68–73; Dubois, *Tombouctou*, pp. 2–4, 10–11; Faidherbe, *Le Sénégal*, pp. 305–306 and passim).

47. Faidherbe, *Le Sénégal*, pp. 328–330; Marc Maurel, "Le Sénégal et la mission Desbordes," *BSGCB* (1881), pp. 409–414, see p. 418. The Senegal (Dakar) railway began in 1881.

francs toward maintenance. Between 1883 and the early 1890s, Bamako remained a frontier town and provisioning station. By the turn of the century, it was still a small post for storing grain and arms.

In the meantime, the Parisian view of Bamako was becoming more complex: the British Foreign Office had decided to settle the fate of the Niger. Now reviving the expansionist paradigm of the revised imagery, Governor Briere de L'Isle (1876–1881), in a letter to Jaureguiberry, ventured that "Bamako ... (was after all) an even more important goal than (Segu)," that is, if the French were to secure the upper Niger. Moreover, for some time Gallieni had argued for a north-south consolidation from the Niger bend to the Guinea Coast, justifying recommendations on two grounds: to provide a north-south outlet to the Atlantic for raw materials from the newly acquired territories intersecting Faidherbe's earlier east-west acquisitions of the 1850s and 1860s; and to forestall British intentions to extend their Sierra Leone holdings to the upper Niger, possibly even to Timbuktu.[48]

In furthering his brief, Gallieni delineated a "quadrilateral" of French-protected territory extending from Timbuktu in the north to Saint Louis in the west, and from Benty in the Southern Rivers to Siguiri in the east. Reviving Faidherbe's "Senegambian Triangle" of 1864—albeit in modified and extended form—Gallieni's "Quadrilateral Policy" once more suggested an exchange of the Gambia for a coastal territory—Assinie, Grand Bassam, perhaps even Gabon.[49] More specifically, Gallieni continued, this vast quadrilateral-like territory, which France was about to acquire, was proving too remote and too difficult to administer from Kayes; in any event the newly constructed Siguiri (Guinea) fort, France's southernmost fortress in the Mande-hinterland, was too remote and unprotected. Closer facilities were needed. Besides, Gallieni warned, sounding further tocsins, the British officer Major Festing had arrived at the Samorian Bissandugu headquarters on a diplomatic mission, alarmingly reminiscent of the visit

---

48. Gallieni, *Deux campagnes*, pp. 620–621; *ASAOF* 1G 50, Gallieni, "Analyse au sujet" (Nango, 10 Sept. 1880), pp. 2–4; *ANSOM* Sén. et Dép. IV Doss. 90 Bis, "Le Sous-Secrétaire d'Etat au Ministère de la Marine et des Colonies au Gouverneur du Sénégal" (Paris, 20 Oct. 1886), pp. 8–9; *ANSOM*, Sén. et Dép. IV Doss. 90 Bis, Gallieni, "Rapport no. 3 ... sur le service vetérinaire, 1887–1888" (Bafulabe, 10 May 1888), p. 24.

49. *ANSOM* Sén. et Dép. IV Doss. 90 Bis, Gallieni "Rapport no. 3 ... sur le service vetérinaire, 1887–1888" (Bafulabe, 10 May 1888), pp. 20–37; *ANMAE*, *1856–1867*, vol. 47, no. 11, pp. 152–157. After 1864, the French raised the question of the exchange of the Gambia again in 1866–1867, 1874–1876, 1880–1881, and 1887–1889.

of the British representative in the Gambia, who had walked away in March 1881, a treaty of friendship in hand with the Almamy of the Futa Jallon. Since the early 1880s, moreover, it was well known that the British were selling arms openly to the Samorians at Sierre Leone, "a flagrant proof," an indignant Peroz postured, that the British intended "the ruin of our colony." British manufactures were even on sale in Timbuktu and surrounding markets. Their intentions on the upper Niger were clear. Without the treaty of Bissandugu signed with the Samorians (23 March 1887), Gallieni sighed with relief, the British could have claimed the upper Niger's entire east bank in much the same way as they had made good their claims to the lower Niger.[50]

Favoring this changing image throughout the late 1880s and early 1890s was the expectation that Bamako's ruined political economies were hovering on the brink of recovery; they would be restored to their "ancient splendor," according to Briere de L'Isle. In any event, complaints about Kayes' unsuitability as France's Sudanese capital were now resounding: The site was unhealthy and the heat intolerable, even more problematic during the wet season; Kayes was too far from the more interior posts, especially Siguiri, where British intervention was feared; with the railway's advent it was no longer important, especially since julaw were now circulating at a faster rate; in any event, the rail station was proving to be too small, lacking storage room; Kayes was now only a gateway to the interior.[51] In August 1892, the Upper Niger was established as

---

50. *ANSOM*, Sén. et Dép. IV Doss. 90 Bis, Gallieni, "Rapport no. 3 ... sur le service vetérinaire, 1887–1888" (Bafulabe, 10 May 1888), p. 18; *ANMAE, 1890–1894*, vol. 123, pp. 13–25, 28–29, 38–51, 55–56, 68–71 and passim. See also Péroz, *Au Soudan Français*, p. 31. Anxious to exclude the British from the Futa Jallon, in 1881, Bayol had concluded a generous treaty with the ruling Alfaya and Soriya houses (5–14 July 1881), allowing them substantial freedoms and a wide diplomatic range, including supplying arms to the Samorians (Winston McGowan, "Fula resistance to French expansion into Futa Jallon, 1889–1896," *JAH*, vol. 22 [1981]: 245–261); Thierno Diallo, "La Mission du Dr. Bayol au Fouta-Djallon (1881) ou la signature du 1er traité de protectorat de la France sur le Fouta-Djallon," *BIFAN*, vol. 34, sér. B (1972): 113–150.

51. *ANSOM* Sén. et Dép. IV Doss. 90 Bis, "Notes sur le fonctionnement de la compatibilté financière et des services des transports fluviaux dans le Soudan français pendant la campagne 1887 à 1888" (Kayes, 20 April 1888), p. 2; *ANSOM* Sén. et Dép. IV Doss. 90 Bis, Gallieni, "Rapport" (Aboard the *Siguiri*, 22 May 1888), pp. 3, 8–9; *ANSOM* Sén. et Dép. IV Doss. 93 Bis, "Routes et ponts: Rapport du Lieutenant Colonel Gallieni, Commandant Supérieur du Soudan français sur le service des travaux pendant la campagne 1887 à 1888" (Aboard the *Siguiri*, 20 May

an autonomous territory, politically and militarily separate from Saint Louis and the colony of Senegal. Enabling administrative infrastructures were set in place with the establishment in 1894 (20 March) of the Ministry of Colonies under the leadership of Eugene Etienne. In 1896 a civil territory—the Circle of Bamako—was recreated with the once small *kafu* as the *chef-lieu*. After the reorganization of the Sudan between 1899 and 1904, and with the Afrique Occidentale Française (AOF) in place, Bamako's "French" identity moved to center stage.

Bamako's "French" Identity:
"Votre Jolie Ville de Bamako, Toute Française"

Needless to say, there was no room for the families in Bamako's new "French" identity. Familial identities were still defined by the state. But because state-society relationships had been radically ruptured, family identities were now in limbo, understood more by function, taxation, and wage-labor value in relation to the new colonial state than by lineage affiliation and valuation in the Mande style. And in the official French mind, the Wagadu heartland had become the stuff from which legends are made.

As Bamako was reinvented, in 1904 the Dakar-to-Bamako railway via Kayes reached its small Bamako station on the upper Niger's west bank, the first train arriving on 12 May 1904. Overall estimated costs for the 496 kilometers linking Kayes to Bamako were approximately 54,550,000 francs (98,288 francs per kilometer at the rate of 55 kilometers per year!). The human cost, difficult to estimate, could only have escalated overall losses.[52] By 1906–1907, the line was extended another 57 kilometers to Kulikoro (total estimate 553 kilometers), the site "where the world began" in

---

1888), pp. 9–10; *ANSOM* Soudan VII Doss. 8, "Le Soudan Français visite du Gouverneur Général M. Roume, Bamako, 8–9 dec. 1903"; *ANMK* K 11, "Fond Ancien, chemin de fer Kayes au Niger: Rapports diverses 1888–1903, le Commandant Joffre Directeur du chemin de fer à Monsieur le Colonel commandant Supérieur du Soudan français" (Kayes, 26 May 1893); *ASAOF* 1G 52, "Brière de L'Isle, Télégramme" (Dakar, 25 June 1880).

52. R. Godfernaux, *Les Chemins de fer coloniaux français* (Paris, 1911), pp. 186–189. Estimated costs in 1905 for the Bamako to Niamey rail was 115,000,000 francs for 1,430 kilometers, or 80,420 francs per kilometer: *ANMK* 1D 243, Digue, "Chemin de fer" (1905), pp. 1–2; Monique Lakroum, "Chemin de fer et réseaux d'affaires en Afrique occidentale: Le Dakar-Niger 1883–1960," 2 vols., Doctorat d'État under the direction of Catherine Coquery-Vidrovitch (Paris VII, 1987), vol. 1, p. 116.

some Mande cosmologies, where Ba Faro, the great river spirit, lived according to another, and where Sumanguru Kante disappeared from the face of the earth after the Battle of Krina, according to a third. In 1923 the Kayes-to-Bamako line was joined to the Senegal railway. An epic saga of about fifty years and 1,159.420 kilometers of rail line had ended. At Kulikoro the French erected a ship-yard.[53]

Between 1905 and 1908 the capital of the Haut-Senegal-Niger was moved from Kayes to Bamako. Anticipating the move, well-informed rumors had been circulating in mercantile circles from as early as 1903 that a move was imminent.[54] By 1907 permanent buildings for administrative services including the governor's palace were constructed at Kuluba (Point F, about 5 kilometers from Bamako)—the twin hillock overlooking the city. By 1909 offices for the Kayes-to-Niger railway were established, together with post and telegraph facilities. Within about five years, construction on the Bamako hospital was completed at Point G, the other twin hillock opposite Kuluba, the site of Sikoro an old Niare village, and where some legends say Jamusadia performed the first rituals as *dugu-kolo-tigi*, claiming the land for posterity. On 25 May 1908 (when Bamako was named the administrative seat of the Haut-Senegal-Niger, replacing Kayes), Marie-Francois Clozel took up his position as lieutenant governor (1908–1915).[55] Kati, about 12 kilometers west of Bamako

---

53. The Bafulabe-Kulikoro section of the railway cost about 49,564,500 francs and a severe toll on lives. The total length of the line from Kayes to Kulikoro was about 553 kilometers.

With respect to the actual railway, the Kayes-Bamako-Kulikoro line required about twenty-six to twenty-seven years for completion. In 1923–1924, it was joined to the Dakar-Thies-Kayes line, thereby getting rid of the unreliable river connection. The total rail line was 670 kilometers from Kidi to Kulikoro (Yacouba Koulibaly, "Le Soudan français dans la guerre 1939 à 1945," Mém. de fin d'études under the direction of M. Kagnoumé Jean Bosco Konaré, l'ENSUP (Bamako, 1981–1982), p. 27. For other related railways: the Conakry-to-Kankan line was opened in 1914; the Abidjan to Bouake in 1912; the Cotonou-to-Save in 1911.

54. *ANMK* 1Q 44, "Rapports commerciaux 1886–1919," see esp. "Rapport 1er trimester" (1904); *ANSOM* Soudan VII 8, "Visite du Gouverneur Générale, 8–9 dec. 1903."

55. For the growth of Bamako as a central place for commerce see the numerous reports in *ANMK* 1Q 44, "Rapports commerciaux Cercle de Bamako, 1886–1919." For the reconstructed town see Villien-Rossi, "Bamako," pp. 379–393. Building construction virtually ceased during World War 1; and although the peace brought renewed initiatives, it was only under the administration of Governor Jean-Henri Terrasson de Fougères (1924–1931) that the city's development really began. Between 1958 and 1960, the Vincent Auriol Bridge (800

in the foothills of the Manding Mountains and former Jara village in the old *kafu*, was established as a military station (1896) (many Niare still reside in Kati). An important livestock and vegetable market, Kati was linked to Bamako by road and rail. To the northwest, Kolokani in the Beledugu—home to the Beledugu warriors and renowned for its Lake Ouegana and large crocodiles—was established as an administrative center. Bamako's population, which in 1883 had been about 600 according to Bayol (1880), had increased tenfold by 1908 when the city became the capital of the Haut-Senegal-Niger.

With France as the "master" of the Niger, and the "mistress" of the Western Sudan with Bamako its "pearl," the old *kafu*'s past needed reinvention; its past should at least match its present importance.[56] Had not Brière de L'Isle predicted in 1880 that Bamako would one day recover its "ancient splendor"?

By 1933 it had. Addressing the Bamako Chamber of Commerce on 26 December 1933 on the fiftieth anniversary of Bamako's conquest, Governor Louis Trentinian informed his audience that "votre jolie ville de Bamako, toute Française" would soon reach new heights. Bamako was about to become "one of the greatest, the most attractive towns of our African empire," he promised the audience, "and you will the have the honor, Gentlemen, to have been among the founders." Then, manipulating the past as Bamako's founders had previously done fifty years before, he noted that Ptolemy's *Geography*, edited in the second century A.D., had been "very useful," having traced the course of the Niger along with "a certain number of localities." By a historical sleight of hand, Bamako (the eighteenth-century *kafu*), had been identified on Ptolmey's second century map! So had Mopti (a nineteenth-century town downriver from Bamako); and Timbuktu (established probably sometime during the eleventh century as a Berber storage camp)! Then, trying to limit the image of an "ancient splendor" fast spinning out of control, Trentinian volunteered that the "Arab" authors of the *Ta'rikh al-Fattash* and the *Ta'rikh as-Sudan* (the Timbuktu *ta'rikhs* were written by local residents: As-Sadi, born in Timbuktu and author of the *Ta'rikh as-Sudan* , had himself been a Jenne *Imam* [c. 1627-c. 1637]), had failed to mention Bamako. An oversight, of course, largely because the "Arabs were mainly interested in the

---

meters) was built (in service in 1961) linking the city with the Badalabugu suburb—housing important government buildings and residential areas. For Point G, see Mamadou Sarr, "La Colline du Point G: Etude morphologique," *EM*, no. 13 (April 1975): 1–27.

56. Jagu-Roche, "Bamako, la perle," pp. 14–18.

northern region and the dynasty of the Askias." "But," he continued, "there are brief passages relative to (Ptolmey's) history of the south, where the Bambara are mentioned" (the bulk of the "Bambara" did not reach the middle and upper Niger regions until about the seventeenth century). Regions farther south on the upper Niger were likewise mentioned, Trentinian continued, notably Kangaba (possibly not in existence before the end of the first millennium), and the village of Kufe or Koufe in the south. Then, recontrolling his runaway imagery, Trentinian once more volunteered that "these references (were) too vague," of course; they should not be further pressed. More importantly, for present considerations, he intoned conclusively, was that Bamako's future had become part of the writing cultures (a fate which the "ignorant Bambara" had so greatly feared). Bamako had finally become a part of history.[57] His audience applauded. Nobody seemed to remember that when recording the *kafu*'s "history" fifty years earlier, Bourouti had denounced his informants' manipulated past as "myth and mystery ... serving only the narrators' interests."

57. *ANMK* 1D 33, "Quelques pages d'histoire," n.d., n.p. See also De Sagazan, "L'Afrique intérieure d'après Ptolémée," *Annales de Géographie* (March-April 1951), p. 118. For a similar manipulated treatment of the past see Borgnis Desbordes, "Un Cinquantenaire: L'Arrivée des Français au Niger 1 février 1883–1 février 1933," *Revue Militaire de l'Afrique Occidentale Française* (April 1933), pp. 33–41.

Conclusion:
Bamako's "French" Identity, or
How Identities Are Formed Revisited

Bamako's "French" Identity

There was little room in Bamako's reinvented identity, "toute française," for the Niare and many other families. Neither was there room in the *kafu*'s reconfigured history, newly aggrandized to serve the colonial image, a history that the French historical imagination had manipulated and upstreamed to Ptolemy and the second century of the present era (see Chapter 5).[1] A search for the families and their identities, reinvented in accordance with changing circumstances, found them in sociological crevices, and in their historical imaginations: With respect to the first, they reappeared in the colonial records as a labor force: "translators," "porters," "spies," and "masons," many identified as "Bambara"; second, they reemerged in the reinvented Wagadu myth, where several families, and not just the Wage, reappeared as "rulers of Wagadu" (see Chapter 1). While it is easy to relate the families' new functional identities to the colonial state and its wage-labor markets, "proving" the Wagadu identity as a by-product of the colonial experience is more problematic. This hypothesis is therefore the template for further study, and nothing more.

Knowing however (from the discourse in Chapter 1) that myths and legends change regionally, situationally and ideologically, or that they continuously respond to particularisms, as well as to present contingencies, and that in the past families manipulated, invented, and reinvented their own legendary identities, it should come as no surprise to learn that oral texts changed in accordance with colonial exigencies. Besides, given the stresses, changes and adjustments of the colonial era, it is probable

---

1. *ANMK* 1D 33, "Quelques pages d'histoire." See also De Sagazan, "L'Afrique intérieure d'après Ptolémée," p. 118.

that more reinventions in the oral literature have occurred since the twentieth century than at any other time in the past. Thus, for the last time in this story I bring back familial identities as they appeared both in myth and history in the late nineteenth and early twentieth century. First, I reconstruct "Bambara" and other "French" identities appearing in the official records of the new colonial state; second, I uncover what lay concealed behind the legend's new retelling. I argue that while the "Bambara" and other colonial identities privileged some young people, a modified Wagadu identity favored many older family members and their love affair with an ethnographic past, real or imagined. With respect to the Niare identity, some ambiguities remained. While Ruault of the artillery infantry had reported them "Bambara" in 1884, Conrard noted the following year that although "Bambara," the Niare were also known as "Marka," at one time "Saracolle" from "Diara" (Jara) in Kingi. Departing Kingi "in 1385," the positivistic Conrard continued, the families settled along the Niger bank (location unnamed).[2] Finally, I bring back ritual, suggesting that the Wagadu identity was probably newly ritualized in accordance with compelling colonial circumstances.

The French "Bambara" Identity

Part 1: Linkages Between the French and the Northern Paradigm

We recall that although Mande-speakers might have been in the Bamako-Beledugu regions since archaic time, it was Bamana in-migrations sometime between the sixteenth and eighteenth centuries that altered the middle and upper Niger's ethnographic cartography and political calculus. While some Bamana carved out cultural spaces at the expense of earlier Soninko and Kagoro residents, others settled with congeners. Within the episteme of the northern paradigm—i.e., the seventeenth-century intellectual categories and imagery designed to separate the "southern animist" from the "northern Islamic" identity—the "animist Bambara" became the Other, at first experientially, subsequently historically realized (see Chapter 2). Thus as "fornicators," "idolaters," and "consumers" of the iniquitous *dolo*, it was not long before the "Bambara" earned the "pagan" sobriquet. We saw how women were accordingly ravaged by the Bambara. Forcing the state of Jenne into tributary status, the "city blessed by God" was sacked by the Bambara. By the late seventeenth century Timbuktu, the Sudan's preeminent entrepot was also vandalized by the Bambara; the

---

2. *ASAOF* 1G 79, Conrard, "Notice" (Bamako, 21 Feb. 1885), p. 3; *ASAOF* 15G 83, Ruault, "Généralités 1880 à 1920" (Bamako, 22 Feb. 1884), p. 18.

generous and scenic Massina abused by none other than the Bambara. Where appearing to "convert," the Bambara was merely mimicking the more "civilized," especially true of the Segovian Bambara who simply "did as they were told ... even lacking understanding."[3]

We also recall that like the Inland Delta and Mande-hinterland, the Mande world was ideologically divided according to the northern paradigm analogically bound into oppositions of Muslim/kaffir, Islamized/infidel, civilized/Bambara, free/slave, trader/animist-farmer, trader/warrior and so on. If in doubt, it was written that the "Malinke" (southerner) was a *dolo*-guzzling "warrior," while the "Wangara," especially the "Wakore" (northern Soninke) was an abstemious "trader."[4] We remember that the first reference to Bambara in the Arabic idiom is in the two seventeenth-century Timbuktu *ta'rikh*s, while Pacheco Pereira's *Esmeraldo de situ orbis* (1506-1508), and Labat's *Nouvelle relation* (1728) are their earliest European references.[5]

We never elaborated on the source of this paradigmatic naming of the Bambara Other. Indeed, given the fluid nature of the evidence, origins may no longer be empirically realizable. For example, recognizing the relatively "open" Bambara identity, Bazin (and Raffenel before him) traced the Kulibaly honorific (as distinct from origins) to Kong, even Bighu in the Gonja region; and while other Kulibaly families have correlated their identities with the Minianka, Bambara populations espousing a southern identity are still commonly found between the Niger and the Bani rivers west of Jenne.[6] In other words, the pejorative image of the problematic "Bambara" could have originated in the south. Except that this seems unlikely. Accordingly, we ask again: Who or what peoples named the "Bambara" along with the pejorative stereotype, especially since we know that the Bambara called themselves *Bamana*, *Banmana*, and *Bamanan* depending on the region?

We surmised before that northern Fulbe, especially those of the *Dina* (i.e., the Massina state), with their *Pulaaku* ("Fulbeness"), or ethno-cultural behavioral code, sharply differentiated the Bambara from other populations, even those among whom they had settled. The Timbuktu Fulbe, as

---

3. *ASAOF* 1G 248, Pérignon, "Monographie" (1899–1900), pp. 259, 321.

4. *Ta'rikh al-Fattash*, pp. 20, note 6, 40, note 2, 65, and note 2.

5. *Ta'rikh as-Soudan*, pp. 172, 223, 274, 276, 280, 411, 418, 420; *Ta'rikh al-Fattash*, pp. 20, 86, 87, 107; Pereira, *Esmeraldo de situ orbis*, p. 67; Labat, *Nouvelle relation*, vol. 3, pp. 257, 334, 359; vol. 4, pp. 85, 87.

6. The honorific "Kulibaly" applies to the Mamari (Biton) Kulibaly lineage (Bazin, "A Chacun son Bambara," pp. 104–105); Raffenel, *Nouveau voyage*, vol. 1, p. 365.

well as the Jawambe and Songhay—cultural brokers to one degree or another—were probably also among early perpetrators of this pejorative coinage. It goes without saying that they were notorious slavers. Jenne's Fulbe and Soninke clerics, notables, and rich traders were similarly among the original name-callers, exacerbated during Ahmadu Shehu's nineteenth-century *Dina* with its capital at Hamdallahi.[7] We recall that the Bambara were associated with these same Fulbe, as well as with desert-side Berberophones (Tamashagh, Sanhaja), possibly also Arabophones (Hassani), and that in the process of linguistic borrowings the Timbuktu Songhay had adopted Soninke and Fulfulde (also Hausa) loan words to identify Mande-speakers (e.g., *Mali, Malinke, Wangara, Wakore*). Given the Fulbe-Songhay-Soninke predilection for naming, it is thus very likely that the Bambara Other earned their "pagan" sobriquet from their northern and desert-side neighbors—especially the exclusive Fulbe from the Massina—who thereby laid the cornerstone of the southern identity.[8]

Others adopting this pejorative namecalling—even if resident farther south—were none other than Islamized Maraka, Sarakolle, and Soninko slavers, notables, and literati identifying more readily with cereal production, urban development, "civilized" merchants, and Islamized scholars, even less (if at all) with "kaffirs" and "slaves." Images were even more firmly etched farther south in the goldmining regions, where some Soninko traders permanently resided. Somono and Bozo river nomads, fisherfolk, and water transporters likewise contributed to the Bambara's Other image. Islamized since beyond living memory, their cultural identities had been crafted in the north, despite the fact that since a great antiquity they had served "pagan" terrestrial lords. With respect to the spread of the Bambara identity, we finally recall that itinerant Islamized traders were largely responsible for a widespread diffusion of the pejorative stereotypes.[9]

---

7. Hammadoun Diallo, "La Prise de Djenné," pp. 21–23; Sanankoua. *Un Empire peul.*

8. *Ta'rikh al-Fattash*, pp. 40 note 2, 65 note 2. In use in the Senegambia was *Soninke*, the western equivalent of *Bambara*. (Quinn, *Mandingo*, p. 53); ASAOF 1G 351, Bobichon, "Note sur le Cercle de Bamako" (Bamako, 20 Feb. 1921), n.p.

9. *ANSOM* Sénégal IV 90 Bis, Vallière, "Rapport sur ... Minamba-Farba" (Bamako, 9 March 1888), pp. 3–6; *ANSOM* Sén. et Dép. IV Doss. 90 Bis, "Campagne 1887 à 1888, Soudan français compte des dépendances de la colonne du Haut Niger" (Kayes, 12 May 1888), pp. 10–11; *ANSOM* Sén. III Doss. 1, Mollien, "Journal du voyage" (Paris, 8 July 1819), p. 10; Insa Coulibaly, "Le Wasulu, un milieu aux potentialités économiques énormes, une zone d'exode rural massif: Tentatives d'explication du paradoxe," Mémoire de fin d'études en Histoire et Géogra-

Linkages between name-callers—Fulbe, Sarakolle, Maraka, Soninke—and the French are all too apparent, explaining in part the French adoption of the "Bambara" nomenclature and identity. Because, ubiquitous among French clerical and skilled hires in the Bamako region after 1883 were none other than youths identified in colonial records as "Marka," "Sarakolle," "Soninke," "Somono" and "Fulbe," whose identity aligned them with the Islamized northern paradigm. Some identified as "Tukulor" also appeared in the record. Not surprisingly, therefore, when colonial circles were redefined in May 1888 and "tribes" named, many Bamana families reemerged in French records as "Bambara."[10] A decade later, on instructions from Governor Clozel, who further "clarified" these "racial" policies, the "tribes" and their "religions" were aligned according to "empirical" observations.[11] Thus, to preexisting images of "farmer," "animist," "*dolo*-consumer," and "slave," French embellishments added "hard-working," "clever," "loyal," "cunning," and "thieving," along with other Bambara "virtues" too numerous to mention. In fact, in an 1884 memo to a successor, Ruault editorialized on the "Bambara's ... notable superiority" compared to "other blacks." On the darker side, however, Ruault noted that the Bambara had "no religion ... no notion of God ... and no sense of the life hereafter ... not even a philosophic doctrine." Possessing no "moral principles" either, the Bambara, whose only language was "force," Ruault continued, should be treated with "great severity." "Indulgence" was mistaken for weakness.[12]

Now also evaluated according to the French style owing nothing to Mande values, filigreed references clarifying the worker's "good/bad" character polished the shiny new image. Thus fully labeled, tabled, and diagrammed as individuals—radically separated from Brevie's "collective identity" or from corporate groups of the great *jo* power association (see Chapters 2 and 3)—family members reappeared as a workforce neatly lined in columns indicating family name, father's name,

---

phie, l'ENSUP (Bamako, 1986), cited in Amselle, *Logiques métisses*, p. 224; Abela de la Rivière, *Les Sarakolé*, p 120.

10. The circle was first created in 1883, and recreated several times thereafter. See *ANSOM* Sén. et Dép. IV Doss. 90 Bis, Gallieni and Vallière, "Délimitation des Cercles" (Bafulabe, 1 May 1888), p. 2; *ANSOM* Sén. et Dép. IV Doss. 90 Bis Vallière "Mémoire" (Siguiri, 15–25 March 1888), pp. 1–55, see esp. p. 34. See also *ASAOF* 1G 32, "Lettre Eugene Mage à Gouverneur" (Saint Louis, 21 June 1866).

11. Delafosse, *Haut-Niger-Sénégal*, vol. 1, p. 151; see also Bazin, "A Chacun son Bambara," p. 119.

12. *ASAOF* 15G 83, Ruault, "Généralités 1880 à 1920" (Bamako, 22 Feb. 1884), pp. 1, 4, 5.

age, educational background, language skills, religion, and work experience, their Bambara (and other "French") identities convincingly "modern." It goes without saying that nowhere in the repertoire was there room for signs that authenticated people "in the Mande style": not Wagadu and the Soninko dispersal, nor Bida the sacred python, nor for that matter Kingi and the sleeping Bemba, not to mention the *siyah* alliance with Biton; and not Seribadia the aged patriarch, nor Jamusadia, Bamako's founder, and not Bamakoni, the sacred crocodile either. Neither was there place for the *jo* and its hallowed gold in this official colonial identity, nor the once-powerful *numuw*, and not even the jeli, or bardic force.

More specifically, among those serving the French was Mamadi Jallo, twenty-eight years old from the Massina, his father Kumba Jallo. Entering the colonial service in 1889 in the ambulance unit, Mamadi appears as a "Bambara"- and French-speaking Fulbe. Also included was Amadu Sumare from the Kayes region, twenty-nine years old, his father Malik Sumare. Entering the French service in 1883 as a political agent and infirmary worker, Amadu was identified as a Fulfulde-speaking Sarakolle. Before that a trader with links to the Senegambia and Saint Louis regions, Amadu's language skills—Wolof, French, and especially Arabic—suggest a certain erudition. Given that "political agents" needed writing skills, it is not unreasonable to suppose that Amadu could have been learned in Islamic sciences, if not a *qadi* (there is no record of Bamako *qadi*), possibly a marabout.[13]

Older than Amadu and Mamdi was the Fulbe Bo Jallo, thirty-seven years old. His father (Samba Jallo), having served the Umarians at Segu, Bo was later chief of the *talibe*, or disciples. With family members still resident in Segu—Bo himself knew the Segu region well—others resided in Bamako and Kayes, the larger family hailing originally from the Kaarta. Entering the colonial service in 1887 as a political agent, Bo was identified as a "Bambara-speaking" Fulbe. (Elsewhere Bo appeared as a "very intelligent Muslim Tukulor" of "intellectual and moral value," who accompanied Archinard to Nioro, Segu, and Bissadugu as chief porter). Also serving was the Islamized Abdullaye Jallo from the Futa Jallon, thirty-five years old his father Mamadu Jallo, his mother Sahimata Keita (one of the few occasions on which a mother's name appears). Recruited in about 1890, Abdullaye was a political courier in the Circle of Kita. Likewise ap-

---

13. *ANMK* 2E 16, "Bulletin de notes des agents politiques, Cercle de Bamako 1881–1894," n.p.; *ANMK* 2E 17, "Bulletin de notes des agents politiques Cercle de Kayes 1890," n.p.

pearing in the record was Abderaman Ture from Bamako, thirty-four years old. A marabout and "Moor" "devoted" to the French (Abderaman had guided the Gallieni Mission to Bamako in May 1880), his father was Jarissa Ture. Joining the service in 1883 as a political agent, later an information agent and tribunal member, Abderaman was in addition a rich trader, who spoke "Sarakolle," and "Bambara."[14]

Among the youngest to be recruited (in this particular selection of records) was Bara Dem, twenty-five years of age (father's identity unknown), a "Muslim Tukulor" from Podor in the Futa Toro. A "precious auxiliary," Bara served in the artillery at Bandiagara (1891–1893) under Captain Marignac, at Timbuktu (1893–1894) under Captain Migotte, and in Nioro under Captains Disdier (1894–1896) and Magasinier (1897). By 1898 Bara was a political agent at Dori, a few months later, a political agent and interpreter at Wagadugu. By 1900 he was identified as the most suitable "political agent for the extension of French influence" among the Mossi. For his pains Bara was named for the Medal of Honor.[15] Also among the early hires, whose identities the French individualized and functionalized, was Karamoko Kulibaly (age unknown), his father Sambadie Kulibaly. A student at the Ecole des Otages at Kayes from 1896 to 1899, Karamoko appears in the records as a French-speaking Bambara. Lassana Simpara (age also unknown) likewise appears as a Sarakolle student at Ecole des Otages at Kayes, 1896–1899. The son of Badara Simpara, Lassana was "Bambara"- and French-speaking, later undertaking a training program at Bamako.[16]

Identified as interpreter, inter alia, was the Islamized Samba Jallo from the Kita region (age unknown), his father Moussa Jallo, his mother a Jakite. Employed until 1882 by the Maison Maurel et Prom at Saint Louis, Sambo later joined the medical corp accompanying Colonels Borgnis Desbordes and Combes, and Lieutenant Frey on their epic journey (1883) to

---

14. *ANMK* 2D 132, "Organisation administrative ... ville de Bamako" (Bamako, 1 Nov. 1902), pp. 15–17; *ANMK* 2E 16, "Bulletin de notes ... Cercle de Bamako" (1881–1894); *ANMK* 2E 43, "Politiques indigènes 1897–1908: Fiches renseignements sur les chefs de Bamako 1897," n.p.; *ANMK* 2E 18, "Bulletin de notes des agents politiques, Cercle de Kita" (1890); *ANSOM* Sén. et Dép. IV Doss. 90 Bis, "Gallieni à M. Le Capitaine Roiffé" (Siguiri, 5 April 1888), pp. 30–34.

15. *ANMK* 2E 22, "Bulletin de notes des agents politiques, Cercle de Ouagadougou, 1900."

16. *ANMK* 2E 16, "Bulletin de notes ... Cercle de Bamako" (1881–1894); *ANMK* 2E 17, "Bulletin des notes ... Cercle de Kayes" (1890); *ANMK* 2E 18, "Bulletin des notes ... Cercle de Kita" (1890); *ANMK* 2E 43, "Notes et fiches ... Bamako" (1897–1908), n.p.

the Niger. By 1888 he was a member of the Niger medical corp. Fluent in "Bambara," Wolof, "Tukulor," and "Malinke," French to a lesser extent, Samba served at Segu with Archinard in 1892. "Devoted" and "zealous," Samba pursued his interpreter's work at Kissidugu until retirement in 1898. Also among interpreters were Samba Ibrahima (age unknown), an "intelligent, devoted Sarakolle," likewise Massa Jara (age unknown), a "clever French-speaking and energetic Muslim Bambara" (elsewhere a "Muslim Bambara" was said to be a contradiction), who served with Colonels Humbert, Archinard, and Combes. In 1902 Massa was appointed chief of the *anciens tirailleurs*, replacing Moussa Sidibe. Among this group as well was Lae Jakite, an "intelligent French-speaking Muslim Fulbe from the Wassulu"—later rewarded for "zeal" and "energy." A *tirailleur* at Saint Louis in 1881, Lae thereafter served in the Frey, Combes and Archinard military campaigns. By the 1890s he was among Bamako's police commissioners, and interpreters for the Bamako Circle. His conduct matching French expectations, Lae was not only rewarded with a Medal of Honor, but also "a weighty authority over his constituency." Serving with him was Bogoba Traore, an "extremely intelligent ... Sarakolle from Buguni." A former slave from Saint Louis (where he learned French), Bogoba in 1894 became interpreter and chief of the "Village de Liberte" at Banankabugu in the Buguni Circle.[17]

Finally, also serving the French in one capacity or another, but coming to a sorry end, was the "refractory political agent" Bandiogu Keita, who inadvisably ran afoul of the administration. Similarly unfortunate was Babo Famoro, a former slave in charge of purchasing grain and animals. The misguided Babo, foolish enough to cross swords with the Siguiri marabouts "and consequently a goodly number of powerful local people" as well, mysteriously disappeared in 1896. Rumor has it that he "went out of his mind," that he was "hiding in the bush," or that "he was dead." Likewise coming to a sorry end was poor Bo Jallo, whom the French later discharged for "drunken indelicacies," and Bogoba Traore who, on being promoted to the chieftaincy of a Bamako quarter, was apparently "robbed blind by relatives." Likewise ending his days in sorrow was the gifted Samba Jallo, dismissed by the French for improprieties although unproven and later dropped. Reinstated in 1898—and now responsible for a

---

17. *ASAOF* 15G 83, Ruault, "Généralités 1880 à 1920" (Bamako, 22 Bamako 1884), p. 14; *ANMK* 2E 43, "Notes et fiches ... Bamako" (1897–1908), n.p.; *ANMK* 2D 132, "Organisation administrative ... ville de Bamako" (Bamako, 1 Nov. 1902), pp. 17–23; *ANSOM* Sén. et Dép. IV Doss. 90 Bis, "Gallieni à M. le Capitaine Roiffé" (Siguiri, 5 April 1888), pp. 30–34.

household of at least twenty-five members—Sambo was removed from the payroll in 1906, deemed "unworthy of further attention."[18]

This proliferation of Islamized local hires identified as Soninke, Sarakolle, Marka, Fulbe and Tukulor in official records fuels the speculation that if the French had already learned of the "pagan Bambara" from Pacheco Pereira (1506–1508), Labat (1728), Park (1796), and Caillie (1827)—not to mention the Timbuktu *ta'rikhs* with which some were familiar—their false knowledge was later substantiated by local hires subscribing to the northern paradigm. All within the twenty and thirty age range, the marital status of these hires was never disclosed, most probably irrelevant to their new "French" identity. But if unmarried and officially resident within cognate kingroups, French hires would still have been "youths" in the Mande style, although the colonizer would have thought otherwise.

However, if these youths developed shiny new identities "in the French style"—complete with first and family names, father's name, age and function—the "Bambara" was far less visible. Tending to reappear in the tabled, mapped and diagrammed records, the Bambara was for the most part grouped among the nameless unknowns, or as a "tribal" statistic according to village, and region. Accordingly, in the 1905 census, the Bambara Other reappeared as approximately 128,322 in number distributed throughout villages in the Bamako Circle, together with 19,804 Malinke, 7,210 Sarakolle, and 5, 832 Fulbe among others. It goes without saying that the Bambara was a "fetishist." By 1909, census figures for Bamako, Kati and Kulikoro were showing 232,811 Bambara, 116,000 Malinke, and 18,524 Marka among others. Predictably, both the Bambara and Malinke were "fetishist." By 1914, the Bamako Circonscription (residence, post, and annex) was showing 109,378 Bambara, 38,000 Malinke, 1,592 Marka, 3,000 Kagoro, 3,000 Wassulunke, and 263 Fulbe. And yes, the Bambara and Malinke were "fetishist."[19]

---

18. *ANMK* 2E 23, "Bulletin de notes des agents politiques, Cercle de Siguiri 1890–1897" (Siguiri, 1890–1897); *ANMK* 2D 132, "Organisation administrative ... ville de Bamako" (Bamako, 1 Nov. 1902), pp. 15–17; *ANMK* 2E 43, "Notes et fiches ... Bamako" (1897–1908), n.p.

19. *ASAOF* 15G 170, Laverdure, "Rapport sur le Conflit markas" (Gorée, 26 June 1905). Statistical data also included other populations, "by race," including Tukulor, Wassulunke, Wolofs, Moors, Somono, etc. Depending on their location and the populations with whom they resided, Kagorow were sometimes identified as Sarakolle, at other times as Fulbe. *ANMK* 5D 53, "Recensement statistiques annuelles: Cercle de Bamako, 1905–1914, Recensement Bamako Cercle 1905"; *ANMK* 5D 53, Recensement de la population, statistiques de Bamako Kati,

Finally as a caveat, my data do not suggest the absence of "Bambara" in the French service. On the contrary, the French frequently turned to the "animist Bambara," who, when disguised as an "Islamized jula," was an ideal spy in Islamized regions where noncomplying marabouts were suspect, or in Islamized trading communities where tax evaders were common. There was, for example, Waraba Konate, a forty-three year old "Malinke and Bambara-speaker," a former slave. Disguised as an "Islamized jula," he reported on errant tax collectors in the Odienne region, and surveyed caravan routes, later spying on marabouts at Sambatiguila. Additionally, there was the "animist" Koberi Keita (further identity undisclosed), who, in Ruault's eyes, deserved special recognition, not to mention the numerous and unnamed "jula spies" reaching Bamako from the right bank, and the Wassulu. Despite disguises, however, spying subterfuges seldom passed unnoticed: Consequently, spies had to be frequently changed.[20] Aside from spying, no specific data explain the Bambara's relative invisibility in the neatly lined columns of auxiliaries. The Bambara's preliterate standing, as opposed to the higher literacy rate among Islamized auxiliaries, may explain his relative under representation in the French labor force in a predominantly Bamanakan region.

Part 2: Linkages Between the
Northern Paradigm and the European Imagination

On learning of the Islamized holographs the French, having already developed their own, were quick to follow these northern initiatives. Ini-

---

Koulikoro, 1909"; *ANMK* 5D 53, "Recensement statistiques annuelles: Cercle de Bamako, 1905–1914 ... Tableau V (1914) ... Tableau VI (1914)." At least one French observer seemed aware that "racial categories" created for official purposes were thoroughly arbitrary. For similar observations for Segu, Timbuktu, and Jenne, see *ANMK* 5D 5, "Recensement de la population du Cercle et de la ville de Tombouctou, 1904–1919, Cercle de Tombouctou, 1904"; *ANMK* 5D 24, "Recensement de la population du Cercle et de la ville de Djenné, 1904–1911"; *ANMK* 5D 45, "Recensement de la population: Cercle de Ségou, 1891–1905."

20. *ASAOF* 15G 83, Ruault, "Généralités 1880 à 1920" (Bamako, 22 Feb. 1884), p. 14; *ANSOM* Sén. et Dép. IV Doss. 90 Bis, "Gallieni à M. Le Capitaine Roiffé" (Siguiri, 5 April 1888), pp. 30–34; *ANMK* 2E 16, "Bulletin de notes ... Cercle de Bamako" (Bamako 1881–1894); *ANMK* 2E 17, "Bulletin des notes ... Cercle de Kayes" (1890); *ANMK* 2E 18, "Bulletin des notes ... Cercle de Kita" (1890); *ANMK* 2E 43, "Notes et fiches ... Bamako" (1897–1908), n. p.; *ANMK* 2E 23, "Agents politiques" (Siguiri 1890–1897), n.p.; *ANMK* 4E 45, "Rapports sur L'Islam ... Cercle de Dédougou" (1913); *ANMK* 2D 132, "Organisation administrative ... Bamako" (Bamako, 1 Nov. 1902), pp. 21–23.

tially transferring French domestications of the northern paradigm and its naming criteria into European imaginations were early voyagers such as Pere Labat (1728), informing the world that the interior was full of Bambara whom Islamized Soninke, or Sarakolle traders, brought as slaves to French trading posts. Some sixty years later, Goldberry (1785 and 1787) confirmed the Bambara's slave image: They were coming in large numbers to French marts in Galam and the Senegambia. Far less "handsome" than the Wolof of Senegal, Goldberry editorialized, the Bambara, the "true negro," strong and robust, spoke a crude language. About ten years later, Park (1796) was introducing his "Bambarran" *jatigi* at Kulikoro to the English-speaking world as a former slave, the "Bambara language as a sort of corrupted Mandingo." Three decades later, Caillie (1827) transplanted the Bambara's "thieving" image into French popular imaginations. It is of interest to note that Caillie was in the hands of Sarakolle guides, one a former Arawan resident and friend of the "Moors." And while on the Mage mission to the Umarian capital at Segu (1863), Dr. Quintin's observation that the Bambara was remarkably resistant to Islam would have raised neither eyebrows nor blood pressures north of Segu.[21]

Further transforming popular images into policy recommendations was none other than the sage Gallieni who, while the Umarians' reluctant guest at Nango (1 June 1880–29 March 1881), composed policy recommendations affecting the so-called superiority of the Sarakolle over the Bambara. Possessed of dynamism, intelligence, and an instinct for commerce the Sarakolle—whose commercial networks extended from the south, the upper Senegal and Niger rivers, to Jenne—were "astute, persuasive, and tenacious." More developed than the Bambara—"perfidious and predatory"—Gallieni favored the Sarakolle as the standard bearers of France's civilization into the interior. With respect to the Gallieni mission, we are once more hardly surprised to learn that among Gallieni's interpreters and guides were Alassane (a Tukulor), Thiama (a Fulbe), Alpha Sega, Abdoulaye, and Abderaman (both Muslims), as well as traders from Saint Louis who "liked the French," not to mention the mission's Tukulor ass-drivers whose identity Gallieni thoughtfully disguised as "Bambara" for the benefit of suspicious and anti-Tukulor Beledugu chiefs whose territories they crossed.[22] Nor is there need to mention the numerous

---

21. Park, *The Travels*, pp. 157, 179; Caillié, *Voyage*, vol. 2, pp. 62, 65–66. Goldberry's reference was to the generic Mande languages (*ANSOM* B4, Walckenaer, *Histoire générale*, vol. 5, "Voyage de Goldberry," pp. 440–441).

22. The Gallieni mission was ambushed by the "Bambara" on 11 May 1880 at Jo in the Beledugu.

Sarakolle suppliers, intermediaries, and informants encountered en route, applauding the French presence—and in the French idiom. And lest his place in mission records pass unnoticed, Valliere echoed the refrain that, despite the "savage" Malinke, it was the Soninke- Sarakolle's "highly developed instinct for trade" that had extended markets throughout the old Mande.[23] As to the Malinke's "fetishism," Valliere was hardly surprised when Bure inhabitants consumed *his* rum as proof of *their* "animist" predilections.[24]

Transferring these images into policies applied farther east was Binger (1892), whose observations would have sounded strangely familiar to northerners and the Muslim literati: "In all the countries visited, the word *Bambara* is a synonym for 'kaffir' or 'infidel.'" He likewise shared as-Sadi's assumptions, no doubt unwittingly, that the Bambara were loose-moraled and "promiscuous."[25] Moreover, his eagerness to "blacken the white spaces" appearing in current maps was matched only by the French cartographers' dislike of spatial blanks. However, cutting through the tangled Segovian traditions, Binger eschewed vituperation of the "fetishist Bambara," providing instead a historical schema. His "Bammana" chronicle and chronology—from 1650 and "Kaladian Kouroubari" to 1861 and the Umarian conquest of Segu—critiqued questionable voices such as Quintin's, when he was on the Mage mission (1863–1866): Challenging Quintin's claim that the "Bammana" reached Segu from Torong, Binger argued instead that they had probably been longtime residents at points closer-in (e.g., Baninko, Bole, and Ganadugu), arriving in the Segu region well before the seventeenth century. Moreover, modifying Quintin's uncritical repetition of the "fetishist" and "refusal to convert" etymology of the Bambara nomenclature, Binger argued instead that Bamana state-building—far from being a retreat from Islam—was in defense of a "fetishist" identity, and Bamana political power. But having avoided the Scylla of one popular etymology, Binger lapsed into the Charybdis of another: that the Bambara's generic name derived from their *tana, bamba,* or *bamma,* the Niger crocodile. The identity of his informants remains unclear, although Mouça Diawara (Moussa Jawara) and Diawe Fonfana were among their ranks, both Islamized, the former a Soninke from the Nioro region, the latter from Dogoofili. Others in Binger's company in-

---

23. Gallieni, *Voyage*, pp. 158, 198, 200–201, 211, 240, 256–257, 290, 322.

24. Volunteers apparently found the drink distasteful (Gallieni, *Voyage*, p. 317).

25. Binger, *Du Niger*, vol. 2, pp. 375, 382, 385–386; *Ta'rikh as-Soudan*, pp. 22, 223, 274, 289, 411, 418, 420; *Ta'rikh al-Fattash*, pp. 20, 106–109.

cluded *tirailleurs* and traders from Kita and Saint Louis, the latter no doubt Muslims.[26]

Not to be outdone, by the turn of the century, French official records were not only reporting that the term "Islamized Bambara" was a contradiction, but they were equating the Bambara's "fetishism" with the Malinke's "resistance to Islam." If the "Bambara" appeared to be "converting," it was because Fulbe propagators were aggressive, and the "Bambara" mindless mimics. For those subscribing to the northern paradigm, French statistics were substantiating these claims; that southerners, including the Malinke, were quite resistant to Islam.[27] At the same time, mixed reports were circulating. Some, on the one hand were confirming Islam's overall "decline" in the west and north, even in Jenne: Due to the French abolition of slavery (1904), children, required to work at home and in the fields were no longer going to Koranic school. Other reports, on the other hand, were hinting darkly at the rise of a "fanatic Islam noir" resistant to colonialism[28] Differences, notwithstanding, still alive and well were ideologies embedded in the northern paradigm, now domesticated by the French. "It is absolutely certain," reported Delafosse in 1912, "that for Sudanese Muslims in general, and in the Niger bend area in particular, the term *Bambara* does not refer to a particular group of people, nor to a special tribe, but to all Sudanese peoples who have remained faithful to their indigenous religion."[29] As to matters affecting the demise of the powerful Umarian state, Fulbe interlocutors in the Massina were informing Lieutenant Caron (1890s) that despite the Bambara revolts—which had shaken the Umarian state to the core—the French could not defeat the *talibe* without Fulbe assistance.[30]

Part 3: Linkages Between the Northern Paradigm and the Academy

If Binger and Delafosse had saved the Bambara from an animist ignominy, the reprieve was but short-lived, because, transferred from popu-

---

26. Binger, *Du Niger*, vol. 1, pp. 1–2, 4, 5–6, 9, 11, 45, and passim; vol. 2, pp. 375, 386.

27. *ANMK* 4E 35, "Politique musulmane" (Bafoulabé, 1897–1914), n.p.; *ANMK* 5D 19, "Recensement de la population du Cercle de Bafoulabé, 1886–1904"; *ASAOF* 1G 248, Pérignon, "Monographie" (1899–1900), p. 259.

28. *ANMK* 1D 32 5, "Etude sur les marabouts" (Bafulabe, 5 July 1894), pp. 1–13; *ANMK* 4E 32, "Rapports sur ... l'Islam" (1908); *ANMK* 4E 35, "Politique musulmane" (Bafulabe, 1897–1914); *ANMK* 4E 36, " Rapport sur l'Islam et les ... Musulmans, Cercle de Bamako" (1897–1911).

29. Delafosse, *Haut-Sénégal-Niger*, vol. 1, p. 126.

30. *ASAOF* 1G 83, "Mission Caron" (1887–1895), p. 29.

lar imaginations into policy recommendations, the Bambara's tarred and feathered image passed virtually unchallenged into intellectual categories. Chanting the same refrain in the 1920s, Monteil reported that "for the Muslim, the Bambara is an infidel, a pagan, (and) a consumer of alcohol; for pastoralists, Moors and Peuls, the Bambara is the cultivator and also the black; for the Semites (sic) and those who claim (this identity), the Bambara is above all the black; for those who hold or once held power, the Bambara is a slave; for all he is the primitive, a socially inferior individual."[31] However, dismissing (like Binger) the flawed etymology of the term *Bambara*—that the Bambara in rebelling against Soninke regional hegemony (prior to the rise of the Segu Bamana state) became those who "refuse all authority" (*u bara bango be la*)—he noted that the nomenclature *Banmana* and its variants applied as well to all blacks; "Banmana," he ventured, was merely a derivative of *ba*, a proto-Pular radical meaning "black." Thus, however many ways Monteil conjured his ethnographic kaleidoscope, the Bambara kept reappearing as a denigrated creature of the Fulbe, and the north's Islamized epistemes, "primitive and socially inferior": Slurring a Muslim with the Bambara sobriquet was worse than an insult. His linguistic and administrative insights passing unchallenged into the academy, or community of learning after World War II, Monteil's imprimatur on the Bambara's fetishist identity entered the Mande historiography.[32] On preparing his valuable monographs on the Bambara of Segu and Kaarta (1924), and the Soninke of Jenne (1932), Monteil's principal informants were Kare Tammoura and Gran Koate, two "Islamized" *jeliw*, both northerners.

Although litanies of name-callers slid through the northern paradigm—and into its domesticated French version—it seems best to cease with Tauxier (1927, 1942) and Dieterlen (1951) whose work did for the Bambara what Kenneth Little did for the Mende of Sierre Leone.[33] Suffice it to say that Tauxier's fieldwork on the Bambara—during his years of service with the AOF between 1905 and 1927—was undertaken in the northern Circle of Niafonke, or Issa-Ber, primarily (on his own admission) a Fulbe circle. His considerable contributions on the origins, and history of the Fulbe before the Umarian wars are still useful.[34] But although Bambara residents had "signed" the Circle's southern spaces (Monteil *had* no-

31. Monteil, *Les Bambara*, p. 9; *ANMK* 1D 38 3, "Monographie ... Djenné, 1909," p. 10.

32. Monteil, *Les Bambara*, pp. 7–11. For Delafosse's view of the Bambara/Banmana, see Delafosse, *Haut-Sénégal-Niger*, vol. 1, pp. 27, 125–126.

33. Personal communication Kenneth Little (Edinburgh, June 1976).

34. Louis Tauxier, *Moeurs et histoire des Peul* (Paris, 1937).

ticed this), there is no clear indication that Tauxier visited the south. Instead, very probably relying on Bambara and "Poullo-Bambara" informants, as well as on a Futanke descendant of the Umarians reaching Segu in 1861, Tauxier (1927), like Monteil before him, favored the Bambara's somewhat savage image. Emphasizing the Bambara's so-called "secret societies," he displayed his "extremely curious information on the Bambara religion" passed on by informants. These insights he supplemented with the earlier works of Pere Henry and Charles Monteil.[35]

In his later *Histoire* (1942)—Tauxier, demurring that his most "definitive" study had finally resolved questions concerning the Bambara's origins, attributed the civilizing of the Bambara to the Fulbe. "It was thought until recently," our author began, "that this powerful dynasty at Segu and Kaarta was of Bambara origin." But it was of Fulbe provenance: "The Peul, having established themselves in Bambara country, reduced its inhabitants to a veritable bondage." The "great dynasty of Mamari Kulibaly," emerging sometime during the early eighteenth century, was nothing less than the product of both races uniting the robustness of the Bambara, with the "distinguished demeanor" of the "Peul."[36]

Finally less problematic, but still displaying traces of the earlier intellectual genealogy, is the work of anthropologist Germaine Dieterlen. Developing her early research in the tradition of Marcel Griaule[37] (whose work still has the power to stir controversy), Dieterlen later opened up the "Bambara's" complex of belief structures and symbolism, the *komo* power association not the least among these.[38] Sharing Griaul's view of the rationality and viability of African cultures (and avoiding Tauxier's poor choice of informants), Dieterlen was served by authentic-looking informants: Bala Diara of Banankoroni, "farmer, hunter, priest and Chief of the *komo* rites"; Dji Diara of Soroba, "farmer, hunter, healer and Chief of the *nama* rites," Bakonimba Koulibali of Soroba, "farmer and Chief of the *komo* rites," Mousa Woulale of Pelengena, a *jeli*, to mention but a few. And

---

35. J. Henry, *L'Ame d'un peuple africain: Les Bambara, leur vie psychique, éthique, sociale, religieuse* (Münster, 1910).

36. Tauxier, *Histoire*, "Preface," pp. v-vi. The Fulbe had claimed in any event that the Bambara state had been established in the seventeenth and eighteenth centuries by a "Fulbe aristocracy." Konaté, "Monographie," p. 10 .

37. Marcel Griaule, *Dieu d'eau. Entretiens avec Ogotemmêli* (Paris, 1948); Marcel Griaule and Germaine Dieterlen, "Signes graphiques des Soudanais," *L'Homme: Cahiers d'ethnologie, de géographie et de linguistique* (Paris, 1952); Marcel Griaule and Germaine Dieterlen, *Le Renard pâle* (Paris, 1965).

38. Dieterlen, *Essai sur la religion*; Germaine Dieterlen and Youssouf Cissé, *Les Fondements*.

unlike Tauxier, who worked mainly in a northern "Fulbe circle," Dieterlen's field-work carried her into the "Bambara" heartland from
Segubugu in the north to Kangaba and the old Mande in the south. Readily she acknowledged abstractions, rational relationships, change and
process in the Bambara's intellectual and cosmological categories. Socially
grounded in pre and proto-history, as well as in meaningful life-experi-
ences, Dieterlen recognized that Bambara metaphysics were also organized, coherent, systematic, and not in any way the series of "incoherent,"
and "disparate elements," which Tauxier and Henry had "conscientious-
ly," but mistakenly portrayed. Bambara metaphysics could even hold
their own in a comparative analysis of the "Mediterranean and Asiatic
systems," she argued.[39]

Yet even while acknowledging the indigenous authenticity of western
Sudanese cultures, Dieterlen noted that "it would be inappropriate to neg-
lect the influences of other Sudanese people on the Bambara (especially
since these Sudanese people) have been in contact with the Mediterranean
Basin since a distant epoch." Appropriately, her first reference was to Islam
and its early introduction into North Africa and the western Sudan. In her
second, a problematic and passing reference, her footnotes quoted P. M.
Schuhl's critique of Griaule's work among the Dogon in which he cautioned against ruling out "an indirect influence of Greek myths on the Sudanese mythology." No critique followed this problematic quote. Was
Dieterlen losing her focus? Finally, citing Tauxier's *Histoire de Bambara* on
the foundations of the "Bambara" states of Kaarta and Segu, Dieterlen
averred that although the "Bambara" claim to have reached Segu from the
Mande, their political systems never developed beyond "little chiefdoms."
Faithful to the Tauxier tradition, she associated the creation of larger states
with the expanding Fulbe regional penetration in the seventeenth century,
when a mixed "local aristocracy" of "Bambara" and "Peul" gave rise to the
Segovian, later the Kaartan state.[40] Although now greatly modified, even
to a certain extent appreciated, Dieterlen's "Bambara" was still the essential "savage" and "primitive" first appearing in the pages of the two Timbuktu *ta'rikhs* approximately two centuries before.

Thus did ideologies within the Islamic northern paradigm—reborn several times across the centuries—finally write the "Bambara" into the pages
of European notebooks. Thus also did European popular imaginations
consume their contents, as Park's importunate companion had literally

---

39. Dieterlen, *Essai sur la religion*, avant-propos and Introduction, pp. xi–xx,
227–230. See especially pp. xiii, xv, xvi and note 1, xvii, 229.
    40. *Ibid.*

consumed "magic" words from the surface of a *saphie* board, washed down by gulps of water (see Chapter 5). And thus did the academy's bearded ones pronounce the French-domesticated northern paradigm as a learned *gris-gris* against the signs of ignorance. Accordingly, the northern paradigm, crafted on the middle Niger's banks and desert-side shores— originally the handiwork of Islamized northerners, literati, and traders seeking kaffir gold and slaves from upper Niger regions, later diffused by long-distance traders—was reified not only on Paris boulevards and in cafes, but it was also mummified in the halls of the academy. Governor Trentinian was correct (see Chapter 5). Passing into the "scientific" historiography, the "Bambara," like Bamako, had become a part of history.

The Re-Birth of the Wagadu Identity

Part 1: Islam, Youth, and Women

If the Bambara identity was being reconstrued according to the colonial state's filigreed configurations, others, especially women, youths and children were also drawn into new identities. So were Bamako's older family members; but with a difference: While some youths increasingly redefined their "French" identities in relation to the individualist and functionalist ideals of the colonial state, older family members protected and elaborated the Mande identity by revising and reinvesting in the past. In other words, older family members did what people the world over compulsively do: They reconfigured their past. As V. Y. Mudimbe reminded us: Colonialism always provoked a "hidden contamination" associated with alien lifestyles and modes of thinking imposed on groups recently deprived of power. As strong tensions developed between "modernity" and "tradition" during the colonial era, he continued, they often led to a nostalgia, reflecting a poor if "golden" image of a mythical past.[41] Given this perspective, it is hardly surprising that the destruction of state power in 1883 evoked a nostalgia for the golden age of Wagadu: "How difficult it is to understand the world," the beheaded serpent, Bida, was heard to say on plunging south to Bure some thirty-three generations earlier. In the south people still say that dried-out river beds are signs that his sacred body passed that way in flight.[42] It would also have been surprising if previous state losses at the hands of deviant youths had not been recalled: Fata Maghan Nyakate had violated a sacred ritual at Wagadu; Bem-

---

41. Mudimbe, *The Invention*, p. 5.
42. Interview Diarra Sylla a metalworker from Nioro (Bamako, 15 May 1983); interview Thiémoko Kanté (Bamako, 4 Jan. 1983).

ba Nyakate had abrogated a ritual taboo at Kingi. More recently, Drave and Ture "sons" and "nephews" had traitorously served in the enemy Samorian forces against the Niare *kafu-tigi*; so had Drave, Ture and Niare sons and nephews served the Gallieni mission in Bamako, the old Mande, the Birgo, and elsewhere. What would the youth do now?

Clearly altering this socio-political alchemy were two factors: first, an "Islam noir," which opposed the French; second, French educational and labor policies affecting the changing role of youth and women. The long history of Islam, its various particularisms and opposition to colonialism in the western Sudan are generally known. Less overtly opposed to colonialism was the older, or "traditional" Islam, in situ in some instances since several centuries. Specifically I am referring to the more "tolerant" traditions of the fifteenth-century Egyptian *alim* (plu.: *ulama*) Jalal al-Din al-Suyuti (d. 1505), whose teachings had reached the Timbuktu mosques by the sixteenth century (see Chapter 2). Not that the Islamic spectrum was polarized between arcane "traditionalists" and progressive "reformists," nor that the al-Suyutti were specifically advocating a "mixed" Islam. Rather, within the widening range of religious experiences occurring across the centuries, the al-Suyutti had come to tolerate regional particularisms on grounds that adapting the *Shari'a* to local exigencies—so long as the integrity of the Sunna, or "Tradition of the Prophet," was maintained—was preferable to conflictual and inter-group aggression, especially between desert-side nomads and their sedentary Sahelian neighbors. The "quietist" al-Suyutti accordingly eschewed the *jihad*, even in the face of the colonized, preferring peace instead.

Likewise less opposed to colonialism in the western Sudan's Islamic particularisms were those associated with the Tawati (southern Algeria) *alim* Muhammad b. Abd al-Karim al-Maghili (d. 1504), al-Suyutti's contemporary. Important to note, however, is that while the al- Suyutti traditions were reasonably flexible on matters affecting mixing, the al-Maghili, who followed their leader's condemnation of Sunni Ali (the fifteenth-century Songhay ruler), were less tolerant of the region's "tyrants" and "wrongdoers," advocating the *jihad* instead. In any event, as Islamic identities shifted, ulama and other Islamic notables often turned pragmatic when seeking interpretations of the Law, selecting instead what appeared most appropriate, if not always ideologically pristine when confronted with historical exigencies. But sometimes wavering between an anti-colonialism and tolerance of the French, "traditionalists" frequently irked the guardian ire of the more militant Islamic practitioners.[43]

---

43. Mervyn Hiskett, *The Development of Islam in West Africa* (New York; Longman, 1984), pp. 15, 16, 34, 36–38, 41, 42, 47, 85, 161, 246, 248, 272, 314, 316–318.

More overtly opposed to colonialism was "Islam noir," associated with the North African "fanatics" and other "disturbers of the peace," according to French observers, who, in policy recommendations separated these offending sentiments from the "traditional Islam," allegedly more passive and quietist.[44] Active mainly in western Sudanese Sufi orders, both the Hamalliyya (especially in the Nioro region during the early twentieth century), and the Sanusiyya were from the outset unambiguously anti-French. The Tijaniyya was also anti-French particularly during the nineteenth-century Umarian wars, although their policies were later modified. Sufi orders tended to attract male youths, women to a lesser extent.

More specifically opposed to the French were the Wahhabiyya. Regarded as "reformist" by the French, and as "foreigners" by some local Malian traditions, the Wahhabiyya called themselves "People of the Sunna and the Book" (*Ahl al-sunni wa' l-kitab*), thereby implying a certain legitimacy. However, by naming them "Wahhabiyya"—after the Arabian *Shaykh* Abd al-Wahhab, active during the first part of the eighteenth century—French Orientalists thereby came to define the terms of an enduring discourse.[45] By the 1920s and 1930s, al-Wahhab's teachings had taken root in the western Sudan, especially in Timbuktu, thanks to the earlier work of Egyptian clerics Jamal al-Afgani, Muhammad Abdu, and the Algerian shaykh Ben Badis, together with itinerant merchants and pilgrims regularly traversing the routes. By 1945 Wahhabiyya religious identities had not only been forged in Mali, but also in the Cote d'Ivoire, even the northern Gold Coast.

Founding the Union Culturelle Musulmane (UCM)—with its sub-Saharan seat at Dakar under the leadership of the Senegalese Shaykh Ture (b. 1925)—the Wahhabiyya established *madrasa*, or Muslim schools, intent on Arabic language and cultural instruction (designed for intellectual and spiritual enlightenment), as well as on other modes of reformist, progressive thought. But hardly a homogeneous movement with unanimity on its

---

44. Marcel Cardaire, *Contribution à l'étude de l'Islam noir*, Mém. no. 2, Institut Français d'Afrique Noire Cameroun (Douala, 1949), vol. 2, pp. 1–119; *Idem, L'Islam et le terroir africain, Etudes soudaniennes* (Kuluba, 1954). For a broader treatment see Vincent Monteil, *L'Islam noir* (Paris, 1964). Some scholar-administrators, including Binger, Clozel and Delafosse, came to realize that Islam was not the "peril" they had once believed. See Christopher Harrison, *France and Islam in West Africa, 1860–1960* (Cambridge University Press, 1988), see especially "Scholar-administrators and the definition of 'Islam noir," pp. 94–117.

45. Centre des Hautes Etudes Administratives sur l'Afrique et l'Asie Modernes (hereafter CHEAM), "Notes et études sur l'Islam en Afrique noire" (Paris, 1962), p. 37.

side, other Wahhabiyya, insisting on the separateness of the "African personality," debated the legitimacy of indigenous chants and dances, even art, insisting that religious experiences and affairs should not be differentiated from social relations. Some even argued for an optional fast, or that daily prayers be reduced to two (since "to work is to pray"), still others even venturing that women, under certain circumstances, deserved a formal education. In Bamako, the Wahhabiyya tended to attract members from the mercantile communities.[46]

Resisting colonial rule through spiritual enlightenment, cultural forms and through education, their schools were expected to counteract the secularism that was polluting the moral environment. Accordingly, we note with interest that approximately 600 students were enrolled in Bamako Wahhabiyya schools by 1961, 160 in Bobo-Julasso by 1958, while in Guinea, al-Hajj Kabine Diane, former director of the Bouake school in the Cote d'Ivoire, was publishing pamphlets on Islamic teachings and faith with an anti-colonial sub-text. Not surprisingly, as the strident anti-colonial tocsins sounded through the western Sudan in the late 1950s, the Wahhabiyya—through the Subbanu, their political arm—together with the Hamaliyya, had already forged the religious wing of the pro-independence Rassemblement Democratic Africain (RDA).[47]

Second, if a more activist and anti-French Islam was operative in some circles, French educational and labor policies were impacting the lives of other youths, women and children. It goes without saying that colonial political economies and public policies were bringing Bamako's youths into the newly developing monetary French-franc economies.[48] Associated with these were wage-labor markets impacting not only on social functions, social structures and behavior, but also on family alliances, even injecting new stresses into preexisting relationships. We saw above the ways in which some young men were drawn into the system and its labor force. Moreover, migratory labor, attracted either out of need or to pay newly imposed taxes brought "strangers" into the region on the basis of different relationships,

---

46. CHEAM, "Notes et études," p. 37; Jean-Loup Amselle, "Le Wahabisme à Bamako, 1945–1983," unpublished paper, pp. 1–14.

47. Louis Brenner, "Constructing Muslim identities in Mali," in Louis Brenner ed., *Muslim identity and social change in sub-Saharan Africa* (Indiana University Press, 1993), pp. 59–78; Lansiné Kaba, *The Wahhabiyya: Islamic reform and politics in French West Africa* (Evanston, 1974), pp. 25–27; Hiskett, *The Development of Islam*, pp. 289–291; Monteil, *L'Islam noir*, pp. 309–311.

48. See the various commercial reports, at least one per quarter, for the Bamako Circle: *ANMK* 1Q 44, "Rapports commerciaux Cercle de Bamako 1886–1919"; see also *ANMK* 1Q 204 (numerous commercial reports 1899–1907).

most importantly the cash nexus—owing little to previous lineage or ritual bonding in the Mande style. And it is probably without coincidence that the French opened their first Bamako school as early as 1884.[49] Here, transforming the political power structure into a dynamic and invisible force operating through children's minds, individual boys from ages six to twelve— said to be minors of "aristocratic" and "notable Islamized families"—were attending a French secular school at Bamako where French language instruction, reading and writing were de rigeur. And as teaching in the great Wagadu myth, the powerful *jo* rituals, and the sacred gold (signs of earlier familial identities and state power) gave way to the secular French curriculum, the French expected that newly internalized values would render youthful minds more tractable. By 1899 several secular schools had opened throughout the Bamako Circle, attended mainly by boys from Islamized families. Hours of instruction—from 6:00 A.M. to 9:00 A.M., 2:30 P.M. to 5:30 P.M., and 7:00 P.M. to 8:30 P.M.[50]—clearly interfered with family routines and the regular ordering of the domestic labor force, where young boys formed an important core. Moreover, drawn into the new political economy, the wage-labor market, and the educational system, to make matters worse, several youths were being empowered for the first time in ways previously unimagined by the old order.[51]

Probably not by coincidence, by the turn of the century school attendance at the French schools showed a decline, even among Bamako's notable and Muslim families: On the one hand, not wanting to be identified as "friends of the French," and indifferent to exhortations on the advantages of the French language, many, including the Niare and the Ture sent "nephews" (slaves, some say) instead of "sons" to French schools; on the other hand, families preferring Koranic schools risked having their children dispatched for several months each year on trade missions "having nothing to do with education, Arabic nor the Koran." In any event, children sometimes took the law into their own hands, playing truant especially in June, the beginning of the planting season.[52]

---

49. *ASAOF* 15G 83, Ruault, "Généralités 1880 à 1920" (Bamako, 22 Feb. 1884), pp. 8–9.

50. *ASAOF* 15G 83, Ruault, "Généralités 1880 à 1920" (Bamako, 22 Feb. 1884), pp. 8–9. Instructional hours varied. For different hours, see *ASAOF* 15G 169 no. 7, "Rapport du Capitaine d'Artillerie de Marine Charnet Commandant le Cercle de Bamako sur les écoles du Cercle" (Bamako, 13 July 1899), pp. 4, 8.

51. Interview Marabout Touré (Bozola-Bamako, 6 Jan. 1980); interview Nana Niaré Dravé (Bamako, 4–5 Jan. 1980); interview Seydou Dravé (Bamako, 7 Jan. 1980).

52. In addition to French history (e.g., the "glorious campaigns" of Napoleon III, 1870–1871), and geography, children, were taught to recognize snow, oak trees,

School enrollments declined still further after the slave emancipation decree of 1904–1905, which theoretically liberated domestic slaves in the western Sudan. Here, families pleading a labor shortage (especially Islamized *horon* families), kept children away from schools. Elsewhere, fleeing slave families contributed further to declining enrollments: Some parents simply left the scene of an erstwhile enslavement, returning instead to some natal land usually farther south, whether in Buguni, Sikasso, or the Wassulu.[53] Elsewhere, opposition to French "progressive" schools was also not wanting. In several Marka towns, for example in Tuba, which boasted twelve or thirteen Koranic schools for 400–500 youths, the Almamy was obdurate: It was of no account that children should "relate" more effectively to the "French authorities," nor that their commercial opportunities be greatly enhanced, nor that they receive a so-called superior understanding of "justice." Farther north in Jenne, French schools were deemed "of little importance." More generally, marabouts predicted darkly that the changing socio-economic and cultural environments would bring an unremitting scholarly decline.[54]

Of even greater concern, as family traditions were contested by the rapidly changing circumstances, were the greater freedoms for women under French protection, threatening the integrity of the marriage institution, the ownership of progeny, property inheritances, the morality of the moral community, and the sacred oathings binding lineages since deep antiquity.[55] As I have shown throughout this discussion, women were not only central to these ancient alliances; they were also essential to larger issues, most importantly (from our perspective) to identities, their multiple configurations, and reconfigurations. This may partly explain why some Maraka slave owners, appalled at the flight of women slaves and children fleeing households, intercepted them en route, even while allowing men to leave. Not surprisingly, by the turn of the century marabouts, julaw,

---

and bears, among other things (*ASAOF* 15G 169 7, Charnet, "Rapport ... sur les écoles du Cercle" [Bamako, 13 July 1899]), pp. 1–8, esp. p. 8; interview Marabout Touré (Bozola-Bamako, 6 Jan. 1980); interview Nana Niaré Dravé (Bamako, 5 Jan. 1980); interview Seydou Dravé (Bamako, 6 Jan. 1980).

53. *ANMK* 1D 33 4, Rougier, "Enquête sur l'Islam" (Banamba, 31 May 1914); *ASAOF* 1G 189, McLeod, "Rapport ... Maracadougou" (Bamako, 1 Oct. 1894); *ANMK* 4E 32, "Rapport sur ... l'Islam" (1908); *ANMK* 1Q 24, "Renseignements sur les maisons de commerce, 1899–1907" (Bamako, 1907); *ASAOF* 15G 170, "Cercle de Bamako: Incidents de Banamba ... 1905."

54. *ASAOF* 1G 189, MacLeod, "Rapport" (Bamako, 1 Oct. 1894), p. 13; *ASAOF* 1G 305, "Sénégambie-Niger Cercle de Djenné" (Jenne, 10 March 1904), pp. 55–59.

55. For a more general discussion, see Labouret, "Les Manding," pp. 63–64.

and especially the Maraka, it was said, were quickening their proselytizing zeal, conceivably enraged at the loss of women and slave property, not to mention an income and a labor force.[56]

Part 2: The Niare and Other Families Revisited

What fate in the meantime had overtaken the Niare families? Conspicuously absent for the most part from the neatly columned Sarakolle-Soninke and Fulbe-Tukulor identities outlined in writing on paper, were the names of Niare youths, ubiquitously absent from functional categories now operationalizing the old *kafu* and beyond. And as events distanced their elders from the new centralizing political power, so did their state-dependent identities languish on the new state's periphery. Conceivably, as indicated above, Niare limited writing—and possibly language—skills could have been the source of their distancing. Doubtless their political loyalty was suspect. And although some Niare youths offered services to the French in the early 1880s, most Niare patronyms appearing thereafter in the records (surprisingly few considering the large family) suggest their roles as local chiefs and magistrates remote from the central power. The supposition, therefore, is that by the 1890s, many Niare "sons" and "nephews"—not to mention "fathers"—had been relegated to local villages assisting the aged and/or infirm chiefly incumbents, whose powers had now been greatly impaired.[57]

Niare patriarchs, now for the most part officially "Bambara" and "fetishist," were accordingly identified with regional villages, erstwhile elements of the now-defunct *kafu*. For example, the "very old" Batigui Niare (d. 1898), Titi's "brother" and chief of Sikoro (in the Bamako Canton), was reportedly jostled about by "nephews and younger brothers exercising the (real) power." His successor, Jyonko Niare (d. 1903)—also "very old, of no intellectual value, inebriated most of the time, and not very enterprising"

---

56. *ANMK* 1D 33 4, Rougier, "Enquête sur l'Islam" (Banamba, 31 May 1914); *ANMK* 5D 24, "Recensement de la population du Cercle et de la ville de Djenné, 1904–1911"; *ANMK* 4E 32, "Rapport sur la situation de l'Islam ... Haut-Sénégal-Niger" (1908), n.p.; *ANMK* 4E 36, " Rapport sur l'Islam et les ... Musulmans, Cercle de Bamako" (1897–1911), n.p.; *ANMK* 4E 3, "Surveillance des personnages religieux" (1910–1912); *ANMK* 4E 9, "Politique musulmane surveillance des personnages religieux: Correspondence avec le Commandant de Djenné 1912–1913."

57. *ASAOF* 15G 83, Ruault, "Généralités 1880 à 1920" (Bamako, 22 Feb. 1884), p. 18; *ANMK* 2E 43, "Notes et fiches ... Bamako" (1897–1908), n.p.; Gallieni, *Voyage*, pp. 248, 337.

(according to official reports)—was equally manipulated by "younger brothers." A member of the Bamako Native Tribunal, Jyonko's "brothers" reportedly led him by the hand to regular sessions (he was apparently blind). Residing elsewhere in small towns and villages, some two to three days' journey from Bamako, other Niare patriarchs joined the rural statistics of the new colonial state. And as the Mande style of composing public business gave way to the French style, not only Titi Niare, the old *kafu* chief, but also regional Niare notables—all "Bambara" and "fetishists"—lost the vestiges of an earlier political power and identity to those who had named them.[58] Thus did many Bambara-Niare notables surrender state office to their erstwhile Islamized clients, and possibly rivals, as well as to onetime Islamized advisors supposedly sometime Niare friends.

Not surprisingly, old Niare-Ture internal rivalries continued. For example, although Jyonke Niare was *chef de ville*, later canton chief after the death of his "brother" Batigui in September 1898, Abdul Jaffar Ture, son of Balaji Ture, was reportedly "uncontested ruler" of Bamako's native quarter. A prosperous merchant held in awe "even by animists," Abdul successfully fended off younger Niare "brothers" claiming their rightful power (see Chapters 2 and 3). In the meantime Ture elders, such as Abderaman Ture and Madani Ture endeared themselves to the French by providing porters, grain and so forth. For their pains, local French administrators requested (July 1906)) the first-class Medal of Honor privileging the devoted Abderaman Ture. And in 1900 when Bamako's population was about 3,800 souls and Jyonke Niare the titular official, Dogofaro Ture was reportedly wielding the real native power. Not all Ture elders were, however, French supporters; and while some refused to pay the tax, Madani Ture, identified in the records as "irascible" and "recalcitrant" refused to cooperate with census-takers, leaving them standing in the sun for days on end. Although some Niare notables later adopted an Islamic identity, the extent to which elders recovered authority, power, and status from their old de facto rivals remains unclear. The 1920s brought no further clarity. Of the local notables appearing on official lists, only three Niare patronyms are listed compared, for example, to the numerous Ture, Konare, Keita, Traore, Jara, Sow, N'Jaye, and so forth. In any event, restricted by the French to familial urban quarters, the Bamako chiefly office was abolished in 1958.[59]

---

58. *ANMK* 2D 132, "Organisation administrative ... ville de Bamako" (Bamako, 1 Nov. 1902), pp. 3–5; *ANMK* 2E 43, "Notes et fiches ... Bamako" (1897–1908).

59. *ANMK* 2D 132, "Organisation administrative ... Bamako" (Bamako, 1 Nov. 1902), pp. 2, 5; Soumaoro, "Etude," p. 11; *ANMK* 2E 43, "Notes et fiches ... Ba-

It goes without saying that the loss of state power seriously undermined not only Niare and Ture identities, but also the many Mande identities dependent on a state affiliation. My hypothesis, therefore, is that for Bamako notables in general and Niare elders in particular, events of the early and mid-twentieth century once more threatened the families with the *via negativa*, liminality, and identity loss. With respect to liminality, I bring back Belgian anthropologist Arnold Van Gennep and his *Les Rites de passage*.[60] Theorized in 1909, Van Gennep was appropriately critiqued by social anthropologists, and the debate has long since been closed.[61] Interesting from our perspective, however, was his elaborated analysis of the liminality of the *rites de passage*, because according to Van Gennep, the state of ritual separation from the group followed by liminality called for a temporary annulment and invalidation of the pre-ritual state of being, behavior, and prescribed norms. Accordingly, while "in passage," or the *via negativa*, the initiate, culturally denuded and socially invisible, was suspended in circumstances somewhat analogized as the void where only the simplest and most rudimentary of preritual systems obtained. Eventually the initiate was reincorporated into a new ritual status and a renewed social identity. Processually, the latter were rendered cognitively real and complete not only because a life-equilibrium had been restored with things past remembered, but also because initiates had been reconnected—from an entirely different perspective, however—to preexisting cultural forms, institutions, and behavioral norms.[62]

But there was more to liminality and the *rites de passage* than the processes of separation and reincorporation. Relatively empty cultural spaces within the ethnographic inventory were parsed into mythic teach-

---

mako" (1897–1908); *ASAOF* 15G 83, Ruault, "Généralités 1880 à 1920" (Bamako, 22 Feb. 1884), p. 18; *ASAOF* 1G 351, Bobichon. "Note sur le Cercle de Bamako" (Bamako, 20 Feb. 1921).

60. Arnold Van Gennep, *Les Rites de passage* (Paris, 1909).

61. Van Gennep's work was critiqued by many (Max Gluckman's and Robert Horton's work withstanding best the test of time), because lacking an adequate comparative social theory, he offered no adequate analysis to explain ritual-prone "tribal societies" as compared to the more resistant "modern" societies. His explanation—that no "semi-civilized mind" was "entirely free from the sacred"—simply begged the question, despite his otherwise "tremendous contribution" according to Gluckman. Max Gluckman, *Essays on the ritual of social relations* (Manchester University Press, 1962), pp. 1–2; Robin Horton, "Ritual man in Africa," *Africa*, vol. 34 (1964): 85–104.

62. Van Gennep, *Les Rites*; Gluckman, *Essays*, pp. 1–52; Evan Zuesse, *Ritual cosmos: The sanctification of life in* African *religions* (Ohio University Press, 1972).

ings, knowledge transfers, and the gnosis of a higher state of spiritual awareness, all richly embossed with signs and sacred rituals. Among these were instruction of the *significata*, including dogma, spiritual doctrine, and sacred theory, all contributing—to one degree or another—to the reconstruction of the ethnographic imagination, an initiatic transcendentalism, a recentered personality, and a restructured identity. Mythic instruction likewise evoked patterned processes, or choreographed modes of reconstituting the past, whether referring to spiritual or secular affairs, to a corpus of creation stories, to the origins of the universe and humankind, or to the beginnings of other living species sharing human ecosystems. All manner of "primitive" knowledge was similarly transmitted in myth, including archaic metaphors likening the known to the unknown. Or, primordial symbols and images became signs explaining the unexplainable, proliferating the conscious and unconscious mind with meaning. Primitive knowledge likewise transmitted abstruse archetypes recalled only through patterned thinking indicating the "must," possibly the "ought to be." With respect to the families, it is of considerable interest that as the century aged, the must and the ought to be came to resemble the Koran's holy writ—(much in the same way as the *jo* among the blacksmiths had come to resemble the tax man, see Chapter 2)—as new Niare elites drew closer to an Islamized identity.

When seen from this perspective, it is not unreasonable to suppose that discontinuities between the persona of the Bamako *kafu*, on the one hand, and the families' state-dependent identity, on the other hand, threatened the older generation—if not the youth to the same extent—with another social marginality and cultural liminality in the *via negativa*. Mitigating this vexing dilemma was the sacred myth—now also Islamized—providing meaning, understood only as worthy of veneration, associated with the holy and the divine, or as signaling against the forbidden. When instructed in the *via negativa* according to these Islamized perspectives, the Wagadu legend became more complex and elaborated than early French administrators had imagined, and more important than earlier observers had understood. Nor, incidentally, had it become a mere cautionary agenda of rational blueprints, and behavioral codes. Nor was it a tale told by an idiot.

Given the circumstances, ironically, or perhaps hardly surprisingly, the older Niare generation did what their genitors and progenitors had done since archaic time: They named themselves according to their new state identity. They named themselves "Bambara." By naming themselves "Bambara," the Niare acquired a "French" identity in association with the new French colonial state. The "grandfathers" could hardly have improved on this! Whether or not weeping and gnashing of teeth were heard as the northern paradigm shifted one more time, remains unclear. Instead, we hear the great Wagadu myth reminding families, primarily the "errant" youth, that they were "Bambara": And that preserving "the Bambara style" was a collective and individual imperative.

As the Niare-Meillassoux version of the great legend makes clear, Amadu Kumba Niare (1883–1964)—concerned that Niare youths were in the process of losing their patrimony—agreed that the "truth" (his word apparently) be written down. Himself a product of the Ecole des Otages, and now (1962–1963) *kun-tigi* (chief) by virtue of descent—he was within Jamusadia's patrilineage—Amadou Kumba was in reality only the paterfamilias *privatus*, the Niare chiefly office having been abolished in 1958. Neither a *burudju-gosila* (genealogist) nor a *jeli*, he had nonetheless memorized the legend, having heard it many times over since childhood. It was clear from his intentions that coming of age in the colonial era, French influences at the Ecole des Otages had been counteracted and contradicted at home by mythic parsings of the Wagadu legend recited at family funerals, chiefly enthronements, and rituals celebrating the *inese*, or cult of the ancestors. His generation having struggled to reproduce a Bambara identity in the face of cultural invasions from the colonial state, Amadu Kumba was now "preserving" (his word apparently) the heritage for those to follow.[63] The mighty myth was being manipulated one more time!

As a matter of interest, when debriefed by their conquerors in 1883, Niare voices (possibly also those who witnessed on their behalf) had spoken more of a homeland in Wagadu, less of being Mande, and certainly not "Bambara." Even their identities seemed ambiguous, at least in the pages of French reporting: Were they "Soninke," "Maraka," "Sarakolle," or "Bambara"? Less than 100 years later, Amadu Kumba was reproducing a mid-twentieth-century version of what it meant to be Bambara—all told as if occurring in archaic time, reminiscent of ancient forms, including an ancient *lex familiaris*, the *privatum consilium*, and the Mande *civitas in parvo*.[64] So much had changed. Nothing had changed.

And so the story ends where it began: with the families—the Niare, the Ture, the Drave, Kulibaly, Jakite, Jara, Keita, Traore, Konate, Dembele, Sissoko, Kante, Sisse, the Dembelle, and the Konare—and their manipulated myths, their particularized identities, and their cultural shifts, the particular within the universal, the same, yet different. Requiring the great Wagadu legend to play out its redemptive role in no way denies or denigrates its sacerdotal nature. Always a religious text, in believers' eyes the

---

63. Meillassoux, "Histoire, pp. 186–187.

64. We recall from Chapter 5 that at the fiftieth anniversary (1933) of the French in Bamako, Governor Trentinian had also reinvented Bamako's history, tracing it to Ptolemey's history of the second century, A.D.

great myth's changing and unchanging ways had never ceased to claim its signs and symbols affecting order, social control, meaning and purpose. Neither had changing-unchanging signs and symbols ceased to communicate in forms appropriated by multiple generations of "Bambara," their signifier-powers always manipulated in control of destructive impulses. Small wonder that in the mid-twentieth century, the great myth's sacred alchemy was once more being sought in pursuit of a Bambara identity: The myth was explaining to the world what it meant to be "Bambara."[65]

In the New World, at the other end of "a large river of salt water," and beyond the land of the *"Toubaubo doo* ... (or) the land of the white people," according to Park's account of Mande geography, was the *"jong sang doo* ... (or) the land where the slaves are sold."[66] Here, "Bambara" still meant "slave," together with "Mandinga," "Mandingo," "Mandinka," and "Malinke."

---

65. For a discussion, see Jean Bazin, "The Past in the present: Notes on oral archaeology," in Bogumil Jewsiewicki and David Newbury, eds., *African historiographies: What history for which Africa?*, (Sage, Beverly Hills, 1986), pp. 59–74.

66. Park, *The Travels*, p. 209.

Maps of Western Africa

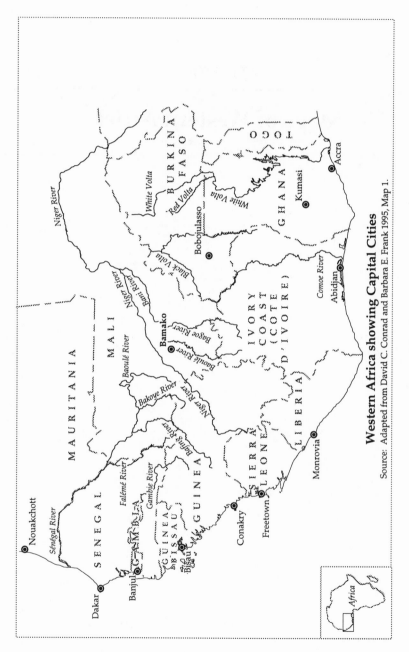

Western Africa showing Capital Cities

Source: Adapted from David C. Conrad and Barbara E. Frank 1995, Map 1.

Map 1

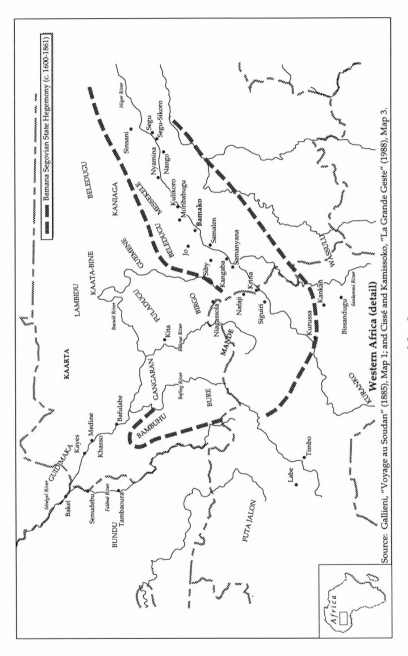

Western Africa (detail)

Source: Gallieni, "Voyage au Soudan" (1885), Map 1; and Cissé and Kamissoko, "La Grande Geste" (1988), Map 3.

Map 2

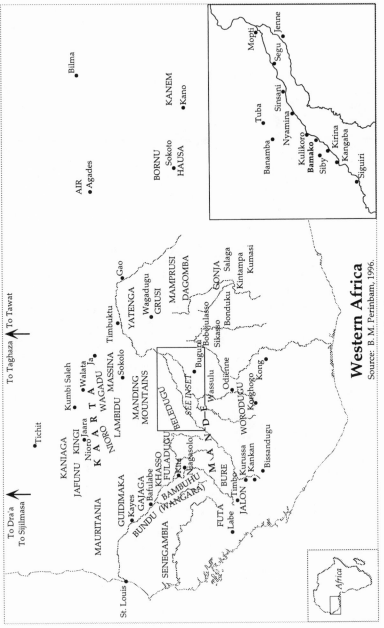

Western Africa

Source: B. M. Perinbam, 1996.

Map 3

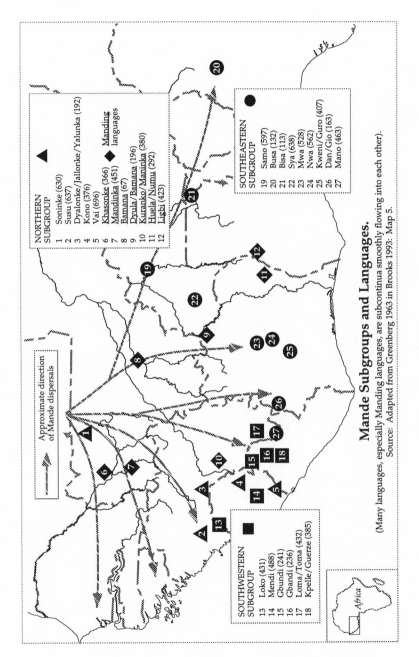

Mande Subgroups and Languages.

(Many languages, especially Manding languages, are subcontinua smoothly flowing into each other).
Source: Adapted from Greenberg 1963 in Brooks 1993: Map 5.

Map 4

NORTHERN
SUBGROUP

1   Soninke (630)
2   Susu (637)
3   Dyalonke/Jallonke/Yalunka (192)
4   Kono (376)
5   Vai (696)
6   Khasonke (366)
7   Mandinka (451)
8   Bamana (67)
9   Dyula/Bamana (196)
10   Kuranko/Maninka (380)
11   Huela/Numu (292)
12   Ligbi (423)

Manding
languages

SOUTHEASTERN
SUBGROUP

19   Samo (597)
20   Busa (132)
21   Bisa (113)
22   Sya (638)
23   Mwa (528)
24   Nwa (562)
25   Kweni/Guro (407)
26   Dan/Gio (163)
27   Mano (463)

SOUTHWESTERN
SUBGROUP

13   Loko (431)
14   Mendi (488)
15   Gbundi (241)
16   Gbandi (236)
17   Loma/Toma (432)
18   Kpelle/Guerze (385)

Approximate direction
of Mande dispersals

Africa

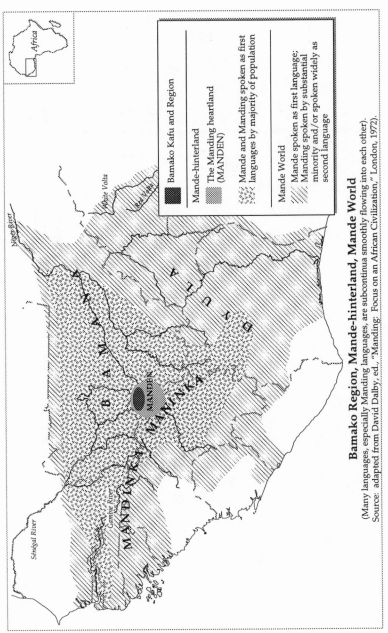

Bamako Region, Mande-hinterland, Mande World

(Many languages, especially Manding languages, are subcontinua smoothly flowing into each other).
Source: adapted from David Dalby, ed., "Manding: Focus on an African Civilization," London, 1972).

Map 5

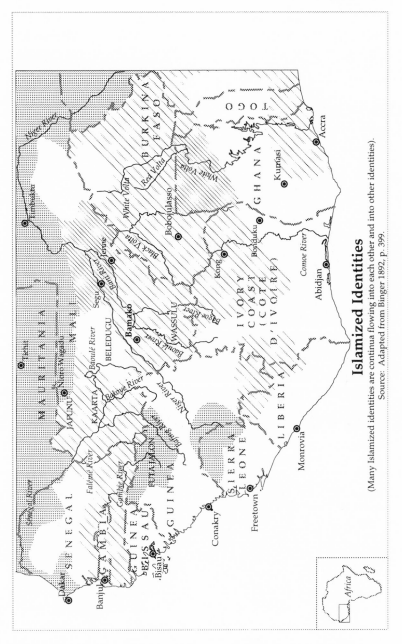

Islamized Identities

(Many Islamized identities are continua flowing into each other and into other identities).
Source: Adapted from Binger 1892, p. 399.

Map 6

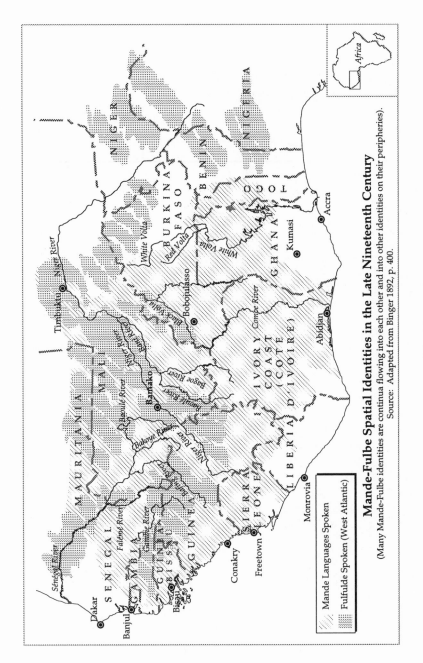

Mande-Fulbe Spatial Identities in the Late Nineteenth Century

(Many Mande-Fulbe identities are continua flowing into each other and into other identities on their peripheries).

Source: Adapted from Binger 1892, p. 400.

Map 7

Bibliography

Articles, Chapters, and Occasional Papers

Adam, M. G. "Légendes historiques du pays de Nioro." *Revue Coloniale*, 1903, pp. 81–98, 232–248, 354–372, 485–496, 602–620, 734–744; 1904, pp. 117–124, 232–248; republished as a brochure (Paris Challamel, 1904), 123 pp.

Amselle, Jean-Loup. "Les Réseaux marchands kooroko." *African Urban Notes*, vol. 5, no. 2 (1970): 143–158.

Amselle, Jean-Loup. "Qu'est-ce qu' un *kafo* ou *jamana*? Le cas du Gwanan ou les faux archaïsmes de l'histoire africaine." *Cahiers de l'Office de Recherche Scientifique et Technique Outre-Mer* (ORSTROM), sér. Sciences humaines, vol. 21, no. 1 (1985): 43–56.

Amselle, Jean-Loup. "L'Ethnicité comme volonté et comme représentation: A propos des Peul du Wasolon." *Annales; Economies, Sociétés, Civilisations* (AESC), vol. 42, no. 2 (1987): 465–489.

Amselle, Jean-Loup. "Un État contre l'état: Le Keleyadugu." *CEA*, vol. 28, (1988): 463–483.

Amselle, Jean-Loup, Z. Dunbya, A. Kuyaté, and M. Taburé. "Littérature orale et idéologie: Les gestes de Jakite Sabashi du Ganan (Wasolon, Mali)." *CEA*, vol. 19, (1979): 381–433.

Anonymous, "Chronique historique de la ville de Bamako." Translated from Arabic by Mallick Yattara, *EM*, no. 20 (Jan. 1977): 62–66.

Appia, Béatrice. "Les Forgerons du Fouta-Djallon." *JSA*, vol. 35 (1965): 317–352.

Ardouin, Claude Daniel. "Une Formation politique précoloniale du Sahel occidental malien: Le Baakhunu à l'époque des Kaagoro." *CEA*, vol. 28 (1988): 443–461.

Arnaud, R. "L'Islam et la politique musulmane française en Afrique occidentale française, suivi de la singulière légende des Soninké," tirage à part du Comité de l'Afrique française (Paris, 1911), pp. 150–151, 155. In 1912, *BCAFRC* reprinted the first part of Arnaud's work, "L'Islam et la politique musulmane française en AOF," in its supplement, *Renseignements Coloniaux* (1912), pp. 2–30, 115–127, 142–154, but not the "Singulère légende." The tirage à part is rare. Arnaud's informant for the legend was a Muslim of the Bathily lineage.

Arnaud, R. "La Singulière légende des Soninké: Traditions orales sur le royaume de Koumbi et sur divers autres royaumes soudanais," in R. Arnaud, *L'Islam et la politique musulmane française en Afrique occidentale française*. Paris, 1911, pp. 144–185.

Balandier, Georges. "L'Or de la Guinée française." *Présence Africaine*, no. 4 (1948): 539–548.

Bathily, Abdoulaye. "La Légende du Wagadu (text soninké de Malamine Tandyan)." *BIFAN*, sér B, vol. 29 (1967): 135–168.[1] This is a new translation of Monteil's version (1953).

Bathily, Abdoulaye. "A Discussion of the traditions of Wagadu with some reference to ancient Ghana including a review of oral accounts, Arabic sources and archaeological evidence," *BIFAN*, sér. B, vol. 37, no. 1 (Jan. 1975): 1–94.

Bathily, Abdoulaye, ed. "Ibrahima Diaman Bathily: Notices socio-historiques sur l'ancien royaume soninké." *Etudes Sénégalaises*, no. 9 (Saint Louis, 1962).

Bathily, I. "Les Diawandés ou Diogoronés." *Education Africaine*, vol. 25 (1936).

Bazin, Jean. "Recherches sur les formations socio-politiques anciennes en pays bambara." *EM*, no. 1 (1970): 12–40.

Bazin, Jean. "Guerre et servitude à Ségou." In Claude Meillassoux, ed., *L'Esclavage en Afrique précoloniale*. Paris, 1975, pp. 135–181.

Bazin, Jean. "La Production d'un récit historique." *CEA*, vol. 19 (1979): 435–483.

Bazin, Jean. "A Chacun son Bambara." In Jean-Loup Amselle and Elikia M'Bokolo, eds., *Au Coeur de l'ethnie: Ethnies, tribalisme, et état en Afrique*. Paris, 1985, pp. 87–127.

Bazin, Jean. "The Past in the present: Notes on oral archaeology." In Bogumil Jewsiewicki and David Newbury, eds., *African historiographies: What history for which Africa?*. Sage, Beverly Hills, 1986, pp. 59–74.

Beckingham, C. F. "The Pilgrimage and death of Sakura, King of Mali." *Bulletin of the School of Oriental and African Studies*, vol. 15, no. 2 (1953): 391–392.

Bernard, R. P. "Bamako, le passé, le présent et l'avenir." *Bulletin des Mission d'Afrique des Pères blancs* (Paris, 1910), pp. 282–291.

Binger, Louis G. "Les Routes commerciales du Soudan Occidental." *Gazette Géographique et l'Exploration* (Paris, 1886), vol. 21, no. 11 (18 March 1886): 201–206; vol. 21, no. 12 (25 March 1886): 221–228.

Binger, Louis G. "Transactions, objets de commerce, monnaie des contrées entre le Niger et la Côte de l'Or." *BSGP*, vol. 12 (Paris, 1889–1890): 77–90.

Binger, Louis, G. "Du Niger au Golfe de Guinée," *BSGP*, vol. 10 (1889): 329–371.

Bléneau, Daniel. "Démographie bamakoise." *EM*, no. 19 (Oct. 1976): 1–36.

Bloch, Marc. "Le Problème de l'or au moyen âge." *Annales d'Histoire Economique et Sociale*, vol. 5 (1933): 1–34.

Bonnel de Mézières, A. "Recherches sur l'emplacement de Ghana (fouilles à Koumbi et à Settah) et sur le site de Tekrour." *Mémoire: Académie des Inscriptions et des Belles-Lettres*, vol. 13 (1920): 227–273.

Borgnis Desbordes, A. "Un Cinquantenaire: L'Arrivée des Français au Niger, 1 février 1883." *Revue Militaire de l'Afrique Occidentale Française* (April 1933), pp. 33–41.

Bouche, D. "Les Villages de liberté en AOF" *Bulletin de l'Institut Français d'Afrique Noire*, sér. B (1949), pp. 491–540; (1950), pp. 135–215.

---

1. *Bulletin de l'Institut Fondamental d'Afrique Noire*. In order to make the distinction clear the earlier title, *Bulletin de l'Institut Français d'Afrique Noire*, is not abbreviated. Both were published in Dakar.

Brasseur, Gérard. "Djenné, centre urbain traditionnel: Evolution de l'habitation rural au Soudan français, Peul et Rimiabé de Seno de Bandiagara." *Conférence des Africanistes de l'Ouest*. Abidjan, 1953.

Brasseur, Gérard. "Bamako, plaque tournante de l'AOF." *France Outre-Mer*, no. 307 (1955): 26–29.

Braudel, Fernand. "Monnaies et civilisations: de l'or du Soudan à l'argent d'Amérique. Un drame méditerranéen." *Annales; Economies, Sociétés, Civilisations* (AESC), no. 1 (1946): 9–22.

Brett, Michael, C. Fyfe, J. Forbes Munro, Andrew Roberts, eds. "The History of the African family," *JAH*, special issue, vol. 24, no. 2 (1983).

Brooks, George E. "Ecological perspectives on Mande population movements, commercial networks, and settlement patterns from the Atlantic wet phase (c.5500–2500 b. c.) to the present." *HA*, vol. 16 (1989): 23–40.

Brunschwig, Henri. "Le Docteur Colin, l'or du Bambouk et la 'colonisation moderne.'" *CEA*, vol. 15 (1975): 166–188.

Burkhalter, Sheryl L. "Listening for silences in Almoravid history: Another reading of 'The Conquest that never was.'" *HA*, vol. 19 (1992): 103–131.

CEA, vol. 28 (1988). Special issue on the Mande.

Chermette, A. "Monument monolithique de la région de Kankan (Haute-Guinée)." *NA*, no. 42 (1949): 3.

Chudeau, Raymond. "Le Grand commerce indigène de l'Afrique occidentale," *Bulletin de la Société Géographique et Commerciale* (1910), pp. 398–412.

Chudeau, Raymond. "Taoudenni et Teghazza d'après les notes du Capitaine Grosdemange." *BCAFRC*, vol. 20 (1910): 13–16.

Chudeau, Raymond. "Note sur l'ethnographie de la région du Moyen Niger." *L'Anthropologie*, vol. 21 (1910): 661–666.

Chudeau, Raymond. "Le Problème du dessèchement en Afrique occidentale." *BCEHSAOF* vol. 1 (1916): 353–369.

Cissé, Youssouf. "La Société des chasseurs malinké." *JSA* vol. 34, no. 2 (1964): 175–226.

Cissoko, Sékéné Mody. "L'Humanisme sur les bords du Niger au XVIe siècle." *Présence Africaine*, vol. 21 (1964): 81–89.

Cissoko, Sékéné Mody. "Famines et épidémie à Tombouctou et dans la boucle du Niger du XVIe au XVIIIe siècle." *BIFAN*, sér. B, vol. 30 (1968): 806–821.

Cissoko, Sékéné Mody. "La Royauté *(mansaya)* chez les Mandingues occidentaux d'après leurs traditions orales." *BIFAN*, sér. B, vol. 31 (1969): 325–338.

Cissoko, Sékéné Mody. "L' Intelligentsie de Tombouctou aux XVe et XVIe siècles." *BIFAN*, sér. B, vol. 31 (1969): 927–952.

Cohen, Abner. "The Origin of trading diasporas." In Claude Meillassoux, ed., *The Development of indigenous trade and markets in West Africa*. Oxford University Press, 1961, pp. 276–278.

Collomb, Dr. "Contribution à l'étude de l'ethnologie et de l'anthropologie des races du Haut-Niger: Les Races du Haut-Niger, Moeurs de la race bambara, les populations du Haut-Niger." *Bulletin de la Société d'Anthropologie de Lyon* (1885 and 1886).

Colombani, F. M. "Le Guidimaka: Etude géographique, historique et religieuse." *BCEHSAOF*, vol. 14 (1931): 365–432.

Conrad, David C. "Searching for history in the Sunjata epic: The case of Fakoli" *HA*, vol. 19 (1992): 147–200.

Conrad, David C. and Humphrey Fisher. "The Conquest that never was: Ghana and the Almoravids, 1076. Part 1, The External Arabic sources." *HA*, vol. 9 (1982): 21–59.

Conrad, David C., and Humphrey Fisher. "The Conquest that never was: Ghana and the Almoravids, 1076. Part 2, The Local oral sources." *HA*, vol. 10 (1983): 53–78.

Daget, J. "Notes sur Diafarabé et ses habitants Bozo." *NA*, vol. 39 (July 1948); pts 1 and 2, pp. 24–26, 31–34.

Daveau, S. "La Découverte du climat d'Afrique tropicale au cours des navigations portugaise (XVe siècle et début du XVIe siècle)." *BIFAN*, sér. B, vol. 4 (1969): 953–988.

De la Rivière, Marie Thérèse Abela. "Les Sarakollés du Mali et leur migration en France." *EM*, no. 7 (Sept. 1973): 1–12.

Delafosse, Maurice. "Monographie historique du Cercle de Bamako." *BCAFRC*, vol. 3 (Paris, 1910): 57–67.

Delafosse, Maurice. "Les Noms des noirs musulmans du Soudan occidental." *Revue du Monde Musulman*, vol. 12 (1910): 257–261.

Delafosse, Maurice. "Les Confréries musulmanes et le maraboutisme dans les pays du Sénégal et du Niger." *BCAFRC* (Paris, 1911): pp. 81–90.

Delafosse, Maurice. "Traditions historiques et légendaires au Soudan occidental traduites d'un manuscrit arabe," *BCAFRC*, vol. 8 (Paris, 1913): 293–306; vol. 9: 325–329; vol. 10: 355–368. This article was reproduced as "Histoire de la lutte entre les Empires de Sosso et de Mandé." *NA*, no. 83 (July 1959): 76–80.

Delafosse, Maurice. "La Question de Ghana et la mission Bonnel de Mézières." *Annuaire et Mémoires du Comité d'Études historiques et Scientifiques de l'AOF* (1916), pp. 40–61.

Delafosse, Maurice. "De l'animisme nègre et sa resistance à l'Islamisation en Afrique occidentale." *Revue du Monde Musulman*, vol. 19 (1922): 121–163.

Delafosse, Maurice. "Terminologie religieuse au Soudan." Extracted from *Anthropologie*, vol. 33 (1923): 371–383.

Delafosse, Maurice. "Le Gâna et le Mali et l'emplacement de leurs capitales." *BCEHSAOF*, vol. 7 (1924): 479–542.

Delafosse, Maurice. "Les Relations du Maroc avec le Soudan à travers les âges." *Hespéris*, vol. 4 (1924): 153–174.

Delafosse, Maurice. "Les Langues du Soudan et de la Guinée." *Les Langues du Monde* (Paris, 1925), pp. 373–845.

DeLuz, Ariane. "Affaires familiales et politiques." In Françoise Héritier-Augé and Elisabeth Copet-Rougier, eds., *Les Complexités de l'alliance: Vol. 3, Economie, Politique, et Fondements symboliques (Afrique)*. Paris: Editions des Archives Contemporaines, 1993, pp. 78–119.

Desplagnes, Louis. "Notes sur l'emplacement des ruines de Ganna ou Gannata, ancienne capitale soudanaise antérieure à l'Islam." *Bulletin de la Société de Géographie de l'AOF*, no. 4 (1907): 298–301.

Dieterlen, Germaine. "The Mande creation myth." *Africa*, no. 27 (1957): 127–134.

Dieterlen, Germaine. "Mythe et organisation sociale au Soudan français." *JSA*, vol. 25 (1955/1956): 38–76, 376–389; vol. 29 (1959): 119–138.

Dieterlen, Germaine, and Z. Ligers. "Notes sur un talisman bambara." *NA*, no. 83 (1959): 89–90.

Dieterlen, Germaine. "Contribution à l'étude des forgerons en Afrique occidentale." *Annuaire de l'Ecole Practiques des Hautes Etudes*, vol. 73 (1965–1966): 1–28.

Dresch, Jean. "La Riziculture en Afrique occidentale." *Annales de Géographie* (1949), pp. 295–314.

Dresch, Jean. "Villes d'Afrique Occidentales." *Outre-Mer*, no. 10 (April-June 1950): 200–230.

Eisenstatd, S., M. Abitbol, M. and N. Chazan. "Les Origines de l'état: Une nouvelle approche." *Annales; Economies, Sociétés, Civilisations*, vol. 38, no. 6 (1983): 1232–1255.

EM, no. 8 (Jan 1974). Special issue on "Le Soudan occidental du paléolithique à la première périod d'instabilité."

Fage, John D. "Ancient Ghana: A review of the evidence." *Transactions of the Historical Society of Ghana*, vol. 3 (1957): 77–98.

Faidherbe, Louis. "Le Soudan français." *Bulletin de la Société de Lille* (1881–1888).

Filipowiak, Wladyslaw. "Contribution aux recherches sur la capitale du royaume de Mali." *Archaeologia Polona*, vol. 10 (1968): 217–232.

Gaden, Henri. Les Salines d'Aoulil." *Revue du Monde Musulman*, vol. 11 (1910): 436–443.

Gaillard, M. "Niani: Ancienne capitale de l'Empire mandingue." *BCEHSAOF*, vol. 6 (1923): 620–636.

Gallieni, Joseph. "Le Capitaine Gallieni à la Société de Géographie de Bordeaux." *BSGCB* (1881), pp. 354–367.

Goody, John R. "The Impact of Islamic writing on the oral cultures of West Africa." *CEA*, vol. 11 (1971): 455–466.

Graves, H. "Bamako, capitale du Haut-Sénégal et Niger." *Questions Diplomatiques et Coloniales*, vol. 23 (Jan.-June 1907): 561–576.

Griaule, Marcel. "Remarques sur une méthode de prospection ethnographique." *NA*, no. 39 (July 1948): 9–11.

Griaule, Marcel. "Le Savoir des Dogons." *JSA*, vol. 22 (1952): 27–42.

Grosz-Ngaté, Maria. "Pouvoir et savoir: La réprésentation de monde mandé dans les oeuvres de Park, Caillié, Monteil et Delafosse." *CEA*, vol. 28 (1988): 485–511.

Hervé, H. "Niani, ex-capitale de l'Empire mandingue." *NA*, no. 82 (April 1959): 51–55.

Hodgkin, Thomas. "Koumbi Saleh and the capital of Ghana." *West Africa*, nos. 21–23 (1953): 243–244.

Hopkins, N. S. "Kita, Ville malienne." *EM*, no. 6 (July 1973): 1–26.

Horton, Robin. "On the rationality of conversion." *Africa: Journal of the International Institute*, vol. 45, nos. 3–4 (1975): 219–225, 373–398.

Hunwick, John O. "Studies in the *Tarikh al-Fattash*: Its authors and textual history." *Research Bulletin*, Centre of Arabic Documentation, University of Ibadan, vol. 5, nos. 1–2 (1969): 57–65.

Hunwick, John O. "The Mid-fourteenth century capital of Mali." *JAH*, vol. 14, no. 2 (1973): 195–208.

Jaeger, P., and Duong-Huu-Thoi. "Grottes à dessins rupestres de la région de Kita (Soudan Français)." *Comptes Rendus de la Conférence Internationale des Africanistes de l'Ouest*, Dakar, 1945, vol. 2 (1951): 313–317.

Jagu-Roche, Pièrre. "Bamako: La Perle de l'AOF." *AOF Magazine*, vol. 20 (1959): 14–18.

Kendall, Martha. "Getting to know you." In David Parkin, ed., *Semantic anthropology* (London, 1982), pp. 197–209.

Kesteloot, Lilyan. "Un Épisode de l'épopée bambara de Ségou: Bakari Dian et Bilissi." *BIFAN*, sér. B, vol. 35, no. 3 (1973): 881–902.

Kesteloot, Lilyan. "Le Mythe et l'histoire dans la formation de l'empire de Ségou." *BIFAN*, sér. B, vol. 40, no. 3 (1978): 578–681.

La Chapelle, F. De. "Esquisse d'une histoire du Sahara occidental." *Hespéris*, vol. 11 (1931): 35–95.

La Roncière, Charles de. "Découverte d'une relation de voyage daté du Touat et décrivant en 1447 le bassin du Niger." *BSGP* (1919), pp. 1–28.

Labouret, Henri. "Les Bandes de Samory dans la Haute Côte-d'Ivoire, la Côte de l'Or et le pays Lobi." *BCEHSAOF*, vol. 8 (1925): 341–355.

Labouret, Henri. "La Parenté à plaisanterie en AOF." *Africa: Journal of the International Institute*, vol. 2 (1929): 244–254.

Labouret, Henri. "Les Manding et leur langue." *BCEHSAOF*, vol. 17 (Jan. 1934): 43–143.

Labouret, Henri, and Moussa Travélé. "Quelques aspects de la magie africaine." *BCEHSAOF*, vol. 10 (1927): 477–545

Lambert, R. "Les Salines de Teguidda n'Tessoum." *BCEHSAOF*, vol. 18 (1935): 366–371.

Lanrezac, H. C. "Au Soudan, la Légende historique," *La Revue Indigène* (1907), pp. 292–296, 380–386, 420–430.

Le Coeur, Charles. "Le Commerce de la noix de kola en Afrique occidentale." *Annals de Géographie* (1927), pp. 143–149.

Lenz, Oscar. "Voyage du Maroc au Sénégal," *BSGP* (1881), pp. 199–226.

Leriche, Albert. "Petites notes sur la sebkha d'Idkil." *Comptes Rendus de la Conférence Internationale des Africanistes de l'Ouest*, II, Bissau, 1947 (1950), 1, pp. 143–150.

Liesegang, G., and K. Sanogo. "Ceramique, tombeau et autres tracés de l' âge du fer à Dogo, Cercle de Bougouni, région de Sikasso." *EM*, no. 21 (April 1977): 48–59.

Lovejoy, Paul E. "Long-distance trade and Islam: The Case of the Hausa nineteenth century trade." *JHSN*, vol. 5, no. 5 (June 1971): 537–548.

Lovejoy, Paul E. "The Bornu salt industry." *IJAHS*, vol. 4 (1979): 629–668.

Lovejoy, Paul E. "Commercial sectors in the economy of the nineteenth century Central Sudan: The trans-Saharan trade and the desert-side salt trade." *AEH*, vol. 13 (1984): 85–116.

Ly, Madina. "Quelques remarques sur le *Tarikh el-Fattach*." *BIFAN*, sér. B, vol. 34 (1972): 471–493.

Mage, Eugène. "Episode d'un voyage au pays de Ségou." *BSGP* (Jan.-June 1867): 72–101.

Marty, Paul. "La Chronique de Oualata et de Néma (Soudan Français)." *Revue des Études Islamiques*, no. 3 (1927): 255–426; no. 4 (1927): 531–575.

Mauny, Raymond. "Niches murales de la maison fouillée à Koumbi Saleh (Ghana)." *NA*, no. 46 (1950): 34–35.

Mauny, Raymond. "État actuel de la question de Ghana." *Bulletin de l'Institut Français d'Afrique Noire*, sér. B, vol. 13, no. 2 (1951): 463–475.

Mauny, Raymond. "La Civilisation de Ghana." *Bulletin de l'Information de l'AOF*, no. 123 (1952): 14–17.

Mauny, Raymond. "Baobabs-cimetières à griots." *NA*, no. 7 (1955): 72–76.

Mauny, Raymond. "Evocation de l' Empire du Mali." *NA*, no. 82 (1959): 33–36.

McDougall, E. Anne. "The Sahara reconsidered: Pastoralists, politics, and salt from the ninth through the twelfth centuries." *AEH*, vol. 12 (1983): 263–286.

McDougall, E. Anne. "Camel caravans of the Saharan salt trade: Traders and transporters in the nineteenth century." In Catherine Coquery-Vidrovitch, and Paul E. Lovejoy, eds., *The Workers of African trade*. Sage, 1985.

McDougall, E. Anne. "Salts of the western Sahara: Myths, mysteries, and historical significance." *IJAHS*, vol. 23, no. 2 (1990): 231–257.

McIntosh, Roderick J. "The Inland Niger Delta before the Empire of Mali: Evidence from Jenne-jeno." *JAH*, vol. 22 (1981): 1–22.

McIntosh, Roderick J. "The Pulse theory: Genesis and accommodation of specialization in the Inland Niger Delta of Mali." *Working Paper*. no. 4, Center for the Study of Institutions and Values, School of Social Services, Houston, Texas, Rice University, March 1988, pp. 1–11.

McIntosh, Roderick J. "Early urban clusters in China and Africa: The arbitration of social ambiguity." *Journal of Field Archaeology*, vol. 18 (1991): 199–212.

McIntosh, Roderick J. and Susan K. McIntosh. "From siècles obscurs to revolutionary centuries in the middle Niger." *World Archaeology*, vol. 2 (1988): 141–165.

McIntosh, Susan K. "A Reconsideration of Wangara/Palolus, Island of Gold." *JAH,.* vol. 22 (1981): 145–158.

McIntosh, Susan K., and Roderick J. McIntosh. "The Early city in West Africa: Towards an understanding." *African Archaeological Review*, vol. 2 (1984): 302–319.

Meillassoux, Claude. "L'Economie des échanges précoloniaux en pays gourou." *CEA*, vol. 3 (1963): 551–576.

Meillassoux, Claude. "Histoire et institutions du *kafo* de Bamako d'après la tradition des Niaré." *CEA*. vol. 4 (1964): 186–227.

Meillassoux, Claude. "The Social structure of modern Bamako." *Africa: Journal of the International African Institute*, vol. 35, no. 2 (April 1965): 125–142.

Meillassoux, Claude. "Les Cérémonies septennales du Kamablon de Kaaba (Mali)." *JSA*, vol. 38, no. 11 (1968): 173–182.

Meillassoux, Claude. "Les Origines de Gumbu (Mali)." *BIFAN*, sér. B, vol. 34 (1972): 268–298.

Meunié, Dj. Jacques. "Cités anciennes de Mauritanie, Tichitt (sic) et Oualata." *Comptes Rendues des Séances, Académie des Inscriptions et des Belles-Lettres* (April–June 1954), pp. 217–226.

Meunié, Dj. Jacques. "Cités caravanières de Mauritanie: Tichite (sic) et Oualata." *JAS*, vol. 27, no. 1 (1957): 19–35.

Mollard, Richard. "Villes d'Afrique Noire." *France Outremer Le Monde Colonial Il-lustré*, no. 254 (Nov. 1950): 367–372, 385–386.

Monod, Théodore. "D' òu provient le sel d'Idjil?" *NA*, no. 47 (July 1950): 89–90.

Monod, Théodore. "Teghaza, la ville en sel gemme." *La Nature*, no. 325 (15 May 1938): 289–296.

Monod, Théodore. "Nouvelles remarques sur Teghaza." *Bulletin de l'Institut Français d'Afrique Noire*, sér. B, vol. 2 (1940): 248–250.

Monod, Théodore. "En marge de la conquête marocaine du Soudan: La Lettre es-pagnole de 1648." In *Mélanges Marcel Cohen*. Paris-La Haye: Mouton, 1970, pp. 459–461.

Monod, Théodore. "Sur quelques constructions anciennes du Sahara occidental." *Bulletin de la Société de Géographie et Archéologie*, vol. 71 (1948/1950): 1–30.

Monteil, Charles. "Le Coton chez les Noirs." *BCEHSAOF*, vol. 9 (1926): 585–684.

Monteil, Charles. "Les Empires du Mali (Etude d'histoire et de sociologie soudanaise)." *BCEHSAOF*, vol. 12 (1929): 291–447. Extracted and republished by G. P. Maisonneuse et Larouse, Paris, 1968.

Monteil, Charles. "Les 'Ghana' des géographes arabes et des Européens." *Hespéris*, vol. 38, nos. 3–4 (1951): 441–452.

Monteil, Charles. "La Légende du Ouagadou et l'origine des Soninké." *Mélanges Ethnographiques*, mém. 23 (Paris, 1953): 361–408.

Monteil, Charles. "Fin de siècle à Médine 1898–1899." *BIFAN*, sér. B, vol. 28, nos. 1–2 (1966): 82–172

Monteil, Vincent. "Chronique de Tichit." *Bulletin de l'Institut Français d'Afrique Noire*, sér. B, vol. 1 (1939): 282–312.

Monteil, Vincent. "Al-Bakrî (Cordoba, 1068), Routier de l'Afrique blanche et noire du nord-ouest." *BIFAN*, sér. B, vol. 30 (1968): 39–116

Montrat, Maurice. "Notice sur l'emplacement de l'ancienne capitale du Mali." *NA*, no. 79 (July 1958): 90–92.

Moraes, Farias, P. F. de. "The Almoravids." *BIFAN*, sér. B, vol. 29, no. 3–4 (1967): 794–878.

Moraes, Farias, P. F. de. "Great states revisited." *JAH*, vol. 15, no. 3 (1974): 479–488.

Mourgues, G. "Le Moyen Niger et sa boucle dans la région de Tombouctou." *BCAFRC* (1932), pp. 351–367, 425–437, 489–549, 564–568, 623–635, 685–694.

Munson, P. "Archaeology and the prehistoric origins of the Ghana empire." Paper presented at the Manding Conference, SOAS, London, 1972.

Museur, Michel. "Un Example specifique d'économie caravanière: L'Echange sel-mil." *JA*, vol. 47 (1977): 48–80.

Neunier, Dominique. "Le Commerce du sel de Taoudeni." *JA*, vol. 50, no. 2 (1980): 133–144.

Niane, Djibril Tamsir. "Mise en place des populations de l'Haute-Guinée." *Recherches Africaines: Etudes Guinéennes*, new ser. no. 2 (1960): 40–53.

Niane, Djibril Tamsir. "Mythes, légendes et sources orales dans l'oeuvre de Mah-moûd Kâti," *Recherches Africaines: Etudes Guinéennes*, new ser. (Jan.-Dec. 1964), pp. 36–42.

Niakaté, Mousa. "Notice historique de Sikasso de 1820 à 1898." *EM*, no. 19 (Oct. 1976): 56–67.

Norris, H. T. "Sanhajah scholars of Timbuctoo." *Bulletin of the School of Oriental and African Studies*, vol. 30, no. 3 (1967): 635–640.

Pageard, Robert. "Notes sur les rapports de 'Senankouya' au Soudan français particulièrement dans les cercles de Ségou et de Macina." *Bulletin de l'Institut Français d'Afrique Noire*, sér. B, vol. 20 (1958): 123–141.

Pageard, Robert. "Note sur les Diawambé ou Diokoramé." *JSA*, vol. 29–30 (1959): 237–256.

Pageard, Robert. "La Parenté à plaisanteries en Afrique occidentale." *Africa*, vol. 12, no. 3 (1959): 244–253.

Pageard, Robert. "La Marche orientale du Mali en 1644, d'après le *Tarikh es-Soudan*." *JSA*, vol. 31, no. 1 (1961): 73–81.

Pageard, Robert. "Note sur le peuplement de l'est du pays de Ségou." *JSA*, vol. 31, no. 1 (1961): 83–90.

Pageard, Robert. "Notes sur les Somonos." *NA*, no. 89 (1961): 17–18.

Pageard, Robert. "Contribution à la chronologie de l'Ouest Africain suivie d'une traduction des tables chronologiques de Barth." *JSA*, vol. 32 (1962): 91–177.

Pageard, Robert. "Une Tradition musulmane relative à l'histoire de Ségou." *NA*, no. 101 (Jan. 1964): 24–26.

Palmié, Stephan. "Against syncretism: 'Africanizing' and 'Cubanizing' discourses in North American *orisa*-worship." In Richard Fardon, ed., *Counterworks: Managing diverse knowledge* (London: Routledge), 1995, pp. 73–104;

Palmié, Stephan. "Ethnogenetic processes and cultural transfer in Afro-American slave populations." In Wolfgang Binder, ed., *Slavery in the Americas*. Würzburg: Königshauser and Neuman, 1993, pp. 337–364.

Pâques, Viviana. "L'Estrade royale des Niaré." *Bulletin de l'Institut Français d'Afrique Noire*, vol. 15, no. 4 (1953): 1642–1654.

Paulme, Denise. "Parenté à plaisanterie et alliance par le sang en Afrique occidentale." *Africa: Journal of the International African Institute*, vol.. 12 (1939): 433–444.

Péfontan, Lt. "Histoire de Tombouctou de sa fondation à l'occupation française (XIIIe siècle—1893)." *BCEHSAOF*, vol. 5 (1922): 81–133.

Perinbam, B. Marie. "Social relations in the Trans-Saharan and Western Sudanese trade." *Comparative Studies in Society and History*, vol. 15, no. 4 (Oct. 1973): 416–436.

Perinbam, B. Marie. "Notes on dyula origins and nomenclature." *BIFAN*, sér. B, vol. 36, no. 4 (1974): 679–690.

Perinbam, B. Marie. "Homo Africanus: Antiquus or oeconomicus? Some interpretations of African economic history." *Comparative Studies in Society and History*, vol. 19, no. 2 (April 1977): 156–178.

Perinbam, B. Marie. "The Juulas in Western Sudanese history: Long-distance traders and developers of resources." In B. K. Swartz and Raymond E. Dumett, eds., *West African culture dynamics: Archaeological and historical perspectives* (Mouton, 1980), pp. 455–475.

Perinbam, B. Marie. "Perceptions of Bonduku's contribution to the western Sudanese gold trade: An assessment of the evidence." *HA*, vol. 13 (986): 295–322.

Perinbam, B. Marie. "Islam in the Banamba region of the Eastern Beledugu, c. 1800 to c. 1900." *IJAHS*, vol. 19, no. 4 (1986): 637–657.

Perinbam, B. Marie. "The Salt-gold alchemy in the eighteenth and nineteenth century Mande world: If men are its salt, women are its gold." *HA*, vol. 23 (1996): 1–21.

Person, Yves. "Le Moyen Niger au XVe siècle d'après les documents européens." *NA*, no. 78 (April 1958): 45–47.

Person, Yves. "Soixante ans d'évolution en pays kissi." *CEA*, vol. 1 (1960): 86–112.

Person, Yves. "Les Ancêtres de Samory." *CEA*, vol. 4 (1963): 125–256.

Person, Yves. "Tradition orale et chronologie." *CEA*, vol. 2 (1962):462–467.

Person, Yves. "La Jeunesse de Samory." *Revue Française d'Histoire d'Outre-Mer*, vol. 58 (1962): 151–180.

Person, Yves. "Samori et la Sierre Leone." *CEA*, vol. 7 (1967): 5–26.

Person, Yves. "L' Empire de Samori selon Péroz." *NA*, no. 113 (1967): 36.

Person, Yves. "Ethnic movement and acculturation in Upper Guinea since the XVth century." *African Historical Studies*, vol. 55, no. 3 (Boston, 1971): 645–658.

Person, Yves, "The Atlantic coast, and the Southern Savannahs (1800–1880)." In J. F. Ajayi, and M. Crowder, eds., *History of West Africa*, vol. 2 (1974), pp. 262–307.

Piétri, Capt. Camille. "Note topographique sur l'itinéraire suivi par la Mission du Haut-Niger, de Kita à Bammako." *BSGCB* (1881), pp. 565–573.

Piétri, Capt. Camille. "Rapport sur la reconnaissance du Ba-Oulé." *BSGCB* (1881), pp. 709-717.

Prudhomme, Cdt. "La Sebkra (sic) d'Idjil (Mauritanie)." *BCEHSAOF*, vol. 8 (1925): 212–216.

Quintin, Aubert. "Etude ethnographique sur le pays entre le Sénégal et le Niger." *BSGP* (Sept. 1881).

Radcliffe-Brown, A. R. "A Further note on joking relationships." *Africa: Journal of the International African Institute*, vol. 19, no. 2 (1949): 133–140.

Renaud, Dr. H.P.J. "La Première mention de la noix de kola dans la matière médicale des Arabes." *Hespéris*, vol. 9 (1928): 43–57.

Roberts, Richard. "Production and reproduction of warrior states: Segu Bambara and Segu Tokolor, c. 1712–1890." *IJAHS*, vol. 13, no. 3 (1980): 389–419.

Rougier, F. "Les Salines de Taodeni." *BCEHSAOF*, vol. 12 (1929): 476–483.

Samaké Maximin. "Tradition orale relative à la formation des Kagfow: L'Exemple de Gonkoro." *EM*, new series, no. 3 (1979): 26–31.

Samaké, Maximin. "Kafo et pouvoir lignager chez les Banmana: L' hégémonie gonkòròbi dans le Cendugu." *CEA*, vol. 28 (1988): 349–353.

Sanneh, Lamin. "The Origins of clericalism in West Africa," *JAH*, vol. 17 (1976): 49–72.

Sarr, Mamadou. "La Colline du Point 'G' Etude morphologique." *EM*, no. 13 (April 1975): 1–27.

Sidibé, Mamby. "Soundiata Keita, héro historique et légendaire, empereur du Manding." *NA*, no. 82 (April 1959): 41–51.

Sidibé, Mamby. "Bamako, ville de rencontre." *Festival Afrique*. July 21, 1958.

Silla, Ousman. "Villes historiques de l'Afrique sahara-soudanaise." *Revue Française d'Etudes Politiques Africaines*, vol. 29 (1968): 25–38. Translated into English in *Africa Quarterly* (New Delhi), vol. 8, no. 2 (1968): 146–157 (Kumbi Saleh, Gao, Jenne, Timbuctu).

Siossat, J. "Les Coutumes des orpailleurs indigènes du Maramandougou." *BCEHSAOF*, vol. 20 (1937): 336–349.

Smith, P. "Les Diakhanké: Histoire d'une dispersion." *Bulletins et Mémoires de la Société d'Anthropologie de Paris*, XIe sér., vol. 8 (1965): 213–262.

Spear, Thomas. "Oral traditions: Whose history?." *HA*, vol. 8 (1981): 165–181.

Szumowski, Georges. "Notes sur la grotte préhistorique de Bamako." *NA*, no. 58 (1953): 35–40.

Szumowski, Georges. "Fouilles à Fatoma (région de Mopti, Soudan)." *NA*, no. 64 (1954): 102–108.

Szumowski, Georges. "Notes sur la grotte de Bamako." Congrès Panafricanist de Préhistorique, *Actes de la IIe Session* (Alger, 1952 [1955]), pp. 673–680.

Szumowski, Georges. "Fouilles à Kami et découvertes dans la région de Mopti (Soudan)." *NA*, no. 76 (1955): 65–69.

Szumowski, Georges. "Sur une gravure rupestre du Niger à Bamako." *Bulletin de la Société Préhistorique* (1955): 651–654.

Szumowski, Georges. "Fouilles de l'abri sous roche de Kourounkorokalé." *Bulletin de l'Institut Français d'Afrique Noire*, sér. B, vol. 18 (1956): 462–508.

Szumowski, Georges. "Fouilles au nord du Macina et dans la région de Ségou." *Bulletin de l'Institut Français d'Afrique Noire*, sér. B, vol. 19 (1957): 224-258.

Szumowski, Georges. "Pseudo tumulus des environs de Bamako." *NA*, no. 75 (1957): 66–73; *NA*, no. 77 (1958): 1–11.

Tautain, Louis. "Etudes critiques sur l'ethnologie et l'ethnographie des peuples du bassin du Sénégal." *Revue d'Ethnographie de Hamy* (1885).

Tautain, Louis. "Note sur les trois langues Soninké, Bamana et Mallinkéou Mandingké (sic)." *Revue de Linguistique et de Philologie Comparée* (Paris, 1887).

Tautain, Louis. "Légende et traditions des Soninké relatives à l'empire de Ghanata, d'après les notes recueillies pendant une tournée de Bamako à Sokoto, Gumba etc. en 1887." *Bulletin de Géographie Historique et Descriptive*, vols. 9–10 (1894–1895): 471–480.

Tauxier, Louis. "Chronologie des rois bambaras." *Outre-Mer* (pt. 1, 2nd trimester, 1930), pp. 119–130; (pt. 2, 3rd trimester 1930), pp. 255–267.

Tellier, G. "Villes d'Afrique: Kayes." *BCAFRC*, vol. 24 (1914): 249–255.

Thomassey, P. "Note sur la géographie et l'habitat de la région de Koumbi Saleh." *Bulletin de l'Institut Français d'Afrique Noire*, sér. B, vol. 13, no. 2 (1951): 438–462.

Thomassey, Paul, and Raymond Mauny. "Campagnes de fouilles de 1950 à Koumbi Saleh (Ghana ?)." *Bulletin de l'Institut Français d'Afrique Noire*, sér. B, vol. 18 (1956): 117–140.

Traoré, Dominique. "Samaniana Bassi." *NA*, no. 34 (1947): 1–3.

Traoré, Dominique. "Sur l'origine de la ville de Bamako." *NA*, no. 35 (July 1947): 26–27.

Traoré, Dominique. "Une Seconde légende relative à l'origine de Bamako." *NA*, no. 40 (Oct. 1948): 7–8.

Traoré, Dominique. "Les Origines de Bamako." *Le Soudan Français*, no. 17 (Dec. 1950): 16–18.

Travélé, Moussa. "Le *Komo* ou *Koma*." *Outre-mer*, vol. 1, no. 2 (1929): 127–150.

Tymowski, Michel. "Le Niger, voie de communication des grands états du Soudan occidental jusqu'à la fin du XVIe siècle." *Africana Bulletin*, vol. 6 (1967): 73–95.

Vallière, Col. François. "Situation politique des états situés entre le Sénégal et le Niger." *BSGCB* (1881), pp. 451–468.

Van Hoven, Ed. "Representing Social Hierarchy: Administrators-Ethnographers in the French Sudan: Delafosse, Monteil, and Labouret." *CEA*, vol. 30 (1990): 178–198.

Vidal, J. "Le Mystère de Ghana." *BCEHSAOF*, vol. 6 (1923): 512–524.

Vidal, J. "Un Problème historque africain au sujet de l'emplacement de Mali (ou Melli) capitale de l'ancien empire mandingue." *BCEHSAOF*, vol. 6 (1923): 251–268.

Vidal, J. "Un Problème historique africain, le véritable emplacement de Mali." *BCEHSAOF*, vol. 6 (1923): 606–619.

Vidal, J. "La Légende officielle de Soundiata, fondateur de l'empire manding." *BCEHSAOF*, vol. 7 (1924): 317–328, 479–542.

Villien-Rossi, Marie-Louise. "Bamako, capitale du Mali." *Outre-Mer*, vol. 16, no. 64 (1963): 379–393.

Villien-Rossi, Marie-Louise. "Les 'Kinda' de Bamako." *Outre-Mer*, vol. 19. No. 76 (1966: 364–381.

Villien-Rossi, Marie-Louise. "Bamako, capitale du Mali." *BIFAN*, sér. B, vol. 28 (1966): 248–380.

Wilks, Ivor. "The Transmission of Islamic learning in the Western Sudan." In Jack Goody, ed., *Literacy in traditional societies.* Cambridge University Press, 1968, pp. 162–195.

Zemp, H. "La Légende des griots Malinké." *CEA*, vol. 6 (1966): 611–642.

Books

Adam, M. G. *Légendes historiques du pays de Nioro* (Sahel). Paris, 1904.

Adams, R. *Nouveau voyage dans l'intérieur de l'Afrique.* Vol. 18. Trans. De Frasans. Paris, 1817.

Ajayi, J.F.A., and Michael Crowder, eds., *History of West Africa.* 2 vols., 2nd ed. New York, 1976.

Al-Kati, Mohammad. *Ta'rikh al-Fattash.* Trans. O. Houdas and M. Delafosse. Paris, 1964.

Amselle, Jean-Loup. *Les Negociants de la savanne: Histoire et organisation sociale desKooroko, Mali.* Paris, 1977.

Amselle, Jean-Loup. *Logiques métisses: Anthropologie de l'identité en Afrique etailleurs.* Paris, 1990.

Amselle, Jean-Loup, and Elikia M'Bokolo, eds., *Au Coeur de l'ethnie: Ethnies, tribalisme, et état en Afrique.* Paris, 1985.

Anonymous. *Notice historique sur le royaume et le Cercle de Ségou.* Edited by order of Colonel de Trentinian. Paris, 1897.

Arcin, A. *La Guinée française.* Paris, 1907.

Arnaud, R. *L'Islam et la politique musulmane française en Afrique occidentale française.* Paris, 1911.

As-Sadi. *Ta'rikh as-Sudan.* Trans. O. Houdas. Paris, 1964.

Ba, Amadou Hampaté, and Jacques Daget. *L'Empire peul du Macina.* Vol. 1 (1818–1853). Paris, 1962.

Ba, Amadou Hampaté, and Jacques Daget. *Jaawambe: Traditions historiques des Peuls jaawambe*. Niamey, 1973?

Barth, Heinrich. *Travels and discoveries in northern and central Africa (1849–1855)*. 5 vols. London, 1858.

Bayol, Jean-Marie. *Voyage en Sénégambie, 1880–1883*. Paris, 1888.

Bazin, Jean, and Emmanuel Terray. *Guerres de lignages et guerres d' états en Afrique*. Paris, 1982.

Benveniste, Emile. *Le Vocabulaire des institutions indo-européennes*. 2 vols. Paris, 1969.

Benveniste, Emile. *Indo-European language and society*. Trans. from the French by Elizabeth Palmer. Miami Linguistic Series, no. 12, University of Miami Press, 1973.

Bérénger-Féraud, Dr. *Les Peuplades de la Sénégambie*. Paris, 1879.

Bernus, Edmond. *Kong et sa région, études eburnéennes*. No. 8. Abidjan, 1960.

Binger, Louis. *Essai sur la langue bambara parlée dans le Kaarta et le Bélédougou suivi d'un vocabulaire*. Paris. 1886.

Binger, Louis. *Du Niger au golfe de Guinée, par le pays de Kong et le Mossi (1877-1889)*. 2 vols. Paris, 1892.

Bird, Charles E., ed., *The Dialects of Mandekan*. Indiana University Press, 1982.

Borgnis-Desbordes, Gustave. *La France dans l'Afrique occidentale*. Paris, 1884.

Boyer, Gaston. *Un Peuple de l'Ouest soudanais: Les Diawara*. Mémoire de l'Institut Français d'Afrique Noire, no. 29. Dakar, 1953.

Brasseur, Gérard. *Les Établissements humains au Mali*, Mémoire de l'Institut Fondamental d'Afrique Noire, no. 83. Dakar, 1968.

Brenner, Louis, ed., *Muslim identity and social change in sub-Saharan Africa*. Indiana University Press, 1993.

Brett-Smith, Sarah C. *The Making of Bamana sculpture: Gender and creativity*. Cambridge University Press, 1994.

Brooks, George E. *Landlords and strangers: Ecology, society, and trade in Western Africa, 1000–1630*. Westview Press, 1993.

Caillié, René. *Voyage à Tombouctou*. 2 vols. Paris, 1985.

Carrière, Frédéric, and Paul Holle. *De la Sénégambie française*. Paris, 1855.

Cissé, Youssouf, and Wa Kamissoko, eds. *La Grande geste du Mali: Des origines à la fondation de l'empire*. Paris, 1988.

Cissé, Youssouf Tata, ed. *Histoire et tradition orale: Projet Boucle du Niger: Actes du Colloque*. Troisième Colloque International de l'Association SCOA. Niamey, 30 Nov.–6 Dec. 1977. Paris, 1980.

Cissoko, Sékéné-Mody. *Histoire de l'Afrique occidentale du moyen-âge et temps modernsVIIe siècle à 1850*. Paris: Presence Africaine, 1967.

Cohen, Abner. *Custom and politics in urban Africa: A study of Hausa migrants in Yoruba towns*. University of California Press, 1969.

Colleyn, Jean-Paul. *Les Chemins de Nya: Culte de possession au Mali*. Paris, 1988.

Conrad, David C., ed. *A State of intrigue: The Epic of Bamana Segu according to Tayiru Banbera*. Transcribed and translated with the assistance of Soumaila Diakité. Oxford University Press, 1990.

Conrad, David C., and Barbara E. Frank, eds. *Status and identity in West Africa: Nyamakala of Mande*. Indiana University Press, 1995.

Cuoq, Joseph M. *Recueil des sources arabes concernant l'Afrique occidentale du VIIIe auXVIe siècle.* Paris, 1975.

Curtin, Philip D. *Economic change in precolonial Africa: Senegambia in the era of the slave trade.* University of Wisconsin Press, 1975.

Dalby, David, ed. *Language and history in Africa.* London, 1970.

David Dalby, ed., *Manding: Focus on an African civilization.* London, 1972.

Dantioko, Oudiary Makan. *Contes et légendes soninké: Soninkan dongomanu do burujunu.* Paris, 1987.

Dantioko, Oudiary Makan. *Soninkara tarixinu: Récits historiques du pays soninké.* Organisation de l'Unité Africaine, Centre d'Etudes linguistiques et historiques par Tradition orale. Niamey, 1985.

D'Escayrac de Lauture. *Mémoire sur le Soudan.* Paris, 1855.

De la Rivière, Marie-Thérèse Abela. *Les Sarakolé et leur emigration vers la France.* Paris, 1977.

De Sanderval, Olivier, J. P. *De l'Atlantique au Niger par le Foutah-Djallon: Carnet de voyage de Olivier de Sanderval.* Paris, 1883.

De Zurara, Gomes Eanes. *Chronique de Guinée.* Trans. Léon Bourdon. Mémoire de l' Institut Français d'Afrique Noire, no. 60. Dakar, 1960.

Delafosse, Maurice. *Esquisse générale des langues de l'Afrique et plus particulièrement de l'Afrique française.* Publication of the Société Anti-Esclavigiste de France. Paris, 1914.

Delafosse, Maurice. *Haut-Sénégal-Niger.* 3 vols. Paris, 1972.

Delafosse, Maurice. *La Langue mandingue et ses dialectes* (Malinké, Bambara, Dioula). Paris, 1929.

Delafosse, Maurice. *Les Frontières de la Côte d'Ivoire et dans les régions limitrophes.* Paris, 1904.

Delafosse, Maurice. *Traditions historiques et légendaires du Soudan occidental.* Trans. from the Arabic. Paris, 1913.

Delcourt, André. *La France et les établissements français au Sénégal entre 1713 à 1763.* Mémoire de l' Institut Français d'Afrique Noire, no. 17. Dakar, 1953.

Diawara, Mamadou. *La Graine de la parole: Dimension sociale et politique des traditions orales du royaume de Jaara (Mali) du XVème au milieu du XIXème siècle.* Stuttgart, 1990.

Dieterlen, Germaine. *Essai sur la religion bambara.* Paris, 1950.

Dieterlen, Germaine, and Youssouf Cissé. *Les Fondements de la société d'initiation du Komo.* Paris, 1972.

Dramani-Issifou, Zakati. *L'Afrique noire dans les relations internationales au XVIe siècle: Analyse de la crise entre le Maroc et le Sonrhaï.* Paris, 1982.

Dubois, Felix. *Tombouctou la mystérieuse.* Paris, 1897.

Dumestre, Gérard. *La Geste de Ségou.* Paris, 1979.

Dumestre, Gérard, and Lilyan Kesteloot. *La Prise de Dionkoloni.* Paris, 1975.

Dupuis-Yakouba (Auguste V. Dupius). *Industries et principales professions des habitants de la région de Tombouctou.* Paris, 1921.

Faidherbe, Louis. *Le Sénégal: La France dans l'Afrique occidentale.* Paris, 1889.

Fernandes, Valentim. *Description de la Côte occidentale d'Afrique (Sénégal) au Cap de Monte, Archipels.* Trans. R. Mauny, Th. Monod, A. Teixera de Mota, Bissau. Mémoire de l'Institut Français d'Afrique Noire, no. 11. Dakar, 1951.

Frey, Henri N. *La Côte occidentale d'Afrique*. Paris, 1890.

Gallais, Jean. *Le Delta intérieur du Niger: Étude de géographie régionale*, Mémoires de l'Institut Fondamental d'Afrique Noire. 2 vols. Dakar, 1967.

Gallieni, Joseph Simon. *Mission d'exploration du Haut-Niger: Voyage au Soudan français (Haut-Niger et pays de Ségou), 1879–1881*. Paris, 1885.

Gallieni, Joseph Simon. *Deux campagnes au Soudan français 1886–1888*. Paris, 1891.

Gardet, Louis. *La Cité musulmane: Vie sociale et politique*. 3rd ed. Paris, 1969.

Geertz, Clifford. *The Interpretation of cultures*. New York, 1973.

Goerg, Odile. *Commerce et colonisation en Guinée, 1850–1913*. Paris, 1986.

Goldbéry, Sylvain. *Fragments d'un voyage en Afrique fait pendant les années 1785, 1786, et 1787*. 2 vols. Paris, 1802.

Goldberry, Silvester. *Travels in Africa in the western parts of the vast continent*. 2 vols. Translated from the French W. Mudford. London, 1808.

Goody, John R., ed. *Literacy in traditional societies: The transmission of Islamic learning in the western Sudan*. Cambridge University Press, 1968.

Goody, Jack. *Production and reproduction: A comparative study of the domestic domain*. Cambridge University Press, 1977.

Goody, Jack. *The Logic of writing and the organization of society*. Cambridge University Press, 1986.

Goody, Jack. *The Interface between the written and the oral*. Cambridge University Press, 1987.

Gomez, Michael A. *Pragmatism in the age of jihad: The precolonial state of Bundu*. Cambridge University Press, 1992.

Gray, William, and Staff Surgeon Dochard. *Travels in western Africa in the years 1818, 1819, and 1821 from the River Gambia through Woolli, Bondoo, Galam, Kasso, Kaarta, and Foolidoo, to the River Niger*. London, 1825.

Griaule, Marcel. *Dieu d'eau: Entretiens avec Ogotemmëli*. Paris, 1948.

Harrison, Christopher. *France and Islam in West Africa, 1860–1960*. Cambridge University Press, 1988,

Henige, David. *The Chronology of oral tradition: Quest for a chimera*. Oxford at Clarendon, 1987.

Henry, Abbé J. *L'Ame d'un peuple africain: Les Bambara*. Munster, 1910.

Hiskett, Mervyn. *The Development of Islam in West Africa*. New York and London, 1984.

Holas, B.. *Le Culte de Zié: Eléments de la religious kono* (Haute Guinée Française). Mémoires de l'Institut Français d'Afrique Noire, no. 39. Dakar, 1954.

Holas, B. *Les Masques kono: Leur rôle dans la vie religieuse et politique*. Paris, 1952.

Hopkins, Anthony G. *An Economic history of West Africa*. New York, 1973.

Hourst. Lieutenant. *Sur le Niger et au pays des Touareg. La Mission Hourst*. Paris, 1897.

Ibn Khaldun. *Histoire des Berbères et des dynasties musulmanes de l'Afrique du Nord*. 4 vols. Trans. from the Arabic de Slane; new trans. P. Casanova. Paris, vol. 1, 1925; vol. 2, 1927; vol. 3, 1934; vol. 4, 1956.

Innes, Gordon. *Sunjiata: Three Mandinka versions*. London, 1974.

Innes, Gordon. *Historical narratives of the Gambian Mandinka*. London, 1976.

Jewsiewicki, Bogumil, and David Newbury, eds., *African historiographies: What history for which Africa*? Sage Publications, 1986.

Johnson, John W. *The Epic of Son-Jara: A West African tradition*. Indiana University Press, 1992.

Kaba, Lansiné. *The Wahhabiyya: Islamic reform and politics in French West Africa*. Evanston, 1974.

Kamissoko, Wa, and Youssouf Tata Cissé, eds. *L'Empire du Mali: Actes du Colloque*.Premier Colloque Internationale de l'Association SCOA de Bamako de 1975. Paris, 1975.

Kamissoko, Wa, and Youssouf Tata Cissé, eds., *L'Empire du Mali: Actes du Colloque*. Deuxième Colloque Internationale de l'Association SCOA de Bamako (12–22 Feb. 1976), 2 vols. Paris, 1977.

Kanya-Forstner, A. S. *The Conquest of the western Sudan: A study in French military imperialism*. Cambridge University Press, 1969.

Kesteloot, Lilyan. *Da Monzon de Ségou épopée bambara*. 4 vols. Paris, 1972.

Keyes, Charles F., ed. *Ethnic change*. University of Washington Press, 1982.

Kopytoff, Igor, ed. *The African frontier: The Reproduction of traditional African societies*. Indiana University Press, 1987.

La Roncière, Charles de. *La Découverte de l'Afrique au moyen âge: Cartographie et explorateurs*. 3 vols. Royal Geographical Society of Egypt: Cairo, vol. 1, 1925; vol. 2, 1925; vol. 3, 1927.

Labat, Jean-Baptiste. *Nouvelle relation de l'Afrique occidentale: Une description exacte du Sénégal et des païs situés entre le Cap Blanc et la Rivière de Serrelionne, jusqu à plus de 300 lieuës en avant dans les terres. L'Histoire naturelle de ces païs, les differentes nations qui y sont répanduës, leurs religions et leur moeurs*. 5 vols. Paris, 1728.

Laitin, David D. *Hegemony and Culture: Politics and religious change among the Yoruba*. University of Chicago Press, 1986.

Laitin, David D. *Language repertoires and state construction in Africa*. Cambridge University Press, 1992.

Launay, Robert. *Beyond the stream: Islam and society in a West African town*. University of California Press, 1992.

Law, Robin, ed. *From slave trade to 'legitimate' commerce: The commercial transition in nineteenth-century West Africa*. Cambridge University Press, 1995.

Le Chatelier, Alfred. *L'Islam en Afrique occidentale*. Paris, 1899.

Lewis, I. M. *Religion in context: Cults and charisma*. Cambridge University Press, 1986.

Lenz, Oscar. *Timbouctou: Voyage au Maroc, au Sahara, et au Soudan*. 2 vols. Trans. Pierre Lehautcourt. Paris, 1886.

Levtzion, Nehemia. *Ancient Ghana and Mali*. London, 1973.

Levtzion, Nehemia, and J.F.P. Hopkins, eds. *Corpus of early Arabic sources for African history*. Cambridge University Press, 1981.

Levtzion, Nehemia, and Humphrey J Fisher. *Rural and urban Islam in West Africa*. Boulder and London: Lynne Rienner, 1987.

Leynaud, Emile, and Youssouf Cissé. *Paysans malinké du Haut-Niger: Tradition et développement rural en Afrique soudanaise*. Bamako, 1978.

Lovejoy, Paul E. *Salt of the desert sun: A history of salt production and trade in Central Sudan*. Cambridge University Press, 1986.

Mage, Eugene. *Voyage au Soudan occidental (1863–1866)*. Paris, 1980.

Marty, Paul. *Études sur l'Islam et les tribus du Soudan*. 4 vols. Paris, 1920.

Marty, Paul. *Études sur l'Islam*. 2 vols. Paris, 1917.

Marty, Paul. *L'Islam en Guinée: Fouta-Diallon*. Paris, 1921.

Matthews, John. *A Voyage to the River Sierra-Leone, on the coast of Africa*. London, 1788/1966.

Mauny, Raymond. *Tableau géographique de l'ouest africain au moyen âge, d'après les sources écrites, la tradition et l'archéologie*. Mémoire de l'Institut Français d'Afrique Noire, no. 61. Dakar, 1961.

McIntosh, Susan K. ed. *Excavations at Jenne-jeno, Kaniana, and Hambarketolo: The 1981 season*. University of California Press, 1995.

McIntosh, Susan K. and Roderick J. McIntosh. *Prehistoric investigation at Jenné, Mali*. 2 vols. Cambridge Monograph in African Archeology, BAR International Series 899 (ii), 1980.

McNaughton, Patrick. *The Mande blacksmiths: Knowledge, power, and art in West Africa*. Indiana University Press, 1988.

Meillassoux, Claude, ed., *The Development of indigenous trade and markets in West Africa*. Oxford University Press, 1961.

Meillassoux, Claude. *Urbanization of an African community: Voluntary associations in Bamako*. University of Washington Press, 1968.

Meillassoux, Claude, ed. *L'Esclavage en Afrique précoloniale*. Paris, 1975.

Meillassoux, Claude. *Femmes, greniers, et capitaux*. Paris, 1975.

Meillassoux, Claude. *Maidens, meal, and money: Capitalism in the domestic economy*. Trans. from the French by Librairie François Maspero. Cambridge University Press, 1981.

Meillassoux, Claude, L. Doucouré, and Simagha. *Légende de la dispersion des Kusa*. (épopée soninké). Dakar, 1967.

Méniaud, Jacques. *Haut-Sénégal-Niger* (Soudan Français). 2 vols. Paris, 1912.

Méniaud, Jacques. *Les Pionniers du Soudan, avant, avec, et après Archinard*. Paris, 1931.

Méniaud, Jacques. *Sikasso ou l'histoire dramatique d'un royaume noir au XIXe siècle*. Paris, 1935.

Miller, Joseph, ed. *The African past speaks: Essays on oral tradition and history*. Kent: England, 1980.

Monnier, Marcel. *Mission Binger: France noire (Côte d'Ivoire et Soudan)*. Paris, 1894.

Monteil, Charles. *Les Bambara de Ségou et du Kaarta*. Paris, 1924/1977.

Monteil, Charles. *Une Cité sudanaise: Djenné, métropole du delta central du Niger*. Paris, 1932.

Monteil, P-L. *De Saint-Louis à Tripoli par le Tchad*. Paris, 1894.

Monteil, P-L. *Une Page d'histoire militaire coloniale: La Colonne de Kong*. Paris, 1902.

Monteil, Vincent. *L'Islam noir*. Paris, 1971.

Mudimbe, V. Y. *The Invention of Africa: Gnosis, philosophy, and the order of knowledge*. Indiana University Press, 1988.

N'Diayé, Bokar. *Les Castes au Mali*. Bamako, 1970.

Niane, Djibril Tamsir. *Sundiata: An Epic of old Mali*. Longmans, Green & Co., 1965.

Niane, Djibril Tamsir. *Recherches sur l'Empire du Mali au moyen âge*. Paris, 1975.

Niane, Djibril Tamsir. *Histoire des Mandingues de l'ouest: Le royaume du Gabou*. Paris, 1989.

Pageard, Robert. *Notes sur l'histoire des Bambaras de Ségou*. Clichy (Seine) 1957.

Pâques, Viviana. *Les Bambara*. Monograph of African Ethnology, published under the patronage of the International African Institute. London, 1954.

Pâques, Viviana. *L'Arbre cosmique dans la pensée populaire et dans la vie quotidienne du North-Ouest Africain*. Travaux et Mémoire de l'Institut d'Ethnologie, Musée de l'Homme. Paris, 1961.

Park, Mungo. *The Travels of Mungo Park*. London, 1907.

Park, Mungo. *Travels in the interior districts of Africa*. New York, 1971.

Penel, J. *Coûtumes soudanaises: Malinké, Sarakolé, Khassonké*. 2 vols. Paris, 1895.

Pereira, Pacheco Duarte. *Esmeraldo de situ orbis*. Trans. and ed. George H. T. Kimble. Nendeln, Liechtenstein, Kraus reprint, 1967 (reprint of 1937 ed.).

Pereira, Pacheco Duarte. *Esmeraldo de situ orbis*. Trans. Raymond Mauny, Bissau, 1956.

Pérignon, Capt. *Haut-Sénégal et Moyen-Niger: Kita et Ségou*. Paris, 1901.

Péroz, Marie-Etienne. *Au Niger: Récits de campagne, 1891–1892*. Paris, 1894.

Péroz, Marie-Etienne. *Au Soudan français: Souvenirs de guerre et de mission*. Paris, 1881.

Person, Yves. *Samori: Une révolution dyula*. 3 vols. Mémoire de l'Institut Fondamental d' Afrique Noire, nos. 80, 89. Dakar, 1968–1975.

Piétri, Camille. *Les Français au Niger*. Paris, 1885.

Pollet, Eric, and Grace Winter, *La Société Soninké (Dyahunu, Mali), Etudes Ethnologiques*. Brussels, 1971.

Quinn, Charlotte. *Mandingo kingdoms of the Senegambia*. London, 1972.

Raffenel, Anne Jean-Baptiste. *Nouveau voyage au pays des nègres*. 2 vols. Paris, 1856.

Raffenel, Anne Jean-Baptiste. *Voyage dans l'Afrique occidentale (1843–1844)*. Paris, 1846.

Rawson, Beryle, ed. *The Family in ancient Rome*. London, and Sydney, 1986.

Roberts, Richard. *Warriors, merchants, and slaves: The state and the economy in the middle Niger valley, 1700–1914*. Stanford University Press, 1980.

Robinson, David. *The Holy war of 'Umar Tal: The western Sudan in the mid-nineteenth century*. Clarendon Press, 1985.

Rouch, Jean. *Contribution à l'histoire des Songhay*. Mémoire de l'Institut Français d'Afrique Noire, no. 29, Dakar, 1953.

Saint-Père, J. H. *Les Sarakollé du Guidimakha*. Paris, 1925.

Sanankoua, Bintou. *Un Empire peul au XIXe siècle: La Diina du Massina*. Paris, 1990.

Searing, James F. *West African slavery and Atlantic commerce: The Senegal river valley, 1700–1860*. Cambridge University Press, 1993.

Soleillet, Paul. *Voyage à Ségou*. Paris, 1887.

Spear, Thomas, and Richard Waller, eds. *Being Maasai: Ethnicity and identity in East Africa*. Ohio University Press, 1993.

Table ronde sur les origines de Kong. Annals de l'Université d'Abidjan 1977, sér. J, vol. 1 Traditions orales 1 à 3 nov. 1975 à Kong. Université Nationale de Côte d'Ivoire, 1977.

Tall, Madina Ly. *L'Empire du Mali*. Paris, 1972.

Tauxier, Louis. *Le Noir de Bondoukou, Koulangos, Dyoulas, Abrons, etc*. Paris, 1921

Tauxier, Louis. *La Religion bambara*. Paris, 1927.

Tauxier, Louis. *Moeurs et histoire des Peuls*. Paris, 1937.

Tauxier, Louis. *Histoire des Bambara*. Paris, 1942.

Tedzkiret en-nisian fi akhbar molouk es-Soudan. Trans. O. Houdas. Paris, 1966.

Tellier, G. *Autour de Kita: Etude soudanaise.* Paris, 1898.

Travélé, Moussa. *Proverbes et contes bambara.* Paris, 1977.

Trimingham, J. S. *A History of Islam in West Africa.* Oxford University Press, 1962.

Trimingham, J. S. *Islam in West Africa.* Clarendon Press, 1959.

Tymowski, Michel. *L'Armée et la formation des Etats en Afrique occidentale au XIXe siècle, Essai de comparaison: L'Etat de Samori et le Kénédougou.* University of Varsovie, 1987.

Urvoy, Y. *Les Basins du Niger.* Mémoire de l' Institut Français d'Afrique Noire, no. 4 Dakar, 1942.

Vansina, Jan. *Oral tradition as history.* University of Wisconsin Press, 1985.

Walckenaer, Baron Charles. *Recherches géographiques sur l'intérieur de l'Afrique septentrionale.* Paris, 1821.

Walckenaer, Baron Charles. *Histoire générale des voyages, ou nouvelle collection des relations de voyages par mer et par terre.* 19 vols. Paris, 1826-1830.

Walckenaer, Baron Charles. *Collection des relations de voyages par mer et par terre en différentes parties d l'Afrique depuis 1400 jusqu' à nos jours.* Paris, 1842.

Webb, James L. A. *Desert frontier: Ecological and economic change along the western Sahel 1600–1850.* University of Wisconsin Press, 1995.

Willis, J. R. *Slaves and slavery in Muslim Africa.* 2 vols. Frank Cass, 1985.

Willis, J. R. *In the path of Allah, The passion of al-Hajj 'Umar: An essay into the nature or charisma in Islam.* London, 1989.

Zahan, Dominique. *Sociétés d'initiation bambara: Le N'domo et le Korè.* Mouton and Paris, 1960.

Zahan, Dominique. *Religion, spiritualité, et pensée africaines.* Paris, 1970.

Malian National Archives

ANMK 1D 2 no. 220, "Mission Monteil, 1890–1891."

ANMK 1D 2 no. 222, "Mission Delanneau: Rapport politique sur la Canonnière 'Niger,' 1895" (Bamako, 1895).

ANMK 1D 5, "Etudes générales: Notice générale sur le Soudan notice sur la région, c. 1895–1899."

ANMK 1D 33 no. 5, "Historique du Cercle de Bamako par Borgnis Desbordes 1880–1890" (n.d., n.p., n.a.).

ANMK 1D 38 no. 2, "Djenné historique 1930, Cercle de Mopti" (n.a., n.p., n.d.).

ANMK 1D 38 no. 3, "Charles Monteil, Etudes générales: Monographie du Cercle de Djenné, 1909."

ANMK 1D 95 Rép. Géog., "Notice historique sur le Bambouck Cercle de Bafoulabé, 1899 (Bafulabe, 4 April 1899).

ANMK 1D 96 Rép. Géog, "Notice sur le Canton de Néré Poste de Kati, Cercle de Bamako, 1902" (Kati, 7 July 1905).

ANMK 1D 97 Rép. Géog, "Notices géographiques historiques topographiques et statistiques Cercle de Bamako Poste Bamako-Kati-Koulikoro, 1902."

ANMK 1D 168, "Lieutenant Greigert, Notice géographique et historique sur la circonscription de Bouna Cercle de Bondoukou" (Buna, 1902).

ANMK 1D 172 C1, "Historique de la Province du Kassémele Cercle de Touba par Lieutenant Curault, 1899."

ANMK 1D 173 C1, "Notice ethnographique et historique de Séguela, 1900 Cercle de Touba" (Seguela, 31 May 1900).

ANMK 1D 174 C1, "Historique du village indépendant de Lodfouko Cercle de Touba par le Lieutenant Curault, 1900."

ANMK 1D 175 C1 n.a., "Rapport ethnographique et historique de la Circonscription de Touba 1900" (Tuba, 7 June 1900).

ANMK 1D 219, "Liste des Missions militaires scientifiques commerciales d'explorations d'études de chemin-de-fer ayant opéré au Soudan de 1875 à 1 jan., 1905."

ANMK 1D 224, "Mission Flatters, Correspondance au sujet des...survivant de la mission...Touaregs du sud, 1895–1896."

ANMK 1D 243, "Mission du Chef de Bataillon Digue, chemin de fer entre Bamako et Niamey" (1905).

ANMK 2D 132, "Organisation administrative de la ville de Bamako; Liste chronologique des Commandants de Cercle de 1883 à 1902; Notes sur les chefs de villages, population 1902" (Bamako, Nov. 1902).

ANMK 2D 135, "Cercle de Bandiagara: Rapport sur la suppression de la résidence de Hombori et la transformation du poste de Mopti en résidence 1906" (Bandiagara, 18 May 1906).

ANMK 2D 163, "Affaires administratives: Notes de service pour les chiefs-lieux Kayes-Bamako, 1905–1908 " (Kayes, 11 August 1905).

ANMK 5D 6, "Recensement population, Correspondance Cercle de Djenné, 1901–1905."

ANMK 5D 11, "Recensement: Correspondance des mouvements de la population du Cercle de Kita, 1900–1905."

ANMK 5D 15, "Recensement: Correspondance des mouvements de la population du Cercle de Nioro, 1893."

ANMK 5D 16, "Mouvements de la population: Liste des chefs de case de la Province du Mérétambaïa ayant quittés leurs villages pour aller s'installer dans les Cercles de Kita et de Dinguiraye Cercle de Satadougou, 1921."

ANMK 5D 18, "Recensement de la population du Soudan au 1 avril 1899."

ANMK 5D 19, "Recensement de la population du Cercle de Bafoulabé, 1887–1907."

ANMK 5D 20, "Recensement de la population du Cercle de Bamako, 1900–1904: Recensement de la population du Soudan, 1899."

ANMK 5D 24, "Recensement de la population du Cercle et de la ville de Djenné, 1904–1911."

ANMK 5D 29, "Recensement de la population du Cercle et de la ville de Kayes, 1887–1904."

ANMK 5D 30, "Recensement de la population: Cercle de Kita, 1890–1905."

ANMK 5D 32, "Recensement de la population: Cercle de Koutiala, 1903–1904."

ANMK 5D 34, "Recensement de la population: Cercle de Médine, 1899–1904."

ANMK 5D 36, "Recensement de la population; Cercle de Nioro, 1904."

ANMK 5D 42, "Recensement de la population Région Ouest Cercles de Kayes Médine: Bafoulabé, Kita, Satadougou, 1899."

ANMK 5D 43, "Recensement des villages Saumonos et Bozos situés sur le territoire de Sansanding, 1901."

ANMK 5D 44, "Recensement du Cercle de Ségou, 1894–1911."

ANMK 5D 45, "Recensement de la population: Cercle de Ségou, 1891–1905."

ANMK 5D 46, "Recensement du Cercle de Siguiri, 1894."

ANMK 5D 47, "Recensement de la population, Cercle de Sikasso, 1904."

ANMK 5D 50, "Recensement de la population du Cercle et de la ville de Tombouctou, 1904–1919: Cercle de Tombouctou, 1904."

ANMK 5D 51, "Soudan 1905–1906, Statistiques de la population: Tableau d'ensemble du Haut-Sénégal-Niger, 1905–1913."

ANMK 5D 52, "Statistiques de la population Cercle de Bafoulabé, 1905–1914: Population de Bafoulabé, 1905."

ANMK 5D 53, "Recensement statistiques annuelles Cercle de Bamako, 1905–1914: Recensement Bamako Cercle 1905."

ANMK 5D 53, "Recensement statistiques annuelles Cercle de Bamako, 1905–1914: Recensement de la population, statistiques de Bamako Kati, Koulikoro 1909."

ANMK 5D 53, "Cercle de Bamako: Etat numérique de la population indigène par race, 1905–1914."

ANMK 5D 55, "Recensement: Statistiques annuelles Cercle de Bandiagara, 1905–1914."

ANMK 5D 56, "Recensement de la population du Cercle de Bougouni, 1894–1904."

ANMK 5D 58, "Recensement: Statistiques de la population Cercle de Bobo-Dioulasso, 1905–1914."

ANMK 5D 59, "Recensement: Statistiques de la population Cercle de Djenné, 1905–1914."

ANMK 5D 67, "Recensement: Statistiques annuelles Cercle de Kayes, 1905–1914."

ANMK 5D 69, "Recensement: Statistiques annuelles Cercle de Kita, 1905–1914."

ANMK 5D 71, "Recensement: Statistiques annuelles Cercle de Koutiala, 1905–1914."

ANMK 5D73, "Recensement: Statistiques de la population Cercle de Mopti, 1909–1914."

ANMK 5D 75, "Recensement: Statistiques de la population Cercle de Nioro, 1905–1914."

ANMK 5D 79, "Recensement: Statistiques annuelles Cercle de Satadougou, 1905–1914."

ANMK 5D 81, "Recensement: Statistiques annuelles du Cercle de Ségou, 1904–1914."

ANMK 5D 82, "Recensement: Statistiques de la population du Cercle de Sikasso, 1905–1914."

ANMK 2E 1, "Politique indigène: Correspondance et rapports Cercle de Bafoulabé, 1897–1908."

ANMK 2E 6, "Politique indigène: Correspondance avec les chefs indigènes Cercle de Kayes, 1887–1911."

ANMK 2E 16, "Bulletin de notes des agents politiques Cercle de Bamako, 1881–1894."

ANMK 2E 17, "Bulletin de notes des agents politiques Cercle de Kayes, 1890."

ANMK 2E 18, Bulletin de notes des agents politiques Cercle de Kita, 1890."

ANMK 2E 22, "Bulletin de notes des agents politiques Cercle de Ouagadougou, 1900."

ANMK 2E 23, "Bulletin de notes des agents politiques Cercles de Siguiri, 1890–1897."

ANMK 2E 43, "Politique indigène: Notes et fiches de renseignements sur les chefs et notables de Cercle de Bamako, 1897–1908."

ANMK 4E, 2 "Politique musulmane, Surveillance des personnages religieux: Correspondance avec le Gouverneur Général, 1901–1912."

ANMK 4E 3, "Politique musulmane, Surveillance des personnages religieux: Correspondence avec le chef du service des postes, 1910–1912."

ANMK 4E 5, "Politique musulmane: Rapport sur l'Islam et les confréries musulmanes Cercle de Bamako, 1903–1912."

ANMK 4E 32, "Politique indigène: Rapport sur la situation de l'Islam dans le Haut Sénégal-Niger, 1908."

ANMK 4E 35, "Politique musulmane: Rapports sur l'Islam et les confréries musulmanes Cercle de Bafoulabé, 1897–1914."

ANMK 4E 36, "Politique musulmane: Rapport sur l'Islam et les confréries musulmanes Cercle de Bamako, 1897–1911."

ANMK 4E 38, "Politique musulmane: Rapport sur l'Islam et les confréries musulmanes Cercle de Bandiagara, 1896–1903."

ANMK 4E 39, "Politique musulmane: Rapport sur l'Islam et les confréries musulmanes Cercle de Beyla, 1896."

ANMK 4E 41, "Politique musulmane: Rapport sur l'Islam et les confréries musulmanes Cercle de Bobo-Dioulasso, 1905–1913."

ANMK 4E 42, "Politique musulmane: Rapports sur l'Islam et les confréries musulmanes Cercles de Bougouni, 1899–1913."

ANMK 4E 44, "Politique musulmane: Rapport sur l'Islam et les confréries musulmanes Cercle de Djenné, 1892–1913."

ANMK 4E 45, "Politique musulmane: Rapport sur l'Islam et les confréries musulmanes Cercle Dédougou, 1913."

ANMK 4E G, "Politique musulmane: Surveillance des personnages religieux" (Correspondence with the Commandant de Djenné, 1912–1915).

ANMK K1-7, "Correspondance du Directeur au Gouverneur du Haut-Sénégal Niger, 1888–1920."

ANMK K 11, "Chemin de fer Kayes à Niger: Rapports diverses, 1888–1903."

ANMK K 17, "Chemin de fer Kayes à Niger: Rapports diverses, 1910–1913."

ANMK K 25, "Tarifs généraux de transports des personnels et marchandises au Soudan et sur le fleuve Sénégal, 1897."

ANMK K 30, "Chemin de fer Kayes au Niger trafic marchandise de gares commerce, 1895–1896."

ANMK K 40, "Chemin de fer: Tarifs généraux et spéciaux pour les transports à grande vitesse et à petite vitesse, 1903."

ANMK K 68, "Chemin de fer Kayes-Niger: Etats des recettes et dépenses, Budgets, 1889–1910."

ANMK K 71, "Statistiques du chemin de fer de Kayes au Niger, 1909–1913."

ANMK K 101, "Travaux publics: Rapports sur les travaux executés dans la colonie du Haut-Sénégal-Niger, 1906."

ANMK K 103, "Travaux publics: Rapports sur les travaux executés Cercle de Bafoulabé, 1903–1908."

ANMK K 104, "Fond Ancien, Travaux publics: Rapports sur les travaux Cercle de Bamako postes de Kati-Banamba et Koulikoro, 1900–1918."

ANMK 2L 8, "Correspondance navigation de Bamako, 1901–1915" (Télégramme) (Bamako, 10 Jan. 1901).

ANMK 1Q 17, "Correspondance commerciale: Cercle de Kita, 1882–1907, Lettre Commandant du Fort à Kita au résident à Niagassolo" (Kita, 17 April 1882).

ANMK 1Q 17, "Correspondance commerciale: Le Capitaine Tellier Commandant le Cercle de Kita à Monsieur le Gouveurneur" (Kayes, 19 April 1897).

ANMK 1Q 22, "Correspondance commerciale: Cercle de Médine, 1887–1907, Lettre au Monsieur Le Commandant Supérieur à Kayes" (Kayes, 27 April 1887).

ANMK 1Q 22, "Correspondance commerciale: Cercle de Nioro, Lettre le Capitaine de Lartigue, Commandant la région du Sahel à Monsieur le Col. Lieut. Gouverneur à Kayes" (25 Dec. 1895).

ANMK 1Q 24, "Renseignements sur les maisons de commerce 1899–1907" (Bamako, 1907).

ANMK 1Q 24, "Correspondance commerciale: Cercle de Nioro, 1892–1911, Lettre Le Capitaine de Lartigue Commandant la Région du Sahel à Monsieur le Gouveurneur à Kayes" (Nioro, 25 Dec. 1895).

ANMK 1Q 28, "Correspondance commerciale: Cercle de Satadougou, 1899–1904."

ANMK 1Q 29, "Correspondance commerciale: Cercle de Ségou, 1898–1909."

ANMK 1Q 44, "Rapports commerciaux: Cercle de Bamako, 1886–1919, Bulletin commercial" (Bamako, Jan. 1886).

ANMK 1Q 44, "Rapports commerciaux: Cercle de Bamako 1886–1919, Bulletin commercial no. 22" (Bamako, 1 May 1887).

ANMK 1Q 44, "Rapports commerciaux: Cercle de Bamako 1886–1919, Bulletin commercial no. 49" (Bamako, 4 July 1887).

ANMK 1Q 44, "Rapports commerciaux" (Niagassolo, Feb. 1889).

ANMK 1Q 44, "Rapports commerciaux: Cercle de Bamako 1886–1919, Bulletin commercial no. 125" (Bamako, April 1891).

ANMK Q 44, "Rapports commerciaux: Cercle de Bamako 1886–1919" (Bamako, 20 Jan. 1899).

ANMK 1Q 44, "Rapports commerciaux: Cercle de Bamako 1886–1919" (Bamako, 1903).

ANMK 1Q 44, "Rapports commerciaux: Cercle de Bamako 1886–1919" (Bamako, 1904).

ANMK 1Q 44, "Rapports commerciaux: Cercle de Bamako 1886–1919" (Bamako, 1905).

ANMK 1Q 44, "Rapports commerciaux: Cercle de Bamako 1886–1919" (Bamako, 1906).

ANMK 1Q 44, "Rapports commerciaux: Cercle de Bamako 1886–1919" (Bamako, 1907).

ANMK 1Q 44, "Rapports commerciaux: Cercle de Bamako 1886–1919" (Bamako, 1908).

ANMK 1Q 44, "Rapports commerciaux: Cercle de Bamako 1886–1919" (Bamako, 1909).

ANMK 1Q 44, "Rapports commerciaux: Cercle de Bamako 1886–1919" (Bamako, 1910).

ANMK 1Q 44, "Rapports commerciaux: Cercle de Bamako 1886–1919" (Bamako, 1886–1911).

ANMK 1Q 44, "Rapports commerciaux: Cercle de Bamako 1886–1919" (Bamako, 1911).

ANMK 1Q 44, "Rapports commerciaux: Cercle de Bamako 1886–1919" (Bamako, 1912).

ANMK 1Q 44, "Rapports commerciaux: Cercle de Bamako 1886–1919" (Bamako, 1913).

ANMK 1Q 44, "Rapport commerciaux: Cercle de Bamako 1886–1919" (Bamako, 1914)

ANMK 1Q 44, "Rapports commerciaux: Cercle de Bamako 1886–1919" (Bamako, 1915).

ANMK 1Q 44, "Rapports commerciaux: Cercle de Bamako 1886–1919" (Bamako, 1916).

ANMK 1Q 44, "Rapports commerciaux: Cercle de Bamako 1886–1919" (Bamako, 1917).

ANMK 1Q 44, "Rapports commerciaux: Cercle de Bamako 1886–1919" (Bamako, 1918).

ANMK 1Q 204, "Renseignements sur les maisons de commerce: Cercle de Bamako, 1899–1907" (Bamako, 1906).

ANMK 1Q 205, "Renseignements sur les maisons de commerce: Cercle de Bafoulabé, 1899–1907" (Bafulabe, 1907).

ANMK 1Q 207, "Renseignements sur les maisons de commerce: Cercle de Bandiagara, 1899–1907" (Bandiagara, 1911).

ANMK 1Q 209, "Renseignements sur les maisons de commerce: Cercle de Bougouni, 1899–1907" (Buguni, 1907).

ANMK 2Q 210, "Renseignements sur les maisons de commerce: Cercle de Djenné, 1899–1907" (Jenne, 1907).

ANMK 1Q 213, "Renseignements sur les maisons de commerce: Cercle de Goumbou, 1899–1907" (Gumbu, 1907).

ANMK 1Q 215, "Renseignements sur les maisons de commerce: Cercle de Kayes, 1903–1907" (Kayes, 1907).

ANMK 1Q 216, "Renseignements sur les maisons de commerce: Cercle de Kita, 1899–1903" (Kita, 1903).

ANMK 1Q 221, "Renseignements sur les maisons de commerce: Cercle de Médine, 1898" (Medine, 1898).

ANMK 1Q 222, "Renseignements sur les maisons de commerce: Cercle de Nioro, 1899–1907" (Nioro, 1907).

ANMK 1Q 223, "Renseignements sur les maisons de commerce: Cercle de Ségou, 1899–1907" (Segu, 1907).

ANMK 1Q 226, "Renseignements sur les maisons de commerce: Région du Sud" (Siguiri, 1899).

ANMK 1Q 227, "Renseignements sur les maisons de commerce: Cercle de Sikasso, 1899–1907" (Sikasso, 1907).

ANMK 1Q 288, "Renseignements sur les maisons de commerce: Cercle de Sokolo, 1899–1907" (Sokolo, 1907).

ANMK 1Q 229, "Renseignements sur les maisons de commerce: Cercle de Tombouctou, 1899–1907" (Timbuktu, 1907).

ANMK 3Q 2, "Demande de concessions de terrains (Bambougou) aurifères, 1896."

ANMK 3Q 3, "Mines: Renseignement sur les régions aurifères du Bambouk, 1896."

ANMK 3Q 5, "Sel-Correspondence, 1897–1899."

ANMK 3Q 7, "Rapport du Capitaine A. Ruby Commandant le Cercle du Lobi sur les gisements aurifères du 'Lobi proprement dit' et leur exploitation par les habitants" (28 Feb. 1901).

ANMK 3Q 7, "Rapport du Capitaine A. Ruby Commandant le Cercle du Lobi sur la question des gisements aurifères du 'Lobi proprement dit' sur les observations faites à ce sujet au cours des opérations de la campagne 1901 à 1902 et sur les travaux de la mission envoyée par la Société du Haut-Niger" (Bobojulasso, 22 May 1902).

ANMK 3Q 12, "Rapport sur le mouvement minier dans la colonie du Haut-Sénégal-Niger, 1909."

ANMK 3Q 13, "Renseignement sur l'industrie minière du Haut-Sénégal-Niger, 1910."

ANMK 3Q 18, "Arête (#1383) du Lieutenant Gouveurneur réglementant le commerce et la circulation de l'or extrait de la colonie, 1918."

ANMK 3Q 19, "Rapport sur le fonctionnement du Service des Mines pendant l'année, 1905."

ANMK 3Q 19, "Rapport sur le fonctionnement du Service des Mines pendant l'année, 1908" (Jan. 1909).

Senegalese Archives

Afrique Occidentale Française

ASAOF Sén. et Dép. 1G 8, "Exploration du Kaarta 1824 à 1829: Rapport de M. Duranton, 1824" (Bakel, 2 April 1824).

ASAOF Sén. et Dép. 1G 8 no. 3, "Duranton, Examen de la situation présente...au Sénégal" (Feb. 1826).

ASAOF Sén. et Dép. 1G 10, "Projet de voyage à Tombouctou par M. M. Berton et Gérardin, 1826 à 1828" (Bakel, 12 April 1826).

ASAOF Sén. et Dép. 1G 12, "Voyage dans le Boundou et la Bambouk par M. Tourette, mineur 1828 à 1829."

ASAOF Sén. et Dép. 1G 22, "Voyage à Timbo par M. Hecquard" (1849–1851).

ASAOF Sén. et Dép. 1G 32, "Mission Mage et Quintin 1863" (Medine, 1 Nov. 1863).

ASAOF Sén. et Dép. 1G 32, "Mission Mage et Quintin: Eugène Mage à M. le Gouverneur" (Saint Louis, 21 June 1866).

ASAOF Sén. et Dép. 1G 46, "Mission Solleillet 1878 à 1879: Rapport sommaire sur le commerce adressé à M. le Gouverneur du Sénégal et dépendances."

ASAOF Sén. et Dép. 1G 50 no. 49, "Mission du Haut-Niger 1880: Lettre Piétri à Gallieni" (Bamako, 9 May 1880).

ASAOF Sén. et Dép. 1G 50 no. 77, "Mission du Haut-Niger 1880: Lettre François Gallieni à Gouverneur à Saint Louis," no. 16 (Makajambugu, 26 April 1880).

ASAOF Sén. et Dép. 1G 50, "Gallieni et Vallière, Mission du Haut-Sénégal 1880: Note sur la situation politique des peuplades des valées du Bafing, du Bakkoy et du Haut-Niger" (Bamako, 9 May 1880).

ASAOF Sén. et Dép. 1G 50, "Mission du Haut-Niger 1880: Lettre Gallieni à Gouverneur" (Nango, 3 July 1880).

ASAOF Sén. et Dép. 1G 50 no. 20, "Mission du Haut-Niger 1880: Lettre François Gallieni à Gouverneur à Saint Louis" (Nango, 7 July 1880).

ASAOF Sén. et Dép. 1G 50, "Mission du Haut-Niger 1880: Lettre Gallieni à Gouverneur" (Nango, 20 August 1880).

ASAOF Sén. et Dép. 1G 50 no. 9, "Gallieni, Mission du Haut-Niger: Analyse au sujet des agissements des Anglais dans le Bassin du Haut-Niger" (Nango, 10 Sept. 1880).

ASAOF Sén. et Dép. 1G 52 no. 6, "Mission de Ségou: Gallieni et Bayol, Note relative à une mission à Ségou, 1880–1881."

ASAOF Sén. et Dép. 1G 52, "Mission de Ségou: Jean-Marie Bayol à. M. Le Commandant Supérieur" (Bakel, 12 June 1880).

ASAOF Sén. et Dép. 1G 52, "Mission de Ségou: Louis Brière de L'Isle, Mission de Ségou Gallieni et Bayol, Télégramme de Gouverneur à Ministre Marine Paris" (Dakar, 25 June 1880).

ASAOF Sén. et Dép. 1G 52, "Mission de Ségou: Jean-Marie Bayol, Télégramme à Gouverneur de Saint Louis no. 314, Ministère des Postes et de Télégraphes" (Saint Louis, 25 June 1880).

ASAOF Sén. et Dép. 1G 52, "Mission de Ségou: Gallieni et Bayol, Télégramme au Gouverneur de Saint Louis" (Salde, 29 June 1880).

ASAOF Sén. et Dép. 1G 52, "Mission de Ségou: Jean-Marie Bayol, Télégramme au Gouverneur à Saint Louis" (29 June 1880).

ASAOF Sén. et Dép. 1G 52 no. 46, "Mission de Ségou: Dr. Jean-Marie Bayol, Gallieni et Bayol, Rapport sur le voyage au pays de Bamako" (Saint Louis, 5 July 1880).

ASAOF Sén. et Dép. 1G 52 no. 46, "Mission de Ségou: Dr. Jean-Marie Bayol, Gallieni et Bayol: Copie sur rapport sur le voyage au pays de Bamako" (Saint Louis, 5 July 1880).

ASAOF Sén. et Dép. 1G 79, Le Capitaine Conrard, "Notice sur l'état de Bammako" (Bamako, 21 Feb. 1885).

ASAOF Sén. et Dép. 1G 79, "Le Capitaine chargé de travaux, Renseignements divers sur Bamako et le pays environnant, 1885" (Bamako, 21 Feb. 1885).

ASAOF Sén. et Dép. 1G 189, "Le Capitaine McLeod, L'Artillerie de Marine Capitaine McLeod adjoint au Comité de Cercle de Bamako sur une tournée faite dans le Maracadougou: Rapport de Mission à la Maracadougou" (Bamako, 1 Oct. 1894).

ASAOF Sén. et Dép. 1G 194, "Dossier sur Tombouctou: Notice sur la région de Tombouctou historique" (c. 1896).

ASAOF Sén. et Dép. 1G 248, "Le Captain Pérignon, Généralities sur les régions du Haut-Sénégal et du Moyen-Niger: Monographie des Cercles de Kita et de Ségou, 1899–1900."

ASAOF Sén. et Dép. 1G 299, n.a., "Sénégambie-Niger: Monographie du Cercle de Bamako, 1903–1904."

ASAOF Sén. et Dép. 1G 299, "Jules Brévié, Monographie du Cercle de Bamako, 1904" (Bamako, 25 April 1904).

ASAOF Sén. et Dép. 1G 305, "Histoire du pays de Djenné depuis les temps les plus reculés jusqu'au 12 avril 1893."

ASAOF Sén. et Dép. 1G 305, "Divisions Administrative du Cercle: Monographie du Cercle de Djenné par l'Administrateur Graffe, 1903–1904."

ASAOF Sén. et Dép. 1G 305, "Gouvernement Général de l'AOF Sénégambie-Niger: Monographie Cercle de Djenné" (Jenne, 10 March 1904).

ASAOF Sén. et Dép. 1G 320, n. a., "Notice sur le Cercle de Ségou, 1904."

ASAOF Sén. et Dép. 1G 322, n. a., "Monographie du Cercle de Sikasso, 1904."

ASAOF Sén. et Dép. 1G 351 no. 23, "Monographie du Soudan: Note sur le Cercle de Bamako établie par l'Administrateur en Chef Bobichon, Commandant de Cercle 1920–1921" (Bamako, 20 Feb. 1921)

ASAOF Sén. et Dép. 1G 351 no. 7 n. a., "Notice historique sur le Cercle de Sikasso, 1921."

ASAOF Sén. et Dép. 1G 351, "Le Commandant le Cercle, Notice sur le Cercle de Bafoulabé" (Saint Louis, 8 Feb. 1921).

ASAOF Sén. et Dép. 15G 66, "Correspondence indigènes 1840–1900: Correspondence avec Tity, Chef de Bamako, 1880 à Colonel Borgnis-Desbordes."

ASAOF Sén. et Dép. 15G 83, "Captaine Ruault, Généralités 1880 à 1920: Affaires politiques et administratives, Affaires diverses" (Bamako, 22 Feb. 1884).

ASAOF Sén. et Dép. 15G 168, "Traités 1821–1899: Le Chef d'escadron d'artillerie Guégan, Commandant la région est à Monsieur le Gouverneur du Soudan français," (Bamako, 19 Oct. 1894).

ASAOF Sén. et Dép. 15G 169 no. 7, "Rapport du Capitaine d'Artillerie de Marine Charnet Commandant le Cercle de Bamako sur les écoles du Cercle" (Bamako, 13 July 1899).

ASAOF Sén. et Dép. 15G 170, "Rapport sur le conflit markas à M. Le Gouvernenr Général Affaires politiques, Incidents de Banamba, dossier du Commandant Laverdure" (Gorée, 15 June 1905).

ASAOF Sén. et Dép. 15G 170, "Cercle de Bamako, Incident de Banamba, dossier du Commandant Laverdure 1905: Rapport sur le Conflit markas" (Gorée, 26 June 1905).

ASAOF Sén. et Dép. 15G 170 no. 20, "Cercle de Bamako, Incident de Banamba, dossier du Commandant Laverdure 1905: Rapport sur le Conflit markas" (Gorée, 11 July 1905).

French National Archives

Section Outre-Mer

ANSOM Sén. III Doss. 1, "Compte rendu du Journal du voyage éxecuté par Monsieur Mollien dans l'intérieur de l'Afrique" (Paris, 8 July 1819).

ANSOM Sén. III Doss. 1, "Instructions pour les seigneurs Brédif, ingénieur de 1ère classe au Corps Royal des Mines et de Chasselus ingénieurs-géographe, envoyés par sa Majestie pour explorer le cours du Sénégal et l'intérièure de cette partie de l'Afrique, jusques aux Royaumes de Galam, Bambouk et Bondou inclusivement, Signé Governor Schmaltz" (Saint Louis, Oct. 1817).

ANSOM Sén. et Dép. XIII Doss. 54 1817 à 1859, "C. Maréchal de Lunéville, à Monsieur le Président du Pouvoir Exécutif, au Citoyen, Président du Conseil du Ministre Chef du Pouvoir éxecutif" (Paris, 1850).

ANSOM Sén. et Dép. XIII Doss. 55, "L. Faidherbe, Agriculture Commerce Industrie 1856 à 1860 Mines du Bambouk Exploitation, 1856 à 1857" (Gorée, 12 July 1856).

ANSOM Sén. et Dép. XIII Doss. 55, "Lettre à M. le Ministre de la Marine et des Colonies" (Paris, 30 Dec. 1857).

ANSOM Sén. et Dép. XIII Doss. 55 (55a), "Le Chef du Bureau, Rapport au Ministre" (Paris, 14 Jan. 1858).

ANSOM Sén. et Dép. XIII Doss. 55 (5b), "Le Chef du Bureau, Rapport au Ministre" (Paris, 29 Jan. 1858).

ANSOM Sén. et Dép. XIII Doss. 55 (5b), "Le Capitaine du Génie Maritz, Rapport au Ministre" (Paris, 2 Feb. 1858).

ANSOM Sén. et Dép. XIII Doss. 55 (5a), "Le Capitaine du Génie Maritz, Rapport au Ministre" (Paris, 3 Feb. 1858).

ANSOM Sén. et Dép. XIII Doss. 55 (5a), "Le Lieutenant Colonel J. Roux, Lettre à Directeur Ministère de la Marine" (Paris, 11 Feb. 1858).

ANSOM Sén. et Dép. XIII Doss. 55 (55c), "Agriculture Commerce Industrie 1856 à 1860, Ministère de l'Algérie et des Colonies" (Paris, Feb. 1859).

ANSOM Sén. et Dép. XIII Doss. 55 (55d), "Lettre de Maritz Capitaine du Génie, Rapport sur l'exploitation des mines d'or du Bambouk" (Saint Louis, 2 August 1859).

ANSOM Sén. et Dép. XIII Doss. 55 (55c), "Faidherbe à M. le Ministre de l'Algérie et des Colonies" (Saint Louis, 14 August 1859).

ANSOM Sén. et Dép. XIII Doss. 55 (55b), "Godfrey de Villiers, Agriculture Commerce Industrie 1856 à 1860, Ministère de l'Algérie et des Colonies" (Paris, 14 Sept. 1859).

ANSOM Sén. et Dép. XIII Doss. 55 (55d), "Lettre de Maritz Capitaine du Génie, Rapport sur l' établissement de Kéniéba et sur l'exploitation projetée des mines d'or à proximité de ce poste" (Kenieba, 20 Oct. 1859).

ANSOM Sén. et Dép. XIII Doss. 55 (55c), "Lettre de Maritz Capitaine du Génie à M. le Gouverneur du Sénégal" (Kenieba, 17 March 1860).

ANSOM Sén. et Dép. XIII Doss. 55 (55c), "Lettre de Maritz Capitaine du Génie à Ministre de l'Algérie et des Colonies" (Saint Louis, 14 April 1860).

ANSOM Sén. et Dép. XIII Doss. 55 (55c), "Faidherbe à M. l'Ingénieur" (Saint Louis, 15 June 1860).

ANSOM Sén. et Dép. XIII Doss. 55 (55c), "Faidherbe à M. Le Ministre de l'Algérie et des Colonies" (Saint Louis, 18 August 1860).

ANSOM Sén. et Dép. IV Doss. 90 Bis, "Borgnis Desbordes et Vallière, Note pour servir à la rédaction des instructions au Colonel Commandant Supérieur du Haut Sénégal" (n.p., 10 Sept. 1886).

ANSOM Sén. et Dép. IV Doss. 90 Bis, "Vallière, Le Sous-Secrétaire au Ministère de la Marine et des Colonies au Gouverneur du Sénégal" (Paris, 20 Oct. 1886).

ANSOM Sén. et Dép. IV Doss. 90 Bis, "François Gallieni, Tarif des rations campagne 1886 à 1887" (Kayes, 16 Feb. 1887).

ANSOM Sén. et Dép. IV Doss. 90 Bis no. 2, "Le Capitaine Tautain, Extraits des rapports politiques venus du Cercle de Bamako" (Bamako, 4 March 1887).

ANSOM Sén. et Dép. IV Doss. 90 Bis no. 4, "Le Capitaine Tautain, Extraits des rapports politiques venus du Cercle de Bamako" (Bamako, 4 June [sic] 1887).

ANSOM Sén. et Dép. IV Doss. 90 Bis no. 5, "Le Capitaine Tautain, Extraits des rapports politiques venus du Cercle de Bamako" (4 June 1887).

ANSOM Sén. et Dép. IV Doss. 90 Bis no. 6, "Le Capitaine Tautain, Extrait des rapports politiques venus du Cercle de Bamako" (Bamako, 5 Aug. 1887).

ANSOM Sén. et Dép. IV Doss. 90 Bis no. 7, "Le Capitaine Tautain, Extraits des rapports politiques venus du Cercle de Bamako" (Bamako, 5 Oct. 1887).

ANSOM Sén. et Dép. IV Doss. 90 Bis no. 8, "Capitaine Extraits des rapports politiques venus du Cercle de Bamako" (Bamako, 16 Sept. [sic] 1887).

ANSOM Sén. et Dép. IV Doss. 90 Bis, "Capitaine Fortin, Rapport sommaire sur les opérations exécutées par la colonne de la Gambie, pendant la campagne contre le marabout Mahmadou Lamine" (Senudebu, 6 Jan. 1888).

ANSOM Sén. et Dép. IV Doss. 90 Bis, "François Vallière, Expédition dans le Grand Bélédougou: Rapport politique adressé à M. le Lieutenant Colonel, Commandant Supérieur" (Bamako, 1 Feb. 1888).

ANSOM Sén. et Dép. IV Doss. 90 Bis, "Rauson, Extraits des rapports venus de Koundou: Rapport politique nov. 1887" (Bamako, 1 Feb. 1888).

ANSOM Sén. et Dép. IV Doss. 90 Bis no. 10, "Campagne 1887 à 1888: Rapport du Lieutenant Colonel Gallieni, Commandant Supérieur du Soudan français sur les opérations militaire exécutés dans le Soudan français pendant la campagne" (1887 à 1888).

ANSOM Sén. et Dép. IV Doss. 90 Bis, "Rapport de la Mission de la Compagnie dans le Bélédougou" (Kita, 26 Feb. 1888).

ANSOM Sén. et Dép IV Doss. 90 Bis, "Le Lieutenant Bonaccorsi à M. Le Chef de Bataillon Commandant la Colonie" (Kangaba, 27 Feb. 1888).

ANSOM Sén. et Dép. IV Doss. 90 Bis, "Le Capitaine Patriarche, Commandant de la Compagnie de Régiment de Tirailleurs sénégalais au Chef de Bataillon...Kayes" (Bamako, 1 March 1888).

ANSOM Sén. et Dép. IV Doss. 90 Bis, "Vallière, Rapport sur l'organisation politique donnée aux états de Mambi situés sur la rive gauche du Niger" (Kangaba, 5 March 1888).

ANSOM Sén. et Dép. IV Doss. 90 Bis, "Capitaine Léjeune, Rapport sur l'opération contre Minamba-Farba (Minambadougou-Farba)" (Keynegue, 7 March 1888).

ANSOM Sén. et Dép. IV Doss. 90 Bis, "Vallière, Rapport sur l'opération de Minamba-Farba" (Bamako, 9 March 1888).

ANSOM Sén. et Dép. IV Doss. 90 Bis, "François Vallière, Expansion territoriale et politique indigène, 1887 à 1888: Mémoire du Cercle de Bammako" (Siguiri, 15–25 March 1888)

ANSOM Sén. et Dép. IV Doss. 90 Bis, "Campagne 1887 à 1888: Le Chef de Bataillon Vallière au Lieutenant Colonel Gallieni, Commandant Supérieur du Soudan français" (Siguiri, 1 April 1888).

ANSOM Sén. et Dép. IV Doss. 90 Bis, "Le Lieutenant Colonel Gallieni, Commandant Supérieur du Soudan français à M. le Capitaine Roiffé, Commandant le poste de Siguiri" (Siguiri, 5 April 1888).

ANSOM Sén. et Dép. IV Doss. 90 Bis, "Gallieni et Vallière, Recolte des fourrages dans les postes du Soudan français" (Siguiri, 6 April 1888).

ANSOM Sén. et Dép. IV Doss. 90 Bis, "Soudan français Service administratif: Note sur le fonctionnement du Service des Approvisionnement et Subsistance dans le Soudan français pendant la campagne, 1887 à 1888" (Kayes, 8 April 1888).

ANSOM Sén. et Dép. IV Doss. 90 Bis, "Notes sur le fonctionnement de la Compatabilité financière et des Services des Transports fluviaux dans le Soudan français pendant la campagne, 1887 à 1888" (Kayes, 20 April 1888).

ANSOM Sén. et Dép. IV Doss. 90 Bis, "François Gallieni et François Vallière, Délimitation des cercles du Soudan français, décision Bafoulabé" (1 May 1888).

ANSOM Sén. et Dép. IV Doss. 90 Bis, "Rapport du Lieutenant Colonel Gallieni, Commandant Supérieur du Soudan français sur les opérations de la colonne du Niger pendant la campagne, 1887 à 1888" (Bafulabe, 4 May 1888).

ANSOM Sén. et Dép. IV Doss. 90 Bis no. 3, "Rapport du Lieutenant-Colonel Gallieni Commandant Supérieur du Soudan français sur le Service vetérinaire le Service du Train et la remonte des saphis dans le Soudan français campagne, 1887 à 1888" (Bafulabe, 10 May 1888).

ANSOM Sén. et Dép. IV Doss. 90 Bis no. 5, "Rapport du Lieutenant-Colonel Gallieni Commandant Supérieur du Soudan français sur le Service administratif du Soudan français pendant le campagne, 1887 à 1888" (Bafulabe, 10 May, 1888).

ANSOM Sén. et Dép. IV Doss. 90 Bis, "Campagne 1887 à 1888 Soudan français: Comptes des dépenses de la colonne du Haut Niger, Campagne (1887 à 1888) 10 dec. 1887 à avril 1888" (Kayes, 12 May 1888).

ANSOM Sén. et Dép. IV Doss. 90 Bis, "Etats des differents traités conclus avec les chefs indigènes du Soudan français et des pays avoisinants campagnes, 1886 à 1887, 1887 à 1888)."

ANSOM Sén. et Dép. IV Doss. 90 Bis, "Gallieni, Rapport sur les opérations militaires exécutées dans le Soudan français, 1887 à 1888" (Aboard the "Siguiri," 20 May 1888).

ANSOM Sén. et Dép. IV Doss. 93 Bis, "Routes et Ponts: Rapport du Lieutenant Colonel Gallieni Commandant Supérieur du Soudan français sur le Service des Travaux pendant la campagne, 1887 à 1888" (Aboard the "Siguiri," 20 May 1888).

ANSOM Sén. et Dép. IV Doss. 90 Bis, "Gallieni, Rapport sur les opérations militaires exécutées dans le Soudan français, 1887 à 1888" (Aboard the "Siguiri," 22 May 1888).

ANSOM Sén. et Dép. IV Doss. 90 Bis, "Le Chef d'Escadron Archinard, Commandant Supérieur du Soudan français à M. le Gouverneur du Sénégal et Dépendances" (Kayes, 3 Nov. 1888).

ANSOM Sén. et Dép IV Doss. 90 Bis, "Service des Travaux Personnel des Travaux campagne, 1887 à 1888" (Bafulabe, 30 Dec. 1888).

ANSOM Sén. et Dép. IV Doss. 90 Bis, "Gouverneur Général à Gallieni, Service vétérinaire: Rapport de fin de campagne, 1888 à 1889" (Paris, 11 Oct. 1889).

ANSOM Sén. et Dép. IV Doss. 93 Bis, "Du Gouverneur Général d'Etat à M. le Lieutenant Colonel Gallieni, Commandant Supérieur du Soudan français" (Paris, 11 Oct. 1889).

ANSOM VI Doss. 1, "Affaires diplomatiques 1889 à 1895 Liberia: Délimination de la Côte d'Ivoire du Soudan et du Liberia, 1892" (Feb.-March 1892).

ANSOM Soudan VII Doss. 3, "Convention passé le 5 avril 1893 entre le Gouverneur du Sénégal et l'Almamy du Bondou" (1893).

ANSOM Soudan V Doss. 2 d, "Marillier, Expéditions militaires 1890 à 1893: Reconnaissance en Bambouk" (Bambuk, March 1894).

ANSOM Soudan 1 Doss. 9, "Louis Edgar de Trentinian, Affaires politiques et indigènes: Exposé de la situation politique intérieure et extérieure des Cercles au 1 juillet 1895" (Kayes, 10 August 1895).

ANSOM Soudan 1 Doss. 9, "Louis Edgar de Trentinian, Rapport (Copie) sur la situation intérieure et extérieure du Soudan au 1 septembre 1895" (Saint Louis, 7 Oct. 1895).

ANSOM Soudan XIII Doss. 11, "Industries diverses le Lieutenant Gouverneur du Soudan français à M. Le Ministre des Colonies à Paris" (Kayes, 4 July 1898).

ANSOM AOF 7 Doss. 4, "Destennave, Occupation et organisation de la Boucle du Niger: Répartition de la défence au temps de paix et en temp de guerre" (Paris, 15 Nov. 1898).

ANSOM AOF VII Doss. 4, "Reorganisation du Soudan, 1896 à 1899, 'Revue Commerciale et Coloniale'" (Paris, 25 Sept. 1899).

ANSOM AOF VII Doss. 4, "Reorganisation du Soudan, 1896 à 1899: Dépêche coloniale no. 940" (1–2 Oct. 1899).

ANSOM Soudan VII Doss. 8, "Le Niger l'importance de sa possession pour la France, 'L'Eclair'" (17 August 1903).

ANSOM Soudan VII Doss. 8, "Le Soudan français: Visite du Gouverneur Général M. Roume" (Bamako, 18 Dec. 1903).

ANSOM B1667, "Binger L.G., *Carnets de Route*, annotés et commentés par Jacques Binger René Bouvier et Pierre Deloncle" (Paris, 1938).

National Archives

Ministère des Affaires Etrangères

ANMAE, Afrique et Colonies françaises, 1780 à 1822, vol. 11. "Mémoire servant à montrer l'importance de la possession de la rivière du Sénégal" (n.d.).

ANMAE, Afrique et Colonies françaises, 1780 à 1822, vol. 11. "Mémoire servant à donner de renseignement sur le pays des mines que nous appelons Bambouk" (n.d.).

ANMAE, Afrique et Colonies françaises, 1780 à 1822, vol. 11. "Mémoire: Moyens à employer par le Ministre pour assurer à la France tous les avantages qu' elle peut tirer d'un établissement près des Mines en Bambouk, 1780."

ANMAE, Afrique et Colonies françaises, 1780 à 1822, vol. 11. "Mémoire no. 5, Moyens de tirer tous les avantages qu' on doit attendrè de nos établissement dans la haute rivière du Senegal indépendement des mines du Bambouk...commerce considerable, 1780."

ANMAE, Afrique et Colonies françaises, 1780 à 1822, vol. 11, "Mémoire no. 13, Contenant le détail et l'estimation de toutes les dépenses nécessaires pour la sûrété et exploitation du commerce de la concession du Sénégal depuis le Cap Blanc jusqu'à la rivière de Sierre Leone inclusivement, 1780."

ANMAE, Afrique et Colonies françaises, 1780 à 1822, vol. 11. Mémoire no. 14, "Détail et estimation de toutes les dépenses qu' exigera l'exécution du projet d'un établissement pour l'exploitation des mines dans le Royaume Bambouk, 1780."

ANMAE, Afrique et Colonies françaises, 1780 à 1822, vol. 11. Mémoire no. 15, "Extrait de deux mémoires contenant l'un le détail et l'estimation de toutes les dépenses nécessaires pour la sûreté et l'exploitation du commerce du Sénégal depuis le Cap-blanc jusqu' à la rivière de Sierre Leone inclusivement, et l'autre le détail et l'estimation de toutes les dépenses qu' exigait le plan d'établissement pour les mines de Bambouk" (n.d.).

ANMAE, Afrique et Colonies françaises, 1780 à 1822, vol. 11. "Mémoire no. 18, sur L'Isle d'Arguin, 1780."

ANMAE, Afrique et Colonies françaises, 1780 à 1822, vol. 11. Mémoire no. 19, "Mémoires et Notes de ce qu' on peut faire pour rendre plus profitable le commerce de la Concession du Sénégal, 1780."

ANMAE, Afrique et Colonies françaises, 1780 à 1822, vol. 11, "Mémoire no. 21, sur le droit qu à la forme de commerce dans tout le cours de la rivière de Gambie ce que les Anglais veulent lui refuser depuis long temps, 1780."

ANMAE, Afrique et Colonies françaises, 1780 à 1822, vol. 11. "Mémoire no. 22, Servant à procurer la consequence de privilège de la Rivière de Serra Lionné par l'étendre de son Commerce, 1870."

ANMAE, Afrique et Colonies françaises, 1780 à 1822, vol. 11. "Mémoire no. 32, Sur le Sénégal, Galam et Bambouc" (n.d.).

ANMAE, Afrique et Colonies françaises, 1780 à 1822, vol. 11. "Mémoire no. 34, Sur les moyens de rendre la Colonie du Sénégal florissante et sur les mésures à prendre pour que cette colonie cesse d'être en peu de temps onéreuse au gouvernement, 1783."

ANMAE, Afrique et Colonies françaises, 1780 à 1822, vol. 11, Mémoire no. 55. "Moyens à employer par le Ministère pour assurer à la France tout les avantages qu' elle doit serrer d'un établissement sur les mines en Bambouk, 1785."

ANMAE, Afrique et Colonies françaises, 1780 à 1822, vol. 11. "Projet d'un nouvel établissement en Afrique, 1816."

ANMAE, Afrique et Colonies françaises, 1780 à 1822, vol. 11, Mémoire no. 93. "Extrait d'un Mémoire ayant pour titre, 'Nouveau système au bien être et à la prosperité de la France par des avantages réciproques, 1819.'"

ANMAE, Afrique et Colonies françaises, 1780 à 1822, vol. 11, Mémoire no. 98. "Itinéraire de Constantine à Tafilet et de Tafilet à Tombouctou 14 aôut, 1822."

ANMAE, Mémoire et Documents Afrique Sénégal et Dépendances, 1773 à 1820, vol. 37. "Reflexions simples et naturelles sur les questions elevées entre la France et l'Angleterre touchant les possessions et le commerce des deux nations sur la Côte occidentalle d'Afrique entre le Cap Blanc et le Sénégal depuis la lession (sic) de cette rivière par art. X du Traité de 1763."

ANMAE, Mémoire et Documents Afrique Sénégal et Dépendances, 1773 à 1820, vol. 37. "Mémoire sur les prétentions de l'Angleterre dans la vue d'empescher (sic) la continuation du commerce et de la traite française à Portendic et à Arguin, 1773."

ANMAE, Mémoire et Documents Afrique Sénégal et Dépendances, 1773 à 1820, vol. 37. "Post script de la main de Monsieur de Boyner à une lettre qu' il a écrite à Monsieur Boniface Gouverneur de Gorée, 11 juin 1773."

ANMAE, Mémoire et Documents Afrique Sénégal et Dépendances, 1733–1820, vol. 37, no. 1, "Lettre Charles Stuart à son Excellence le Marquis Dessolle" (Paris, 23 Aug. 1819).

ANMAE, Mémoire et Documents Afrique Sénégal et Dépendances, 1773 à 1820, vol. 37. "Mémoire sur l'Expédition de Galam" (Paris, 6 Nov. 1819).

ANMAE, Mémoire et Documents Afrique Sénégal et Dépendances, 1856 à 1867, vol. 47, no. 11. "Rapport politique et commercial sur la Côte occidentale d'Afrique et Sierre Leone en particulier, 1865."

ANMAE, Mémoire et Documents Afrique Sénégal et Dépendances, 1843 à 1885, vol. 74. "Côte occidentale 1884, Note pour Monsieur de Largrené Côte occidentale d'Afrique, sept 1843" (Paris, 23 Oct. 1884).

ANMAE, Mémoire et Documents Afrique Sénégal et Dépendances, 1879 à 1881, vol. 75. "Transsaharien Mission Flatters, Soleillet et Choisy: Correspondence 5 aôut 1879–oct. 1879."

ANMAE, Mémoire et Documents Afrique Sénégal et Dépendances, 1879 à 1881, vol. 75. Flatters, "Chemin de fer transsaharien: Mission d'exploration, journal de route" (Wargla, 4 March 1880).

ANMAE, Mémoire et Documents Afrique Sénégal et Dépendances, 1879 à 1881, vol. 75. F. Bernard, "Chemin de fer transsaharien: Mission d'exploration, journal de route" (Wargla, 17 March–18 March, 1880).

ANMAE, Mémoire et Documents Afrique Sénégal et Dépendances, 1879 à 1881, vol. 75. "Commission supérieure pour l'étude des questions relatives à la mise en communication par voie ferrée de l'Algérie et du Soudan Mission M. Paul Soleillet: Rapport à M. le Ministre des Travaux Publics sur le voyage de Saint Louis à l'Adrar" (Dec. 1879–May 1880).

ANMAE, Mémoire et Documents Afrique Sénégal et Dépendances, 1886 à 1889, vol. 122.

ANMAE, Mémoire et Documents Afrique Sénégal et Dépendances, 1890 à 1894, vol. 123. "Le Soudan Français Voyage du Capitaine Binger, 1887-1889. '*Le Temps*,'" pp. 68–69 (Paris, March 1890).

ANMAE, Mémoire et Documents Afrique Sénégal et Dépendances, 1890 à 1894, vol. 123. "Le Sous-Secrétaire d'Etat des Colonies à M. le Ministre des Affaires Etrangères" (Paris, 29 May 1890).

ANMAE, Mémoire et Documents Afrique Sénégal et Dépendances, 1890 à 1894, vol. 123. "Extrait d'un rapport adressé à notre Agent Général au sujet de la Mission Garrett auprès de l'Almamy Samori" (July 1890, received Paris 13 Aug. 1890).

ANMAE, Mémoire et Documents Afrique Sénégal et Dépendances, 1890 à 1894, vol. 123. M. De Lamothe Gouverneur du Sénégal et Dépendances à M. Le Sous-Secrétaire d'Etat des Colonies" (Saint Louis, 5 Oct. 1890).

ANMAE, Mémoire et Documents Afrique Sénégal et Dépendances, 1890 à 1894, vol. 123. "Le Sous-Secrétaire d'Etat des Colonies à M. le Ministre des Affaires Etrangères" (Paris, 23 Oct. 1890).

ANMAE, Mémoire et Documents Afrique Sénégal et Dépendances, 1890 à 1894, vol. 123. Eugène Etienne. "Le Sous-Secrétaire d'Etat des Colonies à M. Le Capitaine Brosselard-Faidherbe chargé de Mission" (Paris, 7 Dec. 1890).

ANMAE, Mémoire et Documents Afrique Sénégal et Dépendances, 1890 à 1894, vol. 123. "Etude géographique sur le Tagant, Alger" (2 Feb. 1891).

ANMAE, Mémoire et Documents Afrique Sénégal et Dépendances, 1892 à 1894, vol 124. "A. Baillat, administrateur du Cercle de la Mellacorée à M. le Gouverneur des Rivières du Sud et Dépendances à Conakry" (Benty, 20 Oct. 1891).

ANMAE, Mémoires et Documents Sénégal et Dépendance, 1892 à 1894, vol. 124. "Le Commandant Supérieur du Soudan français à M. le Sous-Secrétaire d'Etat des Colonies" (Kayes, 11 Sept. 1892).

ANMAE, Mémoires et Documents Sénégal et Dépendance, 1892 à 1894, vol. 124. "M. De Lamothe, Gouverneur du Sénégal et Dépendance à M. le Sous-Secrétaire d'Etat des Colonies" (Paris, 12 Sept 1892).

ANMAE, Mémoires et Documents Sénégal et Dépendance, 1892 à 1894, vol. 124. "Le Sous-Secrétaire d'Etat des Colonies à M. le Ministre des Affaires Etrangères" (Paris, 10 Nov. 1892).

ANMAE, Mémoires et Documents Sénégal et Dépendance, 1892 à 1894, vol. 124. "Le Sous-Secrétaire d'Etat des Colonies à M. le Ministre d'Affaires Etrangères" (Paris, 21 Jan. 1893).

ANMAE, Mémoires et Documents Sénégal et Dépendance, 1892 à 1894, vol. 124. "M. Phipps, Ministre d'Angleterre à M. Hanatoux Directeur des Affaires commerciales" (Paris, 23 Jan. 1893).

ANMAE, Mémoires et Documents Sénégal et Dépendance, 1892 à 1894, vol. 124. "Le Sous-Secrétaire d'Etat des Colonies à M. le Ministre des Affaires Etrangères" (Paris, 2 Feb. 1893).

ANMAE, Mémoires et Documents Sénégal et Dépendance, 1892 à 1894, vol. 124. "Rapport sommaire sur la situation politique de la Guinée française pendant la période du 20 nov. 1892 à jan. 1893."

ANMAE, Mémoires et Documents Sénégal et Dépendance, 1892 à 1894, vol. 124. "Le Sous-Secrétaire d'Etat des Colonies à M. le Ministre des Affaires Etrangères" (Paris, 27 June 1893).

ANMAE, Mémoires et Documents Sénégal et Dépendance, 1892 à 1894, vol. 124. "Le Sous-Secrétaire d'Etat des Colonies à M. le Ministre des Affaires Etrangères" (Paris, 28 July 1893).

ANMAE, Mémoires et Documents Sénégal et Dépendance, 1892 à 1894, vol. 124. "Rapport politique" (Nioro, 31 Dec. 1892, received Paris, 13 March 1893).

ANMAE, Mémoires et Documents Sénégal et Dépendance, 1892 à 1894, vol. 124. "Commandant Supérieur du Soudan français à M. le Sous-Secrétaire d'Etat des Colonies" (Kayes, 1 Nov. 1893).

ANMAE, Mémoires et Documents Sénégal et Dépendance, 1892 à 1894, vol. 124. "Le Sous-Secrétaire d'Etat des Colonies à M. le Ministre des Affaires Etrangères" (Paris, 9 Dec. 1893).

ANMAE, Mémoires et Documents Sénégal et Dépendance, 1892 à 1894, vol. 124. "Le Sous-Secrétaire d'Etat des Colonies à M. le President du Conseil Ministère des Affaires Etrangères" (Paris, 16 Jan. 1894).

ANMAE, Mémoires et Documents Sénégal et Dépendance, 1892 à 1894, vol. 124. "Rapport sommaire sur la situation politique de la Colonie pendant la période du 18 jan. au 18 fev. 1894."

ANMAE, Mémoires et Documents Sénégal et Dépendance, 1890 à 1894, vol. 125. "Etablissement français du Golfe de Guinée, 1888 à 1890, Lettre du Sous-Secrétaire d'Etat des Colonies à Monsieur le Ministre des Affaires Etrangères" (Paris, 22 May 1889).

ANMAE, Mémoires et Documents Sénégal et Dépendance, 1890 à 1894, vol. 125. "Etablissement français du Golfe de Guinée, 1888 à 1890, Lettre du Sous-Secrétaire d'Etat des Colonies à Monsieur le Ministre des Affaires Etrangères" (Paris, 16 June 1890).

ANMAE, Mémoires et Documents Sénégal et Dépendance, 1890 à 1894, vol. 125. "Etablissement français du Golfe de Guinée, 1888 à 1890, Incident de Bondoukou, Note pour le Ministre, Direction Politique Protectorat, 28 juin 1889."

ANMAE, Mémoires et Documents Sénégal et Dépendance, 1890 à 1894, vol. 125. "Etablissement français du Golfe de Guinée, 1888 à 1890, Mission Méniaud du Côte d'Ivoire" (Yacasse, 5 Dec. 1890).

ANMAE, Mémoires et Documents Sénégal et Dépendance, 1890 à 1894, vol. 125. "Etablissement français du Golfe de Guinée, 1888 à 1890, Mission Binger 1892, Rapport politique."

ANMAE, Mémoires et Documents, Sénégal et Dépendance, vol. 127. "Affaires diverses Africa, Conférence de Bruxelles 1889 à 1892, Régime et Commerce des Affaires 1868 à 1895, Lettre du Vice-Consul de France à Liège à Monsieur le Ministre" (Paris, 3 Dec. 1890).

ANMAE, Mémoires et Documents Sénégal et Dépendance, vol. 130, "Possessions Anglaises de la Côte occidentale, 1892, délimitation Franco-Anglaise au Nord de Sierra Leone Mission du Capitaine Brosselard-Faidherbe 1891" (Paris, 1892).

ANMAE, Mémoires et Documents Sénégal et Dépendance, vol. 130. "Possessions Anglaises de la Côte occidentale 1892, Commission de délimination de la Côte d'Ivoire: Rapport du Capitaine Binger sur les opérations de délimination" (Paris, 20 Aug. 1892).

Theses

Bagayogo, D. "Idéologie communautaire, sociétés rurales et associations de culture (cikèton) au Mali." Thèse de doctorat de troisième cycle (Paris, 1982).

Bathily, Mohamadou S. "Les Soninké dans l'histoire du Fuuta Tooro: Introduction à la mise en place et à l'insertion d'une minorité." Mémoire de D.E.A. under the direction of Claude-Hélène Perrot (Paris, 1987).

Camara, Seydou. "La Transmission orale en question: Convention et transmission des traditions historiques au Manden le Centre de Keyla et l'histoire de Minjinjan." Thèse de doctorat d' état under the direction of Emmanuel Terray, 2 vols. (Paris, 1990).

Chastenet, Monique. "L'Etat du Gajaaga de 1818 à 1858 face à l'expansion commerciale française au Sénégal." Mémoire de maîtrise under the direction of Yves Person (Paris, 1975–1976).

Diabaté, Massa Makan. "Essai critique sur l'Épopée Mandingue." Thèse de doctorat de troisième cycle under the direction of Yves Person (Paris, n.d.).

Diabaté, Victor T. "La Région de Kong d'après les fouilles archéologiques: Prospection premiers sondages." Thèse de doctorat de troisième cycle under the direction of Jean Devisse (Paris, 1979).

Diane, Djiba. "Islam en Haute Guinée, 1900–1959." Thèse de doctorat de troisième cycle, under the direction of Yves Person (Paris, 1979–1980).

Dincuff, Antoine. "Kong et Bobo-Dioulasso, capitales Dyoula." Thèse de doctorat de troisième cycle under the direction of Yves Person (Paris, n.d.).

Dosso, Moussa. "Histoire du pays malinké de Côte d'Ivoire: Evolution politique économique et sociale, 1898–1940." Mémoire de maîtrise under the direction of Yves Person (Paris, 1971).

Dramani-Issifou, Zakari. "Les Relations entre le Maroc et l'empire Sonrhaï dans la seconde moitie du XVIe siècle." Thèse de doctorat de troisième cycle under the direction of Jean Devisse (Paris, 1974–1975).

Gaillard, Xavier. "Commerce et production de l'or du Bambouk XVIIe et XVIIIe siècles (d'après les sources françaises)." Mémoire de maîtrise under the direction of Jean Devisse (Paris, 1982).

Goërg, Odile. "Echanges, réseaux, marchés: l' impact colonial en Guinée (mi-XIX siècle à 1913)." Thèse de doctorat de troisième cycle under the direction of Catherine Coquery-Vidrovitch (Paris, 1981).

Joly, Vincent. "Les divers projets de chemins de fer transsahariens, 1870–1900." Mémoire de maîtrise under the direction of Yves Person (Paris, 1975–1976).

Kiethéga, Jean-Baptiste. "L'Exploitation traditionnelle de l'or sur la rive gauche de la Volta noire (Région de Poura-Haut-Volta)." Thèse de doctorat de troisième cycle under the direction of Jean Devisse (Paris, 1980).

Lakroum, Monique. "Chemin de fer et réseaux d'affaires en Afrique occidentale, le Dakar-Niger, 1883-1960." Thèse de doctorat d'état under the direction of Catherine Cocquery-Vidrovitch," 2 vols. (Paris, 1981).

Patinon, Alphonse-Ignace Aikpévi. "Contribution à l'histoire du sel alimentaire dans le Soudan précolonial (fin Xe au début XXe siècles)." Thèse de doctorat de troisième cycle under the direction of Jean Devisse, 2 vols. (Paris, 1986).

Piazza, Michelle. "Le Développement de l'économie coloniale en Guinée française, 1890–1918." Mémoire de maîtrise under the direction of Hubert Deschamps (Paris, 1970).

Renaldo, Claudine. "La Sénégambie à la fin du dix-huitième siècle." Mémoire de maîtrise under the direction of Yves Person (Paris, 1973).

Samaké, Maximin. "Pouvoir traditionnel et conscience politique paysanne: Les Kafow de la région de Bougouni, Mali." Thèse de doctorat de troisième cycle, 2 vols. (Paris, 1984).

Traoré, Bakary. "Etat actuel des connaissance sur les Dyula du Burkina Faso." Mémoire de D.E.A. under the direction of Jean Devisse (Paris, 1985).

Theses
L' École Normale Supérieure
Bamako

Alarba, Ahmadou. "Le Cercle de Gao: Politique coloniale et vie socio-économique (1899–1939)." Mémoire de Fin d'Etudes en Histoire-Géographie under the direction of Madame Parigi, École Normale Supérieure (Bamako, 1975–1976).

Bouaré, Siga. "La Ville de Ségou." Mémoire de Fin d'Etudes en Histoire-Géographie under the direction of M. Patrick Videcoq, École Normale Supérieure (Bamako, 1975–1976).

Camara, Seydou. "Le Manden des origines à Sunjata." Mémoire de Fin d'Etudes en Histoire-Géographie, École Normale Supérieure (Bamako, 1977–1978).

Coulibaly, Insa. "Le Wasulu, un milieu aux potentialitiés économiques énormes, une zone d'exode rural massif: Tentatives d'explication du paradoxe." Mémoire de Fin d'Etudes en Histoire et Géographie, École Normale Supérieure (Bamako, 1986).

Coulibaly, Abdoulaye D. "Séveré, question d'expansion de la ville de Mopti." Mémoire de Fin d'Etudes en Histoire-Géographie under the direction of Madame Kouma Assitan Berthé, École Normale Supérieure (Bamako, 1981–1982).

Coulibaly, Yacouba. "Le Soudan français dans la guerre 1939 à 1945." Mémoire de Fin d'Etudes en Histoire-Géographie under the direction of M. Kagnoumé Jean Bosco Konaré, École Normale Supérieure (Bamako, 1981–1982).

Diabaté, Sidy. "Kankou Moussa Empereur du Mali." Mémoire de Fin d'Etudes en Histoire-Géographie under the direction of Madame Madina Ly, École Normale Supérieure (Bamako, 1973–1974).

Diallo, Hammadoun. "La Prise de Djenné par Archinard en avril 1893." Mémoire de Fin d'Etudes en Histoire-Géographie under the direction of M. Kagnoumé Jean Bosco Konaré, École Normale Supérieure (Bamako, 1976–1977).

Diarra, Brahima. "Du Banimonotie au Cercle de Bougouni: Contribution à l'histoire d'un canton 1667 à 1914." Mémoire de Fin d'Etudes en Histoire-Géographie under the direction of M. Kagnoumé J. B. Konaré, École Normale Supérieure (Bamako, 1974–1975).

Dicko, S. Omar. "La Politique musulmane de l'administration coloniale au Soudan-Français dans la première moitié du XXe siècle (1912 à 1946")." Mémoire de Fin d'Etudes en Histoire-Géographie under the direction of Madame Adama Ba Konaré, École Normale Supérieure (Bamako, 1977–1978).

Guindo, Boubakar Mody. "Les transports routiers de marchandises dans la région de Ségou." Mémoire de Fin d'Etudes en Histoire-Géographie under the direction of M. André Gondolo, École Normale Supérieure (Bamako, 1981–1982).

Konaté, Boubacer. "Monographie historique du Royaume Bambara de Ségou." Mémoire Fin d'Etudes en Histoire-Géographie under the direction of Madame Ly Madina, École Normale Supérieur (Bamako, 1974–1975).

Koulibaly, Yacouba. "Le Soudan français dans la guerre 1939 à 1945." Mémoire de Fin d'Etudes en Histoire-Géographie under the direction of M. Kagnoumé Jean Bosco Konaré, École Normale Supérieure (Bamako, 1981–1982).

Sangare, Oumar. "Les Commerçants à Bamako." Mémoire de Fin d'Etudes en Histoire-Géographie under the direction of M. Voronov, École Normale Supérieure (Bamako, 1976–1977).

Soumaoro, Ismaïla. "Étude d'un quartier de Bamako: Niarela." Mémoire de Fin d'Etudes en Histoire-Géographie under the direction of Monsieur I. M. Albassadjé, École Normale Supérieure (Bamako, 1976–1977).

Touré, Naïny. "L'Amenagement de la ville de Bamako de 1945 à 1973." Mémoire de Fin d'Etudes en Histoire-Géographie under the direction of M. Daniel Bléneau, École Normale Supérieure (Bamako, 1973–1974).

Traoré, Bakary. "Contribution à l'histoire du peuplement du Kala de la fin XVIe au XIXe siècles." Mémoire de Fin d'Etudes en Histoire-Géographie under the direction of Madame Adama Ba Konaré, École Normale Supérieure (Bamako, 1981–1982).

Traore, Yanocot. "La Zone industrielle de Bamako." Mémoire de Fin d'Etudes en Histoire-Géographie under the direction of M. Daniel Bléneau, Normale Supérieure (Bamako, 1973–1974).

Interviews

1980

2–3 Jan.   Seydou Niaré (functionary, Bamako).
3–5 Jan.   Mahmadou Sarr (researcher, Institut des Sciences Humaines, Bamako).
3–10 Jan.   Bani Touré (marabout and instructor, Bozola-Bamako).
4 Jan.   Nana Niaré Dravé (Magistrate at the Tribunal, Bamako).
4 Jan.   Charles Bird (Mande specialist, Bamako).
4 Jan.   Seydou Niaré (functionary, Bamako).
4 Jan.   Batio Touré (functionary, Bozola-Bamako).
5 Jan.   Nana Niaré Dravé (Magistrate at the Tribunal, Bamako).
5–7 Jan.   Mahmadou Sarr (researcher, Institut des Sciences Humaines, Bamako).
5–9 Jan.   Suleyman Dravé (retired functionary, Bamako).
6 Jan.   Seydou Niaré (functionary, Bamako).
8 Jan.   Mahmadou Sarr (Researcher, Institut des Sciences Humaines, Bamako).

1982

23 June   Modibo Diallo (doctoral student at Paris 1)
30 Oct.   Kalifa Coulibaly (merchant, Bamako)
1 Nov.   Djafar Thiam (functionary, Bamako)
3 Nov.   Djafar Thiam (functionary, Bamako)
17 Nov.   Abdulhai Diallo (merchant, Mopti)
17 Nov.   Mahmadou Diallo (merchant, Mopti)
19 Nov.   Alphidi Samounou (merchant, Jenne)
19 Nov.   Mahmadou Oumar Aaba (merchant, Jenne).
19 Nov.   Ahmada Waïgalo (merchant, Jenne)
19 Nov.   Sidi Maïga (merchant, Jenne).
30 Nov.   Alhadji Taudina (merchant, Bamako).
30 Nov.   Modibo Magassa (Bamako).
5 Dec.   Gagni Koita (*jeli*, Bamako).
15 Dec.   Seydou Niaré (functionary, Bamako).

1983

1 Jan.	Thiémoko Kanté (translator, Institut des Sciences Humaines).
8 Jan.	Abdoulaye Touré (Bamako).
7 Feb.	Ali Ongoïba (archivist, Kuluba-Bamako).
7 Mar.	Ali Ongoïba (archivist, Kuluba-Bamako).
10 Mar.	Ali Ongoïba (archivist, Kuluba-Bamako).
10 Mar.	Abdula Gueué (metal worker, Bamako).
12 Mar.	Seydou Doumbia (metal worker and gold dealer, Bozola/Bamako).
12 Mar.	Alpha Touré (gold dealer, Bamako).
15 Mar.	Seydou Camara (researcher, Institut des Sciences Humaines, Bamako).
15 Mar.	Mahmadou Sarr (researcher, Institut des Sciences Humaines, Bamako).
21 Mar.	Massa Makan Diabaté (writer, Bamako).
8 April	Karamogo Touré (former functionary, Bamako).
11 April	Ali Ongoïba (archivist, Kuluba-Bamako).
12 April	Ali Ongoïba (archivist, Kuluba-Bamako).
12 April	El Hajj Mamadou Makadji (merchant, Bamako).
12 April	Bouba Djiré (merchant, Banamba).
13 April	Tiémoko Coulibaly (merchant, Kangaba).
15 April	Karamogo Touré (former functionary, Bamako).
19 April	Bakary Doumbia (metal worker, Bamako).
20 April	Famalé Cissoko (gold miner and metal worker, Bamako).
21 April	Bakary Doumbia (metal worker, Bamako).
30 April	Sibery Kanté (merchant, Bamako).
6 May	Bâ Moussa Coulibaly (metal worker and gold dealer, Mansala).
12 May	Ali Ongoïba (archivist, Kuluba-Bamako).
14 May	Sira Souko (miner, Kalassa).
15 May	Diarra Sylla (traditionalist, Bamako).
16 May	Nouriké Kanté (merchant, Bamako).
16 May	Sibiry Kanté (merchant Bamako region).

About the Book and Author

This groundbreaking book explores the history and the cultural context of family claims to power in Bamako, located in modern-day Mali in West Africa. Perinbam argues that these families manipulated traditional belief systems (including myth, ritual, and ancestral legends) in the quest for political power, economic success, and social status. As a result, Perinbam offers new insights into the processes of Mande social history.

Instead of "Mandingo" rigidities, the author argues that as the families migrated, their ethnographic identities were mediated in accordance with a number of mythic and historical contingencies, most notably the respective states into whose vortex they were drawn. This meant articulating identity in relation to state formation, maintenance, and renewal—and as an ongoing process of meaning sensitive to political, generational, and gender challenges. With the arrival of Europeans in the late nineteenth century and the Mande incorporation into the French colonial state, familial identities adjusted accordingly.

The careful research and original scholarship of *Family Identity and the State in the Bamako Kafu* make it a significant contribution to the histories of West Africa, the African Diaspora, and African-Americans.

B. Marie Perinbam is professor of history at University of Maryland at College Park.

Index

Abdu, Muhammad, 265
Adam, M. G., 72
"Affaires Indigènes," 126
al-Afgani, Jamal, 265
African Frontier, The (Kopytoff), 38–39
Africanus, Leo, 185(n16)
Agriculture, 162, 174(n84), 209
    and Mande-hinterland, 100–101,
        101(n14), 109, 114
    southern, 128
Albreda, 205
Alfaya, Karamoko, 208(n70)
Ali, Sunni, 107
Alliances
    Bamako defensive, 196
    Bamana-speakers and Kong,
        91(n108)
    Bozo-Dogon, 113
    colonialism and, 230, 268
    and cultural diffusion, 78–79
    and endogamy, 60
    French-West African, 220
    identity and family, 13–14, 49–50
    Keita-Niare, 99–100
    Niare/Kulibaly, 85–86, 168,
        168(n67)
    Niare myth and Ture and Drave, 83
    oath—*siyah* and *senankun*, 52,
        52(n19), 77, 85–86, 164–165. *See*
        also Ritual
    political, 148(n20), 160, 161. *See also*
        Political power
    power and marriage, 75–77,
        163–164, 166, 168
    role in Bamako socio-political sys-
        tem, 175, 226
    and social mobilization, 163–167

Almoravids, 61
Amselle, Jean-Loup, 34–35
Animals, domestic, 22(n55), 101, 103n,
        109
    French horse/mule market, 214,
        214(n87)
    livestock trade, 195, 210, 211,
        212–215
Animism, 86–87
    and commodification of gold,
        208–209
    in justifying slavery, 127
    and north/south paradigm,
        105–106, 115–118, 125, 137
    and southern Islamization, 121–124
Arawan, 191(n30)
Archinard, Louis, 221
Architecture, 16
Arnaud, R., 72
As-Sadi, 106, 133, 244

Badis, Ben, 265
Ba family, 17
Bafulabe, 167, 237
Bafulabe Circle, 124
Baghana, 5
Bakhunu, 5, 69
al-Bakri, 6, 62, 183
Bamako (city)
    and colonialism, 156–157, 157(n41)
    European commercial houses in,
        211(n79)
    kindaw in, 95–96
    population, 19
    walls, 162(n52), 169, 169(n70)
Bamako Circle, 17, 17(n42), 98, 242,
        251(n10)

Bamako *kafu*, 80(n87), 149(n23)
  accounts of foundation, 80–82,
    88–93
  and commercial networks, 179–181,
    182, 184–207, 190(n28), 196(n44)
  cultural/family identities in, 2–4,
    11–12, 139
  environment, 22–23
  family/village settlement in, 16–17,
    157–161, 157(n42)
  and the French, 221, 224, 225,
    227–245, 243(n55)
  French schools in, 267–268
  Islam in, 266
  and northern paradigm, 135
  political succession in, 151–152, 155
  population, 255
  relationship with Segu, 168–172
  socio-political organization, 140,
    149–151, 162–167, 173–177, 179,
    226
  state formation, 39, 40, 45–46
  Umarian and Samorian wars and
    defensive alliances, 195–196
Bamana, 80(n88)
  and alliances, 165
  and commerce, 182
  in-migrations, 102–103, 248
Bamanization, 3, 37n, 48, 77–79, 139,
    171–172
Bamba, Samake, 80(n87)
Bambara identity
  construction of, 37–38, 37n, 103–112,
    115, 248–250
  and French colonialism, 247–248,
    251–252, 255–263
  Niare adoption of, 272–273
  See also Northern paradigm
Bambuhu region
  and commerce, 204–205
  and the French, 221–222
  and gold identity, 118
  and Muslims, 89, 167
  political succession in, 155
  poverty in, 128–129
  and slave raids, 125–126, 127(n84)

  socio-political organization in,
    145(n14)
Banamba, 89, 102
  market in, 191–192, 191(n32)
  political succession in, 153
  population, 20
  schools in, 111
Banamba incident (1905), 111
Bangasi, 4
Bani River, 131(n92), 132, 132(n93)
Bari family, 50, 208
  settlement area, 17, 18
Barth, Heinrich, 48, 72
Battle of Krina, 81
Battuta, Ibn, 105, 114, 133
Bayol, Jean-Marie, 236, 241(n50)
Bazin, Jean, 37, 249
Beledugu, 3, 19, 89
  clans and warrior identity, 104
  effect of war on, 210
  and the French, 213, 228, 231,
    232–233, 239
  political power/succession in,
    146(n16), 152–153
  schools in, 111
Belief systems
  Bamako and Segovian, 168
  gold and southern, 118–121
  and identity, 10–11
  Mande views of the French, 227–233
  particularization of, 23–24, 112–113,
    123–124
  in upholding socio-political organi-
    zation, 14, 39, 135, 148
  See also Myth; Northern paradigm;
    Ritual
Berete family, 100
Bernal, Martin, 141(n4)
Berote family, 59(n40)
Beyla, 206, 211
Bida, 118
Bile, Samba, 231
Binger, Louis, 52, 221, 228–229,
    258–259, 265(n44)
Bird, Charles, 12(n26)
Birgo region, 221

Bobo-Julasso, 19, 266
Bonduku, 19
Bonnacorsi, Lieutenant, 233
Boyer, Gaston, 63, 69, 72
Bozo family
    and alliances, 113, 163, 164, 165, 166
    Bamako quarter for, 96
    and commerce, 182
    and identity formation, 83–84, 250
    and northern paradigm, 112
    particularization of belief systems,
        112–113
    ritual sites, 99(n8)
    settlement of Mande-hinterland, 99
    subgroups, 99(n9)
    views of French, 220n
Bozola, 212
Brevie, Jules, 29, 55, 145–147, 162
Briere de L'Isle, Louis, 221, 240
British
    competition with French, 224, 238,
        240–241
    and trade networks, 200, 201, 203,
        206(n65)
Brue, Andre, 222
Buguni, 206
Buna, 167
Bundu, 4
Bure region
    and commerce, 202, 204–205
    and the French, 221–222, 258
    gold identity in, 118, 119, 119(n59)
    grain prices in, 129(n86)
    poverty in, 128–129
    and slave raids, 125–126, 127(n84)

Cadamosto, 207
Caillie, Rene, 21, 34, 131, 184, 207–208,
    234, 257
Camara, Mamadu, 126
Camara family, 18, 119, 125, 167
Caron, Lieutenant, 259
Cayor, 222
Chambonnea, 222
Chasseloup-Labat, Marquis de,
    224(n16)

Chronique du Fouta Sénégalais, 69–70
Chronology, 55–56, 62(n47), 63–64,
    72–73, 73–74, 79
    by Binger, 258
Cisse, Youssouf, 116
Clozel, Marie-Francois, 237–238, 243,
    251, 265(n44)
Cohen, Abner, 27–28, 84
Collomb, Lieutenant, 65, 186–187
Colonialism
    cultural effects of, 26, 263, 266–269,
        271
    Islamic reactions to, 264–266,
        265(n44)
    and misconstruing African identity,
        35–36
    See also French
Commenda, 186
Commerce. *See* Trade
Commercial elites, 125
Communication, 21–22
Conflict, societal
    and family-based states, 175,
        176–177
    and Muslims, 167
    prohibitions in limiting, 161, 165
    See also Political power; Wars
Conrard, Lieutenant, 72, 74(n80), 236,
    248
Cote d'Ivoire, 7, 10, 89, 211, 265
Coulibaly, Tiémoko, 193(n36)
Cults, ethnographic, 84
Cultural forms
    identity and manipulating, 23, 25,
        28, 84–85, 139. *See also* Cultural
        particularisms
    manipulating myth, 55–57
    See also Myth
Cultural particularisms
    in facilitating commerce, 204
    within Islam, 264
    Islam-animist, 86–87, 112–113,
        123–124
    and Mande identity, 15–16
    and Mande migrations, 10–13
Cultural signifiers, 13–16

ancestral homelands as, 9–10
diffusion of, 78–79, 172
maintenance during migrations of,
    8, 11–13
manipulating, 25–26, 85–87,
    273–274
technology as French, 226–227
Curtis family, 201, 223

Daba, 153
Danane, 211
Delafosse, Maurice, 34, 69, 72, 74, 259,
    265(n44)
Delanneau, 152, 153
Dem, Bara, 253
Dembelle family, 16
Desbordes, Gustave Borgnis
    "Bourouti," 4, 199, 221, 237, 239
    and Niare myth, 29, 55, 84, 88, 245
    and Niare-Ture power struggles,
        92
    and Titi Niare, 87, 152, 229
Diane, al-Hajj Kabine, 266
Diara, Bala, 261
Diara, Dji, 261
Diawara, Mamadou, 62, 70, 72–73
Diawara, Mouça, 258
Dieterlen, Germaine, 116, 260,
    261–262
al-Dimashqi, 183
Disease, 22–23
    and domestic animals, 101
Disongo (tribute), 158(n44), 161,
    184(n12)
    Bamako and Segu, 168–169,
        169(n71), 171, 171(n75), 175
    demands to French for, 221
Dochard, Staff Surgeon, 131, 135, 190,
    190(n27), 202, 208, 231, 235
Dogon, 113, 113(n44)
Dokote family, 56
Do ni Kri, 98, 98(n5)
Dra'a valley, 3, 9
Drame family
    and Bamako, 81
    and Kingi myth, 68, 70–71, 71(n69),
        72

Wagadu myth and establishment of,
    64, 66
Drave family, 3
    and alliances, 164
    Bamako quarter for, 95
    and commerce, 187, 196–197, 199
    in Niare myth, 83
    origins, 83(n92)
    settlement area, 16
    slaves of, 162
    and slave trade, 125
Dravela, 95, 212
Dubois, Felix, 235
Dukure family
    dispersal and settlement, 18,
        59(n40), 102
    identity, 19, 48
    as rulers of Bakhunu, 69
Dumbya family
    and *jo* ritual, 118, 118(n57)
    settlement, 100
    tana of, 80(n88)
Dutch, 200

Economy
    Bamako and planning for, 174–175
    currencies, 188
    French effect on, 266–267
    identity and relation to, 33
    of Mande-hinterland, 100–102,
        101(n14), 102(n16), 103
    monetizing, 198, 215, 266
    myth in documenting, 137
    Niger River and north/south devel-
        opment, 131–136
    poverty in south, 128–129
    southern *versus* northern develop-
        ment, 97, 109–110, 114
    and trans-Saharan trade, 107
    war and recovery in Bamako,
        209–210, 215–216
    See also Markets; Trade
Endogamy, 60–61, 60(n42), 85
Environment, 22–23, 100–101
Esmeraldo de situ orbis (Pereira), 249
Etienne, Eugene, 242
Euro-Africans, 201–203, 217

Europeans
commercial houses in Bamako,
211(n79)
competition among, 204, 224, 238,
240–241
and trade networks, 200–203, 200n,
205
See also French

Faamaw, Kulibaly Massassi, 4
Fabes, Mr., 201
Faidherbe, Louis "Fitiriba," 126,
126(n80), 202, 221, 223–224,
223(nn 12, 13), 224(n15), 234,
236–237
Family, 1(n), 144(n11)
alliances and identity, 13–14, 49–50
and Bamako *kafu*, 2–4, 149–150, 173,
175, 176, 179, 226
and colonialism, 242, 247, 271
and commercial networks, 25, 179
and conflict/cooperation, 176–177
endogamy and alliances, 60
and Mande socio-political organization, 140, 143–148, 226
and Roman socio-political organization, 140(n2), 141–142, 141(n5),
142(n6)
settlement in Mande world, 16–19
and shifting identities, 1–2
and social mobilization, 162
in state formation, 24, 40
Famine, 128–129
Famoro, Babo, 254
Faqqus, Mudrik b., 133
Fassi, Muhammad, 68
al-Fazari, 5–6, 62
Fernandes, Valentim, 185(n16)
Fernandez family, 201
Festing, Major, 240
Fodio, Uthman dan, 208(n70)
Fofana family, 19
Fonfana, Diawe, 258
Forage, 212, 215
Fortin, Captain, 192
Fougères, Jean-Henri Terrasson de,
243(n55)

French
adoption of "Bambara" identity, 98,
247–248, 251–252, 255–263
Africans in service to, 252–256
and commercial networks, 136n,
198, 200, 214–215
demands on African economy,
209–210, 215(n89)
document sources, 29–30, 89–90
expansionism and policy, 4,
220–225, 223(nn 12, 13), 224(nn
15, 16), 233–244, 240(n49),
241(n50)
and Mande socio-political system,
124(n75), 156–157, 158, 266–269
Mande views of, 186n, 220, 220n,
221, 227–233
misconstruals by, 25, 219–220, 225,
233–238
and Roman paradigm, 141, 143,
147–148, 148(n21)
Rumi socio-political system,
226–227
trading companies, 222(n11)
Frey, Henri, 236
Freycinet, Charles de, 239
Fuladugu, 4
Fulbe
and alliances, 85–86, 165
and Bambara identity formation,
249–250, 251, 259, 261, 261(n36)
and commerce, 199, 213
ethnography on, 260
and identity shifts/articulations, 11,
48, 49–54, 51(n17), 103
initiation ceremonies, 103n
and northern paradigm, 110
settlement area, 16, 59(n40)
southern views of, 115
and Wagadu myth, 47(n5)
Futa Jallon, 205, 208(n70), 241, 241(n50)
Futa Toro, 208(n70), 222

Gajaaga, 10
Gajaga, 4
Gallieni, Joseph S., 236
and Bamako, 234–235

and Bambara identity, 257–258
cultural accounts by, 80(n86), 128,
    152–153, 197, 197(n48), 221,
    221(n6), 230
and French expansionism, 240
and Jo ambush, 152(n31)
Mande views of, 228, 231–232
reliability of cultural accounts, 34
Gallieni Mission, 29, 84, 88, 92, 151, 239
ambush of, 257(n22)
guides for, 253
Gambia, 222, 240, 240(n49)
Garanke (leather workers), 85(n95)
Gender relations, 120–121, 121(n67),
    188(n23). *See also* Women
Geography (Ptolemy), 244
Ghana, 5, 7
al-Gharnati, Abu Hamid, 183
Gidiume region, 49
Gold
beginnings of trade in, 182(n8)
deposits, 182(n7)
domestic trade in, 180, 192
and the French, 221–222
and international markets,
    119(n60)
market *versus* cosmological value
    for, 182–184, 184(nn 11, 12),
    207–209, 216
mithqal measurement, 133(n97)
in southern identity, 118–121,
    119(n59), 138
Goldberry, Silvester, 155, 234, 257
Gold Coast, 212, 265
Gondiuru, 205
Goree, 19
Grain trade, 195, 210, 211, 212–215,
    215(n89)
Gray, William, 135, 202, 229, 230
Griaule, Marcel, 261
Gringume, 157(n42)
Grosz-Ngate, Maria, 34
Grusi, 10
Guegan, Captain, 237
Guinea, 7, 10, 89
and the French, 221
Islam in, 266

and trade networks, 200–207, 211,
    212, 216–217
Gumbu, 5

Hajj, 120, 121–122, 121(n69), 122(n70)
Hamalliyya, 265, 266
Hausaland, 10
Hawqal, Ibn, 6, 62
Heddle (Charles) family, 201
Henry, Pere, 261
Herding, 101, 109
and the Fulbe, 103, 103n
Histoire (Khaldun), 114
Historical sources
anthropologist-ethnographers,
    30–32, 260–263
on commerce, 185–186, 185(n16)
French documentation, 29–30
oral tradition, 28–29, 30–32
History/historiography
colonialism and myth reconstruc-
    tion, 263, 273–274
European, 141(n4)
French reconstruction of Bamako,
    244–245, 247, 273(n64)
identity studies in, 33–39
and myth-archive comparisons, 97
New World slave, 40–42
Horonw, 14

Ibrahima, Samba, 254
Identity
ancestral homelands in, 9–10
articulating Mande/Fulbe, 47–54
bamanization, 3, 37n, 48, 77–79, 102,
    139, 171–172
Bambara *versus* Wagadu, 247–248,
    263–274. *See also* Bambara
    identity
collective Mande, 9, 23–24, 40–42,
    100
cultural signifiers and, 12–16, 25–26,
    84–87, 273–274. *See also* Cultural
    signifiers
defined, 1
effect of colonialism on, 263
historicizing, 33–39

of principal families, 2–4
and ritual alliances, 85–86
role of myth in, 9, 40, 55, 56–57, 63, 137
and Segovian warfare, 170–172
and spatial settlement, 16–22
and state formation, 39, 45–46
theory and shifts in, 1–2, 27–28, 32–33, 40
See also Northern paradigm; *specific families*
Ideology. *See* Belief systems
al-Idrisi, 183
Ijara, 186–187
Inheritance, 151(n27), 155(n38), 156, 156(n40), 176
Islam
and colonialism, 264–266, 265(n44)
and commerce/traders, 125, 179–180, 186, 187
as identity signifier, 71(n70), 86, 99, 101–102, 105–107
myth and, 26, 83
and *nyamakalaw*, 166, 166(n58)
role in northern paradigm, 137–138, 259
and social mobilization, 165–167
and southern particularism, 123–124
Islamic *jihads*, 12, 46, 208(n70), 264

Ja, 7, 9, 49, 105, 111
Jaby family, 56, 59(n40)
Jakite, Bassy, 81
Jakite, Fade, 126
Jakite, Jan, 126
Jakite, Lae, 254
Jakite, Samanyana, 90
Jakite family
and commerce, 181
identity, 13, 13(n31), 48, 49–50, 50(n13)
settlement area, 17, 18, 50(n15), 59(n40)
Jallo, Abdullaye, 252
Jallo, Bo, 252, 254
Jallo, Mamadi, 252

Jallo, Samba, 253–254, 254–255
Jallo family, 17, 66(n55)
Jallonke speakers, 52
Jamangille, 70, 72
Jambu family, 59(n40)
Jara, Da, 154, 171, 208
Jara, Karamoko, 154
Jara, Massa, 254
Jara, Massatomo, 154
Jara, Monzon, 154, 171, 194, 232
Jara, Ngolo, 86, 171, 174(n83)
Jara, Nyenekoro, 154
Jara family
and alliances, 165
and commerce, 191, 198, 199(n53)
as horse-warriors, 104
settlement area, 16, 18, 159
tana of, 80(n88)
Jarissi family, 59(n40), 69
Jaureguiberry, Jean-Bernard, 221, 239
Jawambe family, 83, 84, 163, 166–167, 199, 250
Jawara family, 70, 196
Jaxaba, 10
Jeliw, 173
Jenne
and Bambara identity formation, 101, 103, 248, 250
commerce and, 134, 197, 212
population, 20
schools/scholars in, 106, 111, 268
and Segu war, 207–208, 208(n70)
Jenne Circle, 112
Jire family, 166
Jomande family, 167
Jo rituals, 13, 116–118, 117(n55), 174
gold in, 119, 138
and north/south paradigm, 115
and particularized belief systems, 112
and state consolidation, 46

Kaarta, 4
and the French, 231
Niare identity and, 48, 49
and northern paradigm, 135
political succession in, 154

socio-political organization in,
146(n16)
war and, 125–126, 210
Kaba family, 50, 165
Kadar, Abdul, 198–199, 199(n53)
Kagoro
identity and Banama in-migration,
102–106
political economy of, 100–102
settlement of Mande-hinterland,
99–100
Kamissoko, Wa, 120, 120(n64), 127–128,
156, 177, 195
Kangaba, 96, 96(n3), 233
Kani, 211
Kaniaga region, 49, 49(n10), 69
Kankan, 19, 205–206, 211
Kante, Sumanguru, 81, 127
Kante family, 18, 85(n95)
Karamoko Drave clan, 196
Kassonke, 144(n10)
Kati, 96, 255
and the French, 243–244
al-Kati, 108
Kayes, 202, 214
and the French, 241
Keita, Bandiogu, 254
Keita, Koberi, 256
Keita, Mansa Musa, 3, 68, 133, 151(n28)
gold and *hajj* by, 120, 120(n64),
121–122, 122(n70)
Keita, Sunjata, 3, 127, 151, 151(n28)
Keita family
and alliances/identity, 13, 18, 165
and the French, 233
interclan rivalries in, 154–155, 175
myth and Mali state foundation,
100
settlement, 16, 18, 99–100, 100(n10)
and slave raids, 125
Kelenga Bozo, 99(n9)
Kerowane, 89, 102, 192
schools in, 111
Keyes, Charles F., 27–28, 84
Khaldun, Ibn, 6, 62, 114, 120(n64),
151(n28)

Khasso, 4
Khassonke, 115
al-Khuwarizmi, 6, 62
Kiba, 102, 111
Kingi, 49, 63, 66–68, 68–73
Kintampa, 19
Kissi, 211
Kita, 234
Kita Circle, 124
Koate, Gran, 260
Kola nut
culture, 210, 217(n77)
trade, 195, 199, 210–212
Kolokani, 244
Komola, 96, 113
Komo rituals, 13, 116, 117–118, 118(n57)
and the Dumbya, 118(n57)
gold in, 119, 121
and Islamized Bozo and Somono,
113
and southern identity, 116, 117(n54)
Konare family, 17
Konate, Waraba, 256
Konate family, 16, 159, 165
Konde family, 100
Kone family, 48, 59(n40), 80(n88)
Kong, 21(n51), 89, 90–91, 91(n108), 167
population, 20, 20(n50)
and textile industry, 211(n78)
Kono, 10, 211
Konyan, 211
Kooroko, 186
Kopytoff, Igor, 38–39
Korhogo, 15
Koulibali, Bakonimba, 261
Kulibaly, Biton (Mamari)
army of, 78(n85)
and Bamako, 184, 185
political succession and, 153
and Segu myth, 73, 74, 75–77
as Segu ruler, 2, 3, 18, 31
Kulibaly, Dekoro, 153
Kulibaly, Karamoko, 253
Kulibaly, Suma, 153
Kulibaly, Sumba, 74, 75, 76, 77
Kulibaly family

identity, 249, 249(n6)
as merchants, 198, 199(n53)
power struggle with Kong region,
91, 93
refugees in Bamako *kafu*, 159,
159(n46)
settlement area, 16, 17
tana of, 80(n88)
Kulikoro, 96, 190–191, 192, 242–243
population, 255
Kumbi, 5, 5(n10), 62
Kumi *kafu*, 152–153, 231
Kumma family, 59(n40)
Kuranko, 10
Kuri, Sissi, 104, 106
Kuri, Suri, 106
Kuri, Turi, 104
Kuyate family, 100, 165
tana of, 85(n95)

al-Laban, Ibn Shaykh, 133
Labat, Jean-Baptiste, 36(n74), 102, 184,
249, 257
Labe, 205
Labor
developing market for, 215, 266
organization of, 162–163, 166–167
Labouret, Henri, 34, 116
Laing, Alexander Gordon, 21, 130
Laitin, David, 78
Lambidu, 67, 74(n79), 88
Language
bilingualism, 190
and identity articulations, 9(n18),
11, 51
Kassonke, 144(n10)
loan words, 52–54, 110, 250
Niare Bamana dialect shift, 78
in political consolidation, 46
regional dialects, 9(n19), 14–15,
14(nn 34, 35), 15(nn 36, 37)
Launay, Robert, 15
Lebanese, 213–214
Lecard, 229
Legal affairs
and family law, 174

and Mande socio-political system,
143, 160
Legend of Wagadu, 4–6, 6(n12)
adultery episode, 67–73, 68(n63),
72(nn 72, 73)
Bamako *kafu* episode, 79–82, 81n
disaster episode, 57–64, 58(n38),
59(nn 39, 40)
Kingi episode, 66–67
as principal identity signifier, 56–57,
247–248, 263–274
sacrifice episode, 64–66, 64(n52)
Segu episode, 73–79, 74(n80)
and social control, 26
Suraka episode, 82–84
Levtzion, Nehemia, 62–63, 70
Leyboun, Madam, 202
Leyboun family, 223
Liberia, 7, 10, 89
and trade networks, 211, 212
Ligby family, 91
Lightburn family, 201, 223
Little, Kenneth, 260
Livestock. *See* Animals, domestic
Lobo, Ahmadu, 208
Lunéville, 145(n14)

Maasai culture, 33
Mage, Eugene, 224, 234, 235
al-Maghili, Muhammad Abd al-Karim,
106, 264
Makadji, El Hajj Mamadou, 193(n36)
Mali, 7, 100
and Niger River, 132–133
Malinke. *See* Maninka
Mandawiyya, al-Abbas, 104, 106
Mande-hinterland, 98
environment, 22–23
family settlement in, 17–18, 88–89,
99–100, 101–102
Niare identity in, 46–51
and north/south paradigm,
107–108
open lineages in, 51–54
Mandekan, 12(n26), 14–15, 14(n35)
Mande world

and north/south paradigm,
     107–108, 249
open lineages in, 51–54
population and settlement in,
     18–23, 88–89
Mandinka, 51, 109
and commerce, 182, 203
Manfara, 123
Maninka (Malinke, Mandingo), 40–42,
     109, 115
al-Maqqari, 185(n16)
Marillier, 145(n14), 155
Marka (pl. Maraka)
and Bambara identity formation,
     110–111, 250, 251
and commerce, 213, 268–269
settlement in, 18
Marka-Sarakolle identity, 3, 3(n4), 48,
     48(n9), 103
Markets
in Bamako, 187–188
and French military campaigns,
     214, 214(n87), 215(n89)
and gold, 182–184
grain, forage, and livestock,
     212–213, 214(n87)
and kola nuts, 210–211, 211(n78)
mercantile families and developing,
     25
middle and upper Niger, 104–105
pre-kafu regional, 181–185
salt, 190–192, 190(n28), 191(n30)
southern, 198(n49)
See also Economy; Trade
Marriage
alliances, 75–77, 163–164, 166, 168
identity and changing traditions of,
     84–85
Massantolo, 231
Massassi, 104
Massina, 4, 49
and Bambara identity, 248
and commerce, 213
war with Segu, 207–208, 208(n70)
Matthews, John, 143, 145(nn 13, 14), 203
Mauny, Raymond, 5(n10), 57
Maurel, Marc, 239

McNaughton, Patrick, 116
Meillassoux, Claude, 30–31, 60, 75
Migrations, population
Bamana arrival in Mande-hinter-
     land, 102–103, 248
and cultural diffusion, 78–79
environmental causes, 22, 61
Mande dispersal, 7–8, 9–10, 46–47,
     47(n3), 59(n40)
Mani-Sumba, 203–204, 204(n61)
Milo River, 132, 132(n94)
Minianka family, 165
Mining identity, 115–116
al-Mokhtar, Al-Hajj Muhammad, 127
Mollien, Gaspard, 155, 206(n65), 228
Monteil, Charles, 34, 116, 260, 261
Moors, 11. See also Islam
Mopti, 212, 244
Moribabugu, 192
Moribugu region, 153
Mosse family, 107, 165
Mudimbe, V. Y., 34, 35, 263
Muslims. See Islam
Myth
conflicting accounts with Niare,
     87–93
and Dumbya, 118
"Epic of Sunjata," 100
manipulating, 45(n1), 55–57, 84,
     247–248, 263–264, 273–274
and Musa hajj, 121–122
and the Niger River, 130
and ritual, 115. See also Ritual
role in identity of, 9, 40, 55, 56–57,
     137
and social control, 26
socialization and, 272
as source, 28–29, 30–32, 55–57
and southern gold/slave identity,
     118, 120
in upholding socio-political organi-
     zation, 148
See also Belief systems; Legend of
     Wagadu

Nani, Mansa Juru Kali, 118
N'Diaye family, 14, 85(n95)

Niare, Amadu Kumba, 30–31, 90(n103), 157, 164, 273
Niare, Batigui, 269
Niare, Biramon, 198
Niare, Biramou, 151–152, 197(n48)
Niare, Bomboli, 198
Niare, Fabile, 151
Niare, Jyokolo, 198
Niare, Jyonko, 269–270
Niare, Madiugu Seriba, 150
Niare, Malassa Bakary, 151
Niare, Seydou, 99(n9)
Niare, Titi, 87, 150, 151–152, 152(nn 30, 31), 173, 197–198, 197(n48), 219(n2), 229–230, 232
Niare (Nyakate) family, 2
  Bamako quarter for, 95
  bamanization of Bamako, 77–79, 84–87, 139
  dynastic claims, 62–63, 68–72
  and the French, 156–157, 221(n7), 247, 267, 269–274
  and identity, 23, 28, 46–54, 124, 248, 272–273
  Islamization of, 71(n70)
  Lambidu myth, 67, 74(n79), 88
  marriage and alliances with, 49–50, 85–86, 164
  as merchants, 197–198, 199(n53)
  and myth/ritual, 26, 28, 56–57, 58–84, 144(n10)
  as rulers of Bamako, 45, 77, 79–83, 88–93, 150–152
  separation of eastern and western, 75, 77
  settlement area, 16, 18, 99
  and slave families, 157–158
  tana of, 58(n38), 80(n88)
Niarela, 95
Nigeria, 48
Niger River, 129–131, 131(n92)
  Delta region, 130(n88)
  political economy and relationship with, 131–134, 132(n95)
  southern ritual relationship with, 97, 138
Niumi region, 155

Nonkon, 153
Nono, 9
Northern paradigm
  effects of, 24, 28, 97–98, 135, 137–138
  French adoption of, 251–252, 255–263
  origins of, 103–116, 133, 248–251
  and southern realities, 121–124, 126–129, 138
Nouvelle relation (Labat), 249
Numuw, 81, 85(n94)
  and political power in Bamako, 173–174
  southerners and, 115–116
Nyakate, Bemba, 67, 71, 72(n73), 264
Nyakate, Fata Maghan, 58–59, 64, 263–264
Nyakate, Jamusadia, 76, 79–81, 85(n94), 150
Nyakate, Mana Maghan, 59, 63, 64, 69, 70–71, 77
Nyakate, Seribadia, 67, 73, 74, 75, 78, 80(n86)
Nyakate, Suleyman Bana, 68, 71
Nyakate family. *See* Niare (Nyakate) family
Nyamakalaw, 14
Nyamina, 111
Nyuaman, Chaman, 153

Odienne, 19, 206, 211
Old Mande, 3, 3(n6)
  political succession in, 154–155, 177
  and trade, 192, 194–195
Oral tradition. *See* Myth
Otherizing
  and Banama in-migration, 102
  and formation of Bambara identity, 24, 37–38, 97–98, 106, 113–114, 137–138, 248

Paques, Viviana, 30, 74, 74(n78)
Park, Mungo, 21, 34
  and Bamako, 29(n61), 234, 235–236
  and Bambara identity, 257

cultural accounts/reports, 123–124,
    125–126, 135, 190–191, 193,
    193(n35), 194, 207
Mande views of, 220n, 227–228, 229,
    230–231
and Niger River, 131
Particularization. *See* Cultural particu-
    larisms
Patrimony, 147–148, 150
Patronyms, 13–14
Pereira, Pacheco, 36, 102, 185(n16), 249
Pietri, Camille, 150, 227, 228, 229, 230,
    232, 235, 236
Political power
    and alliances, 60–61, 75–77,
        148(n20), 160
    in Bamako, 4, 149–150, 173–174
    and colonialism, 26, 156–157, 213,
        269–271
    and concepts of race, 41–42
    and core state, 161
    European observations of Mande,
        143, 144–145
    and knowledge theory, 35, 36
    myth and legitimizing, 57, 58, 59, 72
    and Roman Republic, 141–142
    and state formation, 39
    and succession, 151–156
    See also Socio-political organization;
        State
Pondo Sorogo Bozo, 99(n9)
Population
    Bamako Circle, 17, 17(n43)
    Bamako increases in, 210, 244
    and Bamana in-migration, 103
    declines, 128
    estimates, 104–105, 235, 236
    and French ethnic categories, 255,
        255(n19)
    Mande world, 19–21, 20(nn 49, 50)
    and southern markets, 198(n49)
Portuguese, 200, 201
Prices
    gold, 207, 207(n68)
    grain, 129(n86), 215
    gum, 222(n11)
    salt, 192–193, 193(n35)

Prohibitions
    and limiting conflict, 161, 165
    tana, 58(n38), 80(n88), 85, 85(n95)
Protet, 223(n12)
Ptolemy, 244

al-Qadir, Abd, 208(n70)
al-Qazwini, 183
"Quadrilateral Policy," 240
Quintin, Aubert, 257, 258

Race, 41–42
Raffenel, Anne Jean-Baptiste, 55, 56,
    146(n16), 154, 234, 235
Railways, 227, 238–240, 239nn,
    242–243, 242(n52), 243(n53)
Rassemblement Democratic Africain
    (RDA), 266
Refugees, 159, 170, 210
Religion. *See* Belief systems
Rio Pongo, 202, 205
Rites de passage, 271–272
Ritual
    and gold, 121, 121(n68). *See also*
        Gold
    identity and manipulating, 26, 28,
        40, 84, 139, 248
    and kola nuts, 210
    and rights to natural resources, 81n
    and *rites de passage*, 271–272
    role in Bamako socio-political sys-
        tem, 226
    Roman, 142
    and state maintenance, 173–174
    See also Alliances; *Jo* rituals
Roger, 223(n12)
Roman paradigm, 141, 143, 147–148,
    148(n21)
Roman Republic, 140(n2), 141–142,
    141(n5), 142(nn 6, 8)
Rougier, Ferdinand, 21–22, 152, 153
Ruault, 126, 146(n16), 152, 153, 248, 251

Sacrifice, institutionalized, 58(n37)
Saganogo, 90(n105)
Saharan Walata, 9
Sahel, 5, 9

al-Sahili, Abu Ishaq, 133
Sa'id, Umar Ibn, 136
Saint Louis, 20
Sakho, Mamadu, 126
Sakho family, 48, 56
    settlement area, 18, 101
Salaga, 19
Salt
    and Arawan market, 191(n30)
    as male principle, 120–121,
        121(n67), 188(n23)
    and slave trade, 125
    trade and Bamako, 188–196,
        190(n28), 192nn, 193(nn 35, 36),
        210, 211, 216
Samalen, 181
Samalia, 181
Samanyana, 171, 181, 216
Sambabugu, 232
Samorians, 12, 231
Samorian war, 46, 167
    and Bamako region, 91–92, 195–196,
        209
    and slave trade, 189, 193, 195
    and southern poverty, 128
Sangare family, 17, 18
Sankarani River, 131(n92)
Sanogo, Bamba, 80(n87), 89–90, 90(nn
    103, 106), 91–93, 92(n110)
Sansanding, 234
Sanusiyya, 265
Sarakolle, 101(n14)
    and Bambara identity formation,
        110–111, 250, 251
    and the French, 257–258
Schmaltz, 223(n12)
Schools
    French, 267–268, 267(n52)
    Islamic, 265, 266
    northern identification with, 110, 111
Schuhl, P. M., 262
Segu
    family settlement in, 3, 18
    and the French, 224, 232
    Islamism in, 105
    as military/authoritarian state,
        78–79, 78(n85), 149, 173

Niare identity and, 48, 104
Niare myth and, 73–79
and northern paradigm, 135
political succession in, 153–154
relationship with Bamako, 2, 12,
    168–172
roads to, 96
and taxes/tribute, 171, 171(n75),
    172(n79)
territorial/political hegemony,
    45–46, 81, 168(n65), 204
and textile industry, 211
Umarian takeover, 224(n14)
Segu-Kaarta war, 125–126
Segu-Massina war, 207–208, 208(n70)
Segu-Sikoro, 20, 20(n49)
Senankun, 164–165
Senegal, 221
Senegambia, 4, 10
    French in, 220–225
    and trade networks, 200–207,
        216–217
"Senegambian Triangle," 224, 224(n16),
    240
Settlement
    Bamako *kafu* family/village, 16–17,
        157–161, 157(n42)
    and Mande dispersal, 46–47,
        59(n40), 88–89
    of Mande-hinterland, 17–18, 99–100,
        101–102
    in Mande world, 16–19
    theory, 38–39
    Ture family, 82(n91)
Shehu, Ahmadu, 250
Siby, 155, 181
Sidibe family, 17
Sierre Leone, 7, 10, 89, 211
Sikasso, 19
Silbe family, 70(n67)
Simpara, Lassana, 253
Simpara family, 48, 102, 196
Sinaba (Sinayogo) Bozo, 96
Sinsani, 20, 20(n49), 111
Siracoroba *kafu*, 231
Sisse, Ahmadu Ba Lobo, 4
Sisse, Nyonko, 123–124

Sisse family
    dispersal and settlement, 18,
        59(n40), 102
    identity, 18–19, 48
    and myth, 56, 165
Sissoko, Baba, 56
Sissoko family, 18, 100
Siyah, 52(n19), 77, 85–86, 164
Slavery
    Bamako dealers in, 196–199, 216
    and "Bambara," 111, 257
    domestic trade in, 125–128,
        127(n84), 135, 188–196, 210
    and European trade, 136, 223(n12)
    French emancipation, 163(n53), 268
    and Mande social organization, 14,
        14(n33), 162–163
    northern paradigm in justifying,
        137
    and Segovian wars, 171
Social change, 56, 66, 84–85
Social control, 26, 161
    Bamako and Segovian, 168–172
Socialization
    competition and cooperation in,
        176–177
    and *komo* ritual, 117
    myth in, 272
Social mobilization
    labor organization, 162–163,
        166–167
    ritual alliances and, 163–167
    and warfare, 162, 163
Social stratification, 53
    and myth, 64–66, 65(n53), 85
    and spatial organization, 157–161
Socio-political organization
    and Bamako *kafu*, 140, 149–151,
        157–161, 162–167, 173–176, 179
    Bamako *versus* French, 225–227
    colonial observations of Mande,
        143–147
    north/south paradigm in legitimat-
        ing, 108
    and political succession, 151–156
    Roman, 141–142, 141(n5), 142(nn 6,
        8)

    tri-partite lineage formation, 14
    See also Family; Political power
So family, 17
Sokoto Caliphate, 208(n70)
Solleillet, Paul, 234
Somono family
    and alliances, 165
    and Bambara identity formation,
        112, 250
    identity, 83–84, 113(n45)
    and particularization of belief sys-
        tems, 112–113
    settlement of Mande-hinterland, 99
Songhay
    and alliances, 165
    and Bambara identity formation,
        250
    Niger River and trade in, 134–135
    viceroys in, 134n
Soninke
    and Bambara identity formation,
        110–111, 250
    and Folbe identity shifts/articula-
        tions, 50, 51–54
    and the French, 251
    identity and Banama in-migration,
        102–106
    and Niare identity, 3, 250(n8)
    political economy of, 100–102
    settlement of Mande-hinterland,
        99–100
Sonogo Bozo, 99(n9)
Spatial organization, 157–160
Spear, Thomas, 33
State
    defined, 1
    development by conquest, 136
    formation and the family, 24, 40
    formation of Mande, 10, 261,
        261(n36), 262
    formation theory, 38–39
    maintaining authority of core, 161,
        168–172
    role in identity formation, 2, 45–46,
        55, 135
    role of families in, 140
    segmentary, 24(n56)

See also Political power; Socio-political organization
Succession, political, 144(n12), 151–156, 151(nn 27, 28)
Sudan, 7
Sumare, Amadu, 252
Sumbala, 157–158, 162, 163, 197
    and Bozo alliances, 166
Suraka family, 163, 173, 175
Suraka Talmamane family, 82
Suware, al-Salim, 106(n28)
Suwarian tradition, 106(n28)
al-Suyuti, Jalal al-Din, 106, 264
Sylla family
    and commerce, 196, 199
    dispersal and settlement, 18, 59(n40), 102
    identity, 48, 70(n67)
Symbols
    crocodile imagery, 81
    France and, 226–227
    and kola nuts, 210, 210(n77)
    python/snake, 54, 57, 57(n36), 58(n38)
    siyah as, 77

Tabure, Sidi Muhammad, 68, 68(n61)
Tall, Amadu, 232
Tall, Madina Ly, 108
Tall, 'Umar, 208(n70)
Tall family, 136
Tamari, Tal, 53
Tamentit, 3
Tammoura, Kare, 78(n85), 260
Tangara family, 165
Tappi, 211
Ta'rikh al-Fattash, 59(n39), 68–69, 71, 71(n70), 86, 244
    and northern paradigm, 107–108, 114–115, 249
Ta'rikh as-Sudan, 104, 244
    and northern paradigm, 106, 249
Tautain, Louis-Frédéric, 17(n42), 237
Tauxier, Louis, 53, 116, 120, 260–261
Tawat, 3, 9
Tawatila, 95, 212
Technology, 226–227

Tellier, G., 144–145, 162
Terminology
    and Bamako *kindaw,* 96(n2)
    and "Bambara," 37, 37n, 108, 110
    and "family," 144(n11)
    jula, 220n
    and Mandinga, 40
    ritual terms, 116(n53), 117(n54)
    "Rumi," 219(n3)
    for traders, 180(n2)
    and writing, 227
Textile industry, 102(n16)
    and kola nuts, 211, 211(n78)
Theory
    and cross-cultural methodologies, 33–37
    identity, 27–28, 32–33, 37–39
    knowledge, 35, 36
Tichit, 9
Tie Ceye (Nuhun Bozo), 99(n9)
Tigh, Madam Eliza, 202
al-Tijani, al-Hajj Umar Tall, 12
Tijaniyya, 265
Timbo, 205, 206, 208(n70)
Timbuktu
    and Bambara identity formation, 248, 249–250
    and the French, 244
    population, 20, 20(n50)
    scholarship and, 104, 111
    trade and, 134
Tinkisso River, 131(n92)
Tondibi, 107
Trade
    and cultural diffusion, 78–79
    domestic slave, 125–128, 127(n84), 135, 188–196, 210. *See also* Slavery
    European arms-slave/gold, 136, 136n, 189, 195
    fluctuations in trans-Saharan, 107
    and the French, 222(n11), 223–225, 223(nn 12, 13)
    items, 101(n14), 195, 203, 203(n60), 217, 222(n11). *See also* Salt
    networks and Bamako *kafu,* 179–181, 185–196, 188(n23),

190(n28), 192(n33), 199–200,
    199(n53), 209–217
Niger River and north-south,
    132–133, 134–135
northern identification with, 109, 111
pre-kafu regional markets, 181–185
routes, 184, 192(n34)
Segovian hegemony and, 172
southwestern coastal–northern,
    200–207, 202(n57), 206(n65),
    211–212
See also Economy; Markets
Traders/merchants
    individuals and families of, 82–83,
        180, 185–186, 190–191, 193(n36)
    Islam identity and, 179–180, 187, 190
    partnerships, 186–187
    principal Bamako, 196–199, 212,
        213–214
    southwestern coastal, 201–203
    terminology for, 180(n2)
Transportation
    Niger and tributaries, 131(n92), 132,
        132(nn 94, 95)
Traore, Bogoba, 254
Traoré, Moussa, 147(n18)
Traore family
    and alliances, 165
    as horse-warriors, 104
    identity, 14, 18
    leadership of, 152–153
    as merchants, 198, 199(n53)
    settlement area, 18, 100, 159
Travele, Moussa, 116
Trentinian, Louis, 17(n42), 244–245
Tribute. See Disongo
Tuareg, 107
Tuba, 89, 102, 155(n38)
    and commerce, 192
    schools in, 111, 268
Tuhfat al-Muzzar, 114
Tukulor, 13(n31), 51, 257
Tuleplu, 211
Tunkara family, 165
Ture, Abderaman, 196, 253, 270
Ture, Abdul Jaffar, 196, 270
Ture, al-Habib, 196

Ture, Dogofaro, 270
Ture, Lahaou, 196
Ture, Madani, 270
Ture, Samory, 12, 136
Ture, Shaykh, 265
Ture, Sidi Mohammad, 196
Ture family
    and alliances, 165
    and Bamako political rivalry, 91–92,
        270
    Bamako quarter for, 95
    and commerce, 82–83, 187, 190(n29),
        196, 199
    and the French, 267
    in Guinea, 136
    identity, 3, 14, 18, 82(n91)
    and myth, 82–83, 88–93
    settlement area, 16, 59(n40), 82(n91),
        100
    slaves of, 162
    and slave trade, 125

Ule, Karamoko, 227
al-'Umari, 183, 185(n16)
Umarians, 12
    and the French, 220–221, 232
    and Segu, 224(n14)
Umarian war, 46, 170
    and Bamako, 195–196, 209
    and slave trade, 189, 193, 195
    and southern poverty, 128
Union Culturelle Musulmane (UCM),
    265

Valliere, François
    and Bamako, 237
    and Bambara identity, 258
    cultural accounts/reports, 126, 128,
        146(n16), 149, 155, 195
    Mande views of, 221, 229, 232–233
Van Gennep, Arnold, 271, 271(n61)
Villein-Rossi, Marie-Louise, 30–31
Voltaic region, 89

Wagadu, 5–6, 61–62, 167. See also Leg-
    end of Wagadu
Wago, 56(n32)

al-Wahhab, Shaykh Abd, 265
Wahhabiyya, 26, 265–266
Wakore, 5
Waller, Richard, 33
"Wangara," 48
Wars
and Bamana state development,
104, 109–110
effect on economy, 204, 209–210
Islamic, 12, 46, 208(n70), 264
mobilization for, 162, 163
Segovian, 125–126, 169–172,
207–208, 208(n70)
See also Conflict, societal; Samorian
war; Umarian war
Wassulu, 4, 206, 209
and slave trade, 194–195
Wassulunke, 115
Wattara, Seku, 90
Wattara family, 91, 93
Weapons
British trade in, 206(n65), 241

European arms-slave/gold trade,
136, 136n, 189, 195
Weyaweyanko, 198–199, 199(n53),
212
Wilkinson family, 201, 223
Winterbottom, 127
Women
and colonialism, 268–269
and commerce, 202, 217
French-Mande misunderstandings
regarding, 230
and labor organization, 163
Worodugu, 205, 209
Woulale, Mousa, 261
Writing, 227–230, 252, 256, 269
Wuloni, 231–232

Yatenga, 10
Youth, 263–264, 266, 267–268, 269,
273

Zuenula, 211